# FOREIGN AFFAIRS AND THE CONSTITUTION

# FOREIGN AFFAIRS AND THE CONSTITUTION

by LOUIS HENKIN

The Norton Library

W·W·NORTON & COMPANY·INC·

NEW YORK

COPYRIGHT © 1972 BY THE FOUNDATION PRESS, INC.

First published in the Norton Library 1975 by
arrangement with The Foundation Press, Inc.

Books That Live
The Norton imprint on a book means that in the publisher's
estimation it is a book not for a single season but for the years.
W. W. Norton & Company, Inc.

Library of Congress Cataloging in Publication Data

Henkin, Louis.
    Foreign affairs and the Constitution.

    (The Norton Library)
    Reprint of the ed. published by Foundation Press,
Mineola, N. Y.
    "Cases cited": p.
    Includes index.
    1. United States—Foreign relations—Law and
legislation. 2. United States—Constitutional law.
I. Title.
[KF4651.H45  1975]  342'.73'06  74-31049
ISBN 0-393-00768-5

Printed in the United States of America
1  2  3  4  5  6  7  8  9  0

# CONTENTS

TO ALICE

and Joshua, David, and Daniel

# PREFACE

Volumes about the American Constitution and about American foreign relations abound, but they are two different mountains of books. Those that deal with the Constitution say little about American foreign relations; the others expound, scrutinize, dissect and criticize the international relations, foreign policy, and the "foreign-policy-making process" of the United States, but the controlling relevance of the Constitution is roundly ignored. A constitutional crisis in the conduct of foreign relations besets every generation and fills the journals for a brief time, but how the Constitution governs the conduct of foreign relations does not receive sustained attention or extended exposition.

This was not always so. In earlier days, the constitutional law of American foreign affairs was one, important, integral part of constitutional debate and study. The foreign relations of the future republic were prominent concerns in the deliberations of the Constitutional Convention and in the debates that raged during ratification. They were the subject of essays by Madison, Hamilton and Jay when they wrote the Federalist Papers to promote acceptance of the new Constitution, and of heated polemics later when Hamilton and Madison (and Hamilton and Jefferson) came to see so differently the Constitution and the government it had established. Constitutional issues in the conduct of foreign affairs were disputed learnedly in Presidential messages, Congressional debates, opinions of attorneys-general and writings of leading lawyers. The Supreme Court Reports carried frequent, extended essays on national sovereignty, the law of nations, executive and legislative powers, the Treaty Power, the special role of the courts in foreign affairs. The law of foreign relations received many pages from early commentators on the Constitution (*e. g.*, Story) and in the 19th and early 20th Century treatises (Cooley, Willoughby).

Perhaps the constitutional law of American foreign affairs began to suffer scholarly neglect when, for reasons I suggest later, constitutional lawyers increasingly concerned themselves only with what the Supreme Court was doing, while the Court's contributions in foreign affairs became less frequent. Perhaps it suffered when "public law" expanded to claim much besides constitutional law and international law, and these two fields themselves grew apace and developed into separate expertises of different experts. The constitutional law of foreign affairs, together with international law, became the special domain of those few lawyers who advised the Government in its foreign relations, and it is they who produced the classic treatises and digests—Wharton, Moore, Malloy, Crandall, Hyde, Hackworth and, most recently, Marjorie Whiteman. For the rest, the law of foreign affairs fell somewhere between the constitutional lawyer and the international lawyer, perhaps nearer to the latter, but his credentials in constitutional law were not universally accepted and he was himself less than wholly comfortable with its matter and manner.

In the twentieth century treatises on constitutional law have virtually ceased to appear, and none commands authoritative acceptance;[1] the few that are about tend to look only at that small corner of our field that has caught the attention of the Supreme Court.* Volumes devoted to the law of foreign affairs in particular have not appeared in the void.** There was indeed an excellent study by the late Professor Quincy Wright[2] to which I am much indebted, but it is now fifty years old and much has happened since—in the Constitution, in the institutions and processes of government, in American foreign relations. (Professor Wright wrote in the wake of Versailles: I complete this volume in the quicksands of Vietnam.) Not only have there been at least a dozen innovating Supreme Court decisions since his publication, but its constitutional universe is not ours: the

* Although the issues have been with us from the beginning, the Vietnam controversy finally forced some materials into law reviews and law school casebooks.

** The Law of American Foreign Relations has now been accepted as a "field," including both international law as applied by the United States and the constitutional law particularly relevant to the conduct of foreign affairs. See, e. g., RESTATEMENT (SECOND) OF THE FOREIGN RELATIONS LAW OF THE UNITED STATES (1965) [hereinafter cited as RESTATEMENT]. Sometimes the field is defined to include also statutory and other nonconstitutional materials relating to foreign affairs.

distributions of power between Nation and State and between Congress and the President look different; the safeguards for individual rights have become central; and we have had new problems raising new constitutional questions or framing old questions in new contexts so as to render them effectively new. There have been more recent studies of individual segments, of the powers of the President or of the Congress: in particular, I have drawn heavily on Corwin's study of the Presidency [3] in which the President's role in foreign relations is the subject of one chapter and pervades several others. The particular focus of these studies, however, permits only peripheral vision of the other actors and of the rest of the scene, and some of them are also redolent of an earlier mood, concentrate on earlier problems, antedate several constitutional crises and the latest self-searchings and reexaminations. Most of them reflect the perspectives and insights of the political scientist rather than of the constitutional lawyer.

This volume is designed to begin to fill the need. It is a legal study, although I have attempted to make the text accessible also to those not trained in the law, most of it even to "the general reader." In that cause I ask the indulgence of scholars whom I condemn to turning to the back of the book for citation of authority as well as for the longer illustrative and complementary notes.

I have studied the questions here discussed for fifteen years, as I taught them to classes and seminars at the University of Pennsylvania and Columbia University. At the University of Pennsylvania the seminars were a joint effort with my colleague and friend Professor Covey Oliver, and no doubt much that appears here was learned with and from him. Much was learned too from generations of students. I single out for mention and appreciation some who assisted me directly and extensively: Stuart Licht, J. D. Columbia 1973, as well as Joel Goldberg, J. D. Columbia, 1970, Alan Garfunkel and Michael Stolzer, J. D. Columbia, 1972, and Barbara Black, J. D. Columbia, 1973. Linda Th............ ...................... in various ways. Not least, I am grateful to my friend and colleague Professor Albert J. Rosenthal for reading the manuscript and making many valuable suggestions. Time and facilities for study and writing were provided me by

Columbia University through the Law School and the Institute of War and Peace Studies, with particular assistance from the Ford Foundation. I largely completed this volume during the summer of 1971 as a scholar in-residence at the Aspen Institute for Humanistic Studies.

Over the years I have written about particular pieces of the subject in law reviews and other professional journals.[4] During 1956–57 I examined many of them in the context of *Arms Control and Inspection in American Law*.[5] I have drawn heavily on all these writings and am grateful to the copyright owners for permission to do so.[6]

Louis Henkin

November, 1972

## Notes to Preface

1. The last major, generally cited treatise was W. WILLOUGHBY, PRINCIPLES OF CONSTITUTIONAL LAW OF THE UNITED STATES (2d ed. 1929) [hereinafter cited as WILLOUGHBY].

2. Q. WRIGHT, THE CONTROL OF AMERICAN FOREIGN RELATIONS (1922) [hereinafter cited as WRIGHT].

3. E. CORWIN, THE PRESIDENT, OFFICE AND POWERS 1787–1957 (4th ed. 1957) [hereinafter cited as CORWIN, THE PRESIDENT]. See also his THE PRESIDENT'S CONTROL OF FOREIGN RELATIONS (1917), and THE CONSTITUTION AND WORLD ORGANIZATION (1944). Corwin also edited THE CONSTITUTION OF THE UNITED STATES OF AMERICA: ANALYSIS AND INTERPRETATION, S. DOC. NO. 170, 82d Cong., 2d Sess. (1953). (The later edition, edited by Small and Jayson, is S. DOC. NO. 39, 88th Cong., 1st Sess. (1964).

4. In particular, *The Treaty Makers and the Law Makers: the Niagara Reservation,* 56 COLUM.L.REV. 1151 (1956); *The Treaty Makers and the Law Makers: the Law of the Land and Foreign Relations,* 107 U.PA.L.REV. 903 (1959); *The Foreign Affairs Power of the Federal Courts:* Sabbatino, 64 COLUM.L.REV. 805 (1964); *The Constitution, Treaties, and International Human Rights,* 116 U.PA.L.REV. 1012 (1968); *'International Concern' and the Treaty Power of the United States,* 63 AM.J.INT'L L. 272 (1969); *Vietnam in the Courts of the United States: 'Political Questions,'* 63 AM.J.INT'L L. 284 (1969); *Constitutional Issues in Foreign Policy,* 23 J.INT'L AFF. 210 (1969). Also, *Treaty-Making Powers and their Implementation under a Federal Constitution: The American Experience,* unpublished.

5. Columbia University Press (1958), a study conducted under the auspices of the Legislative Drafting Research Fund, Columbia University.

6. My thanks are due to the Columbia Law Review for permission to draw on my articles in Volumes 56 and 64; to the University of Pennsylvania Law Review and Fred B. Rothman & Co. as regards the articles in Volumes 107 and 116 of the University of Pennsylvania Law Review; to the Columbia University Press for permission to draw on *Arms Control and Inspection in American Law;* to the American Journal of Internatio̲n̲a̲l̲ ̲L̲a̲w̲ ̲f̲o̲r̲ ̲p̲e̲r̲m̲i̲s̲s̲i̲o̲n̲ ̲t̲o̲ ̲d̲r̲a̲w̲ ̲o̲n̲ ̲m̲y̲ ̲a̲r̲t̲i̲c̲l̲e̲s̲ in Volume 69; to the Journal of International Affairs, Columbia University, for permission to draw on my article in Volume XXIII. The full citations are in note 4 above.

# FOREIGN AFFAIRS AND THE CONSTITUTION

# INTRODUCTION

Constitutional government has come to suggest limited government, and the Constitution of the United States is commonly thought of as an edict of limitations on the government of the United States and of the States to protect individual liberty.[1] In fact, in largest part the Constitution is not a charter of liberties but a blue-print for a federal system of government,[2] dividing authority between the nation and the States and distributing the national authority among branches of the national government. Limitations are implied, of course, in these divisions and distributions and in the principles of federalism and the "separation-of-powers" they reflect.* There are also some express limitations on the national government and on the States, including important safeguards for individual liberty, notably in the Bill of Rights and in later amendments.**

* The separation of powers, however, was also designed, at least in part, to safeguard the people's liberties. See Mr. Justice Brandeis, quoted, Introduction to Chapter II, note 2.

** The original Constitution contained a few express limitations and prohibitions on the national government, most of them (in Art. I, sec. 9) to protect state interests (rather than individual freedom); the express limitations on the States also principally protect national interests (Art. I, sec. 10). There are some safeguards for individual rights in the original Constitution, for example provisions requiring a jury trial in criminal cases (Art. III, sec. 2), and prescribing requirements for conviction for treason (Art. III, sec. 3). The principal limitations in favor of the individual are in the Bill of Rights, added by amendment immediately after the Constitution came into ~~f~~ ... ~~the wake~~ ... the wake of the Civil War, in the Thirteenth, Fourteenth and Fifteenth Amendments. See Chapter XI.

Study of the American Constitution tends to neglect—or assume—the constitutional blueprint and concentrate on the limitations and

3

The constitutional blueprint, of course, shapes government, not least the conduct of the nation's foreign relations, and constitutional prohibitions and limitations inhibit foreign affairs as well as other governmental action. And yet, neither those concerned with the Constitution nor they who deal with foreign affairs attend regularly to the applicable constitutional law. The student of American foreign relations is aware, no doubt, that those who daily conduct affairs with other nations derive their authority from the Constitution and perform their functions in a framework of institutions and processes determined by it: the President appoints a new ambassador to Japan, Congress appropriates for foreign aid, the Senate consents to the Nuclear Non-Proliferation Treaty; or, the Secretary of State announces a different American policy in the Middle East, a Congressional committee holds hearings on the desirability of developing anti-ballistic missiles. But few ask whether and where in the Constitution their authority derives, what constitutional prescriptions, if any, they are carrying out, under what restrictions, if any, they act.

In part, no doubt, students of foreign affairs share the common unease with legal inquiries and legal documents. In this instance, I believe, lack of interest reflects, too, the impression that the Constitution and its law do not matter, or perhaps that, like other mechanisms that "work" smoothly, it can be taken for granted. The conduct of foreign relations seems long and far removed from any constitutional origins, confronting no constitutional limitations and generating no constitutional issues. When, re-

prohibitions it contains, largely because these are the focus of cases and controversies in the courts. A student of the Constitution learns to distinguish between two kinds of limitations: since the federal government has limited powers, since each of its branches has defined authority, he asks first whether an act is within the power of the federal government and of the branch that performed it. (This is often a single inquiry since almost all the grants of power to the federal government appear as grants to a particular branch). A separate and subsequent question is whether an action within the domain of the federal government and of the particular branch is nonetheless prohibited by the Constitution, for example because it violates the Bill of Rights.

4

currently, foreign affairs explode in constitutional controversy, it comes as a surprise, and the participants themselves, and other foreign affairs "experts," fumble and mumble in discussing the issues.[3]

Indifference—I dare add ignorance—is not limited to those who might claim lack of legal expertise. The student of the Constitution knows that there are clauses in it that pertain more-or-less directly to foreign affairs, but he can tell you little about them. He too, perhaps, has the sense that the constitutional law of foreign affairs weighs and matters little; but there is much else to deter or deflect him. Students of constitutional law have long been only students of the cases of the Supreme Court, and constitutional issues of foreign affairs rarely come to court.* The courts consider only cases, cases require proper parties and proper issues, and foreign affairs do not ordinarily provide them to the courts' satisfaction. Other judicial doctrines and practices also preclude constitutional decision and discourage constitutional suitors. Claims that would limit the freedom of government to conduct foreign relations, in particular, usually receive short shrift, and some have been declared "political questions" and get no shrift at all. The Supreme Court's jurisdiction is largely discretionary and the occasional foreign-affairs cases that come to its door are not all welcomed. That, as a result, the Court has not developed any confident expertise further encourages judicial abstention and perhaps further discourages might-be litigants.

For other reasons, too, the constitutional issues that trouble the conduct of foreign relations are not those with which constitutional lawyers are familiar. Federalism—once the principal staple of constitutional litigation [4]—rarely raises its head in foreign relations since for these purposes the United States is virtually a unitary state. Because the constitutional allocations of power to conduct foreign affairs are different from those for domestic matters, issues between the President and Congress in foreign affairs are not the same "separation-of-powers" contro-

* See Chapter VIII, pp. 207 *et seq.*

versies that have roiled the governance of domestic affairs. A principal Presidential power, "to make Treaties," has no counterpart in domestic affairs. Even the modest role played by the courts in foreign affairs is different, asserting different judicial authority, maintaining different relations with the political branches, monitoring different limitations on the States.

The fields of constitutional controversy, and the protagonists and the causes they represent, are also different. Since the courts are not the principal arena the contests are fought within and between the political branches of government and are political rather than juridical. Since, usually, private interests are not directly at stake, the causes behind the issues tend to be "political" rather than economic or libertarian. Charges of Presidential usurpation, for a recurrent example, come principally from those who oppose the politics of his policies, as once from isolationist critics "on the right" of Franklin Roosevelt, more recently from anti-interventionist critics "on the left" of Lyndon Johnson or Richard Nixon; constitutional limitations on the Treaty Power are asserted by those who seek to preserve remnants of "States' rights" or to keep the United States free of novel foreign entanglements.

The constitutional law of foreign affairs is also removed from the mainstream of constitutional studies and the focus of constitutional lawyers for yet another reason: the lawyer wants reliable answers and this law often fails to provide any. Generally, all now know, the Constitution is what the Supreme Court says it is,[5] but since the Court has not said much about its foreign affairs aspects, and promises to say little more, many of these have no final, "infallible" arbiter and expositor [6] and are "resolved" only *ad hoc* without resolution in principle. Powerful Presidents and determined Congresses (or Congressmen) take constitutional positions and provide precedents to encourage even their weaker successors, but the issues remain to be fought again some new day. If old and not-so-old Supreme Court constitutional decisions do not escape reexamination,[7] there is even less *stare decisis* for what former Presidents and earlier Congressmen asserted in word or action. And so, major constitutional issues of foreign

6

policy today are at bottom the struggles for constitutional power of our early history. The world is changed, the United States is changed, the institutions of government are changed, the Constitution itself is changed, but the constitutional materials, the Federalist Papers, the debates of Hamilton versus Jefferson or Hamilton versus Madison, remain fresh and relevant and are played back again and again by new voices in new contexts.

I believe, obviously, that the neglect of the constitutional law of foreign affairs is unwarranted and unfortunate. The foreign relations of the United States cannot be understood in the light of the Constitution alone, but they cannot be understood without it, for it continues to shape the institutions and the actions that determine them. If the conduct of foreign relations seems beset by politics rather than governed by law, it is the law of the Constitution that gives the politics its form and much of its content. Even the extra-constitutional institutions and processes which often seem to dominate the conduct of foreign relations are offspring of the Constitution and of needs created by its blueprint for government. If the Constitution says nothing about the President as leader, as "representative of all the people," as chief of his party, as hero or scapegoat, if it says nothing about Congressional committees, seniority or Senatorial courtesy, much of these can be traced to the Constitution, some to its special treatment of foreign affairs.

The constitutional issues of foreign affairs are alive and important. In our day, as with not-infrequent regularity since the beginnings of the nation, foreign relations have echoed and re-echoed with constitutional controversy and have continually generated constitutional law. The public official, the lawyer, the student of foreign affairs, the citizen, cannot afford to ignore them. That the courts are often not available to resolve them renders it more, not less, important that they be understood and publicly debated. Has the President the power to send Marines to the Dominican Republic, or half a million troops to fight in Vietnam? Can he commit the United States, by the Truman Doctrine or the Eisenhower Doctrine or by some secret undertaking to Thailand? What is the constitutional effect of a

Senate resolution declaring that commitments to use American troops abroad can effectively be made only by treaty with the advice and consent of the Senate? Can the President give away American destroyers to the British fighting Hitler, or other materiel to allies of the United States in Korea? Can his sole acts —the Truman Proclamation on the Continental Shelf or Roosevelt's agreement with Litvinov—have the effect of law in the United States? Can Congress disown the President's commitments at Potsdam or Yalta, prevent recognition of Communist China, or compel President Truman to lend millions to Franco Spain? Can Congress deny foreign aid to countries that expropriate American properties, or tell the courts not to give effect to such expropriations? Can the United States adhere to the UN Covenants on Human Rights? Can the State of Oregon refuse an inheritance to a resident of East Germany because his Communist government will not allow an American to inherit there? Can an American be deprived of his citizenship for voting in a foreign election, or be denied a passport and forbidden to travel abroad because he is a Communist? Does a person have any recourse when his suit is dismissed because the defendant has sovereign or diplomatic immunity, or when his claims against a foreign government are disposed of by treaty?

These and many other questions are discussed—I do not say answered—in this volume. Its subject is Foreign Affairs and the Constitution, and it attempts to illuminate the constitutional provisions that deal with foreign relations and the special significance for foreign relations of other constitutional clauses. Implied, of course, is that for this purpose "foreign affairs" can be defined, isolated, grasped, distinguished. That is hardly obvious. In many aspects of national economic life, for example, the domestic and the foreign are thoroughly mixed and unseparable. Domestic influences—say, the political power of particular industries or of ethnic groups—shape foreign policy, and foreign relations have deep domestic consequences even when they do not involve us in war. For constitutional lawyers as for others, the "line" between domestic and foreign affairs is increasingly fluid and uncertain, sometimes unreal, always at most a division of emphasis and degree.* Yet the distinction is basic: for the lawyer, constitutional theories and doctrines depend on it; students of government and politics build other generalizations on that difference; and government officials in every branch, and citizens less or more sophisticated, accept and act on it.

This volume is an essay in law, not in legal history, and it concentrates on where we stand with an eye to where we are going, rather than on where we were or even how we got here. As an essay in constitutional law it must attend particularly to what little the Supreme Court has held or said, and what it has held and said recently, rather less to cases which, although never reconsidered, smell of doctrine of a past day. Where the Supreme Court has not spoken directly, I sometimes attempt to read and extend its mood, but usually I ask more questions than I can answer, and array opposing arguments often without deciding between them. Although what is current is not necessarily new, or abiding, or important, I have given perhaps undue and distorting emphasis to issues that have agitated our times—the constitutionality of the President's actions in Vietnam, the authority of the courts to deny effect to Cuban expropriation of American investments, the use of the Treaty Power to promote international human rights. Such issues having particularly engaged my intellectual interest and sometimes drawn me into intellectual controversy, I have not always refrained from asserting strong convictions or giving confident answers which are not universally shared.

The plan of the book is simple and, because it attempts to focus separately on parts of a web that has few seams, inevitably somewhat artificial. The larger part of it reflects that even in our federal system foreign affairs are national affairs, and that the

---

* Some may find utility in a definition that domestic activities are those about which we do not recognize the right of other government... ...plain. But compare the fate of Art. 2(7) of the UN Charter which purported to deny authority to the UN "to intervene in matters which are essentially within the domestic jurisdiction of any state": it has not kept the UN from at least discussing anything members wished to discuss.

constitutional law of foreign affairs is principally the law of the allocation of authority within the Federal Government. I consider first (Chapter I) insufficiencies in the constitutional blueprint and attempts to explain them, including special theories about the constitutional status of the nationhood of the United States and of the powers of the federal government in foreign affairs.

Chapters II to IV describe the distribution of federal political power in foreign affairs, the powers of the President and of Congress, singly and together, in conflict and cooperation. This part is most important and probably least satisfying. Here are the major issues, real and hypothetical, and the large and abiding uncertainties. Some will ask whether there is constitutional "law" where constitutional text is inadequate, where the Supreme Court is silent, where constitutional Scripture and theoretical argument are invoked by one branch or the other to buttress political power, without any means or hopes for resolution. But if the constitutional law of these chapters is different, it is still constitutional law. The Constitution is not *only* what the Supreme Court says it is, not only what appears in cases. Presidents and Congressmen are under oath to support it and undoubtedly they take their oath seriously. Some issues have been resolved, others have been narrowed. Self-serving constitutional argument can reach far but it is not without limit in language and logic and history and good sense and acceptability and national interest. If the arguments on two or more sides are sometimes equally persuasive, if the constitutional lawyer has few confident answers, he has the same blocks with which the Supreme Court itself must often build, and it usually builds according to the advice of counsel.

A substantial portion of the book is devoted to the constitutional law governing international agreement and cooperation. While the Constitution lists treaty-making among the President's powers, some prefer to see "the treaty-makers" (the President and two-thirds of the Senate) as a special branch of the federal government with special processes raising special questions, including issues about its relation to the other branches. Here, of course, is law particular to foreign affairs and there are some judicial

10

decisions, dicta and substantial "hard law." Here there is contemporary controversy rooted in differences as to the kind of international cooperation that is appropriate and desirable for the United States in today's world. From similar motives I have included here (rather than in the President's chapter) international agreements that are not treaties, whether made by the President on his own authority or jointly with Congress. Also in this part is a small chapter dealing with issues (some real some hypothetical, some weighty some flimsy) suggested by American participapation in the special phenomenon of contemporary international society, the proliferation of international organizations.

Chapter VIII deals with the powers of the judicial branch of the federal government in foreign affairs. References to the courts abound in every chapter, when they have spoken on what the political branches have done; here I bring the courts center stage to examine whether in foreign affairs they play their usual role, whether they play it differently, whether they have additional parts. Chapter IX rounds out national authority in foreign affairs by reflecting on the small but abiding relevance of the States.

Essentially, Chapter X is a second, smaller part of the volume, setting forth the effective constitutional limitations on national power in foreign affairs imposed by the rights and freedoms of the individual. Constitutional law generally is becoming a study less and less of the limitations of federalism and separation of powers, more and more of the safeguards for individuals rights against governmental power.[8] I consider how that law of individual rights applies to the conduct of foreign affairs, which rights are particularly relevant, whether there are on the horizon new safeguards to limit government in its international relations.

Finally, I venture words of summary and evaluation: what is clear and what is uncertain, what is settled and what is in flux, how satisfactory is th........................................................ in and dissatisfactions with an Eighteenth Century Constitution soon 200 years old.

# THE CONSTITUTIONAL BLUEPRINT: FOREIGN
# AFFAIRS AS NATIONAL AFFAIRS

# Chapter I. THE CONSTITUTIONAL AUTHORITY OF THE FEDERAL GOVERNMENT

Foreign affairs are national affairs. The United States is a single nation-state and it is the United States (not the States of the Union, singly or together) that has relations with other nations, and the United States Government that conducts these relations and makes foreign policy.[1]

As the proverbial school boy knows, the Constitution established a "more perfect Union" on pillars of federalism and the separation of powers. It delegated authority and function to the federal government * by vesting legislative powers in Congress, the executive power in the President, the judicial power in a federal judiciary. "The powers not delegated to the United States by the Constitution . . . are reserved to the States respectively, or to the people." (Amendment X)

From the beginning, it was clear, this "more perfect Union" was one sovereign nation and the federal government has main-

---

* The Constitution speaks only of forming "a more perfect Union," not of creating a new government. The powers it vests are the executive, legislative and judicial powers "of the United States," not of the United States Government. (Compare Art. III, sec. 1.). The Constitution contains one reference to "the Government of the United States" (in the "necessary and proper clause," Art. I, sec. 8, cl. 18), and several to "the United States"; the latter seems to denote the national entity, rather than its government. In the Articles of Confederation "the United States in Congress assembled" apparently referred to the colonies acting together in a kind of partnership-entity, and commanded the plural form of the verb; in the Constitution whether "the United States" is singular or plural is not clear.

tained the relations of that nation with other sovereign nations. But the Constitution does not say so expressly or even by indisputable implication. Indeed, where foreign relations are concerned the Constitution seems a strange, laconic document: although it explicitly lodges important foreign affairs powers in one branch or another of the federal government, and denies important powers to the States, many others are not mentioned.

Constitutional lawyers have been troubled by these lacunae and have struggled to explain and to fill them. No explanation has been universally accepted and no proposed principle of constitutional construction has happily supplied what is missing. Different doctrines suggested have different legal and political consequences. Under all of them, however, foreign affairs remain exclusively national.*

Although "the draftsmen could not often assemble the words of a sentence without some reference to the foreign affairs of the little republic to be," [2] very much about foreign relations went without or with little saying. The Constitution does not delegate a "power to conduct foreign relations" to the federal government or confer it upon any of its branches. Congress is given power to regulate commerce with foreign nations, to define offenses against the law of nations, to declare war, and the President the power to make treaties and send and receive ambassadors, but these hardly add up to the power to conduct foreign relations. Where is the power to recognize other states or governments, to maintain or break diplomatic relations, to open consulates elsewhere and permit them here, to acquire or cede territory, to give or withhold foreign aid, to proclaim a Monroe Doctrine or an Open-Door Policy, indeed to determine all the attitudes and carry out all the details in the myriads of relationships with other nations that are "the foreign policy" and "the foreign relations" of the United States? The power to make treaties is granted, but where is the power to break, denounce, or terminate them? The power to declare war is there, but where is the power to make

* The relevance of federalism for American foreign affairs is discussed in Chapter IX.

16

peace, to proclaim neutrality in the wars of others, to recognize or deny rights to belligerents or insurgents? Congress can punish violations of international law but where is the power to assert rights or to carry out obligations under international law, to make new international law or to disregard or violate law? Congress can regulate foreign commerce but where is the power to make other laws relating to our foreign relations—to regulate immigration, or the status and rights of aliens, or activities of citizens at home or abroad affecting our foreign relations? These "missing" powers, and a host of others, were clearly intended for and have always been exercised by the federal government, but where does the Constitution say that it shall be so?

Traditional interpreters of the Constitution have attempted to find the missing powers by traditional doctrines of constitutional construction. Foreign affairs powers expressly granted have been held to imply others: for example, the power to make treaties implies the power to terminate or break them. And some powers taken together have been found to "result" in others: for example, the power to appoint ambassadors and the power to receive foreign ambassadors "result" in the power to do other things involved in maintaining relations with a foreign country.[3] Foreign affairs powers, we shall see, have been spun also from general grants of power and from designations read as grants, for example, the power of Congress to do what is "necessary and proper" to carry out other powers (Art. I, sec. 8), or the provision vesting in the President "the executive Power" (Art. II, sec. 1). Additional powers for the federal government might be inferred from their express denial to the States.*

The attempt to build all the foreign affairs powers of the federal government with the few bricks provided by the Constitution has not been accepted as successful. It requires considerable stretching of language, much reading between lines, and bold ~~~~~~~~ from "the Constitution as a whole," [4] and that still does not plausibly add up to all the power which the federal gov-

---

* U. S. CONST. Art. I, sec. 10. See Chapter IX.

ernment in fact exercises.* Some of the lacunae were filled when the Supreme Court decided that in addition to the enumerated powers and their derivatives the federal government enjoys some powers inherent in the nationhood and sovereignty of the United States. In *The Chinese Exclusion Case*,[5] for example, the Court found that Congress could legislate to exclude aliens because:

> Jurisdiction over its own territory to that extent is an incident of every independent nation. It is a part of its independence. . . . [T]he United States, in their relation to foreign countries and their subjects or citizens are one nation, invested with powers which belong to independent nations, the exercise of which can be invoked for the maintenance of its absolute independence and security throughout its entire territory.

We are not told where in the Constitution the Court found this grant of power, how it is to be justified in the face of the provision that the powers not delegated to the federal government are reserved to the States, which are the powers that "belong to independent nations" ** or how are they to be determined, by whom they can be exercised, how they relate to the powers expressly conferred upon one branch or another of the Federal Government.

* Nor is it consistent with the allocation of function in practice. In the examples given, the explicit power to make treaties is in the President-and-Senate, but the Senate has achieved no role in the "implied power" to break treaties, and the President and Congress each has claimed authority to do it alone. See Chapter V. Similarly, the Senate has a part in appointing Ambassadors but none in controlling their later activities. Perhaps, it might be argued, the powers in question belong to the President, the Senate's role being only ancillary, and the powers implied in them also belong to the President but not necessarily with a corresponding ancillary power in the Senate. See Chapter II, pp. 39–43.

** That other "independent nations" have a particular power may argue that the United States has it, but does not of itself show that it belongs to the federal government: even the governmental powers reserved to the States under the Constitution would in a unitary system of government be subject to national control as inherent in sovereignty.

Some of these difficulties, the anomalous, "spotty" treatment of foreign relations in the Constitution, and perhaps an impression that the Constitution assumes rather than confers foreign relations powers, probably inspired a singular constitutional theory: the powers of the United States to conduct relations with other nations do not derive from the Constitution! Although this theory did not spring new and full blown from the mind of Mr. Justice Sutherland, it finds authoritative expression, almost 150 years after the Constitution was adopted, in his opinion for the Court in *United States v. Curtiss-Wright Export Corp.*[6] In that case, a Joint Resolution of Congress had authorized the President to embargo arms to the countries at war in the Chaco, and imposed criminal penalties for violating such an embargo. President Franklin Roosevelt proclaimed an embargo and the defendant company, indicted for violating it, challenged the Resolution and the Proclamation as entailing an improper delegation of legislative power to the President. Sustaining the indictment, the Supreme Court held that the principles which limit delegation in domestic affairs do not apply equally in foreign affairs.* Justice Sutherland's opinion includes the following essay:[7]

It will contribute to the elucidation of the question if we first consider the differences between the powers of the federal government in respect of foreign or external affairs and those in respect of domestic or internal affairs. That there are differences between them, and that these differences are fundamental, may not be doubted.

The two classes of powers are different, both in respect of their origin and their nature. The broad statement that the federal government can exercise no powers except those specifically enumerated in the Constitution, and such implied ~~~~~~~ ~~ ~~~ ~~~~~~~~~ ~~~ proper to carry into effect the enumerated powers, is

* The issue of delegation in foreign affairs is discussed in Chapter IV, at pp. 119–20.

categorically true only in respect of our internal affairs. In that field, the primary purpose of the Constitution was to carve from the general mass of legislative powers *then possessed by the states* such portions as it was thought desirable to vest in the federal government, leaving those not included in the enumeration still in the states. . . . That this doctrine applies only to powers which the states had, is self evident. And since the states severally never possessed international powers, such powers could not have been carved from the mass of state powers but obviously were transmitted to the United States from some other source. During the colonial period, those powers were possessed exclusively by and were entirely under the control of the Crown. By the Declaration of Independence, "the Representatives of the United States of America" declared the United [not the several] Colonies to be free and independent states, and as such to have "full Power to levy War, conclude Peace, contract Alliances, establish Commerce and to do all other Acts and Things which Independent States may of right do."

As a result of the separation from Great Britain by the colonies acting as a unit, the powers of external sovereignty passed from the Crown not to the colonies severally, but to the colonies in their collective and corporate capacity as the United States of America. Even before the Declaration, the colonies were a unit in foreign affairs, acting through a common agency—namely the Continental Congress, composed of delegates from the thirteen colonies. That agency exercised the powers of war and peace, raised an army, created a navy, and finally adopted the Declaration of Independence. Rulers come and go; governments end and forms of government change; but sovereignty survives. A political society cannot endure without a supreme will somewhere. Sovereignty is never held in suspense. When, therefore, the external sovereignty of Great Britain in respect of the colonies ceased, it immediately passed to the Union. . . .

The Union existed before the Constitution, which was ordained and established among other things to form "a more perfect Union." Prior to that event, it is clear that the Union, declared by the Articles of Confederation to be "perpetual," was the sole possessor of external sovereignty and in the Union it remained without change save in so far as the Constitution in express terms qualified its exercise. The Framers' Convention was called and exerted its powers upon the irrefutable postulate that though the states were several their people in respect of foreign affairs were one. Compare *The Chinese Exclusion Case*, 130 U.S. 581, 604, 606. . . .

. . . .

It results that the investment of the federal government with the powers of external sovereignty did not depend upon the affirmative grants of the Constitution. The powers to declare and wage war, to conclude peace, to make treaties, to maintain diplomatic relations with other sovereignties, if they had never been mentioned in the Constitution, would have vested in the federal government as necessary concomitants of nationality. . . . As a member of the family of nations, the right and power of the United States in that field are equal to the right and power of the other members of the international family. Otherwise, the United States is not completely sovereign. The power to acquire territory by discovery and occupation . . . , the power to expel undesirable aliens . . . , the power to make such international agreements as do not constitute treaties in the constitutional sense . . . , none of which is expressly affirmed by the Constitution, nevertheless exist as inherently inseparable from the conception of nationality. This the court recognized, and . . .

found the warrant for its conclusions not in the provisions of the Constitution, but in the law of nations.

Although Sutherland invoked *The Chinese Exclusion Case* and others, his theory seems different from and more embracing than theirs. The earlier cases found powers inherent in sovereignty to be vested in the federal government "by the Constitution"; Sutherland apparently believed they are extra-constitutional.* The earlier cases seemed to consider that sovereignty provided powers supplementary to those granted; Sutherland apparently considered sovereignty the principal source of foreign affairs power. While the earlier cases said nothing on the matter, Sutherland insisted that these powers were not delegated by the States in the making of the Constitution.[8]

For clarity, I summarize and restate his theory as I understand it, supplying occasional gloss:

—With independence the former colonies became a sovereign nation. The powers of "internal sovereignty" lay with the individual States, but those of "external sovereignty" were with the Union of States acting together.

—The Constitution created a better union and conferred upon it some of the internal powers previously enjoyed by the individual States. It did not confer upon the new union the powers of external sovereignty, for these had already belonged to the Union before the Constitution. The Constitution did not enumerate them; it assumed them, and, in general, dealt with some of them only where there was some reason for doing it: where the locus of the power within the new federal government reflected change from the Articles or had been the subject of con-

---

* Sutherland in fact does not say explicitly that the foreign affairs powers of the federal government are extra-constitutional, only that they "did not depend upon the affirmative grants of the Constitution." But the thrust of his history and his insistence that the States never had powers of external sovereignty seem to imply my reading.

troversy or compromise, for example, which among the branches of the new government shall make treaties.*

—Since the powers of the United States to conduct its foreign relations, and other powers inherent in national sovereignty, do not derive from the Constitution, one cannot identify them exclusively, or even principally, by construction of or inference and extrapolation from constitutional language. In particular, although some of them are mentioned, foreign affairs powers are not "enumerated powers" and are not denied (or reserved to the States) if they are not enumerated; but one must look elsewhere —to political philosophy, to international law and the practices of nations—to determine their full array. And these powers are not subject to doctrines of interpretation and limitation applicable to powers granted by the Constitution, for example those implied in principles of "separation of powers" or "federalism."

Justice Sutherland's theory has not been unanimously acclaimed.[9] His history, in particular, has been challenged, and surely it is not manifestly all his way: there is disagreement whether the Declaration of Independence declared a single sovereign entity or thirteen independent nation-states; there is evidence that, after independence, at least some of the erstwhile colonies, at least for some time and for some purposes, considered themselves sovereign, independent states; even under the Articles of Confederation it is not wholly clear that "the United States" was a sovereign entity rather than a band of sovereigns acting together through the agency of the Congress. But Sutherland's view of the locus of sovereignty between 1776 and 1789 has strong support; [10] and—what Sutherland's critics have largely overlooked—challenging his history does not necessarily destroy

* Perhaps also to remove doubt, especially as it is not always obvious whether some power is an aspect of external or internal sovereignty, *e. g.*, the power to establish rules of naturalization. Sutherland might add that although the States did not have powers ~~of external~~ sovereignty, the Constitution expressly denied these to them (Art. I, sec. 10) out of abundance of caution and to assure doubly against practices which had troubled the Confederation and were among the principal motivations for the Constitutional Convention. See Chapter IX, p. 227.

his constitutional doctrine. Even if it were assumed, contrary to Justice Sutherland, that the States were each independently sovereign up to (or even during) the Articles of Confederation, the crux of Sutherland's theory might yet stand: the States irrevocably gave up external sovereignty, and the United States became one sovereign nation, upon, or by, adopting the Constitution, but tacitly, by implication, outside the framework of the Constitution and its scheme of enumerated delegations.[11] The Constitution, Sutherland might point out, does not explicitly terminate the sovereignty of the States or declare or recognize the United States a nation, does not confer upon the federal government the powers of national sovereignty generally, or specify many of the powers implied in sovereignty. It is reasonable to conclude, he might say, that the Framers intended to deal in full only with the governance of domestic affairs where the distribution between nation and States was new and critical, where the States retained most of the powers and the new central government was to have only what was given it; but, with a few explicable exceptions, they did not deal with, enumerate, allocate powers in foreign affairs where the federal government was to have all.*

Other criticisms of *Curtiss-Wright*, some of which apply as well to the earlier cases looking to sovereignty for federal power, are not as readily avoided. That there were to be principal powers of government outside the Constitution is not intimated in the Constitution itself, in the records of the Convention, or in the Federalist Papers and other contemporary debates. The Sutherland theory, like the earlier cases finding power in sovereignty, carves a broad exception in the historic conception, often reiterated, never questioned and explicitly reaffirmed in the Tenth

* But the explanation for the "exceptions," which I have supplied—that the Framers dealt only with foreign-affairs powers that were allocated differently from the Articles of Confederation or which were the subject of controversy and compromise—does not explain everything: if so, all of the powers of the President should have been enumerated, since he did not exist under the Articles; and why list some of the powers of Congress—*e. g.*, to declare war—which had not been the subject of reallocation or of controversy?

Amendment, that the federal government is one of enumerated powers only.[12]  It means that a panoply of important powers is to be determined from unwritten, uncertain, changing concepts of international law and practice, developed and growing outside the constitutional tradition and our particular heritage.*

Students of the Constitution may choose between the difficulties with Sutherland's theory and the constitutional deficiencies which it supplied,[13] but his opinion, while containing far more than necessary to his decision,** was joined by six other Justices,† has been cited with approval in later cases, and remains

---

* It also lent itself to the argument that these powers inherent in sovereignty are not subject to constitutional limitations, but that argument has not had wide appeal.  See Chapter X, pp. 253–54.

** Sutherland was not looking for new power for the United States or for either the President or Congress, but only to uphold a broad delegation of power by the Congress to the President.  In domestic affairs, such delegation would have raised serious constitutional questions for most of the Justices; Sutherland needed to show only that foreign affairs were different in this respect.  Today, the limitations on delegation are much relaxed even in domestic affairs.  See Chapter IV, p. 119.  Compare note 14, this chapter.

† Only Justice McReynolds dissented, with an opinion of one sentence.  Justice Stone did not participate in the case.  Only six months earlier Sutherland had written the opinion of the Court in Carter v. Carter Coal Co., 298 U.S. 238 (1936), a 5–4 decision, in which he denied the existence of any unenumerated, "inherent" federal powers in domestic matters; the question of inherent power over external affairs, he there said, "is a wholly different matter which it is not necessary now to consider."  *Id.* at 295.

One may wonder how his *Curtiss-Wright* theory received almost unanimous concurrence in a Court so sharply riven by other fundamental constitutional differences.  Of course, in foreign affairs, States' rights were not an issue and other philosophical differences that divided the Court were also irrelevant.  Individual rights had not yet had their luxuriant growth and in any event did not seem threatened by broad foreign affairs powers.  Perhaps, too, the divided Justices were content, even eager, to find one area of agreement.

authoritative doctrine.[14]  If one hesitates to accept its suggestion that foreign affairs powers are extra-constitutional, or that sovereignty and nationhood are principal sources of power, surely it at least reaffirms the earlier cases holding that sovereignty is an additional source of foreign affairs power.†  Before *Curtiss-Wright*, the Court looked to sovereignty to uphold federal "power to acquire territory by discovery or occupation . . . to expel undesirable aliens . . . to make such international agreements as do not constitute treaties in the constitutional sense," [15] to control immigration, to regulate the conduct of American nationals abroad; [16] since then, it has found there the power to register aliens and to regulate travel and other conduct of American citizens which might affect foreign relations.[17]

"Sovereignty" remains available to assure that no federal exercise of power in foreign affairs will fail for want of constitutional support, but sovereignty need not be doctrine for every day. Usually, a power in question could plausibly be inferred from one of the explicit powers of the President or Congress, to which the Court has given imaginative, liberal, expansive (some will say far-fetched) readings, say, the Commerce Power, or the War Powers of Congress and the President, the limits of which have not yet been found.  For, beginning with the judicial revolution in the year following *Curtiss-Wright*,[18] the Constitution has largely ceased to limit the powers delegated to the federal government, in domestic as in foreign affairs, and federalism, as a limitation on national power, survives only by grace of the Federal Government and the political forces it reflects.[19]  The formal safeguards against tyranny * and abuse of governmental power lie in the specific prohibitions of the Bill of Rights and these apply to the conduct of foreign as well as domestic affairs, whether the powers invoked are deemed to come from within or without the Constitution.**

† See Chapter III, pp. 74–76.

* Apart from those inherent in the separation of powers, Introduction to Chapter II, note 2.

** See Chapter X, pp. 253–54.

Whatever the theory, then, there is virtually nothing related to foreign affairs that is beyond the constitutional powers of the federal government, but when one resorts to sovereignty one meets a particular difficulty: † for while the few powers specifically mentioned in the Constitution are assigned—the President makes treaties (with the advice and consent of two-thirds of the Senate), Congress regulates commerce with foreign nations or declares war—we are not told how the undifferentiated bundle of powers inherent in sovereignty is distributed among the federal branches. It seems to have been assumed that they are distributed "naturally", those that are "legislative in character" to the Congress, those "executive" to the President, with apparently, also, a judicial foreign affairs power lodged in the federal courts.[20] Perhaps that assumption is "natural" and "logical," but its principle of division is hardly self-defining.

A similar difficulty, however, is not wholly avoided by more traditional theories as to sources of power in foreign affairs. Of course, if a foreign affairs power is derived by inference or extrapolation from some express power, both lie in the same hands: if the power to receive ambassadors, for example, includes the power to recognize foreign governments, the President who is expressly given the one has the other as well.* But many foreign affairs powers are not clearly implied in particular enumerations and it is often less than obvious whether some power runs with one of the President's or one belonging to Congress: *e. g.,* does the power to proclaim neutrality as regards other people's wars belong to Congress by virtue of its power to declare war and to regulate foreign commerce, or to the President by virtue of his authority in regard to foreign relations and as Commander-in-

---

† In addition, Sutherland's theory, of course, requires, while traditional views avoid, a sharp distinction between domestic and foreign affairs. Compare *e. g.,* Chapter IV, note 11.

---

* But sometimes, apparently, not identically so—as when the President claims the power to terminate treaties on his own authority though he needs the consent of the Senate to make them. See Chapter V.

Chief? Major struggles for power between the President and Congress, then, are about equally intractable under all theories of constitutional power in foreign affairs.

I deal with these and other questions in the following chapters, according to the scheme which the Constitution itself ordained, by inquiring into the powers of each branch of government.

*THE DISTRIBUTION OF POLITICAL POWER*

By *Curtiss-Wright* the basic constitutional doctrine that "the Federal government can exercise no powers except those specifically enumerated in the Constitution" does not apply to foreign affairs.[1] The doctrine of enumerated, delegated powers, however, is an element of the Constitution's federalism, saving state interests, and even those who eschew the far-reaches of *Curtiss-Wright* claim few States' rights in foreign affairs. The Constitution, all know, reflects also other political principles, in particular "separation of powers" and "checks-and-balances," * and these were not primarily safeguards for federalism but postulates of "good government" and bulwarks against tyranny.[2] Whether one finds the mantle of national authority over foreign relations buried in the Constitution or more-or-less outside it, Separation and checks-and-balances govern the conduct of foreign affairs also, but here they look different, have different consequences, raise different issues.

In domestic affairs the principle of Separation is more-or-less clear and its constitutional consequences more-or-less agreed. The Constitution gives legislative power to Congress, executive power to the President, judicial power to the courts. In a word (though requiring many qualifications), the laws and policies of the federal government are made by the Congress (even if largely, now, on Executive initiative), are carried out and enforced by the President, and applied by the courts in particular cases. Constitutionally, the branches are independent of each other, their

---

* "Separation of powers" and "checks-and-balances" are not identical although they are often confused and indeed are intimately related. Separation lodges executive, legislative and judicial functions in different branches of government. That, of course, results in government that is "balanced" rather than concentrated in one body; because different powers are in different hands, they can check each other by failing to cooperate. But the explicit checks-and-balances of the Constitution are the special devices engrafted on, indeed modifying, separation—the President's veto (and the Congress' power to override it) or the need for Senate consent to the President's appointments and treaties. A principal "check" has been judicial review to determine the constitutionality of governmental action. See Chapter VIII.

provinces, generally, have defined, separate, "natural" outlines, and none may usurp another's functions: in the *Steel Seizure Case,* for a famous instance, the Supreme Court seemed to think that seizure of steel mills to prevent disruption of their operations by a labor dispute obviously and inherently required a legislative act and was therefore not to be done by the President on his own authority.[3] Separation has also been held to imply that one branch may not abdicate its functions by delegating them to another.* Separation provides checks-and-balances since each branch is master of its own essential contribution to the common government. In addition, the President has a check on Congress by his veto, which Congress in turn can override by two-thirds vote of each of its houses. (Art. I, sec. 7) There is a check on the President in the requirement of Senate consent to his appointments. (Art. II, sec. 2)

In the governance of foreign relations, too, the political authority of the United States is lodged in the President and Congress, and one or the other, surely the two together, can do on behalf of the United States whatever any other sovereign nation can do.[4] The foreign relations powers also reflect commitment to Separation and checks-and-balances but what each branch can do alone, when the other is silent or even in the face of its opposition, is not determined by any "natural" division. As they have evolved, the foreign relations powers appear not so much "separated" as fissured, along jagged lines indifferent to classical categories of governmental power: some powers and functions belong to the President, some to Congress, some to the President-and-Senate; some can be exercised by either the President or the Congress, some require the joint authority of both. Irregular, uncertain division renders claims of usurpation more difficult to establish and the courts have not been available to adjudicate them. Delegations by Congress to the President have been extensive and constant and *Curtiss-Wright* tells us that in foreign affairs the principle of Separation does not bar them. The special "checks" are also modified: the President has his usual veto

---

* See Chapter IV, p. 119. I speak here of the political branches; of the courts in Chapter VIII.

on foreign affairs legislation but some insist, for example, that he could not veto a declaration of war;[5] the Senate can check the President's treaties as well as his appointments; treaties and acts of Congress, we shall see, can nullify each other in domestic law.*

The constitutional distribution of foreign relations powers is rooted in the antecedents of the Constitution, and grew out of dissension, vacillation and compromise at the Constitutional Convention. Under the Articles of Confederation there was no executive, and Congress was all: it appointed ambassadors, instructed them, received their reports, followed their activities, approved the treaties they negotiated.[6] In the Congress each State had one vote, and major decisions—*e. g.*, engaging in war or concluding treaties—required the assent of nine of the thirteen States.[7] Outside the Congress—*pace* Justice Sutherland—the States were not above some frolics of their own, sometimes sending their own agents abroad, often disregarding the treaties concluded by the Congress with their assent.[8]

The Constitutional Convention was denying powers to the States, but it was also taking some from Congress. The emergence of the President reflected the felt need for an Executive generally, and dissatisfaction with multiheaded diplomacy in particular.[9] But the Framers were hardly ready to replace the representative inefficiency of many with an efficient monarchy, and unhappy memories of royal prerogative, fear of tyranny, and distrust of any one man, kept the Framers from giving the new President too much head. In the process of constitutional negotiation different formulae were considered—different allocations and combinations of authority, different divisions and partitions of function. In the end and over-all, Congress clearly came first, in the longest article, expressly conferring many, important powers; the Executive came second, principally as executive-agent of Congressional policy. Every grant to the President, including those relating to foreign affairs was in effect a subtraction from Congressional power, eked out slowly, reluctantly, and not without limitations and safeguards. Some functions were kept for

* See Chapter V, p. 163.

Congress—"legislative" functions generally, and the power to declare war. Some powers taken from Congress and given to the President were to be checked by the Senate, a part of Congress, to prevent autocratic power (and to give strong reins to the States). Some powers—perhaps they were thought of as merely "duties" or "functions"—were the President's alone, though what they included and how significant they were to be were perhaps not wholly agreed and appreciated, and are not wholly agreed and appreciated today.

How well the blueprint was conceived is still debated almost two centuries later, and how well the machine has worked is a living issue. Perhaps the "contraption" was doomed to troubles from the beginning, for while the Fathers ended the chaos of diplomacy by Congress and of state adventurism, the web of authority they created, from fear of too-much government and through contemporary political compromise, virtually elevated inefficiency and controversy to the plane of principle, especially in foreign relations.

For the Framers, moreover, foreign relations seemed to consist wholly of making or not-making war and making or not-making treaties. Surely, though building magnificently, perhaps better than they knew, the Framers could not foresee what the United States would become, what the world would become. Even in domestic affairs, there are gaps between the "paper powers" and the real powers, between the patterns of Separation and checks-and-balances conceived and those realized. That in foreign relations the division of power was irregular and uncertain has made it the more susceptible to shaping, even distortion, by evolving institutions and by the realities of foreign relations for an expanding, transforming country in a changing world.

Irregular partition has encouraged rivalry and, since the respective allocations are not "natural," well-defined or explicit, has led to tugging for more of the blanket under claim of constitutional right. Concurrent jurisdiction has led to competition for initiative, sometimes to inconsistent policies, without an accepted constitutional principle for resolving them. Division of a common enterprise between independent, competing branches has begotten interference or failure of cooperation and, for the lawyer, issues as to whether cooperation is constitutionally prescribed or interference constitutionally forbidden. Realities have further modified the theoretical divisions, for in the competition of the political branches the President has had most of the advantages and Congress has not always been able to maintain its prerogatives.

The Constitution begins with the powers of Congress. The constitutional law of foreign relations, I believe, must begin with the President.

# *Chapter II.* THE PRESIDENT

Students of American government, and citizens generally, know that American foreign relations are in the charge of the President. Foreign governments believe that it is principally he who determines American policy towards them. The Supreme Court of the United States has described "the very delicate, plenary and exclusive power of the President as the sole organ of the federal government in the field of international relations." [1]

A stranger reading the Constitution would get little inkling of such large Presidential authority, for the powers explicitly vested in him are few and seem modest, far fewer and more modest than those bestowed upon Congress.[2] What the Constitution says and does not say, then, can not have determined what the President can and can not do. The structure of the federal government, the facts of national life, the realities and exigencies of international relations, the practices of diplomacy, have afforded Presidents unique temptations and unique opportunities to acquire unique powers.

In the President's competition with Congress, his advantages have been many, some general (for example, those deriving from his party leadership and control of patronage), others particular to foreign relations. From the beginning the President has been the organ of communication with foreign governments and had control of the channels of information—the voice as well as the eyes and ears of the United States. As Commander-in-Chief he was also its ever-stronger arms. He has been one, and the Con-

many and increasing. Diplomacy by Congress was ineffectual even under the Articles of Confederation when international relations were few and limited, and Congress was unicameral and small; an enlarging Congress could not begin to master the proliferating, complex affairs of a growing country with interests flung far about a growing international society. Unlike Congress, the President is always "in session." He can move quickly and secretly. Whether as a matter of international law or the laws of international politics, he can effectively commit the United States,* and Congress and Congressmen cannot lightly or effectively oppose him.

As a result, in addition to powers which were indisputably the President's by explicit enumeration, many more came to him by accretion, some will say by usurpation never effectively re-captured. Powers which Congress has continued to dispute with-out resolution have been exercised by the President as though the disputes had been resolved in his favor. And Congress itself has found it necessary to delegate to him enormous additional power.

If constitutional language has not determined Presidential pre-eminence, it has not been irrelevant to its achievement. Much of what the President has attained may indeed lie in or between the lines of the Constitution, and all of it has been shaped by what is there. Presidents did not achieve their powers at one blow, and respectable claims to constitutional legitimacy have been compelling weapons in the struggles to acquire and retain them. Despite his predominance, moreover, the President is never whol-ly independent of Congressional cooperation or acquiescence and these are more forthcoming when he holds firmer constitutional ground. Constitutional legitimacy is important to Presidents al-so to maintain a principal source of their power, the confidence of their national constituency, the people of the United States. And though the courts have not been generally available to check alleged Presidential usurpation in foreign affairs, Presidents know that judicial review lies in wait and might yet strike them down. (The ultimate Congressional sanction of impeachment, too, is not wholly a paper weapon.) Presidents, finally, take a solemn oath to execute their office faithfully and to preserve

* On the President's power to commit the United States, see Chap-ter VI.

the Constitution (Art. II, sec. 1, cl. 7), and all of them have undoubtedly taken that oath seriously.[3]

Like the Constitution, I speak of the President as an individual occupying an individual office. Today, all know, the President is the chief officer of the Executive Branch of millions of employees, of whom many thousands are directly involved in the conduct of foreign relations and many thousands more shape them importantly. The vast majority of executive decisions are made, the vast majority of actions are taken, without the participation or even the knowledge of the President. Nonetheless, in principle, the authorized acts of the President's "foreign affairs establishment" are the President's, claim his constitutional power and are subject to his limitations.* But constitutional theory and law, too, cannot blink the realities of the process and one may expect that the Supreme Court would give greater scope to the President's own decision than to one taken by a "middle-level" officer of the Department of State.[4]

## The Constitutional Sources of Presidential Power

For the constitutional lawyer consideration of the President's powers in foreign affairs begins with the language of the Constitution. Of course, if, as Justice Sutherland taught, the authority of the federal government in foreign relations derives from national sovereignty and is basically extra-constitutional, the powers of the President might also have to be sought elsewhere; but one would nonetheless seek in the Constitution some guidance as to which of the nation's sovereign powers are the President's to exercise.

One general theory of Presidential power might eliminate this enquiry or at least radically change its focus. In his Autobiography, written after he left office, Theodore Roosevelt said: [5]

The most important factor in getting the right spirit in my Adminis~~tration~~ ~~was my insistence upon~~

---

* The authority of the President to delegate to subordinates has not raised significant constitutional questions, none that matter in foreign affairs. See Chapter IV, note 97.

the theory that the executive power was limited only by specific restrictions and prohibitions appearing in the Constitution or imposed by the Congress under its Constitutional powers. My view was that every executive officer, and above all every executive officer in high position, was a steward of the people bound actively and affirmatively to do all he could for the people, and not to content himself with the negative merit of keeping his talents undamaged in a napkin. I declined to adopt the view that what was imperatively necessary for the Nation could not be done by the President unless he could find some specific authorization to do it. My belief was that it was not only his right but his duty to do anything that the needs of the Nation demanded unless such action was forbidden by the Constitution or by the laws.

This "stewardship theory," surely, would apply to foreign relations as to other responsibilities of national government, and one might therefore move immediately to consider what the Constitution expressly forbids to the President and what are the powers of Congress which would support prohibitions on his authority. But while Roosevelt's theory might reflect how some Presidents have acted in emergency, it has not been accepted in principle: William Howard Taft, for example—also writing out of office—expressly rejected that "unsafe" notion,[6] and the Supreme Court's opinion in the *Steel Seizure Case* [7] could hardly be squared with it. Even the "stewardship" theory, moreover, would no doubt claim some support in constitutional text.

Article II provides that the President "shall have the Power, by and with the Advice and Consent of the Senate, to make Treaties," and—also subject to the advice and consent of the Senate—to "appoint Ambassadors, other Public Ministers and Consuls"; a subsequent section states that he "shall receive Ambassadors and other public Ministers." On the face of it, this is all the Constitution empowers the President to do in regard to other nations. It is strikingly little. The making of treaties is an important but occasional activity; the appointment of ambassadors is generally less consequential and even more infrequent; and both are powers which the President can exercise only with the consent of the Senate (the former requiring even a two-thirds majority). Receiving ambassadors seems a function rather than a "power," * a ceremony which in many countries is performed by a figurehead. It seems incredible that these few meager grants support the most powerful office in the world and the multi-varied, wide-flung webwork of foreign activity of the most powerful nation in the world.

Since no one believes that the President's powers are only what, on their face, these clauses say, those who resist looking beyond the enumerated grants have had to insist that they are not as flimsy as appears.[8] The powers to appoint and receive ambassadors, they would say, imply power to recognize (or not to recognize) governments and to establish (or not to establish) relations with them; and to modify or terminate relations by withdrawing our ambassador or having a foreign ambassador recalled. It does not fetch too far to infer also power to do all that is involved in relations with other nations: establishing and maintaining channels for intercourse and communication; instructing and informing our ambassadors and receiving their reports, inquiries and recommendations; exchanging information and views with foreign governments. For some it is only another step to conclude that the President must be able to decide also the contents of communications to his ambassadors and to foreign gov-

---

* While making treaties and appointing ambassadors are described as "powers" of the President (Article II, section 2), receiving ambassadors is included in section 3 which does not speak in terms of power but lists things the President "shall" or "may" do.

At least while they were urging ratification of the Constitution, both Hamilton and Madison claimed little for that clause: "This, though it has been a rich theme of declamation, is more a matter of dignity than of authority. It is a circumstance which will be without consequence in the administration of the government. . . ." THE FEDERALIST N̶ . . . (Hamilton). Compare *id.* No. 42 at 302–303 (Madison). Hamilton later saw this and other clauses in Article II, section 3, as sources of power. Compare the "Pacificus-Helvidius" exchange, this chapter, note 9; and see Jefferson, this chapter, note 18.

ernments, *i. e.*, the attitudes and intentions of the United States that constitute American foreign policy. Similarly, some will say, the power to make treaties implies too the power to interpret and implement treaties, scrutinize their operation, even denounce or break them. And if the President can determine the nation's foreign policy by treaty is it not reasonable to infer that foreign policy is his responsibility even when formal international commitment is not involved?

Such arguments are not intrinsically more extravagant than other, established constitutional interpretations, but some of them seem strained and unpersuasive. Those deriving from the power to make treaties or to appoint ambassadors suggest, at most, authority in the President and Senate jointly. What is more, one can with equal plausibility suggest extrapolations and inferences from the enumerated powers of Congress that would lodge control of American foreign policy and relations in that body rather than in the President.*

If constitutional clauses are to support, justify and explain the growth of Presidential power, more must be found. Some more, we shall see, was found in two other clauses which Presidents have turned to use as sources of power in the conduct of foreign relations: the President is "Commander in Chief of the Army and Navy of the United States"; and he "shall take Care that the Laws be faithfully executed." Perhaps because these too seemed insufficient, others sought, and found, a cleaner, larger grant of Presidential power. Alexander Hamilton early insisted that the Constitution expressly vested in the President all authority over foreign relations, with few and clear exceptions.[9] While Article I, he noted, gives to Congress "All legislative Powers *herein granted*" (emphasis supplied), Article II begins: "The executive Power shall be vested in a President of the United States of America." The President, then, is not limited to the powers that are expressly enumerated; he has all of "the executive Power." It included, of course, the authority and responsibility to execute the laws enacted by the legislature; it included in addition a recognized

---

* See Chapter III, pp. 81 *et seq.*

congeries of independent, major, substantive powers "to determine the condition of the nation" in its foreign relations. (The executive power, Hamilton might have added, was not defined because it was well understood by the Framers raised on Locke, Montesquieu and Blackstone.)[10] The enumerations that follow that grant are mere emphasis, some of them, indeed, designed to modify and limit the general grant: for example, the powers to appoint Ambassadors and make treaties are the President's only subject to advice and consent of the Senate.[11]

If the "executive Power" clause constitutes a large grant of power, the accumulation by the President of vast powers in foreign affairs is neither surprising nor improper (and the Constitution ceases to be as strangely inarticulate about foreign affairs as appears).\* But that view, often stated, has been as often challenged; when Hamilton launched it, Madison lashed out at him for attempting to import into the Constitution British monarchical prerogatives.[12] The Supreme Court has not considered it as a possible source of constitutional power to conduct foreign relations,[13] and its use to support other Presidential claims has had a mixed reception. Earlier in this century the Court drew on the "executive Power" clause to support the President's authority to remove a postmaster in disregard of an Act of Congress requiring the Senate's consent for such removal.[14] More recently, in the *Steel Seizure Case,* the Court's opinion pointedly refrained from giving it heed.[15] Indeed, Mr. Justice Jackson—who as Attorney General had justified extended Presidential powers \*\*— concurring, said: [16]

> I cannot accept the view that this clause is a grant in
> bulk of all conceivable executive power but regard it as

---

\* See Chapter I. Justice Sutherland would also have a ready answer as to how the powers inherent in sovereignty are distributed (Chapter I, p. 27): on this view, except as otherwise provided, the Constitution lodged ~~~ ~~~ ~~~ ~~~ ~~~ ~~~ ~~~ the President.

\*\* See especially his famous opinion upholding the "destroyers for bases" agreement, Chapter VI, p. 179.

an allocation to the presidential office of the generic powers thereafter stated.

The few enumerated powers of the President apart, the constitutional lawyer, I fear, will here, too, have the hard choice between the theory that the conduct of foreign affairs, undefined, was indeed "granted in bulk" to the President as executive power, and the need to scrounge among and stretch spare constitutional clauses to eke out full powers which the President commands and many of which he was probably intended to have.[17] The choice made will turn in part on "general principles" and theories of constitutional interpretation, in part, no doubt, on political disposition, even on taste; it will probably not decide concrete issues of Presidential power. "Executive Power" to "transact business" with foreign nations is hardly self-defining and may seem large, but constitutional history is witness that inference and extrapolation from accepted, enumerated powers, too, do not compel narrow conceptions of constitutional authority. Either line of constitutional construction will have to accept that some is denied the President by implication in what is granted to others. All will agree that by constitutional exegesis, by inferences and extrapolations small and large, at least by sanctifying reference to the express grants and the mantle of "executive Power," Presidents have achieved and legitimated an undisputed, extensive, predominant, sometimes exclusive "foreign affairs power," though—like its constitutional underpinnings—its scope and content remain less-than-certain.

## The Scope and Content of Presidential Power

What the President can and cannot constitutionally do in foreign affairs has been in issue from Washington's day. The Supreme Court has decided little and most of that long ago, and precedent, partisan debate and scholarly speculation have yielded only partial resolution. But Presidents continue to act, sometimes to applause, sometimes to grudging acquiescence, sometimes to bitter condemnation and challenge, and action and reaction are also stuff of constitutional law.

In law as in politics what matters is the total of Presidential power rather than the shape and size of its individual components. Constitutionally, every Presidential act stands on all his powers together (as well as those delegated to him by Congress). Presidents need not and do not plead their powers with precision, or match particular act to particular power, and the lawyer is often hard-put to determine even the President's own view as to the reach of his various resources of constitutional authority. But the constitutional sum of Presidential power depends on its parts, and, however imprecisely, analysis measures them singly.

The President's explicit power to make treaties (with the advice and consent of two-thirds of the Senators present) is beyond question, and has its own extensive law (Chapter V.) His powers to appoint ambassadors (with Senate advice and consent) and to receive foreign ambassadors in themselves raise only small issues and need little elaboration, and these are better considered in the context of a broader "foreign affairs power."

## The Foreign Affairs Power: "Sole Organ"

Undefined and undifferentiated invocations of a Presidential "foreign affairs power" alternate with, and may derive from, innumerable references to John Marshall's early characterization: "The President is sole organ of the nation in its external relations, and its sole representative with foreign nations." [18] It is not apparent that either "foreign affairs power" or "sole organ" aspires to legal precision or that they imply different measures of constitutional authority; both have come to describe a constitutional "power," supplementing if not subsuming those specified, supporting a variety of Presidential actions not expressly authorized by the Constitution.

Even narrowly conceived, "sole organ" implies legal authority in the President and legal limitations on others in that only he (not notably. C~~~ ~~~ ~~~ ~~~ ~~~ ~~~ ~~~ ~~~ ~~~ ~~~ foreign govern~~~ ments.* In legal principle as in practice, the President's monopoly

---

* I deal with the limitations on Congress in Chapters III and IV, pp. 87–88, 92–94.

of communication with foreign governments derives in large part from his control of the foreign relations "apparatus." By Article II he appoints "Ambassadors, other public Ministers and Consuls," subject to Senate approval; he fills other offices, created by Congress, in many cases without Senate approval.** Those whose functions are purely "executive" can be removed by him.[19] They report and are responsible to him, he directs and instructs them, and determines what they shall communicate and what they shall withhold.[20]

Beginning with George Washington, Presidents have also appointed innumerable "agents" without asking the Senate, and in some cases have even purported to give them the "personal rank of ambassador." [21] For the most part, these have been sent for particular missions, as John Jay by Washington to negotiate a treaty, or Harry Hopkins by Franklin Roosevelt to develop "lend-lease"; many have been delegates to international conferences, some have gone on fact-finding errands. The constitutional requirement of Senate consent was considered inapplicable because these agents, whatever they were called, were not appointed to permanent "offices," did not serve indefinitely, did not have emoluments of office (often not even compensation), or duties prescribed by the Constitution or by Congress.[22] The practice has not been effectively challenged and is doubtless irreversible, but from time to time the Senate will probably object to particular appointments.

** Article II, section 2, provides that the President shall appoint, with the consent of the Senate, "all other Officers of the United States, whose Appointments are not herein otherwise provided for, and which shall be established by Law; but the Congress may by Law vest the Appointment of such inferior Officers, as they think proper, in the President alone, in the Courts of Law, or in the Heads of Departments." Much of the President's "foreign affairs establishment" is appointed by the President alone, and while many, including all Foreign Service Officers, are subject to Senate approval, it is largely perfunctory. For issues arising out of Senate or Congressional control of executive personnel, see Chapter IV, pp. 116–18 and notes 83–86.

As "sole organ," the President determines also how, when, where and by whom the United States should make or receive communications, and there is nothing to suggest that he is limited as to time, place, form, or forum.* He receives "Ambassadors and other public Ministers" by explicit authorization in Article II, but he also determines how many lesser diplomats shall come and be accredited; and he "receives" heads of state or of government, foreign ministers and special envoys.[23] He also decides whom he will not receive and who shall go home, as when, in a celebrated first instance, Washington demanded the recall of Citizen Genêt.**

Issues begin to burgeon when, as "sole organ" or under his "foreign affairs power," the President presumes to determine also the attitudes, decisions and actions which are the foreign policy of the United States. It has sometimes been said that the President has power to conduct foreign relations but not to make foreign policy.[24] In fact a President could not conduct foreign relations without thereby making foreign policy. But if the division were feasible and meaningful it is contradicted by what Presidents have done and do daily beyond challenge. It is no longer questioned that the President does not merely perform the ceremony of receiving foreign ambassadors but also determines whether the United States should recognize or refuse to recognize foreign governments and whether to maintain or terminate relations with them.† Presidents have established their authority to determine other policy which international usage,

---

* Congress has purported unsuccessfully to control the President's participation in international conferences. See Chapter IV, pp. 112–13.

** ". . . thereby establishing a precedent followed by later Presidents again and again, and more than once in the face of impending war." CORWIN, THE PRESIDENT 182 and notes.

† On several occasions in the past Congress pretended to share in the power of recognit̶i̶o̶n̶ ̶.̶ ̶.̶ ̶.̶ cise it independently; but it was claiming a concurrent power, not denying it to the President. Today Congress recognizes the President's sole and exclusive authority in these matters. See Chapter IV, p. 93.

unhappily, captures in the same, ambiguous word "recognition" —whether to recognize (or not to recognize) new states (*e. g.*, Bangladesh, but not Biafra); the conquest and incorporation of territory (Japanese authority over conquered Manchuria in 1932 or Soviet incorporation of the Baltic republics); especially in earlier times,[25] the status of belligerency or insurgency (Franco's forces in the Spanish Civil War). Hamilton's celebrated exposition of the executive character of foreign relations supported the constitutionality of Washington's proclamation of American neutrality in the war between France and Great Britain. In more recent times "neutrality" has generally been proclaimed pursuant to Congressional resolution, but Presidents have not admitted that they could not act on their own and they have sometimes deviated from Congressional neutrality policy.[26]

The President asserts rights and assumes duties for the United States. In addition to treaties (requiring Senate consent) he makes international agreements of varying importance and formality on his sole authority,* and he acts and speaks the part of the United States in the mysterious process by which customary international law is formed. He claims reparation when another state violates our international rights—when it invades our territory, harasses our ships at sea, infringes our sovereign or diplomatic immunities or privileges or properties, violates treaty obligations, abuses our citizens or confiscates their property. He can stake out new claims for the United States, for example, to acquire territory by discovery or prescription, or to proclaim rights to the mineral resources of our continental shelf.[27] He can also waive our rights, and he can disregard our obligations and

---

* See Chapter VI. Some international obligations of the United States are law of the United States and subject to the President's express duty to see that the laws are faithfully executed. See Chapter V, p. 157. Other undertakings by the United States, however, and the obligations of other states to the United States, have no status as domestic law, and Presidential authority as to them can plausibly be found only in his foreign affairs power. Compare pp. 55–56, 223–24 below.

commit other violations of international law.† It is to the President that other nations turn with claims that the United States has violated their rights, and he can give or deny satisfaction.[28] Even when no rights or obligations are in issue, he responds to other overtures by foreign governments—for example, requests for extradition.[29] He has admitted foreign officials and foreign troops and vessels.[30] And he acts for the United States at its borders even in ways and for purposes that only indirectly involve "foreign policy" or communication and relations with foreign governments: he can exclude aliens; [31] President Grant admitted undersea cables and President Wilson electric current from Canada.[32]

The President surely "makes foreign policy," too, when he declares the attitudes and intentions of the United States in matters that concern other nations. The celebrated "Doctrines" (Monroe's or Truman's or Eisenhower's) or the Open-Door Policy are only famous and dramatic examples; * the President makes and expresses foreign policy, say, by inviting a chief-of-state to visit, or smiling upon a request for a loan, and daily (through his many representatives) in other small deeds and words and gestures toward other nations showing and promising more or less friendliness or hostility. It is foreign policy when Presidents encourage or discourage other governments, or assert displeasure or concern about their policies or actions.

That Presidents have asserted these and other powers related to foreign affairs is not conclusive evidence that they were entitled to do so under the Constitution, and some of their acts and claims have been challenged; ** some can be sustained without

† On the power of the President to interpret and implement treaties, react to their violation by others, or terminate them, see Chapter V, pp. 167–71.

* Presidents have sometimes sought Congressional approval for such doctrines ... they believed they did not need it. See Chapter IV, note 50; compare this chapter, note 42.

** Compare the discussion of the "Commitments Resolution" in Chapter VI, pp. 182–84.

admitting independent Presidential authority because they draw authority from an act of Congress or a treaty. But the broader theories and recurrent practice lend support to the view that the President's powers in foreign affairs are "plenary"—Justice Sutherland's word—and that nothing is inherently outside his domain.[33] His powers are limited, of course, by implications in grants to Congress (see Chapter IV), and by the prohibitions applicable to all acts of government; some of what Presidents have done in the past might today be successfully challenged under the Bill of Rights. (Chapter X)

## The Commander-in-Chief

The President has more than one hat, he wears them at the same time, and he can act under one or another or all together. In addition to his "foreign affairs power" the President is "Commander in Chief of the Army and Navy of the United States," and that clause, too, has inspired independent Presidential initiative in foreign relations.

There is little evidence that the Framers intended more than to establish in the President civilian command of the forces for wars declared by Congress (or when the United States was attacked)—the lesson learned from their unhappy experience with "war by Congress" after independence and under the Articles of Confederation. In the Federalist papers, Alexander Hamilton (later a leading proponent of large Presidential power) depreciated the significance of the Commander-in-Chief clause: [34]

> It would amount to nothing more than the Supreme command and direction of the military and naval forces, as first general and admiral of the Confederacy; while that of the British king extends to the *declaring* of war and to the *raising* and *regulating* of fleets and armies,—all which, by the Constitution under consideration, would appertain to the legislature.

Explicitly, Hamilton was denying to the Commander-in-Chief only those powers expressly granted by the Constitution to Congress. But generals and admirals, even when they are "first," do not determine the political purposes for which troops are to be used; they command them in the execution of policy made by others. Later, however, Presidents found in that clause substantive, "policy-making" authority. Presidents claimed authority to make rules for the government and regulation of the land and naval forces,[35] although that power was explicitly given to Congress (Art. I, sec. 8, cl. 14); they have used troops for political purposes and have even taken action not involving use of the armed forces for "military" reasons.†

Some of the "military" powers which Presidents have asserted derived from and related to war, and the "Commander-in-Chief" clause became a principal foundation for the growth of Presidential "war powers". Lincoln, in particular, in an unprecedented emergency claimed unprecedented powers, and while he asserted them temporarily, pending ratification by Congress, other Presidents have claimed them independently of Congress. Lincoln's powers were exercised during Civil War and largely vis-à-vis the domestic enemy; * later Presidents claimed them as well, perhaps *a fortiori*, during foreign wars and in relation to foreign nations. As Commander-in-Chief in war declared by Congress, the President has exercised full and exclusive control of the conduct of war ** (though how much he could do without authorization from Congress is uncertain and largely academic since he has usually had broad delegations in advance, or ratifications

† Compare notes 30, 41, and 42, this chapter.

* Lincoln, then, could also plausibly rely on his authority to see that the Constitution and the laws of the United States be faithfully executed. See this chapter, note 55. He acted also in warranted expectation that Congress would ratify what he did. Some of Lincoln's acts might afford a precedent for Presidential authority in foreign wars as well, *e. g.*, closing the post offices to treasonable mail, taking money from the treasury, enlarging the Army. See CORWIN, THE PRESIDENT 231, 449. For important initiatives by F.D.R. in World War II, see *id.* at 242 *et seq.*, and note 6, this chapter.

** Including powers to act within the United States in relation to Ame~~ri~~~~ci~~ ~~t~~ ~~··~~ ~~···~~ ~~See~~ CORWIN, THE PRESIDENT 242 *et seq*. See generally C. BERDAHL, WAR POWERS OF THE EXECUTIVE IN THE UNITED STATES 131–34 (1921). As to competition between the President and Congress in the control of the conduct of war, see Chapter IV, pp. 107–108.

soon after). He can exercise the rights which the state-of-war accords the United States under international law in regard to the enemy as well as to neutrals.[36] He has authority to enter into armistice agreements terminating hostilities, although some armistices have had long duration, some have determined the terms of later peace treaties (as with Germany after World War I), and one—in Korea (1953)—has never been replaced by a political peace treaty.* Presumably as Commander in Chief (though perhaps with other supporting authority) Presidents have concluded wartime agreements, as at Yalta and Potsdam, which not only prescribed for the conduct of the war but determined major post-war dispositions. Presidents have occupied and governed enemy territory long after hostilities ceased, and courts established under their authority can try even American citizens.[37]

Without a Congressional declaration of war, the power of the President to use the troops and do anything else necessary to repel invasion is beyond question;[38] Wilson even claimed the right to strike deep in Mexico.[39] The President has power not merely to take measures to meet the invasion, but to wage in full the war imposed upon the United States.[40] In our day of instant war, all assume that the President would have the power to retaliate against a nuclear attack, if only on the theory that retaliation was a form of defense and might prevent or deter a second strike;** probably, he has authority also to anticipate by a preemptive strike an attack he believes imminent.

The Commander-in-Chief clause has also provided the President important authority as regards the wars of others.

* Wilson expressed the view that the armistice he concluded in 1918 was within his constitutional powers and obligated the United States to conclude a peace treaty in accordance with its terms. See S. Doc. No. 120, 66th Cong., 1st Sess. 173 (1919). But compare WRIGHT 241. As to the President's power to end a state-of-war, see Chapter IV, p. 105 and note 37.

** Presumably he has constitutional authority to retaliate even for retribution only. The moral issues in such retaliation have not been widely considered.

Washington's Neutrality Proclamations in the war between England and France, and Franklin Roosevelt's deviations from Congressional neutrality policy to aid those fighting Hitler before we were at war, built in part on power as Commander-in-Chief.* Before we entered World War I Wilson closed a wireless station which would not undertake to abide by naval censorship regulations,[41] and armed merchant vessels for protection against German submarines.[42]

Most controversial have been Presidential assertions of the right to use the armed forces for purposes short of war. Since Jefferson sent the Navy against the Barbary pirates to protect American shipping, Presidents have asserted the right to send troops abroad on their own authority in "more than 125" instances [43] differing widely in purpose and magnitude. The President has frequently directed naval vessels to "show the flag"; he used the Navy to "open up" Japan; sent troops to protect American lives and other interests in China early in the century; stationed troops in the Philippines for common defense; sent marines to Nicaragua in the 1920's to fight "bandits," to Lebanon in 1958 to discourage external intervention, to the Dominican Republic in 1965 to prevent an undesirable government; imposed a naval "quarantine" in 1962 in the Cuban missile crisis.[44] American participation in hostilities in Korea and in Vietnam began on the President's sole authority.

By repeated exercise without successful opposition, Presidents have established their authority to send troops abroad probably beyond effective challenge, at least where Congress is silent, but the constitutional foundations and the constitutional limits of that authority remain in dispute. Such authority no doubt resides somewhere in the government of a sovereign nation; constitutional Scripture does not explicitly grant it to Congress or deny it to the President, and it provides some text to support his initiatives. Some have argued that the Commander-in-Chief can use as he will the forces he commands. But that view of the constitutional design is not persuasive [45] and Presi-

* See this chapter, note 26.

dential acts and their justifications do not support or require it. It is more plausible to urge that while as Commander-in-Chief the President's policy initiatives are limited, he can use the troops he commands in support of his other substantive powers.[46] In modern instances, one can say that President Truman stationed troops in Europe pursuant to his authority to carry out the obligations of the North Atlantic Treaty; President Eisenhower sent Marines to deter intervention by others in Lebanon under his foreign affairs power; President Kennedy sent airplanes to save civilians in the Congo under his authority to protect American citizens abroad.[47] In the result, since a military mission abroad generally supports a foreign affairs purpose, the President's "plenary" foreign affairs power may support uses of the troops as largely as would an unlimited Commander-in-Chief power. That he must rely on another "substantive" power, however, is not only more palatable in constitutional theory, but may make a difference: it rejects the notion that the armed forces are the President's "private army" and requires that their use be for a national purpose within the President's constitutional authority; and the President's inexplicit, undefined foreign affairs power, we shall see, is not wholly impervious to Congressional control.*

## "He shall take Care that the Laws be faithfully executed"

That the President has yet another hat is implied in the common understanding of "executive," and Article II expressly adds: "He shall take Care that the Laws be faithfully executed." Although the words suggest duty and responsibility they have served as a source of power in ways relevant also to foreign affairs.

The principal purport of the clause, no doubt, was that the President shall be a loyal agent of Congress to enforce its laws. For our purposes, then, he is required—and has the power—to assure that Congressional legislation affecting international relations (say, a regulation of foreign commerce) is carried out

---

* I consider below, in Chapter IV, the play between the President's powers and those of Congress, in particular its power to declare war.

as law of the land. Treaties and customary international law, we shall see, are also law of the land and Presidents have asserted responsibility (and authority) to interpret our international obligations and to see that they are "faithfully executed," even when Congress has not enacted implementing legislation.* In the past that authority has been invoked to send troops to various parts of Latin America for purposes short of war when required by treaty;** to extradite persons to a foreign country;[48] to suppress piracy and slave trade;[49] to restore to a foreign government its vessels or other property;[50] to compel Americans to honor the obligations of neutrality, even to intern foreign insurgents when the United States was obligated to do so under an international convention.[51]

The "take care" clause has also been said to justify Presidential action to vindicate rights of the United States under international law.[52] The argument seems to be that since "the Laws" include treaties and international law,† the President has the duty and the power to see to it that foreign nations observe these laws, and he can do so by every means including the use of force, as, for example, against the Barbary pirates.[53] The argument is clever but not compelling. Surely, authority to see that the laws shall be executed means that the President shall enforce the law of the United States [54] (including international law and obligations that constitute United States law) where American law applies, that is, within the United States or in regard to the United States Government or its citizens; [55] there is nothing whatever to suggest that the "take care" clause was intended to extend to violations of international obligations

---

* See Chapter V, pp. 157–58.

** For example, to Panama to maintain the guarantee in the Columbia treaty of 1846, to Mexico (1882–94), Cuba (1903), Haiti (1916); see WRIGHT 217, 227. More recently Presidents claimed authority to send troops to Korea and Vietnam in part pursuant to their responsibilities ~~under~~ obligations under the UN Charter and the South-East Asia Treaty. Compare the debates about sending troops to Europe pursuant to the North Atlantic Treaty, Chapter IV, p. 106.

† See Chapter V, p. 156, Chapter VIII, p. 221.

to the United States, committed outside the United States, by those not subject to the laws of the United States.** In such cases stronger and more persuasive support for Presidential action might be found in a broad foreign affairs power (supplemented by authority as Commander-in-Chief), although reasonable men continue to differ as to whether those powers are strong and persuasive enough.

The authority to see that the laws are faithfully executed is sometimes invoked to support Presidential initiatives exercising rights granted to the United States by treaty, pursuing general policies established by treaty, or exercising discretion in foreign affairs delegated him by Congress. Again, that such initiatives were contemplated by the "take care" clause is less-than-obvious,[56] but that the President has such authority is not now questionable.

## Presidential "Legislation"

The powers we have been discussing authorize the President to perform acts having international character. Although "legislative powers" in foreign affairs (for example, to define and punish piracy) are conferred upon Congress and presumably denied the President,* some of the President's international acts also have domestic effect as law in the United States. The President makes domestic law, we shall see, when he makes a treaty or executive agreement which becomes the law of the land, or when he decides to violate international law, or denounce or break an international agreement, and thereby denies them effect as law of the land.† There are domestic legal consequences when the President decides to recognize or not to recognize a foreign government.[57] President Truman made law when he proclaimed the right of the United States to exploit the re-

---

** Compare the argument that United States courts should refuse to give effect to foreign acts of state which violate international law because international law is part of the law of the United States, Chapter VIII, p. 223.

* See Chapter III, pp. 72–74, Chapter IV, p. 95.

† See Chapters V, p. 155, VI, pp. 184, 188, VIII, pp. 221–22.

sources of her continental shelf. It was law by almost any definition when, on his sole authority, President Washington proclaimed neutrality, or President Truman established occupation law and occupation courts in Germany and subjected American citizens to them.

In these instances governing law of the United States is made or modified as a by-product of international action by the President. No one has suggested that under the President's "plenary" foreign affairs powers he can, by executive act or order, enact law directly regulating persons and property in the United States.** In at least one regard, however—sovereign and diplomatic immunity from the jurisdiction of American courts—the courts have given effect to declarations by the Executive Branch as to an act of Congress or of a legislative agency.

Understanding the cases requires background and context. The courts, we shall see, ascertain and apply international law "as often as questions of right depending upon it are duly presented for their determination." [58] If, in a case before it, a court finds that under international law the defendant (or his property at stake in the case) enjoys immunity from judicial process, it dismisses the proceeding. In deciding whether international law accords immunity in the circumstances, the courts have often sought or received from the Department of State "suggestions" about the identity and status of the defendant or of the property before the court. Sometimes they have received, too, executive expressions of opinion as to what international law required, but while these were accorded "great weight," the courts decided the question of immunity themselves on the basis of their own conclusions as to what international law required. In 1926, in the *Pesaro* case, for example, the Supreme Court concluded that under international law a ship owned and operated by the Italian Government was immune from the jurisdiction of our courts even though the ship was used in the

---

** See Chapter IV, p. 95. Even Wilson's closing of the Marconi station (p. 53 this chapter) might be seen as executing neutrality rather than "legislating." On the President's power to legislate by authority delegated him by Congress see Chapter IV, p. 118.

carriage of merchandise for hire,[59] although the State Department had for some time urged a "restrictive theory" that would accord immunity only for "governmental" not for "commercial" activities of foreign governments.[60]

In 1943, in Ex parte *Republic of Peru,* the Supreme Court struck a very different note. In that case the Department of State had "recognized and allowed" the immunity of a merchant vessel owned and operated by the Peruvian Government. The Court said:[61]

> . . . The [Department of State's] certification and the request that the vessel be declared immune must be accepted by the courts as a conclusive determination by the political arm of the Government that the continued retention of the vessel interferes with the proper conduct of our foreign relations. Upon the submission of this certification to the district court, it became the court's duty, in conformity to established principles, to release the vessel and to proceed no further in the cause.

Two years later, in *Republic of Mexico v. Hoffman,** the Court went on:[62]

> . . . But recognition by the courts of an immunity upon principles which the political department of government has not sanctioned may be equally embarrassing to it in securing the protection of our national interests and their recognition by other nations.
>
> . . . . .
>
> . . . We can only conclude that it is the national policy not to extend the immunity in the manner now suggested, and that it is the duty of the courts, in

---

* In that case a libel *in rem* for collision damage was filed against a vessel owned by the Government of Mexico but operated by a private company under a profit-sharing arrangement with the Mexican Government. The Mexican Ambassador filed a claim of immunity but the State Department's communication only confirmed the facts and expressed no opinion as to the immunity claimed.

a matter so intimately associated with our foreign policy and which may profoundly affect it, not to enlarge an immunity to an extent which the government, though often asked, has not seen fit to recognize.

. . .

The doctrine announced by the Court seems clear and inescapable: the courts would decide the question of immunity in accordance with international law if the Executive wished them to (or said nothing);[63] but if the Executive announced a national policy in regard to immunity generally, or for the particular case, that policy was law for the courts and binding upon them, regardless of what international law might say about it.[64]

In these cases the Supreme Court did not say or intimate that issues of immunity are unique or that the Executive had special powers in regard to them; to support its new doctrine the Court invoked only general Executive powers in foreign affairs. During the same judicial era, the Court also decided *Belmont* and *Pink*,[65] leading cases giving legal effect to an international agreement concluded by the President on his own authority.* In those cases the Court did not appear to give any weight to the fact that Executive policy was contained in an international agreement rather than, as in the immunity cases, in a unilateral Presidential act. In *Pink*, for example, the Court described in broadest terms "The powers of the President in the conduct of foreign relations"; it concluded that "We would usurp the executive function if we held that that decision was not final and conclusive in the courts," that "Effectiveness in handling the delicate problems of foreign relations requires no less." [66] During those years, too, Judge Learned Hand on the Circuit Court of Appeals was prepared to give legislative effect to Executive policy also to modify the doctrine requiring courts to give effect to the "Act of State" of a foreign government in its own territory. He asked whether "our own Executive which is the authority to which we must look as the final word in such matters, has declared that the commonly accepted doctrine

* I deal with these cases at length in Chaptèr VI.

. . . does not apply." Later the Court of Appeals concluded that the doctrine indeed did not apply "In view of this supervening expression of the Executive Policy." [67]

These cases left many questions unanswered. Principally, did they represent some broad principle of Presidential "legislative power" in foreign affairs? [68] If so, how broad was it, and what were its limitations? If not, how were these cases to be distinguished from others where executive action would not be given legislative effect? [69] The Supreme Court has not told us. Indeed, while it has never retreated from either the immunity or the executive agreement cases, it has not reaffirmed them. And a generation after they were decided, in the *Sabbatino* case,[70] the Court took pains to refrain from following Judge Hand's lead to give the Executive controlling say as to the Act of State doctrine. In that case the Court held that the doctrine required American courts to recognize Castro's title to American sugar which he had expropriated, even if the expropriation was in violation of international law. Although that was the rule requested by the Executive Branch, the Court went to lengths to seek novel constitutional doctrine and reestablish Act of State not as national policy promulgated by the Executive but as law created by the federal courts on their own authority.[71] Was the Court merely seizing an occasion to aggrandize judicial power? Or was it now reserving its position as to the earlier view that the President can declare national policy in foreign affairs with legal effect binding on the courts? *

---

* Perhaps the Court now feared the implication, beyond Act of State, that the Executive could legislate; especially, that the courts were subject to *ad hoc* determination controlling the decision of particular cases. Perhaps it was reluctant to have the judiciary appear less-than-independent, its power less than "separate," particularly in regard to the Executive. Perhaps it was reluctant to appear to be the handmaiden of the State Department, abdicating judicial functions and accepting political direction. Perhaps it was reluctant to establish the power of the political branches to determine, define and modify a doctrine that had been judicially developed. Perhaps it was moved by the probability that the policy invoked was made not by the President but by lesser Executive officials.

What was perhaps buried in *Sabbatino* surfaced somewhat in *Zschernig* v. *Miller*.[72] In that case the courts of Oregon, applying a state statute, had denied an inheritance to a resident of East Germany because he did not prove that he would enjoy the inheritance "without confiscation," and that Americans had a reciprocal right to inherit in his country. The Supreme Court reversed, holding that the Oregon statute as applied was "an intrusion by the State into the field of foreign affairs which the Constitution entrusts to the President and the Congress." [73]

The Solicitor General of the United States had informed the Supreme Court that "the Department of State has advised us . . ? that State reciprocity laws, including that of Oregon, have had little effect on the foreign relations and policy of this country"; [74] yet the majority did not feel bound by that view, and even Justice Harlan, who rejected the majority's constitutional doctrine, did not suggest that the Court had to defer to the Executive Branch. Justices Stewart and Brennan "would go further": [75]

> We deal here with the basic allocation of power between the States and the Nation. Resolution of so fundamental a constitutional issue cannot vary from day to day with the shifting winds at the State Department. Today, we are told, Oregon's statute does not conflict with the national interest. Tomorrow it may. But, however that may be, the fact remains that the conduct of our foreign affairs is entrusted under the Constitution to the National Government, not to the probate courts of the several states.

What seems clear is that the Court that established Executive power to dictate to the courts in the immunity cases or to make law by Executive agreement would have seen no need for new doctrines, would not have been reluctant to conclude that judicial authority to declare and apply Act of State is derivative, auxiliary, and subordinate to policy declared by the principal architect of foreign policy, the President. Indeed in *Pink* the Court had said incidentally that the considerations that required giving legal effect to executive agreements also explain the Act of State doctrine. See 315 U.S. at 233.

The Court did not have before it a formal act of the Executive. The friendly interventions of the Solicitor General, the informal statements of State Department views, did not assert that national policy required upholding Oregon's statute, only that such statutes did no harm to the national interest. In the result, however, the Court disregarded the State Department's stated view and substituted its own judgment on issues of foreign policy. Inevitably, it was holding, at least, that the State Department cannot informally legitimize state incursions into foreign policy which, in the Court's view, would be forbidden by the Constitution if there were no relevant federal action.*

In 1972 the Supreme Court had another opportunity to speak to the Executive's "legislative" authority when the State Department sought to modify the Act of State doctrine as the Court and Congress had established it. The Cuban Government had sued to recover assets held by the First National City Bank; the Bank counterclaimed for the value of its properties which Cuba had confiscated. While the case was in the courts the Department of State communicated "a determination by the Department of State that the Act of State doctrine need not be applied" in given circumstances, and its belief that the "doctrine should not be applied to bar consideration of the defendant's counterclaim." The Court of Appeals effectively disregarded the State Department and applied the Act of State doctrine to dismiss the Bank's counterclaim.[76] The Supreme Court reversed,[77] but only three of the five Justices in the majority

---

* Compare the power of Congress to permit state burdens on interstate or foreign commerce, Chapter IX, p. 237.

Perhaps an "activist" Supreme Court was less impressed with Executive expertise and more confident of its own, including its ability to see the long-term needs of the nation which constitutional doctrine represents. Perhaps the Court believed that the courts could better protect the national interest, particularly at some times and in some cases: in *Zschernig* itself, for example, the State Department—long a target of accusations that it was "soft on Communism"—might not have felt free to object to laws and practices directed primarily against the Communist states and involving criticism of Communist ideology and practice.

did so on the ground that the courts should give effect to State Department policy; two Justices who concurred in the judgment, as well as the four dissenting Justices, explicitly rejected the doctrine that the courts are bound to follow the Executive in such cases.[78]

Neither *Sabbatino* nor *Zschernig* overruled either Ex parte *Peru* or *Belmont*: the older cases were not strictly in point and were not mentioned. In the *First National Bank* case a majority refrained from reconfirming the immunity cases and refused to extend them to Act of State, but no Justice in the case rejected them.[79] Nor was the Executive's "legislative power" clearly in issue when the Court in 1971 denied his request for an injunction against publication of the classified "Pentagon Papers." [80] But one reader at least would guess that to the contemporary Supreme Court the older cases represent undue deference to the political branches by the New Deal Court, in reaction to undue resistance earlier that had led to accusations of "government by judiciary," Franklin Roosevelt's "court-packing plan," and the greatest crisis in the Court's history. The recent opinions seem to reflect further thoughts, at least about the language in the older cases, perhaps about law-making by informal, *ad hoc* State Department intervention, possibly about Executive legislation generally;* it might portend reexamination of executive finality even in the immunity cases themselves.

If such change is indeed in the Court's mood, the practical consequences need not be radical. The President and the State Department have not been eager to "legislate," or to intervene *ad hoc* in particular cases. In regard to sovereign immunity, at least, the Department has seemed unbelieving of the power which the Supreme Court said it had,[81] and it has been generally disposed not to inject itself to deny an American plaintiff his day in

---

* At least where, as in *First National Bank,* the Executive acts not by formal Presidential order. And might even State Department action have been found acceptable had it not sought to modify what the Supreme Court had legislated and Congress had arguably reaffirmed? See note 83, this chapter.

court, preferring to leave issues of immunity in particular cases to the courts and perhaps general policy to Congressional legislation.[82]   Although Congress has given the President express authority to make exceptions to the limited Act of State doctrine which Congress enacted, the Executive Branch has not been eager to assume the onus of doing so and defeating the claim of an American citizen against a foreign government.[83]   The Supreme Court's reception of the State Department's effort to modify the Act of State doctrine in the *First National Bank* case is not likely to encourage further efforts.

The cases that have struggled with issues of Presidential legislative power dramatize the special quality of the constitutional law of foreign affairs and the vagaries of judicial incursions that are infrequent and develop no confident mastery.   The New Deal Supreme Court, abjuring the earlier "judicial activism" and espousing self-restraint, extended its deference for "The Government" to the Executive, indeed to unidentified officials of the State Department.   A later Supreme Court has turned its back on the earlier attitude but cannot be too active when its opportunities to intervene are limited and the dangers great if uncertain.   The result is to tear down old guideposts without erecting new ones.   The law student's distinctions between principle, holding, and dictum become critical: we have judicial guidance only on the few issues which the Supreme Court actually decides, and not always there, since *stare decisis* in constitutional cases means little, and less to an activist court.*   Issues of Presidential power, in particular, remain to be fought out in the consciences of the Executive Branch and in the political arena.

In sum, the broader theories and extensive Presidential assertions suggest that the President's powers in foreign affairs are indeed "plenary," and they can be exercised even to make some law in the United States.   Of course, the President cannot do what is forbidden to him, as to all of the United States Government, by the Bill of Rights, and those safeguards have been increasingly invoked and increasingly vindicated, even where for-

* See Introduction, note 7.

eign relations are affected (See Chapter X). Even the broadest theories, moreover, accept that there are major limitations on the President implied in or flowing from grants of power to Congress or the treaty-makers, that some powers can be exercised by the President only when Congress is silent, some only jointly with Congress. I deal with the limitations deriving from Congressional power in Chapter IV (after we consider the powers of Congress), and those that derive from the Treaty Power in Chapter VI.

# *Chapter III.* CONGRESS

If in the competition for power in foreign relations the Presidential office has had inherent advantages, Congress has had other, enormous strengths, not least the history, the conception, and the generous grants of the Constitution.[1] The President had to contend for power in a novel office furnished with few, inarticulate constitutional phrases, compelling him to reach outside the Constitution (as per Justice Sutherland) or for special meanings (as in "the executive Power"). Congress has needed no extravagant, uncommon constitutional interpretations: even its authority deriving from national sovereignty has been secondary to the impressive array of powers expressly enumerated in the Constitution, not least the sole charge of an indispensable and ample purse.

The Constitution confers upon Congress "legislative Powers," set forth principally in Article I, section 8.* Those directly related to foreign affairs are: **

---

* Legislative powers are also conferred on Congress in other articles, *e. g.,* the power to regulate the time, place and manner of holding elections for Representatives and effectively of Senators (Art. I, sec. 4; *cf.* Amendment XVII); to consent to various state acts (Art. I, sec. 10); to create federal offices (Art. II, sec. 2); to establish lower federal courts (Art. III, sec. 1) and regulate the appellate jurisdiction of the Supreme Court (Art. III, sec. 2); to implement the Full Faith and Credit clause (Art. IV, sec. 1); to admit new states (Art. IV, sec. 3); to govern federal territory and other property (Art. IV, sec. 3); to propose constitutional amendments (Art. V). See also the enforcement clauses of various amendments to the Constitution, *e. g.,* Amendments XIII, XIV, XV, XIX, XX, XXIII, XXIV, XXVI ... have recently proved to be rich sources of new power. See p. 77, this chapter.

See p. 77, this chapter.

** One might add the power "To establish an uniform Rule of Naturalization" (clause 4) in which the Supreme Court has seen

To regulate Commerce with foreign Nations, and among the several States, and with the Indian Tribes (Clause 3).

To define and punish Piracies and Felonies committed on the high Seas, and Offences against the Law of Nations (Clause 10).

To declare War, grant Letters of Marque and Reprisal,[2] and make Rules concerning Captures on Land and Water (Clause 11).

And although explicitly the Constitution gives Congress only "All legislative Powers herein granted," Congress, we know, has also an unenumerated "foreign affairs power," the legislative derivative of the powers of the United States inherent in its sovereignty. Congress also has general powers that are indispensable to the conduct of foreign relations, *e. g.,* to tax and to spend for the common defense and the general welfare,[*] to do what is "necessary and proper" to carry out other powers,[**] to appropriate funds from the Treasury.[†]

The powers of Congress are denominated "legislative," as distinguished, in particular, from those "executive." (Under the Articles, whatever executive powers there were had also been exercised by the Congress.) Most of the enumerated powers of

authority also for "specialized regulation of the conduct of an alien before naturalization." Hines v. Davidowitz, 312 U.S. 52, 66 (1941). In other respects, too, foreign nations are not indifferent to our naturalization and nationality laws. Also relevant to foreign relations is the power of Congress to govern territory (Art. IV, sec. 3), including those acquired by conquest or treaty, see this chapter, note 50. The power of Congress to establish federal offices and to authorize the President to fill them without Senate consent (Art. II, sec. 2) has also been used for foreign affairs purposes. See this chapter, p. 77.

[*] "The Congress shall have Power to lay and collect Taxes, Duties, Imposts and Excises, to pay the Debts and provide for the common Defence and general Welfare of the United States . . . ." (Art. I, sec. 8, cl. 1). The power to impose duties on foreign goods might also have been inferred from the power to regulate foreign commerce.

[**] Art. I, sec. 8, cl. 18, *quoted* this chapter, p. 78.

[†] The power is implied in Art. I, sec. 9, cl. 7: "No Money shall be drawn from the Treasury, but in Consequence of Appropriations made by Law . . . ."

Congress are indeed legislative, *i. e.,* they provide authority to make domestic law in the matters indicated. The power to declare war is authority to perform an international act but it has also legislative implications and consequences. Congress has also claimed authority to make foreign policy by resolutions and other actions that do not enact law in the United States.

## Congress as Law-Maker

For some 150 years the meaning and scope of enumerated powers of Congress were a principal fare of constitutional adjudication.[3] Since 1937 the court has given Congress the broadest scope, and some of its powers, including some particularly relevant to foreign affairs, know few limits. Other powers of Congress have been little used but prevailing judicial deference to Congress would doubtless apply to these as well.[4]

### The Commerce Power

From the beginning, the foreign trade of the United States was near the core of its foreign policy and the power to regulate commerce with foreign nations gave Congress a major voice in it.\*
As intervening years brought radical growth and enhanced importance to the international trade of the United States, they brought enhanced importance and radical growth to the Commerce Power of Congress, although the power to regulate foreign commerce was, in the main, the incidental beneficiary of the explosion of the power to regulate interstate commerce.

Long ago Chief Justice Marshall told us that commerce is not merely trade, "it is intercourse."[5] Today, we know, Congress can regulate every aspect of intercourse among States and of an interdependent interstate economy; it can regulate what is in interstate commerce and, largely, what has been or will be in interstate commerce, as well as other intra-state matters that substantially affect interstate commerce; it can regulate intra-state matters when necessary for the effective regulation of interstate

---

\* In addition to direct regulation of foreign commerce by statute, as in tariff laws, Congress has also authorized executive trade agreements. See Chapter VI. Trade can also be regulated by treaty. See Chapter V.

commerce.[6]  No longer subject to serious constitutional challenge, Congress is embarked on unprecedented, far-reaching
regulation of trade and finance, transportation and communication, labor and management, crime and punishment, manners and
morals, even in respects that might seem remote from "commerce" and from "interstate" considerations.[7]  Since 1936 Congress has apparently not approached the limits of its Commerce
Power [8] and many wonder whether there are any limits other
than those in Congressional self-restraint reflecting the restraints
of political forces.

There have been fewer occasions for Congress to act on so
broad a conception of the Commerce Power in regard to foreign
commerce, but there is no reason in law or in fact why it could
not do so.[9]  With perhaps some differences of degree that do not
appear constitutionally material, the international economy is as
interdependent as our own interstate economy.  Local activities
impinge on foreign commerce and require regulation to make
control of foreign commerce effective.  There is room for "police
power" regulation in foreign commerce and in local matters that
affect foreign commerce and intercourse.*

The Commerce Power, then, might be sufficient to support
virtually any legislation that relates to foreign intercourse, *i. e.,*
to foreign relations.[10]  It is principally in that power that Congress has found authority to regulate international shipping, aviation, and old and new media of communication; to impose tariffs
and authorize reciprocal trade arrangements, to grant or deny
more-favored-nation treatment or other preferences, to impose
embargoes on unfriendly countries.**  With a small assist from

* Often interstate and foreign commerce are inextricably intertwined; and local activities that impinge on foreign commerce often
impinge also on interstate commerce and could be regulated on that
ground as well.

**Most favored nation treatment has generally been granted by
treaty, but, for example, Congress legislated to deny such treatment
to Soviet bloc countries.  See the Trade Agreements Extension Act
of 1951, ch. 141, § 5, 65 Stat. 72, 73.  Increasingly trade is the subject
of executive agreement pursuant to Congressional authorization.  See
Chapter VI, p. 176.

the powers "to borrow Money" and "to coin Money, regulate the Value thereof, and of foreign Coin," the Commerce Power supports the part of the United States in a worldwide network of finance and banking.[11]  At one time the Commerce Power was seen also as the basis for Congressional regulation of maritime and admiralty affairs [12] and its control of immigration.[13]  Only the availability of other powers made it unnecessary for the courts to rely exclusively on the Commerce Power or to explore its reaches for other legislative regulation of the international relations of the United States.

## The War Powers

To the Constitutional Fathers, one might guess, the most important power in foreign relations was the power to declare war, and that was given to Congress.  I deal later with the power of Congress to decide for war or peace;  here I consider it only as a source of domestic legislative authority.  For, the Supreme Court has ruled, the power to declare war implies the power to wage war and supports what is necessary and proper to wage war successfully.[14]  We have, then, that congeries of "war powers" under which during the Second World War, for example, Congress totally mobilized the manpower and the resources of this country and regulated even minutiae of the lives of the people.[15]

The legislative war powers, moreover, are not born with the declaration of war nor do they die with the coming of peace. The power to declare and wage war implies power to prepare for war and to act to deter and prevent war: hence, elaborate "peacetime" defense programs entailing not only huge expenditures but detailed regulatory programs,* including, for a few examples, compulsory military service, control of activities related to atomic energy, comprehensive security programs affecting mil-

---

* Defense expenditures are also within the express power of Congress "to lay and collect Taxes  .  .  .  to pay the Debts and provide for the common Defence and general Welfare of the United States  .  .  .  ."  Art. I, sec. 8, cl. 1.  But that clause provides authority only for spending, not for regulatory legislation.  Compare United States v. Butler, 297 U.S. 1 (1936).

lions of employees of the federal government and of government contractors.[16] Congress also has the power to deal with the aftermath and the consequences of war, for example, by providing for the renegotiation of wartime contracts, or the control of prices and rentals years after the fighting ended.[17] The Supreme Court has never declared any limit to the war powers of Congress during war or peace or even intimated where such limits might lie.

Inevitably, what Congress does to wage war, anticipate or prevent war, recover from war, has importance for international relations. Directly, the war powers enable Congress during war to regulate the rights and obligations in the United States of enemies, allies or neutrals, their ships and airplanes, their citizens and their properties, and communication, trade and every form of intercourse with them.[18] In differing degrees in respect of different countries, such regulations could be supported also during the consequences of war that are long with us, and during the chronic state of less-than-peace and eternal defensive vigilance that seems our lot indefinitely. In our day, at least, trade and embargo, transportation and communication, arms programs and foreign aid, indeed whatever might be reached by the power to regulate foreign commerce and intercourse, seem plausibly also within the war powers of Congress.[19]

## *"To Define and Punish"*

The law of nations and the rule of law at sea loomed large in the minds of the Constitutional Framers, hence the explicit grant to Congress of the power to define and punish piracies, felonies on the high seas and offenses against the law of nations.[20] Congress has made it a federal crime to commit piracy as defined by international law and has prescribed punishment for offenses committed at sea, as on American vessels, and more recently in the air, as on American airplanes.[21]

The power to define and punish offenses against the law of nations has been little used and its purport is not wholly clear.[22] Since, in general, traditional international law imposes duties only upon states, not upon individuals, it is not obvious how an individual can commit an offense against the law of nations. Presumably the clause would permit punishment of officials for acts or omissions that constitute violations of international law by the United States, *e. g.,* when they deny fundamental "justice" to an alien, arrest a diplomat, violate an embassy, or fail to carry out a treaty obligation.[23]  The clause would also authorize Congress to enact into national law any international rules designed to govern individual behavior, for example, the laws of war relating to the treatment of prisoners-of-war.[24]  If international law or a treaty of the United States applied directly to individuals, as perhaps happened in the Nuremberg Charter, as might happen some future day pursuant to the Genocide Convention or to human rights covenants,[25] Congress could implement that law by providing for punishment under this clause, though it could also do so amply under other powers discussed below.*

But Congress apparently, and the Supreme Court explicitly, gave the clause a broader meaning.  In upholding a statute that made it a crime to counterfeit foreign currency, the Supreme Court said:

> . . . A right secured by the law of nations to a nation, or its people, is one the United States as the representatives of this nation are bound to protect.  Consequently, a law which is necessary and proper to afford this protection is one that Congress may enact, because it is one that is needed to carry into execution a power conferred by the Constitution on the Government of the United States exclusively. . . .
>
> . . . This statute defines the offence, and if the thing made punishable is one which the United States are required by their international obligations to use due

* *E. g.,* under its power to implement treaties, or its Foreign Affairs Power, this chapter, pp. 74–76.

The "Off——— ————— ————— presumably contemplated legislation rendering such offenses violations of the laws of the United States and punishable as such.  The power to make such offenses international crimes punishable under international authority is discussed in Chapter VII, p. 198.

diligence to prevent, it is an offence against the law of nations.[26]

It is perhaps under such an interpretation of the "Offences clause" that Congress long ago made it a crime to harass diplomats, to impersonate them, to damage the property of foreign governments, or to initiate activities directed against the peace and security of foreign nations.[27]   That power, then, would enable Congress also to enforce by criminal penalties any new international law or obligation the United States might accept, say that American companies shall abide by a new international regime for the sea.   Again, Congress could also implement such undertakings readily under other powers to be considered later.

## The Foreign Affairs Power

Whether under Sutherland's theory, or the narrower implications in *The Chinese Exclusion Case,* Congress derives additional legislative authority from the powers of the United States inherent in its sovereignty and nationhood; [28] the same or a similar power has been invoked as a "power of Congress to deal with foreign relations." [29]   It is this "Foreign Affairs Power," presumably, which supports legislation regulating and protecting the conduct of foreign relations and foreign diplomatic activities in the United States; [30] providing for cooperation with foreign governments, *e. g.,* giving facilities to foreign consuls; [31] or limiting foreign governments, *e. g.,* freezing their assets or forbidding those in default to sell bonds in the United States.[32]   Probably under this power, Congress modified the Act of State doctrine to require American courts in some circumstances to deny effect to acts of foreign governments.[33]   Although other powers have been suggested,* the Foreign Affairs Power might best support Congressional assertions of national sovereignty in territory or in the air-space.   It is presumably under this power that Congress has authorized or approved international agreements on matters that are not within its enumerated powers.[34]

---

* For example, that the power to acquire territory is implied in the expressed power to govern territory, this chapter, note 50.

The Foreign Affairs Power supports the network of immigration laws regulating the entry, sojourn, and departure of aliens,[35] and the law requiring aliens residing in the United States to register.[36] Although the Supreme Court has not expressly held so, presumably this power supports other regulations of aliens, or giving them equality, advantage or disadvantage by comparison with citizens.[37]

The Foreign Affairs Power reaches also conduct of American citizens which affects foreign relations. It is presumably that power which justified a statute depriving an American woman of her citizenship if she married an alien;[38] it was held to support withdrawal of citizenship from one who voted in a foreign election.[39] It apparently permits Congress to provide for extradition to a foreign country even when no treaty requires it.[40]

The Foreign Affairs Power is probably used also in various statutes governing the conduct of Americans abroad. Nothing in the Constitution prevents Congress from exercising its powers outside the United States and, under the applicable enumerated powers, Congress can tax the income of an American citizen living abroad, or require him to return for military service or to testify before an American court.[41] But Congress has also regulated abroad actions which it could not regulate in the United States because they are not within any enumerated powers and are therefore reserved to the States. For example, Congress established an extensive criminal code, to be enforced by court-martial, for dependents of American servicemen and for civilian employees of the military forces living abroad. The Supreme Court struck down the provisions subjecting such civilians to court martial because they denied the accused a jury trial and other constitutional safeguards.[42] It has been commonly assumed, and the Supreme Court intimated, however, that Congress could have such persons returned for trial in civilian courts in the United States.[43] Yet the ~~~~~~~~~~~~~~~~~~~~~~~~~ committed by an American abroad is not within any enumerated power of Congress; the most plausible basis for Congress to reach that conduct is the Foreign Affairs Power, on the theory that the right to regulate the conduct of nationals abroad is inherent in sovereignty, or that such conduct might affect our foreign relations.[44]

No one knows the reaches of the Foreign Affairs Power of Congress. In a bold (perhaps too-bold) article I wrote with confidence that the Foreign Affairs Power would support legislation on any matter so related to foreign affairs that the United States might deal with it by treaty: [45] the rights of foreign governments and their officials, diplomats and consuls; the rights of foreign nationals in commerce, friendship and navigation in the United States; extradition; taxation and trade rights of Americans abroad; the status of American military forces in other countries and of foreign forces in the United States; and a host of reciprocal rights, or rights conditioned on reciprocity.[46] Less confidently, I argued, just as the Commerce Power reaches all, no matter how local, that is or affects interstate or foreign commerce, perhaps the Foreign Affairs Power reaches any matter, no matter how domestic, which in our interdependent times affects our foreign relations, including our "image" and influence abroad, even, say, race, or poverty, or the alienation of youth.

In *Missouri* v. *Holland,* Mr. Justice Holmes said: "It is obvious that there may be matters of the sharpest exigency for the national well being that an act of Congress could not deal with but that a treaty followed by such an act could. . . ." [47] But Holmes wrote half a century ago, before the explosion of Congressional powers. Today, there is surely no warrant for confident assertion that there is any matter relating to foreign affairs that is not subject to legislation by Congress.

## General Congressional Powers

The vast legislative powers of Congress that relate particularly to foreign affairs do not begin to exhaust its authority to make law affecting foreign relations. Congress has general powers that, taken together, enable it to reach virtually where it will in foreign as in domestic affairs, subject only to constitutional prohibitions protecting individual rights. The power to tax (Art.

I, sec. 8, cl. 1) has long been a power to regulate through taxation, and could be used to control, say, foreign travel, as it has gambling or narcotics. Major programs depend wholly on the "Spending Power" (in the same clause)—to "provide for the common Defence and general Welfare of the United States"— and it has been used in our day for billions of dollars in foreign aid.[48]  Other, specialized powers also have their international uses: Congress has authorized a network of international agreements under its postal power (Art. I, sec. 8, cl. 7), and there are international elements in the regulation of patents and copyrights.[49]  The express power to govern territory (Art. IV, sec. 3) may imply authority to acquire territory, and Congress determines whether territory acquired shall be incorporated into the United States.[50]  Congress can exercise "exclusive Legislation" in the nation's capital, its diplomatic headquarters (Art. I, sec. 8, cl. 17).  The power to acquire and dispose of property has supported lend-lease and other arms programs, and sales or gifts of nuclear reactors or fissionable materials.[51]  The passing assertion that the President can make appointments to offices "which shall be established by Law" (Art. II, sec. 2, cl. 2) gives Congress the power to create and control the Executive bureaucracy, including largely the foreign affairs establishment.*  By implication in the Constitution's grant of maritime jurisdiction to the federal judiciary (Art. III, sec. 2), Congress can legislate maritime law,[52] and it can doubtless extend that law in, under or above the seas, a power that will have new importance as the seas become increasingly hospitable to human activity.  The authority in the Thirteenth Amendment to implement the abolition of slavery enables legislation cooperating in international suppression of slavery.  The Fourteenth Amendment enables Congress to maintain the equal protection of the laws and the due process of law required of the States, and supports laws that have given to aliens in the United States basic rights that more than satisfy what international law requires and nations ask of the United States.[53]

* See Chapter IV, p. 116.

The final clause of Article I, section 8, gives Congress the power:

> To make all Laws which shall be necessary and proper for carrying into Execution the foregoing Powers, and all other Powers vested by this Constitution in the Government of the United States, or in any Department or Officer thereof.

Through most of our history, and in most respects, the courts have interpreted that clause in the light of Marshall's celebrated dictum:

> Let the end be legitimate, let it be within the scope of the constitution, and all means which are appropriate, which are plainly adapted to that end, which are not prohibited but consist with the letter and spirit of the constitution, are constitutional.[54]

The "necessary and proper" clause has loomed large in Congressional authority, justifying varied, imaginative initiatives for carrying out the many powers of Congress, whether enumerated or "inherent." [55] For the conduct of foreign relations the clause has additional significance, since it empowers Congress to carry out not only its own powers but all those vested in "the Government of the United States, or in any Department or Officer thereof." In that clause, Justice Holmes found the basis for his landmark opinion in *Missouri* v. *Holland* upholding a statute implementing a treaty which, it was assumed, Congress could not have enacted in the absence of treaty.[56] Laws for carrying into execution the President's powers might include also those that support the President's foreign affairs establishment, that punish interference with his freedom of action (as by the old Logan Act forbidding "private diplomacy"), that protect foreign diplomacy in the United States.* Indeed one can readily build a plenary power of Congress to enact laws in regard to foreign affairs as necessary and proper to carry into execution the President's plenary powers to conduct foreign affairs.**

---

* See notes 27 and 30, this chapter.

**The argument has been made that when Congress acts to carry out the President's powers it ought not be able to enact legislation

One necessary and proper power of Congress, as important as any for the conduct of foreign relations, is that implied in the provision that "No Money shall be drawn from the Treasury, but in Consequence of Appropriations made by Law." (Art. I, sec. 9, cl. 7.) While, we shall see,† Congress usually feels legally, politically, or morally obligated to appropriate funds to maintain the President's foreign affairs establishment and to implement his treaties and other foreign undertakings, Congress can readily refuse to appropriate when it believes the President has exceeded his powers. Even when the President acts clearly within his powers, Congress decides the degree and detail of its support: it determines ultimately the State Department's budget, how much money the President shall have to spend on the armed forces under his command, how much he can agree to contribute to the United Nations.* Since the President is always coming to Congress for money for innumerable purposes, domestic and foreign, Congress and Congressional committees can use appropriations and the appropriations process to bargain also about other elements of Presidential policy in foreign affairs. Because the President usually cannot afford to veto appropriations acts they are favorite vehicles for "conditions" and other riders imposed on unwilling Presidents.**

## "Non-legislative" Powers of Congress

Congress can mold if not determine the foreign policy of the United States through its vast legislative powers, including the "quasi-legislative" powers to spend and appropriate funds. In

he does not approve, for example by overriding his veto. Congress might reply that it acts in support of the power of the Presidency not of a particular President, and the views of the present incumbent are not controlling.

† See Chapter IV, pp. 108–109, Chapter V, pp. 161–62.

* For possible distinctions between voluntary and obligatory con- ~~~~~~~ to international organizations, see Chapter IV, p. 115.

** Presidents have failed to obtain an "item veto," the right to veto one item without vetoing the whole enactment. See Chapter IV, p. 113.

addition, the Constitution leaves to Congress the most momentous non-legislative decision in foreign policy, the power to declare war.†

## The Power to Declare War

For the Framers, surely, war or peace was the paramount decision in foreign policy.[57] War terminates relations with the enemy, and abrogates or suspends treaty obligations and the bulk of rights and duties under international law.* Traditionally, it has also altered relations with all other nations, often modifying their treaties, and imposing on them the choice of neutrality or belligerency and the consequences of that choice.[58] Constitutionally, war suspends some provisions and gives others a different cast,[59] and, we have seen, provides Congress (and the President) with a formidable arsenal of powers to mobilize the lives and other resources of the country for war.

The Founders considered the power to declare war too important to entrust to the President alone, or even to him and the Senate, and gave it to Congress (or left it there, as under the Articles of Confederation).** There have been suggestions that the power of Congress was intended to be only a formal power to declare formal wars, and that wars can be fought by the President on his own authority if they are not "declared." That view is without foundation: the Constitution gave Congress the power to decide the ultimate question, whether the nation shall or shall not go to war.[60] It is true that our five declarations of war were requested by Presidents and that no such request has been de-

---

† The non-legislative character of a declaration of war has been cited for an argument that would deny the President power to veto such a declaration. See Introduction to Chapter II, p. 33.

* For the effect of war on treaties, see Chapter V, note 134.

** Under the Articles of Confederation, Article IX, Congress had "the sole and exclusive right and power of determining on peace and war." But that of course was not directed at a president, since there was none, but was designed to deny the war power to the individual States.

nied; it is true that Presidents can pursue policies and conduct foreign relations in ways that will lead to war, and that the hand of Congress may also be forced, or declaration of war become academic, if the United States were attacked. (See Chapter IV.) Nonetheless, the constitutional power to decide whether to go to war lies with Congress. There is no foundation either for the view that Congress can decide for war only by formal declaration: Congress can decide, and has decided, to wage war formally or informally, expressly or by implication, in advance or by subsequent ratification, by legislation or resolution, even merely by appropriating funds for the conduct of war. The Supreme Court recognized undeclared war against France in 1800 and our undeclared Civil War. Congress has on numerous occasions asserted the power to authorize the use of force by resolution rather than by declaration.[61]

The power to decide for war surely implies also a corollary power to decide that war should end. While, ordinarily, wars are ended by treaty, Congress declared an end to both World Wars by resolution when treaties failed.[62]

## Foreign Policy Short of War

That Congress was expressly given the powers of war and peace, to regulate commerce—intercourse—with foreign nations, and other large legislative powers pertinent to foreign affairs, early led to claims that Congress had all the powers of the nation in foreign relations other than those explicitly conferred on the President (alone or with the Senate). Congress, not the President, it was said, or at least Congress as well as the President, can determine "the condition of the nation," [63] the grand designs of its foreign policy as well as the attitudes that shape day-to-day relations with other nations.

Especially in earlier times, Congress in fact declared national policy other than by legislation or declaration of war. In 1794, and on several occasions thereafter, Congress proclaimed the neutrality of the United States in regard to the wars of others.[64] In 1798, Congress resolved "that the United States are of right freed and exonerated from the stipulations" of treaties with

France, and on other occasions it directed the President to terminate treaties.* In the nineteenth century one or both Houses pretended to some part in recognizing the independence of several Latin American republics, and Congress did in effect recognize the independence of Cuba in 1898.[65] Although treaties to that effect had been negotiated, they were not ratified and Congress instead resolved to annex Texas, and later Hawaii.[66] Congress has issued directives to Presidents and instructions to delegates to international conferences; and in numerous cases it sought to control or influence foreign relations by "riders" and other conditions.** Congress has authorized or approved international agreements on matters not within its enumerated powers.† In one famous instance, in 1864, the House of Representatives resolved sweepingly that

> Congress has a constitutional right to an authoritative voice in declaring and prescribing the foreign policy of the United States, as well in the recognition of new Powers as in other matters; and it is the constitutional duty of the executive department to respect that policy, not less in diplomatic negotiations than in the use of national forces when authorized by law; and the propriety of any declaration of foreign policy by Congress is sufficiently proved by the vote which pronounces it; . . . .[67]

The best known, farthest-reaching argument for a plenary Congressional power is probably that made by "Helvidius" (Madison) in his challenge to "Pacificus" (Hamilton) who had supported President Washington's power to proclaim neutrality in the war between France and Great Britain.[68] Basically, with variations, the argument is that Congress is the principal organ

---

* 1 Stat. 578 (1798). See Chapter V, p. 169. The power to terminate a treaty internationally is not to be confused with the power of Congress by legislation to make law for the United States in disregard of existing treaty obligations. *Id.* at p. 163.

** See Chapter IV, p. 113.

† See Chapter VI, pp. 174–75.

of government and has all its political authority, in foreign affairs as elsewhere, except that specifically granted to the President (alone or with the Senate). The determination of foreign policy and the control of foreign relations lay with Congress under the Articles of Confederation and, with particularized exceptions, the Constitution left them there. The powers of Congress are not limited to domestic "law-making," narrowly conceived: witness, to Congress is expressly given the most important foreign affairs power, the power to declare war, which can effectively terminate all relations with the enemy and modify relations with others.* That power surely includes the power to decide not to go to war, as by a proclamation of neutrality; it must include also the power to determine national policy generally, for these might determine war or peace.

Adding to Madison's arguments, one might note, too, that even war apart the enumerated powers of Congress are not in fact limited to domestic law-making. Congressional regulations of foreign commerce are not exclusively domestic laws;** and Congress can authorize or approve international agreements which are not legislative in character.† Is it not significant, too, that the power to consent to wars or compacts by the States with foreign governments was given to Congress, not to the President? †† Building on Sutherland one might add that the powers of the United States inherent in its sovereignty, including the authority to make foreign policy, apparently reside in Congress, the principal repository of the sovereign power; [69] indeed, the Court has usually invoked the sovereignty of the United States

---

* See p. 80.

** The powers to spend, to borrow money, to support an army and navy are also not plainly "legislative" in character.

† See Chapter VI, pp. 173–75.

†† "No State shall . . . . . . . . . . . . . . . . the Consent of Congress, lay any Duty of Tonnage, keep Troops, or Ships of War in time of Peace, enter into any Agreement or Compact with another State, or with a foreign Power, or engage in War, unless actually invaded, or in such imminent Danger as will not admit of delay." Art. I, sec. 10, cl. 3.

to support an act of Congress.*  In sum, the argument concludes, in foreign affairs as elsewhere, the President is only the executive agent of Congress: Congress makes foreign policy and the President conducts foreign relations in the light of that policy. At least, Congress has concurrent power to "resolve" foreign policy, and its power is superior and should control inconsistent Presidential action.

The merits of arguments for "plenary" Congressional authority in foreign affairs—including powers claimed by the President as within his "executive Power" as "sole organ"—are debatable and continue to be debated.[70]  That Congress is the principal repository of the external sovereignty of the United States is not obvious and would surely be denied by Presidents; surely they would deny that any national sovereignty which Congress might represent includes full authority over foreign relations.  The grant to Congress of power to decide for war gives it respectable claim to related authority, say to end war, or determine the status of territory gained in war; perhaps, too, to decide to stay out of the wars of others and proclaim national neutrality.  But, as a matter of constitutional construction, control of war and peace will not (*pace* James Madison) obviously reach to give Congress blanket authority "to make foreign policy."  The fact is that, increasingly, the large part of foreign policy is less-than-intimately related to war-and-peace.  Happily, war has not been common in the life of the United States and war on Congressional initiative has been even less frequent.  While, in theory, the power to declare war can give Congress great influence even when it is not exercised, one cannot say that Congress has importantly shaped the foreign policy of the United States through the unexercised "uses" of that power.

Nonetheless, except for those to whom the vesting of "the executive Power" in the President constitutes an explicit grant of control over foreign relations, the theoretical arguments for Congressional primacy, or at least concurrent authority, are not less persuasive than those for the President.  But in our history

* See pp. 26, 74–76 above.  In what is perhaps dictum, however, the Supreme Court found in sovereignty also Executive power to exclude aliens, Chapter II, note 31.

84

Congressional claims collided with and recoiled before the President's claims to exclusive authority. The President prevailed in part because in the nineteenth century, surely, American foreign policy did not readily court war and its relation to war became increasingly hypothetical; even more because foreign policy depended effectively on communication and commitment, expressed or tacit, to other nations, and the President was effectively "the *sole* organ" of the United States while Congress, vis-à-vis other nations, remained effectively "deaf and dumb." [71] Congress did win, early, the battle of neutrality proclamations, and since President Washington's day neutrality has been determined by Congress—perhaps because proclamation of neutrality is in substantial measure a decision not to go to war, perhaps, too, because neutrality was addressed also to American citizens and depended directly on legislation to make it effective. The power of Congress to resolve an end to war can also be accepted as a necessary implication of its authority over war-or-peace. For the rest, Congress itself has effectively reduced its claims, and early precedents for Congressional authority to make policy other than by legislation have been limited or abandoned and explained away.[72] Resolutions of policy are indeed adopted by one or both Houses of Congress but usually they are only "sense resolutions" (discussed below) not purporting to establish or declare the policy of the United States or to direct or control the President. No doubt wider claims will again be made and power might be effectively redistributed, but today Congress can assert with confidence, in addition to its spending and law-making powers, only the power to go to war and the rimlands of that power.*

---

* The power of Congress to join with the President to conclude international agreements, as a procedure alternative to a treaty by President-and-Senate, also remains well established (see Chapter VI, p. 173), but that authority is not challenged by Presidents and is indeed invoked, at least by the President who joins in such agreements. Compare the suggesti~~........~~ ~~................~~
an international act they represent the full sovereignty of the United States (Introduction to Chapter II, note 4) or that in the Treaty Power the Constitution accepted Senate consent as a lesser safeguard, but that approval of an agreement by the whole Congress is effective *a fortiori*, Chapter VI, note 9.

Especially with the changing character of war, the allocation to Congress of the power to decide for war while foreign relations are conducted largely by the President has led to competition for power and has engendered doubts about the viability and wisdom of the constitutional distribution. (See Chapter IV).

## The Political Influence of Congress

Assuming that Congress has little power in that narrowing area that does not involve legislation or spending or the implications of its war powers, it can exercise tremendous influence even on such policy—by non-legislative riders to legislation or appropriations, by "sense resolutions," by the formal and informal actions of Congressional committees, by the interventions and expostulations of individual Congressmen. For Presidents need Congress, have to get along with them, must take their views into account; and Congressmen often reflect public opinion and can create opinion for or against Presidential policies.

Since Congress may not communicate with foreign governments, resolutions directly addressed to foreign governments are technically objectionable: once, President Grant even vetoed a resolution saying thanks to foreign governments for their congratulations upon our First Centennial as a nation![73] But resolutions by one or both Houses of Congress expressing the "sense" of the Congress about some international matter, or calling on the President to do something, have long been with us and Presidents cannot lightly disregard them.[74] They are particularly significant when they reflect national public opinion, or when they imply that Congress might support its "sense" by adopting or denying actions or appropriations that are within its powers. Presidents and Secretaries of State have had to tell other governments that even Congressmen have freedom of speech, but that singly, or even together in non-legislative resolutions, they do not speak for the United States nor are their statements of any legal effect: Secretary Seward disowned a House Resolution attacking French activities in Mexico during our Civil War;[75] Secretary Dulles disowned an address by Senator

John F. Kennedy promoting Algerian independence.[76] On the other hand, the Executive has been known to encourage, even inspire, sense resolutions to strengthen his position vis-à-vis other nations, claiming that he must take account of the views of Congress and of public opinion which Congress reflects.

The power of Congress to investigate is implied in its power to legislate and should be related to that function, but there is no way of keeping Congress close to its legislative last, and virtually any subject can be investigated to determine whether legislation *might* be desirable or even permissible.[77] In any event, whether in connection with particular legislation, appropriations, appointments, or under undefined and undifferentiated investigative power, Congressional committees and individual Congressmen have opportunities to inquire, cross-examine, expose, criticize, even harass and threaten executive officials engaged in the conduct of foreign policy, and the need to justify to Congressmen is a not-insignificant influence on Executive policy.

Informal extra-constitutional powers and actions also give Congress—or some Congressmen—tremendous influence. Chairmen of important committees, party leaders, other influential legislators are not to be ignored, and, especially if their support should later be needed for formal action, they will be informed and consulted.[78] Congressmen engage in making foreign policy when they are appointed to delegations to international conferences.* In our times, ready travel, instant international communication and foreign "monitoring" of our Congressional processes bring Congressmen's voices into foreign offices and to foreign peoples. Spending programs give Congressmen official reasons for investigation around the world, and neither foreign officials nor American diplomats will deny them access or refuse to talk with them.

Like the powers of the President, like other powers of Congress, those related to foreign affairs are, of course, limited by the Bill of Rights; they are subject also to limitations on Con-

---

* The practice no longer raises constitutional questions under Art. I, sec. 6, cl. 2. See Chapter V.

gressional power expressed in the Constitution, some of which have some relevance to foreign affairs: for example, Congress may not impose a tax or duty on articles exported from any State, or give a preference to the ports of one State over those of another.[79] Limitations on Congressional power are also implied in grants of power to the President, to the courts, some even in powers reserved to the States.

There are also limitations implied in the principle of separation of powers. The changing character of American foreign relations has enhanced the powers of both President and Congress but it has not made them independent of each other, nor has it made it easier to separate their powers or determine their respective limits. The result, of course, is hardly to prevent conflict or assure cooperation.

# Chapter IV. SEPARATION OF POWERS: CONFLICT AND COOPERATION

Both the President and Congress command vast powers in foreign affairs, but the distribution between them, even as originally conceived, surely as now realized, is not what it is in domestic affairs. While the classic separation of executive from legislative functions obtains in some measure, we have seen also a division of the power to "legislate" foreign policy between the two political branches.* The President makes foreign policy by his conduct of foreign relations generally, by international acts as "sole organ" or as Commander-in-Chief, by international agreements, by assertions of rights for the United States or resistance or concession to the claims of others, by "doctrines" announcing national intentions, by occasional domestic regulations, in some circumstances even by direction to the courts. Congress makes foreign policy by regulating foreign commerce and intercourse and by other domestic laws, by spending, by declaring and waging war, by authorizing or approving executive agreements, by some resolutions of national policy related to its war power. In a sense there is also a division of executive function: the President carries out the foreign policy he makes as well as that made by Congress, but Congress "executes" the President's policies, too, by implementing legislation and appropriation of funds.

---

* I deal here with conflict and cooperation between Congress and the President. Conflict and cooperation between the Congress and "the Treaty-Makers" are left to Chapter V, and the relation of Congress to executive agreements is in Chapter VI.

For one attempt to define the distribution of authority between President and Congress in foreign affairs, see WRIGHT 335–36.

The respective powers of President and Congress are established in the large, but the division I have described has not been accepted in all respects by all Presidents and all Congresses at all times, and in any event the generalizations leave ample areas of uncertainty. In principle as in fact, recurrent competition for power has punctuated relations between President and Congress, throwing up the dominant, least-tractable constitutional issues of American foreign relations. That the Constitution is especially inarticulate in allocating foreign affairs powers; that a particular power can with equal logic and fair constitutional reading be claimed for the President or for Congress; that the powers of both President and Congress have been described in full, even extravagant adjectives ("vast," "plenary"); that instead of a "natural" separation of "executive" from "legislative" functions there has grown an irregular, uncertain division of each— all have served and nurtured political forces inviting to struggle. Recurrent disputes have derived in particular from the separation—shades of Clausewitz! *—of power to conduct foreign relations and make foreign policy, acquired by the President, from the power to decide for war, lodged in Congress. Conflict has been compounded also by the uncertain reach of the authority of the Commander-in-Chief, in war or in peace. Since, generally, these "boundary disputes" have not been resolved in court,[1] they remain unresolved in principle and if the President has succeeded in winning most of them in fact, Congressional "irredentism" runs deep and erupts in almost every Congressional generation. Practice and sometimes even constitutional doctrine have been shaped by personal or partisan and other political relations between particular Presidents and particular Congresses (or Congressmen), sometimes too by particular issues: Lincoln and both Roosevelts effectively took power from fearful or friendly Congresses; the Vietnam war stirred Congressmen to reassert authority and confront the President.

* "[W]ar is not merely a political act, but also a real political instrument, a continuation of political commerce, a carrying out of the same by other means." 1 CARL VON CLAUSEWITZ, ON WAR [1832] Bk. 1, Ch. 1, § 24, at 23 (8th Rev. ed. 1966). Compare John Quincy Adams, this chapter, note 33.

Issues as to the respective bounds of President and Congress apart, the Constitution's division of an indivisible process requires peaceful co-existence if not active cooperation between the political branches, and in innumerable ways every day the conduct of foreign relations reflects and depends on their combined actions.[2]   Routine cooperation, of course, goes unnoticed and raises neither political nor constitutional issues.*   But joint operation by substantially independent branches cannot wholly escape conflict, and the exceptional prerogatives of the President and the exceptional subordination of the Congress in foreign affairs have bred tendencies which engender controversy.[3]   The Executive is sometimes carried away by ready initiative, by expertise, responsibility and the security of secrecy, to invade where Congress has its claims—for example, by "going it alone" to the brink of war and beyond (as some think happened in Vietnam in the 1960's).   Congress, frustrated by separation from the means and channels of diplomacy, distrustful of executive assertions of expertise, sensitive to domestic implications or responding to domestic "pressures," is sometimes tempted to tie the President's constitutional hands.

Particular allocations of power have evoked particular resistance.   Congress has not been content merely to make domestic laws and to pay the President's bills; it has especially resented Presidential *faits accomplis* committing the United States before the world and compelling Congress to rubber-stamp his initiatives.   Presidents, in turn, have resented their dependence on Congress for money and implementing legislation, Congressional efforts to exploit that dependence for limiting Executive prerogative, and its control of the Executive's foreign affairs establishment.   There have been claims by each branch that the other refused cooperation which the Constitution commands or actively hampered the exercise of constitutional powers. Presidents have challenged the constitutionality of special extra

---

* There have been complaints of "excessive cooperation" in the form of undue delegation of authority to the President by Congress. See pp. 119–20 below, this chapter.

legislative devices developed by Congress to oversee Executive activity.

## Competition for Power

Because in domestic affairs the respective powers of President and Congress are allocated explicitly and according to an expressed principle, they are generally recognized as "exclusive," denied to the other branch: the executive power belongs to the President, the legislative to Congress, and the President cannot exercise legislative power or Congress executive power.[4] Even with this clear division, issues have arisen as to where some power lies, and there have been claims by one branch to authority admittedly possessed also by the other.* The absence of a comprehensive, "natural" division in foreign affairs excluding the other branch has been a strong invitation to compete for power or to claim a concurrent authority.

In the competition for power in foreign affairs, the principal issues have resulted from Presidential initiatives invoking one or more of his "plenary" powers, resisted by Congress citing its "plenary" powers; but Presidents have also accused Congress of "poaching." Sometimes each has claimed exclusive power, sometimes the power to act as well as the other; occasionally the branches acted differently if not inconsistently and each sought to prevail.

For the constitutional lawyer the questions are: What are the inherent limits of particular powers, and what limitations upon the powers of one branch are implied in those granted to the other? Is a particular power "exclusive" or might it be exercised also by the other branch, and which shall prevail if their acts conflict?

### Exclusive Powers of the President

Although in foreign affairs the allocation of power between President and Congress conforms to no "natural" separation of executive and legislative powers, the domains of President and Congress are, for the most part, distinct and exclusive, as they

* See p. 104 below.

are in domestic matters. Even for proponents of maximum Congressional authority,† the expressed, unambiguous grants to the President leave no doubt that he, not Congress, can make treaties, appoint or receive ambassadors, command the armed forces, see that the laws are faithfully executed. For many years now, Congress has not seriously doubted either that the President is the sole organ of communication with foreign governments: Congress may not give or receive communications on behalf of the United States, or negotiate with foreign governments, or "conduct foreign relations." [5]   Like Madison, however, Congressmen —usually in rhetoric and declamation—recurrently deny that the President can "make foreign policy" on his own authority; even more often they claim at least that Congress can make foreign policy concurrently with the President.*

Effectively, that view has not prevailed, and accepted Presidential authority implies limitations on Congressional power that can be stated with some confidence.**   Its legislative and spending powers apart, Congress can determine national foreign policy only in respects expressly confided to it by the Constitution, and the plausible penumbra of these explicit grants: it can go to war, or end war, or abstain from war and proclaim neutrality, and it can join the President in making international agreements.  But it cannot itself (or effectively direct the President to) recognize foreign states or governments, or establish or regulate or break relations with them, or terminate treaties, or proclaim "doctrines," or determine present and future policies or attitudes of the United States, though it may express its "sense" and request or exhort the President.

It has been suggested [6] that some limitations on Congressional powers are implied in the Treaty Power, that the Constitution

† See Chapter III, pp. 82–84.

* See Chapter III, p. 84 and note 70.

** See Chapter III, pp. 84–85.  Some of the express limitations on Congress in the original Constitution (as distinguished from the Bill of Rights and later Amendments) also have relevance for foreign affairs.  See Chapter III, note 79.

intended that some action be taken or policies established only by treaty, not by act of Congress.* There is little basis for that view. Of course, Congress cannot bind the United States internationally and surely it cannot legislate obligations for other nations. Also, some matters which might be the subject of international agreement—say, recognition, or a promise of friendship—are indeed the domain of the President, not of Congress. But there is nothing to suggest that any matter apparently within the ambit of Congressional power is to be regulated instead only by the President and Senate and only with the cooperation of a foreign power; that some acts can be done or policies established only bilaterally by binding international agreement but not unilaterally by the United States.** Rather, Congress can legislate domestically on any matter which might be regulated by treaty, and Congress can do for the United States her part of what might ordinarily be done by treaty: *e. g.,* acquire and incorporate territory, end wars, prescribe terms for the settlement of claims or the extradition of persons; it can even approximate international agreements by legislation based on reciprocity.[7]

## Exclusive Powers of Congress

Broad assertions and extravagant adjectives, some of them supported by the Supreme Court, might leave the impression that the President can exercise virtually all the national political pow-

---

* The suggestion may originate in the fact that, in the past, some matters commonly dealt with by international agreement did not appear to be within the enumerated powers of Congress (compare Mr. Justice Holmes, p. 76); now it is accepted that Congress has power to legislate in all matters affecting foreign affairs. *Ibid.* Of course, the President and Senate can proceed to regulate differently by treaty and prevail over prior legislation. See p. 163.

The converse, that matters within the domain of Congress cannot be the subject of a treaty, is considered (and rejected) in Chapter V, p. 148.

** That Congress and the President can join to make international agreements fully equivalent to a treaty in international as in domestic law also tends to deny that the Constitution gave the treaty-makers a domain from which Congress is excluded. See Chapter VI, p. 175.

er in foreign affairs, at least concurrently with Congress. In fact, large areas have never even been claimed by him. In principle, it would be difficult for a President to dispute that by vesting in Congress "all legislative Powers herein granted" and granting it a comprehensive array of specific powers, the Constitution barred the President from exercising these powers even as regards foreign affairs.* Whatever, then, he might do by treaty or other international agreement (Chapters V, VI), he cannot unilaterally regulate commerce with foreign nations,[8] or make domestic laws punishing piracy or defining offenses against the law of nations,** or declare war.† Equally, he cannot exercise, even for foreign affairs purposes, the general powers allocated to Congress: he cannot regulate patents or copyrights or the value of money, or establish post offices, or dispose of American territory or property; †† he cannot enact necessary and proper laws to carry into execution the powers of Congress or even his own powers, for example, criminal laws to enforce an arms embargo.[9]

---

* Except, perhaps, under theories like Theodore Roosevelt's that the President can do anything not forbidden by the Constitution or by the laws. Chapter II, p. 39.

Other limitations on the President's powers are clearly implied: he can make "treaties" but not that which is not a treaty (Chapter V, p. 142); he can make treaties or appoint ambassadors with the consent of the Senate, but not without that consent. But compare Chapter VI, p. 175, and Chapter II, p. 45.

Foreign governments are generally entitled, and required, to treat as authoritative what the President does in relation to them, regardless of possible constitutional limitations upon his authority. Compare Chapter V, note 36, Chapter VI, note 21.

** In the Nuremberg Charter and its counterparts, the President in effect joined to define new offenses against the law of nations, but he did that by international agreement, and he did not purport to make them offenses against the United States punishable as criminal laws in American courts. Compare Chapter VII, p. 200.

† The relation of the President's powers to those of Congress as regards making war is discussed at p. 99.

†† As regards the President's power to dispose of United States property by executive agreement, see Chapter VI, p. 180.

He cannot spend money on his own authority for foreign aid, or draw funds from the Treasury, without Congressional appropriation, to build an embassy.[10]   Presumably, the unexpressed lawmaking powers of Congress deriving from national sovereignty are also generally denied to the President: he cannot enact general immigration laws by executive order.**

Even in domestic matters, however, there is apparently a "twilight zone" clearly within the constitutional domain of Congress in which the President could also act.   When the Supreme Court held that President Truman had no authority to seize the steel mills during a labor dispute to keep them running, it appeared that a majority of the Court would have upheld the President if Congress had not propounded a different and inconsistent policy.[11]   In foreign affairs, surely, where Congress has spilled over into what is admittedly the President's domain, the fact that Congress can act in some respect does not, of itself, prove that the President could not; Presidents, we have seen, have acted unilaterally in some matters which Congress might undoubtedly have regulated.   Which powers, then, belong to Congress exclusively?   What foreign affairs actions can be taken only by Congress?

The President was denied power by the Supreme Court in a few aged or aging cases having some relation to foreign affairs.   In 1814, the Supreme Court (by Chief Justice Marshall) held that the President could not confiscate the property of alien enemies in time of war without authorization from Congress, and a Congressional declaration of war alone did not constitute such authorization.[12]   In issue was the President's power as Commander-in-Chief during war, not his foreign affairs powers; the property was seized in the United States, there were no relations with the enemy, and relations with other nations were not involved. Marshall wrote long before Lincoln established virtual Presidential autonomy in war and before other aggrandizements of Presidential power; later, during the Civil War, the Supreme Court in

---

** But apparently the President (as well as Congress) can exclude aliens. See Chapter II, p. 37.

effect rejected much of what Marshall had written when it upheld seizures pursuant to Lincoln's blockade.[13]  A principal theme
of Marshall's opinion, moreover, was that war between nations
did not ordinarily engage their civilian nationals and the private
property of such nationals.[14]  Since then nations have learned
total war, and recognized the importance to the conduct of such
war of new kinds of property controlled by new kinds of aliens,
particularly large alien companies;  in the World Wars Congress
authorized comprehensive confiscations of enemy property.[15]
If, then, a war-time President some future day proceeded to seize
alien enemy properties without Congressional authorization,
it is unlikely that the courts would interfere, and surely they
would not write as Marshall did about the narrow implications
of a Congressional declaration of war or the narrow limits of
Presidential war-power.  The Supreme Court might again reject,
however, what Marshall in fact rejected—the seizure of a private
vessel by a local United States attorney claiming the mantle of
Executive authority but apparently bearing no Presidential decree or authentic Presidential decision.

In 1851, the Supreme Court (by Chief Justice Taney) held that
while the President, as Commander-in-Chief, could temporarily
occupy and control conquered territory, only a treaty or act of
Congress could annex it to the United States.[16]  Taney, too, spoke
of Presidential war-power still in its infancy, of a subordinate
President and a dominant Congress.  Today, the President's powers as Commander-in-Chief in declared wars know few constitutional limits, and the Supreme Court has not yet found any on
his power in occupied territory.*  His matured foreign affairs
powers, too, might well give him authority to claim for the United
States what the forces he commands had conquered.[17]  But the
power to determine the permanent domestic status of acquired
territory, with its far-reaching irreversible consequences, might
still be for Congress alone, to which are expressly granted related

---

* The President's power to seize, occupy and govern enemy territory
is well established.  See Chapter II, p. 52.  Compare p. 105, this
chapter.

powers to govern territory and admit new States (Article IV, Sec. 3).*

In this century, in 1936, the Supreme Court (by Justice Sutherland) held that the President did not have authority to extradite an American citizen when not required to do so by treaty or statute.[18]   One might ask whether the Supreme Court which gave effect to Executive policy in the immunity cases and upheld executive agreements [19] would have refused to honor a Presidential agreement providing for extradition, or a President's unilateral declaration of national policy favoring extradition, perhaps even a President's decision *ad hoc* to extradite a particular person.   But the tides of governmental power in general, and of executive power in particular, have again receded, unmistakably if in unknown degree, especially before the realities of the bureaucratic process and the rising claims of individual rights.**   A contemporary court, too, might insist that extradition of a United States citizen for a criminal trial abroad should be based on national policy, not on the possible caprice of a "working-level" official of the State Department signing the name of the Secretary of State.

There is also a more recent case, *Kent* v. *Dulles*.   In that case the Supreme Court held that Congress had not authorized the Department of State to withhold a citizen's passport (and thereby deny his right to travel) because of his alleged Communist beliefs and associations.   The Court did not consider whether the President might have authority to deny passports and the right to travel abroad on his own constitutional authority.   But talking of the right to travel abroad, the majority said: [20]

> If that "liberty" is to be regulated, it must be pursuant to the law-making functions of the Congress. *Youngstown Sheet & Tube Co.* v. *Sawyer, supra.*

---

* The President could, of course, annex territory by treaty.   See Chapter V.   Compare the power of Congress to decide whether territory acquired by the United States shall be "incorporated" into the United States or remain "unincorporated".   See Chapter III, note 50.

** Compare Chapter II, p. 60 *et seq.*

The reference to *Youngstown* (the *Steel Seizure Case*) strengthens the implication that the Court thought the President could not regulate the right to travel abroad on his own authority.

These few Supreme cases apart, there are other matters as to which Presidents, without conceding exclusive powers to Congress in principle, have accepted it in fact. Although Washington proclaimed neutrality on his own authority and Hamilton justified it on principles that have largely prevailed in other respects, Presidents have in practice conceded to Congress the power to decide to be neutral, as equivalent to a power to decide not to go to war.† Similarly, Presidents have not claimed the power unilaterally to declare peace, as distinguished from an armistice.

In all, then, whatever the President might do during authorized war or by international agreement, Congress alone can spend, authorize war, legislate and regulate generally within the United States, even in matters regarding foreign affairs. The courts will be particularly reluctant to uphold unilateral executive acts that impinge on individual rights; they might be less unsympathetic to unilateral acts of some urgency that impinge only on economic activities and property rights, particularly of corporations.* *Ad hoc* "legislation" for particular individuals and circumstances, and "suggestions" to the courts in particular cases, have also become suspect, and, if they survive, will be limited to matters like sovereign and diplomatic immunity that directly involve a foreign government and diplomatic relations with it, and are particularly the concern of the Executive.**

† See Chapter II, p. 53; Chapter III, p. 85.

* This generalization might deny Wilson's power to impose censorship in support of neutrality, unless supported in legislation, Chapter II, p. 53. Presidential decisions to admit cables or electric current (Chapter II, p. 49) might pass as a form of control of communications with the outside world only indirectly regulating domestic private rights; one might distinguish them also because they affect only ~~economic rights.~~ The Supreme Court has elsewhere built constitutional doctrine distinguishing between economic regulation and intrusions on "preferred" freedoms. See Chapter X, pp. 256–57.

** See Chapter II, pp. 56–64.

*Where exclusive powers meet: committing the nation to war.*[21]

That there are accepted zones of exclusive authority for President and Congress has not prevented political controversy and constitutional confusion in "frontier areas," particularly between the President's conduct of foreign relations, including the use of force for foreign policy purposes,† and the power of Congress to decide for war. Perhaps because Presidents of both major political parties have repeatedly asserted large power and commanded Congressional and public support, it is commonly accepted, usually also by most Congressmen, that the President can conduct our foreign relations and can deploy American forces for foreign policy purposes, at least when Congress is silent. On the other hand, no President has disputed that, unless war is thrust upon the United States, Congress alone has the authority to decide that the United States shall go to war.[22] Unhappily, the line between war and lesser uses of force is often elusive, sometimes illusory, and the use of force for foreign policy purposes can almost imperceptibly become a national commitment to war. Even when he does not use military force, the President can incite other nations or otherwise plunge or stumble this country into war, or force the hand of Congress to declare or to acquiesce and cooperate in war.[23] As a matter of constitutional doctrine, however, one can say confidently that a President begins to exceed his authority only if he wilfully or recklessly moves the nation towards war, and a responsible President, loyal to his constitutional oath, should stop, or seek the authorization of Congress.[24] Some might ask, even, that the President seek Congressional approval for policies that might conceivably lead to war,[25] but foreign policy and international relations do not permit infallible prescience or fine judgments, and a President can insist that the "line" between war and foreign policy by means short of war is the constitutional imperative delimiting his domain from that of Congress.

In the realities of national life, however, that constitutional issue is becoming hypothetical for it is increasingly difficult to make an authentic case that the President has taken the country

† See Chapter II, pp. 53–54.

Separation of Powers

into war without Congressional authorization in advance or ratification soon after. Presidents cannot use the armed forces for long in substantial operations without Congressional cooperation; surely any action that can properly be called war depends on Congressional appropriations and other forms of approval, expressed or implied. Presidents who fought these wars inevitably sought Congressional approval and invariably obtained it.

In substantial measure, I believe, failure to accept these political realities and their relevance for constitutional principle confused a major controversy of our time, the Vietnam war.[26] In the light of piles of precedent hardening into doctrine, it is difficult to fault on constitutional grounds the Presidents who began to support South Vietnam by various forms of aid short of war.* Even with sad hindsight to show how these early steps were "inevitably" to lead the United States into war, one cannot make a case that the Presidents usurped Congressional authority, especially since those early measures too, in fact, had the approval of Congress. In time, however, Vietnam—like Korea a decade earlier [27]—became what surely must be called a war within the meaning of the Constitution, and it was not for the President to wage it on his sole authority. He needed the approval of Congress, and the question—a different question, with different constitutional undertones—was whether he had it. For constitutional purposes it seems indisputable that he did, in the "Tonkin Resolution," in repeated Congressional appropriations, and in an express declaration by Congress of "its firm intentions to provide all necessary support for members of the Armed Forces of the United States fighting in Vietnam." [28]

That, as some later claimed, Congress did not appreciate what it was doing, or that its hand was forced to do it, is constitutionally immaterial. (In other cases, too, Presidents have been charged with forcing the hand of Congress or misleading Congress into declaring or authorizing war.) [29] It would be constitutionally material if _____, the resolutions did not authorize full-scale war, that the President misinterpreted them and exceeded the authority they granted; there is no evidence,

* See Chapter II, pp. 53–54.

101

however, that Congress (as distinguished from some Congressmen) thought so,[30] and Congress had the power and many opportunities to tell the President so, and did not seize them.† (The Tonkin Resolution itself expressly reserved the power to withdraw the authorization it granted by concurrent resolution.) [31] Congress also had the power to withhold appropriations, at least to make them with disclaimer and protest, and to check the President in other ways; and surely it could have readily and justifiably done so if it believed he had exceeded the authority granted him. Similarly, that Congress could not muster a majority to terminate or redefine the President's authority;[32] that it could not openly break with the President without jeopardizing major national interests; that it could not discontinue support for the war because it "could not let the troops down"—these do not indicate that Congress did not authorize or continue to support the war; rather, they show that, and why, Congress did. (I deal later with Congressional authority to limit the President's conduct of the war.)

For the constitutional lawyer, as for the citizen, then, it is important to distinguish in these controversies between appeals to the Constitution and complaints against it. The claim on Vietnam, properly, was less that the President usurped power than that the Constitution gave him "excessive" power; or, since Congress had authority to check the President, that the constitutional distribution does not work because, in the end, the restraints on the President are not effective.[33] Many were really asking whether, in essential respects, we have a desirable system for conducting foreign relations.*

Unhappiness about Vietnam led Congress to seek remedies for what some thought to be the constitutional problems it reflected. In 1972 the Senate passed "The War Powers Act," [34] which provided that in the absence of a declaration of war "the

---

† As a matter of constitutional doctrine Congressional inaction cannot always, or usually, be deemed consent, but consent once given remains effective unless it expires or is terminated.

* See Chapter XI.

Armed Forces of the United States may be introduced in hostilities, or in situations where imminent involvement in hostilities is clearly indicated by the circumstances," only in the face of an armed attack on the United States or its armed forces, to protect American nationals pending their evacuation, or pursuant to specific statutory authorization. Use of the Armed Forces in the circumstances indicated must be promptly reported to Congress in writing, and cannot be sustained beyond thirty days unless "the continued use [of the armed forces] in such hostilities or in such situation has been authorized in specific legislation enacted for that purpose  . . . ." Congress may terminate the use of force prior to the thirty-day period.

Congress can surely prescribe for future uses of force in situations amounting to war. As regards hostilities "short of war," it may be that, although the President can use force if Congress is silent, Congress can forbid or regulate even such uses of force, if only on the ground that they might lead to war. Presidents, however, are likely to deny the control of Congress in such cases.[35]

Whether such legislation would effectively restrain the President is a different question. A President who wished to act could exploit its ambiguities and uncertainties, notably the meaning of "hostilities," and when "imminent involvement" in them is "clearly indicated." Of the numerous recent "uses" of force, only Korea and Vietnam would have been clearly covered. Had such legislation been in effect, President Truman would perhaps have acted anyhow, but might have been impelled to seek Congressional approval within thirty days. Vietnam was expressly authorized, and, presumably, any Tonkin Resolution would have clearly authorized hostilities beyond thirty days as well. Of course, such legislation might serve to discourage a hesitant President, promote policies of non-action, and enable him to shift the responsibility for action or inaction to Congress

In our day, the changing character of war, and the extraordinary acerbity of international relations, have given also a new cast to competition between the President and Congress. "Cold war" was a metaphor carrying all the dangers of metaphor, but the phrase inevitably stirred echoes of older constitutional controversies. Is cold war sufficiently like "hot war" to suggest that major decisions as to whether to "declare" it, wage it, or end it belong to Congress? Or is the crux of cold war that it is not war and is not even likely to lead to war, that it is by definition foreign policy short of war and therefore the responsibility of the President, except to the extent that its "conduct" depends on domestic legislation and spending? Or, perhaps, is it constitutionally, as some have thought it is politically, *sui generis*, further eroding distinctions between domestic and foreign affairs, and calling for extraordinary Presidential leadership but demanding special forms of cooperation rather than checks-and-balances? The broad constitutional issue was not debated but it colored particular issues of conflict and cooperation, discussed below.*

## Concurrent Powers

Although the President and Congress have large exclusive powers which each alone can exercise, there is clearly some uncertain zone in which each might act, at least when the other has not acted. For the reasons generally favoring Executive initiative, Presidents have successfully claimed to duplicate powers of Congress more often than Congress has been able to act in what is indubitably the President's domain, though exactly how much Congressional power Presidents could exercise on their own authority cannot be determined since they exercise so much by delegation from Congress. The courts, we have seen, have recognized the authority of the President to direct them in regard to sovereign and diplomatic immunity, some thought also in Act of State, subjects which are also proper subjects for Congressional legislation. The President can apparently exclude aliens, as Congress surely can. Presidents have "legislated," as no doubt Congress could, "at the border," *e. g.*, to admit international cables or electric power. President Truman claimed rights in the Continental Shelf which Congress could have done, just as it declared national sovereignty over air space. Presidents have not conceded in principle that they could not proclaim or implement neutrality, and Congress has not admitted that it could not terminate treaties

---

* Compare pp. 113–14 below, and Chapter XI.

or direct the President to do so. Concurrence results where the President's powers as Commander-in-Chief overlap those of Congress to make the necessary rules for the government and regulation of the land and naval forces. No one can disentangle the war powers of the two branches,[36] including their powers to act towards the enemy, toward neutrals, and foreign nationals; there are suggestions that Presidents, like Congress, can determine to end hostilities.[37] The Supreme Court held that Presidential courts in occupied Germany after the Second World War could exercise jurisdiction over an American civilian for whom Congress had in effect provided trial by court-martial.[38]

Concurrent power often begets a race for initiative and the President will usually "get there first." When the President acts and Congress is silent, there is often a justifiable presumption that Congress has acquiesced in, even approved, what the President has done; if so, the action is supported by the constitutional powers of both branches.* A President is less likely to remain silent when Congress acts in what he considers his domain, but his failure to veto Congressional legislation or to protest other Congressional initiatives might also imply acquiescence and mute any objection that Congress lacks constitutional authority.

Concurrent authority inevitably carries the possibility of conflicting assertions of power and the constitutional lawyer must consider who prevails as a matter of law. Mr. Justice Jackson provided a suggestive formula: [39]

1. When the President acts pursuant to an express or implied authorization of Congress, his authority is at its maximum, for it includes all that he possesses in his own right plus all that Congress can delegate . . . .

2. When the President acts in absence of either a Congressional grant or denial of authority, he can only rely upon his ~~~~~~~~ ~~~~~~ ~~~~~~ powers, but there is a zone of twilight in which he and Congress may have

* Compare the suggestion that the President always acts by tacit acquiescence of Congress, Chapter II, note 17.

concurrent authority, or in which its distribution is uncertain  .  .  .  .

3.  When the President takes measures incompatible with the expressed or implied will of Congress, his power is at its lowest ebb, for then he can rely only upon his own constitutional powers minus any constitutional powers of Congress over the matter.  .  .  .

That the area of concurrent power seems to involve largely Presidential pretensions where Congressional authority is clear would suggest that Congress should usually prevail in case of conflict, no matter which branch acted first.[40]  So, surely, the President is bound to follow Congressional directives in regard to neutrality or the landing of submarine cables.[41]  Even where the President's authority is clear and perhaps primary, his acts will bow before an act of Congress for purposes of domestic law: the President is bound by, and the courts will give effect to, Congressional legislation modifying the Act of State doctrine, or regulating the extradition of inhabitants of the United States, or the admission of foreign forces, perhaps even diplomatic immunities.*

More difficult to resolve in principle have been recurrent conflicts of authority as regards the use of American forces abroad. In 1940 President Roosevelt sent troops to Greenland and Iceland in the face of legislation that seemed to forbid it.[42]  In the famous "Troops to Europe" debates of 1950–51, Congress considered, and the President resisted, limitations on the number of troops the United States could station in allied countries in time of peace. Congressmen cited Congressional authority to raise armies and to spend money for the common defense, and saw troops in Europe as intimately related to its powers of war-and-peace.  The Presi-

---

* Compare Chapter III, pp. 74–76.  But by treaty the President can effectively repeal a statutory provision, Chapter V, p. 163.  And, perhaps the immunity cases (Chapter II, p. 57) mean that even in the face of an Act of Congress, the courts should follow the President's instructions, at least *ad hoc*, to dismiss a proceeding which he says would jeopardize relations with the state involved.  But compare State Department proposals for legislation to regulate diplomatic and sovereign immunity, Chapter II, note 79.

dent, invoking authority as Commander-in-Chief and foreign affairs powers, argued, in effect, that troops are stationed abroad not for making war but for not making war, *i. e.*, for deterrence, or for general political influence. In the end, the limitations were not formally imposed but the constitutional issue was not resolved.[43]

## Concurrent powers during war

Constitutional conflict between President and Congress in time of war has been virtually unknown until Vietnam.* Congress has either delegated virtually unlimited powers in advance, or later ratified what Presidents have done, and it has not otherwise attempted to limit the President in the conduct of war. But issues of Congressional authority over the conduct of war agitated our political discourse in the latter part of the Vietnam war. In 1970, when President Nixon sent troops into Cambodia, he claimed that it was not a new war (requiring new Congressional approval) but an aspect of the same war, and realistically—as well as literally—within the terms of the original authorization.[44] But members of Congress, unhappy with that extension of the war and fearful of further extensions, some of them indeed desiring to terminate the war entirely, sought to repeal the original resolution authorizing war in Indochina and to limit the continuation of war by forbidding expenditures for certain purposes and beyond prescribed dates.[45] The President purported to acquiesce in the repeal of the Tonkin Resolution, claiming he could continue planned operations under his authority as Commander-in-Chief, but challenged the right of Congress to control the conduct of war once authorized, whether directly or by imposing conditions on expenditures.

Constitutionally, in my view, the President was wrong. The power of Congress to declare war is the power to decide for war

---

* There has never been an instance of Congress declaring a war which the President did not ~~want to fight. But President Cleveland is reported to have said~~ in 1897 that if Congress declared war on Spain on account of Cuba he would refuse to order the Army and Navy to fight. See 2 R. McElroy Grover Cleveland 249–50 (1923), cited in Corwin, The President 438–39, n. 95.

or peace, and should imply the power to unmake war as well as to make it.[46] In the political context of Vietnam-Cambodia repeal of the Tonkin Resolution did not in fact constitute a Congressional decision to end the war.[47] But a clear resolution to that effect would have bound the President [48] and he could not have properly insisted on prosecuting the war thereafter.

Less confidently, whatever the President can do short of war, in war his powers as Commander-in-Chief are subject to ultimate Congressional authority to "make" the war, and Congress can control the conduct of the war it has authorized. (One might suggest, even, that the President's powers during war are not "concurrent" but delegated by Congress, by implication in the declaration or authorization of war.)* It would be unthinkable for Congress to attempt detailed, tactical decisions, and as to these the President's authority is effectively supreme. But, in my view, he would be bound to follow Congressional directives not only as to whether to continue the war, but whether to extend it to other countries and other belligerents, whether to fight a limited or unlimited war,[49] today, perhaps, even whether to fight a "conventional" or a nuclear war.

## Issues in Cooperation

Separation and division of powers were not designed to make the political branches autonomous, and the conduct of foreign relations depends on their continuing cooperation. That complementary action is called for does not always assure it in practice, and there have been doctrinal differences about the nature of cooperation and the obligation to accord it.

### The Obligation of Congress to Cooperate

The President requires Congressional appropriation of funds for the maintenance of his foreign affairs establishment, for the expenses of conducting foreign relations generally, for special foreign policy actions and programs (including the use of troops short of war), for carrying out obligations of the United States under international agreements. Foreign policy and foreign re-

---

* Compare Brown v. United States, p. 96 above, and note 12, this chapter.

lations generally, and international agreements in particular, may also require implementation and support by domestic legislation.[50] Is there constitutional obligation to provide the money and the legislation, or was Congress intended to exercise an independent "checks-and-balances" judgment and possible veto?

The issue arose early, and has remained, as regards the obligation of Congress to implement a treaty, and periodically Congressmen continue to assert their independence in principle.[51] In fact, Congress has rarely refused to adopt the laws or appropriate the funds required to implement an international undertaking,* though Congress might differ with the President as to how much money or what laws were required. Congress has also generally refrained from drawing its purse strings to frustrate other activities that are clearly the President's prerogative, as by refusing to appropriate for the salary of an Ambassador or the expenses of an embassy, for participating in international conferences, or even to pay the costs of sending the Navy on a foreign policy mission far removed from war.[52] But especially since Congress never concedes and periodically resists the suggestion that the President can "make foreign policy" without the consent of the Senate or the approval of both Houses, it would surely deny that it has no discretion but to pass laws or appropriate funds to implement Presidential policy generally.[53]

In recent times a similar issue has arisen in the special context of foreign assistance. It has been argued that increasingly foreign policy takes the form of spending programs; that bilateral aid (and contributions to multilateral assistance programs) in particular are essential elements in contemporary foreign policy and for the United States essential indicia of friendly relations with many countries; that decisions as to aid are therefore properly the President's responsibility and Congress can no more refuse the President appropriations for foreign assistance than for maintaining an embassy.[54]

---

* See Chapter V, p. 161; but compare note 79, this chapter. Congress has been less hesitant to compel the United States later to dishonor obligations, by enacting legislation inconsistent with them. See p. 163 below.

Here the argument for Congressional independence is surely stronger. Foreign assistance seems not merely an appropriation of funds to implement policies which are primarily the President's responsibility but a form of spending for the general welfare of the United States, and it is difficult to accept that the President should command a power expressly conferred upon Congress. (Art. I, sec. 8, cl. 1) Congress can exercise its other expressed powers—for example, to regulate foreign commerce—in ways inconsistent with Presidential designs, and favorable trade terms loom as large in contemporary foreign relations as direct financial assistance. Whether and how much to spend, moreover, depends inevitably on national taxes (determined by Congress) and other income, and on choices and priorities that go far beyond foreign affairs and are admittedly for Congress ultimately to determine. However unhappy the consequences of division of authority in this context, one must conclude that Congress could insist on its spending power as on other express powers, and in foreign, as in domestic matters, can spend (or not spend) according to its views of the general welfare of the United States.

## The President's Obligation to Execute the Laws

A somewhat similar issue as to obligation to cooperate arises when Presidents refuse to execute Congressional laws relating to foreign affairs which they could not afford to veto or which were repassed over their veto, or were approved by a predecessor President. Early Presidents claimed that the constitutional provision that "He shall take Care that the Laws be faithfully executed" gave them discretion not to execute enactments that, in their view, were unconstitutional,[55] and in foreign affairs a President might raise the particular objection that Congress was invading his domain.[56] More recently, it has been asserted generally that the complexities of government, limited executive resources, and constitutional independence, permit the President discretion as to which laws he should execute first,[57] and even whether some law should be executed at all. Presidents have

110

claimed, in particular, that authorizations and appropriations of funds are not mandatory and they are free to "impound funds" and spend less or not to spend at all.[58]

It is doubtless true that many laws, including many that authorize or appropriate funds (especially for programs initiated by the President), can properly be interpreted as leaving the President discretion as to whether or not to act or to spend; surely, he need not spend all that is appropriated if the job can be done for less. But other laws, including some spending programs, are clearly intended to be mandatory and, as to these, it is difficult to build a persuasive argument that "He shall take Care that the Laws be faithfully executed" gives him discretion not to execute them.[59] Presidential authority not to execute some Congressional mandates would have to be found in some other constitutional power: the argument might be that Congress cannot impose foreign policy on the President and the President's "primacy" in foreign relations gives him special discretion as to whether and how to execute laws relating to foreign affairs.* As regards spending programs, in particular, the argument would amount to saying that even if Presidents cannot command Congress to spend for foreign affairs purposes,[60] Congress in turn cannot make foreign policy by spending where the President does not wish to. That may be what President Truman had in mind when he declared that a provision directing him to make a loan to Franco's Spain was unconstitutional and he would treat it as only an authorization to do so. (In fact he lent Spain the money.) The issue of principle remains unresolved.

---

* As regards funds for weapons, Presidents may also be asserting special authority as Commander-in-Chief even in the face of the express grant to Congress of the power "To raise and support Armies . . ." and "to provide and maintain a Navy" (Art. I, sec. 8). The argument would be that modern weapons have an essential strategic significance for deterring an enemy and defending the nation, and the President has independent authority to defend the United States against attack, Chapter II, p. 52. The President might also argue that the strategic balance is essential to his ability to conduct foreign relations.

## *"Executive Privilege"*

Presidents are frequently charged with failure to cooperate when they deny to Congress or its committees information or documents, whether to preserve "confidentiality" of operations within the Executive Branch, or because the Executive believes that they should be "classified" and concealed in the national interest.[61]  In regard to foreign relations, in particular, Presidents often claim that disclosure would jeopardize national policies, offend some friendly nation, or otherwise embarrass the United States in its relations with other nations.  "Executive privilege" was asserted by President Washington to withhold from the House of Representatives papers relating to the negotiation of the Jay Treaty,[62] but while he justified that in part because the House had no constitutional function in the making of treaties, later Presidents refused documents and information which were indisputably relevant to legitimate Congressional concerns.[63]

This issue, too, has not been resolved in principle,[64] but in fact Presidents have prevailed.[65]  Congress has never sought to enforce its demands by threat of criminal sanction or citation for contempt against executive officials.[66]  In foreign affairs, in particular, Congress has itself recognized limitations, for while it has long demanded reports of all executive departments, it has requested them of the State Department only "if not incompatible with the public interest." [67]  But Presidents have been careful not to deny Congress lightly, or too often.[68]

## Interference

Separation of powers has also contributed to charges, usually by the President against Congress, of unconstitutional "interference."  Differing conceptions of their respective constitutional authority have sometimes led Congress to enjoin the President in matters which he deemed not its business: Congress has directed Presidents to negotiate or to denounce treaties; [69] once Congress directed President Grant to notify certain diplomatic and consular establishments "to close their offices." [70]  A known dead letter, still on the statute books (since 1913), provides: [71]

> Hereafter the Executive shall not extend or accept any invitation to participate in any international con-

gress, conference, or like event, without first having specific authority of law to do so.

Presidents have been sensitive to such encroachments,* have usually protested, and often disregarded them.

## *"Unconstitutional conditions"*

Congress has attempted to influence the conduct of the President, and of other governments, by imposing "conditions," especially on spending and appropriations. Favorite vehicles for various such "riders," not always germane, have been the annual appropriations acts (in recent years also the foreign assistance acts) which Presidents must have and cannot afford to veto because they object to incidental provisions.

The constitutional lawyer would distinguish between different appropriations and between different conditions. If Congress cannot properly withhold appropriations for the President's activities, it ought not be able to impose conditions ** on such appropriations.[72] Even when Congress is free not to appropriate, it ought not be able to regulate Presidential action by conditions on the appropriation of funds to carry it out, if it could not regulate the action directly. So, should Congress provide that appropriated funds shall not be used to pay the salaries of State Department officials who promote a particular policy or treaty, the President would no doubt feel free to disregard the limitation,[73] as he has "riders" purporting to instruct delegations to international conferences.[74]

The constitutional answers might be different as regards the conditions which Congress has been imposing in the annual foreign assistance acts. There are in effect "conditions" in every such act, when Congress designates countries to receive aid

---

* Sometimes, too sensitive, even to harmless Congressional resolutions. Compare President Grant's protest when Congress adopted a resolution thanking certain foreign nations for their congratulations for the centennial of the United States. Chapter III, p. 86, and note 73.

** In every appropriation there is, of course, an implied condition that funds be used for the purpose for which they are appropriated.

(thereby denying aid to others), allocates foreign aid by categories or limits the number of countries to be assisted.[75] In several acts Congress also imposed qualifications and requirements for designated recipients. In 1954, for example, Congress provided that none of the funds authorized shall be used to assist a government "committed by treaty to maintain Communist rule in Asia"; it declared also that there shall be no delivery of military goods bought with foreign aid funds to signatories of the European Defense Community Treaty until they had all ratified the treaty.[76] The Foreign Assistance Act of 1961,[77] as amended, barred or restricted: aid to Cuba, to any country which assisted Cuba, to unfriendly and Communist countries, to the United Arab Republic, to countries that seized U.S. fishing vessels in international waters, to those that traded or permitted ships flying their flag to trade with Cuba or North Vietnam, to those that sold certain materials to the Communist Bloc, to countries whose military expenditures materially interfered with their development. In 1963, the First Hickenlooper Amendment forbade foreign assistance to any country that nationalized American properties without prompt, adequate and effective compensation.[78]

Presidents have resented these conditions and sometimes resisted them, challenging their validity. Surely, to give to some and not to others, to extract concessions from recipient nations, to threaten to terminate spending as an international sanction, can seriously affect relations with the aggrieved nations, and Presidents understandably deplore Congressional "interference." * But Congress has insisted and Presidents have reluctantly accepted that in foreign affairs as in domestic affairs, spending is expressly entrusted to Congress and its judgment as to the general welfare of the United States, and it can designate the recipients of its largesse and impose other conditions upon it.**

---

* Congress has itself sometimes recognized the President's claims and authorized him to waive the conditions in some circumstances. Compare notes 65 and 77, this chapter.

** See p. 110 above. Congress might be saying that it is for the general welfare of the United States to assist some governments and not others, or even the same government if it follows certain policies

The distinction I have drawn between obligatory appropriations and voluntary spending would apply also to appropriations to international organizations. If Congress is obliged to implement treaty obligations it must appropriate what the United States is obliged to pay, for example its share of the regular budget of international organizations, and ought not be able to impose conditions on such appropriations.[79] On the other hand, Congress can claim that voluntary contributions to special programs require an exercise of its spending power and it can spend or not spend, or spend on conditions.[80] But Congress cannot impose conditions which invade Presidential prerogatives to which the spending is at most incidental, or which violate individual rights; for example, in contributing to a special program of an international organization, Congress ought not be able to instruct the Executive as to how to vote on issues before the organiza-

but not if it follows others. Where the conditions seek to induce some action (or inaction) by the recipient, the argument could be made that Congress cannot use the spending power to "buy up" regulatory authority it does not otherwise have. Compare the disagreement between majority and dissent as to conditions on spending in United States v. Butler, 297 U.S. 1 (1936). Though the *Butler* case was carefully distinguished, the broader power of Congress largely prevailed in the *Social Security Cases*, Steward Machinery Co. v. Davis, 301 U.S. 548 (1937), and Helvering v. Davis, 301 U.S. 619 (1937). In the foreign aid cases moreover (unlike *Butler*), Congress is not trying to regulate domestic activities that are otherwise under the jurisdiction of the States; it is not "buying" State power and distorting the federal system.

The argument against conditions designed to induce Presidential action would be much stronger—if, say, Congress conditioned foreign assistance on the President's appointing X as foreign aid administrator. That condition is no doubt improper, but would it fall, and would the appropriation then stand unconditionally? The President is probably not free to disregard improper conditions and make the contribution for the United States unless one can assume that Congress would have made the contribution unconditionally if it had known its conditions would fail. Compare the discussion of improper conditions on Senate consent to treaties, Chapter V, p. 135. Of course, Congress can effectively impose even such conditions informally.

tion unrelated to that contribution, or insist that certain persons be denied employment there.[81]

Sometimes Congress has escaped political conflict and attenuated constitutional objections by giving the President authority to waive conditions or limitations.[82]

## Congressional Control of the Foreign Affairs Establishment

One source of conflict and confusion, in foreign as in domestic affairs, has been Congressional control over the organization and personnel of the Executive Branch. The Constitution (Article II, Section 2) provides that the President

> shall nominate, and by and with the Advice and Consent of the Senate, shall appoint Ambassadors, other public Ministers and Consuls, Judges of the supreme Court, and all other Officers of the United States, whose Appointments are not herein otherwise provided for, and which shall be established by Law: but the Congress may by Law vest the Appointment of such inferior Officers, as they think proper, in the President alone, in the Courts of Law, or in the Heads of Departments.

That provision has raised questions, real or hypothetical, many of which apply also to officers conducting foreign affairs. It seems accepted that the Senate can only consent or refuse to consent to the President's appointments; it cannot consent with conditions (as it can in consenting to treaties).[83] That view apparently reflects the assumption that conditions could only invade the powers of the office or limit its term, and these are either prescribed by the Constitution, established by law, or reserved to the President's discretion. But it is not obvious why the Senate could not grant consent on other kinds of condition, for example that the appointee divest himself of certain financial holdings or that he learn French or Swahili. In the realities of political life, of course, the Senate can informally impose any conditions, simply by withholding consent until the President gives satisfaction, but it would not be surprising if the Senate began also to impose conditions formally. If so, there would be no consent if the conditions were not met, and Presidents would probably accept them as the price of consent rather than consider the appointment rejected.[84]

The quoted requirement that appointment to offices not expressly provided in the Constitution be "established by Law," means that while the President appoints the members of the Executive Branch engaged in foreign affairs, Congress creates many of the offices to which they are appointed. And although "Ambassadors, other public Ministers, and Consuls," are expressly mentioned in the Constitution and would appear to occupy offices not "established by Law," Congress has in fact acquired control of the entire foreign service and has subjected it to detailed regulation, determining their number, prescribing their table of organization, defining their functions, setting qualifications and terms of employment.[85] Presidents are probably entitled to disregard qualifications that are so detailed as to constitute virtually a direction to appoint particular persons.[86] The Supreme Court has upheld the President's power to remove officers who exercise the President's "executive power," even if they were confirmed by the Senate, even within the term of office fixed by Congress, even if Congress forbade their removal without Senate consent.[87] And officers protected by Civil Service and other legislation could no doubt be assigned to other duties.

Controversy has also flared when Congress directed the actions of members of executive departments, claiming the power to decide what is necessary and proper to see that its laws are executed, while the President asserted authority to direct them otherwise. In the *Kendall* case,[88] the Supreme Court ordered the Postmaster-General to pay out money as directed by Congress although President Jackson told him not to pay. The Court said:

> There are certain political duties imposed upon many officers in the executive department, the discharge of which is under the direction of the President. But it would be an alarming doctrine, that congress cannot im-
> ~~... ...y executive officer any duty they may~~
> think proper, which is not repugnant to any rights secured and protected by the constitution; and in such cases, the duty and responsibility grow out of and are

subject to the control of the law, and not to the direction of the President.

In the conduct of foreign affairs the lines of authority are tangled, since executive officials carry out both laws enacted by Congress—for example, tariff or immigration legislation—and "political duties" under the direction of the President.[89] It is commonly accepted, for example, that the authority which Congress gives consular officers to issue visas pursuant to the Immigration Laws is not reviewable by the Department of State, or, presumably, even by the President,[90] though if that view conforms to the theory of the *Kendall* case it does not necessarily reflect the realities of foreign service in the Executive Branch.

As in domestic affairs, if to a lesser degree, Congress has also lodged foreign affairs functions in administrative agencies which have enjoyed some independence of the President, for example the Tariff Commission.[91] The successive bodies administering foreign aid have illustrated vividly how Congress can keep control of foreign affairs activities, particularly those heavily dependent on "spending." Yet even in such bodies the lines of responsibility and control are impossible to unravel,[92] for Presidents often use their personnel also for activities other than those assigned them by Congress.* And whatever it could theoretically do under the *Kendall* doctrine, Congress has frequently recognized the indivisible character of foreign relations and the special prerogatives of the President in regard to them, and has given the President ultimate discretion.[93]

### Issues in Delegation

The conduct of foreign relations is permeated by a special form of "cooperation," involving not the conjunction of separate powers of President and Congress, but Presidential actions pursuant to Congressional power delegated to him. When the President acts by Congressional authority he has the sum of their powers and can be said "to personify the federal sovereignty," [94] and in foreign affairs, surely, he then commands all the political au-

---

*E. g.*, Averell Harriman, who while head of the Mutual Security Agency also served the President as a personal trouble shooter.

thority of the United States. But the separation of powers has been held to forbid abdication by one branch to another and to imply, therefore, limitations on delegation. Uneasy Congresses have themselves sought to mitigate the dangers of delegation by special devices to revoke or limit delegated authority, or to oversee the President's discretion in carrying it out, which Presidents have challenged as impermissible.

## "Excessive" Delegation

That the separation of powers forbids excessive, unguided, uncontrolled delegation by Congress to the President is doctrine that still has some life in domestic affairs.[95] In foreign affairs it has never had much: whatever else *Curtiss-Wright* said, it specifically held that "within the international field" Congress may "accord to the President a degree of discretion and freedom from statutory restriction which would not be admissible were domestic affairs alone involved." [96] If, as we saw, Sutherland's essay in reaching his decision is not wholly compelling,* one might find sufficient reasons for the Court's conclusion in the realities of the foreign affairs process, for, from the beginning, reluctant Congresses have felt compelled to delegate to Presidents the largest discretion with minimal guidelines to carry out the most general legislative policy. That the President's own powers are "plenary" and include some legislative authority, that the di-

---

* That the foreign affairs powers of the federal government derive from national sovereignty, and are perhaps extra-constitutional, does not tell us whether one branch can delegate its component of that sovereign power to another. Indeed, since it seems agreed that the sovereign foreign affairs power is divided between President and Congress along lines not unrelated to those expressed in the Constitution, one might conclude that the principle of the separation of powers and the constitutional limitations it implies are not irrelevant. At least, one should ask whether the reasons that support Separation generally apply in some measure to the conduct of foreign affairs. Sutherland treated the issue in th~~~~~~~~~~~~~~~~~~~~~~~~~~ not consider whether the arms embargo could be imposed by the President on his own authority, with Congress enacting criminal penalties as necessary and proper to carry out the President's embargo. But perhaps that is what he had in mind. See this chapter, note 9.

vision of authority to make foreign policy is irregular and uncertain, tend to reduce any doctrinal objections to delegation: often a strong argument can be made that what Congress has delegated to the President was within his power to do on his own authority. If there remain some theoretical limitations on Congressional delegation even in foreign affairs, no one has persuasively stated what they are and apparently no actual delegation by Congress has approached them.

Recently, however, the Supreme Court has seemed again disposed to consider the question where the delegated power impinges on individual rights, for example the right to travel abroad.* In such cases, indeed, the pre-New Deal limitations on delegation in domestic matters may be alive and well, and applicable even in regard to foreign affairs.[97]

## Controlling Delegated Authority: the "Legislative Veto"

The need to delegate vast powers to the President has often left Congress uneasy and it has sought to circumscribe the powers delegated, supervise and impose conditions on their exercise, limit their duration and require the President to seek renewal of his mandate. Sometimes Congress has insisted on making explicit what is not being granted to the President, perhaps implying an opinion that he does not have such power on his own authority either. In the United Nations Participation Act, for example, Congress provided:

> [N]othing contained in this section shall be construed as an authorization to the President by the Congress to make available to the Security Council . . . armed forces, facilities or assistance in addition to the forces, facilities and assistance provided for in [an agreement subject to the approval of Congress].[98]

A different limitation is expressed in the Trade Agreements Extension Act:

> The enactment of this Act shall not be construed to determine or indicate the approval or disapproval by the

* See p. 98 above and Chapter X, p. 257.

Congress of the Executive Agreement known as the General Agreement on Tariffs and Trade.[99]

Sometimes Congress has provided that executive action pursuant to delegation shall lie before Congress for a time before going into effect, so as to give Congress the opportunity to veto it by new legislation; such "waiting periods" have not been seriously challenged.[100] Constitutional controversy has been generated, however, when, to avoid the difficulties of repealing or modifying delegations by ordinary legislative process (requiring a majority of both houses and subject to Presidential veto), Congress developed extraordinary machinery.[101] In the Lend-Lease Act, for example, Congress provided that the President's authority shall end if the two houses of Congress so provided by concurrent resolution, which does not require the President's consent and is not subject to his veto.[102] Foreign aid statutes have provided that aid to a particular foreign country could be terminated by concurrent resolution.[103] The Neutrality Act of 1939 provided that the President shall issue a proclamation putting various provisions of the Act into effect whenever he "or the Congress by concurrent resolution," finds that there is a foreign war and that U.S. interests require the protection.[104] Congress has even purported to subject Executive action to "oversight" or veto by one House of Congress, by particular Congressional Committees, even by a committee chairman.[105]

Such "infra-legislative" controls of the Executive have been challenged on various grounds. Presidents have objected to any repeal or modification of legislation other than by the normal legislative process. Concurrent resolutions for legislative purposes (as distinguished, say, from "sense" resolutions) would seem to violate the express Constitutional requirement of Presidential approval for every "Order, Resolution, or Vote to which the Concurrence of the Senate and the House of Representatives may be necessary." (Article 1, Section 7.)[106] "Legislative veto" in any form has been said to violate the separation of powers in that either it seeks to legislate by less than both Houses of Congress and Presidential approval, or it arrogates to Congressional bodies executive functions and the President's express power to see that the laws are faithfully executed.[107]  The argument for Congress is presumably that when the President executes Congressional laws or exercises delegated authority he is the agent of Congress and subject to any controls his principal deemed necessary.  By the devices described, Congress is not repealing or modifying the original legislation but is exercising powers reserved in that legislation.  Surely Congress should be able to recapture powers it delegates to the President without the consent of the agent.[108]

None of these Congressional devices has been authoritatively reviewed by the Supreme Court, and they continue to roil relations between the President and Congress.  In some instances Presidents, unwilling to veto important legislation, have challenged the Congressional control and announced that they would disregard it, or treat it as only exhortation; sometimes, Presidents have felt compelled to comply, if only under protest.

In the realities of national and international life, of course, these issues of constitutional power are often not drawn sharply. Lawyers' arguments about the implications of Separation sometimes reflect as much as they determine conflict or cooperation between President and Congress; but they test the respective bargaining powers of the two branches and shape the compromises that emerge.  Since the courts are usually unavailable to define or circumscribe the powers of either branch, their joint powers are virtually without limit except in self-restraint, while their respective powers depend on what each can seize, and on relations between them.  The President has won most of the battles not because his constitutional arguments are necessarily stronger but because his temptations and opportunities have been greater, because he has had all the advantages of "sole organ," and foreign policy is effectively what he communicates to other nations. If increasingly Congress can also see and hear for itself, its means are even now not wholly effective; today it succeeds in being heard around the world, but its voice is diffuse, and restrained by historic limitations, by the customs of international life, and by the reluctance to have the United States speak uncertainly and in a confusion of different voices.  Even in circumstances where Congress can effectively frustrate national attitudes and intentions expressed or intimated by the President, Congress cannot—without making our international life impossible—readily "repeal," contradict or derogate from what the President said.

In reality even more surely than in principle, then, Congress is not free to refuse to appropriate funds for an embassy to a country which the President insists on recognizing; to prevent the President from using the armed forces for limited foreign policy purposes; to fail to implement formal or informal undertakings to other nations. But neither can the President take Congress wholly for granted or disregard its known sentiments and those of its constituents, for he needs the cooperation of Congress generally and for his foreign policy in particular, and Congress has known to convert that need into power, creating a check and a balance not provided by the letter of the Constitution. In the end, while insisting on its constitutional autonomy, Congress has generally sensed that in the strange contraption which the Fathers created for conducting foreign policy, the Congress are the rear wheels, indispensable and usually obliged to follow, but not without substantial braking power.

Constitutional issues of conflict and cooperation abound also but take special forms as regards the special power of the President to make treaties and other international agreements. I deal with them in the course of the following chapters.

*THE CONSTITUTIONAL LAW OF INTERNATIONAL COOP-ERATION*

The foreign affairs of the United States include many acts of international cooperation, frequently in the form of international law, treaties or other international agreements, and various international organizations. These have engendered a large and discrete segment of the constitutional law of foreign affairs.

"The United States," the first Chief Justice, John Jay, said, "by taking a place among the nations of the earth, [became] amenable to the law of nations." [1] Although the Constitution does not say that expressly, it is implied in the provision conferring upon Congress power to define and punish offenses against the law of nations, and in various references to Ambassadors, treaties, war, and other international acts and relations that depend on international law. The Constitution is wholly silent, however, about the respective powers and responsibilities of the federal branches in regard to international law, the respective rights and obligations of the Nation and the States, or the relation of international law to United States or state law. International organizations as we know them did not exist when the Constitution was written and were not anticipated. Only treaties are explicitly dealt with, and these too, not as regards their international obligation and character, but only as to who shall make them on behalf of the United States and what shall be their effect as domestic law in the United States.

The constitutional blueprint for these formal forms of international cooperation is different from that for unilateral foreign affairs actions. Treaties are made by "the treaty-makers"—the President and two-thirds of the Senators present—in unique combination. International agreements, it has developed, can also be made by the President-and-Congress in joint action also without parallel. The President alone also makes agreements which have constitutional status, perhaps greater than that of his unilateral acts. Sepa... ...ecks and balances, conflict and cooperation, interference and delegation, appear here too, but differently. Participation in international organization has raised issues about the relation of American institutions to international

127

institutions and of constitutional rights and obligations to international responsibilities.*

* Customary international law is effectively law for the courts; I deal with it principally in that context, in Chapter VIII, p. 205.

# Chapter V. TREATIES AND THE TREATY POWER

For the Constitutional Fathers the foreign relations of the new republic consisted largely of treaties to be concluded or not concluded with other countries; and who shall have the power to make treaties, and their status when made, were questions of special concern to them.[1] They were eager to abandon treaty-making by Congress which, under the Articles of Confederation, appointed negotiators, wrote their instructions, followed their progress, approved or rejected their product. They were not eager for the United States to conclude treaties lightly or widely, and were disposed to render it difficult to make them.[2] They were concerned to end the anarchy that prevailed under the Articles and to assure that treaties made by the United States would be honored by the individual States.[3]

And so, the Constitution gave the power to make treaties to the President but only with the advice and consent of two-thirds of the Senators present (Article II, section 2); it expressly forbade treaty-making by the States (Article I, section 10); it provided that, like the Constitution itself and the laws of the United States, treaties shall be the supreme law of the land and binding on the States (Article VI, section 2). The Framers did not stop to distinguish treaties from other international agreements or commitments.* They did not prescribe what purposes treaties might serve or suggest limitations upon them. They did not anticipate and resolve conflict between treaties and the Constitution or between treaties and laws, or competition for power between the treaty-makers and the l————

* A distinction between treaties and "Agreements or Compacts" with a foreign state is implied in the limitations imposed on the States, Article I, section 10. See Chapter IX, p. 228. Compare Chapter VI.

## The Treaty-Making Process

Article II, section 2 of the Constitution provides[4] that the President

> shall have Power, by and with the Advice and Consent of the Senate, to make Treaties, provided two thirds of the Senators present concur.

Although it is the President, then, who makes treaties, and the power to make them is listed in the article dealing with executive power; although treaty-making has often been characterized as an executive function (in that special sense in which the conduct of foreign relations is executive),* constitutional writers have considered the making of treaties to be different from other exercises of Presidential power, principally because of the Senate's role in the process, perhaps too because treaties have particular legal and political qualities and consequences. Hamilton suggested that treaty-making might be seen as a function of a fourth branch of government, the President-and-Senate (in its executive character).[5] Contemporary writings sometimes refer to "the treaty-makers."

The President's part in treaty-making seems clear. He appoints and instructs the negotiators and follows their progress in negotiation. If he approves what they have negotiated, if he has the advice and consent of the Senate, he can ratify, "make" the treaty.**

---

* See Chapter II, pp. 42–43. On the other hand, later, at least, Madison in the first Helvidius letter said: ". . . there are sufficient indications that the power of treaties is regarded by the constitution as materially different from mere executive power, and as having more affinity to the legislative than to the executive character." 6 J. MADISON, WRITINGS 138 (Hunt ed. 1910), Chapter II, note 12. That under the Articles treaties were the responsibility of Congress is not revealing since Congress had both executive and legislative functions.

** The Senate gives consent to ratification, the President ratifies, but even the Supreme Court has erroneously referred to the Senate's action as "ratification." B. Altman & Co. v. United States, 224 U.S. 583, 600–601 (1912); Wilson v. Girard, 354 U.S. 524, 526 (1957).

It is the Senate's part that has raised questions and issues. As originally conceived, no doubt, the Senate was to be a kind of Presidential council affording him advice throughout the treaty-making process and on all aspects of it—whether to enter negotiations, who shall represent the United States, what should be the scope of negotiations, the positions to be taken, the responses to be made, the terms to be accepted.[6] Almost from the beginning, however, Presidents found that conception of the Senate's function uncongenial, perhaps unworkable; the Senate, for its part, also rejected it, seeking to deliberate and pass judgment rather than to advise.[7] After Washington did it once,[8] no President has talked to the Senate about a forthcoming treaty, nor has advice often been sought or given by exchange of messages.[9] As the Senate has grown, surely, its advice could not easily be sought before the President began to negotiate and at every new development in some distant, complex negotiation.

In a word, the Senate does not formally advise on treaties before or during negotiations, and failure of such advice no doubt has sometimes led to failure of later consent. Presidents have developed informal substitutes, consulting Senate leaders or the chairman and other members of its Foreign Relations Committee. In our day Presidents have appointed Senators to delegations negotiating treaties so that they will contribute their sense of what the Senate will accept, and later deter and disarm Senate opposition.* In a well-known modern instance, Senator Vanden-

Exchange of ratifications binds the United States internationally; that it becomes effective retroactively as of the time of signature (Haver v. Yaker, 9 Wall. 32 (U.S.1869)) is no longer the accepted understanding. For domestic purposes the treaty becomes law only upon proclamation by the President. *Ibid.*

* In the past there was controversy about the practice, in part because the Constitution (Art. I, sec. 6, cl. 2) provides: "No Senator or Representative shall, during the Time for which he was elected, be appointed to ~~~~~~~~~~~~~~~~ under the Authority of the United States, which shall have been created, or the Emoluments whereof shall have been encreased during such time; and no Person holding any Office under the United States, shall be a Member of either House during his Continuance in Office." When President Madison appointed

berg was encouraged to promote a resolution in which the President was "advised of the sense of the Senate" that the United States should conclude a North Atlantic treaty.[10]

The requirement of Senate consent is an important "check" on Presidential power to make foreign policy by treaty; inevitably, it has bred controversy. A case has been made that often in our history the Senate denied consent not because it thought the proposed treaty would contravene the national interest, but from motives of partisan politics: a Senate controlled by the opposition party might withhold its consent from a significant treaty in order to deny a President political advantage, especially in an election year.[11]  Once, Secretary of State John Hay, bloody from encounters with the Senate, said that he "did not believe another important treaty would ever pass the Senate." [12]  President Wilson's searing experience with the Treaty of Versailles confirmed the Senate's appellation as "grave-yard of treaties."  There have been proposals to eliminate at least the need for concurrence by two-thirds of the Senators present, the assumption that a Senator voting "no" is *"ipso facto* twice as well informed and weighty as one of his colleagues who votes 'yes.' " [13]

In recent years, in part as a result of better coordination by the Executive Branch, few treaties have been rejected by the Senate.[14]  But a box-score of consents and rejections tells less than the whole story of the Senate's impact on treaty making.  Treaties are not fungible: one rejection of a Treaty of Versailles * is not balanced by consent to ten extradition treaties.  And if

a Senator and a Representative to serve on the commission to negotiate peace with Great Britain in 1814 they resigned from Congress. There was recurrent controversy over the constitutionality of the practice of appointing members of Congress to delegations, again during the McKinley Administration, and the practice was abandoned, to be revived after the Treaty of Versailles fiasco.  Those opposed to using Senators to negotiate treaties have argued also that it later prevented independent Senate consideration of the treaty.  See WRIGHT 251. It is now common practice and no longer challenged.

* In an attempt to avoid the onus of patently rejecting the Treaty of Versailles, the Senate purported to consent, but with numerous and radical reservations.

the Senate has become more sensitive to the onus of explicitly rejecting what the United States and other nations have labored to conclude, it has not hesitated to let treaties gather dust on Senate shelves.* Presidents, moreover, have avoided sending treaties to the Senate when its consent seemed improbable or might require a struggle which the President was not prepared to undertake. Negotiators have always kept clearly in mind that the treaties they produce will have to be acceptable to the Senate and meet its objections, political or constitutional, partisan or substantive, real or pretended.

The requirement of Senate consent provides "slippage" and opportunity for second thoughts. Presidents have refused to send to the Senate treaties already negotiated; they have withdrawn treaties from the Senate before it acted; they have refused to ratify treaties to which the Senate consented; they have refrained from pressing for Senate consent to treaties submitted by their predecessors.[15] For its part the Senate has sometimes given or denied consent and then reconsidered its action.[16] While there is no authoritative decision on the question, the Senate can probably withdraw, modify or interpret its consent before the President has concluded the treaty.[17]

In many cases the Senate has given its consent with reservations.[18] Whether the Senate insists on a modification in the terms of a treaty, or on a particular interpretation of it, or on some limitation of its consequences, reservation usually requires renegotiation, to the dismay of Presidents and the impatience of other governments,[19] but all now accept this additional obstacle in the American treaty process. The constitutional authority

* This is more likely to happen to a multilateral treaty where no particular nation negotiated it with the United States and is waiting for the United States to ratify it, e. g., the Genocide Treaty which has been before the Senate from 1949 to 1972. (But see note 71, this chapter.)

It has been ~~ ... ~~ the Senate should either consent or reject and that withholding action is "of questionable propriety." WRIGHT 253. The practice is well established, however, and makes it possible readily to pick a treaty from the Senate table years after it was put there.

of the Senate to impose reservations has not been seriously questioned.[20]  If the Senate can give or withhold consent it can also give its consent on condition that changes be made.  Or, one might say, the Senate withholds consent from the treaty presented to it but indicates what revised treaty will earn its consent, and gives it in advance to a treaty as so revised.  (Of course, the President might decide not to "make" the treaty that is satisfactory to the Senate.) [21]

The Senate has sometimes imposed conditions that seek not modification of the international obligations of the treaty but some control of its effect in the United States.*  In an extended and unedifying controversy with several Presidents, the Senate consented to United States adherence to general arbitration conventions only on condition that any specific submission to arbitration thereafter also obtain the consent of the Senate.[22]  The Senate has sometimes insisted that a treaty should not take effect, or that action shall not be taken under it by United States officials, without prior approval of Congress.[23]  There are reservations requiring the President to perform some domestic act.[24] On several occasions the Senate provided that nothing in the treaty shall enhance the powers of the President; in a recent instance the Senate expressed its intent also that nothing in the treaty shall add to, or subtract from, the reach of the powers of Congress.[25]

The legal effect of such "reservations" has been seriously debated in only one instance, involving a treaty with Canada to divide the waters of the Niagara River.  In the United States there were divisions of opinion and interest as to the regime that should govern the exploitation of our share of the waters.  Had the treaty been ratified without more, these waters would have been subject to general federal legislation governing waters belonging to the United States for which no special provision was made.  In consenting to ratification of the treaty, the Senate resolved that the United States reserves the right to provide for

---

* Some speak of Senate "amendments" to describe reservations that seek a change in the treaty obligations as distinguished from other conditions.

redevelopment of its share of the waters by act of Congress, and no such redevelopment should be undertaken until specifically authorized by Act of Congress. Both the United States and Canada treated this provision like other reservations; the President asked Canada to accept it and Canada—though somewhat mystified—did.[26]

Some who wished to see the treaty come into effect without the Senate's limitation argued that the reservation had no legal effect: it was not a proper treaty provision since it contained no element of international obligation.[27] That objection, of course, does not relate to the Senate's part in the treaty-making process; it would apply as well if the same provision had been inserted by the negotiators in the original treaty. (I discuss that objection below).* But the arguments failed to consider the effect of the Senate proviso as a condition to its consent. If the Senate gave its consent only on condition that the United States share of the waters should await disposition by Congress, the treaty could take effect only subject to that condition. If the Senate's condition did not operate to prevent the treaty from coming into effect, it is questionable whether the President had authority to ratify the treaty until Congress adopted the implementing legislation called for by the Senate, and whether his ratification in disregard of the Senate's condition was constitutionally effective.[28] Similarly, when the Senate gives consent to a treaty on condition that officers appointed by the President pursuant to the treaty shall be appointed only with Senate approval, the President who proceeds to ratify the treaty has been deemed obligated to conform to the condition.[29]

A different question is whether the Senate can impose conditions unrelated to the treaty itself. While the Senate has never attempted to do so, one may ask hypothetically whether, say, it can tell the President that it will consent to a treaty only if he dismisses his Secretary of State. Perhaps such conditions were contemplated, perhaps the Senate that made them would be abusing its power, and indeed it seems incredible that a Senate

* See pp. 143, 160–61.

would put such a condition, at least formally and publicly. But since the Senate can withhold its consent for no reason, perhaps it can withhold it for any reason, and a President may have to buy that consent at whatever price and in whatever form the Senate asked. It would be particularly difficult to conclude that when the Senate imposes a condition which is not "proper," the President can disregard the condition, treat the Senate's consent as unconditional and proceed to ratify the treaty.

Sometimes the Senate can be persuaded to achieve clarification or even some modification of a treaty provision without entering a reservation, by expressing instead its "understanding" of the provision.[30] If that understanding is communicated to the other party and is accepted or acquiesced in there is no issue and the treaty need not be reopened.[31] There is danger, however, of failure of communication that may engender doubt and controversy as to whether the parties agreed to the same terms.[32]

Once the Senate has consented, the President is free to make (or not to make) the treaty and the Senate has no further authority in respect of it. Attempts by the Senate to withdraw, modify or interpret its consent after a treaty is ratified have no legal weight; nor has the Senate any authoritative voice in interpreting a treaty or in terminating it.* Of course, in its legislative capacity as one of the two houses of Congress (as distinguished from its executive role as treaty-maker) the Senate participates in whatever Congress can do about treaties.**

---

* See p. 167. A Senate resolution explaining its understanding of a treaty to which it had previously consented without reservation was without legal effect. Fourteen Diamond Rings v. United States, 183 U.S. 176 (1901). But if, as a condition of its consent to a treaty, the Senate should reserve special powers to interpret or terminate the treaty, a President might have to accord it that role or refuse to ratify the treaty because he cannot meet its conditions. Compare the reservation to the Versailles Treaty, notes 23, 24, this chapter.

** See pp. 161, 163 below.

## Constitutional Restrictions on the Treaty Power

The Constitution does not expressly impose prohibitions or prescribe limits on the Treaty Power, nor does it patently imply that there are any.[33] No provision in any treaty has been held unconstitutional by the Supreme Court and few have been seriously challenged there.[34] It is now settled, however, that treaties are subject to the constitutional limitations that apply to all exercises of federal power, principally the prohibitions of the Bill of Rights; numerous statements also assert limitations on the reach and compass of the Treaty Power.*

Once, indeed, there was extant a myth that treaties are equal in authority to the Constitution and not subject to its limitations. The doctrine, propagated even by eminent authority, found its origins, no doubt, in the language of the Supremacy Clause (Article VI, section 2):

> This Constitution, and the Laws of the United States which shall be made in Pursuance thereof; and all Treaties made, or which shall be made, under the Authority of the United States, shall be the supreme Law of the Land . . . .

Reading that language, Mr. Justice Holmes said:[35]

> Acts of Congress are the supreme law of the land when made in pursuance of the Constitution, while

---

* It is a different question whether a treaty that exceeds any of these limitations is binding in international law, whether the other party to the treaty can be charged with knowledge of our constitutional limitations, whether the United States can defend against an international claim on the ground that the treaty was outside the power of the treaty makers or prohibited to them by the Constitution. It is now accepted that a treaty made in violation of a nation's constitution is nevertheless binding upon it unless the violation is "fundamental" and the other party knew or had reason to know the lack of authority to make it. For various formulations of that conclusion compare 1 L. OPPENHEIM, INTERNATIONAL LAW (Lauterpacht 8th ed. 1955) 887–90; 2 C. HYDE, INTERNATIONAL LAW 1385 (2d ed. 1945); RESTATEMENT § 123; Vienna Convention on the Law of Treaties, May 23, 1969, arts. 46, 47, reprinted in 63 AM.J.INT'L L. 875, 890 (1969). Compare Chapter VI, note 21.

treaties are declared to be so when made under the authority of the United States. It is open to question whether the authority of the United States means more than the formal acts prescribed to make the convention.

Holmes read "in pursuance of" the Constitution to mean "consistent with its substantive prohibitions" and that phrase has been generally so interpreted; [36] if so, the language does indeed lend itself to his dictum. Long before he wrote, however, that curious language of the Supremacy Clause had been explained otherwise: to the Framers, "in pursuance of" the Constitution meant—or meant also—"following its adoption," and they wished to provide that treaties made before the adoption of the Constitution (principally the treaties with France and Great Britain that were being resisted in some States) should also be the law of the land and binding on the States.[37]

Perhaps Holmes did not know of that suggestion; perhaps he did not accept it. Perhaps he thought that if the Framers were seeking only to maintain the supremacy of preexisting treaties they might readily have designed explicit language to that end; it can be argued that preexisting treaties were fully taken care of in the phrase "treaties made or which shall be made," [38] and that there must have been another purpose in the failure to require that treaties be "pursuant" to the Constitution. One can suggest reasons why the Framers might have intended not to subject treaties to any constitutional limitations. They might have thought that in its international relations the United States should be equal and sovereign, not hampered by restraints that limit what the federal government can do within the national family.* It might have appeared particularly unacceptable that

---

* Compare, for example, the suggestion that the powers essential to the common defense "ought to exist without limitation . . . . The circumstances that endanger the safety of nations are infinite, and for this reason no constitutional shackles can wisely be imposed on the power to which the care of it is committed." THE FEDERALIST No. 23 (Hamilton). The Netherlands Constitution (Article 63) apparently accepts treaties that deviate from constitutional limitations applicable to acts of parliament.

an individual be able to assert his particular grievance in order to have a treaty declared unconstitutional by the courts, frustrate important national interests and invite perhaps grave international consequences.[39]

Such arguments have in fact been made but, long before the suggestion lightly dropped by Holmes, the Supreme Court pronounced (albeit in dictum) that the Treaty Power does not extend "so far as to authorize what the Constitution forbids." [40] Holmes himself stressed that the treaty he was considering "does not contravene any prohibitory words to be found in the Constitution." [41] Congress has always assumed that there were limits on the Treaty Power for, from the beginning, it gave the federal courts jurisdiction over suits "where is drawn in question the validity of a treaty." [42] The treaty-makers themselves have thought they were subject to limitations.[43] In our day, during the extensive and intensive debates on the Bricker Amendment, no one claimed that treaties were free of constitutional limitations: those who objected to making that clear by constitutional amendment insisted that it was clear enough without amendment.[44]

In 1957, Mr. Justice Black laid the issue to rest: [45]

> . . . no agreement with a foreign nation can confer power on the Congress, or on any other branch of Government, which is free from the restraints of the Constitution.

> . . . The prohibitions of the Constitution were designed to apply to all branches of the National Gov-

It is not obvious that the Framers saw in the Constitution any limitations applicable to treaties. Compare Rawle note 33, this chapter. The limitations of the original Constitution were principally those implied in federalism and the separation of powers and these are hardly relevant to the Treaty Power. Even the original Amendments, which became the Bill of Rights, were not obviously relevant to treaties and the only provision that ~~~~~~~~~~~~~~~~~~~~~~~~~, is in ~~~~ addressed to Congress only. See p. 254 below. The limitations of Article I, section 9, probably apply to treaties but it is not clear that the Framers contemplated that. Compare p. 140 and note 46, this chapter.

ernment and they cannot be nullified by the Executive
or by the Executive and the Senate combined.

The prohibitions set forth in Article 1, section 9, then,
though contained in the article devoted principally to Congress
and following immediately upon the catalogue of its powers,
would doubtless be held to apply to treaties as well: [46] a treaty
cannot grant a title of nobility, or lay a duty on articles exported from any State, or give preference to the ports of one State
over those of another. Treaties, surely, are also subject to more
important prohibitions, notably in the Bill of Rights, protecting
individual rights.* I deal with these in Chapter X.

## Scope and Limits of the Treaty Power

The Constitution does not define "Treaties": the Framers, apparently, saw no need to define what was well known to international law and practice.[47] Nor does the Constitution provide
that some matters cannot be dealt with by treaty or that particular dispositions are beyond the authority of the treaty-makers.† From our constitutional beginnings, however, there have
been assertions that the Treaty Power was limited by implications in the character of treaties and of the Treaty Power, in
other provisions of the Constitution, in the Constitution as a
whole, in the philosophy that permeates it and the institutions

---

* Even the First Amendment expressly addressed to Congress, and
the prohibitions implied elsewhere, *e. g.*, in the citizenship clause of the
Fourteenth Amendment. See Chapter X, pp. 253–54.

An argument might be made that these prohibitions do not limit
the power to make treaties, but only forbid giving them effect as
law of the United States; that conceptual distinction will generally
have no consequence in fact, since Presidents will not make treaties
that would be unenforceable. Whether these prohibitions apply outside the United States, see Chapter X, p. 266.

† By contrast, the Articles of Confederation provided that no treaty
should restrain state legislatures "from imposing such imposts and
duties on foreigners as their own people are subjected to, or from
prohibiting the exportation or importation of any species of goods
or commodities whatsoever." Art. IX. Compare Rawle, note 33, this
chapter. On the right to prohibit the importation of slaves by treaty,
compare note 46, this chapter.

it established—notably in the separation of powers among the branches of the federal government and the division of authority between that government and the States.[48]   In the Supreme Court, the best known statement of implied limitations on the Treaty Power is probably that of Mr. Justice Field in *Geofroy* v. *Riggs*: [49]

> .   .   . The treaty power, as expressed in the Constitution, is in terms unlimited except by those restraints which are found in that instrument against the action of the government or of its departments, and those arising from the nature of the government itself and of that of the States.  It would not be contended that it extends so far as to authorize what the Constitution forbids, or a change in the character of the government or in that of one of the States, or a cession of any portion of the territory of the latter, without its consent.   .   .   . But with these exceptions, it is not perceived that there is any limit to the questions which can be adjusted touching any matter which is properly the subject of negotiation with a foreign country.

These and similar dicta,[50] I stress, were expressed while the Court was upholding an exercise of the Treaty Power, and each statement was asserting the fullness of that power rather than restrictions upon it.  Only cautious phrases, like *"properly* the subject of negotiation with a foreign country," suggest possible limitation, but with the exceptions Field mentioned (changes in the character of government, cession of state territory) there is no indication that any of the Justices had in mind any particular limitation or any category or principle of limitation.

Jefferson, however, early "codified" a series of limitations in his *Manual of Parliamentary Practice*: [51]

> By the Constitution of the United States this department of legislation is confined to two branches only ~~of the ordinary~~ legislature—the President originating and the Senate having a negative.  To what subjects this power extends has not been defined in detail by the Constitution;  nor are we entirely agreed among

ourselves. 1. It is admitted that it must concern the foreign-nation party to the contract, or it would be a mere nullity, *res inter alios acta.* 2. By the general power to make treaties, the Constitution must have intended to comprehend only those subjects which are usually regulated by treaty, and can not be otherwise regulated. 3. It must have meant to except out of these the rights reserved to the States, for surely the President and Senate can not do by treaty what the whole Government is interdicted from doing in any way. 4. And also to except those subjects of legislation in which it gave a participation to the House of Representatives. This last exception is denied by some on the ground that it would leave very little matter for the treaty power to work on. The less the better, say others. . . .

As the final sentence perhaps implies, Jefferson was no friend of the Treaty Power.[52] The limitations he enumerates would leave little room for treaties,[53] and have long proved to be bad "guesses," and notable evidence that ours has not become a Jeffersonian Constitution.* But all the limitations he cited have also been suggested by others, some again quite recently; I consider them, and others, on their merits.

## Limitations inherent in the "character" of treaties

Since the Constitution speaks of "Treaties" without more, it may be said to incorporate the definition of treaties in international law and practice, for example: "a formal instrument of agreement by which two or more States establish or seek to establish a relation under international law between themselves." [54] One limitation implied in such definition is perhaps what Jefferson had in mind in his first clause: a treaty "must concern the foreign nation party to the contract, or it would be a mere

---

* In many other respects this manual (based on British parliamentary practice) prepared by Jefferson for his own use as presiding officer of the Senate, is still recognized as authoritative and underlies the current rules of both Houses of Congress.

nullity, *res inter alios acta.*" A treaty, then, must be a *bona fide* agreement between states, not a "mock marriage," nor a unilateral act by the United States to which a foreign government lends itself as an accommodation in order to bring it within the United States Treaty Power. So if, to circumvent the House of Representatives and the States, a uniform divorce law for the United States alone were written into "a treaty" and Canada cooperated in the scheme by signing its name to it, it would not be a treaty under international law, and therefore not a treaty under the Constitution.\* This, let it be clear, is a hypothetical example of a hypothetical limitation: no "agreement" made by the President and Senate has ever been challenged as a "psuedo-treaty." †

## Limitations implied in federalism

The principal attacks on the scope of the Treaty Power flew banners of federalism and "States' rights."

The Constitution denies the States the power to make treaties and gives them no part in the national treaty-making process.[55]

---

\* Under international law Canada might perhaps be estopped from questioning its character as a treaty, if somehow it had an interest to do so; constitutionally one could nonetheless argue that it is beyond the power of the treaty-makers. This is not to suggest that a constitutional treaty requires "consideration," some *quid pro quo* between the parties. Constitutionally as well as internationally, there are *bona fide*, valid unilateral treaties, where the undertakings are all by one party to the other, as for example, in peace treaties; unlike the hypothetical mock-treaty, these are, and are intended to be, international acts with international consequence. This "limitation" on the Treaty Power is, but should not be, confused with a different alleged requirement that a treaty deal with a matter that is of "international concern." See p. 151 below.

† In the Niagara Treaty debates, p. 135 above, it was argued that the Senate Reservation accepted by Canada did not have status as a treaty provision under the Constitution because it did not "concern Canada." B̲ ̲ ̲ ̲ ̲ ̲ ̲ ̲ ̲ ̲ ̲ ̲ ̲ ̲ ̲ claimed that it was not *bona fide* or that Canada agreed to it from improper motives to help circumvent the separation of powers of the United States Government. The argument there seemed closer to that implied in the "international concern" requirement and I consider it in that context. See Chapter V, note 91.

Of course, the Treaty Power responds to the concerns of federalism in that the President, the principal treaty-maker, is elected by a process reflecting our origins as a union of States, and, especially, that the Senate, the other participant in the treaty process, has been particularly representative of the States and of state interests.[56] But States have sometimes also seen an interest in asserting limitations on the Treaty Power as on other exertions of federal authority. At bottom, their argument was that made in Jefferson's Manual—that treaties could not deal with matters reserved to the States, as contemplated by the constitutional scheme and expressly provided in the Tenth Amendment.[57] The claim was repeatedly made and repeatedly rejected by the Supreme Court, finally and definitively in *Missouri* v. *Holland*,[58] perhaps the most famous and most discussed case in the constitutional law of foreign affairs.

The background of the case is relevant. In 1913 Congress enacted a law to regulate the hunting of migratory birds.[59] Two lower federal courts declared the statute invalid because not within any enumerated power of Congress, and the Department of Justice feared that the statute might meet the same fate in the Supreme Court.[60] Someone suggested, however, that migratory birds were a subject of concern to other nations as well, for example, Canada; and if the United States and Canada agreed to cooperate to protect the birds, Congress could do what it had done, under its power to do what is necessary and proper to implement the treaty. The treaty was made, the statute enacted,[61] and the Supreme Court so held.

*Missouri* v. *Holland* involved the validity of the act of Congress, not the validity of the treaty itself, but if "the treaty is valid there can be no dispute about the validity of the statute under Article I, § 8, as a necessary and proper means to execute the powers of the Government." [62] Holmes stated the argument of the State of Missouri and disposed of it:

> It is said that a treaty cannot be valid if it infringes the Constitution, that there are limits, therefore, to the treaty-making power, and that one such limit is

that what an act of Congress could not do unaided, in derogation of the powers reserved to the States, a treaty cannot do. An earlier act of Congress that attempted by itself and not in pursuance of a treaty to regulate the killing of migratory birds within the States had been held bad in the District Court. . . .

Whether the two cases cited were decided rightly or not they cannot be accepted as a test of the treaty power. . . . It is obvious that there may be matters of the sharpest exigency for the national well being that an act of Congress could not deal with but that a treaty followed by such an act could, and it is not lightly to be assumed that, in matters requiring national action, "a power which must belong to and somewhere reside in every civilized government" is not to be found. . . . What was said in that case with regard to the powers of the States applies with equal force to the powers of the nation in cases where the States individually are incompetent to act. We are not yet discussing the particular case before us but only are considering the validity of the test proposed. With regard to that we may add that when we are dealing with words that also are a constituent act, like the Constitution of the United States, we must realize that they have called into life a being the development of which could not have been foreseen completely by the most gifted of its begetters. It was enough for them to realize or to hope that they had created an organism; it has taken a century and has cost their successors much sweat and blood to prove that they created a nation. The case before us must be considered in the light of our whole experience and not merely in that of what was said a hundred years ago. The treaty in question does not cont~~ ~~~~ ~~~~y prohibitory words to be found in the Constitution. The only question is whether it is forbidden by some invisible radiation from the general terms of the Tenth Amendment. We must consider what this country has become in deciding what that Amendment has reserved.[63]

Holmes's eloquence needs no applause but it may have distracted attention from the core of his argument.[64] What he said, simply, was that the Constitution delegated powers to various branches of the federal government, not only to Congress; the Treaty Power was a delegation to the federal treaty-makers in addition to and independent of the delegations to Congress. Since the Treaty Power was delegated to the federal government, whatever was within it was not reserved to the States by the Tenth Amendment. Many matters, then, may be "reserved to the States" as regards domestic legislation but not as regards international agreement. They are, one might say, left to the States subject to defeasance if the United States should decide to make a treaty about them.

The argument is clear and indisputable and disposes of Jefferson and others who have made Missouri's claim before and since.[65] Without asking whether Congress could regulate such matters in the absence of treaty, the Court has consistently upheld the validity and supremacy of treaty provisions dealing with matters as local as the right to inherit land or to engage in local trade.[66] And yet, the argument has recurred in various guises and, even after *Missouri* v. *Holland,* even official American negotiators continued to assert that the United States could not by treaty regulate, say, armaments manufacture, because manufacture was a local activity reserved for regulation by the States.[67] More recently United States representatives have sometimes supported "federal-state clauses" setting obligations for federal states different from those of unitary states, sometimes with arguments reflecting constitutional "reserved rights" limitations on the treaty-making powers.[68]

Eventually, the implications of *Missouri* v. *Holland* were recognized and understood, but not necessarily welcomed. They were particularly objectionable to those who feared "newfangled" treaties in which the United States might accept common international standards of governmental behavior applicable also towards its own citizens, for example international human rights covenants. Between 1952 and 1957, there was a concerted effort bearing the name of Senator Bricker to amend the Constitution in order, in particular, to "overrule" *Missouri* v. *Holland*.[69] The principal clause of the principal version of the Bricker Amendment would have provided that "A treaty shall become effective as internal law in the United States only through legislation which would be valid in the absence of treaty." Congress, then, would have no power to enact pursuant to a treaty what it could not enact apart from treaty, thus effectively cutting the Treaty Power down to the size of Congressional power. The amendment's proponents did not recognize, however, that *Missouri* v. *Holland* had already lost its importance: its principal point, that there were "matters of the sharpest exigency for the national well being that an act of Congress could not deal with but that a treaty followed by such an act could," ceased to be true in fact, for with expanding Congressional power there were virtually no matters of any exigency —including human rights legislation—that Congress could not deal with even in the absence of treaty.[70] Since the Bricker controversy, further extensions of the powers of Congress to enact human rights legislation, by new readings of the Thirteenth and Fourteenth Amendments,* render it even clearer that the Bricker Amendment would not have effectively barred adherence to the treaties at which it aimed. For our purposes, however, I note that the amendment was not adopted and its failure only reaffirmed *Missouri* v. *Holland*.[71]

*Missouri* v. *Holland*, I stress, did not say that there were no limitations on the Treaty Power in favor of the States, only that there were none in any "invisible radiation" from the Tenth Amendment. The Constitution probably protects some few States' rights, activities, and properties against any federal invasion, even by treaty.** Although it is not obvious why there should be such a limitation, or where in the Constitution it is to be found, Mr. Justice Field ⸻⸻⸻ said that without a

* See Chapter III, p. 77 and note 53.

** See generally Chapter IX, p. 245.

State's consent its territory could not be ceded to a foreign country.[72] Because "The United States shall guarantee to every State in the Union a Republican Form of Government" (Article IV, section 4), the treaty-makers presumably could not modify the republican form of government of the States.[73] "A well-regulated militia, being necessary to the security of a free State" (Amendment II), and since the States are expressly reserved the right to train the militia and appoint its officers (under Congressional regulation) (Article I, section 8, clause 16), perhaps the United States could not agree to abolish all state militia, for example in a treaty for general and complete disarmament.[74] There are perhaps remnants of state sovereign immunity that might stir questions about a treaty—say a disarmament agreement with inspection provisions—that violates the Statehouse.[75]

## Limitations deriving from the separation of powers

Because the President and the Congress compete for power in the conduct of foreign relations, because the treaty-makers are the President and one house of Congress but not the other, because treaties, we shall see, often have effect as law like acts of Congress, it was inevitable that questions should arise about the relations between this "Fourth Branch of Government" and the Congress, and not surprising that these relations might suggest limitations on the scope of the Treaty Power. Early in our history members of the House of Representatives argued that treaties could regulate only that which could not be otherwise regulated (Jefferson's second clause);[76] and they could not deal with matters that were in the domain of Congress since that would exclude the House from its rightful legislative role (Jefferson's fourth clause).*

* Any such limitations in favor of the House (or of the Congress as a whole) might presumably be satisfied by associating the House (or the Congress as a whole) in the treaty-making process. Compare an analogous suggestion as regards the States, p. 151, and note 57, this chapter.

Like many issues about the treaty power this one, too, arose with the Jay Treaty, the first treaty concluded under the Constitution. See 1 BUTLER, THE TREATY POWER 422 *et seq.*

In one sense, no regulation which can be accomplished by treaty can be achieved by act of Congress, since only a treaty can create a system of regulation entailing international obligations: † legislation conditioned on reciprocity might approximate such a treaty but would bind neither the United States nor the other nation.[77] But if Jefferson's second limitation means more, and—like his fourth—would outlaw treaties on matters as to which Congress could legislate domestically, it would virtually wipe out the Treaty Power, as Jefferson himself recognized: under contemporary views of the powers of Congress there is little—or nothing—that is dealt with by treaty that could not also be the subject of legislation by Congress.[78]

Even in Jefferson's day, as he noted, this limitation was hardly accepted by all; it has now been long dead. Treaties have dealt with many matters that were also subject to legislation, *e. g.*, tariffs and other regulations of commerce with foreign nations; on many subjects treaties and acts of Congress have been alternative means of regulation, one by agreement, the other unilaterally, sometimes on condition of reciprocity.[79] (A different question, discussed below, is whether the treaty-makers can themselves execute such treaties or require acts of Congress to give them effect). The House of Representatives has frequently bristled, but its exclusion from the treaty process was the clear constitutional plan, and the House could not command the cooperation of the Senate and the President to accept modifications of their privileged prerogatives.[80] The House had to find consolation in that the treaty-makers voluntarily left some subjects to regulation by Congress (*e. g.*, international tariffs and trade),* and that it has some say also when, as often, the

---

† Even a unilateral treaty, containing only undertakings by the United States, would create an irrevocable international obligation, which is not accomplished by an act of Congress to the same effect. Compare Calhoun, quoted note 49, this chapter.

---

For political rather than constitutional reasons Presidents and Senates have also accepted that trade and tariff agreements should generally be by executive agreement based on the authority of both houses of Congress rather than by treaty. See Chapter VI, p. 176.

President must come to Congress as a whole to seek appropriation of funds or other implementation of a treaty. Presidents have also learned to take account of House sensibilities informally by consulting its leaders about major treaties.

While the Treaty Power is not limited by the powers of Congress,* it is assumed to be subject to other radiations from the separation of powers. It has been stated that a treaty cannot increase, diminish, or redistribute the constitutional powers of the branches of the federal government or delegate them to others—say, the power of Congress to declare war, or the President's command of American forces, or a court's exercise of judicial power, or indeed the power of the treaty-makers to make international agreements for the United States.[81] These examples are almost wholly hypothetical, but such issues have been raised, particularly in regard to United States participation in international organizations; I consider them in that context (Chapter VII).

Some have found in the separation of powers a different limitation, that a treaty cannot "bargain away" the powers of any of the branches—say, the power of Congress to impose a tariff or declare war. That argument is fallacious. Any treaty commitment by the United States "bargains away" its earlier right to do the contrary, usually by act of Congress or the President: a treaty which grants free entry for goods makes it unlawful, under international law, for Congress to exercise its constitu-

---

In 1961, Congress even purported to direct the President to "accelerate a program of negotiating treaties for commerce and trade, including tax treaties, which shall include provisions to encourage and facilitate the flow of private investment." Foreign Assistance Act of 1961 § 601(b) (2), 75 Stat. 424, 438, 22 U.S.C. § 2351(b) (2) (1970). But trade is still sometimes governed by general provisions in treaties like "most-favored nation" clauses.

* The judicial power, too, does not prevent a treaty whereby the United States and Great Britain would confer upon each other's courts jurisdiction over offenses committed on the other's vessels on the high seas. 19 OP.ATT'Y GEN. 644 (1890). For argument that the judicial power of the United States can devolve only on courts established by Congress (and not presumably by treaty), see Chapter VII, p. 199.

tional powers to impose duties or imposts; a treaty which gives immunities from judicial process to member representatives to the United Nations has "bargained away" some authority of the Executive, the Congress, the federal courts, and their counterparts in every state and city. But such self-limitations are what many treaties are about, presumably in exchange for some advantage to the United States. A treaty, moreover, does not dispose of constitutional power: internationally the United States retains the power (not the right) to violate its treaty obligations; constitutionally, the President and Congress can exercise their powers even in violation of a treaty undertaking.* Congress, for example, could authorize aggressive war in violation of the UN Charter or raise and support an army in violation of a disarmament agreement.

## Domestic matters, not of "international concern"

In their doctrine, at least, those who sought limitations on treaties in the separation of powers were not restricting federal power, only the authority of the President-and-Senate alone to adhere to certain treaties. Limitations based on federalism, on the other hand, would deny federal power, but presumably their object, too, was not to avoid those international undertakings but to prevent federal aggrandizement and diminution of state authority.[82] (In theory, the United States could adhere to those treaties with the consent of all the States.) Arguments from both Separation and federalism, however, probably carried strands of deeper objection, of resistance to too-much-government, including too-much-government by agreement with other nations. With some, moreover—perhaps with Jefferson as with Senator Bricker—limitations on the Treaty Power supported particular resistance to unnecessary, novel "entanglements" with other countries, reflecting a desire to maintain for the United States a sacrosanct zone of isolation, autonomy, "privacy," freedom from foreign scrutiny. And so when it was said that with

---

* See generally, HENKIN, ARMS CONTROL 30–33 and corresponding notes. I deal further with this question in relation to United States participation in international organizations, Chapter VII below.

federalism nor separation of powers provided any significant limitation on the Treaty Power, a different limitation was conceived: under the Constitution only matters of "international concern" are permissible subjects for treaties.[83] That limitation has been widely accepted, and some have invoked it to oppose adherence by the United States to modern international undertakings, *e. g.*, human rights covenants.[84]

The antecedents of the doctrine are not wholly clear [85] but its modern underpinnings are remarks that sprang full-blown from the mouth and mind of Charles Evans Hughes in 1929: [86]

> . . . I should not care to voice any opinion as to an implied limitation on the treaty-making power. The Supreme Court has expressed a doubt whether there could be any such. That is, the doubt has been expressed in one of its opinions. But if there is a limitation to be implied, I should say it might be found in the *nature* of the treaty-making power.
>
> What is the power to make a treaty? What is the object of the power? The normal scope of the power can be found in the appropriate object of the power. The power is to deal with foreign nations with regard to matters of international concern. It is not a power intended to be exercised, it may be assumed, with respect to matters that have no relation to international concerns.
>
> . . . . .
>
> So I come back to the suggestion I made at the start, that this is a sovereign nation; from my point of view the nation has the power to make any agreement whatever in a constitutional manner that relates to the conduct of our international relations, unless there can be found some express prohibition in the Constitution, and I am not aware of any which would in any way detract from the power as I have defined it in connection with our relations with other governments. But if we attempted to use the treaty-making power to deal with matters which did not pertain to our external

relations but to control matters which normally and appropriately were within the local jurisdictions of the States, then I again say there might be ground for implying a limitation upon the treaty-making power that it is intended for the purpose of having treaties made relating to foreign affairs and not to make laws for the people of the United States in their internal concerns through the exercise of the asserted treaty-making power.

Hughes was not speaking *ex cathedra*, either as Secretary of State (which he had long ceased to be) or as Chief Justice (which he had been designated but had not yet become).[87] Much of his argument dealt with the political advisability of making treaties on some subjects rather than with constitutional power to make them. But, perhaps because he became Chief Justice shortly thereafter; perhaps because the constitutional law of foreign relations has so little authoritative, hard, "case" law and is driven to rely on other "authority"; perhaps because some were eagerly seeking constitutional limitations on the Treaty Power—the Hughes address was quickly and uncritically seized, shorn of Hughes's own *caveats* and limitations, and accepted as authority. It has been incorporated in the case books, taught to students, invoked in a lower court opinion,[88] enshrined, in first place and in black letters, in the Restatement of the Law of United States Foreign Relations.*

It may be that Hughes was merely echoing Jefferson's requirement that a treaty be a *bona fide* agreement between the United States and another country: by hypothesis, a *bona fide* treaty deals with a foreign nation about matters "which pertain to our external relations," which are of mutual, "international concern." But Hughes has been interpreted to mean that

---

* Section 117(1). The Restatement's comment continues however: "Matters of international concern are not confined to matters ~~~~
~~~~ concerned with foreign relations. Usually, matters of international concern have both international and domestic effects, and the existence of the latter does not remove a matter from international concern."

some matters are not appropriate subjects for agreement with another country because they are our own affair and not the legitimate "concern," not the "business" of any other country.[89] I know no basis for reading into the Constitution such a limitation on the subject matter of treaties.* (Nor would I know any basis for determining which matters are and which are not the proper "business" of other countries.) If there are reasons in foreign policy why the United States seeks an agreement with a foreign country, it does not matter that the subject is otherwise "internal," that the treaty "makes laws for the people of the United States in their internal concerns," or that—apart from treaty—the matter is "normally and appropriately . . . within the local jurisdictions of the States." Any treaty that has any effect within the United States, including the traditional treaties of friendship and commerce, are specifically designed to change the law of the United States that might otherwise apply, e. g., the rights of aliens here.[90] As other laws of the United States become of interest to other countries they are equally subject to modification by treaty if the United States has foreign policy reasons for negotiating about them.

If there is any basis for the Hughes doctrine,† and if it bars some hypothetical agreement on some hypothetical subject, sure-

---

* Such a constitutional doctrine would have made Senator Bricker's struggle to amend the Constitution largely unnecessary, legally as well as politically.

† At the least, the Hughes doctrine should have a change of name. "International concern" suggests an objective standard as to what matters do, or should, or properly may, concern nations generally. Especially since international law and practice know no such conception, note 83 this chapter, there is no basis for finding it in the use of the word "treaties" or in the grant of the Treaty Power, in the Constitution. While Hughes used the phrase "international concern" he used other, better phrases even more frequently. He spoke of the power to make an agreement "that relates to the conduct of our international relations," not to deal with matters "which did not pertain to our external relations." He proposed "a limitation upon the treaty-making power that it is intended for the purpose of having treaties made relating to foreign affairs." (Later, as Chief Justice, he also

ly it is not relevant where it has been invoked—to prevent adherence by the United States to international human rights conventions.[91] Human rights have long been of international concern and the subject of international agreements—in the treaties of hundreds of years ago guaranteeing religious freedom, in the minority treaties of the 19th Century and Post-World War I, in the human rights provisions of World War II treaties, in the UN Charter, in human rights arrangements now in effect in several regions of the world, in the UN covenants on human rights, on the elimination of racial discrimination, and on other specific rights.[92]

For the United States parallel human rights undertakings have obvious foreign relations purposes.[93] In part, she is concerned to maintain leadership in international affairs by proving that she deserves it, by her behavior at home and her willingness to join in cooperative international efforts. In larger part, she is concerned to see minimum standards observed in other countries in order to safeguard her own standards, to promote conditions that are conducive to American prosperity and to American interests in international peace and security. Of obvious "international concern" to this country, for example, would be an international convention fixing high labor standards or outlawing slavery or forced labor, if it were adopted by the nations with which the United States competes to sell manufactured goods in the world markets. Other human rights are also of authentic international concern for the United States, witness apartheid in South Africa, events not long ago in Communist countries, in Nigeria, in India and Pakistan, in Cyprus, and other actual or potential situations where the treatment of individuals or minority groups is relevant to war and peace.

The United States, then, does not adhere to human rights covenants in order to distort or circumvent our constitutional sys-

spoke of the treaty ~~ ... ~~ ... ~~ ... properly
pertain to our foreign relations." Santovincenzo v. Egan, 284 U.S. 30, 40 (1931).) To say that a treaty must have a foreign relations purpose is indeed implied in the word "treaties" and in the constitutional framework, though that might go without saying.

tem, to legislate greater human rights for its own citizens by treaty rather than by act of Congress or to take additional matters from the States into the federal domain; she adheres to such covenants in order to modify the behavior of other governments in ways that affect American interests. To get other nations to undertake to observe higher standards and to give the United States the right to request compliance with those standards, the United States is prepared to pay the price of undertaking to apply similar standards in the United States and to recognize the right of other nations to request American compliance.

## Treaties As Law of the Land

I have been discussing the constitutional requirements for making treaties, and alleged constitutional limitations on the international obligations which the United States can assume by treaty. The Constitution also prescribes the place and effect of treaties in the law of the United States.

### Self-Executing and Non-Self-Executing Treaties

In Western parliamentary systems, generally, treaties are only international obligations, without effect as domestic law; [94] it is for the parliament to translate them into law, or to enact any domestic legislation necessary to carry out their obligations. The Constitution established a different regime. The Supremacy Clause (Article VI, section 2) provides:

> This Constitution, and the Laws of the United States which shall be made in Pursuance thereof; and all Treaties made, or which shall be made, under the Authority of the United States, shall be the supreme Law of the Land; and the Judges in every State shall be bound thereby, any Thing in the Constitution or Laws of any State to the Contrary notwithstanding.

That clause, designed principally to assure the supremacy of treaties to state law, has been interpreted to mean also that treaties are law of the land of their own accord and do not re-

quire an act of Congress to translate them into law.* Chief
Justice Marshall said:

> A treaty is in its nature a contract between two na-
> tions, not a legislative act. It does not generally effect,
> of itself, the object to be accomplished, especially so
> far as its operation is infra-territorial; but is carried in-
> to execution by the sovereign power of the respective
> parties to the instrument.

> In the United States a different principle is estab-
> lished. Our constitution declares a treaty to be the law
> of the land. It is, consequently, to be regarded in
> courts of justice as equivalent to an act of the legisla-
> ture, whenever it operates of itself without the aid of
> any legislative provision. . . .

Not all treaties, however, are in fact law of the land of their
own accord. Marshall continued:

> . . . But when the terms of the stipulation
> import a contract, when either of the parties engages
> to perform a particular act, the treaty addresses it-
> self to the political, not the judicial department; and
> the legislature must execute the contract before it can
> become a rule for the Court.[95]

In the United States, then, treaties designed to have domestic
consequences can be either "non-self-executing," requiring an
act of Congress to carry out the international obligation; † or
"self-executing," and without any legislative intervention the

* As an original matter one might have asked whether the purpose
of achieving the supremacy of federal treaties required that they
become law automatically, and whether indeed that was the purpose
and purport of the Supremacy Clause: the supremacy of treaties
would have been achieved even if they required Congressional legislation to give them domestic effect as law. Marshall's statement, however, is established law.

† Strictly, if a treaty is not self-executing it is not the treaty but
the implementing legislation that is effectively "law of the land."
Sometimes the implementing legislation gives the treaty itself legal
effect or incorporates it by reference.

Executive and the courts will accord to claimants the benefits promised by the United States.†† Whether a treaty is one or the other is ordinarily a domestic question,† in the first instance for the Executive, who must decide whether to "take care" that the treaty is "faithfully executed" * as law or to seek implementation by Congress; ultimately, for the courts, which must decide whether they should give the treaty effect as law if there has been no legislative implementation. The courts have considered that to be a matter of interpretation of the agreement,** but agreements have often been drafted without attention to that question so that it may be difficult to determine what was contemplated.*** In particular instances, United States

†† A treaty is not law of the land until proclaimed and the persons affected given notice of it. See REV. STAT. sec. 210; *cf.* Haver v. Yaker, 9 Wall. 32 (U.S.1869). Hence, a secret treaty can not be law of the land while it is secret. Compare note 9, this chapter.

A self-executing treaty when proclaimed, or a non-self-executing treaty when implemented by Congress, supersedes state law automatically, without awaiting its repeal or other action by the States. Compare Ware v. Hylton, 3 Dall. 199, 236–37 (U.S.1796) (Chase, J.)

It has sometimes been suggested that the obligations of other nations in a treaty with the United States are also the law of this land and therefore enforceable against them by claimants in American courts. That interpretation of the Supremacy Clause is not supported by its history and I know of no authority for it. Compare Chapter II, p. 55, Chapter VIII, pp. 223–24.

† The Bricker Amendment did not purport to limit the power to make treaties; but by rendering all treaties non-self-executing, and denying Congress the power to implement certain treaties in domestic law, it would have effectively prevented the federal government from making them.

* Art. II, sec. 3. Chapter II, p. 55.

** They will, therefore, give the Executive views on the question "great weight," p. 167 below.

*** Other parties to a treaty, of course, prefer that a treaty be self-executing in the United States in order that they may enjoy rights under it immediately upon proclamation, without awaiting legislative implementation. Whether a treaty is self-executing or not, the obligation of the United States becomes effective with exchange of ratifica-

negotiators have been careful to make clear that the treaty will require Congressional implementation: in the North Atlantic Treaty, for example, it was accepted by all parties that no events would put the United States automatically at war; if war were called for, Congress would have to declare it.[96] On numerous occasions, the Senate provided by reservation that the treaty shall not take effect as domestic law but shall be implemented by Congress.[97]

Some obligations, it is accepted, cannot be executed by the treaty itself.†† A treaty cannot appropriate funds: the Constitution expressly provides that "No Money shall be drawn from the Treasury, but in Consequence of Appropriations made by Law," and a treaty is apparently not law for this purpose;[98] any financial undertaking by the United States, then, requires appropriation by Congress. A treaty cannot itself enact criminal law: enforcement of treaty obligations by penal sanction can be effected only by Congress.[99] It has often been said, too, that the United States cannot declare war by treaty, only by res-

tions, and if the treaty is not self-executing the President is obliged to seek legislative implementation promptly. Sometimes a treaty may undertake only to seek domestic legislation, with the possible interpretation that if legislation is sought bona fide the obligation of the United States is discharged even if the legislature should refuse.

†† It has been suggested that treaties that deal with matters on which Congress could legislate cannot be self-executing. Compare CORWIN, THE PRESIDENT 195. There is no basis for that view and it does not reflect constitutional practice. In the numerous instances in which acts of Congress were held to supersede treaty provisions (p. 163 below), there was no suggestion that the treaty was not law anyhow since it could not be self-executing. (The doctrine that statutes and self-executing treaties have equal stature, and the later in time prevails, itself contradicts this suggestion.) Today, since any subject of a treaty is probably also within Congressional power (p. 76 above) the suggestion would virtually eliminate self-executing treaties. But Congress has often insisted that treaties modifying tariffs are not self-executing and require Congressional implementation, and the Executive has generally acquiesced. CRANDALL, TREATIES 195–200; see note 110, this chapter. In recent years tariffs have been the subject of executive agreements authorized by Congress or requiring Congressional implementation. See Chapter VI, p. 176.

olution of Congress,[100] though it is not clear why that power is denied to the treaty-makers when other enumerated powers of Congress are not. That question is, and is likely to remain, academic: no treaty of the United States has ever been designed to put the United States into a state of war without a declaration by Congress.†

The status of a treaty as law of the land derives from and depends on its status as a valid, living treaty of the United States. It is not law of the land for either the President or the courts to enforce if it is not made in accordance with constitutional requirements, or is beyond the power of the President and Senate to make, or violates constitutional prohibitions. It is not law of the land if it is not an effective treaty of the United States internationally because it is not binding,[101] or is invalid under international law, or because it has expired, or has been terminated or destroyed by breach, whether by the United States or the other party.*

Legal effect has been given, however, to incidental provisions in a treaty (or in Senate reservations upon consenting to it) which themselves contain no international obligations,[102] for example, a provision that a treaty shall not be self-executing in the United States; ** or that territory acquired under the treaty shall not be automatically "incorporated" into the United States but shall await the disposition of Congress.[103] Perhaps such provisions are considered penumbral to the treaty, sharing in its character as law of the land; perhaps the Treaty Power implies ancillary authority to regulate the incidental concomitants

---

† It has been argued, however, that pursuant to United States undertakings in the UN Charter, President Truman had authority to send troops to fight in Korea when called upon to do so by resolution of the Security Council. See Chapter IV, notes 22, 27.

* See p. 167 below. For the effect of termination of a treaty on legislation implementing it, see note 105, this chapter.

** Compare the Niagara Reservation, p. 134 above. A provision that the treaty shall not go into effect at all until Congress acts is not simply a domestic limitation since it affects the international obligations of the treaty as well. See Henkin, *Niagara* 1169–75.

and consequences of a treaty, and such regulations, whether in the original treaty or imposed by the Senate, also have effect as law. Whatever the theory, surely the Constitution does not prevent the treaty-makers from limiting their own authority and the consequences of their own acts in order to cooperate with Congress and enhance its legislative opportunities.[104]

## Congressional Implementation

When a treaty requires implementation by domestic legislation or an appropriation of funds to carry out United States obligations, only the Congress can supply them. As *Missouri* v. *Holland* confirmed, Congress has the power to do what is "necessary and proper" to implement a treaty even if its action was not within other Congressional powers.[105] But as early as the Jay Treaty, debate flared as to whether Congress is constitutionally and morally obligated to implement treaties.[106] In a draft for Washington's message to the House of Representatives, Hamilton wrote:

> . . . the House of Representatives have no moral power to refuse the execution of a treaty which is not contrary to the Constitution, because it pledges the public faith; and have no legal power to refuse its execution because it is a law—until at least it ceases to be a law by a regular act of revocation of the competent authority.[107]

In the House, on the other hand, Representatives, including Madison, saw in this division of power an element of checks and balances and insisted on the right (if not the duty) of Congress to determine independently the desirability of appropriations or legislation.[108] The House resolved:

> . . . when a Treaty stipulates regulations on any of the subjects submitted by the Constitution to the power of Congress, it must depend, for its execution, as to such stipulations, on a law or laws to be passed by Congress. And it is the Constitutional right and duty of the House of Representatives, in all such cases, to deliberate on the expediency or inexpediency of carrying

such Treaty into effect, and to determine and act thereon, as, in their judgment, may be most conducive to the
public good.[109]

Like some other constitutional debates this one, too, has not
been resolved in principle.[110]  Hamilton's position would obviously make for a more efficient system, for otherwise treaty-makers
might find that they had negotiated treaties but could not assure that the United States would carry them out; effectively,
Presidents would have to consult the House of Representatives
and perhaps obtain its formal consent prior to ratification.
Separation and checks-and-balances, on the other hand, were
dear to the Constitutional Fathers, and many of them were
still on the scene when implementation of the Jay Treaty passed
the House only barely and after bitter debate.  Since then,
though Congressmen have continued to assert their power and
right not to do so, Congresses have not in fact failed to carry
out international obligations.  They have responded, no doubt,
to a sense of duty to carry out what the treaty-makers promised,
to a reluctance to defy and confront the President especially
when he can no longer retreat, to an unwillingness to make the
American system appear undependable and ludicrous.  But the
independence of the legislative process (subject only to the regular Presidential veto) has given Congress opportunities to interpret the need for implementation and to shape and limit it
in important details; Congress has not always given the President exactly the laws he asked for or as much money as he said
a treaty required.  And Congress has on various occasions later
enacted laws inconsistent with treaty obligations.*

---

* See p. 163 below.  It has been argued that since, as we shall see,
Congress has the power to "repeal" a treaty, it should have the power
to refuse to implement it.  The cases are distinguishable.  The power
of Congress to enact domestic legislation inconsistent with an earlier
treaty is deemed an exercise of its independent power to make domestic
laws; and usually such enactments come from a later Congress.  To
say that Congress can refuse to implement a treaty in the first instance would destroy the independence of the Treaty Power, and give
the House of Representatives a voice in treaty-making not intended
for it; it would also put an unusual premium on self-executing treaties,
p. 156 above.

## Conflicting Treaties and Acts of Congress

Since treaties are law of the land, since treaties often deal with matters that are also the subject of Congressional legislation, it can happen (and has happened) that a treaty and an act of Congress might enact inconsistent law.** The legal consequence has been long settled by the Supreme Court:

> By the Constitution a treaty is placed on the same footing, and made of like obligation, with an act of legislation. Both are declared by that instrument to be the supreme law of the land, and no supreme efficacy is given to either over the other. When the two relate to the same subject, the courts will always endeavor to construe them so as to give effect to both, if that can be done without violating the language of either; but if the two are inconsistent, the one last in date will control the other, provided always the stipulation of the treaty on the subject is self-executing.[111]

As an original matter, the equality as law of treaties and federal statutes seems hardly inevitable; surely, there is no basis for it in the Supremacy Clause which the Supreme Court invoked. That clause says only that treaties and statutes are both law of the land, and both supreme over state laws and binding on state courts; it does not follow that they are equal to each other. (3 and 2 are both "supreme" to 1 but are not equal.) Indeed, the Supremacy Clause obviously did not intend to assert the equality of all supreme federal law for it lists the Constitution as well as laws and treaties as supreme law of the land, and surely laws and treaties are not equal as law to the Constitution. The Supremacy Clause apart, it has been argued that Congress is the paramount legislator and its statutes should

** The issue arises only for self-executing treaties. Since a non-self-executing treaty is not law of its own accord, any inconsistency between such a treaty and an Act of Congress is, as regards domestic law, an inconsistency ~~~~~~~~~~~~~~~~~~~~~~~~~~~~ the statute implementing the treaty. Since both are the work of Congress there is less doctrinal difficulty in insisting that the later repeals the earlier, even if one is pursuant to a treaty and may even be constitutionally required of Congress.

prevail as law in the United States in the face of a treaty even if the treaty came later.[112] (The treaty-makers then would have to seek new legislation to repeal the old, and—as in some parliamentary systems—might have to do so before the treaty is ratified so that they could assure United States compliance.) Supporters of this view note also that there is only one case in which the Supreme Court held that a treaty provision repealed an earlier statute, and that was a "liquor prohibition" statute which had notoriously low estate, was widely disregarded and was about to be repealed.[113]

On the other hand one might well have argued to the contrary, that a treaty should prevail even in the face of a subsequent statute.[114] The international obligations of the United States are the responsibility of the treaty-makers. The Senate was given a part in the process but the House, and Congress as a whole, were purposely denied any say. Congress, we have seen, probably has a constitutional obligation to implement the treaties which the President and Senate make; it is anomalous to accord it power to disregard a treaty obligation, compel its violation, and put the United States in default.[115]

Whatever the arguments, the equality of statutes and treaties in domestic law seems established, and acts of Congress inconsistent with earlier treaty obligations are regularly given effect by the courts.[116] That is not to say, as is often erroneously said, that Congress can "repeal" a treaty: [117] Congress is not acting upon the treaty, but, exercising one of its legislative powers, it legislates without regard to the international obligations of the United States. Such legislation does not affect the validity of the treaty and its abiding international obligations, though it compels the United States to go into default.

### Enforcement

Responsibility for carrying out treaty obligations falls on the President under his foreign affairs powers, and it is upon him that foreign governments will call when there is failure in compliance by the United States. If a treaty entails domestic regulation and is not self-executing, or if it requires appropriation of funds, the President has to seek Congressional action. Self-executing treaties, and other treaties after they are implemented by Congress, are subject to the President's duty to see that the laws are faithfully executed.† Responsibility is also a source of authority, for a treaty gives the President powers he might not otherwise have: for example, if without a treaty a President cannot extradite an accused citizen to a foreign land, the treaty gives the President authority to do so.[118] Without Senate concurrence he can make additional agreements contemplated by the treaty, and probably others which he considers necessary and proper for giving effect to it.*

Many treaty obligations can be carried out by the Executive Branch. Undertakings that are, or are translated by Congress into, domestic law are executed by the President like other laws of the United States, including, if necessary, by the use of federal marshals and the armed forces.[119] When a treaty is relevant to a case before a court, the Executive can intervene, if only as *amicus curiae*, to call the obligations of the United States to the court's attention. The Executive Branch has also communicated with state governors and legislatures to prevent actions that might violate international obligations of the United States.

Where private rights are at stake, the courts have often enforced the treaty obligations of the United States, particularly to prevent or undo violations by the States.** In general, an aggrieved person can seek relief from violation of a treaty by state officials through a declaratory judgment or injunction from an appropriate state or federal court; [120] or, when prosecuted or sued under a state statute, he can assert in his defense that the

† See Ch. II, p. 55. But acting under other constitutional power, notably his foreign affairs powers, the President can terminate or break treaties, thereby abolishing or modifying their effect as domestic law. See pp. 168, 171 below.

See Chapter VI, p. 176 below.

** Federal violations are less frequent and if they are national policy by the President or Congress the courts will not give effect to the treaty. See p. 171 below.

statute is inconsistent with a treaty.* If necessary, he can usually carry his case to the Supreme Court for a final decision, as in the early *Ware* v. *Hylton,* where the Court allowed a British creditor to collect from a Virginia debtor, holding that the Virginia statute discharging the debt fell before the treaty that promised that such debts would be paid; [121] on several occasions the Supreme Court struck down state provisions denying or taxing inheritance to an alien as inconsistent with treaty obligations.[122]

Or take the well-known case of Mr. Asakura. Officials of the City of Seattle prosecuted Asakura, a Japanese national, for operating a pawnshop in violation of an ordinance making it illegal for an alien to do so. Asakura defended on the ground that as to him the ordinance was invalid, since a treaty between the United States and Japan provided that the citizens of each country shall have the right to carry on trade in the territory of the other on the same terms as citizens of the host country. Although his claim was rejected by the state courts, the Supreme Court upheld it on appeal. The Court said:

> The rule of equality established by it [the treaty] cannot be rendered nugatory in any part of the United States by municipal ordinances or state laws. It stands on the same footing of supremacy as do the provisions of the Constitution and the laws of the United States. It operates of itself without the aid of any legislation, state or national; and it will be applied and given authoritative effect by the courts.[123]

Consider, however, a more recent, less happy instance, also involving a treaty with Japan. In order to promote local products to the disadvantage of foreign competition, South Carolina required merchants selling Japanese textiles to advertise that they were doing so, a requirement that was probably in violation of a provision in the Treaty of Commerce, Friendship and Navigation between the United States and Japan. Like Asakura,

---

*As in *Asakura,* below. Treaties will be given effect by the courts, superseding inconsistent state law, in other kinds of proceedings as well, *e. g.,* the cases in note 122, this chapter.

a merchant wishing to sell Japanese textiles without posting the offending advertisement might have obtained a judgment nullifying the state statute; or he could have disregarded the State's requirement and the treaty would have effectively prevented his conviction for violating it. But no merchant appeared willing to challenge the requirement, political persuasion was not effective for some time, and the State Department helplessly expressed regret to the Japanese Government.[124]  The Federal Government did not seek the assistance of the courts although there is support for the view that, even without specific authorization from Congress,[125] federal courts, under general jurisdictional statutes, could entertain a suit by the Attorney General or the Secretary of State to enjoin treaty violations by state officials or private interference with treaty rights.[126]

## Interpretation

The obligation and authority to implement or enforce a treaty involve also the obligation and authority to interpret what the treaty requires. For international purposes, no doubt, the President determines the United States position as to the meaning of a treaty.*  Domestically, too, since the President has usually the principal, often the sole, responsibility to execute a treaty, the treaty means what he says it means. But Congress, too, has occasion to interpret a treaty when it considers implementing legislation or other legislation on the same subject; [127] the courts also interpret treaties in cases before them. Both Congress and the courts have claimed the right to interpret a treaty independently, even while admitting that the Executive's interpretation is entitled to "great weight." [128]  It could happen, then, that Congress and the courts would in effect apply treaty provisions different from those that bind the United States internationally—another cost of the separation of powers.

## Breach and Termination of Treaties

The United States sometimes has the right to terminate a treaty by its own terms, at some prescribed time after giving

---

* Subject to any "understanding" imposed by the Senate in its consent to ratification, p. 136 above.

notice of its intention to do so (*e. g.,* the Nuclear Test Ban of 1963).[129]  Treaties can be terminated by more or less formal agreement of the parties.  The international law of treaties permits termination for important breach by the other side, or because of a fundamental change in circumstances (the principle of *rebus sic stantibus*).[130]  International law also recognizes the power—though not the right—to break a treaty and abide the international consequences.

No doubt, the Federal Government has the constitutional power to terminate treaties on behalf of the United States in all these ways and circumstances:  neither the declaration in the Supremacy Clause that treaties are law of the land, nor anything else in the Constitution, denies the United States these powers inherent in its sovereignty.  But while the Constitution tells us who can make treaties, it does not say who can unmake them.

At various times the power to terminate treaties has been claimed for the President, the President-and-Senate, the Congress.[131]  Presidents have claimed authority, presumably under their foreign affairs power, to act for the United States to terminate treaties, whether in accordance with their terms, or in accordance with or in violation of international law.  Franklin Roosevelt, for example, denounced an extradition treaty with Greece in 1933 because Greece had refused to extradite the celebrated Mr. Insull;  in 1939 he denounced the Treaty of Commerce, Friendship and Navigation with Japan.[132]  Without formal termination, Presidents in conducting foreign relations have acted contrary to treaty obligations, even where the treaty had domestic effect as law of the land, sometimes inviting the other party to terminate the treaty.*

---

* While the President has the duty to see that the laws, including treaty-law, are faithfully executed, that duty presumably ceases to exist when the treaty ceases to exist because the President acted under his constitutional authority in another capacity to destroy it.  See p. 160 above.  Compare the constitutional authority of the political branches to act without regard to international law, Chapter VIII, p. 222, and the power of Congress to legislate contrary to treaty, p. 163 above.

In principle, one might argue, if the Framers required the President to obtain the Senate's consent for making a treaty, its consent ought to be required also for terminating it, and there is eminent dictum to support that view.[133] But perhaps the Framers were concerned only to check the President in "entangling" the United States; "disentangling" is less risky and may have to be done quickly, and is often done piecemeal, or *ad hoc*, by various means or acts. In any event, since the President acts for the United States internationally he can effectively terminate or violate treaties, and the Senate has not established its authority to join or veto him.*

Congress, we know, has some power effectively to breach treaties. While it is probably required to pass legislation necessary and proper to implement treaty obligations, it could refuse to do so, put the United States in default, perhaps compel the President to terminate the treaty or induce the other party to do so; often it can achieve these ends too later, by enacting legislation inconsistent with treaty obligations.** Congress can also declare war and terminate or suspend treaty relations with the other belligerent.[134]

In the past, Congress purported also to denounce or abrogate treaties for the United States or to direct the President to do so. Those instances, no doubt, reflect the recurrent claims of Congress to general powers to make foreign policy, as well as particular arguments that the maintenance or termination of treaties is intimately related to war-or-peace for which Congress has sole responsibility.[135] But Congressional resolutions have no effect internationally unless the President adopts and com-

---

* The Senate might perhaps reserve a right to denounce a particular treaty as a condition of its consent to it. In 1919 the Senate entered a reservation to the Versailles Treaty that would have authorized its denunciation by concurrent resolution. 59 CONG.REC. 5423 (1919). See p. 136.

** If a treaty is not self-executing Congress need only repeal its implementing legislation leaving the treaty obligation thereafter unfulfilled.

municates them, and while some Presidents have chosen to comply with Congressional wishes, others have disregarded them.[136]

In recent times issues as to who has authority to terminate treaties have not arisen. The United States has not been frequently disposed to terminate treaties, perhaps because the part of treaties in American foreign relations has changed. Second World War agreements were not formal treaties and were not terminated; they lapsed or disintegrated. While the number and subjects and dispositions of treaties since the War have proliferated and varied, "political" treaties by the United States have been few; and these were largely the product of United States initiative (*e. g.*, NATO, SEATO), and neither Presidents nor Congresses wished to terminate them before their agreed term. Tensions between the United States and other countries (*e. g.*, Cuba) also did not impel the United States to terminate treaties with them. In general, surely, President and Congress have not differed as to the desirability of maintaining existing treaties.

If issues as to who has power to terminate treaties arise again, however, it seems unlikely that Congress will successfully assert the power. Especially with the changed character of war and its place in international relations, Congress will probably be unable to claim plausibly that the maintenance or termination of treaties is intimately related to war or peace; a President who wishes to maintain a treaty will doubtless treat a Congressional denunciation or directive to terminate as only a hortatory "sense resolution." (Politically of course, the President could not lightly disregard the sense of Congress especially if both houses have joined, claimed constitutional power, and publicly proclaimed a call for radical action.)

The power to terminate a treaty is a political power: courts do not terminate treaties, though they may interpret political acts or even political silences to determine whether they implied or intended termination.[137] If there is a breach of a treaty by the other party, it is the President not the courts who will decide whether the United States will denounce the treaty, consider itself liberated from its obligations, or seek other relief or none at all.[138]

Nor do courts sit in judgment on the political branches to prevent them from terminating or breaching a treaty.[139]  Where fairly possible, the courts will interpret actions of the President or of Congress to render them consistent with international obligations, but both President and Congress can exercise their respective constitutional powers regardless of treaty obligations, and the courts will give effect to acts within their powers even if they violate treaty obligations or other international law.*

* For that reason, for example, attempts to enjoin Executive action in Vietnam on the ground that it violated United States obligations under the UN Charter were misconceived.  Compare Chapter VIII, pp. 214, 221–22;  Chapter XI, p. 274;  compare generally Chapter IV, pp. 100 *et seq.*

# Chapter *VI*. OTHER INTERNATIONAL AGREEMENTS

Since our national beginnings Presidents have made some 1300 treaties with the consent of the Senate; they have made many thousands of other international agreements without seeking Senate consent.[1] Some were authorized or approved by joint resolution of Congress; many were made by the President on his sole authority.

The Constitution does not expressly confer authority to make international agreements other than treaties,* but executive agreements, varying widely in formality and in importance, have been common from our early history. Where does the President find constitutional authority to make them? How does one distinguish an agreement which can be approved by the President with the approval of Congress, or on his own authority, from one requiring Senate consent? Are executive agreements subject to the same constitutional limitations as treaties, or to others? Do they have the same quality as law of the land, the same supremacy to state law, the same equality with acts of Congress?

## Congressional-Executive Agreements

Agreements made by joint authority of the President and Congress have come about in different ways. Congress has authorized the President to negotiate and conclude agreements on particular subjects, reciprocal trade, lend-

---

* The Constitution does provide for "Agreements or Compacts" between States and foreign powers, with the consent of Congress. Art. I, sec. 10. See Chapter IX, p. 229.

lease, foreign assistance, nuclear reactors.[2] Congress has authorized the President to conclude particular agreements already negotiated, as in the case of the Headquarters Agreement with the United Nations and various multilateral agreements establishing international organizations, *e. g.*, UNRRA, the International Bank and the International Monetary Fund, the International Refugee Organization.[3] In some instances Congress has approved Presidential agreements by legislation or appropriation of funds to carry out their obligations.[4]

Constitutional doctrine to support Congressional-Executive agreements is not clear or agreed. The Constitution expressly prescribes the treaty procedure and nowhere suggests that another method of making international agreements would do as well.[5] Congress, also, has no authority to negotiate with foreign governments; it can not, then, delegate any to the President.[6] One might say that Congress can join its legislative powers in regard to the subject matter to the President's authority to negotiate with foreign governments,[7] but international agreements are primarily international acts and make domestic law only incidentally. Many agreements, moreover, make no domestic law at all, and some of the agreements authorized or approved by Congress, *e. g.*, for participation in some international organizations, deal with matters that are not within any enumerated power of Congress or even its unenumerated power to legislate in matters relating to foreign affairs. Some have denied,[8] therefore, any power in President-and-Congress to make international agreements on matters not within the legislative powers of Congress.* Others have urged that even if neither the Pres-

---

* In *Missouri* v. *Holland* Holmes said that there may be matters of the sharpest exigency for the national well being that an act of Congress could not deal with. Chapter III, p. 76, Chapter V, p. 145. In such cases, Congress could legislate only in support of a treaty, and presumably also in support of an executive agreement based on the President's constitutional authority, but it had no legislative power that would supply any deficiency in the President's constitutional authority to make such agreements. A broad power for Congress to legislate domestically on foreign affairs is now accepted but it, too,

ident nor Congress alone has authority to support a particular international agreement, together they embody the national sovereignty in international relations and can exercise all the powers inherent in such sovereignty, including the power to make international agreements.[9]

Neither Congresses nor Presidents nor courts have been troubled by these conceptual difficulties and differences. Whatever their theoretical merits, it is now widely accepted that the Congressional-Executive agreement is a complete alternative to a treaty: the President can seek approval of any agreement by joint resolution of both houses of Congress instead of two-thirds of the Senate only.[10] Like a treaty, such an agreement is the law of the land, superseding inconsistent state laws as well as inconsistent provisions in earlier treaties, in other international agreements or acts of Congress.[11]

The Congressional-Executive agreement had strong appeal some years ago as an alternative to the treaty method. By permitting approval of an agreement by simple majority of both houses, it eliminates the veto by one-third-plus-one of the Senators present which in the past had effectively buried important treaties. It gives an equal role to the House of Representatives which has long resented the "undemocratic" anachronism that excludes it from the treaty-making process. Especially since so many treaties require legislative implementation if only by appropriation of funds, it assures approval of the agreement by both houses before ratification, virtually eliminating the danger that the House of Representatives might later refuse to join in giving effect to the agreement. It simplifies the parliamentary process: a treaty goes to the Senate for consent and, often, to the Senate again and to the House for implementation; a Con-

would not supply any lack in Presidential authority as regards matters which have no domestic legal import.

There have been ~~~ ~~~~~~ ~~~~~~~ ~~~~~~ ~~~~~~~~~ ~~ ~~~~~~~~ ~~
cause the Senate can be deemed to give consent to the agreement by implication when it votes for a Joint Resolution to approve it. But formal and conceptual objections apart, approval by joint resolution does not require a two-thirds vote. Compare note 9, this chapter.

gressional-Executive agreement can go to both houses in the first instance, and "consent" and implementation achieved in a single action. It eliminates issues about self-executing and non-self-executing agreements and about the consequences of inconsistency between international agreements and statutes: all such agreements are "executed" by Congress, every agreement has Congressional sanction, and the joint resolution approving it, clearly, can repeal any inconsistent statutes.

Despite these advantages, the Congressional-Executive agreement has not effectively replaced the treaty. No doubt the Senate has been jealous for its special prerogatives, and perhaps the Framers' reasons for excluding the House remained persuasive to the Senate and the President, even to some members of the House itself.[12] Perhaps the Executive has not pressed the alternative method of making international agreements because the Senate has proved sufficiently responsible and "internationalist," often more so than the House has been in other contexts, and there appeared no important agreement which could command a majority but not two-thirds of the Senate and which the President was willing to fight for through both houses. Perhaps enthusiasm for an alternative to the treaty method fell victim to the Bricker controversy in which "internationalists" who had earlier scorned the treaty process now found themselves resisting efforts to cripple it. But the constitutionality of the Congressional-Executive agreement is established, it is used regularly at least for trade and postal agreements, and remains available to Presidents for general use should the treaty process again prove difficult.

## "Sole" Executive Agreements

Presidents have made numerous international agreements contemplated by a treaty, or which they considered appropriate for implementing treaty obligations, and no one seems to have questioned their authority to make them.[13] Perhaps it is assumed that Senate consent to the original treaty implies consent to supplementary agreements;[14] perhaps by such agreements the President takes care that the treaty is faithfully executed.*

* Compare Chapter II, p. 55.

Constitutional issues and controversies have swirled about executive agreements concluded by the President wholly on his own authority. Without the consent of the Senate, the approval of Congress, or the support of a treaty, Presidents from Washington to Nixon have made many thousands of agreements, of different degrees of formality and importance, on matters running the gamut of American foreign relations. (The World War II agreements at Yalta and Potsdam [15] and more recent agreements in South-east Asia are only dramatic and controversial examples.) Periodically, Senators (in particular) have objected to some agreements,[16] and the Bricker Amendment sought to curtail or regulate them,* but the power to make them remains as vast and its constitutional foundations and limits as uncertain as ever.

No one has doubted that the President has the power to make some "sole" executive agreements. As Commander-in-Chief, for example, he can make armistice agreements, and, viewed broadly, that power might support many other agreements as well, including war-time commitments on territorial and political issues for the post-war, as at Yalta and Potsdam.** But the Supreme Court has found Presidential authority to make international agreements that would reach much farther. In *United States* v. *Belmont*, speaking of the "Litvinov Agreement" on the occasion of United States recognition of the Soviet Union, Mr. Justice Sutherland said: [17]

> . . . The recognition, establishment of diplomatic relations, the assignment, and agreement with respect thereto, were all parts of one transaction, resulting in an international compact between the two governments. That the negotiations, acceptance of the assignment and agreements and understandings in respect thereof were

* See Chapter V, p. 147.

** See Chapter II, p. 52. Agreements as to post-war dispositions were obviously relevant to the tasks and commitments of the various allies in the conduct of war as to which the President's authority is unquestioned.

within the competence of the President may not be doubted. Governmental power over internal affairs is distributed between the national government and the several states. Governmental power over external affairs is not distributed, but is vested exclusively in the national government. And in respect of what was done here, the Executive had authority to speak as the sole organ of that government. The assignment and the agreements in connection therewith did not, as in the case of treaties, as that term is used in the treaty making clause of the Constitution (Article II, § 2), require the advice and consent of the Senate.

A treaty signifies "a compact made between two or more independent nations with a view to the public welfare." . . . But an international compact, as this was, is not always a treaty which requires the participation of the Senate. There are many such compacts, of which a protocol, a modus vivendi, a postal convention, and agreements like that now under consideration are illustrations. . . .

*Belmont* involved an agreement incidental to recognition of the Soviet Union, and Sutherland's opinion gave some emphasis to that fact. Recognition is indisputably the President's sole responsibility, and for many it is an "enumerated" power implied in the President's express powers to appoint and receive Ambassadors.* *Belmont*, then, might hold only that the President's specific and exclusive powers (principally those in respect of recognition, and his powers as Commander-in-Chief) support agreements on his sole authority. But, we have seen, the whole conduct of our foreign relations is exclusively the President's, and that authority, too, has been said to be expressly "enumerated," in the clause vesting the "executive Power." ** Sutherland in fact seemed to find authority for the Litvinov Agreement not in the President's exclusive control of recognition policy but

* See Chapter II, p. 41, Chapter IV, p. 93.

** See Chapter II, p. 42.

in his authority as "sole organ," his "foreign affairs power" which supports not only recognition but much if not most other foreign policy.[18]

There have indeed been suggestions, claiming support in *Belmont*, that the President is constitutionally free to make any agreement on any matter involving our relations with another country, although for political reasons—especially if he will later require Congressional implementation—he will often seek Senate consent.[19] As a matter of constitutional construction, however, that view is unacceptable, for it would wholly remove the "check" of Senate consent which the Framers struggled and compromised to write into the Constitution.[20] One is compelled to conclude that there are agreements which the President can make on his sole authority and others which he can make only with the consent of the Senate,[21] but neither Justice Sutherland nor any one else has told us which are which.[22]

The Supreme Court has not held any executive agreement *ultra vires* for lack of Senate consent nor has it given other guidance that might define the President's power to act alone.* Members of the Senate—the principal "victim" of sole executive agreements—have periodically charged Presidential usurpation but have not asserted plausible limits to Presidential power,** and Presidents have not confessed constitutional error or promised to behave differently in the future. The practice of Presidents, too, has not reflected any principle of limitation, for they have made numerous agreements across the range of American foreign relations.[23] In 1817, the Rush-Bagot Agreement disarmed the Great Lakes.[24] *Root-Takahira* and *Lansing-Ishii* defined American policy in the Far East. A Gentlemen's Agreement with Japan (1907) limited Japanese immigration into the United States. Theodore Roosevelt put the bankrupt customs houses of Santo Domingo under American control to prevent

---

* But ~~ ~~ ~~ *Reidacker* case, p. 187 this chapter, Chapter IV, p. 98.

** See note 16, this chapter. Compare the "Commitments Resolution," p. 181 below.

European creditors from seizing them. McKinley agreed to contribute troops to protect Western legations during the Boxer Rebellion and later accepted the Boxer Indemnity Protocol for the United States. Franklin Roosevelt exchanged over-age destroyers for British bases.* Potsdam and Yalta shaped the political face of the world after the Second World War. Many Presidents have concluded agreements settling claims between the United States and foreign governments.[25]

Whatever limitations the Constitution imposes on the subject matter of treaties ** would apply, surely, to executive agreements as well. But at least one of the limitations we considered —and discarded—in regard to the Treaty Power has been asserted to apply nevertheless to executive agreements.† In 1953, in the *Capps* case,[26] Chief Judge Parker of the United States Court of Appeals for the Fourth Circuit refused to give effect to an executive agreement regulating the export of potatoes by Canada to the United States. (The Supreme Court, expressly declining to consider the questions that concern us, affirmed on other grounds.) Judge Parker might have limited himself to holding, as he did, that the executive agreement could not prevail in the face of an earlier inconsistent act of Congress,†† but he also said:[27]

> The answer is that while the President has certain inherent powers under the Constitution such as the power pertaining to his position as Commander in Chief of Army and Navy and the power necessary to see that the laws are faithfully executed, the power to regulate interstate and foreign commerce is not among the powers

* The President's power to make that agreement was supported in a famous opinion by Attorney General Jackson. 39 Op.Att'y Gen. 484 (1941).

** See Chapter V, pp. 140 *et seq.*

† I deal here with suggested limitations on the power to make executive agreements, leaving for later related limitations on the status of executive agreements in domestic law.

†† Compare pp. 185–86 below.

> incident to the Presidential office, but is expressly vest-
> ed by the Constitution in the Congress. . . .

Judge Parker's suggestion,[28] it should be clear, would not only deny to many executive agreements effect as domestic law in the United States; it denies the President's power to make them at all. His argument is unpersuasive. It takes the narrowest view of the President's power,** not even mentioning his foreign affairs powers. Judge Parker finds the President has no power because Congress does. If the President cannot make agreements on any matter on which Congress could legislate, there could be no executive agreements with domestic legal consequences, since, we have seen, the legislative power of Congress has few and far limits. If Judge Parker denied the President the power to make executive agreements only as to matters on which Congress has "express" powers to legislate, he was drawing a line between express and implied powers of Congress that makes little sense for any purpose. In either event it is difficult to see why the powers of Congress to legislate are any more relevant to determine the scope of Presidential power to commit the United States by executive agreement than by treaty.*

Judge Parker's dictum does not accord with the practice either before or since he wrote: Presidents have made executive agreements on matters as to which Congress could legislate, notably international trade.[29] Others have suggested other limitations: a sole executive agreement can be only "temporary" or of short duration; or, it can be effective only for the term of the President who makes it.[30] None of these or similar suggestions has any apparent basis relevant to the scope of Presidential power generally, or to the Treaty Power, where any limitations on the power to make executive agreements should lie. One

---

** Judge Parker decided the case at the height of the Bricker Amendment controversy and ~~~~~~~~~~~~~~~~~~~~~ supporters of the Amendment by reducing the "threat" of a broad Presidential power to make executive agreements.

\* Compare Chapter V, pp. 147–48.

might suggest that the President must go to the Senate with "important" agreements,[31] but even that "definition" would have at least one major qualification: executive agreements have been used for some very important agreements where either or both parties desired that the agreement remain confidential.[32]

Periodically, the Senate has attempted to assert its authority and call Presidents to order but these efforts, too, have foundered on difficulties of definition and on Presidential primacy in foreign affairs. Consider, for a recent instance, the fate of Senator Fulbright's "National Commitments Resolution" of 1969 that grew out of the unhappy involvement in Vietnam. As introduced, it would have

> *Resolved*, that it is the sense of the Senate that a national commitment by the United States to a foreign power necessarily and exclusively results from affirmative action taken by the executive and legislative branches of the U.S. Government through means of a treaty, convention, or other legislative instrumentality specifically intended to give effect to such a commitment.[33]

Only a "sense resolution" was proposed but it had little chance of being adopted, and none that any President would heed it, for it purported to deny all sole executive agreements whatever. Emergencies apart, and the need for private if not secret diplomacy apart, daily foreign relations and daily foreign policy inevitably involve "commitments," if only in informal, urgent, ad *hoc* "agreements." No President could avoid them if he wished; the Constitutional system would not last a month if he sought Senate or Congressional consent for every one of them. The "Commitments Resolution" suffered also deeper difficulties. For what troubled the Senators particularly were not executive agreements, even those like Potsdam and Yalta that had become a focus of unhappiness, regret and partisan recrimination, but political commitments that are not legally binding at all but effectively pledge the faith and "credit" of the United States nonetheless.

In the end, the resolution was sharply limited by defining "national commitment" as

> the use of the armed forces of the United States on foreign territory, or a promise to assist a foreign country, government, or people by the use of the armed forces or financial resources of the United States, either immediately or upon the happening of certain events.[34]

Even as so limited, however, the resolution is not likely to determine Executive behavior. While no President has ever obligated the United States to go to war, and no responsible President is likely to do so, Presidents have claimed and Congresses have accepted the power to send troops abroad for purposes short of war; if Presidents can do so unilaterally it is difficult to deny them the power to undertake to do so by executive agreement or "commitment." On the other hand, Presidents as well as foreign-government "promisees" have always been aware that agreements "to commit the financial resources" of the United States depend directly and immediately on appropriations by Congress.* The resolution was obviously intended as a warning to Presidents and as a reminder to foreign governments that the Senate for its part reserves its right not to implement Presidential commitments, and it may effectively serve that end. But while Presidents as well as foreign governments know the difference between political commitments and legal obligations and are well aware of the braking powers of Congress, they know, too, that in the end Senates and Congresses, while theoretically free to disown such commitments, cannot do so lightly.

While the issue of Presidential power to make executive agreements or commitments has no legal solution, political forces have mitigated its theoretical rigors. The President has to get along with the Congress and with the Senate in particular, and he will not lightly risk antagonizing it by disregarding what it

---

* While Congress ha~~s~~ ~~generally~~ ~~felt~~ ~~obliged~~ ~~to~~ ~~appropriate~~ ~~funds~~ ~~re~~quired by treaty (Chapter V, p. 161), it might not sense the same obligation if it considered the agreement or commitment improper; but since the United States would be "committed" Congress would be pressed to carry out the undertaking.

believes are its constitutional prerogatives. As the record of the Senate in regard to treaties improves, the temptation to circumvent it is reduced. Often the President will be careful to use the treaty form so as not to risk subsequent challenge to the authority of the agreement, especially if it is to have effect as domestic law and its validity might be questioned in the courts. Often the treaty process will be used at the insistence of other parties to the agreement because they believe that a treaty has greater "dignity" than an executive agreement, because its constitutional effectiveness is beyond doubt, because it will "commit" the Senate and the people and make its subsequent abrogation or violation less likely.

If an agreement is within the President's power there seem to be no formal requirements as to how it must be made. It can be signed by the President or on his behalf; it can be made by Secretaries of State, Ambassadors, or lesser authorized officials; and there is no reason why it must be formal or even written.

## Executive Agreements as Law of the Land

One suggestion has had it that while the President can surely make some executive agreements, and perhaps even any agreement on any subject related to foreign affairs, such agreements are like treaties only in their international obligation. Congress, then, is presumably obligated to implement them,[*] but, unlike treaties, they are never self-executing and cannot be effective as domestic law unless implemented by Congress.[35]

If there was ever any basis for that view, the *Belmont* case surely rejects it as general doctrine. In the Litvinov Agreement involved in that case, the Soviet Union had assigned to the United States all claims by Soviet Russia against American nationals, among them some against New York banks based on accounts of Russian nationals which the Soviet Government had nation-

---

[*] See Chapter V, p. 161; also Chapter IV, p. 108. But Congress would probably disclaim obligation to implement some agreements on the ground that they were invalid for lack of Senate consent.

alized. Earlier the Soviet Government had tried to recover these claims in court, but the New York courts held that it was against the policy of the State of New York to give effect to confiscations of assets situated in the State.[36] When the Litvinov Agreement assigned these claims to the United States, the Federal Government sought to recover these bank accounts for itself, but the state courts held that the United States stood no better than its assignor the Soviet Union and that the public policy of New York still barred recovery. The Supreme Court reversed, Mr. Justice Sutherland saying: [37]

> Plainly, the external powers of the United States are to be exercised without regard to state laws or policies. . . . And while this rule in respect of treaties is established by the express language of cl. 2, Art. VI, of the Constitution, the same rule would result in the case of all international compacts and agreements from the very fact that complete power over international affairs is in the national government and is not and cannot be subject to any curtailment or interference on the part of the several states. [Citing *Curtiss-Wright.*] In respect of all international negotiations and compacts, and in respect of our foreign relations generally, state lines disappear. As to such purposes the State of New York does not exist. . . .

Again, it has been suggested that the doctrine of the *Belmont* case gives supremacy over state law only to executive agreements intimately related to the President's power of recognition, and that even such agreements will supersede only state public policy not formal state laws. Neither of these limitations was expressed—or implied—in *Belmont*, or in the *Pink* case decided five years later by a reconstituted Supreme Court.[38] While *Pink* makes much of the relation of the Litvinov assignment to the recognition of the Soviet Government, the language and the reasoning of both cases would apply as well to any executive agreement and to any state law.

At least some executive agreements, then, can be self-executing and have some status as law of the land.[39] As with treaties,

185

of course, a self-executing executive agreement would surely lose its effect as domestic law in the face of a subsequent act of Congress. On the other hand, in the *Capps* case, we saw, an intermediate federal court held that an executive agreement—unlike a treaty—could not prevail against an earlier act of Congress; the Supreme Court expressly declined to consider that question.[40] Yet many of the arguments why a treaty supersedes an earlier statute apply as well to executive agreements.[41] The Supreme Court built its doctrine that treaties are equal to and can supersede acts of Congress on the Supremacy Clause of the Constitution, and, under *Belmont*, executive agreements, too, are supreme law of the land. If one sees the Treaty Power as basically a Presidential power (albeit subject to check by the Senate) there is no compelling reason for giving less effect to agreements which he has authority to make without the Senate. If one accepts Presidential primacy in foreign affairs in relation to Congress, one might allow his agreements to prevail even in the face of earlier Congressional legislation.* If one grants the President some legislative authority in foreign affairs—as in regard to sovereign immunity **—one might grant it to him in this respect too.[42]

Of course, the *Belmont* case may reflect doctrine of an earlier Supreme Court age when "the Government," could do no or little wrong, particularly in foreign affairs.† While the Court is not likely to reconsider the holding that state law must bow before

---

* In most instances, it might be argued, the statute would be of a general character and might be of an earlier time. As with treaties, moreover, Congress could prevail by reenacting its statute. The issue, then, comes down to a choice of "presumption" or "burden of going forward": the rule of the *Capps* case would bar effect to an executive agreement until Congress modified its earlier statute; a contrary rule would allow the President to prevail until Congress reasserted its earlier policy. Of course, in theory a President and a Congress might engage in a continuing round of overruling each other, but that is not likely to happen.

** See Chapter II, p. 56.

† Compare Chapter II, pp. 63–64.

a valid executive agreement,* it might look again at some of its enthusiastic language. It will doubtless look again and harder at any executive agreement which impinges on private rights in the United States,** for even at about the time of *Belmont*, even executive actions not inconsistent with an act of Congress were not sacred if they threatened private freedoms. Except on that ground it is difficult to understand why only a year before *Belmont* the Supreme Court held that the President did not have the power to extradite Mr. Neidecker to France when there was no treaty or act of Congress requiring it.[43] The Court did not deal with the case as involving an executive agreement but, surely, at least an informal agreement was inevitably involved.[44] Was the Court rejecting an *ad hoc* agreement making law for a particular case? † Would it have refused effect also to a formal executive agreement of general applicability? (Chapter X.)

## Customary International Law

Treaties and other international agreements provide a major part of the international rights and obligations of the United States but many of them lie in unwritten customary law: the status of states in international society; the concepts of sovereignty, national territory, nationality; the fundamentals of property, contract and tort between nations; the law of treaties itself, including the principle *pacta sunt servanda*, that international agreements create obligations and should be observed; the responsibility to aliens in the United States and the rights of Americans abroad, and many others.[45]

---

* The tendency is rather to limit the States even further where foreign relations are concerned. Compare, *e. g.*, Zschernig v. Miller, 389 U.S. 429 (1968), Chapter IX, p. 238.

** Compare Ch⸻ ⸻, p. 88, Chapter X, p. 253.

† The Litvinov Agreement in *Belmont* and *Pink* also made law *ad hoc*, for known, defined claims, but in issue was only property, not "preferred freedoms." Chapter X, pp. 253, 256–57.

The United States found much customary law at its birth as a nation † and international law has influenced national behavior since. It is principally the President, "sole organ" of the United States in its international relations, who is responsible for the behavior of the United States in regard to international law, and who participates on her behalf in the indefinable process by which customary international law is made, unmade, remade. He makes legal claims for the United States and reacts to the claims of others; he performs acts reflecting views on legal questions and justifies them under the law, in diplomatic exchange, in judicial or arbitral proceedings, in international organizations or in the public forum. Congress, state legislatures and even state officials also impinge on foreign relations governed by law, for example in determining and giving effect to the rights of aliens in the United States or of foreign vessels off our coasts; and Federal and state courts are major makers of international law when they determine what that law requires in order to decide a case before them.* But these other actors play on the domestic scene only; the President represents what they do to the rest of the world and can seek to justify them under international law or confess violation.

International law is law for the United States and, we shall see, it is also law of the United States to be applied by the courts. (Chapter VIII). But the Constitution does not forbid Congress or the President to exercise their powers in disregard of customary international law as it does not invalidate their violations of treaties and international agreements.**

Like treaties,*** executive agreements and customary international law bow before Constitutional prohibitions, notably those of the Bill of Rights, but some Constitutional safeguards are interpreted to take account of the principles of international law which antedate the Constitution. (See Chapter X).

† See Introduction to Chapter V, note 1.

*See Chapter VIII, p. 221.

** See pp. 221–22 below.

*** See Chapter V, p. 137.

# Chapter VII. INTERNATIONAL ORGANIZATION

The constitutional powers to make treaties and other international agreements have seen new uses in the spectacular development of multilateral diplomacy and the mushrooming of international organization. The United States has been a member of almost a hundred international organizations differing widely in scope and function, from the United Nations to, say, the Cape Spartel Lighthouse.[1] They differ, too, in their structures and procedures, in the obligations they impose on the United States, in the degree to which they impinge on activities of her government, her officials and her citizens. Such new uses of international agreements have suggested new constitutional questions and framed old questions in new contexts.

In fact, international organizations and arrangements in being, and those which the United States has seriously considered, raise no significant constitutional difficulties. The United States has adhered to them by treaty or by executive agreement approved by Congress.* They deal with matters clearly of "foreign policy concern" ** and, generally, contain undertakings by the United States that do not differ in kind from those in its traditional bilateral treaties. They raise no issues under the Bill of Rights because they impinge directly only on the United

---

* The United States joined many organizations by treaty, some by Congressional-Executive agreement. See Chapter VI, note 3. If the President attempted to join an organization by sole executive agree-
[torn] would soon have to seek Congressional approval at least in the form of an appropriation to pay the United States contribution to the organization.

** Compare Chapter V, p. 151.

States Government itself (not on individual citizens) and neither "the United States," nor any branch of its government, nor any federal official in that capacity, has constitutional rights to freedom of speech or of silence, to security from unreasonable searches or seizures, to equality or liberty or property or due process of law. (See Chapter X.)

Constitutional obstacles even worth discussing arise only when international organization begins to acquire attributes of government and to impinge directly on the lives and activities of the inhabitants of the United States, or on state government. In such cases one might have to consider whether a treaty or agreement has improperly delegated powers or functions of the federal government to supranational, international, or foreign bodies; has violated the separation of powers by transferring functions among the branches of the United States Government, or has imposed inappropriate functions upon them; has infringed upon any abiding sovereignty of the States; or has denied rights to individuals by subjecting them to foreign authority, or to regulations which the United States itself could not impose.

No international organization to which the United States is now party seriously stirs any of these issues, but since the questions have been raised I shall indicate why that is so for the principal organizations. I consider also constitutional objections that might be evoked by arrangements that are periodically proposed and which might be considered by the United States some future day.

## The United Nations

By treaty implemented by acts of Congress and of the President,[2] the United States has adhered to the United Nations Charter, is a member of the United Nations Organization, and a "Permanent Member" having special rights and obligations in the Security Council.[3] The Charter forbids the United States to use or threaten force against other states [4] and requires it to cooperate with the Organization in maintaining international peace and security and in promoting social and economic ends.[5]

By the Charter of the UN, then, the United States has given up the right to go to war at will.[6] Some have asked whether these undertakings are consistent with the Constitution, which clearly contemplated that the United States might go to war and gave Congress the power to decide to do it. The Charter denies also the constitutional powers of the President to send troops abroad for purposes inconsistent with those of the United Nations.

Such objections misconceive the character of treaties and their place in the constitutional pattern. In every treaty undertaking the United States limits its right to do what it could do freely in the absence of treaty, what is within the constitutional power of some branch of the Federal Government to do. The power to wage war or use other force has no greater constitutional sanctity than other powers, and no greater immunity to limitation by treaty, whether a bilateral treaty of alliance, friendship or non-aggression, or the United Nations Charter establishing general international law. Moreover, we have seen, the UN Charter does not deprive the Congress or the President of constitutional power: both the Congress and the President continue to have their powers—though not the right under international law—to declare war, use force or otherwise act in violation of the UN Charter, as they can disregard other international obligations.*

A different question is whether by adhering to the UN Charter the treaty-makers have delegated powers of Congress or of the President to an international body.[7] The argument is that the Security Council can direct the United States to take action not determined by Congress or the President and which they may be unwilling to take. And if the United States should yet conclude "Article 43 agreements" to place troops at the disposal of the Security Council,[8] the Council (rather than the President or Congress) could send American troops to war.†

* See Chapter V, p. 151

† A related objection is that the Charter commits the United States to war in certain circumstances, and that can be done only by act of Congress, not by treaty. In fact, the UN Charter does not commit the United States to go to war unless the Security Council orders

These objections, too, are not substantial. One complete answer is that the United States has a veto: [9] every such action by the Council, then, would have the concurrence of the President acting under his own vast powers in foreign relations and pursuant to a treaty of the United States implemented by Congress.[10] Another sufficient answer is that even the mandatory decisions of the Security Council cannot be enforced against the United States: as with any other international obligation, the United States has the ultimate decision as to whether it will or will not comply—whether it will or will not go to war, allow its troops to be used by the UN, impose sanctions, break diplomatic relations.[11] (I deal with other UN "legislative" and regulatory powers below.)

## NATO

American participation in NATO [12] raises the same and other questions. Has the United States delegated the power to declare war to others? Do the treaty and the organization it created impinge in other ways on the powers of the President or of Congress?

Again, these questions do not appear serious. The North Atlantic Treaty does not purport automatically to put the United States into war in given circumstances.* Rather, it provides that if an armed attack occurs against one party, every other party shall take forthwith "such action as it deems necessary, including the use of armed force"; and that provision shall be "carried out by the Parties in accordance with their respective constitutional processes." [13] No doubt the treaty imposes the obligation to go to war in some circumstances but that is no different from other treaty undertakings that are to be carit, and the United States could prevent such an order by its veto. In any event the Constitution does not forbid a treaty that commits the country to war, although it may preclude a provision that would automatically put the country into war in certain circumstances. See Chapter V, p. 159–60, and this chapter, pp. 192–93.

---

*Compare Chapter V, pp. 159–60, and note 100.

ried out by the President or Congress, and which they can refuse to honor.

Nor are there unconstitutional delegations in international command arrangements or deployments of troops. The principal NATO commander, who has always been an American, is under orders not of the President of the United States but of the NATO Council; in the Council, however, the United States has a veto in principle (in the requirement of unanimity), and the dominant voice in fact.[14] Even if United States troops served under foreign command, it could hardly stir constitutional difficulties for the President, temporarily and revocably, to put troops under an allied command in a common cause as was done in both World Wars. The arrangements would have the approval of the President and would be subject to his continuing control, and he could terminate them at any time even if that should involve breach of an international agreement.

## International Regulatory Agencies

Every international organization "legislates," if only the annual budget and rules for the governance of the organization.[15] Many also have broader legislative or regulatory authority.*

* In the UN, in addition to the comprehensive authority of the Security Council to "legislate" in maintaining peace, the Council and the General Assembly make law when they interpret their own authority or the obligations of members under the Charter, and members have found themselves effectively bound in ways they had not intended and do not desire. The Assembly has asserted the right to assess members for various purposes including its peace-keeping efforts and economic and social programs; it has interpreted the Charter as establishing human rights standards which some members at least deny and resist.

For the United States, the Senate, of course, never consented to these interpretations but it can be deemed to have consented to the system that produces them. (There is no Senate consent to later interpretations of any treaty by the President or the courts.) Of course, the United States can refuse to accept these interpretations or to abide by them. General Assembly Resolutions have also purported to declare international law for members, and the United States has rejected some of these assertions. Compare, for example, the

The UN General Assembly can adopt rules for the administration of trust territories, and the Security Council for strategic trust territories (of which there has been only one, administered by the United States).[16] The International Monetary Fund limits the extent to which a government can modify the rate of exchange of its currency.[17] The International Civil Aviation Organization (ICAO) promulgates "international standards and recommended practices."[18] Some organizations fix prices, as under the Commodity Agreements—wheat, sugar, coffee.[19]

One can make a case that international organizations have substantial legislative power, and something of a case that they sometimes create law for the United States; there is little case for finding in any of these instances an unconstitutional delegation by the United States of the legislative power of Congress. In most existing instances "legislation" by an international organization is only a recommendation or exhortation which the United States is not bound to accept.* In the few organizations that formally have power to make binding regulations, the United States has either a veto, the benefits of "weighted voting" or other special voting arrangement that render it difficult for any regulation to be established without its concurrence.** These "legislative" or "regulatory" bodies, then, are essentially forums for negotiating agreements; and it could hardly make a constitutional difference that U.S. representatives reach international agreement within some organ of an international organization rather than by negotiating a formal agreement in a plenipotentiary conference. For constitutional purposes, the "agree-

---

resolution declaring the use of nuclear weapons illegal, G.A.Res. 1653, 16 UN GAOR Supp. 17 at 4–5, UN Doc. A/5100 (1962).

*WHO "regulations," for example, are voluntary and adopted by the United States only if the appropriate federal officials decide it. ILO conventions on labor standards also are only recommended to the United States and would become binding only if formally adhered to by the United States.

** As in the International Monetary Fund, the International Bank for Reconstruction and Development, the Wheat Agreement and the Fishery conventions, notes 17 and 19 this chapter.

ments" produced in these organizations are effectively Presidential agreements. Or, they can be seen as implementations of the original treaty establishing the organization and giving it "regulatory" powers; in consenting to that agreement the Senate may be said to have consented in advance to any regulations authorized by the agreement.[20]

But even if an organization can assess or impose law upon the United States against its will, it is not exercising powers that belong to Congress, for it is not exercising the "legislative Powers herein granted." * (Article 1, section 1). It is creating law *for* the United States not *of* the United States, international law for the government, not domestic law for its inhabitants. Like law made by treaty, that made by international organizations creates international obligation which the United States might be required to implement in this country; again, the United States can refuse to enact that law and incur a violation.

For similar reasons, other arrangements and organizations that have been the subject of more-or-less serious negotiation would not create constitutional difficulties for the United States, though particular forms and details might be troublesome. Under proposals for "General and Complete Disarmament," for example, the United States could agree to abolish existing armies and armaments, and to refrain from the raising of armies, and from the manufacture, possession or research and development of armaments in the future.[21] It could agree to create a complex international organization to provide comprehensive inspection that would abolish the secrecy of governmental operations, require full reporting, and subject government installations, activities and files to unlimited surveillance, and its officials to international interrogation. Within large limits it could subject the activities of its citizens also to relevant, reasonable limitations and surveillance like those imposed by Congress through domestic regulatory programs. Issues of improper delegation could be wholly avoided if international authority, regulation and administration were brought to bear only on the Gov-

* Clearly, the legislative powers of the United States. Compare Article III, section 1, discussed p. 196 below.

ernment of the United States rather than directly on individuals in the United States.

Consider, even, the original Acheson-Lilienthal plan for the international development and control of atomic energy.[22] That proposal might have given to an international authority power to regulate the activities not only of the Government of the United States but of mining companies, manufacturers, scientists, laborers, and citizens generally. A body with such powers and functions, it would have been argued, would be exercising governmental authority within the United States, assuming functions of the President and Congress. Again, constitutional objections would have been eliminated if the United States Government stood between the international authority and the individual, if the requirements of the Authority were imposed upon the Government of the United States and implemented and enforced by the Government in the same ways as other treaty obligations or the regulations of its own administrative agencies. (Of course, some regulations might have been challenged as violating individual rights and liberties. Compare Chapter X.)

## International Judicial Tribunals

United States participation in international judicial tribunals would raise similar as well as additional issues.[23] The United States is a party to the Statute of the International Court of Justice [24] and was a party to the Nuremberg Charter.[25] There are international courts, commissions, and committees that consider charges of violation of human rights.[26] There have been proposals for international criminal tribunals.

Article III, section 1, of the Constitution provides:

The judicial Power of the United States, shall be vested in one supreme Court, and in such inferior Courts as the Congress may from time to time ordain and establish. The Judges, both of the supreme and inferior Courts, shall hold their Offices during good Behaviour, and shall, at stated Times, receive for their Services, a Compensation, which shall not be diminished during their Continuance in Office.

That article defines and allocates "the judicial Power of the United States," the power to administer law and justice under the authority of the United States for persons subject to her jurisdiction and laws. When the United States accepts the jurisdiction of the International Court of Justice, or of other judicial or arbitral bodies that decide cases or controversies between nation-states, she is not delegating to those tribunals any of the judicial power of the United States.[27] Nor would United States participation in such tribunals raise issues under provisions in Article III and in the Bill of Rights requiring due process of law and particular safeguards in criminal proceedings. The Bill of Rights, like the rest of the Constitution, safeguards individuals; it accords no rights to the Government of the United States. International tribunals with jurisdiction over controversies between states do not apply criminal law, and their proceedings are not "criminal proceedings." The prohibitions and safeguards of the Constitution govern only the United States Government,* not an international body exercising international functions, even if the United States is party to it.[28]

The United States, then, could accept the jurisdiction of a tribunal like the European Human Rights Court with jurisdiction over complaints of human rights violations brought by other states. She could even, it would seem, adhere to a court that could hear complaints against the United States by individuals, including her own citizens or residents.[29] Nothing in the Constitution, we have seen, prevents the United States from undertaking international obligations in regard to her own citizens and residents; ** nothing prevents the United States from submitting her observance of such obligations to scrutiny and judgment by an international tribunal. There seem to be no compelling constitutional reasons why the relations between the United States and her citizens could not be subject to both the laws and courts of the United States and to international law ad-

---

* And, to a large extent, the States of the United States. Chapter X, p. 269.

** See Chapter V, pp. 155–56.

ministered by international tribunals exercising international judicial power.

Proposals for international tribunals superimposed on national judicial systems have raised different issues. In the days of the Hague conferences, when international arbitration and adjudication were a principal focus of hopes for a better world, one proposed convention would have established an international prize court to hear appeals from national prize courts.[30] The United States, it was argued, could not adhere to such arrangements: appeals to the international court directly from lower federal courts would deny the appellate jurisdiction of the Supreme Court; appeals from the Supreme Court to the international court would be inconsistent with its being the *Supreme* Court.[31] To meet such objections the Convention was modified to provide for a new action in the international court instead of appeal from the national courts.[32] Other proposals for appeal from national courts to international tribunals were also modified to avoid constitutional issues for the United States: national courts would be required instead to certify questions of international law or treaty interpretation to an international tribunal, with final decision of the whole case left to the domestic court; should United States courts fail to accept the international court's answer in some case, the United States would be in violation of the treaty and required to compensate those aggrieved.[33]

## International Criminal Courts

Periodically there have been proposals for international courts to enforce international criminal law against individuals,[34] in past times for piracy, slave-running, arms smuggling; more recently, for waging aggressive war, genocide and other gross violations of human rights, or hijacking airplanes. Although the United States has never seriously considered adhering to any such court, lawyers have pondered the constitutional implications of the various proposals.

If an international criminal court sat outside the United States and imposed punishment outside the United States, it would not be exercising judicial power or other governmental authority of the United States. The United States could adhere to such tribunals, agree that American nationals might be tried by them, and even extradite persons for such trials.[35] Constitutional issues would appear, however, if an international court were to sit in the United States, apply law to acts committed in the United States by citizens or residents of the United States, and execute punishment in the United States. The objection might be made that only American law can apply in the United States, and criminal laws only if enacted by Congress (or by the States); and that only American courts can try persons for violations of law in the United States, and such courts must be established by Congress (or by the States).[36] If, perhaps, criminal courts could also be created by treaty, they must still be American courts, their judges must be appointed by the President with the consent of the Senate and assured of life tenure and undiminished compensation,[37] and their proceedings must include trial by jury and the other safeguards of the Bill of Rights.[38]

The crux of that argument—that under the Constitution only the law of the United States can apply to acts committed in the United States, and only courts of the United States can sit here in judgment on such acts—is not, however, always and necessarily so. Foreign consuls have long enforced the criminal laws of their countries in the United States, for example against visiting seamen even when their acts are also subject to American law and the jurisdiction of American courts.[39] Under the NATO Status of Forces Agreement, allied soldiers and civilian dependents and defense employees in the United States can be tried by allied military courts for acts committed here, even when these are also violations of American law and triable in our courts.[40] Similarly, during World War II, Congress permitted allied forces in the United States to try their troops by military tribunal, authorized United States courts to order witnesses (presumably even American citizens) to appear before these tribunals, and made contempt of such tribunals or perjury before them federal crimes.[41] While the constitutionality of such hospitality to foreign criminal law has never been considered by the Supreme Court, there is no reason to believe that the Court would forbid it. Those tribunals do not apply the law of the United States or exercise judicial power of the United States, but act under authority granted them by their own laws; the United States, in effect, agrees not to apply its laws and its jurisdiction, and to allow the foreign government to exercise its jurisdiction on American territory instead of taking the accused home or elsewhere for trial.[42]

Similarly, one might argue, there is nothing in the Constitution that forbids the United States to permit an international tribunal to apply international law to acts committed by individuals in the United States, including American citizens and residents.[43] It would be international law that governed their acts and was being applied by the international tribunal; international judicial power which the tribunal was exercising; international punishment that was imposed and executed by international authority. The tribunal would not be exercising governmental authority of the United States but the authority of the international community, of a group of nations of which the United States was but one and acting in the same capacity as others not as territorial sovereign.[44]

Some of the constitutional objections I have considered and the constitutional justifications they have invoked must appear artificial, almost grotesque.* It is difficult to accept that United States participation in contemporary forms of multi-national cooperation should depend on "technicalities" about "delegation," "judicial power" and "case or controversy," and on forms and devices to satisfy them. The Framers did not presume to anticipate what the interests of the United States require today, and surely they did not presume to prevent it. They did insist on a few basic safeguards—respect for the political process, the integrity of national institutions, the rights of the individual.

---

* From the point of view of constitutional law, there are other ways of looking at international tribunals applying criminal law to Americans in the United States, and other, more technical arguments both for and against full participation by the United States. Some of them are suggested in HENKIN, ARMS CONTROL, Chapter VIII.

International organization, in sum, raises no constitutional difficulties when it imposes international obligations for the United States to carry out in accordance with its normal constitutional procedures. Novel arrangements might raise significant issues if they distorted domestic institutions or impinged substantially and directly on individuals in the United States, particularly if they deprived persons of their flourishing civil rights and liberties; but no international institutions entailed such domestic intrusions in the past, and none is now in prospect. If one appeared, if the United States should decide that participation in such an organization was in the national interest, the constitutional issues would have to be decided without precedent and on the basis of very general principles that hardly compel the answer. Like many constitutional questions, these cannot be decided with confidence, surely not hypothetically, divorced from a particular proposal and context. Political as well as legal doubts could of course be eliminated by constitutional amendment, but often, even without that slow, uncongenial process, creative legal imagination can find ways and suggest means to bring such arrangements largely within a dynamic, flexible, hospitable Constitution.

*FEDERAL JUDICIAL POWER*

# Chapter VIII. THE COURTS IN FOREIGN AFFAIRS

Foreign relations are political relations conducted by the political branches of the federal government. At times, however, they come into court. The ordinary business of courts, too, sometimes involves or affects American foreign relations.

An independent judiciary applying the written Constitution is a hallmark of American government. The courts have successfully established their final and "infallible" authority to impose their readings of the Constitution on the political branches of the federal government as well as on the States,[1] as they monitor the separation of powers and the divisions of federalism, and protect individuals, minorities, even majorities, against too-much government.

Judicial review is the most dramatic function of American courts but it is not their principal or their most important activity; even judicial review is incidental to the real business of the courts—to decide cases between parties, to administer civil and criminal justice, to regulate the complex administration of government. In the course of that business they interpret and apply law made by the federal political branches and by the States. In interpreting law, of course, they make law. They also make law explicitly. The Common Law, woven magnificently over centuries by the judges of England, was received by the colonies and maintained by the States, the judges continuing to add and change. When legislatures intervened to codify or modify the judges continued to apply their art to carry out and fill out legislative policy and purpose. The federal courts, too, applied the common law, in the federal territories and in cases between citizens of different States.[2] The courts have also found in the Constitution or in acts of Congress directives to them to develop law for given subjects and purposes.

That courts make law, once radical "realism," is now commonplace; now it is necessary realism to emphasize the limits of judicial law-making. The law they make is still only "interstitial": [3] even in interpreting the Constitution, even the Supreme Court cannot be heedless of the constraints of language, history and politics.[4] Judicial review and judicial legislation render the American courts probably the most independent and powerful in the world, but "government by judiciary" is a polemical exaggeration.[5] The judiciary is still "the least dangerous branch",[6] having principally braking power, and even that cannot always be applied and is not always effective, especially in matters of transnational import. The powers of the courts, including judicial review, are also contained by the character of the judicial function and by particular constitutional limitations: under Article III, the courts of the United States exercise only the judicial power of the United States, carry out only judicial functions, decide only "cases" or "controversies" and only those committed to their jurisdiction by the Constitution or by law. Political forces further curtail in fact the part courts might play in theory.

The scope and the limitations of judicial power largely apply to state courts as to federal courts, in foreign affairs as elsewhere. But foreign affairs make a difference. The courts are less willing than elsewhere to curb the political branches and have even developed doctrines of special deference to them.[*]

---

[*] Compare the courts' view that they are bound by Executive assertions of immunity (Chapter II, p. 56) and will give great weight to Executive interpretations of treaties (Chapter V, p. 167) or determinations of international law.

Judicial review, the "political question" doctrine (p. 210 below), the respect generally due by the courts to executive actions and determinations, can be seen as aspects of "separation of powers" between the Executive and the Judiciary. Judicial-Executive "separation" is sometimes modified by Congress. Compare La Abra Silver Mining Co. v. United States, 175 U.S. 423, 459–61 (1899), where the Court held that Congress could ask the courts to decide a question of fraud

They have asserted judicial power to develop doctrines to safeguard the national interest in international relations against both judicial interference and invasion by the States. They have a special role on behalf of the nation to give effect to obligations of international law.

The judicial part in foreign affairs is prescribed in Article III, section 2, particularly:

> The judicial Power shall extend to all Cases, in Law and Equity, arising under this Constitution, the Laws of the United States, and Treaties made, or which shall be made, under their Authority;—to all Cases affecting Ambassadors, other public Ministers and Consuls; . . . to Controversies . . . between a State, or the Citizens thereof, and foreign States, Citizens or Subjects.
>
> In all Cases affecting Ambassadors, other public Ministers and Consuls, and those in which a State shall be Party, the supreme Court shall have original Jurisdiction. In all the other Cases before mentioned, the supreme Court shall have appellate Jurisdiction, both as to Law and Fact, with such Exceptions, and under such Regulations as the Congress shall make.[7]

As contemplated by Article III, the federal courts have exercised jurisdiction of suits by foreign ambassadors (and suits against them when not inconsistent with international law), of cases to which foreign consuls are parties, and of suits by States against aliens.[8] Their principal participation in foreign affairs, however, is in cases arising under the Constitution, laws or treaties, involving various parties and matters: a company challenges the validity or application of a tariff; an airline invokes the Warsaw Convention to limit its liability to the victim of an accident; an alien challenges state laws that deny him employment or inheritance; a soldier seeks to enjoin the Secretary of

underlying a claim against Mexico which the Executive might itself have decided. Compare also the Second Hickenlooper Amendment, this chapter, note 55.

Defense from sending him to Vietnam. The courts review the activities of federal administrative agencies (*e. g.*, the Immigration Service, the Civil Aeronautics Board or the National Maritime Commission), the foreign activities of the Department of Commerce and the Treasury, of coastal and border States relating to foreign neighbors or those of New York State and New York City to the United Nations.

## Judicial Review

Thanks to both constitutional and political limitations, the paramount judicial prerogative of invalidating acts of the political branches has not loomed large in the conduct of foreign relations.* A major obstacle has been the requirement of "case or controversy": constitutional issues cannot come before the courts unless raised by one who has "standing" to make a "justiciable" claim in an actual case [9] against a proper, available defendant.[10] (It was in regard to foreign affairs that the Justices told President Washington they could not give him advisory opinions.)[11] The President cannot bring a judicial proceeding to challenge alleged usurpations by Congress, nor can Congress (or a Congressman) sue to enjoin alleged usurpations by the President, for these would be political and not justiciable claims.† A State cannot complain in court of a breach of the constitutional compact,[12] nor can a citizen, *qua* citizen, complain that the constitutional system of government is being distorted.[13] Only an individual (or corporation) aggrieved in his person or property by an act of the political branches can challenge it as beyond the power of the federal government or of the acting branch.[14] Most of foreign policy and foreign affairs, however, including most

---

* I have found no case in which the Supreme Court invalidated a statute, treaty, or executive act intimately related to foreign affairs on the ground that it was beyond the power of the federal government; recently some have been struck down because they violated individual rights. See this chapter, note 16, and Chapter X.

† Congressmen have sought to challenge Presidential action in Vietnam on the ground that he usurped their legislative authority. See *Mitchell et al.* v. *Nixon et al.*, D.D.C., April 7, 1972. It is not likely that these claims will be heard.

acts that have raised serious constitutional issues, do not impinge directly on private interests. It is difficult even to concoct hypothetical cases in which the courts would decide whether Congress had constitutional authority, say, to recognize the independence of Cuba from Spain, or the President the power to commit the United States to the Yalta and Potsdam agreements without Senate consent. In practice, surely, few "boundary disputes" between Congress and the President in regard to foreign affairs have come to court: even the perennial issues as to the President's power to send troops abroad, which might perhaps have been challenged by an individual about to be sent, did not reach the courts during the 175 years before the bitter days of Vietnam.[15]

Jurisdictional limitations apart, resort to the courts is unlikely if claimants and their lawyers see little hope of winning, and the courts have evinced no disposition to frustrate national foreign policy. Long before the modern constitutional revolution gave the Federal Government virtually full powers in domestic matters,[16] its accepted monopoly in foreign affairs discouraged constitutional controversy based on States' rights, and the few claims made were quickly proved hopeless.[17] Issues of separation of powers fared little better. Usually, the courts could find that the President and Congress were in fact acting together and— as in *Curtiss-Wright*—were not disposed to limit their cooperation.* Even when one branch—usually the President—was clearly acting alone, the courts have been loath to find "usurpation," perhaps because they thought his powers "plenary", perhaps because in the silences of the Constitution they could find few standards to justify and guide judicial intervention; perhaps because in foreign relations in particular, they thought, cooperation and conflict had to be worked out between the President and Congress and the courts could not contribute much to their accommodation.** The Supreme Court itself has also been

* See Chapter IV, p. 119.

** See Chapter IV. But compare the cases finding lack of Presidential authority, pp. 96–99.

able to avoid frustrating political action yet without affirming its validity, by exercising the discretion it has in most cases to deny *certiorari* and refuse to hear the case.[18]

As in domestic affairs, the Supreme Court has been more willing to scrutinize foreign affairs actions alleged to violate individual rights, although national interest in foreign relations, as the Court sees it, no doubt weighs heavily in the balance of competing claims. (See Chapter X.) Here, too, however, judicial review rarely spends itself for, reluctant to invalidate political action, the courts are likely to stretch, narrow or bend words to avoid the rigors of a statute or Executive order, or to find that it did not authorize what had been done under it.[19] Such gymnastic construction, of course, does not limit constitutional power, but it casts the onus on the Congress or the President expressly to authorize what has been challenged and warns them of possible constitutional difficulties.

On the other hand, judicial review has flourished in its other manifestation as the courts have staunchly upheld the supremacy of treaties and of acts of Congress or of the President over inconsistent state action. Even where the political branches have not acted, judicial readings of and into a spare, laconic Constitution, to find what the judges believe our foreign relations require, have led them to protect foreign commerce against "undue" burdens by the States, and other foreign relations against other state intrusions. (Chapter IX.)

## "Political Questions"

Judicial review of the conduct of foreign relations has faced an additional obstacle: the courts have elevated judicial abstention to a principle that the courts will not decide "political questions," and issues of foreign affairs have been cited as prime examples and a principal justification of the doctrine.[20]

That there is a constitutional "political question" doctrine is not disputed, but there is little agreement as to anything else about it—its constitutional basis; whether abstention is required or optional; how the courts decide whether a question is "political," and which questions are. Some have insisted that the courts may abstain only when they must, when as a matter of fair construction the Constitution has denied the courts authority to review a particular case or kind of case; others have seen in the doctrine "something greatly more flexible, something of prudence," giving the courts a substantial measure of discretion to consider or avoid a question.[21] Mr. Justice Frankfurter, the Supreme Court's leading modern proponent of the doctrine, inveighed against "Disregard of inherent limits in the effective exercise of the Court's 'judicial Power'" which "not only presages the futility of judicial intervention" but may well impair "the Court's position" and "The Court's authority": [22] it is not clear whether he was saying that in such cases the Constitution requires the courts to abstain, or that they have discretion to do so, if only the general discretion of an equity court to deny relief.

The Supreme Court took occasion to reexamine the doctrine in 1962, in *Baker* v. *Carr*.[23] Mr. Justice Brennan found that the doctrine has "attributes which, in various settings, diverge, combine, appear, and disappear in seeming disorderliness." [24] After discussing previous cases, he concluded:

> "It is apparent that several formulations which vary slightly according to the settings in which the questions arise may describe a political question, although each has one or more elements which identify it as essentially a function of the separation of powers. Prominent on the surface of any case held to involve a political question is found a textually demonstrable constitutional commitment of the issue to a coordinate political department; or a lack of judicially discoverable and manageable standards for resolving it; or the impossibility of deciding without an initial policy determination of a kind clearly for nonjudicial discretion; or the impossibility of a court's undertaking independent resolution without ... ....ng lack of the respect due coordinate branches of government; or an unusual need for unquestioning adherence to a political decision already made; or the potentiality of embarrassment from

multifarious pronouncements by various departments on one question." *

The majority of the Court seemed to conclude from the earlier cases, including notably foreign affairs cases, that the courts must abstain on some issues (where there is "a textually demonstrable commitment of the issue to a coordinate political department"); and should, or may, abstain on others, when in its judgment abstention is required by the limitations of the judicial function, or for the sake of proper relations with the other branches or of the national interest.** But the Court's selection and summary of the precedents did not reduce the confusion which they had engendered, for it failed to recognize that "po-

---

* 369 U.S. at 217.  Later the Court reiterated the criteria which it distilled from earlier cases:

.  .  .  We have no question decided, or to be decided, by a political branch of government coequal with this Court.  Nor do we risk embarrassment of our government abroad, or grave disturbance at home if we take issue with Tennessee as to the constitutionality of her action here challenged.  Nor need the appellants, in order to succeed in this action, ask the Court to enter upon policy determinations for which judicially manageable standards are lacking.  369 U.S. at 226 (footnotes omitted).

** Justice Brennan said:

.  .  .  There are sweeping statements to the effect that all questions touching foreign relations are political questions. Not only does resolution of such issues frequently turn on standards that defy judicial application, or involve the exercise of a discretion demonstrably committed to the executive or legislature; but many such questions uniquely demand single-voiced statement of the Government's views.  Yet it is error to suppose that every case or controversy which touches foreign relations lies beyond judicial cognizance. Our cases in this field seem invariably to show a discriminating analysis of the particular question posed, in terms of the history of its management by the political branches, of its susceptibility to judicial handling in the light of its nature and posture in the specific case, and of the possible consequences of judicial action.  369 U.S. at 211–12 (footnotes omitted).

litical questions" had been used in different cases in different senses to describe different kinds of questions as to which the functions of the courts were different.

The doctrine of political questions is constitutionally significant only as an ordinance of extraordinary judicial abstention, particularly if it prevents judicial review of a claim that the federal political branches have failed to live up to constitutional requirements or limitations. In such a case the courts would say, in effect: "It may be that, as the petitioner claims, the political branches have indeed violated the Constitution, but in this instance their action raises a question not given to us to review; only political remedies are available." [25]

Despite common impressions and numerous citations, there are in fact few cases, and apparently no foreign affairs case, in which the Supreme Court ordained or approved such judicial abstention from constitutional review or from deciding some other question that might have led to a different result in the case.* In the foreign affairs cases commonly cited the courts did not refrain from judging political actions by constitutional standards; they judged them but found them constitutionally not wanting. If the Court sometimes spoke of the special quality of foreign relations and the need for the nation to speak with one voice, it did so not to support judicial abstention but to explain the broad constitutional powers granted the President or Congress. In no case did the Court have to use the phrase "political questions," and when it did, it was using it in a different sense, saying in effect: "We have reviewed your claim and we find that the action complained of involves a political question, one that is within the powers granted by the Constitution to the political branches to decide. The act complained of violates no constitutional limitations on that power, either because the Constitution imposes no relevant limitations, or because the action is amply within the limits prescribed. We give effect to what

---

* In principle, presumably, courts may, or must, abstain on "political questions" in any case, not only where constitutional issues are raised.

the political branches have done because they had political authority under the Constitution to do it." [26]

Thus, for example, when the political branches asserted the sovereignty of the United States, or denied the sovereignty of a foreign power, in particular territory, the courts have not abstained, but have followed the political branches on these "political questions" because they had made decisions that were theirs to make.[27] To whom the territory in question belonged as a matter of international law was irrelevant: the President (or the Congress) was not constitutionally forbidden to make a claim contrary to international law or even to violate it, and his actions were "law of the land" binding on the courts.* Or, when the President decides to recognize or not to recognize a foreign agreement, the courts do not abstain from reviewing his action; they give effect to it because recognition is a political act within the President's constitutional powers.[28]

There is, then, no Supreme Court precedent for extraordinary abstention from judicial review in foreign affairs cases.[29] Lower courts, however, invoked the political question doctrine to justify abstention from considering constitutional issues arising out of the Vietnam war. In several cases, plaintiffs raised two principal issues. One was whether the actions of the United States in Vietnam violated international law, in particular the treaty obligations assumed in the Kellogg-Briand Pact and the UN Charter.[30] The courts properly refused to consider that question because it was immaterial, and would not control the disposition of the case: the Constitution does not prohibit the political branches, acting within their powers, to disregard treaties or other obligations of international law.[31] Plaintiffs also claimed that the President had exceeded his constitutional power by engaging in war not declared by Congress; several courts held that the political question doctrine required or permitted them not to decide that question.[32]

The Supreme Court has refused to review these cases. The constitutional issue which the lower courts refused to decide is,

---

* See Chapter VI, p. 188, and this chapter, pp. 221–22.

of course, "political" in a deep sense, but so is every claim that the President (or Congress) has exceeded his powers to a petitioner's detriment.[33] If the political question doctrine means that the courts must abstain only when, as a matter of fair construction, the Constitution says they must, there is no basis for refusing review in these cases. But if, as Justice Brennan seemed to say, though the Supreme Court had not in fact so held, the political question doctrine includes a right (or an obligation) for the courts to refrain from deciding constitutional cases from "prudence," the courts in the Vietnam cases could claim, in Justice Brennan's words, "an unusual need for unquestioning adherence to a political decision already made," and "the potentiality of embarrassment from multifarious pronouncements by various departments on one question." On that view, courts should not consider issues of war and peace, or other questions as to which a decision adverse to the political branches could have grave consequences for the national interest, where indeed the President might feel compelled not to heed the courts.* They might refuse, in particular—as in the Vietnam cases—to step into major confrontation between the President and the Congress to protect the Congressional domain when Congress itself can but will not do it.**

This broader view of the political question doctrine would give the judiciary, in theory, discretion to "sit out" major foreign affairs cases,† but it is not likely to be exercised often, and hard-

---

* Or, as Professor Bickel suggests, this chapter, note 21, the Court's anxiety may be "not so much that judicial judgment will be ignored, as that perhaps it should be, but won't."

** See Chapter IV, pp. 99 *et seq.*, 107–108.

† In time, presumably the Supreme Court would lay down standards or lines to guide the discretion of the lower courts.

Though the doctrine is judge-made, to the extent that it is not required by the Constitution it can probably be modified or regulated by Congress. Compare the control of Congress over the jurisdiction and rules of the courts. Congress has also modified the Act of State doctrine, this chapter, note 55, but there Congress merely determines the applicable law, while modification of the political question doctrine would compel the courts to act where they do not deem it appropriate.

ly to avoid a claim that a foreign-policy action denies individual liberty under the Bill of Rights. (See Chapter X).

## Judicial Legislation

In foreign affairs as elsewhere, the courts make law implicitly when they determine and interpret the applicable law to decide cases before them. Judicial legislation by interpretation is fundamental and dispositive when the courts develop the law of the Constitution,* and their constitutional constructions have importantly influenced foreign relations and sometimes built a continuing role for the courts, for example to monitor state burdens on foreign commerce or intrusions into foreign relations.** The courts have ample scope and influence, too, when they read and apply statutes, treaties, other international agreements or executive acts, or, we shall see, when they find customary international law.

The federal courts have made and developed law explicitly in several parts of the federal domain, claiming authorization to do so from Congress or from the Constitution,[34] and partaking of their supremacy to state law. While Congress has not delegated law-making authority to the courts in foreign affairs,[35] the Constitution readily supports, for example, the power of federal judges to make maritime law since the judicial power of the United States extends "to all Cases of admiralty and maritime Jurisdiction"; and maritime law was (and has remained) largely judge-made.[36]

Federal courts have also made other law relevant to foreign affairs but, until recently at least, its constitutional basis and status have been less clear. The courts have determined the principles of customary international law † and the requirements of

---

* Some constitutional clauses, *e. g.*, the due process clause, have been largely filled by the courts. See Chapter X, pp. 255–57.

** See Chapter IX.

† See this chapter, p. 221. Strictly, in applying international law, the courts are supposed to be finding rather than making the law and must look to what others consider the law to be. While that was

international comity; [37] rules to decide which of conflicting laws of different countries should govern a transnational transaction; the rights of foreign governments to sue in domestic courts and the effect to be given here to judgments of foreign courts.† But unlike the maritime law and other law made by direct authority of Congress or the Constitution, this other law made by the federal courts was commonly deemed to be only their particular "finding" of the common law and did not enjoy federal supremacy; and the States were free to go their own way. [38] Indeed, in cases involving suits between citizens of different states, where a federal court must apply the law of the State in which it sits, it appeared that the federal courts would have to apply the law as determined by the local state courts even on these matters affecting foreign affairs. [39]

All that, I believe, changed when the Supreme Court decided the *Sabbatino* case. [40] In that case a financial agent of the Cuban Government sued in the federal courts to recover the proceeds of a sale of sugar. The defendant denied the Cuban Government's title to the sugar, alleging that it belonged to a company largely owned by Americans and had been confiscated in violation of international law. The lower federal courts held that although under the Act of State doctrine courts were not to sit in judgment on the acts of foreign states performed in their own territory, they did not have to give effect to Premier Castro's expropriation of American sugar because it violated international law. [41] On appeal the Supreme Court reversed, holding that the Act of State doctrine applied even as to acts that violated international law. *

said, too, of the common law, *e. g.*, by Mr. Justice Story in Swift v. Tyson, 16 Pet. 1, 18–19 (U.S.1842) (a view rejected in Erie R. R. v. Tompkins, 304 U.S. 64, 79–80 (1938)), the judges have been substantially less free to follow their own bent in determining customary international law.

† Local federal ~~court~~ ................................ ~~common law applicable~~ in the District of Columbia and other federal territories.

* At least "in the absence of a treaty or other unambiguous agreement regarding controlling legal principles." 376 U.S. at 428.

What is of interest here is the basis on which the Court reached its decision, and what it said in reaching it. After concluding that the Act of State doctrine was not required by notions of sovereignty, by international law, by the political question doctrine, or by anything in the Constitution, the Court said: [42]

> The act of state doctrine does, however, have "constitutional" underpinnings. It arises out of the basic relationships between branches of government in a system of separation of powers. It concerns the competency of dissimilar institutions to make and implement particular kinds of decisions in the area of international relations. The doctrine as formulated in past decisions expresses the strong sense of the Judicial Branch that its engagement in the task of passing on the validity of foreign acts of state may hinder rather than further this country's pursuit of goals both for itself and for the community of nations as a whole in the international sphere. . . . Whatever considerations are thought to predominate, it is plain that the problems involved are uniquely federal in nature. If federal authority, in this instance this Court, orders the field of judicial competence in this area for the federal courts, and the state courts are left free to formulate their own rules, the purposes behind the doctrine could be as effectively undermined as if there had been no federal pronouncement on the subject.
>
> . . .
>
> However, we are constrained to make it clear that an issue concerned with a basic choice regarding the competence and function of the Judiciary and the National Executive in ordering our relationships with other members of the international community must be treated exclusively as an aspect of federal law. . . .

The Court claimed no delegation or authorization from Congress, and seemed carefully to avoid seeking support in Executive authority; [43] it found implied in the Constitution an independent power for the federal courts to make law on their own authority.[44]  It was the federal judiciary that decided that the foreign relations of the United States required the Act of State doctrine, and the judiciary that was deciding, in *Sabbatino*, that the foreign relations of .the United States did not permit exception for acts of state that violate international law.[45]  And, of course, like other federal law this is one of those "enclaves of federal judge-made law which bind the States." [46]

In the result, in the Court's reasoning and dicta and their implications, *Sabbatino* establishes foreign affairs as a domain in which federal courts can make law with supremacy.  There ought to be little doubt, then, that in the established areas of judicial law-making, law that is substantially related to foreign affairs—the determination of customary international law and comity for judicial purposes; * guidelines for the interpretation of treaties and the meaning of particular treaty provisions; the principles of (international) conflicts-of-laws; rules as to access of foreign governments to domestic courts and the treatment of foreign judgments [47]—the federal courts can make law for their own guidance and can decide also whether federal interests require that the States conform to them.  It follows that state decisions regarding such supreme judge-made federal law raise federal questions subject to review by the Supreme Court if Congress so provides.[48]

Later cases will have to answer the more difficult question, whether and which new subjects are also within the legislative power of the federal courts.  The Court in *Sabbatino* noted that the Act of State doctrine "concerns the competency of dissimilar institutions to make and implement particular kinds of decisions in the area of international relations." [49]  Act of State is a doctrine particularly for the guidance of the courts, and it is about its own "engagement in the task of passing on the validity of foreign acts" that the Judicial Branch felt competent and justifi... ...express its "strong sense" that such involvement may hinder rather than further national and broader interests

* See p. 222 below.

in international relations.[50]    Act of State is an element of the
law of conflicts-of-law in multi-national transactions where the
political branches hardly tread and courts have never waited for
the political branches to make law or to ask the judges to make
it.[51]    But can the courts make law without invitation of the political branches on foreign affairs questions not the specialty of
courts, indeed on any matter in which the political branches
could legislate? †    Only the courts can tell us but one may expect that without limiting their power in principle, they will
legislate sparingly.[52]

In *Sabbatino*, Congress was silent and the President and the
Supreme Court arrived at the same conclusion; [53] concurrent
power here brought neither conflict, nor competition for initiative, nor a reach for new power to fill a vacuum of authority.
But the legislative power of the courts in foreign affairs is concurrent and surely it is subordinate to that of Congress.[54]  (Congress has in fact legislated to modify the *Sabbatino* doctrine
of Act of State and the courts have applied the statute.) [55]  Judicial legislation would also bow to a treaty; * would it give
less respect to executive agreements ** or Presidential declarations of policy?  Foreign policy is largely made by the President and the "intrinsically federal" character of foreign relations on which the Court relied in *Sabbatino* is substantially
Presidential.  Judge-made law, the courts must recognize, can
only serve foreign policy grossly and spasmodically;  their attempts to draw lines and make exceptions must be bound in
doctrine and justified in reasoned opinions, and they cannot provide flexibility, completeness, and comprehensive coherence.[56]
In the *First National City Bank* case, we know, most of the
Justices expressed their distaste for *ad hoc* direction by the
State Department, but a majority of the Court in fact reached

---

† If so the courts might have the powers of both Congress and the
President, but limited, as is all judicial legislation, by the *ad hoc*,
random character of judicial law-making.

* *A fortiori*, since even Congressional legislation bows to treaty.
See Chapter V, p. 163.

** Compare Chapter VI, p. 184.

the result the State Department asked for.† Might the Court yet accept, even welcome, formal, general declarations of policy approved by the President, not in the context of a particular case?

### Customary International Law

American courts also make foreign relations law when they determine and apply customary international law.[57] Although how it got there is not agreed,[58] international law is part of the law of the United States and will be given effect when it is "self-executing" in character. In the oft-quoted language of Mr. Justice Gray in *The Paquete Habana*: [59]

> International law is part of our law, and must be ascertained and administered by the courts of justice of appropriate jurisdiction, as often as questions of right depending upon it are duly presented for their determination.

In that case the Supreme Court held that under international law fishing vessels belonging to enemy nationals were exempt from capture by armed vessels of the United States and could not be condemned and sold as prize of war. In innumerable cases, state and federal courts have dismissed proceedings against foreign governments, their diplomats, vessels or other property, because international law gave them immunity from judicial process.[60]

Like treaties, customary international law is law for the Executive and the courts to apply,* but the Constitution does not

---

† Compare Chapter II, pp. 62–63.

* A statute or treaty of the United States will be given effect in American courts in disregard of an earlier principle of customary international law, but although a treaty will supersede an earlier federal statute (Chapter V, p. 163) it has not been decided whether a newly developed principle of customary international law can be applied by the courts in disregard of an earlier statute, treaty or executive action. If the Executive accepts the new unwritten principle by some public act, the latter might have legislative effect and "repeal" an earlier executive act or treaty (which the President can

forbid the President (or the Congress) to violate international law, and the courts will give effect to acts within the constitutional powers of the political branches without regard to international law.[61]   On the other hand, the courts have enforced international law against lower federal officials not directed by the President to disregard international law.[62]

In regard to the States, however, the constitutional status of customary international law has not been as clear as that of treaties.   While the Supremacy Clause expressly declares treaties to be the law of the land and expressly establishes their supremacy over state law, it does not mention customary international law.   The courts have said that it is "part of our law" but it is not patently part of the "laws of the United States"; it is not, strictly, federal law made by the federal government but the law of the international community to which the United States contributes only in an uncertain way and to an indeterminate degree, and much customary international law was created before the United States existed.*   The States have indeed given effect to international law but it was long assumed that they did so because international law was state law, part of the common law received by them from Great Britain and retained as their colonial heritage.[63]   But if for the States customary international law has only the status of their common law, the state courts can decide for themselves what international law requires;   and like other common law it is presumably subject to modification or repeal by the state legislature.   Unlike ques-

terminate).   But an earlier act of Congress might still prevail; compare the discussion of executive agreements inconsistent with earlier acts of Congress, Chapter VI, p. 186.

* Strictly, of course, a treaty, too, is not made only by the federal government but by it together with one or more foreign governments. But treaties do not have to qualify as "Laws of the United States" since they are expressly mentioned in the Supremacy Clause.

Customary international law of vintage antedating the U. S. Constitution would have an additional obstacle since the Supremacy Clause speaks of U. S. law "pursuant to" the Constitution.   Compare Chapter V, p. 137.   One might argue perhaps that such customary law has been reaffirmed, in effect, since the Constitution.

tions arising under treaties, moreover, issues of customary international law would not raise federal questions and could not be appealed to the Supreme Court for final adjudication.[64] Fifty states could have fifty different views on some issue of international law while the federal courts might have still another view. Indeed, not only would the States be free to disregard the views of the federal courts, but in cases where a federal court is required to apply the law of the State in which it sits it would have to apply the State's view on disputed questions of international law.[65]

The implications of *Sabbatino*, however, and recent constitutional writings support a better, more orderly view. Determination and application of international law are integral to the conduct of foreign relations and are the responsibility of the federal government. In the absence of federal statute, treaty, or authoritative Executive action,[66] international law is determined, "made," by the federal courts as though it were federal law, and their views bind the state courts.[67] Issues of international law that arise in the state courts, then, are federal questions and can be appealed to the Supreme Court; and the Supreme Court can determine and establish a single, uniform rule of customary international law for state as well as federal courts.

That international law is the law of the United States means that, as in the case of treaties, American courts will give effect to the obligations of the United States under customary international law; at the behest of affected private parties,* courts will prevent violations of international law by the States or by lower federal officials. The doctrine itself gives no one rights, remedies, or defenses against a foreign government for its violation of international law. That has not always been understood. Thus, when Castro's Cuba expropriated American properties, probably in violation of international law, it was urged that the courts of the United States must refuse to give effect to these ~appropriations, and must reject claims by the Cuban government

---

* Or, as regards state violations, of federal officials. Compare Chapter V, p. 167.

of title to the property, and even afford a remedy to the victims against Cuba.[68] The argument overlooked that while international law is part of the law of the United States, the law of the United States has no application to what Castro did in Cuba. In the absence of special treaties, moreover, international law establishes rights, duties and remedies only for states against states; Castro's violations, then, might be an "international tort" against the United States giving rights and remedies to the United States, but not to any private victims. International law itself, finally, does not require any particular reaction to violations of law; specifically, in the present context, it does not require nations to refuse effect to violations by other nations. Whether and how the United States wished to react to such violations are domestic, political questions: the courts will not assume any particular reaction, remedy, or consequence.[69] Of course, Congress could legislate that the courts should refuse to recognize Castro's title or should give a remedy against him (and might incorporate by reference the norm of international law to guide the courts) but it would not be international law but the federal statute that gave the courts their mandate.[70]

The contribution of the courts to foreign policy and their impact on foreign relations are significant but not large. The Supreme Court in particular intervenes only infrequently and its foreign affairs cases are few and haphazard. The Court does not build and refine steadily case by case, it develops no expertise or experts; the Justices have no matured or clear philosophies; the precedents are flimsy and often reflect the spirit of another day. But the supporting part of the courts is indispensable and inevitable and if their competence and equipment for making foreign policy is uncertain, they can be improved by stronger, continuing guidance by Congress and, perhaps, by the President.

# THE ABIDING RELEVANCE OF FEDERALISM

# Chapter IX.   THE STATES AND FOREIGN AFFAIRS

—"The states are unknown to foreign nations;   .   .   ."
—"It was one of the main objects of the constitution to make us, so far as regarded our foreign relations, one people, and one nation;   .   .   ."
—".   .   .   in respect of our foreign relations generally, state lines disappear.   As to such purpose the State   .   .   .   does not exist."

So said three Supreme Court Justices known for their sensitivity to the claims of the States in the federal system, at different times during more than 100 years; [1] the same was said in different ways by justices and commentators before, between, and since, without dissent from even the most ardent champions of States' rights.[2]

Even in the Articles of Confederation the States had left themselves little independent authority in foreign relations, and eliminating that little was a principal purpose of the Constitutional Fathers.*   Whether, as *Curtiss-Wright* said, the States never had international sovereignty, or gave it up when they

---

* Under the Articles "Each state retains its sovereignty, freedom and independence, and every Power, Jurisdiction and right, which is not by this confederation expressly delegated to the United States, in Congress assembled." (Art. II.)   The delegates to the Congress were appointed annually by the state legislatures, and each State had one vote.   But the States were expressly denied the power, without the consent of Congress, to send or receive embassies, enter into agreements with any foreign state, or engage in wars, or ~~~~~~~~~~~~~~~~~~ would interfere with any treaty made by Congress.   (Art. VI.)   The Congress was given "the sole and exclusive right and power of determining on peace and war," of sending and receiving ambassadors and concluding treaties and alliances.   (Art. IX.)

accepted the Constitution, they have none under the Constitution. Federalism, then, appeared irrelevant to the conduct of foreign affairs even before it began to appear to be a wasting force in American life generally—before we became one nation economically, and moved toward welfare government disregarding state lines, before the power of the States was theirs only by grace of Congress and by political realities rather than constitutional compulsion.[*]

Foreign relations are national relations. The language, the spirit and the history of the Constitution deny the States authority to participate in foreign affairs, and its construction by the courts has steadily reduced the ways in which the States can affect American foreign relations. And yet, despite many light, flat statements to the contrary, the foreign relations of the United States are not in fact wholly insulated from the States, are not conducted exactly as though the United States were a unitary state. In constitutional theory, the States are not irrelevant, playing a small part of their own, and even limiting somewhat the plenary authority of the Federal Government. In political fact, States and state interests help select those who conduct our federal relations and substantially shape the foreign policy they make.

## State Exclusion from Foreign Affairs

By *Curtiss-Wright* [3] the Federal Government would have all the foreign relations powers, and the States none, even if the Constitution had said nothing. In fact, the Constitution explicitly denies the States the principal foreign affairs powers, other limitations are clearly implied, and still others have been distilled by the courts.

### Express Limitations

Article I, section 10, is a catalogue of prohibitions and limitations for the States, and most of them relate to foreign affairs:

> No State shall enter into any Treaty, Alliance, or Confederation; grant Letters of Marque and Reprisal;

[*] See especially Chapter III, pp. 69 et seq.

coin Money; emit Bills of Credit; make any Thing but gold and silver Coin a Tender in Payment of Debts; pass any Bill of Attainder, ex post facto Law, or Law impairing the Obligation of Contracts, or grant any Title of Nobility.

No State shall, without the Consent of the Congress, lay any Imposts or Duties on Imports or Exports, except what may be absolutely necessary for executing it's [sic] inspection Laws: and the net Produce of all Duties and Imposts, laid by any State on Imports or Exports, shall be for the Use of the Treasury of the United States; and all such Laws shall be subject to the Revision and Controul of the Congress.

No State shall, without the Consent of Congress, lay any Duty of Tonnage, keep Troops, or Ships of War in time of Peace, enter into any Agreement or Compact with another State, or with a foreign Power, or engage in War, unless actually invaded, or in such imminent Danger as will not admit of delay.

Most of these prohibitions are as clear as words can make them and have raised no issues, but some beg interpretation and invite at least hypothetical questions, and a few have engendered controversies and cases.

The provision that a State shall not lay a duty or impost on imports or exports, except what may be "absolutely necessary" for executing its inspection laws, has required interpretation of principal terms. The Court early decided that a tax on the importer was a tax on the import, that an import remained an import immune to tax while it remained the property of the importer in the "original package." [4] An export became an export when the article entered "into the export stream that marks the start of the process of exportation." [5]

That treaties are absolutely forbidden to the States but compacts and agreements are permitted with the consent of Congress [6] requires distinguishing the two classes of agreement, but no helpful, authoritative distinction has emerged. No agreement by a State with a foreign power has been challenged as a forbidden treaty.[7] It might be sufficient to invalidate an agreement with a foreign country if a State were indiscreet enough to call it a treaty, or to conclude it with all the formalities associated with treaties.[8] Looking rather to the substance of the agreement, one early writer suggested that treaties deal with "subjects of great national magnitude and importance, and are often perpetual, or for a great length of time," but Story found this "at best a very loose and unsatisfactory exposition,"; his own suggestion, that the prohibition of the Constitution applies "to treaties of a political character," has not met unanimous acclaim either.[9] One can perhaps do no better than to itemize kinds of agreement which the Framers probably considered to be treaties forbidden to the States, *e. g.*, agreements of alliance or confederation, war or peace, cession of territory.*

Whatever the distinction the Framers contemplated, whatever motivated them to entrust the national interest to Congressional surveillance as to some agreements but not others,** the different constitutional treatment has lost all practical significance. It is difficult to believe that Congress would withhold consent from an agreement of which it approved because it was properly a forbidden treaty, or that an agreement to which Congress consented would be invalidated for that reason.[10] In fact, the States have asked, and Congress has given, consent to few foreign agreements, and none that apparently involved local intrusion on matters of national policy. Congress has consented to an agreement by the State of New York with Canada to establish a port authority to operate a bridge across the Niagara River.[11] It authorized Minnesota to enter a highway agreement with the Province of Manitoba.[12] It approved the Northeastern Interstate Forest Fire Protection Compact among several States and

* Compare the efforts to distinguish treaties from executive agreements, Chapter VI, pp. 179–81.

** The Articles of Confederation, by contrast, did not draw this distinction and the making of treaties (and confederations or alliances) was also forbidden "without the consent of the United States in congress assembled." See Articles VI, IX.

contiguous Canadian provinces.[13]   It authorized the Civil Defense Administrator to "give all practicable assistance to States in arranging, through the Department of State, mutual civil defense aid between the States and neighboring countries."[14] The St. Lawrence Seaway project, in which the federal government, States and Canadian authorities participated, may be seen as including a state compact with Congressional consent, but federal participation gives that agreement special character and directly safeguards national interests.[15]

The "Agreement or Compact" clause itself has also produced issues.[16]   In *Holmes* v. *Jennison*,[17] the only case in which the Supreme Court considered that clause in respect of state agreement with a foreign power, the Justices divided as to whether there had been any "agreement."   Holmes, a resident of Canada, was indicted for murder there but fled to Vermont.   Although there was no effective extradition treaty between the United States and Great Britain (then responsible for Canada's foreign relations), the Governor of Vermont signed a warrant for Holmes's arrest and his extradition to Canada.   On writ of habeas corpus, the Supreme Court of Judicature of Vermont upheld the Governor.   Holmes's appeal to the Supreme Court of the United States was dismissed because the Court was equally divided,[18] but, among other arguments, Chief Justice Taney (for himself and three other Justices) said: [19]

> .   .   .   The word "agreement," does not necessarily import any direct and express stipulation; nor is it necessary that it should be in writing. If there is a verbal understanding, to which both parties have assented, and upon which both are acting, it is an "agreement." And the use of all of these terms, "treaty," "agreement," "compact," show that it was the intention of the framers of the Constitution to use the broadest and most comprehensive terms;   and that they
> ~~anxiously desired~~ to cut off all connection or communication between a state and a foreign power:   and we shall fail to execute that evident intention, unless we give to the word "agreement" its most extended signifi-

cation; and so apply it as to prohibit every agreement, written or verbal, formal or informal, positive or implied, by the mutual understanding of the parties.
. . .

. . . The Constitution looked to the essence and substance of things, and not to mere form. It would be but an evasion of the Constitution to place the question upon the formality with which the agreement is made. The framers of the Constitution manifestly believed that any intercourse between a state and a foreign nation was dangerous to the Union; that it would open a door of which foreign powers would avail themselves to obtain influence in separate states. Provisions were therefore introduced to cut off all negotiations and intercourse between the state authorities and foreign nations. If they could make no agreement, either in writing or by parol, formal or informal, there would be no occasion for negotiation or intercourse between the state authorities and a foreign government. Hence prohibitions were introduced, which were supposed to be sufficient to cut off all communication between them.

In a separate opinion Mr. Justice Catron seemed agreed that if the extradition had in fact been asked by Canadian authorities, the Governor's action would have constituted an agreement with Canada that required the consent of Congress. On the record in the case, however, he assumed (as Taney did) that there was no request by Canadian authorities, and for him there was therefore no agreement, only a unilateral action by Vermont which the Constitution did not forbid.[20] Three other Justices concluded virtually without discussion that there was no agreement between Vermont and Canada within the meaning of Article I, section 10.[21]

*Holmes* v. *Jennison* dealt with extradition, historically a subject of national policy, usually made by reciprocal international agreement;[22] and all the Justices seemed agreed that a clear, formal compact or agreement on that subject between Vermont and Canada would have required Congressional consent. But neither Taney's essay nor any of the other opinions suggests that the subject or the particular disposition of it made any difference: agreement between a State and a foreign authority on any subject is forbidden unless Congress consents. Later, in a case involving an interstate (not a foreign) compact, the Court held that, despite the general constitutional language, agreements or compacts require the consent of Congress only when they tend "to the increase of political power in the States, which may encroach upon or interfere with the just supremacy of the United States." [23] Since the same language applies to foreign compacts, one might adapt the Court's distinction and conclude that Congressional consent is required only if a foreign agreement tends to give a State elements of international sovereignty, interferes with full and free exercise of federal authority, or deals locally with a matter on which there is or might be national policy. Whether by so narrowing the constitutional requirement of Congressional consent, or because consent was assumed, state and local authorities have in fact entered into agreements and arrangements with foreign counterparts without seeking consent of Congress, principally on matters of common local interest such as the coordination of roads, police cooperation, and border control.[24] The State and the City of New York have arrangements with the United Nations about the UN Headquarters and its personnel, and with permanent missions to the UN of various foreign governments.[25] An interstate compact to facilitate the interpleader of other parties to judicial proceedings, which contemplates adherence by foreign governments and their component units, also appears not to have obtained the consent of Congress.[26]

Effectively, whether an agreement or compact requires Congressional consent will often be determined by the State.[27] If it proceeds without consent, and if Congress learned of it and were moved to act ~~~~~~~~~, Congress would doubtless prevail,* but ordinarily the State's judgment would not be reviewed

---

* If the reason why some agreements can be concluded by States is that the consent of Congress may be assumed, Congress can of

unless some aggrieved private interest challenged the agreement in court.

## Implied Limitations

Some limitations on the States are indisputably implied in the explicit prohibitions of Article I, and some of the grants of power to the federal government as clearly imply that the States do not have those powers.[28] Article I, section 10, for example, does not expressly forbid the States to appoint Ambassadors to foreign nations, but such a prohibition can be inferred from the provisions forbidding States to make treaties and granting the President the executive Power and the power to appoint Ambassadors.*

## "Commerce with foreign nations"

International trade and intercourse are of course commonly regulated by federal statute or treaty and these are supreme law binding on the States. A fertile source of limitation on state action has been the Supreme Court's early conclusion that in addressing to Congress the power "to regulate commerce with foreign Nations, and among the several States," the Constitution also spoke words of prohibition to the States: [29] the Constitution did not leave the States wholly free to act in regard to

---

course act to reject such agreements. Even on the view that the Constitution itself permits some compacts regardless of Congressional approval or acquiescence, rejection by Congress might still prevail: the courts might well hold that the line between agreements requiring Congressional consent and those that do not is itself for determination by Congress. Compare Frankfurter and Landis, this chapter, note 9.

* That the exchange of ambassadors and negotiation with foreign powers are forbidden to the States by implication from the grants to the federal government, see Taney's opinion in Holmes v. Jennison, 14 Pet. 540, 575, 577 (U.S.1840). But since the States may make foreign agreements with the consent of Congress (and some even without such consent, this chapter, p. 233), they must have the right to negotiate with foreign governments or their subsidiary units to achieve such agreements. It has not been suggested that States must obtain Congressional consent to begin negotiations.

interstate or foreign commerce until prevented by a supreme act of Congress, for Congress could not anticipate or deal with the myriads of state actions that might infringe the national interest.[30] The prohibitions implied in the Commerce Clause, of course, are determined in the first instance by the States, subject to judicial review, and the power of the courts to protect the nation and the other States against self-seeking "balkanizations" by any State has long been accepted as a basic safeguard of the federal system.[31]

What the Commerce Clause forbids and what it permits the States has splintered the Supreme Court, and has filled volumes of law, not all of it clear or consistent. No one has claimed that the Commerce Clause denies to the States more than it grants to Congress: what is not within the Commerce Power of Congress is surely not forbidden to state regulation. But, it was agreed from the beginning, what Congress might do under the Commerce power is not *ipso facto* forbidden to the States;[32] surely, not all that Congress could reach today with the long, long arm of the Commerce Power * is foreclosed to state regulation if Congress is silent. The Supreme Court, then, has had to develop doctrines to distinguish an area susceptible to federal regulation in which States will be tolerated from one from which they are excluded. Long ago, in the *Cooley* case, Mr. Justice Curtis announced:[33] "Whatever subjects of this power are in their nature national, or admit only of one uniform system, or plan of regulation, may justly be said to be of such a nature as to require exclusive legislation by Congress."

The *Cooley* doctrine is still cited but it clearly has not proved an adequate touchstone: few "subjects" are in their "nature" either wholly "national" or wholly local, and to many issues of State "interference" with commerce the *Cooley* doctrine is simply irrelevant. Later the Court toyed with and abandoned distinctions between direct and indirect burdens on commerce.[34] Today ~~two doctrines~~ govern and it is not wholly clear how they are related and which will be applied. One has

---

* See Chapter III, p. 69.

it that "reconciliation of the conflicting claims of state and national power is to be attained only by some appraisal and accommodation of the competing demands of the state and national interests involved." [35]  Balancing state and national interests is easier to ask than to execute with confidence or consistency, and much depends of course on who balances and with what scales.[36]  In other cases the Court seems to decide merely whether a state burden on interstate commerce is "unreasonable" or "undue," weighing the effect on commerce but not necessarily the local interest.[37]  There is also one clear "subdoctrine", applied without regard to the magnitude of the burden on commerce, or the balance of national and local interests:  the Court will not tolerate state regulations that exclude out-of-state commerce, that overtly discriminate against it, that favor local economic interests, as by barring foreign sellers or buyers or otherwise limiting competition from beyond the State.[38]  Although the States may favor some local interests other than economic welfare—for example, the health and safety of its citizens— even regulations for these purposes might not stand if the Court believes that a less burdensome means than that used was available and that discrimination against out-of-state commerce lurks in the regulation.[39]

In largest part, the cases defining the implied prohibitions of the Commerce Clause deal with state regulation of interstate commerce, since most States have greater opportunities and temptations to impinge on commerce with other States than with foreign countries.  But nothing in the cases suggests, and there is no reason to believe, that they and the various doctrines do not apply equally to foreign commerce.[40]  The Court, then, will not tolerate state regulations that exclude foreign persons or foreign goods, that discriminate against foreign buyers or sellers, that set up tariffs or other obstacles to transportation or trade or to other forms of intercourse with foreign nations. Surely the Court will be as sensitive to burdens on foreign as on interstate commerce and in any balancing the Court might find even that the national interest in protecting foreign commerce has additional weight, that local regulation is particularly suspect when it impinges on the foreign policy and the foreign relations of the United States.

The Court has also built into the Commerce Clause a complex, technical, not wholly rational edifice of limitations and permissions governing state taxation of interstate and foreign commerce.[41] The constitutional law implied in that structure can not be explained by any *"Cooley* Doctrine" distinguishing subjects "in their nature national" or local, by differences between substantial and insubstantial burden, or even by a general principle of balancing, although the Court is obviously trying to achieve some accommodation between the principle that out-of-state commerce should contribute to the costs of state government and the need to protect it from "undue" burdens of taxation. Again, discrimination against out-of-state commerce is forbidden and the Court has been sensitive, too, to burdens of multiple taxation on the same property or activity. Again, most of the relevant law has been made in interstate cases and, again, it doubtless applies also to foreign commerce.[42] Again, one might expect that the courts would be especially sensitive to taxes on foreign commerce which might burden the foreign relations of the United States and are often tantamount to a duty or impost (or a tax on exports) that are expressly forbidden to the States.

Under its power to regulate foreign commerce Congress can, of course, bar state regulations which the courts would tolerate if Congress were silent. It is also established doctrine that Congress can permit the States to regulate commerce in ways that could not stand were Congress silent.[43] So far as the Commerce Clause is concerned, then, Congress could authorize the States to exclude foreign commerce, to discriminate against it, to impose heavy burdens upon it, to satisfy minor local interests at the price of major obstacles to such commerce, to establish a patchquilt of local idosyncrasies. But such _____ _____ are infrequent domestically, and rare as regards foreign commerce.

*State "intrusion" in foreign affairs*

The limitations on state regulation or taxation of foreign commerce were found implied in the Commerce Clause. The Court never asked whether such state actions might run afoul also of some larger principle limiting the States in matters that relate to foreign affairs. Such a larger principle—how large is yet to be determined—has now become part of the Constitution.

Until 1968 there was no sign of such a principle.[44] In the government of their affairs, States have variously and inevitably impinged on American foreign relations. They regulate and tax commerce with foreign nations. They regulate the rights of aliens. Even laws that apply identically to aliens and citizens might invite issues with foreign governments, but States have also singled out aliens for special treatment, subjecting them to registration, limiting their right to own or inherit property, to work, to engage in trade and professions, to direct or own stock in domestic corporations, to use state recreational and other facilities. State courts apply state law and policy in deciding whether domestic law or foreign law should apply to a transnational transaction; whether to give effect to a foreign act of state that imposed a tax or penalty, or was criminal in character, or confiscated property outside its territory; whether to enforce the judgment of a foreign court.[45] Some of these state regulations have indeed been struck down because they violated the Fourteenth Amendment, or because they were inconsistent with federal policy as expressed in a treaty, statute, executive act, or judicial decision. But it was never suggested that they might run afoul of an implicit constitutional limitation barring state impingement on the federal domain of foreign relations even when the federal government had not acted.[46] Indeed, in *Clark* v. *Allen,* upholding a California statute that allowed an alien to inherit in the State only if his country permitted Americans to inherit, the Supreme Court rejected such a claim as "far fetched." [47]

In 1968, the Supreme Court decided *Zschernig* v. *Miller.*[48] Pursuant to state statute, the Oregon courts had denied an inheritance to a resident of East Germany because he could not satisfy them that his country allowed Americans to inherit estates in that country, and that the East German heir would receive payments from the Oregon estate "without confiscation, in whole or in part." In a brief *amicus curiae* before the Supreme Court the United States Department of Justice said that the federal government "does not contend that the application of the Oregon escheat statute in the circumstances of this case unduly interferes with the United States' conduct of foreign relations." [49] The Supreme Court, however, reversed the state court, finding "an intrusion by the State into the field of foreign affairs which the Constitution entrusts to the President and the Congress." [50]

This is new constitutional doctrine. No doubt, an act of Congress or a treaty, probably an executive agreement, perhaps an official executive declaration, possibly even a rule made by the federal courts, could have forbidden what Oregon purported to do. Here there was no relevant exercise of federal power * and no basis for deriving any prohibition by "interpretation" of the silence of Congress and the President. The Court tells us that the Constitution itself excludes such state intrusions even when the federal branches have not acted.[51]

*Zschernig* v. *Miller*, then, imposes additional limitations on the States but what they are and how far they reach remains to be determined. While political branches might prescribe for particular cases or even provide some guidelines, as under the Commerce Clause, it will be largely for the courts and will take many years and many cases to develop the distinctions and draw the lines that will define the new limitations on the States. There are perhaps some intimations in that the Court expressly refused to overrule *Clark* v. *Allen,* adding: [52]

---

The Supreme Court, too, was not purporting to legislate federal substantive law. Compare *Sabbatino*, Chapter VIII, p. 218; it found that the Constitution preempted the field for the Federal Government and told the States to stay out.

. . . At the time *Clark* v. *Allen* was decided, the case seemed to involve no more than a routine reading of foreign laws.

. . .

The Government's acquiescence in the ruling of *Clark* v. *Allen* certainly does not justify extending the principle of that case, as we would be required to do here to uphold the Oregon statute as applied; for it has more than "some incidental or indirect effect in foreign countries," and its great potential for disruption or embarrassment makes us hesitate to place it in the category of a diplomatic bagatelle.

As we read the decisions that followed in the wake of *Clark* v. *Allen*, we find that they radiate some of the attitudes of the "cold war," where the search is for the "democracy quotient" of a foreign regime as opposed to the Marxist theory. The Oregon statute introduces the concept of "confiscation," which is of course opposed to the Just Compensation Clause of the Fifth Amendment. And this has led into minute inquiries concerning the actual administration of foreign law, into the credibility of foreign diplomatic statements, and into speculation whether the fact that some received delivery of funds should "not preclude wonderment as to how many may have been denied 'the right to receive' . . . ."

That kind of state involvement in foreign affairs and international relations—matters which the Constitution entrusts solely to the Federal Government—is not sanctioned by *Clark* v. *Allen*.

It may be, then, that *Zschernig* v. *Miller* excludes only state actions that reflect a state policy critical of foreign governments and involve "sitting in judgment" on them.[53] Even if so limited, the new doctrine might cast doubts on the right of the States to continue to invoke their own "public policy" in trans-

national situations.* Or is the Court suggesting different lines
—between state acts that impinge on foreign relations only "indirectly or incidentally" and those that do so directly or pur-
posefully? [54] Between those that "intrude" on the conduct of
foreign relations and those that merely "affect" them? Difficulties with similar formulae in the Commerce Clause cases may
yet lead instead to doctrines like those that grew there: certain impingements on foreign affairs are excluded because national uniformity is required; infringements are barred if they
discriminate against or unduly burden our foreign relations; the
Courts will balance the State's interest in a regulation against
the impact on American foreign relations.

The *Zschernig* doctrine does not, of course, substitute the
judgment of the federal courts for that of the federal political
branches; it asserts only the authority of the courts to strike
down state acts when the political branches have not acted. In
the Commerce Clause cases, we saw, the Court recognized the
right of Congress to permit burdens on commerce which would
have been invalid had Congress not spoken. While in *Zschernig*
the Court seemed to hold that a communication expressing State
Department toleration of the Oregon law was not enough to
validate it, it was perhaps resisting *ad hoc* direction to the courts
in particular cases. It is difficult to believe that the Court would
find constitutionally intolerable state intrusions on the conduct
of foreign relations which the political branches formally approve or tolerate.** Domestic considerations apart, there might
be foreign relations reasons why the political branches might
deem it desirable to leave some matters to the States rather
than deal with them by formal federal action.[55]

---

* See p. 238, this chapter. It would presumably forbid also sense
resolutions on foreign policy, though these are not law and could not
be invalidated, but state legislatures presumably cannot be prevented
or enjoined f--- ---- ------- -----. Some old state resolutions on foreign
affairs are cited in WRIGHT 264–65 n. 5 (1922). The practice continues. Compare p. 247 below.

** Compare Chapter II, p. 61.

## Exclusion by Federal Supremacy

A major limitation on state action relating to foreign affairs is rooted in the Supremacy Clause. Treaties and laws of the United States are expressly declared to be the supreme law of the land, and will supersede inconsistent state law. Innumerable federal statutes regulating interstate and foreign commerce, for example, have invalidated laws that were otherwise within the authority of the State. Laws denying employment to an alien have been held inconsistent with "the right to work for a living in the common occupations of the community" implied in the decision of Congress to admit him to this country.[56] Treaties, we know, imposed on Missouri international regulation of migrating birds; invalidated Virginia's laws sequestering debts of its citizens to British creditors, or denying alien rights to inherit local land; required Seattle to permit Japanese to run pawn shops.[57] Executive agreements on the President's sole authority, and law made by the courts under their judicial power, also enjoy such supremacy: New York's policy to deny effect to Soviet confiscations was overturned by Roosevelt's executive agreement with Litvinov; the Act of State doctrine of the federal courts will bind the state courts as well.* The States are also bound by public international law and, under the better view, what international law requires is a federal question as to which state courts must follow the federal lead and are subject to review by the Supreme Court.**

The supremacy of federal law does more than supersede inconsistent state law. In many instances the Court has found that a federal regulation bars even identical, consistent, or supplementary state regulations because the federal government "occupied the field," "preempted" state regulation. In such cases, the Court avoids finding that the state action violates some substantive provision of the Constitution, finds instead a purpose in the federal regulation to exclude the State, and places the onus for invalidating state law on the political branches.[58]

* See *Belmont*, Chapter VI, p. 185, and *Sabbatino*, Chapter VIII, p. 219.

** See Chapter VIII, p. 223.

Whether a federal regulation was designed to exclude consistent state regulation is not always obvious or easy to determine, but the Court has attempted to suggest some guidelines for finding such a purpose: [59]

> . . . Such a purpose may be evidenced in several ways. The scheme of federal regulation may be so pervasive as to make reasonable the inference that Congress left no room for the States to supplement it. . . . Or the Act of Congress may touch a field in which the federal interest is so dominant that the federal system will be assumed to preclude enforcement of state laws on the same subject. . . . Likewise, the object sought to be obtained by the federal law and the character of obligations imposed by it may reveal the same purpose. . . . Or the state policy may produce a result inconsistent with the objective of the federal statute. . . .

In *Hines* v. *Davidowitz*,[60] the Court struck down Pennsylvania's alien registration law although it was wholly consistent with the federal alien registration law, because, it found, Congress had occupied the field and told the States to stay out. The Court said: [61]

> . . . Consequently the regulation of aliens is so intimately blended and intertwined with responsibilities of the national government that where it acts, and the state also acts on the same subject, "the act of Congress, or the treaty, is supreme; and the law of the State, though enacted in the exercise of powers not controverted, must yield to it." And where the federal government, in the exercise of its superior authority in this field, has enacted a complete scheme of regulation and has therein provided a standard for the registration of aliens, states cannot, inconsistently with the purpose of Congress, conflict or interfere with, curtail or complement, the federal law, or enforce additional or auxiliary regulations. . . .

. . .

. . . . And whether or not registration of aliens is of such a nature that the Constitution permits only of one uniform national system, it cannot be denied that the Congress might validly conclude that such uniformity is desirable. . . . Having the constitutional authority so to do, it has provided a standard for alien registration in a single integrated and all-embracing system in order to obtain the information deemed to be desirable in connection with aliens. When it made this addition to its uniform naturalization and immigration laws, it plainly manifested a purpose to do so in such a way as to protect the personal liberties of law-abiding aliens through one uniform national registration system, and to leave them free from the possibility of inquisitorial practices and police surveillance that might not only affect our international relations but might also generate the very disloyalty which the law has intended guarding against. Under these circumstances, the Pennsylvania Act cannot be enforced. . . .

While to date the Supreme Court has attributed preemption only to acts of Congress, there is no reason why a treaty, an executive agreement, a judicial doctrine or any federal regulation could not also be construed as closing the field to state regulation.[62]

### The Uses of the States in Foreign Affairs

That foreign affairs are national affairs means that ultimate, supreme authority over them is in the national government and that States may not intrude upon them with initiatives and policies of their own. But inevitably, the States touch foreign affairs even in minding their proper business, since aliens live or do business in the State pursuant to its laws and seek the aid of its courts, and citizens bring transnational affairs within its jurisdiction.* While, in principle, all these local contacts

---

* Increasingly, indeed, even apparently "domestic" matters wholly within the State acquire relevance to foreign affairs. Compare the

244

with foreign affairs might be brought under national control by federal law or international agreement, that could not begin to be done and there has never been any disposition to begin to do it. Federal authority in foreign affairs as in other national affairs, then, remains essentially interstitial and the lives and affairs of aliens and the transnational business of citizens remain largely subject to state laws and legal institutions.

The federal government has also given or left to the States a substantial part in the implementation of national foreign policy. Congress has left to the States at least concurrent authority to implement some United States obligations under treaties and international law.[63] It has never sought to deprive state courts of all jurisdiction, or to authorize removal from them, even of cases directly involving foreign governments or diplomats, treaties, or other international matters.[64]

## States' Rights Limitations on National Policy

If, despite the principles of federalism, the States have been effectively excluded from foreign affairs, federalism has suggested some reciprocal limitations, deriving from States' rights, on federal powers to conduct foreign relations. In general, the Tenth Amendment ("The powers not delegated to the United States by the Constitution . . . are reserved to the States . . .") has been dismissed as stating "but a truism that all is retained which has not been surrendered." [65] Yet it has remained the symbol of States' rights and of the doctrine of limited, enumerated, federal powers, a guide to interpreting constitutional grants of power to the federal government and an influence for limiting them.[66] In regard to foreign affairs, however, the Supreme Court has repeatedly rejected limitations based on "invisible radiations" from that Amendment.[67] The Amendment was circumvented in principle when the Court accepted that the Federal Government has foreign affairs powers not expressly enumerated in the Constitution: * little was left

discussion of treaties dealing with human rights or other "domestic" matters, Chapter V, p. 155.

* See Chapter I.

of it in fact when the courts recognized vast powers in Congress,[68] and federal powers to make treaties and executive agreements, to do other executive acts, and make law through judicial power, without regard to reserved States' rights.

Whatever the States retain in regard to foreign affairs as a matter of constitutional right must be found in other doctrines. There are dicta by Justices and by writers asserting hypothetical limitations on federal power, including its foreign affairs powers, in specific constitutional guarantees to the States and in implied state sovereignty and inviolability. Justices have said that a treaty cannot cede State territory without its consent; presumably, the United States could not, by treaty or by statute for international purposes, modify the republican character of state governments or, perhaps, abolish all state militia.* Under the Eleventh Amendment foreign governments and their nationals cannot sue a State in the courts of the United States without its consent.[69] There is also something more left, too—how much cannot be said with confidence—of the sovereign immunity of the States, that would presumably limit federal regulation under foreign affairs powers as well. State immunities have shrunk radically and state activities are generally subject to federal regulation.[70] But Mr. Justice Frankfurter said:[71]

> . . . There are, of course, State activities and State-owned property that partake of uniqueness from the point of view of intergovernmental relations. These inherently constitute a class by themselves. Only a State can own a Statehouse; only a State can get income by taxing. These could not be included for purposes of federal taxation in any abstract category of taxpayers without taxing the State as a State.

While state immunity to federal taxes might be most plausible since least restrictive of federal authority—the Federal Government can get revenue other than by taxing the States—an earlier dictum had it generally that the Federal Government cannot "destroy the [State] nor curtail in any substantial manner

* See Chapter V, pp. 147–48.

the exercise of its powers." [72]   In principle, then, the strictly "governmental" activities of the States might have some immunity from federal foreign affairs regulation.[73]   And there are old cases that deny the power of the Federal Government to impose duties and functions on state officials.[74]

## Political Limitations of Federalism

If the constitutional limitations in favor of the States are few and largely hypothetical, the federal system gives the States opportunities to affect foreign relations, not necessarily in happy, constructive ways.   State actions (or inactions) can violate the obligations of the United States under international law, as when they "deny justice" or fail to provide basic protections to aliens. States and state officials may fail to carry out obligations to foreign countries or their citizens, may deny aliens treaty rights or fail to prevent private persons from invading them.   And federal remedies—principally through the federal courts—may not be available or effective, or take inordinately long.[75]   If the States will often heed informal State Department intercession in support of our international obligations, the Department will usually have less influence to prevent embarrassing "sense resolutions" of state legislatures on foreign issues.

The principal influence of the States in foreign relations derives from the constitutional framework of government and the political forces that animate it.   Much of our foreign relations does not affect the States or local interests directly, and state governors and legislatures are often indifferent to and even ignorant of major national foreign policies.   But where foreign affairs begin to touch the States, whether in their particular economic interest (as in issues of free trade versus protectionism), or even in small matters of pride or prejudice or principle, the plenary powers of the national government take on all the colors of federalism.   The President has a national constituency and is chief of a national party, but both are built of local blocks and he can not be impervious to their qualities and interests.   His diplomatic representatives are, or are made, acutely aware of our federal character—as when they hesitate to negotiate about "local matters," or insist on adding "federal-state" clauses that are constitutionally unnecessary but politically attractive.* The Senate still substantially represents the States and has often protected their interests and adopted their views, as when it refused consent to treaties that would allow aliens to practice the professions regardless of state requirements, or conventions that would regulate the rights of American citizens.[76] The House of Representatives represents the people, but it is the people of the States,[77] and is often even more "parochial" than the Senate, obstructing "enlightened," "internationalist" federal regulation in behalf of interests that are even less than statewide.

What has been said about federalism generally still has ample relevance even in regard to foreign relations:

> . . . The continuous existence of the states as governmental entities and their strategic role in the selection of the Congress and the President are so immutable a feature of the system that their importance tends to be ignored. . . . The actual extent of central intervention in the governance of our affairs is determined far less by the formal power distribution than by the sheer existence of the states and their political power to influence the action of the national authority.
>
> . . .
>
> . . . Far from a national authority that is expansionist by nature, the inherent tendency in our system is precisely the reverse, necessitating the widest support before intrusive measures of importance can receive significant consideration, reacting readily to opposition grounded in resistance within the states.[78]

* See Chapter V, p. 146.

# THE LIMITS OF CONSTITUTIONAL POWER

# Chapter X.  INDIVIDUAL RIGHTS AND FOREIGN AFFAIRS

The Constitution was ordained and established by "We the People of the United States" but the people are not the subject of the Constitution:  the individual, even *qua* citizen, is mentioned infrequently and he appears in constitutional law not laden with duties, responsibilities, opportunities or even "rights," but principally as the beneficiary of limitations imposed on government.[1]  Here, too, then, I am concerned with the individual not as an actor in the nation's foreign relations, or even as a member of the chorus, but as the object of constitutional limitation on foreign policy and process.  How the United States behaves towards individuals, alien as well as citizen, moreover, is increasingly of legitimate interest to other nations, and the constitutional rights of individuals become a condition of American foreign policy.

In the original conception, the Constitution was to support individual rights principally by assuring good government.  No doubt the separation and allocation of powers within the central government and the division of authority between it and the States were designed for the good of "the people" and consequently of every individual;[2]  and an aggrieved individual can invoke the aid of the courts to maintain the constitutional system of government.*  In the original Constitution, however, there were few guarantees of individual rights or liberties.[3]  And, although the Bill of Rights was added immediately, it did not quickly and radically transform the character of the Consti-
̶t̶u̶t̶i̶o̶n̶ ̶.̶.̶.̶ ̶t̶h̶e̶ ̶c̶o̶n̶t̶e̶n̶t̶ ̶o̶f̶ constitutional law:  there was hardly a case during more than a hundred years in which the courts

* See Chapter VIII, p. 208.

invalidated federal action on the ground that it violated an individual's constitutional rights.*

All that, we know, has changed.[4] Today, the courts hardly monitor the separation of federal powers and there are few States' rights left to be protected against federal invasion; only maintaining federal supremacy against state challenge remains a staple of judicial vindication of the constitutional "system." Increasingly, on the other hand, the courts have invoked, extended and intensified the protections of the Bill of Rights, and for the courts, at least, the Constitution has become primarily a bulwark for the individual against governmental excess. Constitutional guarantees for individual rights also help assure compliance by the United States with international obligations, notably in the treatment of aliens, increasingly also under the growing international law of human rights. Inevitably, of course, these constitutional rights restrict foreign policy, preventing what the United States might wish to do alone, limiting even some forms of international cooperation.

Nothing in the Constitution suggests that the rights of individuals in respect of foreign affairs are different from what they are in relation to other exercises of governmental power. But special constitutional theories and peculiarities of constitutional language about foreign relations, their high place in national policy and interest, the asserted needs of extraordinary freedom of action for those who conduct them, the different constitutional issues they raise and the different contexts in which these arise, have engendered views that individual rights and protections are fewer and narrower than elsewhere. While these views have not prevailed in principle, constitutional protections for individuals sometimes do have a particular, different look.

### Applicability of Constitutional Safeguards

That, under *Curtiss-Wright*, federal foreign relations powers inhere in sovereignty and are perhaps extra-constitutional might

* The only case in the Supreme Court before the Civil War was the *Dred Scott Case* which invalidated the Missouri Compromise on the ground that it denied a slave owner his property without due process of law. Scott v. Sandford, 19 How. 393 (U.S.1857).

suggest that they are not subject to constitutional limitations, even to safeguards for individual rights.[5] That conclusion is hardly compelled, since the framers of the Bill of Rights might well have sought to protect the people even against excesses in the exercise of sovereign, extra-constitutional powers. In any event that view has no support whatever. *Curtiss-Wright* itself exempts foreign relations only from the rigors of limitations on delegation inherent in the separation of powers; it did not suggest that other constitutional limitations were also inapplicable, and it expressly said that the President's plenary power in foreign affairs, "of course, like every other governmental power, must be exercised in subordination to the applicable provisions of the Constitution." * Later, while upholding a statute depriving a man of his citizenship for voting in a foreign election, the Court said:

> Broad as the power in the National Government to regulate foreign affairs must be, it is not without limitation. The restrictions confining Congress in the exercise of any of the powers expressly delegated to it in the Constitution apply with equal vigor when that body seeks to regulate our relations with other nations.[6]

Nor is any particular exercise of foreign affairs power exempt from limitations in favor of individual rights. Arguments, based on the language of the Supremacy Clause, that treaties

---

* 299 U.S. at 320.

In addition to the safeguards of the Bill of Rights, concern for individual rights engenders other judicial limitations on the conduct of foreign relations. Despite the claims of foreign relations the Court uncovered a constitutional immunity from involuntary expatriation. See this chapter, note 6. Generally prepared to give full sway to the plenary foreign affairs powers of President and Congress, the Court has tended to become less expansive about them when they are exercised in ways that impinge on individual rights. Compare the narrow reading of the necessary and proper clause in the court-martial cases, Chapter III, note 54, and the return to stricter limitations on Congressional delegation of authority in the passport cases, Chapter IV, p. 98, and notes 96, 97. Compare the limitation on Executive extradition, Chapter IV, p. 98.

are not subject to constitutional prohibitions are now well at rest.* Although the First Amendment provides that "Congress shall make no law" abridging freedom of speech, press, religion, assembly or petition, these are equally safe from infringement by treaty, Executive agreement or action, or court order.[7]

## The Bill of Rights

In principle, then, the Bill of Rights limits foreign policy and the conduct of foreign relations as it does other federal activities.** The President, for example, would not make a treaty that forbids teaching or advocating racial superiority because it would probably violate the First Amendment.[8] Largely on the basis of that Amendment, the Supreme Court refused the Executive Branch an injunction against press-publication of the classified "Pentagon Papers."[9] The constitutional provisions that afford fair criminal procedures apply also to persons charged with violating foreign affairs statutes, even to foreign nationals accused of espionage.[10] The United States could not adhere to an international criminal court without considering the relevance of the rights assured to those accused of crime in the Fourth, Fifth, Sixth and Eighth Amendments.† Since the Bill of Rights generally protects aliens equally with citizens,[11] it satisfies (and probably exceeds) standards of "justice" required by international law,[12] or special protections promised in treaties, e. g., the "bill of rights" for the accused under the NATO Status of Forces Agreement.[13] But, by that token, the United States could not abridge these basic alien rights, say in retaliation for mistreatment or to promote better treatment of Americans abroad. Foreign governments, however, and probably foreign diplomats in their official capacity, have no constitutional rights, and there are no constitutional obstacles, say, to tapping wires of foreign embassies.[14]

Even the "preferred freedoms" of the First Amendment,[15] moreover, are not absolute but are "balanced" against, and might be outweighed by, important public interests.[16]  One may expect that the national interest in war and peace and even lesser concerns of foreign relations would have important weight in any balance.  So, for example, courts have upheld prohibitions on picketing foreign embassies.[17]  Hypothetically, it is far from obvious that they would bar, say, a statute or treaty that forbids publication of matter inciting to war or seriously exacerbating international relations, or private research related to nuclear or biological weapons.[18]  Similarly, the Fourth Amendment affords important protection to the "right of the people to be secure in their persons, houses, papers, and effects," but only "against unreasonable searches and seizures"; [19]  the national interest in maintaining an important disarmament system and in gaining required inspection rights in other countries might render "reasonable" some intrusive inspections of private establishments and records.[20]

### Due Process

The Fifth Amendment includes the provision that "No person shall be   .   .   .   deprived of life, liberty, or property without due process of law."  In regard to foreign relations as to other matters, "due process of law" requires fair procedures for aliens as for citizens, for corporations as for persons, in civil as in criminal proceedings, before administrative bodies and in courts.[21]  But an alien seeking admission to the United States is due no process beyond the consideration and decision by the designated administrative officer.[22]  An alien in the United States, however, is entitled to a fair administrative hearing and the Government must prove by clear, unequivocal and convincing evidence that he is deportable on the grounds provided by Congress.[23]

"Procedural due process" has never been held to require that a legislature afford hearings to those who might be affected by contemplated legislation, or that administrative agencies grant hearings before promulgating rules or regulations.[24]  To date, no process has been "due" either as regards the "legislative" acts of the Executive in respects affecting foreign relations, whether under his own constitutional authority or by delegation from Congress: whether the Executive acts by general order or in a particular case,[25] a person cannot demand a hearing as of constitutional right before the Executive Branch determines that the party he is suing is entitled to diplomatic or sovereign immunity; that an arms embargo or a tariff should be imposed in particular circumstances or in regard to particular goods; that the Act of State doctrine should apply to give effect to a foreign confiscation of his property.[26]

It is long established that "due process" limits also the substance of what government can do.* The day is gone, of course, when the Supreme Court used the due process clause to strike down economic regulations on the ground that deviations from *laissez faire* deprived persons or corporations of property or of the "liberty" to contract at will.[27] There is in it still a requirement, however vague and variable with reference to time and circumstance, that a law—and presumably also any official act, including an international agreement—"shall not be unreasonable, arbitrary or capricious, and that the means selected shall have real and substantial relation to the object sought to be attained."[28] No economic regulation has been held by the Supreme Court to run afoul of that standard since it was formulated in 1934, and strong presumptions giving the legislature the benefit of every doubt make it unlikely that many will.[29] Foreign relations regulations or international agreements are surely no more vulnerable to such objections than domestic prohibitions or regulations that adversely affect the economic rights of one or of many. No court would hold that restrictions on trade with Cuba or Communist China or Rhodesia or the Republic of South Africa denied due process because they inflicted financial losses. No court would heed the claim of an arms manufacturer that an arms control agreement deprived him of the liberty to carry on

---

*It is the Due Process Clause, also, which is invoked when a party challenges acts of either political branch as beyond its constitutional powers, whether because they usurp powers reserved to the States or invade the domain of another branch of the federal government. See p. 208, and note 14, Chapter VIII.

his trade or of his property interest in his business or his patents.[30]

"Substantive due process" protects also a person's "liberty," and here, increasingly, the constitutional limitation is greater and judicial deference to the political branches far less.[31] In 1958, the Court held [32] that the right to travel abroad is "a part of the liberty of which the citizen cannot be deprived without due process of law," and avoided a constitutional decision only because "we will not readily infer that Congress gave the Secretary of State unbridled discretion to grant or withhold it." * More recently, the Court invalidated a statutory provision making it a crime for members of certain communist organizations to obtain or use passports, because that "too broadly and indiscriminately restricts the right to travel and thereby abridges the liberty guaranteed by the Fifth Amendment." [33] As regards time-of-war, however, the Court upheld unprecedented invasions of liberty and property, even far more drastic than later appeared necessary, as in the sad chapter of the relocation of American citizens of Japanese ancestry.[34] And to date the Court has continued to hold that not only has an alien no constitutional right to be admitted to the United States, but that even one long resident here can be deported for whatever reasons seem proper to Congress.[35]

## Equal Protection of the Laws

The Bill of Rights contains no explicit guarantee of equal protection of the laws. The Supreme Court has held, however, that substantive due process effectively requires it of the Federal Government as the Fourteenth Amendment expressly requires it of the States.[36]

Equal protection does not command identical laws applied identically to all; it ordains only that distinctions and classifications be relevant and reasonable, not invidious. Holmes once deprecated some cl. . . .

---

* Later, however, the Court upheld the State Department's authority, under the same broad delegation, to refuse to issue a passport valid for travel to Cuba. Zemel v. Rusk, 381 U.S. 1 (1965).

resort of constitutional arguments," [37] and, as in regard to substantive due process, the Supreme Court long gave to government the benefit of every presumption and every doubt.[38]  In
recent years, however, eager to find constitutional support for
appealing claims but reluctant to revive the "disreputable" substantive due process, the Court began to give new vitality instead to equal protection.  While it remains unavailable to challenge distinctions in social and economic regulation, as to some
"fundamental rights"—voting, interstate travel, welfare support,—the Court held that distinctions can be justified only by a
"compelling state interest." [39]

Whether in its traditional implications or in its recent special
significance for "fundamental rights," the need to afford equal
protection of the laws does not importantly hamper the conduct
of foreign relations.  Distinctions between foreign and domestic
matters permeate constitutional law and the Court would no
doubt tend to uphold regulations reflecting them.  Distinctions
which our national policy makes among nations raise no issues
of equal protection since foreign governments have no constitutional rights in the United States.  While foreign nationals in
the United States are entitled to equal protection,[40] discriminations among aliens of different nationality apparently raise no
constitutional difficulties if they reflect different agreements between the United States and their countries, or reciprocity for
treatment of Americans in those countries; probably, even, when
designed to implement general United States policy towards the
alien's government, as when assets of Chinese or Cuban citizens
were frozen in time of discord with their countries.

On the other hand, the courts would presumably strike down
discriminations against aliens of particular nationality that do
not reflect national foreign policy,[41] as they have those based on
race.[*]  While in the past many discriminations between citizen

---

[*] As regards admission to the United States discriminations based
on national origin were the foundation of our immigration laws for
many years until 1965.  The Supreme Court never considered their
constitutionality and it is not clear that any one had standing to challenge them.

and alien—for example, those barring aliens from various public employment [42]—have been accepted as "reasonable", increasing judicial resistance to such discriminations by the States (discussed below) suggests that the requirement of citizenship for federal jobs, rights, privileges or opportunities will be increasingly scrutinized and some of them will not survive.

### *"Taking" and "Just Compensation"*

There is also some protection, and perhaps great promise, in the final clause in the Fifth Amendment, that private property shall not "be taken for public use, without just compensation." That clause has obvious significance for foreign relations when an alien's property is taken by eminent domain,[43] or any person's property is taken to build an embassy or for some other foreign relations use. It may also be acquiring larger relevance, for the Court has been moving the line between what is and what is not a "taking," and what is and what is not a public "use."

Every governmental regulation that prohibits or limits the use of property or a person's ability to earn income—for example, fire and health regulations, zoning restrictions, limitations on wages or prices—can be said to be "taking" someone's property for a public use. No one, however, would today claim that such regulations require that those adversely affected be compensated;[44] there must be a "taking" for "use". But even as confined to their more literal sense those terms are not self-defining. In 1944, in the *Caltex* case,[45] a majority of the Supreme Court held that the United States had to pay for oil taken in the Philippines by American armed forces for their use during the Second World War, but it did not have to pay for oil they destroyed to keep it from falling into enemy hands. In 1946, in *Causby* v. *United States*,[46] a majority of the Court held that when, in peacetime, United States military aircraft regularly flew low over a farmer's property, frightening his chickens and ~~...~~ his egg business, the United States had partially "taken" the farmer's airspace and owed him compensation under the Fifth Amendment. The difference between *Caltex* and *Causby* (and between majority and dissent in each case) may appear to be a difference between more-or-less literal and more-or-less "sophisticated" interpretations of "taking" and of "public use"; at bottom, of course, they represent differences as to whether economic loss resulting from a national policy shall be suffered wholly by those directly affected or borne by the community as an element in the cost of that policy.†

The question for the future is whether expanding concepts of "taking" and "use", and judicial disposition to widen the constitutional policy of distributing the cost of national endeavor, might extend to include some "incidental" costs of foreign relations and foreign policy. Consider the famous case of *Ware* v. *Hylton*, decided in 1796.[47] During the War of Independence a Virginia statute provided that any monies owing by Virginia citizens to British creditors might be paid instead to the State, and declared that the debts shall thereby be discharged. Later the peace treaty with Great Britain reaffirmed all debts to British creditors and required that they be paid.* The Supreme Court held that although Hylton had paid his debt into the Virginia Treasury, he had to pay his British creditor as required by the treaty.

To make Hylton pay twice seems an obvious deprivation of property without substantive due process of law, but for the Supreme Court that did not invalidate the treaty. Perhaps the Court did not yet consider that the due process clause imposed substantive limitations.** Probably the Court assumed that the citizen would be relieved of the dual burden. Mr. Justice Cushing suggested that Virginia was bound "in justice and honor, to

† *Caltex* perhaps reflects also a special reluctance to compensate one, corporate victim of war when "the strange arithmetic of chance" left so many others without recourse for their losses.

* The Framers had that provision in particular in mind when they established the supremacy of preexisting treaties over state laws. Chapter V, p. 138.

** The first and only application of substantive due process before the Civil War was in the *Dred Scott* case, which in fact invalidated a statute implementing a treaty. See p. 252.

indemnify the debtor, for what it in fact received." [48]   But Mr.
Justice Chase had a different idea:

> That Congress had the power to sacrifice the *rights*
> and *interests* of *private* citizens to secure the safety
> and prosperity of the public, I have no doubt; but the
> immutable principles of justice; the public faith of the
> States, that confiscated and received *British* debts,
> pledged to the debtors; and the rights of the debtors
> violated by the treaty; all combine to prove, that ample
> compensation ought to be made to all the debtors who
> have been injured by the treaty for the benefit of the
> *public*.   This principle is recognized by the Constitu-
> tion, which declares, "that *private* property shall not be
> taken for *public* use without *just compensation*." [49]

There is no evidence that Hylton sought or obtained compensation from the United States, and there is no later case awarding compensation for any "taking" by treaty.   In 1952, however,
in a case involving an act of Congress (not a treaty), the Court
gave some support to the old suggestion of Justice Chase.   In
*Cities Service Co.* v. *McGrath*,[50] the Court upheld the power of
Congress to authorize the Alien Property Custodian to "seize"
certain obligations owned by an enemy alien, and collect them
from the obligor, where the latter was in the United States but
the negotiable debenture was not and therefore could not be
physically taken.   The Court said that if the obligor should in
the future be compelled by a foreign court to make payment on
the debenture to a holder in due course, the obligor would be entitled to compensation from the United States under the Fifth
Amendment to the extent of any double liability.   ".   .   .
[O]nly with this assurance against double liability can it fairly
be said that the present seizure is not itself an unconstitutional
taking of petitioners' property." [51]

The opinions quoted lend support to the view that making
someone pay twice for some overriding foreign relations purpose,
while not constitutionally impermissible, constitutes a taking for
a public use that requires just compensation; and, perhaps, if
no compensation is forthcoming the original taking becomes un-

lawful as a deprivation of property without due process of law. But double payment, surely, is not the only form of deprivation of property, and *Ware* v. *Hylton*, in particular, involved a treaty provision unique in our history. What of the common international agreements that affect private property rights not by reinstating claims against Americans that have been paid, but by nullifying claims by Americans that have not been paid?

International agreements settling claims by nationals of one state against the government or nationals of another are established international practice reflecting traditional international theory. For while a private claimant may be able to recover under the laws of his country or that of the debtor (or even of some third country), in international law the individual and his debt have no independent existence: his claim is only a right of his government against that of the debtor. For international law and diplomacy, then, what begins life as a debt between individuals of different nationality is, or becomes, automatically a debt between governments, and governments have dealt with such private claims as their own, treating them as national assets and as counters in international bargaining. Agreements have lumped or linked claims deriving from private debts with others that were intergovernmental in origin, and concessions in regard to one group might be set off against concessions in the other or against larger political considerations unrelated to debts. Except as an agreement might provide otherwise, international claims settlements generally wipe out the underlying private debt, terminating any recourse under domestic law as well.

The United States has been party to many such settlements, terminating claims of Americans against another state or its citizens, usually in exchange for a lump sum payment to the United States.[52] Some agreements established machinery for hearing and awarding individual claims against the lump sum payment; others said nothing about payment to individuals and payment by the foreign government was made into the Treasury of the United States; but Congress usually provided that private claims affected by the agreement should be examined and paid in full or on a *pro rata* basis. The United States has sometimes disposed of the claims of its citizens without their consent, or even without consultation with them, usually without exclusive regard for their interests, as distinguished from those of the nation as a whole.[53]  There was no assurance that the lump sum settlement was the best "deal" that could have been gotten, that it was a fair deal, that claims of citizens were not sacrificed to some other national interest;  surely one could not be certain that the private party recovered the full "value" of his claim.

Particularly instructive is the story of the "French Spoliation Claims."  By treaty in 1800 the United States renounced claims of American shipowners against France arising out of alleged spoliations;  France, in turn, effectively forgave the United States for alleged breach of a treaty undertaking to support France in war against Great Britain.[54]  Here, there was no cash payment to the United States in liquidation of the claims of the shipowners, but, clearly, the United States had "taken" and "used" them to offset claims against the United States, yet for eighty-five years Congress failed to appropriate funds to compensate the American claimants.[55]

No one has successfully argued in the Supreme Court that in purporting to dispose of private claims, in the details of a particular settlement, in the procedures established for making awards to private claimants, in Congressional legislation providing (or failing to provide) for award and payment, the United States deprived the original claimants of property without due process of law, impaired the obligation of their contracts[56] or appropriated their claims for a public purpose and was obligated to pay them just compensation for any loss.[57]  The Court has refused to scrutinize any settlement and has affirmed that Congress has discretion to decide whether and how and to what extent to compensate the original creditors.[58]  Perhaps the Court refused to see these settlements as involving any "taking" of property.  Perhaps it took the international theory at face value concluding that since usually the claimant had no assured rights against a foreigner, even less against a foreign government, the United States did not deprive him of anything.  Perhaps the

263

Court thought that what was involved was the political judgment of the negotiators that the settlement was in the national interest,[59] usually too in the best interest of the claimants, and no court could effectively review that judgment or analyze and weigh its components.* But in a famous case arising out of the French Spoliation Claims, the Court of Claims in effect gave Congress an advisory opinion, saying:[60]

> . . . But in the negotiation of 1800 we used "individual" claims against "national" claims, and the set-off was of French national claims against American individual claims. That any Government has the right to do this, as it has the right to refuse war in protection of a wronged citizen, or to take other action, which, at the expense of the individual, is most beneficial to the whole people, is too clear for discussion. Nevertheless, the citizen whose property is thus sacrificed for the safety and welfare of his country has his claim against that country; he has a right to compensation, which exists even if no remedy in the courts or elsewhere be given him. A right often exists where there is no remedy, and a most frequent illustration of this is found in the relation of the subject to his sovereign, the citizen to his Government.
>
> It seems to us that this "bargain" (again using Madison's word), by which the present peace and quiet of the United States, as well as their future prosperity and greatness were largely secured, and which was brought about by the sacrifice of the interests of individual citizens, falls within the intent and meaning of the Constitution, which prohibits the taking of private property for public use without just compensation.

A hundred years ago, the Court of Claims could give no relief since Congress had not provided any. Now Congress has given the Court of Claims jurisdiction of all claims for just com-

---

* There were also technical obstacles to recovering a judgment for just compensation since it requires an appropriation by Congress and in every instance Congress had indicated all that it was prepared to do.

pensation under the Fifth Amendment, and has been automatically appropriating funds to pay that court's judgments.[61] Now, too, we have seen, the Supreme Court has shown a willingness to read "take" and "use" in the Fifth Amendment more "realistically." Will it also begin to see such takings behind the legal and diplomatic fictions of international claims settlements and, at least in some cases, allow the Court of Claims to assess the claim and award a judgment for any difference between its value and what the claimant eventually receives?[62] In other contexts, too, might the Court move the line between "regulation" and "taking" and hold, say, that a treaty that requires terminating an arms business, confiscating drugs or ploughing-under poppy fields, or giving up "rights" acquired by oil companies in coastal waters, entails some taking of property for a public use, and a loss that should be borne by the community as part of the cost of the nation's foreign policy?

Changing notions of fairness and reasonableness may yet engender constitutional rights where none had existed in regard to other foreign affairs regulations as well. He who sues a sovereign or a diplomat will have his suit dismissed because international law gives the defendant immunity from suit. In tort cases, often, the defendant is insured and will not assert his immunity, but where he does the plaintiff is left without his day in court, and often without a remedy. This has been international law and the law of the land before the Constitution and has remained so, and until international law and practice change it seems unlikely that the Constitution will come to protect the plaintiff (though Congress might do so voluntarily). But perhaps in new situations, where history does not bar the plaintiff, *e. g.*, when immunities are accorded to international organizations, their officials and member representatives, by treaty;[63] or where the plaintiff can claim that international law does not require the immunity but immunity is "suggested" by the United States because it is required by American foreign policy interests "—might the Constitution yet be read to require that

---

* See Chapter II, p. 59 above. Might such a claim be made even when the plaintiff has his day in court but the law applies some special

the plaintiff be afforded another remedy or be compensated by the United States? [64]

## The Constitution Abroad

In 1891, the Supreme Court upheld the conviction of a seaman, John Ross, for killing a ship's officer on an American ship in Japanese waters. He had been tried by an American consul authorized by Congress to prosecute and try Americans for violations of certain American Laws. Ross challenged the validity of his trial because it had not provided the safeguards of criminal process required by the Bill of Rights, but the Court did not attempt to construe and apply the relevant clauses of the Constitution. It concluded rather, that "The Constitution can have no operation in another country." [65] Ross, then, was entitled to a fair trial but not to the specific protections of the Constitution.

Why the Justices thought the Constitution was "territorial," like a deity of old, is not clear.* Perhaps they assumed that to have been the intention of the Framers. Perhaps they thought that some or all of the Constitution's provisions were not appropriate or could not be effective elsewhere.

Whatever its original rationale, that doctrine is dead. In *Reid* v. *Covert* [66] the Court held that Congress could not provide trial by court martial abroad for the wife of a member of the armed forces, because Congress had no power to deprive a civilian of constitutional rights to a jury trial and other procedural safeguards. The plurality opinion of Mr. Justice Black dismissed *Ross* as "a relic from a different era."[67] Later cases

doctrine like Act of State which results in a judgment different from what might have issued if the sensibilities of a foreign government were not at stake? Compare pp. 255–56 above, and note 26, this chapter.

* Perhaps the Justices considered that applying the Constitution in another country would somehow violate her sovereignty. The act of Congress authorizing consular prosecution and trial, and the conduct of the trial, were not such a violation since the country consented by treaty. But it has never been considered a violation of sovereignty for a state to apply its laws to its nationals in the territory of another state even without the latter's consent. Compare Chapter III, p. 75.

confirmed Black's view that wherever it acts the United States "can only act in accordance with all the limitations imposed by the Constitution." [68]

There are nonetheless obvious and inevitable differences in the extent to which individual rights limit the foreign policy of the United States at home or abroad. In the United States virtually all the safeguards of the Constitution apply to all who are here—citizens, alien residents, even those sojourning temporarily or in transit. Abroad, constitutional protection for the individual against governmental action is enjoyed by American citizens,[69] perhaps also by alien residents of the United States who are temporarily abroad.[70] But an inhabitant of a foreign country presumably cannot invoke the Constitution when he is aggrieved, say, by discrimination in American trade or immigration policy, when a consul capriciously denies him a visa,[71] or when a military purchasing agent refuses to buy from him on account of his race; someone in Vietnam, surely, could not object that the President of the United States had no constitutional authority to wage war there. The courts of the United States in fact will not be available to foreign nationals abroad for raising such claims, despite the general language of the statutes establishing jurisdiction.[72] It is only abroad, moreover, that the United States acts in capacities to which the usual constitutional safeguards do not apply. When the United States exercises authority as an occupying power, for example, the President, as Commander in Chief, may establish courts for the trial of crimes committed there, and even American citizens may be tried in such courts without jury trial or other safeguards provided in the Bill of Rights.*

---

* Madsen v. Kinsella, 343 U.S. 341 (1952), Chapter II, note 37, Chapter IV, note 38. Although Justice Black dissented in that case, he later distinguished it in his opinion in *Reid* v. *Covert*; and it was not overruled in any of the later cases, Chapter III, note 42. The change in the composition and disposition of the Court since those cases suggests that the *Madsen* case might have renewed vitality. The issue, happily, is academic since the United States is no longer an occupying power anywhere. Compare analogous issues that might arise in unincorporated territories, p. 268 below.

A related but different issue was involved in the famous controversy at the turn of the century, "whether the Constitution follows the Flag." There, of course, the question was not whether the Constitution applies abroad but whether newly acquired territories were still "abroad" for constitutional purposes, or had become a part of the United States. In the *Insular Cases* a majority of the Supreme Court held that the Constitution did not apply fully in territories acquired by conquest and cession from Spain, until Congress "incorporated" them into the United States; [73] in "unincorporated" territories, only "fundamental" constitutional rights applied, but, for example, American authorities did not have to provide indictment by grand jury or trial by jury. In his plurality opinion in *Reid* v. *Covert*, Mr. Justice Black distinguished these cases "in that they involved the power of Congress to provide rules and regulations to govern temporarily territories with wholly dissimilar traditions and institutions . . .," but in any event "neither the cases nor their reasoning should be given any further expansion." [74]

The likelihood that the United States will acquire new territories in the years ahead seems remote, and it is not out of the question that some territories now "unincorporated" will achieve independence, incorporated status, or even statehood. Today, despite the aspersions cast on them, the *Insular Cases* continue to govern the United States in such unincorporated territories as Guam and the Trusteeship Islands in the Pacific. It remains to be seen, however, whether the content of the "fundamental rights" that obtain there will expand. In regard to the States of the United States, for example, it had once been established doctrine that the Constitution required of them only respect for fundamental rights, but the Court has now held that almost all the provisions of the Bill of Rights are indeed "fundamental." * If so, is an individual now entitled to them also in an unincorporated territory? Or will the Court continue to apply there the concept it has now rejected for the States, concluding that what is fundamental for the people of unincorporated territories, who have different traditions from a different civilization, are only those rights that are "basic to a free society," that are "implied in the concept of ordered liberty," the denial of which would "shock the conscience"? [75]

## The States and Individual Rights

I have been discussing individual rights that limit the freedom of the Federal Government to conduct foreign relations. The States do not conduct foreign relations, but the extent to which they can influence them * is also limited by constitutional safeguards for individual rights. Increasingly, the rights of the individual against infringement by the States have become virtually identical with those protected against the Federal Government. The original Constitution forbids the States *ex post facto* laws, bills of attainder, and laws impairing the obligation of contracts (Article I, section 10, clause 1). And while the Bill of Rights did not apply to the States,[76] virtually all of its provisions now do, having been "incorporated" in the Fourteenth Amendment.[77] The due process clause of that Amendment, in particular, affords procedural and substantive protections identical to those that by the same clause in the Fifth Amendment govern the Federal Government.**

It is particularly important to the conduct of foreign relations that the Fourteenth Amendment forbids the States to deny to any person the equal protection of the laws, and discriminations and distinctions which might be reasonable if made by the Federal Government might yet constitute denials of equal protection if established by a State.† The Equal Protection Clause has long protected aliens against state discriminations denying them equal right to common employment.[78] New doctrine giving new vitality to the equal protection clause has rendered alienage a "suspect classification" and requires a "compelling state interest" to support discriminations against aliens.[79] The alien has also found protection against the States in supreme federal law,

* See Chapter IX.

** See p. 255 above.

† See pp. 258–59 above.

principally the Civil Rights Acts, and Congressional protection held to be implied in the Immigration Laws admitting aliens to residence in the United States.[80]· In 1971 the Supreme Court held that a State may not deny an alien equal treatment as regards welfare assistance.[81]  And despite earlier cases suggesting the contrary,[82] the Constitution (or the unspoken will of Congress) may yet be read to require the States to allow aliens to practice law or medicine or hold public employment.

Aliens and other individuals have also found protection against state regulation in constitutional provisions not directly promoting individual rights, for example in the limitations of the Commerce Clause, in federal supremacy and preemption, in the new doctrine forbidding state intrusion into foreign relations. (Chapter IX).

# Chapter XI. CONCLUSION: OUR EIGHTEENTH CENTURY CONSTITUTION

"Your Constitution, sir, is all sail and no anchor." [1] If Macaulay's *mot* appears not quite *juste* as regards the Constitution as a whole, it would not be wholly inapt or unjust as applied to the prescriptions for the conduct of foreign relations. That is not because the Constitution has become so different from what it was: although, indeed, one cannot look twice in the same Constitution, and our own times have seen two periods of radical constitutional mutation, the constitutional law of foreign affairs has not changed wildly. It is not even, at bottom, that the conceptions of the Framers are insufficient to this day, although, obviously, the United States is changed, the world is changed, and relations between them are changed, in ways that "could not have been foreseen by the most gifted of its begetters." [2] The principal difficulty has been that, from the beginning, the compromises, irresolutions, oversights, and intentional silences of the Constitution left it unclear who had sail and who had rudder, and, most important, where is command. Inevitably the ship has been less than "tight" and the voyage often rocky, especially in the recurrent turbulences of international waters. In our day the uncertainties have been particularly troubling, perhaps only from our too-close perspective, perhaps because the stuff of foreign relations today seems to render ambiguity of authority and responsibility more dangerous.

The uncertainty should not be exaggerated: much is clear, and the relations of the United States are conducted every minute of every day with respectable efficiency within the constitutional framework. The President conducts foreign relations, and no one challenges his authority and responsibility even when

Congresses resolve and Congressmen travel and talk and televise. The President largely makes foreign policy, even if Congresses and Congressmen do not refrain from telling him what it ought to be. There is generally little disposition even to challenge his uses of troops for foreign relations purposes where they are not likely to become involved in fighting. At the other end of the axis, Congress alone clearly adopts domestic legislation, regulates foreign commerce, authorizes spending and appropriates money and—happily not often—makes war.

Of the uncertainties I have described in this volume many are lawyer's uncertainties and not unimportant to individuals occasionally affected by them, but they do not imply tension in the conduct of government or disturbance to relations with other nations. Whether the courts shall make law, in what circumstances, within what limits—as in Act of State; what respect judges owe to Executive declarations and suggestions, as in regard to sovereign immunity; what intrusions by the States the courts shall tolerate when the political branches have not spoken, as in inheritance laws to beat Communism with—none of these is beyond effective control if the political branches desire it. Even false, exasperating "issues," *e. g.*, whether, under the Constitution, the United States can adhere to human rights treaties, have not raised serious differences within the political branches or with other countries and have not been the important obstacles to new forms of international cooperation.*

Some of the uncertainties, no doubt, will be resolved by the courts. To some extent judicial diffidence in relation to foreign affairs has been the product of conceptualisms about sacrosanct "sovereignty," of unexamined assumptions reflected in incantations about "war and peace," of set habits of thought about international relations, about how they are conducted, about the "proper" role of courts in regard to them. But intellectual and judicial fashions change, and activist courts will strain at re-

---

* Even some of the issues of Separation, *e. g.*, executive privilege or Presidential impounding of funds (Chapter IV), do not themselves seriously disturb the process for conducting foreign relations though they often reflect turbulence in that process.

straints imposed by their predecessors. In a nation turning inward to face deep domestic problems, the old constitutional assumptions that foreign affairs are different and special may not survive unexamined. But, I believe, they will survive, essentially. Courts will not begin to intervene lightly in the foreign policy process. They will continue to protect the nation and extend the remedies available to it against frolics by the States, and they are not likely to keep their doors closed for long to claims of individual rights and freedoms affected by foreign relations. In such cases they will erode requirements of standing, attenuate the doctrine of political questions, enlarge the protections of the Bill of Rights. Even when "it is only money," they are likely to extend rights to compensation for losses resulting from foreign policy so that its costs will be borne not by the fortuitous "victim" alone but by the general taxpayer.

The abiding uncertainties lie principally—almost wholly—in the separation, distribution, fragmentation of powers between the President and Congress (or between President and Senate). Despite cycles of "isolation" and "intervention," despite recurrent assertions by Congressmen, the division of powers in the conduct of foreign relations is not, has not been, and cannot be what it is in domestic affairs. If it were possible to distinguish and divide "making foreign policy" from "conducting foreign relations," it is not the distinction and division lived by for soon 200 years. The President makes foreign policy patently—in recognizing states and governments and maintaining diplomatic relations with them, in asserting rights for the United States and reacting to the claims of others, in executive agreements, in "doctrines", declarations and commitments. He makes foreign policy in fact in the attitudes revealed and implied by what we say and what we do every minute of every day to every nation. On the other hand, the Constitution clearly gave Congress the ultimate foreign relations power, the power to go or not to go to war, major legislative powers integral to foreign policy (*e. g.*, to regulate foreign commerce), and a spending power that has become a principal tool in foreign as in domestic affairs. The division of power to make foreign policy between two branches

273

sometimes pulling in different directions, and, in particular, the separation of power to decide for war or peace from the power to make other foreign policy (and to use force short of war), have bred failures of cooperation and mutual interference, inefficiency, duplication and frustration, conflict and confusion.

Some of the uncertainties and conflicts, no doubt, arise out of different constitutional interpretations that might in theory be resolved: I do not think that they will soon be. The difficult issues come in clusters and during crises, in the context of a Cuba (1898) or Vietnam (1970), and those conditions are not conducive to constitutional deliberation. For their own part Congresses and Presidents are not more likely to resolve the issues than they have been, and each will no doubt continue to claim prerogatives in principle even when yielding them in practice. The courts, despite sometimes-misguided efforts to compel them to do so (as on Vietnam),* are not likely to step into in-

---

* Compare the state statutes designed to circumvent the Supreme Court's discretion on certiorari and "compel" it to hear objections to the constitutionality of the Vietnam War. The Massachusetts statute (1970 Laws, c. 174), for example, authorized the Attorney General to bring a proceeding in the name of the State alleging Presidential usurpation of Congressional power. (It sought, in effect, to persuade the Court to overrule Massachusetts v. Mellon, 262 U.S. 447 (1923), which held that a State's objection to Congressional usurpation was not justiciable.) Of course the original jurisdiction of the Supreme Court is also, in fact, optional and the Supreme Court refused the case. Massachusetts v. Laird, 400 U.S. 886 (1970). See Chapter VIII, note 12.

These statutes and proceedings were, in my view, misguided. They rang of the Eighteenth Century Kentucky and Virginia Resolutions and invoked reactionary and hopeless arguments of State rights to challenge federal policy. If the Court wished to consider the questions raised it had had ample opportunity to do so. Chapter VIII, notes 8, 18. If impelled to hear the issues, it might have held them to be political questions, Chapter VIII, p. 210. If it decided them on the merits, it would almost surely have upheld the legality of the President's action because authorized by Congress. Chapter IV, p. 101. Possibly the proponents did not wish to have the issues decided and indeed hoped the Court would not decide them, but sought to publicize and dramatize the issues in order to mobilize public support in opposition to the war.

tense confrontations between President and Congress, or inhibit either when the other does not object. Whether from the sense that the boundary between Congress and President (and between Senate and President, between executive agreement and treaty, between commitment and agreement), cannot be defined by law, whether from realization of the inherent limitations of judicial power or from prudence, whether under a doctrine of "political questions" or by other judicial devices and formulae for abstention, courts will not make certain what was left uncertain, will not curtail the power of the political branches, will not arbitrate their differences. Then, in time, the issues will recede, stirring neither controversy nor case. If the courts do speak to separation occasionally,* they will speak only delphically; hard cases will make as little law as possible,[3] as the Justices reach for the narrowest grounds; and the struggle and uncertainty will continue. The few old cases will remain, unreviewed and largely irrelevant. The Justices will not build and refine steadily case by case, will not develop clear philosophies, expertise or experts, only that confident sense that the deepest ills of the constitutional system are not theirs to cure.

Much of the controversy in the conduct of foreign affairs, moreover, is not due to constitutional uncertainty and issue, but is what the Constitution intended, and many differences between Congress and the President are not of constitutional dimension even when the Constitution is invoked in ritual incantation. If Congress refuses to authorize an ABM program requested by the President, or the President vetoes a tariff adopted by Congress, or the Senate refuses consent to a human rights treaty negotiated by the President, the controversy may

---

* As in the *Steel Seizure Case*, Chapter IV, p. 96, not strictly a foreign affairs case, and not one where Congress was deeply committed. While Congress had not granted the President power to seize plants in a labor dispute, while some Justices treated Congressional inaction as denying that power, Congress was not obviously and unalterably opposed to President Truman's initiative, and the Court's opinions deal with the President's powers as a legal question not as a political controversy.

be bitter but it does not involve competition for constitutional power—only the kind of conflict prescribed by the Constitution when it separated powers and subdivided functions. When the President exercises power which he holds concurrently and subject to the power of Congress, there may be controversy when Congress repudiates his initiative but it is not constitutional controversy. Neither are there constitutional issues for our purposes when the complaint is not that the Constitution has been violated but that it is not working very well.

That, I believe, was the lesson of the national *crise* over Vietnam that assumed the appearance of a constitutional crisis, and evoked soul-searching examination of the adequacy of the Constitution and proposals for its amendment. In my view Vietnam showed that, in important cases, "usurpation" of authority, as between the President and Congress, is not the real issue. Separation of powers, particularly the divisions of power in foreign relations, have always carried invitation to cooperation as well as to conflict, but the complexities of government have increased mutual dependence, making it virtually impossible for one branch long to pursue a course to which the other objects strongly. Surely, Presidents cannot use troops for any extended time and purpose, whether in war or far short of war, without Congressional acquiescence. And Congress cannot "sit it out," for whether it wishes or not, it shares responsibility if only because it has authority. The real complaint about Vietnam was not that the President usurped constitutional power but that, acting within his powers, he virtually compelled Congress to go along. That was a complaint against the Constitution. It is not the only respect in which in our constitutional system, one branch has been able to compel cooperation by another, or to use its dominance in one area to exact concessions in others, and that may even be what the Fathers contemplated.

The constitutional system for the conduct of foreign relations has chronic ailments. Some have asked whether, despite political modifications and adaptations, the constitutional framework, designed for a small new nation and reflecting 18th century political compromises and 18th century concern to prevent too-

strong government,* is sufficient to the United States today.[4]
There have been, and there are every day, numerous suggestions
for amending the Constitution, many only cosmetic, some radical; ** none seems clearly necessary or desirable, none seems
clearly worth the effort, few are likely to materialize in our
amendment-resisting Constitution.† For the conflict, confusion,
uncertainty, frustration, inefficiency and occasional national

---

* More than fifty years ago, Henry Adams said: "The fathers had
intended to neutralize the energy of government and had succeeded,
but their machine was never meant to do the work of a twenty-million
horse-power society in the twentieth century, where much work
needed to be quickly and efficiently done. . . . bad machinery
merely added to friction." THE EDUCATION OF HENRY ADAMS 375
(1918).

** The recurrent proposal to give the House an equal voice with
the Senate in treaty-making has much to commend it in principle but
is not directed at any problem that matters today, and is not likely to
be adopted. While the Senate has sometimes graciously granted the
House equality, it will not forego its privileged status as of right and
irrevocably. Presidents too are not eager to erect additional obstacles
to treaty making. More important, the amendment is unnecessary.
The Senate has not in recent years been a graveyard of treaties; there
have been few instances where one might expect that a treaty which
could not get the consent of two-thirds of the Senate would obtain a majority of both Houses; and, above all, the Constitution already effectively permits approval of international agreements by resolution of
Congress. See Chapter VI, p. 173.

† In almost 200 years there have been 26 amendments. The first
ten were part of the original "package," the price of ratification of
the Constitution; the thirteenth, fourteenth and fifteenth constituted
the peace treaty of the Civil War; the eighteenth (prohibition) and
the twenty-first largely canceled each other. Some of the rest are
patching or picayune, surely reflecting no major modification of the
system, *e. g.*, the twenty-fourth, outlawing the poll tax when it was
virtually defunct and about to be invalidated even without amendment.
(Compare Harper v. Virginia Board of Elections, 383 U.S. 663 (1966).)
Apart from the difficult process involved, one reason why the Constitution has hardly been amended is, no doubt, that without amendment the Supreme Court has read it differently as great need arose.
*E. g.*, NLRB v. Jones & Laughlin Steel Corp., 301 U.S. 1 (1937), Chapter III, note 6; Brown v. Board of Education, 347 U.S. 483 (1954).

detriment that comes from the "irregular" division of powers in the conduct of foreign relations will not be cured by tinkering or even by major surgery. If those who can amend the Constitution were all willing, if they could all agree on changes to be made, I do not believe they would succeed: the boundaries between President and Congress are fluid and cannot be defined or redefined; foreign affairs are not in fact separable and the machinery for running them cannot be isolated from the rest of government; nor could one transplant a new organ for the conduct of foreign affairs leaving the rest of the body politic as is.

I do not suggest that our system is the best of all possible systems or that it is working well, only that it cannot be effectively improved by constitutional amendment. Perhaps that reflects an impression that without constitutional amendment we muddle through, and a perhaps-tired conclusion that that is the best one can hope for in human government. Conflict never quite becomes all-out war, confusion is not quite chaos, frustration does not grind government to a standstill. Like the proverbial "love-hate" marriage, that of Congress and President goes on: that the tensions continue and recur, that the arguments, constitutional and political, repeat and reecho, may only suggest that it will go on. There are—and will be—strong Presidents and weak ones, assertive Congresses and acquiescent ones. The President wields power with few limits when Congress does not resist or protest; * Congress sometimes asserts power even when the President does resist or protest. At bottom, between as well as during controversies, each needs the other, and each knows how to convert the other's need into power. If reality, including the two-party system, has modified the theoretical separation of powers, if Congress has not been as successful in maintaining its prerogatives, if it cannot readily prevent, repeal, contradict or derogate from Presidential policy, occasional road blocks and threats of more serious ones, coupled with periodic

* President Truman is quoted as having said that the President's powers would have made Caesar or Genghis Khan or Napoleon bite his nails with envy. See C. ROSSITER, THE AMERICAN PRESIDENCY 30 (1960); see also U. S. PUBLIC PAPERS OF THE PRESIDENTS OF THE UNITED STATES: HARRY S. TRUMAN, 1952–53 1061 (1966).

reclamations of Congressional power, remind Presidents and other governments that ours is a unique, home-built contraption.

That under a less-than-certain and less-than-happy constitutional arrangement, the conduct of foreign relations continues to function is due in substantial part to infra- or extra-constitutional arrangements and accommodations. Congress has made its part more effective by various devices: standing committees and subcommittees, special committees, even joint committees of both Houses, are now permanent elements in the foreign policy machinery, and consultation between them and officials of the executive branch are integral to the foreign policy process. Committee staffs in particular observe, consult, negotiate with members of the Executive Branch daily and help shape executive decisions as well as legislation and other Congressional assertions of policy. Collaboration and coordination have become at least slogans, although the two branches are not always agreed on their import and the obligations they imply.

The quest must be for more and better cooperation, consultation, accommodation, by better legislative-executive *modi vivendi et operandi*. Vietnam, in particular, persuaded many that separating the authority to go to war from the authority to use other means of foreign policy has proved, or has become, unworkable, and that there is need to develop and improve institutions and procedures to mitigate the deficiencies of that constitutional conception.[5] Here "checks"—as by giving one branch a veto on the other—do not work very well. The need is for built-in "balances," for arrangements and procedures that will assure appropriate roles for both in the making of foreign policy. The Executive must learn to conduct foreign relations with less secrecy and greater responsibility. Congress must have a timely, honest, meaningful role, and the flow of information to fulfill it. Congress's part cannot be equal to the President's, but the constitutional conception (as well as the impulsions of a democratic foreign policy) suggest that the degree and kind of Congressional participation should increase as the means of foreign policy begin to include uses of force and to approach a national commitment to war, and as the cost of policy begins to loom large in the competition for national resources. But Congress will have to assert and demand a role. "Only Congress itself can prevent power from slipping through its fingers." [6]

Of course, cooperation is a good thing, and cooperation is surely better than conflict. In the history of our foreign affairs, periods of competition and cooperation have alternated, although since the Second World War, developing institutions, political forces, and the growing complexity of foreign relations have enhanced cooperation. But the Framers thought they had good reasons for prescribing limits to cooperation, even some conflict. If effective government, in foreign relations as elsewhere, requires cooperation, democratic government, in foreign relations as elsewhere, abhors Congressional abdication and often enjoins it to provide loyal opposition.[7] The President provides initiative and efficiency, and these are not to be depreciated. But the Congress is the more representative branch and brings to bear the influences of public opinion, diversity, concern for local and individual rights. At its best, of course, there is a counterpoint of Presidential expertise and some inexpert Congressional wisdom, producing foreign policy and foreign relations not always efficient but supporting larger, deeper national interests.

Whether by constitutional amendment or by new arrangements within or without the Constitution the quest must be for improved operation and cooperation, not for limitations on national responsibility or national power. One tragedy of Vietnam, I believe, was the impulse it gave to an impatient tendency to deal with political mistakes not by improving procedures and selecting better officials but by denying power to offices and institutions so they can be safely entrusted to mediocrity. We have not yet escaped the "republican tendency of reducing executive power." [8] "We fear to grant power and are unwilling to recognize it when it exists." [9] A dozen years ago, in a related context, I wrote: [10]

Many will have deep sympathy for those who dream of old days thought good, or better; who yearn for decentralization even in foreign affairs and matters of international concern, for limitations on federal power, for increase in the importance of the States; who thrill to a wild, poignant, romantic wish to turn back all the clocks, to unlearn the learnings, until the atom is unsplit, weapons unforged, oceans unnarrowed, the Civil War unfought. The wish remains idle, and the effort to diminish power in this area for fear that it may not be used wisely is quixotic, if not suicidal. It is not the moment to attempt it when all ability, flexibility, wisdom are needed for cooperation for survival by a frightened race, on a diminishing earth, reaching for the moon.

We have since reached the moon, but the lesson is yet to be learned.

There is a better known and more flattering judgment on the American Constitution than Macaulay's. Gladstone said: [11]

But, as the British Constitution is the most subtle organism which has proceeded from the womb and the long gestation of progressive history, so the American Constitution is, so far as I can see, the most wonderful work ever struck off at a given time by the brain and purpose of man.

There is no reason to believe that he excluded from his judgment the mechanism which the Framers struck off for the conduct of foreign relations. Today, after another hundred years of "progressive history," we can still accept his flattery, with a wry smile.

# NOTES

# ABBREVIATED CITATIONS

BUTLER, THE TREATY POWER
[C. BUTLER, THE TREATY-MAKING POWER OF THE UNITED STATES (1902)].

CORWIN, THE PRESIDENT
[E. CORWIN, THE PRESIDENT: OFFICE AND POWERS 1787–1957 (4th rev. ed. 1957)].

CRANDALL, TREATIES
[S. CRANDALL, TREATIES THEIR MAKING AND ENFORCEMENT (2d ed. 1916)].

ELLIOT'S DEBATES
[J. ELLIOT, ed., DEBATES IN THE SEVERAL STATE CONVENTIONS ON THE ADOPTION OF THE FEDERAL CONSTITUTION (1896)].

FALK, VIETNAM
[R. FALK, ed., THE VIETNAM WAR AND INTERNATIONAL LAW (1968–72)].

FARRAND
[M. FARRAND, THE RECORDS OF THE FEDERAL CONVENTION OF 1787 (rev. ed. 1937)].

THE FEDERALIST
[THE FEDERALIST, B. F. Wright ed., (1961)].

HAYDEN, TREATIES
[HAYDEN, THE SENATE AND TREATIES, 1789–1817 (1920)].

HEARINGS, NATIONAL COMMITMENTS
["U. S. Commitments to Foreign Powers," *Hearings on S. Res. 151 before the Senate Committee as Foreign Relations,* 90th Cong., 1st Sess. (1967)].

HEARINGS, SEPARATION OF POWERS
[*Hearings Before the Subcommittee on Separation of Powers of the Senate Committee on the Judiciary,* 90th Cong., 1st Sess. (1967)].

HENKIN, ARMS CONTROL
[L. HENKIN, ARMS CONTROL AND INSPECTION IN AMERICAN LAW (1958)].

Henkin, *Niagara*
[Henkin, *The Treaty Makers and the Law Makers: The Niagara Reservation,* 56 COLUM.L.REV. 1151 (1956)].

HOLT
[W. HOLT, TREATIES DEFEATED BY THE SENATE (1933)].

MALLOY, TREATIES

[W. MALLOY, TREATIES, CONVENTIONS, INTERNATIONAL ACTS, PROTOCOLS AND AGREEMENTS BETWEEN THE UNITED STATES OF AMERICA AND OTHER POWERS 1776–1909 (1910)].

McCLURE, INTERNATIONAL EXECUTIVE AGREEMENTS

[W. McCLURE, INTERNATIONAL EXECUTIVE AGREEMENTS: DEMOCRATIC PROCEDURE UNDER THE CONSTITUTION OF THE UNITED STATES (1941)].

MOORE, DIGEST

[J. B. MOORE, DIGEST OF INTERNATIONAL LAW (1906)].

Nobleman, ANNALS

[Nobleman, *Financial Aspects of Congressional Participation in Foreign Relations,* 289 ANNALS OF THE AMERICAN ACADEMY OF POLITICAL SCIENCE 145 (1953)].

RESTATEMENT

[AMERICAN LAW INSTITUTE, RESTATEMENT OF THE LAW (SECOND), FOREIGN RELATIONS LAW OF THE UNITED STATES (1965)].

RICHARDSON

[J. RICHARDSON, A COMPILATION OF THE MESSAGES AND PAPERS OF THE PRESIDENTS (1897 ed.)].

S. REP. NATIONAL COMMITMENTS

[SENATE COMMITTEE ON FOREIGN RELATIONS, NATIONAL COMMITMENTS, S.REP. No. 797, 90th Cong., 1st Sess. (1967)].

S. REP. SEPARATION OF POWERS

[SENATE COMMITTEE ON THE JUDICIARY, SEPARATION OF POWERS, S.Rep. No. 91–549, 91st Cong., 1st Sess. (1969)].

STORY, COMMENTARIES

[J. STORY, COMMENTARIES ON THE CONSTITUTION OF THE UNITED STATES (3d ed. 1858)].

WILLOUGHBY

[W. WILLOUGHBY, PRINCIPLES OF CONSTITUTIONAL LAW OF THE UNITED STATES (2d ed. 1929)].

WRIGHT

[Q. WRIGHT, THE CONTROL OF AMERICAN FOREIGN RELATIONS (1922)].

NOTES, INTRODUCTION, pp. 3 to 11.

1. I draw here on my article, *Constitutional Issues in Foreign Policy*, 23 J.INT'L AFF. 210 (1969).

2. But compare Mr. Justice Jackson concurring in Youngstown Sheet & Tube Co. v. Sawyer, 343 U.S. 579, 653 (1952): "That instrument must be understood as an Eighteenth-Century sketch of a government hoped for, not as a blueprint of the Government that is."

3. Compare the literature churned up by the Vietnam controversy. See Chapter IV, note 26.

4. See, for example, my article, *Some Reflections on Current Constitutional Controversy*, 109 U.PA.L.REV. 637, 638–50 (1961).

5. Writing between his two terms of service on the Supreme Court, Charles Evans Hughes said: "We are under a Constitution, but the Constitution is what the judges say it is, and the judiciary is the safeguard of our liberty and property under the Constitution." See C. E. HUGHES, ADDRESSES 185 (2d ed. 1916).

6. "We are not final because we are infallible, but we are infallible only because we are final." Mr. Justice Jackson concurring in Brown v. Allen, 344 U.S. 443, 540 (1953). Compare Cooper v. Aaron, 358 U.S. 1 (1958).

7. In constitutional questions, "when convinced of former error, this Court has never felt constrained to follow precedent." Smith v. Allwright, 321 U.S. 649, 665 (1944). In recent years the Court has been freely reexamining past decisions.

8. See, Henkin, *Some Reflections on Current Constitutional Controversy*, this Introduction, note 4.

NOTES, CHAPTER I, FEDERAL AUTHORITY, pp. 15 to 27.

1.  The "capacity to enter into relations with other States" is usually considered an essential qualification of statehood under international law. See, *e. g.*, Article 1 of the Convention on Rights and Duties of States, Montivideo, 1933, 49 Stat. 3097, T.S. No. 881.

2.  J. ROGERS, WORLD POLICING AND THE CONSTITUTION 14 (1945).

3.  See, *e. g.*, WRIGHT 132–34. Compare: "The Constitution confers absolutely on the government of the Union, the powers of making war, and of making treaties; consequently, that government possesses the power of acquiring territory, either by conquest or by treaty." American Ins. Co. v. Canter, 1 Pet. 516, 542 (U.S.1828). *Cf.* Cohens v. Virginia, 6 Wheat. 264, 415–16 (U.S.1821). Story speaks of powers that result not merely from aggregating enumerated powers but "from the aggregate powers of the national government." As an example he cites jurisdiction over conquered territory: "This would perhaps rather be a result from the whole mass of the powers of the national government, and from the nature of political society, than a consequence or incident of the powers specially enumerated." 2 J. STORY, COMMENTARIES ON THE CONSTITUTION 148 (5th ed. 1891), [hereinafter, STORY, COMMENTARIES]. See also Strong, J., in Legal Tender Cases, 12 Wall. 457, 534–35 (U.S.1870). But *cf.* 1 WILLOUGHBY § 54; compare note 5, this chapter.

It has been argued that all foreign affairs relate to war and peace and, except for what is expressly given the President, are the responsibility of Congress implied in or resulting from its power to declare war. Compare Chapter III, p. 83.

4.  And many, many variations on that theme, most often Marshall's reminder that "it is *a constitution* we are expounding." McCulloch v. Maryland, 4 Wheat. 316, 407 (U.S.1819).

5.  130 U.S. 581, 603–604 (1889). A year later the Court found that as a nation the United States had authority under international law to acquire territory by discovery and occupation and to exercise jurisdiction over it. Jones v. United States, 137 U.S. 202, 212 (1890). Compare Story, note 3, this chapter.

6.  299 U.S. 304 (1936). Sutherland had special interest and expertise in foreign relations. He had been United States Senator from the State of Utah and a member of the Senate Foreign Relations Committee, and had delivered lectures published as CONSTITUTIONAL POWERS AND WORLD AFFAIRS (1919). In 1909 he had written an article anticipating the distinction he here propounded: THE INTERNAL AND EXTERNAL POWERS OF THE NATIONAL GOVERNMENT, S.DOC.NO. 417,

61st Cong., 2d Sess. (1910). According to one writer, "a careful check indicates that the whole theory [of *Curtiss-Wright*] and a great amount of its phraseology had become engraved on Mr. Sutherland's mind before he joined the Court, waiting for the opportunity to be made the law of the land. The circumstances show that he had preformed opinions on the subject and that when he spoke in the *Curtiss-Wright* decision, he did little to reexamine his long cherished ideas." Levitan, *The Foreign Relations Power: An Analysis of Mr. Justice Sutherland's Theory*, 55 YALE L.J. 467, 478 (1946). For Sutherland's sources, see this chapter, note 10.

7. 299 U.S. at 315–18. The italics are Justice Sutherland's; some of his citations are omitted.

8. In other cases, it is not clear whether, according to my distinction, the Court is talking *Chinese Exclusion* or *Curtiss-Wright*: e. g.: "As a nation with all the attributes of sovereignty, the United States is vested with all the powers of government necessary to maintain an effective control of international relations." Burnet v. Brooks, 288 U. S. 378, 396 (1933). Or: "But there may be powers implied, necessary or incidental to the expressed powers. As a government, the United States is invested with all the attributes of sovereignty. As it has the character of nationality it has the powers of nationality, especially those which concern its relations and intercourse with other countries." Mackenzie v. Hare, 239 U.S. 299, 311 (1915). Compare Legal Tender Cases, 12 Wall. 457, 555 (U.S. 1870) (concurring opinion, Bradley, J.), with Perez v. Brownell, 356 U.S. 44, 58 (1958), quoted this chapter, note 14.

Sutherland's view need not depend on whether the Constitution was a compact among the States or among the people of the States. Compare McCulloch v. Maryland, 4 Wheat. 316, 403 (U.S.1819) (Marshall, C. J.). See also Chisholm v. Georgia, 2 Dall. 419, 471 (U.S.1793); Martin v. Hunter's Lessee, 1 Wheat. 304, 324–25 (U.S.1816).

9. See, *e. g.*, Levitan, *The Foreign Relations Power: An Analysis of Mr. Justice Sutherland's Theory*, this chapter, note 6.

10. Farrand reports that at the Constitutional Convention James Wilson of Pennsylvania "could not admit that when the colonies became independent of Great Britain they became independent also of each other." He read the Declaration of Independence to mean that they became independent "not *Individually* but *Unitedly*," and "were confederated as they were independent." 1 M. FARRAND, THE RECORDS OF THE FEDERAL CONVENTION OF 1787, at 324 (Rev. ed. 1966) [hereinafter cited as FARRAND]. Sutherland quotes King of Massachusetts: "The States were not 'sovereigns' in the sense contended for by some." 299 U.S. at 317. See also Mr. Justice Paterson in Penhallow v. Doane, 3 Dall. 54, 81 (U.S.1795); Chisholm v. Georgia, 2 Dall. 419, 470 (U.S.

1793). For other materials supporting Sutherland's position see Professor Richard Morris's testimony before a master in United States v. Maine, No. 35 Original, U.S.Sup.Ct., October Term 1972. He concludes that most of those who addressed themselves to the question at the Constitutional Convention, most of the early Justices of the Supreme Court, and the principal Founding Fathers took the "nationalist" view.

For materials on the other side see generally Van Tyne, *Sovereignty in the American Revolution: An Historical Study*, 12 AM.HIST.REV. 529 (1907); See also the array of opposing views in C. BUTLER, THE TREATY-MAKING POWER OF THE UNITED STATES §§ 137–41 and §§ 142–43 (1902) [hereinafter cited as BUTLER, THE TREATY POWER]. Essentially, the case against Sutherland consists of Luther Martin's statement, FARRAND 323; Mr. Justice Iredell in *Penhallow*, 3 Dall. at 94, who might have granted that in war the Continental Congress "stood, like Jove, amidst the deities of old, paramount, and supreme" (Paterson, J., *id.* at 81), but thought that Congress had power because the States delegated it. Compare Mr. Justice Chase in Ware v. Hylton, 3 Dall. 199, 224, 231; also Marshall, C. J., in Gibbons v. Ogden, 9 Wheat. 1, 187 (U.S.1824); and the discussion of the nature of the Confederation in THE FEDERALIST No. 43 (Madison); also Talbot v. The Commanders, 1 Dall. 95, 99 (High Ct. of Err. and App., Pa.1784); People v. Gerke, 5 Cal. 381, 385 (1855).

The language of the Declaration lends some support to the view that thirteen independent sovereign states were declared, and some States followed with individual declarations of their own independence. See also the assertions of sovereignty in early state constitutions, *e. g.*, CONN.CONST.PREAMBLE (1776); MASS.CONST. part. I, art. IV (1780); N.H.CONST. part I, art. VII (1784). The Articles of Confederation provided: "Each state retains its sovereignty, freedom and independence, and every Power, Jurisdiction and right, which is not by this confederation expressly delegated to the United States, in Congress assembled." (Article II).

Some of the States appointed agents and negotiated with foreign countries for money and arms. See, *e. g.*, Benjamin Franklin's complaint against their competition with his efforts, in a letter to the Congressional Committee of Foreign Affairs, dated May 26, 1779, quoted in 3 F. WHARTON, THE REVOLUTIONARY DIPLOMATIC CORRESPONDENCE OF THE UNITED STATES 192 (1889). (Apparently the practice did not wholly stop with the Articles of Confederation which forbade the States, without the consent of Congress, to send or receive "any embassy" (Art. VI).) Although individual States did not, it seems, conclude treaties with foreign countries, the treaties with France in 1778 were executed between "The Most Christian King, and the thirteen United States of North America" (the word "thirteen" is omitted from one of the treaties), each of them mentioned by name, and they were ratified by each of the individual States; in various respects the terms of the treaties seem to treat each of the thirteen as a separate sovereign. 1 W. MALLOY (ed.), TREATIES, CONVENTIONS, INTERNATIONAL ACTS, PROTOCOLS AND AGREEMENTS BETWEEN THE UNITED STATES OF AMERICA AND OTHER POWERS 1776–1909, S.DOC. No. 357, 61st Cong., 2d Sess. at 468, 479 (1910) [hereinafter cited as MALLOY, TREATIES]. Later, the Continental Congress adopted a resolution to instruct its negotiators "That these United States be considered in all such treaties, and in every case arising under them as one nation, upon the principles of the Federal constitution." 3 SECRET JOURNALS OF CONGRESS 452, March 26, 1784. See J. G. Davis's notes to Samuel Miller's LECTURES ON THE CONSTITUTION OF THE UNITED STATES 53–54 (Davis ed. 1891); Davis's notes at 36–58, were perhaps a source of Sutherland's theory; compare also 1 WILLOUGHBY 90, 514–16.

On the whole there is perhaps no disagreement that under the Articles the States retained no external sovereignty. It is not agreed whether the States had sovereignty before the Articles, whether under the Articles they could have gained (or regained) sovereignty at will, whether sovereignty passed directly from the United States under the Articles to the United States under the Constitution. On these questions, too, Sutherland may have the better of the argument for from independence nationhood seems to have been the dominant pattern and manifestations of state autonomy exceptional. Of course, at what time the United States became one state in international society has had only historic interest since events and actions prior to 1789 ceased to raise issues, but some States have recently claimed that they had had sovereignty then as a basis for claiming title to sea-bed off their coasts. Compare the arguments in the *Maine* case, *supra*.

11. Compare Taney, C. J.: "The states, by the adoption of the existing Constitution, have become divested of all their national attributes, except such as relate purely to their internal concerns." Holmes v. Jennison, 14 Pet. 540, 550 (U.S.1840). Compare note 14, this chapter.

12. Between *The Chinese Exclusion Case* and *Curtiss-Wright* the Court had rejected claims of federal power inherent in sovereignty where foreign affairs were not at issue. Kansas v. Colorado, 206 U. S. 46 (1907) (dismissing U.S. petition to intervene on ground it had inherent legislative authority to appropriate navigable waters). Compare *Ex parte* Quirin, 317 U.S. 1, 25 (1942) ("Congress and the President, like the courts, possess no power not derived from the Constitution.")

13. At one time, the people of the United States divided sharply on issues of national power, reflecting in part different views as to the sources of power; certainly the kind of opinion written, in some cases perhaps too the result, would have been different for different lawyers. Whether the United States could acquire the Philippines, for example, seemed to some at the time to depend on whether the powers of the United States derived exclusively from the Constitution and its enumerations or might be sought also in international law and practice. See, *e. g.*, E. STAWWOOD, A HISTORY OF THE PRESIDENCY: 1897–1916 26 (1916).

14. Later restatements, however, tacitly avoid some of Sutherland's "underpinnings." In *Perez* v. *Brownell*, for example, the Court, by Mr. Justice Frankfurter, said: "The States that joined together to form a single Nation and to create, through the Constitution, a Federal Government to conduct the affairs of that Nation must be held to have granted that Government the powers indispensable to its functioning effectively in the company of sovereign nations." 356 U.S. 44, 57 (1958), *overruled* in Afroyim v. Rusk, 387 U.S. 253 (1967). Neither the dissent in *Perez* nor the overruling majority in *Afroyim* questioned the *Curtiss-Wright* element in Frankfurter's opinion. Mr. Justice Jackson, concurring in *Youngstown Sheet & Tube Co.* v. *Sawyer*, referred to Sutherland's essay as "dictum," 343 U.S. 579, 635–36 n. 2 (1952). See Chapter III, p. 75 and note 39.

15. 299 U.S. at 318, citing Jones v. United States, 137 U.S. 202, 212 (1890); Fong Yue Ting v. United States, 149 U.S. 698, 705 *et seq.* (1893); B. Altman & Co. v. United States, 224 U.S. 583, 600–601 (1912).

16. The Chinese Exclusion Case, 130 U.S. 581 (1889); United States v. Bowman, 260 U.S. 94 (1922); compare Burnet v. Brooks, 288 U.S. 378 (1933).

17. Hines v. Davidowitz, 312 U.S. 52 (1941); Perez v. Brownell, 356 U.S. 44 (1958), *overruled* in Afroyim v. Rusk, 387 U.S. 253 (1967); Zemel v. Rusk, 381 U.S. 1 (1965).

18. *Cf.* N.L.R.B. v. Jones & Laughlin Steel Corp., 301 U.S. 1 (1937), Chapter III, notes 6, 8, and West Coast Hotel Co. v. Parrish, 300 U.S. 379 (1937); in a few years, also United States v. Darby, 312 U. S. 100 (1941), and Wickard v. Filburn, 317 U.S. 111 (1942); see Chapter VIII, note 16. Since then the Court has extended the powers of Congress to new reaches, *e. g.*, Heart of Atlanta Motel v. United States, 379 U.S. 241 (1964) (commerce clause); Katzenbach v. McClung, 379 U.S. 294 (1964) (commerce clause) (Chapter III, note 7); Katzenbach v. Morgan, 384 U.S. 641 (1966) (Fourteenth Amendment); South Carolina v. Katzenbach, 383 U.S. 301 (1966) (Fifteenth Amendment); Jones v. Alfred H. Mayer Co., 392 U.S. 409 (1968) (Thir-

teenth Amendment).   See Chapter III, note 53;  Chapter X, p. 252.
While in cases limiting the power of Congress to provide trial by court-
martial the Court seemed to narrow the scope of the "necessary and
proper" clause, it was in effect only sustaining the jury requirement of
the Bill of Rights.   See Chapter III, note 54.   Only the power to extend the right to vote in state elections to eighteen year olds has been
denied Congress.   Oregon v. Mitchell, 400 U.S. 112 (1970).

19.   Compare Henkin, *Some Reflections on Current Constitutional
Controversy*, 109 U.PA.L.REV. 637, 645–46 (1961).

20.   Compare Banco Nacional de Cuba v. Sabbatino, 376 U.S. 398
(1964), Chapter VIII, p. 217.   That the Court thought executive power readily distinguishable from legislative power, see Youngstown
Sheet & Tube Co. v. Sawyer, 343 U.S. 579 (1952), discussed in Introduction to Chapter II, p. 32, and in Chapter IV, p. 96.

NOTES, INTRODUCTION TO CHAPTER II, DISTRIBUTION OF POWER, pp. 31 to 35.

1. 299 U.S. 304, 316 (1936).

2. "The doctrine of the separation of powers was adopted by the Convention of 1787, not to promote efficiency but to preclude the exercise of arbitrary power. The purpose was, not to avoid friction, but, by means of the inevitable friction incident to the distribution of the governmental powers among three departments, to save the people from autocracy." Mr. Justice Brandeis dissenting in Myers v. United States, 272 U.S. 52, 293 (1926). See also Madison in THE FEDERALIST NOS. 47, 51. Compare Madison: ". . . if there is a principle in our constitution, indeed in any free Constitution, more sacred than another, it is that which separates the legislative, executive, and judicial powers." 1 ANNALS OF CONG. 604 (1789); see also *id.*, at 516–17.

Madison devoted one of the Federalist papers to showing that "unless these departments be so far connected and blended as to give to each a constitutional control over the others, the degree of separation which the maxim requires, as essential to a free government, can never in practice be duly maintained." THE FEDERALIST NO. 48 at 343 (Madison). Compare: "The actual art of governing under our Constitution does not and cannot conform to judicial definitions of the power of any of its branches based on isolated clauses or even single Articles torn from context. While the Constitution diffuses power the better to secure liberty, it also contemplates that practice will integrate the dispersed powers into a workable government. It enjoins upon its branches separateness but interdependence, autonomy but reciprocity." Mr. Justice Jackson concurring in Youngstown Sheet & Tube Co. v. Sawyer, 343 U.S. 579, 635 (1952). Compare also *Ex parte* Grossman, 267 U.S. 87, 119–20 (1925).

3. Youngstown Sheet & Tube Co. v. Sawyer, 343 U.S. 579 (1952). That, at least, was the view of Justice Black in an opinion for a majority of the Court, though some of that majority seemed to go along on other grounds. Compare the concurring opinions of Frankfurter and Jackson, *id.* at 593, 634, discussed Chapter IV, note 11. That Separation requires the branches to be "forever separate and distinct" and forbids usurpation, see also Springer v. Philippine Islands, 277 U.S. 189, 201–202 (1928); *cf.* Kilbourn v. Thompson, 103 U.S. 168, 182, 190–91 (1881).

But compare Mr. Justice Holmes dissenting in *Springer*, at 209: "The great ordinances of the Constitution do not establish and divide fields of black and white. Even the more specific of them are found to terminate in a penumbra shading gradually from one extreme to the other." And compare note 2 this Introduction.

4. Subject, of course, to the limitations of the Bill of Rights. That acting together Congress and the President can exercise all federal political powers, *cf.* Hamilton v. Dillin, 21 Wall. 73, 88 (U.S.1875); Wilson v. Shaw, 204 U.S. 24, 32 (1907). Acting together the President and Congress can do what neither can do alone—for example, make international agreements fully equivalent to a treaty. See Chapter VI, p. 173.

5. It has been argued that the power of Congress to declare war is not a legislative power and can be exercised without the concurrence of the President. See, *e. g.*, Senator Morgan of Alabama, 28 CONG. REC. 2107 (1896); *contra*, C. BERDAHL, WAR POWERS OF THE EXECUTIVE IN THE UNITED STATES 95 (1921); see generally Baldwin, *The Share of the President of the United States in a Declaration of War*, 12 AM.J.INT'L L. 1 (1918). The issue has remained hypothetical since all declarations of war were made in response to Presidential request. On the relation of the President's authority to that of Congress as regards waging war see pp. 100, 107, Chapter IV.

6. And even before the Articles. See, *e. g.*, Mr. Justice Paterson in Penhallow v. Doane, 3 Dall. 54, 80 (U.S.1795).

7. ARTICLES OF CONFEDERATION, Arts. V, IX.

8. See Chapter I, p. 23 and note 10. The "retrograde from unity" and the inability of the Continental Congress to enforce its treaties are described in 1 BUTLER, THE TREATY POWER §§ 164, 165 (1902). Unhappiness with state disregard of treaties was repeatedly voiced at the Constitutional Convention (see 1 FARRAND 164, 171, 316; 3 *id.* at 113, 548), and was a particular impetus to the explicit establishment of the supremacy of treaties. (Art. VI, sec. 2; see Chapter V.)

9. Compare generally C. THACH, THE CREATION OF THE PRESIDENCY, 1775–1789 (1923).

NOTES, CHAPTER II, THE PRESIDENT, pp. 37 to 65.

1. United States v. Curtiss-Wright Export Corp., 299 U.S. 304, 320 (1936). Similar statements abound.

2. For a good survey of the President's powers in foreign affairs, with attention to selected issues, see CORWIN, THE PRESIDENT, Chapter V; his other chapters are not irrelevant. Antecedents and early constitutional conceptions of the office are discussed in his Chapter I.

3. For an early appeal to the President's conscience, compare Marbury v. Madison, 1 Cranch 137, 165–66 (U.S.1803).

4. See Chapter VIII, pp. 220–21. Compare the suggestion of Harlan, J., dissenting, in *The Pentagon Papers Case* that the courts should give effect to classifications of documents if made by the Head of the Department. New York Times Co. v. United States, 403 U.S. 713, 757–58 (1971), Chapter X, note 9.

5. T. ROOSEVELT, AN AUTOBIOGRAPHY 371–72 (MacMillan ed. 1914).

6. W. H. TAFT, OUR CHIEF MAGISTRATE AND HIS POWERS 143–47 (1916). See also 45 CONG.REC. 6067–69 (1910) (remarks of Senators Borah and Bacon) and 54 CONG.REC. 863–82 (1917) (remarks of Senator Work). But President Truman seemed to echo Theodore Roosevelt in 2 MEMOIRS 472–73 (1956); he doesn't even suggest that he is limited by what Congress forbids him.

An even more radical view of Presidential power, at least in time of war, was expressed by Franklin D. Roosevelt in his famous message demanding that Congress repeal a provision of the Emergency Price Control Act:

> I ask the Congress to take this action by the first of October. Inaction on your part by that date will leave me with an inescapable responsibility to the people of this country to see to it that the war effort is no longer imperiled by threat of economic chaos.
>
> In the event that the Congress should fail to act, and act adequately, I shall accept the responsibility, and I will act.
>
> The President has the powers, under the Constitution and under Congressional acts, to take measures necessary to avert a disaster which would interfere with the winning of the war.
>
> I have given the most thoughtful consideration to meeting this issue without further reference to the Congress. I have determined, however, on this vital matter to consult with Congress. . . .
>
> The American people can be sure that I will use my powers with a full sense of my responsibility to the Constitution and

to my country. The American people can also be sure that I shall not hesitate to use every power vested in me to accomplish the defeat of our enemies in any part of the world where our own safety demands such defeat.

When the war is won, the powers under which I act automatically revert to the people—to whom they belong.

88 Cong.Rec. 7044 (1942), quoted and discussed in Corwin, The President 250–52.

7. Youngstown Sheet & Tube Co. v. Sawyer, 343 U.S. 579 (1952). But some of the Justices who constituted the majority, though they joined Justice Black's opinion, apparently considered that Congress had in fact tacitly forbidden the President to seize the steel mills. See Chapter IV, note 11.

8. Some of the arguments that follow are in Wright 146–50.

9. In his famous "Pacificus" letter supporting Washington's power to proclaim neutrality. See 7 A. Hamilton, Works 76, 81 (Hamilton ed. 1851).

The debate between "Pacificus" and "Helvidius" (Madison) is set forth and discussed in E. Corwin, The President's Control of Foreign Relations 8–27 (1917). He also reproduces there an early-twentieth-century replay, between Senator Spooner and Senator Bacon, *id.* at 169–204. See also 60 Cong.Rec. 1417–21 (1906).

10. Montesquieu saw two different kinds of executive power: "*la puissance exécutrice des choses qui dépendent du droit des gens, et la puissance exécutrice de celles qui dépendent du droit civil.*" By the former, "*il fait la paix ou la guerre, envoit ou reçoit des ambassades, établit la sureté, prévient les invasions.*" 1 Montesquieu, De L'Esprit des Lois, Livre XI, C. VI (Amable LeRoy, ed.) (Lyon, 1805). He, as well as Rousseau and Blackstone, saw foreign relations as properly the function of the monarch. Compare Blackstone, Commentaries * 253–54. Locke spoke of the "federative" power as distinct from the executive power but saw them as belonging in the same hands. The Second Treatise of Civil Government, Chapter XII, §§ 143–48 (Gateway ed. 1968). Vattel, however, noted that some rulers are obliged to take the advice of a senate, or of the representatives of the nation. The Law of Nations, Book II, Chapter XII; Book III, Chapter I; Book IV, Chapter II (Ingraham ed. 1883). Blackstone, Locke and Montesquieu are quoted in Corwin, The President 416–18. In The Federalist No. 75, at 476, Hamilton said that the power to make treaties seems "to form a distinct department, and to belong, properly, neither to the legislative nor to the executive."

Jefferson, too, hardly an exponent of expansive constitutional construction or of large Presidential power, wrote: "The transaction of business with foreign nations is *Executive altogether*. It belongs, then, to the head of that department except as to such portions of it as are specially submitted to the Senate. *Exceptions are to be construed strictly.*"    5 T. JEFFERSON, WRITINGS 162 (Ford ed. 1892) (emphasis in original).

11.    Hamilton continued:

The enumeration ought therefore to be considered, as intended merely to specify the principal articles implied in the definition of executive power; leaving the rest to flow from the general grant of that power, interpreted in conformity with other parts of the Constitution, and with the principles of free government.

The general doctrine of our Constitution then is, that the *executive power* of the nation is vested in the President; subject only to the *exceptions* and *qualifications*, which are expressed in the instrument. (Emphasis in original).

7 HAMILTON, WORKS 76, 81. See also J. Q. Adams in THE JUBILEE OF THE CONSTITUTION 70–71, 76 (1839).

12.    6 J. MADISON, WRITINGS 138, 147–50 (Hunt ed. 1910).    Madison insisted that under the Constitution foreign relations are rather legislative in character, pointing to the powers of Congress to regulate foreign commerce and declare war; even the treaty power, he said, is more legislative than executive.    Compare Chapter III, p. 82 and Chapter V, p. 130.    Earlier, however, in 1789, in the House of Representatives, Madison had argued that the power to remove officials was "in its nature" an "executive power" belonging to the President. See 1 ANNALS OF CONG. 378–80, 461–64 (1789).    Compare Chief Justice Taft in the *Myers* case, this chapter, note 14.

Madison's reply to Hamilton was apparently instigated by Jefferson.    See 6 JEFFERSON, WRITINGS 338 (Ford ed. 1892.)    Perhaps Jefferson was rejecting not Hamilton's reading of the "executive power" clause, which Jefferson also seemed to accept (see this chapter, note 10), but Hamilton's attempt to put so much power into it. Or perhaps Jefferson, like Madison (and indeed like Hamilton, in reverse, compare this chapter, p. 41), had changed his views.    See generally CORWIN, THE PRESIDENT 177–82.

For others opposing Hamilton's reading of the "executive Power" clause see the Senate debate, note 9 this chapter; and compare the statements of Webster and Calhoun quoted in CORWIN, THE PRESIDENT at 321–22.    Taft, who later, as Chief Justice, invoked "executive power" in *Myers*, had rejected it as a blanket grant of foreign affairs powers.    See Taft, this chapter, note 6, at 73, 140, 144.

13.    But compare the Court's finding that there is an inherent executive power to exclude aliens, this chapter, note 31.    And compare the discussion of Presidential power in New York Times Co.

v. United States, 403 U.S. 713 (1971), for example in the opinion of Marshall, J., concurring, *id.* at 740.

14. Myers v. United States, 272 U.S. 52, 128 (1926). But *cf.* Holmes, J., dissenting, *id.* at 177, and McReynolds, J., dissenting, *id.* at 178, 183. And see note 19, this chapter.

Compare Kansas v. Colorado, 206 U.S. 46, 81–82 (1907), where Mr. Justice Brewer based an argument similar to Hamilton's on the absence of the words "herein granted" in Article III, to support a broad judicial power.

15. Youngstown Sheet & Tube Co. v. Sawyer, 343 U.S. 579 (1952). Only Chief Justice Vinson dissenting says: "The whole of the 'executive power' is vested in the President," and speaks of "This comprehensive grant of the executive power." *Id.* at 681–82.

16. 343 U.S. at 641. See also Mr. Justice Douglas concurring, *id.* at 632.

17. In the *Steel Seizure Case*, 343 U.S. at 634–35, Mr. Justice Jackson also said:

> A judge, like an executive adviser, may be surprised at the poverty of really useful and unambiguous authority applicable to concrete problems of executive power as they actually present themselves. Just what our forefathers did envision, or would have envisioned had they foreseen modern conditions, must be divined from materials almost as enigmatic as the dreams Joseph was called upon to interpret for Pharaoh. A century and a half of partisan debate and scholarly speculation yields no net result but only supplies more or less apt quotations from respected sources on each side of any question. They largely cancel each other. And the court decisions are indecisive because of the judicial practice of dealing with the largest questions in the most narrow way.
> (Footnote omitted.)

Those who insist that foreign relations are primarily the responsibility of Congress, Chapter III, p. 81, might argue that when Congress has not said no, the President acts by tacit delegation from Congress. Compare the argument that in some cases Congress silently authorizes the States to regulate commerce. See, *e. g.,* Southern Pacific Co. v. Arizona, 325 U.S. 761, 768 (1945), citing Dowling, *Interstate Commerce and State Power,* 27 VA.L.REV. 1 (1940), Chapter IX, p. 235. But the latter argument developed because the Constitution gave Congress the power to regulate commerce, and tacit delegation by Congress could explain why States can do some things that are admittedly regulations of commerce. While there may be instances where tacit delegation by Congress to the President is a reasonable inference from circumstances (*cf.* United States v. Midwest Oil Co.,

236 U.S. 459 (1915)), in general the President purports to act in foreign affairs on his own authority. In some cases, admittedly, his power is secondary to that of Congress and bows to it when conflict occurs. See Chapter IV, p. 104.

18. Marshall's statement in the House of Representatives, 10 ANNALS OF CONG. 613 (1800), reprinted in 5 Wheat.Appendix note 1, at 26 (U.S.1820), has been repeatedly cited and invoked by the Supreme Court, *e. g.*, in United States v. Curtiss-Wright Export Corp., 299 U.S. 304, 319 (1936). Marshall was justifying an extradition to Great Britain of one Jonathan Robbins, assumed to be an American citizen; since a request for extradition involved "a national demand made upon the nation" it could only be made on the President since he was the sole channel of communication.

Compare Jefferson's letter to the French Minister Genêt:

> [The President] being the only channel of communication between this country and foreign nations, it is from him alone that foreign nations or their agents are to learn what is or has been the will of the nation; and whatever he communicates as such, they have a right, and are bound to consider as the expression of the nation, and no foreign agent can be allowed to question it. . . .

6 T. JEFFERSON, WRITINGS 451 (Ford ed. 1895).

Literally, at least, both Marshall and Jefferson spoke of the President as the sole organ of communication and did not imply any power to make foreign policy. Substantive power was later read into the phrase, *e. g.*, by Sutherland in *Curtiss-Wright*, 299 U.S. at 319–21, quoted this chapter, p. 37. Earlier, in justifying the President's treaty-making role, Hamilton had referred to "the constitutional agency of the President in the conduct of foreign negotiations." THE FEDERALIST No. 75, at 477.

19. And Congress could not constitutionally ordain otherwise. Myers v. United States, 272 U.S. 52 (1926), this chapter note 14. Andrew Johnson invited impeachment and was nearly convicted when he removed his Secretary of War Stanton in the face of the Tenure of Office Act of 1867. See CORWIN, THE PRESIDENT 64–66 and notes. The Supreme Court in *Myers* expressly upheld President Johnson, 272 U.S. at 164–76.

*Myers* has not been followed as to an appointee to an office which is not "purely executive," "who occupies no place in the executive department and who exercises no part of the executive power vested by the Constitution in the President." Humphrey's Ex'r v. United States, 295 U.S. 602, 627–28 (1935); Wiener v. United States, 357 U.S. 349 (1958).

20. Even from Congress, see Chapter IV. On the right to withhold from the public see *The Pentagon Papers Case*, Chapter X, note 9.

The authority of the President over his department of foreign affairs was recognized by the first Congress;

> That there shall be an Executive department, to be denomi- . nated the Department of Foreign Affairs, and that there shall be a principal officer therein, to be called the Secretary for the Department of Foreign Affairs, who shall perform and execute such duties as shall from time to time be enjoined on or intrusted to him by the President of the United States, agreeable to the Constitution, relative to correspondences, commissions or instructions to or with public ministers or consuls, from the United States, or to negotiations with public ministers from foreign states or princes, or to memorials or other applications from foreign public ministers or other foreigners, or to such other matters respecting foreign affairs, as the President of the United States shall assign to the said department; and furthermore, that the said principal officer shall conduct the business of the said department in such manner as the President of the United States shall from time to time order or instruct.

Act of July 27, 1789, 1 Stat. 28–29.

Congress also supported the President's monopoly on communications by the early "Logan Act" entitled "An Act to Prevent Usurpation of Executive Functions," making it a crime for any person to correspond with a foreign nation with an intent to influence its conduct in relation to a controversy with the United States. Act of January 30, 1799, c. 1, 1 Stat. 613 (now 18 U.S.C. § 953 (1970)); see Chapter III, note 30. See Warren, *Memorandum on the History and Scope of the Laws Prohibiting Correspondence with a Foreign Government*, S.DOC.NO. 696, 64th Cong., 2d Sess. (1917), and CORWIN, THE PRESIDENT 183–84 and notes.

21. Attorneys General early upheld the President's power to appoint special agents without Senate confirmation. See, *e. g.*, 1 OP. ATT'Y GEN. 65, 186, 204–206, 212–13 (1855). In the first century of the nation's existence more than 400 Presidential agents were appointed. S.DOC.NO. 231, 56th Cong., 2d Sess., part 8, at 337–62 (1901); H.R.DOC.NO. 387, 66th Cong., 1st Sess., part 2, at 5 (1919). The Senate has sometimes denied the President's power to appoint persons to negotiate agreements or carry on diplomatic negotiations without having them confirmed by the Senate. See Chapter V, note 24. Presidential agents are often paid out of the President's "contingency fund" for which he does not have to account. See 31 U.S.C. §§ 54, 107 (1970). See, generally, Wriston, *The Special Envoy*, 38 FOREIGN AFFAIRS 219 (1960); H. WRISTON, EXECUTIVE AGENTS IN AMERICAN FOREIGN RELATIONS (1929).

22.   Compare note, p. 45, this chapter.

23.   U.S.CONST. art. II, sec. 3.   That includes "all possible diplomatic agents which any foreign power may accredit to the United States." 7 OP.ATT'Y GEN. 209 (1871).   Compare *In re* Baiz, 135 U.S. 403, 431–32 (1890).

24.   That was Madison's view in his "Helvidius" letter, this chapter, note 12.   See Chapter III, p. 82, and especially note 70.   But President Truman is reported to have said, "I make American Foreign Policy."   L. KOENIG, THE CHIEF EXECUTIVE 211 (1964).   See generally Chapter IV.

25.   Traditional international law required neutrality of those who sought its benefits but a nation could lawfully decide to become a belligerent.   It can be argued that the laws of neutrality and belligerency have been modified if not superseded by the UN Charter outlawing war.   See Chapter VII, note 6.

That the President has authority to recognize belligerency, see, *e. g.*, Secretary of State John Quincy Adams quoted in Wright, *The Power to Declare Neutrality Under American Law*, 34 AM.J.INT'L L. 302, 308 (1940).   See The Prize Cases, 2 Black 635, 670 (U.S.1862) (President can accord a status of belligerency to those who attack the United States); *cf.* United States v. Palmer, 3 Wheat. 610, 643 (U.S. 1818).   Members of Congress have differed on the President's authority, some denying it because such recognition had commercial and other domestic consequences.   See, *e. g.*, 28 CONG.REC. 2121; for the opposite view, see *id.* at 2164.   Some thought that the power to recognize belligerency or the independence of foreign nations is a "joint power."   *Id.* at 3078.   See also Hale, *Power to Recognize the Independence of a New Foreign State*, S.DOC.NO. 56, 54th Cong., 2d Sess. 28 (1897).

26.   Washington ordered prosecutions for transgressions of neutrality as violations of international law.   11 Stat. 753 (App.1859), 1 MESSAGES AND PAPERS OF THE PRESIDENTS 148–49 (Richardson ed. 1897) [hereinafter cited as RICHARDSON].   The word "neutrality" was ultimately omitted from Washington's proclamation by way of concession to Jefferson.   See Letter to James Madison, June 23, 1793, 6 T. JEFFERSON, WRITINGS 315–16 (Ford ed. 1895).   While the Act of 1794 can be seen as domestic legislation implementing and effectively ratifying Washington's neutrality proclamation, later Presidents eschewed declaring neutrality on their own authority and Congress has since both declared and implemented neutrality.   See Chapter III, pp. 81 and 85, and note 64.

That F. D. Roosevelt deviated from Congressional neutrality policy, compare CORWIN, THE PRESIDENT 202–204, 238–39.   Compare his decision to send troops to Greenland and Iceland, apparently in the face of legislation forbidding it.   See Chapter IV, p. 106.

Some might find in the *Curtiss-Wright* case, quoted Chapter I, p. 19, an implication that the President might have imposed an arms embargo on his own authority; surely, he could not have enacted criminal penalties for its violation. See Chapter IV, p. 95.

27. See Presidential Proclamation No. 2667, Sept. 28, 1945, 10 FED. REG. 12303 (1945); see generally L. HENKIN, LAW FOR THE SEA'S MINERAL RESOURCES (1968). While the President can act to acquire territory under international law he probably cannot, acting alone, incorporate such territory into the United States. See Chapter IV, p. 97.

28. "That the President's control of foreign relations includes the settlement of claims is indisputable." Frankfurter, J., concurring in United States v. Pink, 315 U.S. 203, 240 (1942). Compare the majority opinion, *id.* at 229. The President, however, probably cannot dispose of United States property without authority from Congress. See Chapter IV, p. 95, and compare Chapter VI, p. 180.

The President accounts to other nations for the treatment of their nationals in the United States, but the protection of aliens in fact depends largely on the judiciary and on the States. Compare 1 OP. ATT'Y GEN. 25 (1792); 3 OP.ATT'Y GEN. 253 (1837). See Chapters VIII, IX.

29. But the Supreme Court has denied the President's power to extradite on his own authority, Chapter IV, p. 98. An Attorney General rendered the opinion that in the absence of treaty the President could extend to the German Government the privilege of taking the testimony of prisoners in federal prisons but not in state prisons. 17 OP.ATT'Y GEN. 565 (1883).

Presidential responses to foreign overtures often can be seen as involving informal executive agreements. Compare Chapter VI, p. 187.

30. Compare Tucker v. Alexandroff, 183 U.S. 424, 435 (1902):
    While no act of Congress authorizes the executive department to permit the introduction of foreign troops, the power to give such permission without legislative assent was probably assumed to exist from the authority of the President as commander-in-chief of the military and naval forces of the United States.

An Attorney General ruled that the President could admit British flying students and authorize their instruction at United States Army Air Corps training centers. 40 OP.ATT'Y GEN. 58 (1941).

31. In upholding a broad delegation to the President of power to exclude aliens, the Supreme Court said:
    . . . The exclusion of aliens is a fundamental act of sovereignty. The right to do so stems not alone from legislative power but is inherent in the executive power to control the

> foreign affairs of the nation. . . . When Congress pre-
> scribes a procedure concerning the admissibility of aliens, it
> is not dealing alone with a legislative power. It is imple-
> menting an inherent executive power.

United States *ex rel.* Knauff v. Shaughnessy, 338 U.S. 537, 542 (1950).
Later the Court reiterated that "the power of exclusion of aliens is
also inherent in the executive department of the sovereign." *Id.* at
543. The Court seemed to say not merely that the Executive can bar
aliens whose entry is unauthorized by law, but that the policy, the
"law" to exclude aliens, can be made by the President alone, at least
when Congress has not legislated otherwise. But admission, especially for extended sojourn, might be a legislative responsibility.

32. See 22 OP.ATT'Y GEN. 13 (1898); 30 OP.ATT'Y GEN. 217, 221
(1913). See also CORWIN, THE PRESIDENT 196–97, 436–37. Congress
later gave the President authority to license and regulate cables, ch.
12, 42 Stat. 8 (1921), *as amended,* 47 U.S.C. §§ 34–39 (1970).

Congress has enacted comprehensive legislation giving the President
large authority as regards the certification of carriers for foreign air
transportation. The Supreme Court said:

> Congress may of course delegate very large grants of its
> power over foreign commerce to the President. . . . The
> President also possesses in his own right certain powers con-
> ferred by the Constitution on him as Commander-in-Chief
> and as the Nation's organ in foreign affairs. For present
> purposes, the [President's] order draws vitality from either
> or both sources. Legislative and Executive powers are pooled
> obviously to the end that commercial strategic and diplomatic
> interests of the country may be coordinated and advanced
> without collision or deadlock between agencies.

Chicago & Southern Air Lines v. Waterman S. S. Corp., 333 U.S. 103,
109–10 (1948); also *id.* at 111.

33. Writing in 1908, Professor Woodrow Wilson, generally a sup-
porter of Congressional power, said: "One of the President's powers is
. . . his control, which is very absolute, of the foreign relations
of the nation." W. WILSON CONSTITUTIONAL GOVERNMENT IN THE
UNITED STATES 77–78 (1908).

34. THE FEDERALIST NO. 69, at 446 (Hamilton). Later, however,
Hamilton castigated President Jefferson for insisting that he "was
unauthorized by the Constitution, without the sanction of Congress,
to go beyond the line of *Defense*" against the Barbary States. Compare Jefferson in 1 RICHARDSON 326, with 7 A. HAMILTON, WORKS
745–48 (Hamilton ed. 1851). In *The Prize Cases,* 2 Black 635, 668

(U.S.1863), the Supreme Court supported Hamilton. See WRIGHT 286–89.

35. In 1863 Lincoln promulgated the rules of the Lieber Commission, in General Orders No. 100, reprinted in 3 THE WAR OF THE REBELLION: A COMPILATION OF THE OFFICIAL RECORDS OF THE UNION AND CONFEDERATE ARMIES, ser. III (Scott ed. 1901).

"The power of the executive to establish rules and regulations for the government of the army, is undoubted." United States v. Eliason, 16 Pet. 291, 301 (U.S.1842). In that case, however, the President had established regulations pursuant to an act of Congress. *Cf.* Smith v. Whitney, 116 U.S. 167, 180–81 (1886). But see Kurtz v. Moffitt, 115 U.S. 487, 503 (1885), where the Court gave effect to regulations providing rewards for apprehension of deserters, promulgated on the President's own authority.

36. See Fleming v. Page, 9 How. 603, 615 (U.S.1850). See also Mitchell v. Harmony, 13 How. 115 (U.S.1851); United States v. Russell, 13 Wall. 623 (U.S.1871); Totten v. United States, 92 U.S. 105 (1875); *In re* Yamashita, 327 U.S. 1 (1946). See WRIGHT 196. But *cf.* Brown v. United States, 8 Cranch 110 (U.S.1814), Chapter IV, p. 96. More recently the Supreme Court has avoided examining the reach of the President's powers as Commander-in-Chief in time of war, finding in each case that there had been Congressional authorization or approval. See, *e. g.*, Hirabayashi v. United States, 320 U.S. 81, 92 (1943); *Ex parte* Quirin, 317 U.S. 1, 29 (1942).

37. Without according them the constitutional protections enjoyed by the accused in criminal proceedings in the United States, and even where Congress provided an alternative means of trial, by court-martial. Madsen v. Kinsella, 343 U.S. 341 (1952), Chapter IV, p. 105. See also Cross v. Harrison, 16 How. 164 (U.S.1853); Dooley v. United States, 182 U.S. 222 (1901); Santiago v. Nogueras, 214 U.S. 260 (1909). But compare the later cases limiting courts-martial in time of peace, Chapter III, note 42.

38. That was clearly contemplated by the Framers (see Chapter III, note 60), and repeatedly done by Presidents since the beginning. "If a war be made by invasion of a foreign nation, the President is not only authorized but bound to resist force by force." The Prize Cases, 2 Black 635, 668 (U.S.1862). The Supreme Court has held that "the authority to decide whether the exigency has arisen, belongs exclusively to the president, and . . . his decision is conclusive upon all other persons." Martin v. Mott, 12 Wheat. 19, 30 (U.S.1827). See also The Prize Cases, *supra* at 670. No doubt the consent of Congress to war in the event of invasion or attack could be assumed. In 1795 Congress expressly authorized the President to call forth the

militia whenever "the United States shall be invaded, or be in imminent danger of invasion." 1 Stat. 424.

It has been suggested that the President can go to war also in the case of an attack on an ally, but that would not appear to be within this exception to Congressional power as originally conceived. In such a case the President might claim to be acting pursuant to the treaty of alliance, but such treaties have usually provided for United States action in accordance with constitutional procedures, contemplating apparently recourse to Congress for a declaration of war. See Chapter V, p. 159, Chapter VII, p. 192. Compare Chapter IV, p. 100.

39. See CORWIN, THE PRESIDENT 404.

40. Compare The Prize Cases, 2 Black 635, 668 (U.S.1862).

41. See 30 OP.ATT'Y GEN. 291 (1914), justifying closing the Marconi station under both the foreign affairs and Commander-in-Chief powers to implement American neutrality under international law. Corwin suggests that there was authority for Wilson's act in a Congressional statute, ch. 287, 37 Stat. 302 (1912), but Attorney General Gregory did not rely on it. See CORWIN, THE PRESIDENT 197. Today the action would raise serious questions under the First Amendment. See Chapter X, p. 254.

42. Wilson said he had the power to arm American merchant vessels in defense against German submarines but wished Congressional support. When a proposed Congressional resolution died in a Senate filibuster, Wilson proceeded on his own authority. See E. CORWIN, THE PRESIDENT'S CONTROL OF FOREIGN RELATIONS 152–56 (1917); WRIGHT 294–96. Wright thought Wilson had authority also under existing legislation.

43. The numbers vary widely depending on the principle of inclusion. See *Background Information on the Use of United States Armed Forces in Foreign Countries,* 1970 Revision by the Foreign Affairs Division, Legislative Reference Service, Library of Congress, for the Subcommittee on National Security Policy and Scientific Development of the House Committee on Foreign Affairs, 91st Cong., 2d Sess. 15 *et seq.* and Appendices I and II. For earlier lists under the same title see H.R.REP.NO.127, 82nd Cong., 1st Sess. 55–62 (1951); also, *Authority of the President to Repel the Attack in Korea,* Department of State Memorandum of July 3, 1950, 23 DEP'T STATE BULL. 173 (1950); J. ROGERS, WORLD POLICING AND THE CONSTITUTION 56 *et seq.,* 93–123 (1945). *Cf.* Memorandum by J. R. Clark, State Department Solicitor, *Right to Protect Citizens in Foreign Countries by Landing Forces* (Government Printing Office, 3d Rev. ed. 1934).

44. In numerous instances Presidents sought and obtained Congressional approval; in some there was later ratification. See *Background Information on the Use of United States Armed Forces in*

*Foreign Countries,* this chapter, note 43 at 32–37; CORWIN, THE PRESIDENT 223–24; WRIGHT 293–99; and see Chapter IV, p. 99.

45.   Jackson, J., concurring in the *Steel Seizure Case,* agreed that "Commander-in-Chief" is "something more than an empty title" but expressly rejected the suggestion that it vests the President with "power to do anything, anywhere, that can be done with an army or navy." 343 U.S. 579, 641–42 (1952). But compare W. H. TAFT, OUR CHIEF MAGISTRATE AND HIS POWERS 94–95 (1916):

> The President is the Commander-in-Chief of the army and navy, and the militia when called into the service of the United States. Under this, he can order the army and navy anywhere he will, if the appropriations furnish the means of transportation.

That the power to wage war is given to Congress provides one limitation on the President's use of the armed forces but some argue that that is the only limitation. Compare Chapter IV, p. 99.

There have been small constitutional issues about the President's use of the militia. Article I, section 8, clause 15, gives to Congress the power "to provide for calling forth the Militia to execute the Laws of the Union, suppress Insurrections and repel Invasions," and Article II, Section 2 makes the President Commander-in-Chief of the militia "when called into the actual Service of the United States." Even after the militia was organized into the National Guard and was made available for service outside the United States, the Attorney General expressed the opinion that the President could send the state militia outside the United States only when necessary to repel invasion. 29 OP.ATT'Y GEN. 322 (1912). Later Congress provided that the militia could be "federalized" and automatically transformed from state militia into national forces; Presidents, then, can use them abroad for other purposes. *Cf.* Selective Draft Law Cases, 245 U.S. 366 (1918); Cox v. Wood, 247 U.S. 3 (1918). Compare the discussion as to whether the United States could agree to abolish the state militia by a disarmament treaty, Chapter V, p. 148.

46.   So long as he stays short of war. Chapter IV, p. 99. Compare Secretary of State Acheson: "Not only has the President the authority to use the armed forces in carrying out the broad foreign policy of the United States and implementing treaties, but it is equally clear that this authority may not be interfered with by the Congress in the exercise of powers which it has under the Constitution." "Assignment of Ground Forces of the United States to Duty in the European Area," *Hearings by Sen. Comm. on Foreign Relations and Armed Services,* 82d Cong., 1st Sess. 92–93 (1951). But compare SEN. COMM. ON FOREIGN RELATIONS, WAR POWERS, S.REP.NO.606, 92d Cong. 2d Sess. (1972).

47.   The power to use force to protect citizens abroad was recogognized in Durand v. Hollins, 8 F.Cas. 111 (No. 4186) (C.C.S.D.N.Y. 1860); see also *In re* Neagle, 135 U.S. 1 (1890), this chapter, note 52, and statute there cited.   See CORWIN, THE PRESIDENT 194–204 and notes.   The right to protection abroad has been said to be one of the "privileges and immunities of citizens of the United States."   Slaughter-House Cases, 16 Wall. 36, 79 (U.S.1872).

In early days the United States Navy was often an auxiliary of the foreign affairs establishment used for *ad hoc* foreign purposes including the ferrying of American diplomats, as in nineteenth century China.

48.   Doubts about Presidential authority to extradite pursuant to treaty without Congressional authorization (see, *e. g.*, Mr. Justice Catron in *In re* Kaine, 14 How. 103, 112 (U.S.1852)), have long been resolved: see Valentine v. United States *ex rel.* Neidecker, 299 U.S. 5 (1936); Fong Yue Ting v. United States, 149 U.S. 698, 714 (1893); *cf.* United States v. Robins, 27 F.Cas. 825 (No. 16,175) (D.C.S.C. 1799), and John Marshall's statement in the House of Representatives, note 18, this chapter.   The President probably had authority pursuant to treaty (even without Congressional authorization) to return deserting seaman, but not, it has been said, in the absence of treaty.   See Chapter IV, note 18.   Treaties on that subject were terminated and are no longer made.   Ch. 153, 38 Stat. 1164, 1184 (1915). See WRIGHT 195.

Story is reported to have said that the President did not have authority to carry out awards of foreign consuls based on treaty in the absence of Congressional legislation.   See 2 J. B. MOORE, DIGEST OF INTERNATIONAL LAW 298 [hereinafter cited as MOORE, DIGEST]; 5 *id.* 223.   It is unlikely that his view would be followed today, but the question is academic since Congress has enacted legislation giving the courts authority to enforce them.   See 22 U.S.C. § 258a (1970).   Compare Chapter VII, note 39.

49.   See WRIGHT 192–94, 296.

50.   See, *e. g.*, 1 OP.ATT'Y GEN. 560, 566, 570–71 (1822); S.EXEC. DOC. NO. 123, 26th Cong., 2d Sess. 379, 384, 853, 1288, cited in CORWIN, THE PRESIDENT 437.

51.   See *Ex parte* Toscano, 208 F. 938 (S.D.Cal.1913).   See also notes 26 and 41, this chapter, and WRIGHT 196.

52.   Compare State Department Solicitor J. R. CLARK, RIGHT TO PROTECT CITIZENS IN FOREIGN COUNTRIES BY LANDING FORCES 44–48 (3d rev. ed. 1934); Wright, *Constitutional Procedure in the United States for Carrying Out Obligations for Military Sanctions*, 38 AM.J. INT'L L. 678, 680, 684 (1944); Mathews, *The Constitutional Power of the President to Conclude International Agreements*, 64 YALE L.J.

345, 360 n. 88, 365 n. 107, 367 & nn. 115, 118–20 (1955). Writers
have not distinguished between a) authority to carry out the obligations of the United States under treaty or customary law (which can
plausibly be found in the "take care" clause); b) authority to exercise rights reserved to the United States by international law or given
it by treaty (see this chapter, note 56); and c) authority to compel
other states to carry out their international obligations to the United
States.

Sometimes cited is Mr. Justice Miller in *In re* Neagle, 135 U.S. 1
(1890). Neagle, a United States deputy marshall detailed to act as
bodyguard for Justice Field, was charged with killing an assailant.
He sought habeas corpus under a statute authorizing the writ for persons detained "for an act done or committed in pursuance of a law of
the United States." The Court held that although he was appointed
on the authority of the Executive without statutory authorization,
Neagle's act was committed "in pursuance of a law of the United
States." Speaking of the "take care" clause, Mr. Justice Miller asked,
rhetorically (at 64):

> Is this duty limited to the enforcement of acts of Congress
> or of treaties of the United States according to their *express
> terms,* or does it include the rights, duties and obligations
> growing out of the Constitution itself, our international rela-
> tions, and all the protection implied by the nature of the gov-
> ernment under the Constitution? (Emphasis in original.)

The suggestion that the President's power to execute the laws em-
braces also "the rights . . . growing out of . . . our international relations" was of course dictum. Miller did proceed to
narrate how the Secretary of State intervened to obtain the release
from foreign internment of Martin Koszta who had declared his intention to become an American citizen, and the opinion seems to imply that diplomatic protection as in that case was an exercise of the
"take care" clause. But Miller did not say that in such cases the President "executes" international law; more likely he had in mind that
diplomatic protection was one of the privileges of American citizenship and it is that "law" which the President was executing. See
this chapter, note 47. And Congress had expressly authorized the
use of any means "not amounting to acts of war" to obtain the release of American citizens unjustly detained. Expatriation Act of July
27, 1868, ch. 249, 15 Stat. 223, 224, 22 U.S.C. § 1732 (1970). Surely
nothing in Miller's opinion implies that the "take care" clause would
support the use of force against other kinds of violations of international law abroad. (Compare Lamar, J., dissenting, 135 U.S. at 84–
85, who seemed to derive the power to intervene by threat of force on
behalf of Martin Koszta in that "the Constitution . . . expressly

commits all matters pertaining to our diplomatic negotiations to the treaty-making power.")

53. Jefferson's use of force against the Barbary Pirates is often cited as an exercise of his power to see that international law is faithfully executed. International law gave the United States the right to act against pirates, a right which the President could exercise; but it seems strained to say that the President was exercising authority to see that the pirates complied with international law. Compare Chapter III, notes 21 and 24. Apart from authority under his foreign affairs powers and as Commander-in-Chief he apparently had authority from Congress and was therefore executing American law. 2 Stat. 129 (1802).

54. Compare 29 OP.ATT'Y GEN. 322 (1912). Madison wrote about the President's power of "executing the *national* laws" (emphasis added). 1 J. MADISON, THE CONSTITUTIONAL CONVENTION OF 1787, at 52–53 (Hunt ed. 1908). The President has no constitutional authority to execute the laws of the States or of any foreign government.

55. *E. g.*, The Paquete Habana, 175 U.S. 677 (1900); Berizzi Bros. Co. v. S. S. Pesaro, 271 U.S. 562 (1926). See Chapter VIII. Under international law the United States can prescribe law also for aliens abroad but only under the "protective principle," *i. e.*, in special circumstances to protect state interests, *e. g.*, to punish espionage or counterfeiting of U. S. currency, and perhaps in selected cases subject to "universal jurisdiction," *e. g.*, piracy or "war crimes." See generally 1 L. OPPENHEIM, INTERNATIONAL LAW § 147 (Lauterpacht 8th ed. 1955).

Lincoln indeed built his war powers on the "take care" clause combined with his authority as Commander-in-Chief, but, since no right to secede was recognized, he was seeking to enforce not international law but the Constitution and laws of the United States within the United States against inhabitants of the United States. See p. 51.

56. William Howard Taft, when Secretary of War to President Theodore Roosevelt, urged that the "take care" clause authorized the President to intervene to maintain order in Cuba because in the Platt Amendment to the treaty with Cuba the Cuban government had consented to such intervention. See W. H. TAFT, OUR CHIEF MAGISTRATE AND HIS POWERS 85–88 (1938). Compare his view that the President had authority to govern in the Panama Canal Zone pursuant to treaty when Congress failed to provide for such government. *Id.* at 83–85. In that instance, Congress having authorized the building of the Canal, and government in the Zone being necessary to that end, the President's authority to govern can be said to derive from his responsibility to execute the Act of Congress. Congress, moreover, knew and acquiesced and later ratified.

The rights of the United States under international law include all that is not forbidden to her by customary law or treaty (*cf.* The S.S. "Lotus," [1927] P.C.I.J., ser. A, No. 9, in 2 M. HUDSON, WORLD COURT REPORTS 20 (1935)), constituting, then, the mass of actions and policies of the United States that make up or impinge on her foreign relations. These indeed are largely within the President's foreign affairs authority, but they hardly seem to be within his responsibility to see that the law, even international law, is faithfully executed. Rights granted the United States by treaty are also perhaps in the President's discretion to exercise under his foreign affairs power but these too do not seem law he is to see "faithfully executed." The President probably has authority also to further national policy established in treaties of the United States, but, again, it does not seem plausible to say that in such cases he is "faithfully executing" the law of the United States, though there, as when he is given discretion (not directive) by Congress, he may be said to be exercising "executive" power.

57. *E. g.,* Oetjen v. Central Leather Co., 246 U.S. 297 (1918); Russian Socialist Federated Soviet Republic v. Cibrario, 235 N.Y. 255, 139 N.E. 259 (1923); see Banco Nacional de Cuba v. Sabbatino, 376 U.S. 398, 408–12 (1964).

58. The Paquete Habana, 175 U.S. 677, 700 (1900), discussed in Chapter VIII, p. 221.

59. Berizzi Bros. Co. v. S. S. Pesaro, 271 U.S. 562 (1926).

60. After the First World War, noting that increased "state trading" by other governments claimed the benefits of immunity while American private enterprise could not, the State Department urged that the United States refuse to grant immunity to vessels of foreign governments used for commercial purposes, and to governments themselves as regards claims arising out of commercial transactions. The Attorney General of the United States rejected the proposal, asserting in effect that sovereign immunity was a question of international law and that international law knew no such distinction; the sovereign was immune regardless of the nature of the claim against him, and his vessels and other property were immune regardless of the public purpose for which they were used. See 2 G. HACKWORTH, DIGEST OF INTERNATIONAL LAW 429–30 (1941). Later, the view of the State Department was, in effect, adopted by Judge Mack in the lower court in The Pesaro, 277 F. 473 (S.D.N.Y.1921). When Judge Mack's decree was vacated for other reasons, the issue came anew before Judge Augustus N. Hand who took a contrary position, 13 F.2d 468 (S.D.N.Y. 1926); he was affirmed by the Supreme Court which found that international law accorded immunity to such vessels as well. See the previous note.

A quarter of a century later, in the "Tate Letter," the State Department announced that henceforth it would follow the "restrictive" theory of immunity. 26 DEP'T STATE BULL. 984 (1952). It has refused, however, to extend that doctrine to permit attachment and seizure or execution on the property of a foreign government, even when it was used for commercial purposes. See letter of Secretary of State to Attorney General, referred to in New York & Cuba Mail S.S. Co. v. Republic of Korea, 132 F.Supp. 684, 685 (S.D.N.Y.1955).

61. 318 U.S. 578, 589 (1943).

62. 324 U.S. 30, 36, 38 (1945).

63. Compare *Ex parte* Muir, 254 U.S. 522 (1921); Berizzi Bros. Co. v. S. S. Pesaro, 271 U.S. 562 (1926). Compare also Victory Transport, Inc. v. Comisaria General de Abastecimientos y Transportes, 336 F.2d 354 (2d Cir. 1964), *cert. denied,* 381 U.S. 934 (1965).

64. It is possible, but difficult, to read Stone's opinions in these cases as announcing only that the Executive had determined what international law required of the United States and that his views of international law are binding on the courts. The courts have often said that, when necessary to the decision of the case before them, they interpret what international law, or a particular treaty, requires, though they will give "great weight" to Executive views. See Chapters V, p. 167, Chapter VIII, p. 223. Nothing in the sovereign immunity cases rejects or modifies that doctrine. Stone was apparently giving effect not to Executive views of international law but to "national policy" on immunity even if it was contrary to, or not based on or related to international law. The Court's doctrine has been criticized particularly by those who were reluctant to see what had been a question of international law converted into a question of national policy. See, *e. g.,* Jessup, *Has the Supreme Court Abdicated One of its Functions?* 40 AM.J.INT'L L. 168 (1946).

65. United States v. Belmont, 301 U.S. 324 (1937); United States v. Pink, 315 U.S. 203 (1942). The opinion in *Belmont* was written by Sutherland; Stone concurred but thought it was not necessary to consider the effect of the agreement. He took that position also in *Pink* where he dissented because, he said, the agreement did not purport to give the United States better rights than the Soviet Union would have had.

66. 315 U.S. at 229–30.

67. Bernstein v. Van Heyghen Frères, 163 F.2d 246 (2d Cir. 1947), *cert. denied,* 332 U.S. 772 (1947). In that case the plaintiff sought to recover damages for the loss of his shipping company, which the Nazis had compelled him to transfer (when he was still a German national) pursuant to the anti-Jewish Nuremberg laws, and which was later sold to the defendant, a Belgian corporation. Judge Hand found

312

that under the Act of State doctrine the courts of the United States could not sit in judgment on the Nazi laws applied in German territory, and had to give them effect. In the course of deciding, however, Judge Hand found it relevant to inquire "whether since the cessation of hostilities with Germany our own Executive, which is the authority to which we must look for the final word in such matters, has declared that the commonly accepted [Act of State] doctrine . . . does not apply." 163 F.2d at 249. After examination he concluded that the Executive had not lifted the restraints of Act of State. The Circuit Court ruled the same way in a later case involving similar facts, Bernstein v. N. V. Nederlandsche-Amerikaansche Stoomvaart-Mattschappij, 173 F.2d 71 (2d Cir. 1949).

Seizing Judge Hand's hint, Bernstein addressed an inquiry to the Department of State, and the Department wrote a letter saying:

". . . The policy of the Executive, with respect to claims asserted in the United States for the restitution of identifiable property (or compensation in lieu thereof) lost through force, coercion, or duress as a result of Nazi persecution in Germany, is to relieve American courts from any restraint upon the exercise of their jurisdiction to pass upon the validity of the acts of Nazi officials." Letter of Acting Legal Adviser Tate, April 13, 1949, 20 DEP'T STATE BULL. 592, quoted in Banco Nacional de Cuba v. Sabbatino, 376 U.S. 398, 419 (1964).

The Court of Appeals, quoting the Department's letter, then decided that the Act of State doctrine would not apply "In view of this supervening expression of the Executive Policy," and revised its mandate. Bernstein v. N. V. Nederlandsche-Amerikaansche Stoomvaart-Maatschappij, 210 F.2d 375, 376 (2d Cir. 1954). (The case was later settled and did not reach the Supreme Court.)

But compare the views of Judge Irving Lehman of the New York Court of Appeals in Anderson v. N. V. Transandine Handelmaatschappij, 289 N.Y. 9, 20, 43 N.E.2d 502, 507 (1942). And see this chapter, notes 77–78.

For a discussion of Act of State in other contexts see Chapter VIII, p. 217.

68. *Cf.* THE FEDERALIST NO. 64, cited with approval in United States v. Pink, 315 U.S. 203, 230 (1942): "All constitutional acts of power, whether in the executive or in the judicial department, have as much legal validity and obligation as if they proceeded from the legislature." (Jay was speaking of the treaty power.)

There may be an additional issue in that the Court was giving legislative effect not to a formal act of the President but to the views of the State Department asserted in a particular case. Does the State

Department in effect have power to make law *ad hoc* for specific cases, whereas Congress probably cannot constitutionally pass special legislation for a particular case? As to whether the State Department is granting "due process" to the plaintiffs who are effectively being denied a day in court, see Chapter X, p. 256.

69. Some distinctions might be attempted. Perhaps executive agreements, involving international obligations like those in treaties, have more claim to domestic legal status than unilateral acts of the President. See Chapter VI, p. 184. In the immunity cases, perhaps the State Department should be followed because immunity is a sensitive issue applicable to all countries and involves the reciprocal rights of the United States abroad. Act of State also involves delicate issues of sitting in judgment on the acts of friendly foreign governments. In both kinds of cases the Department is in effect deciding United States positions on doctrines of international law or comity. Compare note 81 below; see Chapter VIII. (Would the same judicial deference be required if the State Department urged that failure to dismiss a suit against a foreign tourist, say the son of a foreign Chief of State, would seriously impair our foreign relations?) The immunity cases, moreover, require dismissing a suit; Act of State, too, is a special doctrine for judicial guidance in choosing the appropriate law in a transnational transaction. Neither attempts to regulate the activities of private persons or establish rules of substantive law to determine their rights.

70. Banco Nacional de Cuba v. Sabbatino, 376 U.S. 398 (1964), *rev'g* 307 F.2d 845 (2d Cir. 1962), *aff'g* 193 F.Supp. 375 (S.D.N.Y. 1961), discussed in Chapter VIII, p. 217.

71. In the Supreme Court, the Executive Branch appeared *amicus curiae* to urge that the lower courts be overruled, and the Act of State doctrine applied. It warned that judicial interference might adversely affect the foreign relations of the United States and, in particular, that it would jeopardize diplomatic efforts to vindicate broader American interests including the rights of other Americans who had suffered Cuban expropriation. See Brief pp. 12, 22 and Argument of Deputy Attorney General Katzenbach, 32 U.S.L.W. 3158 (Oct. 29, 1963). That Act of State was executive policy might reasonably have been inferred also from long executive acquiescence in the doctrine and from the very limited and guarded waiver of it in the *Bernstein* case, note 67 above. See Henkin, *The Foreign Affairs Power of the Federal Courts: Sabbatino*, 64 COLUM.L.REV. 805, 821–23 (1964).

72. 389 U.S. 429 (1968). See Chapter IX, p. 238.

73. 389 U.S. at 432.

74. Memorandum for the United States at 5. The Solicitor General continued: "Appellant's apprehension of a deterioration of inter-

national relations, unsubstantiated by experience, does not constitute the kind of 'changed circumstances' which might call for a re-examination of *Clark v. Allen* [an earlier case in which the Court had upheld a California reciprocal inheritance statute]."

Later in a brief *amicus curiae* the Solicitor General said that the Government "does not . . . contend that the operation of the Oregon escheat statute in the circumstances of this case unduly interferes with the United States' conduct of foreign relations." Brief for the United States as *amicus curiae* at 6 n. 5.

Of these statements by the Executive Branch, the opinion of the majority of the Court said simply:

> The Government's acquiescence in the ruling of *Clark v. Allen* certainly does not justify extending the principle of that case, as we would be required to do here to uphold the Oregon statute as applied; for it has more than "some incidental or indirect effect in foreign countries," and its great potential for disruption or embarrassment makes us hesitate to place it in the category of a diplomatic bagatelle. 389 U.S. at 434–35.

75. 389 U.S. at 443 (concurring opinion).

76. At its first consideration, the Court of Appeals had applied the Act of State doctrine to dismiss a counterclaim by First National for the value of properties confiscated by the Cuban Government. Banco Nacional de Cuba v. First National City Bank of New York, 431 F.2d 394 (2d Cir. 1970). While the case was before the Supreme Court on petition for certiorari, the Legal Adviser of the State Department addressed his letter to the Supreme Court. (The full text of the letter appears in the subsequent opinion of the Court of Appeals, 442 F.2d at 536–38.) The Supreme Court vacated the judgment and remanded the case to the Court of Appeals for reconsideration in light of that letter. 400 U.S. 1019 (1971). The Court of Appeals reaffirmed its earlier decision saying that *Bernstein* should be narrowly construed and confined to its facts—the act of state of a defunct Nazi government. Virtually without considering whether it was free to do so, it simply disregarded the State Department letter and applied its own views (and those of the Supreme Court in *Sabbatino*) as to what the Act of State doctrine should be. 442 F.2d 530 (1971). Judge Hays dissented sharply, following *Bernstein*. *Id.* at 538.

77. First National City Bank v. Banco Nacional de Cuba, 406 U.S. 759 (1972).

78. Mr. Justice Rehnquist (joined by Chief Justice Burger and Mr. Justice White) said:

> . . . We conclude that where the Executive Branch, charged as it is with primary responsibility for the conduct of

315

foreign affairs, expressly represents to the Court that application of the act of state doctrine would not advance the interests of American foreign policy, that doctrine should not be applied by the courts. . . .

. . . The only reason for not deciding the case by use of otherwise applicable legal principles would be the fear that legal interpretation by the judiciary of the act of a foreign sovereign within its own territory might frustrate the conduct of this country's foreign relations. But the branch of the government responsible for the conduct of those foreign relations has advised us that such a consequence need not be feared in this case. The judiciary is therefore free to decide the case free from the limitations that would otherwise be imposed upon it by the judicially created act of state doctrine. 406 U.S. at 768.

I note that even these three Justices said that the "judiciary is therefore free"; the implication seems to be not that the courts must adopt the Executive view on the act of state doctrine but that since the Executive says that the doctrine is unnecessary in the circumstances the courts are free not to apply it if *they* think it unnecessary or undesirable. The dissenting justices rejected the *Bernstein* doctrine explicitly and would have followed *Sabbatino*. Douglas and Powell, JJ., concurring, refused to apply it, Douglas saying it should not "govern here," and Powell that he would be "uncomfortable" with it. (Douglas, J., would establish a special rule for counterclaims; Powell concurred because he basically disagreed with *Sabbatino*).

79. But *cf.* Mr. Justice Brennan, dissenting, 406 U.S. 789 n. 13 (1972).

80. New York Times Co. v. United States, 403 U.S. 713 (1971), discussed in Chapter X, note 9.

81. When in the "Tate Letter," 26 DEP'T STATE BULL. 984 (1952), note 60, this chapter, the State Department adopted the restrictive theory of immunity, it said: "It is realized that a shift in policy by the executive cannot control the courts, but it is felt that the courts are less likely to allow a plea of sovereign immunity where the executive has declined to do so." *Id.* at 985. The statement seems inconsistent with Stone's opinions. Was the Department saying that it did not intend to lay down binding policy, only to assert a view of international law which it would follow but as to which the courts were free to make their own determination? Was the Department being coy, or reluctant to accept the responsibility? Was it uncertain about the continuing validity of what the Supreme Court had said? The Supreme Court has never had occasion to consider the effect of that letter but lower courts have applied it.

The Restatement also seems to doubt that the Court meant what it said. See RESTATEMENT OF THE LAW (SECOND), THE FOREIGN RELATIONS LAW OF THE UNITED STATES, Reporters' Note § 72, at 226–28 (1965).

82. The Department has considered proposing legislation on sovereign immunity. See Belman, *New Departures in the Law of Sovereign Immunity*, 1969 PROC.AM.SOC.INT'L L. 147.

83. Under the Second Hickenlooper Amendment, Pub.L.No. 88–633, 78 Stat. 1009, 1013 (1964), *as amended*, 22 U.S.C. § 2370(e) (2) (1970), Chapter VIII, note 55, the President can insist that the courts apply Act of State even where the Amendment would otherwise bar it. The Executive has not yet exercised that right in any case. Of course, if he should do so he would not be legislating on his own authority but by authority of Congress.

NOTES, CHAPTER III, CONGRESS, pp. 67 to 88.

1. Scholarly writing about Congress and foreign affairs includes R. DAHL, CONGRESS AND FOREIGN POLICY (1950); J. ROBINSON, CONGRESS AND FOREIGN POLICY-MAKING (Rev. ed. 1967); *Congress and Foreign Relations,* ANNALS OF THE AMERICAN ACADEMY OF POLITICAL AND SOCIAL SCIENCE (1953); H. CARROLL, THE HOUSE OF REPRESENTATIVES AND FOREIGN AFFAIRS (1958). There are also specialized volumes, *e. g.,* those on the Senate's part in treaty-making, cited in Chapter V.

2. This is a dead power. No letters of marque or reprisal have been issued by the United States since before the Civil War. The European powers agreed to end privateering in the Declaration of Paris (1856). See F. PIGGOTT, THE DECLARATION OF PARIS, 1856 (1919).

3. See generally, *e. g.,* my article, *Some Reflections on Current Constitutional Controversy,* 109 U.PA.L.REV. 637, 638–40 (1961). Since that article was written the Court has found new powers for Congress, especially in the enforcement clauses of the Civil War Amendments. See this chapter, p. 77, and note 53.

4. There have been infrequent use and little judicial examination, for example, of the power of Congress to consent to state compacts with foreign nations, or to other state acts covered in Article I, section 10, clause 3. Compare Chapter X.

5. Gibbons v. Ogden, 9 Wheat. 1, 189 (U.S.1824).

6. N.L.R.B. v. Jones & Laughlin Steel Corp., 301 U.S. 1 (1937); United States v. Darby, 312 U.S. 100 (1941); United States v. Sullivan, 332 U.S. 689 (1948); McDermott v. Wisconsin, 228 U.S. 115 (1913); Wickard v. Filburn, 317 U.S. 111 (1942); The Shreveport Case, 234 U.S. 342 (1914); and see the following note.

7. It can regulate the transportation of people and things across state lines for economic ends or for "police power" reasons of health, safety, morals, and other public welfare; the wages of a maintenance man in a building that houses small manufacturers whose goods cross state lines, or the compensation of a clerk hurt at her desk in the office of a railroad company; the amount of wheat a farmer grows for his own consumption; the labeling by a local pharmacist of drugs that had once come from another state; racial discrimination by "local" hotels and restaurants. See United States v. Darby, this chapter, note 6; Lottery Case, 188 U.S. 321 (1903); Hoke v. United States, 227 U.S. 308 (1913); Kirschbaum Co. v. Walling, 316 U.S. 517 (1942); Reed v. Pennsylvania R.R., 351 U.S. 502 (1956); Wickard v. Filburn, this chapter, note 6; United States v. Sullivan,

this chapter, note 6; Heart of Atlanta Motel v. United States, 379 U.S. 241 (1964); Katzenbach v. McClung, 379 U.S. 294 (1964). See also Electric Bond & Share Co. v. SEC, 303 U.S. 419 (1938) (upholding statute forbidding the use of instrumentalities of interstate commerce and of mails by unregistered companies); Kentucky Whip & Collar Co. v. Illinois Central R.R., 299 U.S. 334 (1937) (upholding statute prohibiting transportation of convict made goods into a State in violation of its law); Gooch v. United States, 297 U.S. 124 (1936) (statute forbidding transportation in interstate or foreign commerce of kidnaped persons).

The Economic Stabilization Act of 1970, Pub.L.No. 91–379, Title II, § 202(a), 84 Stat. 799 (1970), *as amended,* Pub.L.No. 92–15, § 3, 85 Stat. 38 (1971), 12 U.S.C.A. § 1904 (1970), *as amended,* (Supp. 1972) authorizes the President "to stabilize prices, rents, wages and salaries. . . ." No constitutional support for the legislation is cited, and although the principal source of Congressional power must be the Commerce Clause the statute does not mention interstate commerce or limit the President's power to matters in or affecting such commerce. Nonetheless, one may expect that the courts will uphold its validity without attempting even to narrow its scope. See Amalgamated Meat Cutters & Butcher Workmen of North America v. Connally, 337 F.Supp. 737 (D.C.D.C.1971), where the petitioner did not even challenge the power of Congress to act, only its broad delegation to the President, which the three-judge court upheld.

8.  The last Supreme Court decision invalidating an act of Congress as beyond the Commerce Power was Carter v. Carter Coal Co., 298 U.S. 238 (1936). The revolution came with N. L. R. B. v. Jones & Laughlin Steel Corp., 301 U.S. 1 (1937). See generally Stern, *The Commerce Clause and the National Economy 1933–46,* 59 Harv.L.Rev. 645 (1946).

9.  It has been argued, indeed, that the powers given to Congress in regard to foreign commerce exceed those for interstate commerce, since the latter were at the expense of the reserved powers of the States while control of foreign commerce is an aspect of federal power over foreign relations. See, *e. g.,* the dissenting opinion in Lottery Case, 188 U.S. 321, 373–74 (1903); Brolan v. United States, 236 U.S. 216, 222 (1915). It is generally accepted, however, that the power of Congress is the same as regards both. See License Cases, 5 How. 504, 578 (U.S.1847); Pittsburgh & Southern Coal Co. v. Bates, 156 U.S. 577, 587 (1895). Some of the cases defining the Commerce Power involved foreign commerce, *e. g.,* Buttfield v. Stranahan, 192 U.S. 470 (1904); The Abby Dodge, 223 U.S. 166 (1912); Weber v. Freed, 239 U.S. 325 (1915); Brolan v. United States, *supra*; Trustees of University of Illinois v. United States, 289 U.S. 48 (1933). Compare

Armement Deppe, S. A. v. United States, 399 F.2d 794 (5th Cir. 1968), *cert. denied*, 393 U.S. 1094 (1969), where the Court of Appeals found Congressional power to regulate shipping contracts among foreigners that affected United States commerce.

10.  Chief Justice Marshall in Gibbons v. Ogden, note 5, this chapter, at 193, said that the power of Congress comprehends "every species of commercial intercourse between the United States and foreign nations."

11.  Art. I, sec. 8, cl. 2 and cl. 5.  These Congressional powers supply authority for international agreements on these matters; even United States adherence to international organizations like the International Bank for Reconstruction and Development and the International Monetary Fund was authorized by Congress rather than effected by treaty.  See the Bretton Woods Agreements Act, ch. 339, 59 Stat. 512 (1945).  On the power of Congress to authorize international agreements generally, see Chapter VI, p. 173.

12.  See The Lottawanna, 21 Wall. 558, 577 (U.S.1875).  But compare The Belfast, 7 Wall. 624, 640 (U.S.1869), and *In re* Garnett, 141 U.S. 1, 12 (1891).

13.  See Nishimura Ekiu v. United States, 142 U.S. 651, 659 (1892); Head Money Cases, 112 U.S. 580, 591–96 (1884).  Other support for the power of Congress to regulate immigration might be implied in Article I, section 9: "The Migration or Importation of such Persons as any of the States now existing shall think proper to admit, shall not be prohibited by the Congress prior to the Year one thousand eight hundred and eight . . . ."  But that clause referred to the importation of slaves, a form of property clearly within the power to regulate foreign commerce; the immigration of free persons is not as obviously "foreign commerce," and later cases preferred to find Congressional authority over immigration in the powers inherent in sovereignty.  See this chapter, p. 75.

14.  See Hirabayashi v. United States, 320 U.S. 81, 93 (1943); Home Building & Loan Assoc. v. Blaisdell, 290 U.S. 398, 426 (1934); United States v. Macintosh, 283 U.S. 605, 622 (1931) ("the plenary power to wage war with all the force necessary to make it effective").  See also Chase, C. J., in *Ex parte* Milligan, 4 Wall. 2, 139 (U.S.1866) ("all legislation essential to the prosecution of war with vigor and success").  Chief Justice Marshall listed the power "to declare and conduct a war" as one of the enumerated powers of Congress.  McCulloch v. Maryland, 4 Wheat. 316, 407 (U.S.1819).  On Sutherland's view that the power to wage war was inherent in sovereignty, see Chapter I, p. 21, Congress might claim legislative power in that source also.  Compare Mr. Justice Paterson in Penhallow

v. Doane, 3 Dall. 54, 80–81 (U.S.1795), on the war power of the Continental Congress, Chapter I, note 10.

15.  Young men were drafted into military service and sent to distant battles; property was taken for the war (subject to compensation) and property of alien enemies was sequestered (without compensation); the economy of the nation was regulated, with production, prices, wages, rents controlled, and the most local of businesses subjected to scrutiny to assure compliance with the war program.  Special restrictions were imposed on basic freedoms of speech and press, of domestic and international travel.  Alien enemies were interned. The Supreme Court even acquiesced in a less-than-glorious page in our history when military officials imposed special restrictions on American citizens of Japanese ancestry, interned them, relocated them far from their homes.  Korematsu v. United States, 323 U.S. 214 (1944). Compare the vast legislative powers exercised by the States during the Revolutionary War.  CORWIN, THE PRESIDENT 453–55.

In effect the war power also gives Congress the power to acquire territory by conquest, see American Ins. Co. v. Canter, 1 Pet. 516, 542 (U.S.1828); see this chapter, note 50.

16.  The Supreme Court has not considered the validity of some of these programs but I have little doubt they would be upheld.  Compare Ashwander v. TVA, 297 U.S. 288, 327–28 (1936); Silesian-American Corp. v. Clark, 332 U.S. 469, 476 (1947); see 2 STORY, COMMENTARIES, § 1185, at 104.  In Martin v. Mott, 12 Wheat. 19, 29 (U.S.1827), Story said that "the power to provide for repelling invasions includes the power to provide against the attempt and danger of invasion, as the necessary and proper means to effectuate the object."

Compulsory military service was upheld during the First World War in Selective Draft Law Cases, 245 U.S. 366 (1918).  The validity of federal security programs in principle has been assumed. Compare Greene v. McElroy, 360 U.S. 474 (1959).  Some of these programs no doubt find support in other powers of Congress as well, *e. g.*, the power to "raise and support Armies," and to "provide and maintain a Navy," Art. I, sec. 8, cl. 12 and cl. 13.  Security programs for federal employees can be supported also by the power of Congress to establish executive offices, Art. II, sec. 2.  Compare Chapter IV, p. 116.

17.  Woods v. Miller Co., 333 U.S. 138 (1948); Lichter v. United States, 334 U.S. 742, 755, 757–58 (1948); *cf.* Hamilton v. Kentucky Distillers & Warehouse Co., 251 U.S. 146 (1919).  Alien enemies could be kept in internment even after the fighting stopped.  Ludecke v. Watkins, 335 U.S. 160 (1948).  But see Mr. Justice Jackson concurring in Woods v. Miller, *supra*, at 146–47, stressing the dangers of this "open-ended" view of the war-powers.

18. Even in ways that violate international law, since the Constitution does not forbid Congress to disregard international law. See Chapter VIII, pp. 221–22. The power to deal with alien enemies was asserted as early as the Alien Enemy Act of 1798, 1 Stat. 577, and even its opponents did not doubt that the power to enact it was implied in the power to declare war. See generally the *Ludecke* Case, this chapter, note 17.

19. Compare The Chinese Exclusion Case, 130 U.S. 581, 606 (1889).

20. Art. I, sec. 8, cl. 10. The Articles of Confederation gave Congress exclusive power to appoint courts for the trial of piracies and felonies committed on the high seas. Article IX. At the Constitutional Convention, it was decided that "felonies" and "law of nations" were too vague and should require definition by Congress. 1 J. ELLIOT, DEBATES IN THE SEVERAL STATE CONVENTIONS ON THE ADOPTION OF THE FEDERAL CONSTITUTION 246 (1866) [hereinafter cited as ELLIOT'S DEBATES].

21. Piracy as defined by the law of nations is punishable under 18 U.S.C. § 1651 (1970). See also 49 U.S.C. § 1472(i) (1970). A statute punishing "piracy, as defined by the law of nations" was held sufficiently explicit. United States v. Smith, 5 Wheat. 153 (U.S.1820).

22. For the view that the "law of nations" included more than is encompassed in contemporary public international law, and included also, at least, private international law, see, *e. g.*, Rheinstein, *The Constitutional Bases of Jurisdiction*, 22 U.CHI.L.REV. 775, 802–17 (1955).

23. Including state officials. Compare the statutes that punish acts under color of state law that violate constitutional rights, *e. g.*, 18 U.S.C. §§ 242, 245 (1970). As regards some applications of that legislation, Congressional power derives from the enforcement clauses of the Fourteenth Amendment. Compare, *e. g.*, United States v. Guest, 383 U.S. 745 (1966).

24. Congress was held to have defined such offenses by reference, in the Articles of War. *Ex parte* Quirin, 317 U.S. 1, 27–28 (1942). Compare *In re* Yamashita, 327 U.S. 1, 26 (1946) (dissenting opinion).

Violations of fishing regulations of international administrative agencies are violations of federal law in some circumstances. See, *e. g.*, The Whaling Convention Act of 1949, ch. 653, 64 Stat. 421 (1950), 16 U.S.C. §§ 916–916*l* (1970), implementing the Convention for the Regulation of Whaling, Dec. 2, 1946, 62 Stat. 1716 (1948), T.I.A.S. No. 1849, 161 U.N.T.S. 72. Perhaps these are also offenses against the laws of nations; they are surely punishable under the "necessary and proper" clause, p. 78 above.

There is an old conceptual dispute as to whether piracy is an international crime, an offense against the law of nations, or whether international law merely permits nations to apply national laws against piracy even though it ordinarily permits them to apply their laws only to acts committed in their territory or to their own nationals. See W. BISHOP, INTERNATIONAL LAW, CASES AND MATERIALS 461 (3d ed. 1971). Compare Chapter II, note 55.

25. Convention on the Prevention and Punishment of the Crime of Genocide, *adopted* December 9, 1948, 78 U.N.T.S. 277; International Covenant on Economic, Social and Cultural Rights, *opened for signature* December 16, 1966, G.A.Res. 2200, 21 U.N. GAOR Supp. 16, at 49, U.N.Doc. A/6316 (1966): International Covenant on Civil and Political Rights, *id.* at 52. The Nuremberg principles have not been incorporated in any multilateral treaty but they were unanimously approved by the General Assembly, G.A.Res. 161, U.N.Doc. A/236 at 1144 (1946). Article VI of the Genocide Convention provides:

> Persons charged with genocide or any of the other acts enumerated in Article III shall be tried by a competent tribunal of the State in the territory of which the act was committed, or by such international penal tribunals as may have jurisdiction with respect to those Contracting Parties which shall have accepted its jurisdiction.

No such international tribunals have been established, and none are in prospect. See Chapter VII, p. 198, and note 34.

26. United States v. Arjona, 120 U.S. 479, 487–88 (1887). Earlier, Story seemed to read the clause to the same effect:

> It is obvious, that this power has an intimate connection and relation with the power to regulate commerce and intercourse with foreign nations, and the rights and duties of the national government in peace and war, arising out of the law of nations. As the United States are responsible to foreign governments for all violations of the law of nations, and as the welfare of the Union is essentially connected with the conduct of our citizens, in regard to foreign nations, congress ought to possess the power to define and punish all such offences, which may interrupt our intercourse and harmony with and our duties to them. 2 STORY, COMMENTARIES § 1165, at 95.

See generally Fredman, Comment, *The Offenses Clause: Congress' International Penal Power*, 8 COLUM.J.TRANSNAT'L L. 279 (1969).

Statutes like that in *Arjona* can also be supported today under the Commerce Power, the Foreign Affairs Power, perhaps even the War Power.

27. Anyone who swears out a writ or executes process against a foreign diplomat may be guilty under United States law as a "violator of the laws of nations and a disturber of the public repose." Ch. 9, 1 Stat. 117 (1790), *as amended*, 22 U.S.C. §§ 252–54 (1970). It is an

offense to assault a foreign diplomat "in violation of the law of nations," 18 U.S.C. § 112. See also 18 U.S.C. § 915 (impersonation of foreign diplomats, consuls or officers); 18 U.S.C. § 962 (arming a vessel against a friendly nation); 18 U.S.C. § 956 (conspiracy to injure property of foreign government). Compare 22 U.S.C. §§ 461–65 (offenses against the declared neutrality of the United States). See also Frend v. United States, 100 F.2d 691 (D.C.Cir.1938) (upholding prohibition on picketing of embassies), and Greenberg v. Murphy, 329 F.Supp. 37 (S.D.N.Y.1971) (barring picketing of UN).

28. See Chapter I. But *cf.* Brennan, J., concurring in Kennedy v. Mendoza-Martinez, 372 U.S. 144, 195–96 (1963): ". . . under our Constitution, only a delimited portion of sovereignty has been assigned to the Government of which Congress is the legislative arm. To say that there inheres in United States sovereignty the power to sever the tie of citizenship does not answer the inquiry into whether that power has been granted to Congress." The Court, he said, can assume that Congress has this power only on "some sense of the inevitable fitness of things." *Id.* at 196.

The Court has never considered how the powers inherent in national sovereignty are divided among the branches. But in upholding an act of Congress requiring an American citizen to return to give testimony in a federal court, the Supreme Court said: "What in England was the prerogative of the sovereign in this respect, pertains under our constitutional system to the national authority which may be exercised by the Congress by virtue of the legislative power to prescribe the duties of the citizens of the United States. It is also beyond controversy the one of the duties which the citizen owes to his government is to support the administration of justice by attending its courts and giving his testimony whenever he is properly summoned. . . . And the Congress may provide for the performance of this duty and prescribe penalties for disobedience." (Citations omitted). Blackmer v. United States, 284 U.S. 421, 437–38 (1932). See also Mackenzie v. Hare, 239 U.S. 299, 311 (1915).

A power fully equivalent to the "sovereignty" or "foreign relations" power of Congress might be built from several powers of Congress, or as "necessary and proper" to carry out the foreign affairs powers of the President. See this chapter, p. 78. See generally Henkin, *The Treaty Makers and the Law Makers: The Law of the Land and Foreign Relations*, 107 U.PA.L.REV. 903, 913 *et seq.*, especially 915 n.26 (1959).

29. Perez v. Brownell, 356 U.S. 44, 59 (1958), discussed in this chapter, note 39.

30. Compare the legislation, supportable also by other powers, this chapter, note 27. And see the Logan Act, Ch. 1, 1 Stat. 613 (1799),

as amended, 18 U.S.C. § 953 (1970), imposing criminal penalties for Americans who carry on "correspondence or intercourse" with any foreign government with intent to influence its conduct in relation to a dispute with the United States or to defeat the measures of the United States.

31.  22 U.S.C. §§ 256–58a (1970).  Compare Chapter VII, note 39.

32.  See, *e. g.*, Johnson Debt Default Act of April 13, 1934, ch. 112, 48 Stat. 574, *as amended*, 18 U.S.C. § 955 (1970).  Such legislation is presumably also within the Commerce Power.

33.  See the Second Hickenlooper Amendment, now in 22 U.S.C. § 2370(e) (2) (1970).  In Banco Nacional de Cuba v. Farr, 383 F.2d 166, 182 (2d Cir. 1967), *cert. denied,* 390 U.S. 956 (1968), *rehearing denied,* 390 U.S. 1037 (1968) (Chapter VIII, note 55), the Court of Appeals found ample Congressional power for such legislation in the commerce clause supported by the necessary and proper clause, and additional authority in the power to define and punish offenses against the law of nations.  See Chapter VIII, p. 220 and Chapter II, note 83.

34.  See Chapter VI, p. 173.  That this authority of Congress is presumably based on its Foreign Affairs Power, see my article *The Treaty Makers and the Law Makers: The Law of the Land and Foreign Relations,* 107 U.Pa.L.Rev. 903, 926–29 (1959).

35.  The Chinese Exclusion Case, 130 U.S. 581 (1889); Fong Yue Ting v. United States, 149 U.S. 698 (1893); see also United States *ex rel.* Knauff v. Shaughnessy, 338 U.S. 537 (1950); *cf.* Hines v. Davidowitz, 312 U.S. 52 (1941); Galvan v. Press, 347 U.S. 522 (1954).

36.  8 U.S.C. § 1302 *et seq.* (1970).  In Hines v. Davidowitz, 312 U.S. 52 (1941) the Supreme Court held that since Congress had provided for the registration of aliens, Pennsylvania could not.  See Chapter IX, p. 243.

37.  *E. g.*, in times past, exemptions from military service.  But see now 50 U.S.C. § 456(a) (1) (App.1970).  And compare p. 77 this chapter, and Chapter X.

In Hines v. Davidowitz, 312 U.S. 52, 62–63 (1941), Mr. Justice Black said: "When the national government by treaty or statute has established rules and regulations touching the rights, privileges, obligations or burdens of aliens as such, the treaty or statute is the supreme law of the land."  He added that "the regulation of aliens is . . . intimately blended and intertwined with responsibilities of the national government."  *Id.* at 66.  But *cf.* Stone's dissent, *id.* at 76, denying a general power in Congress to regulate aliens.  The law now seems clear that for many if not all purposes the power to regulate aliens flows from the power to admit them, and both depend on the Foreign Affairs Power.  *Cf.* Takahashi v. Fish & Game Comm'n, 334

U.S. 410 (1948), and Graham v. Richardson, 403 U.S. 365 (1971). See Chapter X.

Compare the act authorizing war-time allies to exercise court-martial jurisdiction over their troops in the United States, Service Courts of Friendly Foreign Forces Act, ch. 326, 58 Stat. 643 (1944), 22 U.S.C. §§ 701–706 (1970); *cf.* North Atlantic Treaty Status of Forces Agreement, June 19, 1951, [1953] 4 U.S.T. 1792; T.I.A.S. No. 2846. See Chapter VII.

38.  Ch. 2534, § 3, 34 Stat. 1228 (1907).  Mackenzie v. Hare, 239 U.S. 299 (1915).  Compare this chapter, p. 76.  As applied to naturalized citizens, such regulations might be seen also as conditions of naturalization under Congress' power to "establish an Uniform Rule of Naturalization," Art. I, sec. 8.  But compare the following note.

39.  Perez v. Brownell, 356 U.S. 44 (1958).  That case was later overruled, Afroyim v. Rusk, 387 U.S. 253 (1967), on the ground that Congress cannot take away a man's citizenship against his will.  In Rogers v. Bellei, 401 U.S. 815 (1971), the Court held that Congress can withdraw derivative citizenship conferred by statute.  See Chapter X.  In none of these cases did any one doubt that the subject was within the powers granted to Congress.  I know no basis for the denials of Congressional power (in the absence of treaty) expressed in THE CONSTITUTION OF THE UNITED STATES OF AMERICA, ANALYSES AND INTERPRETATION 477 (Small & Jayson eds., 1964).  Compare Chapter I, note 14.

There are loose suggestions that the power to expatriate is implied in the power of Congress to establish a "uniform Rule of Naturalization" but while expatriation in given circumstances might be imposed as a condition of naturalization (see *Bellei, supra*), it is difficult to find in that clause the power to cancel the citizenship of one who has it by birth.

40.  See Valentine v. United States *ex rel.* Neidecker, 299 U.S. 5, 8–9 (1936); Grin v. Shine, 187 U.S. 181, 191 (1902).  The power of Congress to deport aliens would seem to support also their extradition (even in the absence of a treaty obligation), but extradition of a citizen of the United States would have to be justified in a broad Foreign Affairs Power.

41.  Blackmer v. United States, 284 U.S. 421 (1932); United States v. Bowman, 260 U.S. 94 (1922).  *Cf.* Kawakita v. United States, 343 U.S. 717 (1952); Steele v. Bulova Watch Co., 344 U.S. 280 (1952).  But in *Blackmer* the Court seemed to draw on sovereignty for authority to compel the citizen to return to the United States.  See note 28, this chapter.

Ordinarily laws of Congress are construed to apply only in the United States.  See American Banana Co. v. United Fruit Co., 213 U.S. 347, 357 (1909); Robertson v. R.R. Labor Board, 268 U.S. 619, 622

(1925); but *cf.* Blackmer v. United States, *supra*; Vermilya-Brown Co. v. Connell, 335 U.S. 377 (1948). For other statutes that apply to American citizens abroad, see, *e. g.*, 18 U.S.C. § 2381 (treason); 18 U.S.C. §§ 793–94 (espionage); 18 U.S.C. § 1621 (perjury); 18 U.S.C. § 953 (the Logan Act, forbidding private diplomacy, note 30, this chapter); see also 26 U.S.C. § 7201 (tax evasion).

42. Reid v. Covert, 354 U.S. 1 (1957); Kinsella v. United States *ex rel.* Singleton, 361 U.S. 234 (1960); Grisham v. Hagan, 361 U.S. 278 (1960); McElroy v. Guagliardo, 361 U.S. 281 (1960). Compare O'Callahan v. Parker, 395 U.S. 258 (1969), with Relford v. Commandant, U.S. Disciplinary Barracks, 401 U.S. 355 (1971); *cf.* United States *ex rel.* Flemings v. Chafee, 330 F.Supp. 193 (E.D.N.Y. 1971), *aff'd*, 458 F.2d 544 (2d Cir. 1972), *cert. granted*, 407 U.S. 919 (1972).

The "Offences clause" expressly authorizes Congress to define and punish felonies on the high seas. Congress can also legislate maritime law, regulate navigable streams, and govern territory belonging to the United States. Since 1790, for example, Congress has made it a crime to commit murder and other felonies "upon the high seas, or in any river, haven, basin, or bay, out of the jurisdiction of any particular state. . . ." Act of April 30, 1790, ch. 9, § 8, 1 Stat. 112, 113–14; *cf.* 18 U.S.C. § 1652 (1970).

43. Compare Kinsella v. United States *ex rel.* Singleton, 361 U.S. 234, 246 (1960); United States *ex rel.* Toth v. Quarles, 350 U.S. 11, 21 (1955).

44. International law recognizes the right of a state to apply its laws to its nationals anywhere but, with minor exceptions, forbids the exercise of legislative authority over others outside its territory. See 1 L. OPPENHEIM, INTERNATIONAL LAW 331–33 (Lauterpacht 8th ed. 1955). See Chapter II, note 55.

It has been suggested that where there is a treaty permitting the United States to try and punish certain offenses committed in a foreign country, Congress can legislate against such offenses under its power to do what is necessary and proper to implement the treaty. See Chapter V, p. 144. But generally such treaties merely *permit* the United States to apply its laws to these persons, and it is not obvious that the penal statutes are "necessary and proper" to implement such permissive treaties and give Congress legislative powers it would not otherwise have. Compare the North Atlantic Treaty Status of Forces Agreement, June 19, 1951, [1953] 4 U.S.T. 1792, T.I.A.S. No. 2846, and the cases rejecting court-martial authority, this chapter, note 42. Compare the annotated Constitution (Small & Jayson eds.) this chapter, note 39 at 477. Compare also the suggestion that Congress can prescribe the "duties of citizens" in *Blackmer v. United States,* quoted this chapter, note 28.

45.   Henkin, *The Treaty Makers and the Law Makers: The Law of the Land and Foreign Relations,* 107 U.PA.L.REV. 903, 920–30 (1959). On that view, surely, this power renders redundant other powers of Congress, *e. g.,* to define offenses against the law of nations, perhaps even the Foreign Commerce Power and the War Power.   That of course is the implication of Sutherland's statement in *Curtiss-Wright* that if these powers had not been mentioned in the Constitution they would nonetheless belong to the United States as inherent in its sovereignty. See Chapter I, p. 21.

46.   I have argued, too, that any matter, including the human rights of her own citizens, is a valid subject for a treaty if the United States concludes it for foreign relations purposes.   See Chapter V, p. 155.

The argument that any matter appropriate for a treaty is *ipso facto* within the foreign affairs power of Congress would also support the common view that Congress can repeal as domestic law even a treaty dealing with matters not within the enumerated powers of Congress. See my article, the previous note, at pp. 929–30; see Chapter V, note 117.

As regards reciprocal legislation, see, for example, the Nolan Act, ch. 26, 415 Stat. 1313 (1921), Robertson v. General Electric Co., 32 F.2d 495 (4th Cir. 1929), *cert. denied,* 280 U.S. 571 (1929).   As the opinion in the *Robertson* case tells, Congress used reciprocal legislation as a substitute for a treaty with Germany to which the Senate failed to consent.   (Germany, in its turn, also adopted legislation.)   For a partial collection of reciprocal statutes by Congress, see Henkin, *The Treaty Makers and the Law Makers: The Law of the Land and Foreign Relations,* 107 U.PA.L.REV. 903, 921 n. 41 (1959).

47.   252 U.S. 416, 433 (1920), *discussed in* Chapter V, p. 144.

48.   As long ago as 1806, Congress appropriated $50,000 for the "wretched sufferers" of an earthquake in Venezuela.   See 31 ANNALS OF CONG. 458 (1817).   (Lend-lease, perhaps foreign aid, too, could be supported also by the War Power.)

"[T]he power to spend [is] subject to limitations," United States v. Butler, 297 U.S. 1, 66 (1936).   In that case the Supreme Court struck down payments to farmers who agreed to curtail production, as an attempt to "purchase" acquiescence to a regulation that was not within the enumerated powers of Congress.   But the Court affirmed Hamilton's view that the Spending Power is an independent power with independent purposes: Congress can spend for purposes other than those included in its enumerated legislative powers.

No spending program or appropriation has been successfully challenged as not for "the common Defence or general Welfare," and clearly "general Welfare" has been interpreted with the widest latitude. Of course, spending programs are particularly difficult to challenge since a federal taxpayer, *qua* taxpayer, has standing to challenge expenditures only on the ground that they contravene "specific constitutional limitations imposed upon the . . . taxing and spending power" and to date that has been found only in the Establishment of Religion clause. Flast v. Cohen, 392 U.S. 83, 102–103 (1968); compare Frothingham v. Mellon, 262 U.S. 447 (1923).

The Spending Power is not to be confused with the "Appropriations Power," the power of Congress to appropriate funds necessary and proper to carry out any of its substantive powers and those of other branches of government, expressly referred to in Art. I, sec. 9. See this chapter, p. 79.

49. See, *e. g.*, 39 U.S.C. §§ 505, 506 (1970) (authorization for international postal agreements). For legislation dealing with international patent regulation see, *e. g.*, 35 U.S.C. §§ 102, 119, 184 (1970); compare also, 15 U.S.C. § 1126 (1970) (trademark regulation); 17 U.S.C. § 107 (1970) (copyright regulations).

The power of Congress to issue and protect patents and copyrights is in Article I, sec. 8, cl. 8; trademarks are regulated under the Commerce Power. Compare the Trade-Mark Cases, 100 U.S. 82 (1879), with the Lanham Act of 1946, ch. 540, 60 Stat. 428, *as amended*, 15 U.S.C. § 1051 *et seq.* (1970).

50. President Jefferson and others seemed to have doubts about the constitutionality of the Louisiana Purchase but their concern was not where in the federal government the power to acquire territory lay but whether the United States could acquire additional territory at all. That doubt has long been laid to rest. See, *e. g.*, Mr. Justice Jackson concurring in Youngstown Sheet & Tube Co. v. Sawyer, 343 U.S. 579, 638 n. 5.

The United States has the power to acquire territory by conquest or treaty. See American Ins. Co. v. Canter, 1 Pet. 516, 542 (U.S. 1828); Mormon Church v. United States, 136 U.S. 1, 42 (1890). The Supreme Court there suggested that Congress can acquire and govern such territories by virtue of the powers inherent in the sovereignty of the United States, *ibid.*; 1 Pet. at 542–43, 546. But Congress also has the express power "to make all needful Rules and Regulations respecting the Territory, or other Property belonging to the United States." Art. IV, sec. 3, cl. 2. That power, and the power to admit new States (*Id.*, cl. 1), might be held to imply for Congress authority to acquire territory by any necessary and proper means; but some argued that the territory clause referred only to territory then already belonging to the United States.

In the *Insular Cases* the Supreme Court upheld and applied provisions in a peace treaty leaving to Congress the future status of territories ceded to the United States. Downes v. Bidwell, 182 U.S. 244 (1901). That Congress can decide whether territory should be "incorporated" in the United States or remain "unincorporated," see also Dorr v. United States, 195 U.S. 138 (1904); Balzac v. Puerto Rico, 258 U.S. 298 (1922). For the status of individual rights in such territories, see Chapter X, p. 268.

Although of relatively small importance today, the power of the United States to acquire territory through discovery was recognized in Jones v. United States, 137 U.S. 202 (1890). The power may become important once again if the United States should claim territorial rights in space or additional rights in or under the seas. Compare the Truman Proclamation on the Continental Shelf, Chapter II, note 27, and the Congressional declaration of national sovereignty in air space, 49 U.S.C. § 1508(a) (1970); *cf.* Braniff Airways v. Nebraska State Board, 347 U.S. 590, 596 (1954). Resolutions of the United Nations have declared that neither of these environments is subject to national appropriation. Declaration of Legal Principles Governing the Activities of States in the Exploration and Use of Outer Space, G.A.Res.1962, 18 U.N. GAOR Supp. 15, at 15, U.N.Doc. A/5515 (1963); Declaration of Principles Governing the Sea-Bed and the Ocean Floor, and the Subsoil Thereof, Beyond the Limits of National Jurisdiction, G.A.Res. 2749, 25 U.N. GAOR Supp. 28, at 24, U.N. Doc. A/8097 (1970). The U.S. has accepted that principle as to outer space, by treaty. See Treaty on Principles Governing the Activities of States in the Exploration and Use of Outer Space, Including the Moon and Other Celestial Bodies, Jan. 27, 1967, Art. 2, [1967] 18 U.S.T. 2410, T.I.A.S.No.6347; and limits of national jurisdiction in the seas are still to be redefined.

51. The power to dispose of property is explicit in Art. IV, sec. 3, cl. 2. Ashwander v. TVA, 297 U.S. 288 (1936), might be read to imply that Congress can acquire property only for purposes that come within its other powers, but that would include its foreign affairs power as well. In United States v. Gratiot, 14 Pet. 526, 537 (U.S. 1840), the Court said that the power of Congress to deal with or dispose of U.S. property "is . . . without limitation." See also Alabama v. Texas, 347 U.S. 272, 273–74 (1954).

The power of eminent domain—an aspect of the property power, supported by the "necessary and proper clause," and implied in the requirement of "just compensation" in Amendment V (Chapter X, above)—can be used for foreign affairs purposes as for others. Compare United States *ex rel.* TVA v. Welch, 327 U.S. 546 (1946); Berman v. Parker, 348 U.S. 26 (1954).

52.  See United States v. Bevans, 3 Wheat. 336 (U.S.1818); The
Propeller Genesee Chief v. Fitzhugh, 12 How. 443 (U.S.1851); Southern Pacific Co. v. Jensen, 244 U.S. 205, 215 (1917); Note, *From Judicial Grant to Legislative Power: The Admiralty Clause in the Nineteenth Century,* 67 HARV.L.REV. 1214 (1954).  The property power,
this chapter, notes 50–51, would support Congressional authority to
deal with the territorial sea, its bed, and resources.  See United States
v. California, 332 U.S. 19 (1947); Alabama v. Texas, 347 U.S. 272
(1954).  Congress has also legislated for the continental shelf of the
United States in the Outer Continental Shelf Lands Act, ch. 345, 67
Stat. 462 (1953), 43 U.S.C. § 1331 *et seq.* (1970).  See generally L.
HENKIN, LAW FOR THE SEA'S MINERAL RESOURCES (1968).

53.  See Chapter X, note 12.  Congress can also regulate the rights
of aliens under its Foreign Affairs Power, p. 75 above.

The rights to equal protection and due process apply to aliens as well.
See Chapter X, pp. 255, 258.  After the Civil War Congress enacted
basic civil rights legislation applicable to "all persons," including aliens.
Act of April 9, 1866, ch. 31, 14 Stat. 27, reenacted in the Enforcement
Act of 1870, ch. 114, 16 Stat. 140, codified in REV.STAT. §§ 1977–91
(1874), now 42 U.S.C. §§ 1981 *et seq.* (1970).  See Comment, *The Alien
and the Constitution,* 20 U.CHI.L.REV. 547 (1953).

The power of Congress under the Fourteenth Amendment has been
extended to new reaches in Katzenbach v. Morgan, 384 U.S. 641 (1966);
United States v. Guest, 383 U.S. 745 (1966); but *cf.* Oregon v. Mitchell,
400 U.S. 112 (1970).  See Chapter I, note 18.  The Thirteenth Amendment has been interpreted to give Congress authority to remove whatever it deems to be a badge of slavery, for example, private discrimination in housing against blacks; Jones v. Alfred H. Mayer Co., 392
U.S. 409 (1968).  Both the Thirteenth and Fourteenth Amendments,
then, can now support wide civil rights legislation.  The vast powers
of Congress under the Fifteenth Amendment to eliminate racial discrimination in voting (South Carolina v. Katzenbach, 383 U.S. 301
(1966)) are also not without significance for American foreign relations in view of contemporary international interest in racial discrimination.

54.  McCulloch v. Maryland, 4 Wheat. 316, 421 (U.S.1819).  But
compare Mr. Justice Clark in Kinsella v. United States *ex rel.* Singleton,
361 U.S. 234, 247 (1960): "The latter clause is not itself a grant of
power, but a *caveat* that the Congress possesses all the means necessary to carry out the specifically granted 'foregoing' powers of § 8 'and
all other Powers vested by this Constitution. . . .'  As James Madison explained, the Necessary and Proper Clause is 'but merely a declaration, for the removal of all uncertainty, that the means of carrying
into execution those [powers] otherwise granted are included in the

grant.'" But compare the opinion of Mr. Justice Whittaker, *id.* at 259; Mr. Justice Harlan, *id.* at 253–55. It is fair to assume that the Court took a limited view of the necessary and proper clause in those cases only in order to safeguard the right to a jury trial for persons not themselves in the armed services. See this chapter, note 42. After those cases, the Court again reverted to Marshall's broad view of the clause, *e. g.*, in United States v. Oregon, 366 U.S. 643 (1961); and *cf.* Relford v. Commandant, U. S. Disciplinary Barracks, 401 U.S. 355, 362–63 (1971). See generally GUNTHER & DOWLING, CONSTITUTIONAL LAW, CASES AND MATERIALS 420–23 (8th ed. 1970).

55. See, *e. g.*, Legal Tender Cases, 12 Wall. 457, 556 (U.S.1870) (Justice Bradley, concurring); United States v. Arjona, 120 U.S. 479, 487 (1887) p. 73 this chapter. Although literally the clause confers the power to implement only "the foregoing Powers, and all other Powers vested by this Constitution," Congress can doubtless implement also the powers of the United States inherent in sovereignty. Compare: ". . . Congress has broad power under the Necessary and Proper Clause to enact legislation for the regulation of foreign affairs." Kennedy v. Mendoza-Martinez, 372 U.S. 144, 160 (1963).

56. 252 U.S. 416, 432 (1920). See Chapter V, p. 144. Holmes himself would probably not have held the statute regulating migratory birds beyond the powers of Congress even in the absence of treaty, but he had to carry his brethren who did not share his view of the Commerce Power. See his dissent in Hammer v. Dagenhart, 247 U.S. 251, 277 (1918). Today the Commerce Power alone reaches beyond what even Holmes, I guess, would have then accepted.

57. For the view that traditional war between states is no longer "done," and has lost its prime place in the conduct of foreign policy, see L. HENKIN, HOW NATIONS BEHAVE 134–41 (1968). Compare Chapter II, note 25.

58. See generally, 2 L. OPPENHEIM, INTERNATIONAL LAW, Part I, Chapter 2 (II) at 301–35, and Part III (Lauterpacht 7th ed. 1952). See Techt v. Hughes, 229 N.Y. 222, 128 N.E. 185, *cert. denied,* 254 U.S. 643 (1920); compare Chapter V, note 134. For the argument that the UN Charter has changed all that, see Chapter II, note 25.

59. The Third Amendment provides in effect that in time of war soldiers may be quartered in private homes without the consent of the owner, if prescribed by law.

The Fifth Amendment provides that in time of war persons in the militia may be tried for crime without grand jury indictment, and the same exception has been read into the jury trial requirement in Amendment VI. The power to try military personnel generally by court martial is different in time of war from what it is in time of peace. Compare the cases in note 42, this chapter; compare *Ex parte Quirin*, 317 U.S. 1 (1942).

60. See, *e. g.*, *Talbot* v. *Seeman* in which Chief Justice Marshall stated: "The whole powers of war [were] by the constitution . . . vested in congress." 1 Cranch 1, 28 (U.S.1801). See also Marshall in *McCulloch* v. *Maryland*, quoted in this chapter, note 14. See generally Chapter IV and the materials on the Vietnam war there at pp. 100–103, 107–108.

It was originally proposed that Congress be given the power "to make war." 2 FARRAND 168. The language was changed, it appears, only so as not to deny the President power to make war when necessary to repel invasion. *Id.* at 318. See Chapter IV, p. 107. Although today war, except in self defense against armed attack, is forbidden by the UN Charter, Congress remains constitutionally free to declare war in violation of the UN Charter or other international law. See Chapter V, p. 163; Chapter VII, p. 191.

61. It has been suggested that a formal declaration of war is constitutionally required because the Framers wished to make going to war difficult and to assure public awareness and support for the war. I know no basis for this suggestion, and it does not reflect 18th century attitudes. Compare CORWIN, THE PRESIDENT 200–201.

Even after Vietnam was undeniably a war, and national controversy about it had begun, the Senate Committee holding hearings on the National Commitments Resolution affirmed: "The committee does not believe that formal declarations of war are the only available means by which Congress can authorize the President to initiate limited or general hostilities. Joint resolutions such as those pertaining to Formosa, the Middle East, and the Gulf of Tonkin are a proper method of granting authority. . . ." S.REP.NO.797, 90th Cong., 1st Sess. 25 (1967).

Increasingly in our day wars are being fought without declaration, perhaps because wars are illegal under the UN Charter, perhaps because nations seek to avoid the traditional consequences of declared war on relations with third nations or even with some of the belligerents. Compare the Nixon statement, Chapter IV, note 23. For early Congressional authorization of hostilities other than by declaration of war, see, *e. g.*: ch. 48, 1 Stat. 561 (1798), ch. 60, *id.* at 572 (France); ch. 4, 2 Stat. 129 (1802) (Tripoli); ch. 90, 3 Stat. 230 (1815) (Algiers). For recent authorizations see, *e. g.*: ch. 4, 69 Stat. 7 (1955) (Formosa); Pub.L.No.85–7, 71 Stat. 5 (1957) (Middle East); Pub.L.No.87–733, 76 Stat. 697 (1962) (Cuban quarantine); H.Con.Res. 570, 76 Stat. 1429 (1962) (Berlin). And see the Tonkin Resolution, Chapter IV, note 28. For a comparison of these resolutions see 110 CONG.REC. 18428–29 (1964). For an earlier authorization compare J.Res.No.10,

38 Stat. 770 (1914), quoted in CORWIN, THE PRESIDENT 439 n. 96. That Congress intended undeclared limited war against France in 1798–1800, see Bas v. Tingy, 4 Dall. 37, 39, 40–41, 43, 45 (U.S.1800); Talbot v. Seeman, 1 Cranch 1 (U.S.1801).

Congress ratified Presidential wars in the Civil War, in Korea, perhaps also in the Mexican War, where the Congressional declaration in terms recognized that war existed. See Chapter IV, note 23. The Supreme Court upheld subsequent Congressional ratification as fully effective in The Prize Cases, 2 Black 635, 670–71 (U.S.1862). And see the discussion of Vietnam, Chapter IV, pp. 100–103. Subsequent ratification has been given the effect of prior authorization in other contexts, *e. g.*, Mitchell v. Clark, 110 U.S. 633, 640 (1884); United States v. Heinszen & Co., 206 U.S. 370 (1907). Subsequent ratification may be merely by appropriation of funds. Wilson v. Shaw, 204 U.S. 24 (1907); Isbrandtsen-Moller Co. v. United States, 300 U.S. 139, 147 (1937); Brooks v. Dewar, 313 U.S. 354, 360–61 (1941); Hirabayashi v. United States, 320 U.S. 81, 91 (1943); Fleming v. Mohawk Wrecking & Lumber Co., 331 U.S. 111, 116 (1947). But *cf. Ex parte* Endo, 323 U.S. 283, 303 n. 24 (1944).

62.  Ch. 40, 42 Stat. 105 (1921); ch. 519, 65 Stat. 451 (1951). Under Article IX of the Articles of Confederation, Congress had "the sole and exclusive right and power of determining on peace and war" but there Congress had the treaty power as well. A motion to give Congress the power to make peace was voted down in the Constitutional Convention, 2 FARRAND 319, 540–41; Story says that it was assumed that peace would be made by Treaty. STORY, COMMENTARIES § 1173, at 98. WRIGHT, at 292, questioned the propriety of ending World War I by Congressional resolution repealing the Declaration of War, but the power to end the state of war by resolution is now well established. See Commercial Trust Co. v. Miller, 262 U.S. 51, 57 (1923): "[T]he power which declared the necessity is the power to declare its cessation and what the cessation requires. The power is legislative." See also Ludecke v. Watkins, 335 U.S. 160, 168–69 (1948); see Mathews, *The Termination of War*, 19 MICH.L.REV. 819, 833–34 (1921). Compare the discussion of the repeal of the Tonkin Resolution, Chapter IV, pp. 107–108 and note 47.

63.  The phrase is Hamilton's in The Pacificus letters but he considered that it was the President who could determine the condition of the nation. See Chapter II, p. 43.

64.  See Chapter XLI, 1 Stat. 372 (1794); also *id.* at 400; the last neutrality act was that of 1939, ch. 2, 54 Stat. 4, 22 U.S.C. § 441 (1970); principal provisions of the 1939 Act were repealed in 1941, ch. 473, 55 Stat. 764.

65. J.Res.No.24, 30 Stat. 738 (1898). In 1882 Congress adopted "An Act to establish diplomatic relations with Persia." Ch. 399, 22 Stat. 301. For Congressional statements asserting Congressional control of recognition, see 1 G. HACKWORTH, DIGEST OF INTERNATIONAL LAW 162–63 (1940). See generally Bakker, *Congress and the Power to Recognize*, in 3 COLUMBIA ESSAYS IN INTERNATIONAL AFFAIRS, THE DEAN'S PAPERS, 1967, at 403 (1968). And see note 67, this chapter.

66. 5 Stat. 797 (1845) (Texas); 30 Stat. 750 (1898) (Hawaiian Islands). The treaty with Texas had been rejected by the Senate, principally to avoid war with Mexico. The Senate did not vote consent to the treaty with the Hawaiian Republic but it supported a Joint Resolution to approve the annexation. See CRANDALL, TREATIES 135–38.

67. CONG.GLOBE, 38th Cong., 2d Sess. 65–67 (1864). The resolution—in response to Seward's statement to France that Congress does not speak for the United States, this chapter, p. 86—is also set forth in the cousre of Hale's memorandum on the power of Congress to recognize the independence of a new foreign state; the memorandum recites various efforts by Congress to act in foreign affairs during the 19th century. S.DOC.NO.56, 54th Cong., 2d Sess. 47 (1897).

68. See Chapter II, note 12.

69. Compare Blackmer v. United States, quoted this chapter, note 28. In a famous debate in 1906 with Senator Spooner (see Chapter II, note 9), Senator Bacon said: "Congress and not the President is supreme under the Constitution in the control of our foreign affairs." And "the Constitution has invested Congress with almost all the prerogatives of sovereignty." 40 CONG.REC. 2132, 2134 (1906).

70. For a contemporary replay of Madison and Senator Bacon, see Fulbright, in *Hearings on Separation of Powers before the Subcomm. on Separation of Powers of the Senate Comm. on the Judiciary,* 90th Cong., 1st Sess. 43–44 (1967). Senator Fulbright recognized that the conduct of foreign relations was the responsibility of the President but believed that Congress had the power to make foreign policy, and he was concerned about the erosion of its authority and responsibility. While recognizing some overlap between shaping foreign policy and conducting foreign relations, *e. g.*, in foreign aid, Fulbright said:

> The criteria of responsible and constructive debate are restraint in matters of detail and the day-to-day conduct of foreign policy, combined with diligence and energy in discussing the values, direction, and purpose of American foreign policy. Just as it is an excess of democracy when Congress is overly aggressive in attempting to supervise the conduct of policy, it is a failure of democracy when it fails to participate ac-

tively in determining policy objectives and in the making of significant decisions. *Id.* at 52.

See also Senator Fulbright's statements in "U. S. Commitments to Foreign Powers," *Hearings on S.Res. 151 Before the Senate Comm. on Foreign Relations,* 90th Cong., 1st Sess. 79–80, 183–84 (1967); Senator E. McCarthy, *id.* at 33. See also an earlier statement by Senator Morse: . . . "under our Constitution foreign policy does not belong to the President of the United States and the Secretary of State. They are but the administrators of the people's foreign policy." 107 CONG.REC. 6575 (1961).

71. In denying the sovereignty of the States, King (of Massachusetts) said: "Considering them as political Beings, they were dumb, for they could not speak to any forign (sic) Sovereign whatever. They were deaf, for they could not hear any propositions from such Sovereign." 1 FARRAND 323.

72. The abrogation of the treaty with France in 1798 has been characterized as, in the circumstances, a partial declaration of war. Compare Bas v. Tingy, 4 Dall. 37 (U.S.1800); CORWIN, THE PRESIDENT 435 n. 75. See Chapter V, note 136. Congressional recognition of Cuban independence in 1898 (this chapter, note 65) followed President McKinley's reference of the Cuban question to Congress and formed a "package" with the declaration of war against Spain. See 30 Stat. 364, 738 (1898).

For the principal powers denied to Congress see Chapter IV, p. 92.

73. 9 RICHARDSON 438–86 quoted in CORWIN, THE PRESIDENT 430–31 n. 46. See also WRIGHT, 278–83. But *cf.* 24 DEP'T STATE BULL. 556–57 (1951) (reaction of Secretary of State Acheson to Senate resolution expressing friendship for the Soviet people during the Berlin crisis of 1951). For some references to Congressional expressions of policy and different reactions of different Presidents see WRIGHT, *supra;* CORWIN, *supra* at 183–84, 192–93, 433–35 n. 66. Increasingly, of course, foreign governments monitor Congressional proceedings and are fully aware of Congressional views and sentiments. Compare, for example, text at notes 75 and 76, this chapter.

In the past, at least, attempts by foreign governments to talk directly to Congress or Congresssmen or the American people were sorely resented. Compare the reaction to the communication by the German Embassy published in American newspapers, Telegram from Mr. Bryan, Secretary of State, to Mr. Gerard, Ambassador in Germany, May 13, 1915, [1915 Supp.] FOREIGN REL.U.S. 393, 395 (1928). Foreign governments still tend to be discreet but Congress has invited formal addresses by foreign statesmen (usually at Executive instigation) and Congressmen have been known to invite discussion with foreign diplomats, sometimes to the helpless unhappiness of the Executive Branch.

74. Congressional resolutions whether or not expressed as sense resolutions have sometimes effectively become national policy: for example, the Lodge Resolution in 1912 barring the Western Hemisphere to foreign powers for military and naval purposes, even when done through quasi-public corporations. S.Res. 371, 62d Cong., 2d Sess., 48 CONG.REC. 10046–47 (1912). (It was directed against a reported attempt by a Japanese company to establish a coaling station in Mexico.) Sometimes Congress has resolved to condemn Executive actions: *e. g.*, on Feb. 7, 1894, the House adopted a resolution condemning "the action of the United States minister in employing United States naval forces and illegally aiding in overthrowing the constitutional Government of the Hawaiian Islands." 26 CONG.REC. 2001–2002 (1894). Compare the resolution of the House condemning "Polk's war" cited Chapter IV, note 23.

Contrary to common assumption, the President is not always more "internationalist" than Congress. In 1927 Coolidge failed to heed a Senate Resolution favoring arbitration of the oil dispute with Mexico. See S.Res. 327, 69th Cong., 2d Sess., 68 CONG.REC. 2233 (1927). For a report on the propriety of the House of Representatives expressing itself on foreign affairs, see H.R.REP. No. 1569, 68th Cong., 2d Sess. 10 (1925).

75. WRIGHT 279–81; 6 MOORE, DIGEST 497–98.

76. 37 DEP'T STATE BULL. 142 (1957), in response to French objections to Kennedy's statements, 103 CONG.REC. 10780 *et seq.* especially at 10788 col. 1 (1957).

77. Compare Watkins v. United States, 354 U.S. 178 (1957); Barenblatt v. United States, 360 U.S. 109 (1959).

78. It is reported, for example, that in July 1949, Secretary of State Marshall promised the Senate Foreign Relations Committee that there would be no recognition of Communist China without consultation with the Committee. See D. CHEEVER AND H. HAVILAND, AMERICAN FOREIGN POLICY AND THE SEPARATION OF POWERS 11 (1952). Compare Chapter VI, note 10.

79. Art. I, sec. 9, clauses 5 and 6. For the suggestion that the "export clause" should be interpreted as forbidding also more sophisticated controls designed for domestic economic purposes, see Note, *Constitutionality of Export Controls*, 76 YALE L.J. 200 (1966). Compare Fairbank v. United States, 181 U.S. 283 (1901) (stamp tax on export bill of lading); United States v. Hvoslef, 237 U.S. 1 (1915) (tax on marine charter parties); Thames & Mersey Marine Ins. Co. v. United States, 237 U.S. 19 (1915) (tax on marine insurance policy on exports). The Constitutional Convention apparently assumed that the

"export clause" limited only commercial regulation and would not prohibit an embargo under the war power. 2 FARRAND 361–62. The provision prohibiting port preferences was designed to prevent preferences between ports based on their location in different States; it does not forbid discriminations between individual ports generally. Louisiana Public Service Comm'n v. Texas & N. O. R. R., 284 U.S. 125, 131 (1931).

Clause 1 of section 9 was designed to deny Congress the power to prohibit the importation of slaves before 1808, or to impose a tax or duty of more than ten dollars per slave. See this chapter, note 13. Clause 7 contains the provision that "No money shall be drawn from the Treasury, but in Consequence of Appropriations made by Law; and a regular Statement and Account of the Receipts and Expenditures of all public Money shall be published from time to time."

There are hypothetical foreign policy consequences also in the provision forbidding the grant of titles of nobility, or requiring the consent of Congress for any American official to accept "any present, Emolument, Office, or Title, of any kind whatever, from any King, Prince, or foreign State." (Clause 8).

As regards matters as to which Congressional power derives from the sovereignty of the United States as determined by international law, it has been argued that such powers cannot be exercised in violation of international law; the argument is not persuasive since sovereignty includes the power (not the right) to act in violation of international law and obligation. See Chapter V, p. 151, Chapter VIII, pp. 221–22.

NOTES, CHAPTER IV, SEPARATION OF POWERS, pp. 89 to 123.

1. Issues of Separation do not often come to court. See Chapter VIII. When they do, the Supreme Court can often avoid questions of respective power; finding that President and Congress concurred the Court had to consider only the powers of both together. See, *e. g.*, Chicago & Southern Air Lines v. Waterman S.S. Corp., 333 U.S. 103, 109–10, 112–14 (1948); Hirabayashi v. United States, 320 U.S. 81 (1943); compare *Ex parte* Quirin, 317 U.S. 1 (1942); United States v. Curtiss-Wright Export Corp., 299 U.S. 304 (1936). But compare the cases discussed later in this chapter at pp. 96–99.

2. "Legislative and Executive powers are pooled obviously to the end that commercial strategic and diplomatic interests of the country may be coordinated and advanced without collision or deadlock between agencies." Chicago & Southern Air Lines v. Waterman S.S. Corp., 333 U.S. 103, 110 (1948), quoted Chapter II, note 32.

3. Sometimes there are issues as to whether a President's act claiming Congressional authority was in fact authorized by Congress. Compare Executive Order 11387 of January 3, 1968, 33 Fed.Reg. 47, limiting the transfer of capital abroad. The President claimed authority in a 1917 statute giving him authority in time of war or proclaimed emergency; a Senate subcommittee thought the Executive order was a usurpation of Congressional authority. See SENATE COMM. ON THE JUDICIARY, SEPARATION OF POWERS, S.REP.No.91–549, 91st Cong., 1st Sess. 16 (1969) [hereinafter cited as S.REP., SEPARATION OF POWERS].

4. As the Supreme Court held in invalidating President Truman's seizure of the steel mills. Justice Black's opinion for the Court made much—some think too much—of an obvious and inherent difference between legislative and executive power. See p. 96 this chapter. Compare also Kent v. Dulles, quoted p. 98, this chapter; and Mr. Justice Black dissenting in Zemel v. Rusk, 381 U.S. 1, 20–21 (1965).

Congress, in turn, cannot invade the Executive's power of appointing officials, Art. II, sec. 2, cl. 1 (see p. 116, this chapter), or his power to remove some officials, p. 117, this chapter. Neither can Congress usurp his power to pardon criminal offenders. Art. II, sec. 2, cl. 2. *Ex parte* Garland, 4 Wall. 333 (U.S.1866); see U. S. v. Klein, 13 Wall. 128 (U.S.1871); *Ex parte* Grossman, 267 U.S. 87 (1925). But Congress has power to grant a general amnesty. Brown v. Walker, 161 U.S. 591, 601 (1896).

5. See Chapter III, p. 85. But Congress has participated in inter-parliamentary bodies. See, *e. g.*, Interparliamentary Union Acts, 22 U.S.C. §§ 276–276k (1970).

6. Compare, *e. g.*, Calhoun, 29 ANNALS OF CONG. 529–32, quoted Chapter V, note 49.

7. See Chapter III, note 46.

8. Compare the Executive Order limiting transfers of capital, this chapter, note 3.

The Supreme Court held that the President had power as Commander-in-Chief to impose tariffs on goods coming into Puerto Rico and the Philippine Islands from the United States while the islands were under occupation, but that such authority terminated when the treaty with Spain came into effect ceding these territories to the United States. Dooley v. United States, 182 U.S. 222 (1901); Lincoln v. United States, 197 U.S. 419 (1905), *reaffirmed,* 202 U.S. 484 (1906). (Congress, however, could ratify his acts and give them retroactive effect. United States v. Heinszen & Co., 206 U.S. 370 (1907).) In those cases, of course, when the island became United States territory, any duties on goods passing between them and other parts of the United States would not be within any foreign affairs authority of the President.

9. Especially since the "necessary and proper" clause (Art. I, sec. 8, cl. 18) gives Congress the power to implement the powers of the President. See p. 78 above; compare, generally, J. HART, THE ORDINANCE MAKING POWERS OF THE PRESIDENT OF THE UNITED STATES Chapter IX (1925). Compare also the dissenting opinion in the *Steel Seizure Case,* note 11 this chapter, that argued the President's power to seize the steel mills as a means of executing various laws and other federal authority.

The *Curtiss-Wright* case, Chapter I, p. 19, might be read to imply that the President might have imposed an arms embargo on his own authority; but he could not have prosecuted violators unless an act of Congress prescribed penalties for such violation. See p. 95, this chapter; Chapter V, note 99; Chapter VII, note 36.

10. President Lincoln apparently incurred obligations of two million dollars without Congressional authorization or appropriation. Few believe he had Constitutional authority to do so, but his acts were later ratified by Congress. For that and other instances of Presidential expenditure without authorization, or Presidential "overdraft" or diversion of funds to other purposes, see L. WILMERDING, THE SPENDING POWER (1943), cited in CORWIN, THE PRESIDENT 399–400.

11. See the various opinions in Youngstown Sheet & Tube Co. v. Sawyer, 343 U.S. 579 (1952). In 1952, while American troops were fighting in Korea, a labor dispute in the steel industry led the union to

give notice of a nation-wide strike. A few hours before the strike was scheduled to take effect, President Truman issued an Executive Order reciting that steel was indispensable to the production of weapons, and that the President believed that work stoppage would jeopardize the national defense; he directed the Secretary of Commerce to take possession of most of the steel mills and keep them running. The President reported the action to Congress but Congress took no action.

Affirming a lower court decision, the Supreme Court declared the seizure to be beyond the President's power because it was an exercise of "legislative" power. See also Douglas, J., concurring, *id.* at 630. But three justices dissented, and four of the six justices in the majority relied heavily, if not exclusively, on the fact that the President's action was inconsistent with Congressional policy, Congress having provided a different procedure for handling such strikes and indeed having refused to adopt a provision authorizing plant seizures. It is not unfair to assume that the majority of the Justices in the case would have upheld the President's power had Congress not acted at all. Mr. Justice Jackson, concurring, wrote explicitly of "a zone of twilight in which he and Congress may have concurrent authority, or in which its distribution is uncertain." *Id.* at 647, quoted this chapter, pp. 105–106.

Compare United States v. Midwest Oil Co., 236 U.S. 459 (1915); La Abra Silver Mining Co. v. United States, 175 U.S. 423, 459–61 (1899); Myers v. United States, 272 U.S. 52, 161 (1926); also Little v. Barreme, 2 Cranch 170, 177 (U.S.1804). But the much-cited Hale memorandum, S.Doc.No.56, 54th Cong.2d Sess. 4 (1897), argued that the Constitution did not intend "to place any given power in two or all three branches of the Government concurrently." Madison, in his second Helvidius letter (see Chapter II, note 12) said: "A concurrent authority in two independent departments, to perform the same function with respect to the same thing, would be awkward in practice, as it is unnatural in theory."

*Youngstown* has not been considered a "foreign affairs case." The President claimed to be acting within "the aggregate of his constitutional powers," but the majority of the Supreme Court did not treat the case as involving the reach of his foreign affairs power, and even the dissenting justices invoked only incidentally that power or the fact that the steel strike threatened important American foreign policy interests.

12. Brown v. United States, 8 Cranch 110 (U.S.1814). Story had ruled to the contrary on circuit in the court below, and sitting on the Supreme Court he adhered to his view that the President had the power unless Congress denied it. *Id.* at 129, 145, 149 *et seq.* It is not clear whether Story's view was that during wars declared by Congress

the President had authority flowing automatically from his constitutional power as Commander-in-Chief, or that Congress had conferred it upon him implicitly by its declaration of war. Story admitted that Congress could have denied or limited the President's powers. Compare this chapter, p. 107 and note 49.

13. The Prize Cases, 2 Black 635 (U.S.1862). Even before the Civil War, the Court recognized the power of military authorities to seize or destroy private property in case of military necessity, even of citizens, subject to compensation. *Cf.* Mitchell v. Harmony, 13 How. 115, 134 (U.S.1851). For later cases, compare United States v. Russell, 13 Wall. 623 (U.S.1871); Totten v. United States, 92 U.S. 105 (1875); see 40 OP.ATT'Y GEN. 250, 253 (1942). And compare Chapter X, p. 259. President Lincoln's Emancipation Proclamation may be seen as asserting even larger Executive authority but that was later ratified by the Thirteenth Amendment.

I do not consider here limitations on Presidential war-power in favor of citizens within the United States. See, *e. g.*, *Ex parte* Milligan, 4 Wall. 2 (U.S.1866), which held, after the war, that a loyal citizen could not be tried by court martial where civilian courts were functioning. See generally Chapter X.

14. See 8 Cranch at 124–29.

15. See Trading With the Enemy Act of 1917, ch. 106, 40 Stat. 411, as amended by the First War Powers Act, 1941, ch. 593, § 301, 55 Stat. 839. *Cf.* Silesian-American Corp. v. Clark, 332 U.S. 469 (1947); Uebersee Finanz-Korp. v. McGrath, 343 U.S. 205 (1952).

16. Fleming v. Page, 9 How. 603 (U.S.1850).

17. Compare the Truman Proclamation claiming for the United States the natural resources of its Continental Shelf, Chapter II, p. 48. Previous attempts to deal with the matter by legislation died in committee. S.J.Res. 208, 75th Cong., 1st Sess., 81 CONG.REC. 8882, 9236, 9548 (1937) (Senator Nye); S.J.Res. 24, 76th Cong., 1st Sess., 84 CONG.REC. 70 (1939) (Senator Nye); S.J.Res. 83, *id.* at 1976 (Senator Walsh); H.R.J.Res. 176, *id.* at 1646, 6235 (Rep. Hobbs); H.R.J.Res. 181, *id.* at 1850 (Rep. O'Connor).

18. Valentine v. United States *ex rel.* Neidecker, 299 U.S. 5 (1936). In that case, the extradition treaty with France provided that neither party "shall be bound" to extradite its own nationals. The Court said that there being no treaty obligation the President had no authority to extradite an American citizen.

In 1825, President J. Q. Adams took the position that he had no authority to extradite a fugitive because the applicable extradition treaty was no longer in force. See letter quoted by Mr. Justice Thompson in Holmes v. Jennison, 14 Pet. 540, 582–83 (U.S.1840); see also Taney's opinion, *id.* at 574, discussed in Chapter IX, p. 231. But Lincoln extradited Arguelles to Spain on his own authority. See Chapter VI, note 16.

Attorney General Cushing was of the opinion that the President could not return deserting seamen in the absence of a treaty. 6 OP. ATT'Y GEN. 148, 209 (1871). But compare the Supreme Court's statement that the Executive has the power to exclude aliens from the United States, Chapter II, note 31.

19. See Chapter II, p. 57; Chapter VI, p. 184. But the executive agreements given effect in those cases involved only money, not rights of a citizen accused of crime.

Any extradition might be seen as involving an *ad hoc* agreement with the foreign country, and might seem readily within the President's powers to conclude executive agreements. See Chapter VI, p. 187. It might be argued, however, that the Act of Congress which provides procedures for implementation "[w]henever there is a treaty or convention for extradition . . . " ch. 645, § 3184, 62 Stat. 822 (1948), as amended 18 U.S.C. § 3184 (1970), implies that there shall be no extradition in the absence of treaty. As to whether an executive agreement can prevail in the face of an inconsistent statute, see Chapter VI, p. 186.

20. 357 U.S. 116, 129 (1958). The four dissenting Justices did not consider the President's independent authority, having found that Congress had authorized denying passports in such cases. 357 U.S. at 130. Compare Zemel v. Rusk, 381 U.S. 1 (1965), with United States v. Laub, 385 U.S. 475 (1967); see this chapter note 97 and Chapter X. For the *Youngstown* case see this chapter notes 4 and 11.

21. I draw here on my article *Constitutional Issues in Foreign Policy*, Preface note 4.

22. Under the Hamilton Plan at the Constitutional Convention the Executive was to have "the direction of war when authorized or begun." 1 FARRAND 292.

For a collection of statements by Presidents, especially early Presidents, asserting that only Congress can commit the nation to war, see Wormuth, *The Vietnam War: The President versus the Constitution*, in 2 THE VIETNAM WAR AND INTERNATIONAL LAW 711 (1969), edited for the American Society of International Law by Professor Richard Falk [hereinafter cited as FALK, VIETNAM]; and Lawyers Memorandum, *Indochina: The Constitutional Crisis*, 116 CONG.REC. 15,410–16 (1970). Also, SENATE COMM. ON FOREIGN RELATIONS, NATIONAL COMMITMENTS, S.REP.NO.797, 90th Cong., 1st Sess. 9–12 (1967) [hereinafter cited as S.REP. NATIONAL COMMITMENTS].

President Truman seemed to consider Korea different because he acted pursuant to a UN resolution. See Note, *Congress, The President, and the Power to Commit Forces to Combat*, 81 HARV.L.REV. 1771, 1791–

Notes, Chapter IV

92 (1968), reprinted in 2 FALK, VIETNAM at 616, 636–37; see remarks of Truman and Acheson in 23 DEP'T STATE BULL. 3, 5–6 (1950); see *Authority of the President to Repel the Attack in Korea*, 23 DEP'T STATE BULL. 173. But see this chapter, note 27.

23. Hamilton anticipated that the President exercising his powers might

> affect the exercise of the power of the legislature to declare war. Nevertheless, the executive cannot thereby control the exercise of that power. The legislature is still free to perform its duties, according to its own sense of them; though the executive, in the exercise of its constitutional powers, may establish an antecedent state of things which ought to weigh in the legislative decisions . . . .
>
> While, therefore, the legislature can alone declare war, can alone actually transfer the nation from a state of peace to a state of hostility, it belongs to the "executive power" to do whatever else the law of nations, cooperating with the treaties of the country, enjoin in the intercourse of the United States with foreign powers. Letters of Pacificus No. 1, 7 A. HAMILTON, WORKS 83–84 (Hamilton, ed. 1851), Chapter II, note 9.

Compare the House Resolution of 1848 referring to the Mexican war "unnecessarily and unconstitutionally begun by the President of the United States." CONG.GLOBE, 30th Cong., 1st Sess. 95 (1848). There have been somewhat similar accusations against F. D. Roosevelt as regards World War II. For the view that Franklin Roosevelt exceeded his powers in 1940–41 see SENATE COMM. ON FOREIGN RELATIONS, 91st CONG., 2d SESS., *Documents Relating to the War Power of Congress, the President's Authority as Commander-in-Chief and the War in Indochina* 15 (Comm. Print 1970). And compare CORWIN, THE PRESIDENT 202–204. Corwin concludes (at 204): "A summary history of the wars in which the United States has engaged since the adoption of the Constitution will concede to Congress that policies and views advanced within its walls were primarily responsible for two of these wars, the War of 1812 and the war with Spain. But our four great wars . . . were the outcome of presidential policies in the making of which Congress played a distinctly secondary role."

Earlier Wright (at 286–89) pointed out that even Congressional declarations of war have been, in terms, recognitions of war; compare also Ch. 4, 2 Stat. 129 (1802). But perhaps Congress was merely seeking to put the onus for starting the war on the enemy. Apparently only the Declaration of War in 1812 followed substantial debate in Congress (24 ANNALS OF CONG. 1631–83 (1812)). For an accusation that Theodore Roosevelt was trying to force Congress to declare war, see Senator Morgan's speech, 38 CONG.REC. 426, 434–41 (1904), some of it quoted in CORWIN, THE PRESIDENT 438.

President Nixon, while a private citizen, said that "there will never be another declaration of war . . . that time is gone." Interview, WETA–TV Channel 26, Nov. 27, 1967, quoted in Wallace, *The President's Exclusive Foreign Affairs Powers over Foreign Aid,* 1970 DUKE L.J. 293, 309. But perhaps he meant only that even wars authorized by Congress would be fought without formal declaration.

24. Andrew Jackson said that the President should seek Congressional approval for policy that would probably lead to War. 4 RICHARDSON 1484.

25. Compare C. BERDAHL, THE WAR POWERS OF THE EXECUTIVE IN THE UNITED STATES 27–30 (1921).

26. The Vietnam War produced a spate of articles and memoranda dealing with the constitutional authority of the President to fight in Vietnam. Most of them are reprinted in FALK, VIETNAM; constitutional issues are dealt with especially in volumes 2 and 3. See, in particular, Note, *Congress, the President, and the Power to Commit Forces to Combat,* this chapter, note 22. See also *Symposium on United States Action in Cambodia,* 65 AM.J.INT'L L. 1 (1971); *United States Intervention in Cambodia: Legal Analyses of the Event and its Domestic Repercussions,* 50 B.U.L.REV. 1 (1970); *Hammarskjöld Forum: Expansion of the Vietnam War into Cambodia—the Legal Issues,* 45 N.Y.U.L.REV. 625 (1970); *Legality of United States Participation in the Vietnam Conflict: a Symposium,* 75 YALE L.J. 1084 (1966); *Brief for Constitutional Lawyers: Committee on Undeclared War as Amicus Curiae, Massachusetts v. Laird,* 17 WAYNE L.REV. 67 (1971); Comment, *The President, Congress and Power to Declare War,* 16 KAN.L. REV. 82 (1967); Kurland, *Impotence of Reticence,* 1968 DUKE L.J. 619; Malawer, *The Vietnam War Under the Constitution,* 31 U.PITT.L.REV. 205 (1969); Faulkner, *War in Vietnam: Is it Constitutional?* 56 GEO.L.J. 1123 (1968); *Legal Memorandum on the Amendment to End the War,* 116 CONG.REC. 16,120 (1970); *The War in Southeast Asia: A Legal Position Paper, id.* at 17,090; *Symposium of Lawyers on Indochina,* May 20, 1970, *id.* at 17,387; *Lawyer's Memorandum, Indochina: The Constitutional Crisis,* Part I, *id.* at 15,410 and Part II, *id.* at 16,478; E. Rostow *et al., Letter on Constitutional Authority of President in Using American Troops, id.* at 18,338.

27. In Korea, President Truman acted without advance authorization from Congress. Presumably, he claimed authority to act in the first instance to protect American lives and property; then, pursuant to the UN Security Council resolution, in implementation of the UN Charter (a treaty of the United States) and the UN Participation Act

adopted by Congress. See note 22, this chapter. Some questioned whether the Charter and the Act authorized the President ever after to go to war at the behest of the UN especially when, as in this case, UN action was taken at the request of the United States, effectively of the Executive Branch. Compare Chapter VII, p. 191. President Truman acted in emergency and there was early consultation with Congressional leaders; the circumstances perhaps gave him the right to expect Congressional ratification; and Congress did approve and ratify, implicitly, by appropriation of funds and renewal of the Selective Service Laws with full knowledge and the intent to approve what the President was doing.

The Korean war also produced debate, but only a few Congressmen expressly challenged the President's authority. See, *e. g.*, SENATE COMM. ON FOREIGN RELATIONS AND COMM. ON ARMED SERVICES, POWERS OF THE PRESIDENT TO SEND THE ARMED FORCES OUTSIDE THE UNITED STATES, 82d Cong. 1st Sess. (1951); 96 CONG.REC. 9228–31, 9232–33, 9268–69, 9320, 9322–23, 9327–29, 9538–39, 9647–49 (1950). See generally G. PAIGE, THE KOREAN DECISION (1968).

28. Pub.L.No.90–5, § 401, 81 Stat. 5 (1967).

In the Tonkin Gulf Resolution, Pub.L.No.88–408, 78 Stat. 384 (1964), ". . . the Congress approves and supports the determination of the President, as Commander in Chief, to take all necessary measures to repel any armed attack against the forces of the United States and to prevent further aggression." Section 2 of the Resolution provides: "The United States regards as vital to its national interest and to world peace the maintenance of international peace and security in southeast Asia. Consonant with the Constitution of the United States and the Charter of the United Nations and in accordance with its obligations under the Southeast Asia Collective Defense Treaty, the United States is, therefore, prepared, as the President determines, to take all necessary steps, including the use of armed force, to assist any member or protocol state of the Southeast Asia Collective Defense Treaty requesting assistance in defense of its freedom." Compare the testimony of Undersecretary of State Nicholas Katzenbach, 113 CONG. REC. 23390–92 (1967), also in "U. S. Commitments to Foreign Powers," *Hearings on S.Res. 151 before the Senate Comm. on Foreign Relations,* 90th Cong. 1st Sess. 77 *et seq.* (1967) [hereinafter cited as *Hearings, National Commitments*]. See generally J. GALLOWAY, THE GULF OF TONKIN RESOLUTION (1970).

For appropriations to support the Vietnam War, see *e. g.*, The Supplemental Defense Appropriation Act of May 7, 1965, Pub.L.No.89–18, 79 Stat. 109; Defense Appropriations Act of 1970, Pub.L.No.91–171, § 638, 83 Stat. 486 (1969).

That Congress had authorized the Vietnam War was held in Orlando v. Laird, 443 F.2d 1039 (2d Cir. 1971), *cert. denied,* 404 U.S. 869 (1971).

29. Compare note 23, this chapter.

30. Both supporters and opponents of the Resolution seemed to recognize that the President was being authorized to go to war if he thought it necessary. Compare, *e. g.,* Senator Fulbright, 110 CONG. REC. 18409 (1964), with Senator Morse, *id.* at 18430.

Senator Fulbright who piloted the Resolution through the Senate later said: "Figuratively speaking, we did not deal with the resolution in terms of what it said and in terms of the power it would vest in the Presidency; we dealt with it in terms of how we thought it would be used by the man who occupied the Presidency. Our judgment turned out to be wrong, but even if it had been right, even if the administration had applied the resolution in the way we then thought it would, the abridgment of the legislative process and our consent to so sweeping a grant of power was not only a mistake but a failure of responsibility on the part of the Congress." He appeared to be of the view that the Resolution constituted an unconstitutional delegation by Congress to the President of the war power. See "Separation of Powers," *Hearings Before the Subcomm. on Separation of Powers of the Sen. Comm. on the Judiciary,* 90th Cong., 1st Sess. 47 (1967) [hereinafter cited as *Hearings, Separation of Powers*]. Some would characterize it an authorization to carry hostility as far as the President deemed necessary, including full-scale war.

For extended debates as to what the Tonkin Resolution authorized, see the exchanges between Undersecretary of State Katzenbach and several Senators, in *Hearings, National Commitments,* 82 *et seq.*

31. Section 3 of the Resolution, note 28 this chapter, provides: "This resolution shall expire when the President shall determine that the peace and security of the area is reasonably assured by international conditions created by action of the United Nations or otherwise, except that it may be terminated earlier by concurrent resolution of the Congress."

32. See, *e. g.,* the tabling on March 1, 1966, of amendments offered by Senators Morse and Gruening, which would have repealed the Tonkin Resolution and barred the use of draftees in Southeast Asia without Congressional consent. The vote was 92–5 against the Morse Amendment and 94–2 against the Gruening Amendment. 112 CONG.REC. 4404, 4406 (1966). See also various attempts to have Congress limit U.S. involvement in Cambodia and set a date for withdrawal of U. S. troops, note 45, this chapter. On the effect of the later repeal of the Tonkin Resolution, see this chapter, p. 108 and note 47.

33.   Compare John Quincy Adams' reference to "that error in our Constitution which confers upon the legislative assemblies the power of declaring war, which, in the theory of government, according to Montesquieu and Rousseau, is strictly an Executive Act." Later he referred to the "absurdity" of "having given to Congress, instead of the Executive, the power of declaring war." 4 MEMOIRS OF JOHN QUINCY ADAMS 32 (C. F. Adams ed. 1875). It appears, however, that he thought that practice had effectively corrected this error.

That "short of war" is not an effective constitutional standard see Jones, *The President, Congress and Foreign Relations*, 29 CALIF.L. REV. 565, 579 (1941).

34.   S. 2936. See S.REP. NO. 606, 92d Cong., 2d Sess. (1972). The House of Representatives did not act on the measure during the 92d Congress.

35.   See Acheson, quoted Chapter II, note 46.

36.   Compare Taney's effort in *Ex parte* Milligan, 4 Wall. 2, 139–140 (U.S.1866).

37.   No one doubts the power of the President (and Senate) to end war by treaty. The Supreme Court has said that " 'the State of War' may be terminated by treaty or legislation or Presidential proclamation." Ludecke v. Watkins, 335 U.S. 160, 168 (1948). It is not clear whether the Court meant by Presidential proclamation on his own authority. Wilson denied the President's power to end war by proclamation. See C. ROSSITER, THE SUPREME COURT AND THE COMMANDER IN CHIEF 79 & n. 23 (1951). So did Madison in the first Helvidius Letter, 6 J. MADISON, WRITINGS 148 (Hunt ed. 1910), Chapter II, note 12; see note 47, this chapter. Blackstone thought that the power to decide for war and the power to make peace should be in the same hands, but for him they would both be lodged in the Executive, the Monarch. 1 BLACKSTONE, COMMENTARIES * 257–58. Compare: "It should therefore be difficult in a republic to declare war; but not to make peace." 2 STORY, COMMENTARIES § 1171, at 97.

Perhaps, since Congress has the power to decide that the U.S. should go to war, the President ought not be able to say that it should not, or should not remain at war, in effect repealing the declaration of war. Compare the proposal at the Constitutional Convention that would have denied the President a role in making peace treaties, Chapter V, note 4. Perhaps it is not the power to end war that is denied the President alone, but to conclude the political and territorial arrangements that sometimes go with peace, especially any involving the territory of the United States. Compare Fleming v. Page, this chapter, p. 97. Presidents can perhaps effectively end a state of war merely by resuming diplomatic relations with the former enemy.

38. Madsen v. Kinsella, 343 U.S. 341 (1952). The Court apparently concluded that Congress did not intend to preclude the alternative means, trial by occupation court. But *cf.* United States *ex rel.* Hirshberg v. Cooke, 336 U.S. 210 (1949) (since Congress did not authorize it, the Navy could not court-martial for an offense committed during prior enlistment).

39. Youngstown Sheet & Tube Co. v. Sawyer, 343 U.S. 579, 635–37 (1952) (Jackson, J., concurring).

40. This would unquestionably be true if the act of Congress followed. Compare the power of Congress to supersede even treaty provisions as domestic law, Chapter V, p. 163.

General statements cast doubt on the President's authority to supersede an Act of Congress, *e. g.*: "No power was ever vested in the President to repeal an Act of Congress," United States v. Clarke, 20 Wall. 92, 112–13 (U.S.1874). And see cases in the following note. But *cf.*, United States v. Midwest Oil Co., 236 U.S. 459 (1915). Treaties prevail over an earlier act of Congress (Chapter V, p. 163) and some argument has been advanced that even executive agreements might supersede an inconsistent statute. See Chapter VI, p. 186.

In the *Steel Seizure Case* the concurring Justices held, in effect, that the President could not act inconsistently with an earlier act of Congress. See note 11, this chapter.

41. Gelston v. Hoyt, 3 Wheat. 246, 330–33 (U.S.1818), held that the President could not authorize revenue officers to seize a vessel for violating neutrality when the statute authorized seizure only by the military. Compare Little v. Barreme, 2 Cranch 170, 177–78 (U.S. 1804). See also The Orono, 18 F.Cas. 830 (No. 10,585) (C.C.Mass. 1812), and President's Proclamation Declared Illegal, 19 F.Cas. 1289 (No. 11,391) (C.C.N.C.1812).

In 1898, the Acting Attorney General thought that the President had concurrent power to control the landing of foreign submarine cables, subject to Congressional supremacy. 22 OP.ATT'Y GEN. 13. In United States v. Western Union Telegraph Co., 272 F. 311 (S.D. N.Y.1921), *dismissed*, 260 U.S. 754 (1922), the President was denied the power to exclude an Atlantic cable by a company claiming a license under an act of Congress. In 1941, Attorney General Jackson held that the President was barred by statute from transferring certain "mosquito boats" to a foreign power even by executive agreement. 39 OP.ATT'Y GEN. 484 (1941). See Chapter VI, note 42.

42. Congress had provided that members of the forces inducted under the Selective Service Act might be sent only to U. S. territories or in the Western Hemisphere. Ch. 720, § 3(e), 54 Stat. 886 (1940). Roosevelt acted by executive agreement; see the discussion, Chapter VI, note 42, as to whether executive agreements stand better than uni-

latral executive acts, and whether an executive agreement can prevail in the face of an earlier act of Congress.

Compare the statute authorizing detail of small numbers of forces to China subject to the proviso that "United States naval or Marine Corps personnel shall not accompany Chinese troops, aircraft, or ships on other than training maneuvers or cruises." Ch. 580, 60 Stat. 539 (1946). Once Congress also purported to limit the President's use of the armed forces for law enforcement in the United States, Ch. 263, § 15, 20 Stat. 152 (1878), as amended, 18 U.S.C. § 1385 (1970). For Congressional efforts to control the use of troops by withholding appropriations see note 52, this chapter.

Other conflicts between the President's powers as Commander-in-Chief and Congressional powers have not been frequent, but in 1867 Congress purported to take away some of President Johnson's powers as Commander-in-Chief and vest them in General Grant. See debate, CONG.GLOBE, 39th Cong., 2d Sess. 1851–55 (1867); ch. 170, §§ 2, 6, 14 Stat. 486, 487 (1867); see generally A. MCLAUGHLIN, A CONSTITUTIONAL HISTORY OF THE UNITED STATES 662 (student's ed. 1935); and compare the *Hirshberg* case this chapter, note 38.

43. Instead, the Senate adopted what was largely a "sense" resolution, approving the dispatch of four divisions, calling on the President to consult with both foreign affairs committees before sending troops abroad under the North Atlantic Treaty, requiring Congressional approval for any policy involving the assignment of troops abroad and for sending any additional troops, and requesting Presidential reports on the implementation of the North Atlantic Treaty. S.Res. 99, 82nd Cong., 1st Sess., 97 CONG.REC. 3282–83 (1951). President Truman said that while he did not need Congressional approval he would consult with members of the Senate Foreign Relations Committee and the Armed Services Committee before sending troops to the North Atlantic Treaty area. See N. Y. Times, Jan. 12, 1951. Compare the "Commitments Resolution," Chapter VI, pp. 182–83.

A Senate Report quoted at length (and seemed to accept) an Executive memorandum supporting Presidential authority to send troops abroad. S.Rep.No.175, 82d Cong., 1st Sess. (1951). See also "Assignment of Ground Forces of the United States to Duty in the European Area," *Hearings on S.Res. 99 and S.Con.Res. 18 Before the Sen. Comm. on Foreign Relations and the Comm. on Armed Services*, 82d Cong., 1st Sess. (1951); SENATE COMM. ON FOREIGN RELATIONS AND COMM. ON ARMED SERVICES, POWERS OF THE PRESIDENT TO SEND THE ARMED FORCES OUTSIDE THE UNITED STATES, 82d Cong., 1st Sess. (1951).

For an earlier debate on the constitutionality of Congressional efforts to control the President's use of the armed forces see, *e. g.*, the extended debates on the Lend-Lease Bill, recounted in Jones, *The President, Congress, and Foreign Relations,* 29 CALIF.L.REV. 565, 582–84 (1941) ; CORWIN, THE PRESIDENT 132–38.

44. See Rehnquist, *The Constitutional Issues—Administration Position,* 45 N.Y.U.L.REV. 628 (1970) (*Hammarskjöld Forum: Expansion of the Viet Nam War into Cambodia—The Legal Issues*), reprinted in 3 FALK, VIETNAM 175. See the text of the Tonkin Resolution, note 28, this chapter.

45. See the McGovern-Hatfield Amendment "to end the war" (S. Amend. 862), rejected by the Senate, 116 CONG.REC. 30683 (1970), and the Cooper-Church Amendment (S. Amend. 620) to limit U. S. involvement in Cambodia, adopted by the Senate, *id.* at 22251, but failed in conference. See CONGRESSIONAL QUARTERLY, WEEKLY REPORT 3008–12 (Dec. 18, 1970). In 1971, however, the supplemental foreign aid authorization which the President signed into law included a provision that the funds authorized shall not be used to finance the introduction of U. S. combat troops or any U. S. military advisers into Cambodia. Special Foreign Assistance Act of 1971, Pub.L.No.91–652, §§ 7, 84 Stat. 1943 (1971), 22 U.S.C.A. § 2411 and note (Supp.1972).

Several attempts were made in the first session of the 92d Congress to add a troop withdrawal amendment to the bill extending the draft. The Senate adopted Senator Mansfield's amendment (S. Amend. 214) which urged the President to set a final date for withdrawal contingent upon the release of all prisoners of war. 117 CONG.REC. S9718. The amendment, a non-binding expression of policy, was rejected by the House, 117 CONG.REC. H5943, and was dropped in conference. See CONGRESSIONAL QUARTERLY, WEEKLY REPORT 2665 (Dec. 25, 1971).

46. Compare Chapter III, notes 14, 60, 61.

47. Its repeal (Pub.L.No.91–672, § 12, 84 Stat. 2055 (1971)) could properly be interpreted only as withdrawing authority for new military actions in the area in the future. That Congress repealed the resolution while appropriating funds for continuance of the war and rejecting resolutions for its termination could leave no doubt that repeal was not intended as the equivalent of a resolution to terminate the war. Compare Da Costa v. Laird, 448 F.2d 1368 (2d Cir. 1971), *cert. denied,* 405 U.S. 979 (1972).

48. Compare Madison's Helvidius Letter no. 1, Chapter II, note 12: "Those who are to *conduct a war* cannot in the nature of things, be proper or safe judges, whether *a war ought* to be *commenced, continued,* or *concluded.*"

49. Congress decided to fight a limited war against France at the end of the eighteenth century and the Supreme Court recognized that

it could do so.  Bas v. Tingy, 4 Dall. 37 (U.S.1800) ; Talbot v. Seeman, 1 Cranch 1 (U.S.1801), Chapter III, note 61.

Compare: "The sovereignty, as to declaring war and limiting its effects, rests with the legislature.  The sovereignty, as to its execution, rests with the president.  If the legislature do not limit the nature of the war, all the regulations and rights of general war attach upon it." Story, J., dissenting in Brown v. United States, 8 Cranch 110, 153–54 (U.S.1814).  See also *id.* at 145: ". . . congress (for with them rests the sovereignty of the nation as to the right of making war, and declaring its limits and effects) . . ." At 147: "If, indeed, there be a limit imposed as to the extent to which hostilities may be carried by the executive, I admit that the executive cannot lawfully transcend that limit . . . ." And at 149: "If any of such acts are disapproved by the legislature, it is in their power to narrow and limit the extent to which the rights of war shall be exercised . . . ." And see Marshall, C. J., quoted Chapter III, notes 14, 60.

But *cf. Ex parte* Milligan, 4 Wall. 2, 139 (U.S.1866): "This power [of Congress] necessarily extends to all legislation essential to the prosecution of war with vigor and success except such as interferes with the command of the forces and the conduct of campaigns.  That power and duty belong to the President as Commander-in-Chief." I assume that the Court's dictum of exception applies to detailed, tactical decisions on the conduct of the war.  But *cf.* C. BERDAHL, THE WAR POWERS OF THE EXECUTIVE IN THE UNITED STATES 116–17 (1921).

During the War of 1812, soon after the declaration of war, the House passed a bill authorizing the President to ". . . occupy and hold, the whole or any part of East Florida, including Amelia Island, and also those parts of West Florida which are now in possession and under the jurisdiction of the United States." 24 ANNALS OF CONG. 1684–85 (1812) ; 23 ANNALS OF CONG. 323–24 (1812) [1811–1812].  A Senate amendment proposed authorization to occupy Canada also.  *Id.* at 325.  The whole bill died in the Senate, *Id.* at 326.

During the Mexican War, a House resolution demanding the withdrawal of American troops to the east bank of the Rio Grande was defeated 137–41.  CONG.GLOBE, 30th Cong., 1st Sess. 93 (1847).  A similar resolution calling for the withdrawal of American forces from Mexico to "defensive positions" was tabled.  *Id.* at 179.

Congress early asserted its authority to investigate the conduct of war, as in the famous case of General St. Clair.  During the Civil War Congress established a committee to investigate the conduct of the war that asserted substantial authority.  See Pierson, *The Committee on the Conduct of the Civil War*, 23 AM. HISTORICAL REV. 550 (1918).  The committee was the subject of controversy but no one at the time seemed to challenge Congressional authority to scrutinize the conduct of the war, on constitutional grounds.

It has even been suggested that the President could not veto Congressional restrictions or termination of hostilities. Ratner, *The Coordinated War Making Power,* 44 S.CALIF.L.REV. 461, 478 (1971).

50. Presidential authority, perhaps obligation, to propose legislation can be found in Article II, section 3: "He shall from time to time give to the Congress Information of the State of the Union, and recommend to their Consideration such Measures as he shall judge necessary and expedient. . . ." On the potentialities of "the legislative leadership of the President" in foreign affairs, see Jones, *The President, Congress, and Foreign Relations,* 29 CALIF.L.REV. 565, 567–75 (1941).

Presidents have sought Congressional authorization even when they might perhaps have acted on their own authority. Mr. Justice Jackson suggested that that was sound and prudent policy especially if their action might face judicial review. Youngstown Sheet & Tube Co. v. Sawyer, 343 U.S. 579, 647 n. 16 (1952). Presidents have also sought Congressional endorsement of policy, sometimes in vain for many years, as for the Monroe Doctrine. Cf. D. PERKINS, THE MONROE DOCTRINE 1826–1867, at 217–23 (1933).

51. For a contemporary assertion of autonomy for the power of the purse generally, see the Statement of Senator Morse (erstwhile professor of law), *Hearings, Separation of Powers* 57, 63–64.

52. An effort in 1842 to delete funds for a Minister to Mexico was defeated. CONG.GLOBE, 27th Cong., 1st Sess., Appendix, 513–14 (1842). For a more recent effort, in 1940, to compel the severance of diplomatic relations with the Soviet Union, see 86 CONG.REC. 1172–79, 1192 (1940). See generally Nobleman, *Financial Aspects of Congressional Participation in Foreign Relations,* 289 ANNALS OF THE AMERICAN ACADEMY OF POLITICAL AND SOCIAL SCIENCE 145 (1953) [hereinafter cited as Nobleman, ANNALS]. Compare the discussion of conditions on appropriations, pp. 113–16, this chapter.

It is accepted that Theodore Roosevelt sent the fleet around the world and compelled Congress to appropriate funds to bring it back. See CORWIN, THE PRESIDENT 137. In 1912, after Senator Root objected to it as unconstitutional, the Senate defeated an amendment to an appropriation bill that would have forbidden the use of the funds for supporting troops outside the United States or sending or returning them. 48 CONG.REC. 10921–30 (1912). A Congressional rider to a 1969 statute provided that none of the funds appropriated by the Act "shall be used to finance the introduction of American ground combat troops into Laos or Thailand." Pub.L.No.91–171, § 643, 83 Stat. 487 (1969). Compare this chapter, note 42. For other instances see CORWIN, THE PRESIDENT 136–37, 401–404. See generally E. CARPER, THE DEFENSE APPROPRIATION RIDER (1960).

53. Nevertheless, a Senate subcommittee has concluded: "To a large extent, it appears that much of the 'power of the purse' has shifted from Congress to the President." SENATE COMM. ON THE JUDICIARY, SEPARATION OF POWERS, REP.NO.549, 91 Cong., 1st Sess. 12 (1969).

54. See generally Wallace, *The President's Exclusive Foreign Affairs Powers over Foreign Aid,* 1970 DUKE L.J. 293, 453.

55. See, *e. g.,* Jefferson, Letter to Mrs. John Adams, Sept. 11, 1804, in THE WRITINGS OF THOMAS JEFFERSON 310–11 (Ford ed. 1897). Compare Jackson, 3 RICHARDSON 1144–45; Lincoln, First Inaugural Address, 7 RICHARDSON 3206, 3207, 3210–11.

But *cf.* Curtis's argument on behalf of President Johnson in his impeachment proceedings, CONG.GLOBE, 40th Cong., 2d Sess. (Supp.) 126–27 (1868).

56. Compare Curtis's argument, cited in note 55.

57. See, *e. g.,* Vinson, C. J., dissenting in Youngstown Sheet & Tube Co. v. Sawyer, 343 U.S. 579, 700 (1952). Compare United States v. Midwest Oil Co., 236 U.S. 459 (1915), this chapter note 11.

58. . . . . This term describes a variety of actions which may be taken by the executive branch with respect to the expenditure of funds appropriated by Congress. 'Impounding' may result from directions by the President to the head of an agency to refuse to spend or to delay the expenditure of appropriated funds, from the issuance of such an order by the agency head himself, or from a decision by the Bureau of the Budget 'apportioning' a part or all of the appropriations as reserves.

The effect of such actions is to restrict the use of funds below the level authorized and appropriated by Congress and thereby to affect adversely the implementation of a public activity or program established by Congress. In its most extreme form, "impounding" affords the President the equivalent of an "item veto" which may be exercised to restrict or to halt programs of which he disapproves. In effect, impounding grants to the President his own 'power of the purse' which may effectively frustrate congressional decisions and enacted law. The impounding power was first asserted by President Roosevelt in 1941, in an effort to defer public works projects he considered nonessential in view of the war emergency. Congress continued to appropriate funds for these projects and the President did not wish to veto entire appropriations bills. Accordingly, he directed the Bureau of the Budget to place the funds for these projects in reserves unavailable for expenditure by the agencies.

In more recent years, impoundment has been used primarily in the national defense area. Among the most well-known examples are the B–70 bomber program and the nuclear frigate construction. In the domestic field, highway construction and aid to impacted schools have been subject to executive impounding. S.REP., SEPARATION OF POWERS 12–13.

In 1948, Truman refused to spend about $800 million to expand the Air Force. Eisenhower refused to expend funds to maintain the full strength of the Marine Corps. See M. RAMSEY, IMPOUNDMENT BY THE EXECUTIVE DEPARTMENT OF FUNDS WHICH CONGRESS HAS AUTHORIZED IT TO SPEND OR OBLIGATE 4 (Library of Congress Legislative Reference Service, 1968). For the controversy involving the effort to direct the President to build the "RS 70" airplane, see H.R. REP.NO.1406, 87th Cong., 2d Sess. 3–9 (1961); compare 108 CONG. REC. 4714 (1962). See *Hearings, Separation of Powers* 28–29, 40. See generally "Executive Impoundment of Appropriated Funds," *Hearings Before the Subcomm. on Separation of Powers of the Senate Comm. on the Judiciary,* 92d Cong., 1st Sess. (1971); Miller, *Presidential Powers to Impound Appropriated Funds: An Exercise in Constitutional Decision Making,* 43 N.CAR.L.REV. 502 (1965); Fisher, *Presidential Impoundment of Funds,* 38 GEO.WASH.L.REV. 124 (1960); Davis, *Congressional Power to Require Defense Expenditures,* 33 FORDHAM L.REV. 39 (1964).

59. Compare Kendall v. United States *ex rel.* Stokes, 12 Pet. 524, 612–13 (U.S.1838):

It was urged at the bar, that the postmaster general was alone subject to the direction and control of the president, with respect to the execution of the duty imposed upon him by this law; and this right of the president is claimed, as growing out of the obligation imposed upon him by the constitution, to take care that the laws be faithfully executed. This is a doctrine that cannot receive the sanction of this court. It would be vesting in the president a dispensing power, which has no countenance for its support, in any part of the constitution; and is asserting a principle, which, if carried out in its results, to all cases falling within it, would be clothing the president with a power entirely to control the legislation of congress, and paralyze the administration of justice.

To contend that the obligation imposed on the president to see the laws faithfully executed, implies a power to forbid their execution, is a novel construction of the constitution, and entirely inadmissible.

In another context (in his famous Proclamation on Nullification) President Jackson said: "The laws of the United States must be executed. I have no discretionary power on the subject; my duty is emphatically pronounced in the Constitution." 3 RICHARDSON 1217.

60. Section 3(d) of the Mutual Security Act of 1952, ch. 449, 66 Stat. 141, included: "Not less than $25,000,000 of the funds made available [under specified sections] shall be used for economic, technical, and military assistance to Spain in accordance with the provisions of this Act." President Truman said, *inter alia*: "I do not regard this provision as a directive, which would be unconstitutional, but instead as an authorization, in addition to the authority already in existence under which loans to Spain may be made. . . . Money will be loaned to Spain whenever mutually advantageous arrangements can be made . . . and whenever such loans will serve the interest of the United States in the conduct of foreign relations." 23 DEP'T STATE BULL. 517 (1950). Compare the appropriation for China despite Presidential objection, China Aid Act of 1948, ch. 169, Title IV, 62 Stat. 158–59 (authorization); ch. 685, *id.* at 1056 (appropriation); see Nobleman, ANNALS 160.

61. The President is expressly required to give Congress "from time to time" "Information of the State of the Union", (Art. II, sec. 3), and State of the Union messages have included major declarations of policy, *e. g.*, the Monroe Doctrine. Congress also requests reports from the President on numerous subjects, including many relating to foreign affairs, *e. g.*, the annual report on the United Nations. See generally REPORTS TO BE MADE TO CONGRESS, H.R.DOC.NO.23, 87th Cong., 1st Sess. (1961).

The Continental Congress established a Department of Foreign Affairs and provided that "any member of Congress" shall have access to all its papers "provided that no copy shall be taken of matters of a secret nature without the special leave of Congress." See Wolkinson, *Demands of Congressional Committees for Executive Papers*, 10 FED. BAR J. 103, 328 (1949). That department, however, was a department of Congress, there being no executive branch.

For opinions strongly upholding executive privilege, see 40 OP. ATT'Y GEN. 45 (1941); 41 *id.* at 507, 525–31 (1960). An early, historical article on "executive privilege" is Warren, *Presidential Declarations of Independence*. 10 B.U.L.REV. 1 (1930). See also CORWIN, THE PRESIDENT 110–18, 182–83, 427–30. For more recent writings, see, *e. g.*, Berger, *Executive Privilege v. Congressional Inquiry*, 12 U.C.L.A.L.REV. 1044, 1288 (1965); Bishop, *The Executive's Right of Privacy: An Unresolved Constitutional Question*, 66 YALE L.J. 477 (1957); Collins, *The Power of Congressional Committees of Investigation to Obtain Information from the Executive Branch: The Argu-*

*ment for the Legislative Branch,* 39 GEO.L.J. 563 (1951); Hruska, *Executive Records in Congressional Investigations—Duty to Disclose —Duty to Withhold,* 35 NEB.L.REV. 310 (1955); Kramer & Marcuse, *Executive Privilege—A Study of the Period 1953–1960,* 29 GEO.WASH. L.REV. 623, 827 (1961); Schwartz, *Executive Privilege and Congressional Investigatory Power,* 47 CALIF.L.REV. 3 (1959); Younger, *Congressional Investigations and Executive Secrecy: A Study in the Separation of Powers,* 20 U.PITT.L.REV. 755 (1959). Compare Henkin, *The Right to Know and the Duty to Withhold: The Case of the Pentagon Papers,* 120 U.PA.L.REV. 271 (1971).

62. 1 RICHARDSON 186–88.

63. The President has even refused to disclose information to the Senate about a treaty. See CORWIN, THE PRESIDENT, 182–83, 428–29 n. 41. Many instances of Presidential refusal are collected in 40 OP. ATT'Y GEN. 45 (1954); see also Kramer & Marcuse, this chapter, note 61.

Congress apart, the Supreme Court has recognized the need for Executive secrecy in foreign relations, see, *e. g.,* United States v. Curtiss-Wright Export Corp., 299 U.S. 304, 320 (1936); Chicago & Southern Air Lines v. Waterman S. S. Corp., 333 U.S. 103, 111 (1948); Zemel v. Rusk, 381 U.S. 1, 17 (1963). Compare Totten v. United States, 92 U.S. 105, 107 (1875). In *Jencks* v. *United States,* the Supreme Court required the Government to make witnesses' reports available to the accused or drop the prosecution. 353 U.S. 657 (1957). In *United States* v. *Reynolds,* a suit against the United States, the Court found a governmental privilege in the circumstances but suggested that if it appeared necessary the trial judge would inspect the documents to determine whether they were privileged. 345 U.S. 1 (1953). And compare the various opinions in New York Times Co. v. United States, 403 U.S. 713 (1971), Chapter X, note 9; also Mr. Justice Douglas dissenting in Gravel v. United States, 408 U.S. 606, 637–46 (1972).

In *Marbury* v. *Madison* the Attorney General claimed the right to refuse to divulge to the courts anything relating to his official transactions while he was acting as Secretary of State. Although Chief Justice Marshall said that the Attorney General was required to communicate what was being asked, Marshall accepted the privilege in principle. He said: "There was nothing confidential required to be disclosed. If there had been he was not obliged to answer it; and if he thought that anything was communicated to him in confidence he was not bound to disclose it." 1 Cranch 137, 143–45 (U.S.1803).

64. For a Congressional view, see HOUSE COMM. ON GOVERNMENT OPERATIONS, EXECUTIVE BRANCH PRACTICES IN WITHHOLDING INFORMATION FROM CONGRESSIONAL COMMITTEES, H.R.REP.NO.2207, 86th

Cong., 2d Sess. (1960); and compare Collins, note 61, this chapter. An executive view is in SUBCOMM. ON CONSTITUTIONAL RIGHTS OF THE SENATE COMM. ON THE JUDICIARY, THE POWERS OF THE PRESIDENT TO WITHHOLD INFORMATION FROM THE CONGRESS—MEMORANDUM OF THE ATTORNEY GENERAL, 85th Cong., 2d Sess., Parts I and II (Comm.Prints 1958 and 1959).

Even Congressional Committees have sometimes recognized that the Executive has the legal right to refuse information under the "doctrine of executive privilege". See, *e. g.*, S.REP.NO.1761, 86th Cong., 2d Sess. 22 (1960); compare also the Senate Report quoted in *Curtiss-Wright*, 299 U.S. at 319, quoted Chapter V, note 7.

In 1948 the House passed a joint resolution purporting to require the Executive to furnish any information required by Congressional Committees, H.R.J.Res. 342, 80th Cong., 2d Sess., 94 CONG.REC. 5821 (1948). In the Senate the resolution died in Committee. Although a House Resolution "directed" the Secretary of State to transmit "full and complete information" with respect to any agreements or commitments between President Truman and The British Prime Minister, at least some Representatives agreed that it was within the President's province to refuse to divulge the information if he considered it would be incompatible with the national interest. See, *e. g.*, 98 CONG. REC. 1205, 1215 (1952).

65.  The Foreign Assistance Act of 1961, Pub.L.No.87–195, § 634 (c), 75 Stat. 455, as amended, 22 U.S.C. § 2394(c), (d) (1970), required that certain documents and information be given to Congress or disbursements of aid cease. Congress usually does not press this device to a showdown, and waives noncompliance if the President certifies that he has forbidden disclosure and gives his reasons for so doing. *Ibid.* See also Mutual Security Appropriations Act of 1960, Pub.L.No.86–383, § 111(d), 73 Stat. 720; Mutual Security Act of 1960, Pub.L.No.86–472, § 201(a), 74 Stat. 134–35; Mutual Security and Related Agencies Appropriation Act of 1961, Pub.L.No.86–704, § 101(d), 74 Stat. 778 (1960). But compare Mutual Security Act of 1959, Pub.L.No.86–108, § 401(h), with § 401(i), (j), and (m), 73 Stat. 254. On the constitutionality of such provisions, compare 41 OP.ATT'Y GEN. 507 (1960). Compare HOUSE COMM. ON GOVERNMENT OPERATIONS, AVAILABILITY OF INFORMATION FROM FEDERAL DEPARTMENTS AND AGENCIES, H.R.REP.NO.818, 87th Cong., 1st Sess. (1961).

66.  The President himself is not subject to subpoena, mandamus or injunction by the courts. See Mississippi v. Johnson, 4 Wall. 475 (U.S.1867). He could not be held in contempt by Congress but it could, of course, impeach him.

Congress might be able to cite a federal official for contempt. Compare Jurney v. MacCracken, 294 U.S. 125 (1935); Anderson v. Dunn,

6 Wheat. 204 (U.S.1821); compare also Groppi v. Leslie, 404 U.S. 496 (1972). But if he acted on Presidential orders the President would doubtless protect him: even after a change of administration an Attorney General is not likely to prosecute for the crime of contempt of Congress (2 U.S.C. § 192 (1970)) an executive official who had acted under Presidential orders.

It is believed 'that failure of an official to give information to Congress led to his rejection by the Senate when he was later nominated to a cabinet post. See Exec.Rep.No.4, 86th Cong., 1st Sess., 105 CONG.REC. 9982–87 (1959); also *id.* 10271, 10907–28; Zinn, *Extent of the Control of the Executive by the Congress of the United States*, HOUSE COMM. ON GOVERNMENT OPERATIONS, 87th CONG., 2d SESS., 19 n. 7 (Comm.Print, 1962)..

67.  See United States v. Curtiss-Wright Export Corp., 299 U.S. 304, 321 (1936). See the famous remarks of Senator Spooner, 40 CONG.REC. 1420 (1906):

> It is a Department which from the beginning the Senate has never assumed the right to direct or control, except as to clearly defined matters relating to duty imposed by statute and not connected with the conduct of our foreign relations. We *direct* all the other heads of departments to transmit to the Senate designated papers or information. We do not address directions to the Secretary of State, nor do we direct requests, even, to the Secretary of State. We direct requests to the real head of that Department, the President of the United States, and, as a matter of courtesy, we add the qualifying words, "if in his judgment not incompatible with the public interest."

68.  It is reported that Presidents Kennedy and Johnson directed that the Executive Branch cooperate with Congress and avoid denying information to its committees except where absolutely necessary.

One writer has said: ". . . on the whole, a good case can be made out for the proposition that the present imprecise situation is, in fact, reasonably satisfactory. Neither the executive nor the Congress is very sure of its rights, and both usually evince a tactful disposition not to push the assertion of their rights to abusive extremes. Of such is the system of checks and balances." Bishop, 66 YALE L.J. at 491 (1957), note 61, this chapter.

It has been suggested that only the President himself should be able to assert Executive privilege, and only the House (or Senate) itself, by formal resolution, ask for information which the Executive branch would withhold. Maass, *Hearings, Separation of Powers* 197.

Compare the suggestion of Mr. Justice Harlan in *The Pentagon Papers Case,* New York Times Co. v. United States, 403 U.S. 713, 757 (1971), that the courts should examine only whether the subject is within the Executive's competence and whether the head of the Executive Department himself certifies to the need for secrecy.

69. See Chapter V, pp. 150, 169 and note 136.

70. Grant objected and persuaded Congress to withdraw. See 9 RICHARDSON 4331–32.

71. Ch. 149, 37 Stat. 913 (1913), 22 U.S.C. § 262 (1970). Congress is free, of course, to request or "call upon" the President or to express its sense that something be done or not done, Chapter III, p. 86. A sense resolution introduced by Senator Joseph McCarthy in June, 1955, that before a "Big Four summit meeting" is held there should be agreement to discuss the status of countries under communist control, was defeated by a vote of 77–4. S.Res. 116, 84th Cong., 1st Sess., 101 CONG.REC. 8723–25, 8933–60 (1955).

The Trade Expansion Act of 1962, Pub.L.No.87–794, § 243, 76 Stat. 878 (1962), 19 U.S.C. § 1873 (1970), required the inclusion of members of Congress on delegations to negotiate trade agreements. Such a provision may claim justification in that the agreements are negotiated upon Congressional authority (Chapter VI, p. 173), but Presidents will reject it in principle as interference with their appointive powers or negotiating authority.

72. Compare p. 108 this chapter. That Congress cannot impose "unconstitutional conditions" on appropriations, see 41 OP.ATT'Y GEN. 230 (1955). *Cf.* Butler v. United States, 297 U.S. 1, 74 (1936); Frankfurter, J., concurring in United States v. Lovett, 328 U.S. 303, 329 (1946); Lovett v. United States, 104 Ct.Cl. 557, 593 (1945) (Madden, J. concurring); CORWIN, THE PRESIDENT 401–404 n. 64; Herblock Cartoon facing 41 CALIF.L.REV. 566 (1953). For a noted veto message by President Hayes objecting to House of Representatives conditions to an appropriation, see 9 RICHARDSON 4482–83, quoted in CORWIN, THE PRESIDENT 138.

73. Representative Findlay proposed "to shut off the salaries of any State Department personnel who might use their official time to advance" the nuclear nonproliferation treaty, but his amendment did not get very far. See *Hearings, National Commitments* 235–36. If Congress cannot remove an executive officer (note 87, this chapter) it cannot do so by denying his salary. Compare United States v. Lovett, 328 U.S. 303, 329 (1946) (Frankfurter, J., concurring).

74. For example, Joint Resolution of May 15, 1924, ch. 155, 43 Stat. 119, 120, authorized an appropriation for a delegation to the International Opium Conference. Congress provided that: ". . . the representatives of the United States shall sign no agreement which

does not fulfill the conditions necessary for the suppression of the habit-forming narcotic drug traffic as stated in the preamble." (The conditions related to: 1) the designation of certain opium uses as "illegitimate" and 2) the control of the production of raw opium.) The American Delegation heeded the Congressional conditions (perhaps because its chief was the chairman of the House Foreign Affairs Committee and had himself proposed the conditions); when these proved unacceptable to other governments the Delegation withdrew from the Conference. But the delegates to a later Opium Conference in 1931 disregarded the conditions. See Nobleman, ANNALS 156 and authorities cited.

In 1826, an attempt to add a rider instructing the delegation to a Panama Conference was defeated. Daniel Webster opposed the rider arguing that while Congress was free to refuse to appropriate funds to implement foreign policy, it could not attach conditions to such appropriations. See Hale Memorandum, S.DOC.NO.56, 54th Cong., 2d Sess. 37–40 (1897).

Compare the statement of Senator Borah in regard to the Commander-in-Chief power: "Undoubtedly the Congress may refuse to appropriate and undoubtedly the Congress may say that an appropriation is for a specific purpose. In that respect the President would undoubtedly be bound by it. But the Congress could not, through the power of appropriation, in my judgment, infringe upon the right of the President to command whatever army he might find." 69 CONG. REC. 6760 (1928) quoted in CORWIN, THE PRESIDENT 403–404.

75. But compare Wallace, this chapter, note 54.

76. See Mutual Security Act of 1954, ch. 937, §§ 105(b) (1), 121, 68 Stat. 835, 837.

In 1950 the House passed an amendment to terminate assistance to the United Kingdom so long as Ireland remained partitioned, but the amendment died in conference. See 96 CONG.REC. 4344–48, 7221–25 (1950) (conference report on amendments to the Economic Cooperation Act of 1948).

77. Foreign Assistance Act of 1961, Pub.L.No.87–195, § 620, 75 Stat. 444–45, as amended, 22 U.S.C. § 2370(a), (f), (n), (o), (p), (s) (1970). See also the Mutual Defense Act of 1951 which suspended aid to any country permitting shipment of embargoed materials to the U.S.S.R. unless the President found that "unusual circumstances indicate that the cessation of aid would clearly be detrimental to the security of the United States." Ch. 575, § 103(b), 65 Stat. 646; Foreign Assistance Act of 1948, ch. 169, § 103, 62 Stat. 138 (1948).

Congress has also required that 50% of all our assistance be shipped in American vessels. See Act of August 26, 1954, ch. 936, 68 Stat. 832, as amended, 46 U.S.C. § 1241(b) (1) (1970).

There are other provisions that are not directives, for example that the President "consider" terminating assistance to a country that permits or fails to prevent mob action against United States property. See Foreign Assistance Act of 1967, Pub.L.No.90–137, § 301(f) (1), 81 Stat. 459, 22 U.S.C. § 2370(j) (1970).

78. The First Hickenlooper Amendment is sec. 301(e) of the Foreign Assistance Act of 1963, Pub.L.No.88–205, 77 Stat. 386, as amended, 22 U.S.C. § 2370(e) (1) (1970); compare related provisions in the Inter-American Development Bank Act, Pub.L.No.89–6, 79 Stat. 24 (1965), as amended, 22 U.S.C. § 283*l*(c) (1970). (The Second Hickenlooper Amendment, Pub.L.No.88–633, § 301(d), 78 Stat. 1013 (1964), as amended, 22 U.S.C. § 2370(e) (2) (1970), contained in the Foreign Assistance Act of 1964, is a modification of the Act of State doctrine (Chapter VIII, p. 220), not a condition on spending, and has no relation to foreign assistance.)

79. Congress once established "ceilings" on the amounts that could be appropriated for the payment of annual contributions to various international organizations. Of course, if the international organization proceeds to assess the United States for more than the Congressional ceiling, the United States is, internationally, in default. Later Congress legislated instead to forbid any U. S. representative to commit the U. S. to contribute more than 33.33% of the budget of any organization to which the legislation applied; this, of course, does not prevent an international organization from imposing a higher assessment. The power of Congress to instruct delegates to international organizations in this respect is as questionable as in respect of any other international act or negotiation. See H.REP.No.1257, 81st Cong., 2d Sess. 7–8 (1950); ch. 651, 66 STAT. 550–51 (1952). See generally, Nobleman, ANNALS 160–63.

Compare also sec. 110, ch. 328, 67 Stat. 372 (1953), which prohibits the use of appropriated funds to pay any U. S. contribution "to any international organization which engages in the direct or indirect promotion of the principle or doctrine of one world government or one world citizenship"; and S.REP.No.309, 83d Cong., 1st Sess. p. 7 (1953) in which a Senate Committee recommended legislation that would have cut off U. S. contributions to the UN if Communist China were admitted to membership.

In 1971 Congress placed the United States in default when it refused to appropriate funds to pay its obligations to the International Labor Organization.

80. Compare the provision in sec. 107(b) of the Foreign Assistance Act of 1966 that the President "shall seek to assure" that no U. S. contribution to the UN Development Program should go to the Castro regime. Pub.L.No.89–583, 80 Stat. 800 (1966), as amended, 22 U.S.C.

§ 2221(b) (1970). Compare sec. 107(c) which provides that contributions to the United Nations Relief and Works Agency for Palestine Refugees should be made only on condition that the Agency "take all possible measures to assure that no part of the United States contribution" be used to assist any refugee receiving military training as a member of the "so-called Palestine Liberation Army." 22 U.S.C. § 2221(c).

81.  Sometimes there are "suggestions" by committees or members. Compare those to the United States Representative to the International Bank for Reconstruction and Development to vote against a loan to Greece. *Hearings on Proposed World Bank Loan to NIBID of Greece before the Subcommittee on International Finance of the House Comm. on Banking and Currency*, 90th Cong., 2d Sess. 17–18, 26 (1968).

In the 1950's, the Department of State, under pressure of Congressional committees, arranged for "advisory screening" of American citizens for employment in the UN and other international organizations. See *e. g.*, SUBCOMMITTEE TO INVESTIGATE THE ADMINISTRATION OF THE INTERNAL SECURITY ACT AND OTHER INTERNAL SECURITY LAWS OF THE SENATE COMMITTEE ON THE JUDICIARY, REPORT ON ACTIVITIES OF UNITED STATES CITIZENS EMPLOYED BY THE UNITED NATIONS 82d Cong., 2d Sess. (Comm.Print 1953). See 31 DEP'T STATE BULL. 279, 354 (1954).

82.  Compare this chapter, note 65.

83.  Compare 3 OP.ATT'Y GEN. 188 (1837); CORWIN, THE PRESIDENT 78, 366 n. 32. Compare Chapter V, pp. 133–36.

There have also been issues arising out of the President's power to make recess appointments. Attorneys General have expressed the view that under Article II, section 2, clause 3, permitting him to fill vacancies "that may happen during the Recess of the Senate," he can make a recess appointment even when the vacancy occurred earlier while the Senate was in session. See CORWIN, THE PRESIDENT 78–79, 366–67 n. 34.

84.  Compare the discussion of consent to treaties in Chapter V, pp. 133–36. Presidents have insisted that the Senate cannot withdraw its consent once given, at least after the commission of office has been signed. On one occasion the Supreme Court avoided the issue by holding that the Senate had acted in violation of its own rules. United States v. Smith, 286 U.S. 6 (1932); see CORWIN, THE PRESIDENT 76–77. Withdrawal of consent after an appointee has taken office would of course be in effect an attempt to remove him from office; see note 87 below.

85.  Until 1855 Congress merely appropriated lump sums—"for the support of such persons as he shall commission to serve the United

States in foreign parts" (1 Stat. 128 (1790)), or, later, for the "expenses of the intercourse between the United States and foreign nations" (3 Stat. 422 (1818)). (But in those days appropriations for departments dealing with domestic affairs were also general and brief.) Even the early statutes, however, fixed maximum salaries for specified diplomatic ranks, *e. g.*, 1 Stat. 128 (1790). Then (in ch. 133, 10 Stat. 619) Congress began to assign definite diplomatic ranks to representatives to named countries, with specified compensation and given qualifications (including a requirement of U. S. citizenship). Attorney General Cushing gave the opinion that such legislation by Congress was beyond its authority and could only be recommendatory, 7 OP.ATT'Y GEN. 186, 217, 242 (1855); but Presidents have long ago conceded. Even the distinction between the ranks mentioned in the Constitution (Ambassadors, other public Ministers and Consuls), as to which the President claimed autonomy, and other personnel in offices created by Congress, has effectively disappeared. The first comprehensive regulation of the Foreign Service was the Rogers Act of 1924, ch. 182, 43 Stat. 140. It was overhauled in the Foreign Service Act of 1946, ch. 957, 60 Stat. 999, and is now in 22 U.S.C. § 801 *et seq.* (1970). For a small recognition of the President's "inherent authority," see 22 U.S.C. 811a. Compare the President's acquired power to appoint special agents (without Senate consent), Chapter II, p. 46.

For an essay on Congressional control of federal offices generally, see Mr. Justice Brandeis dissenting in Myers v. United States, 272 U.S. at 264–74 (1926).

86. In one famous instance Congress, in creating posts in the Judge Advocate's Department of the Army, provided that "one such vacancy, not below the grade of major, shall be filled by the appointment of a person from civil life, not less than forty-five nor more than fifty years of age, who shall have been for ten years a judge of the Supreme Court of the Philippine Islands, shall have served for two years as a captain in the Regular or Volunteer Army, and shall be proficient in the Spanish language and laws." Ch. 134, § 8, 39 Stat. 169 (1916). There was only one person in the world who met those "qualifications," and he got the job. In 1884 Congress passed a bill which authorized the President "to nominate, and by and with the consent of the Senate to appoint Fitz John Porter" to the position of Colonel in the Army. But President Arthur vetoed the bill on the ground that if it was mandatory it usurped the President's power of appointment and if merely a recommendation it does not belong on the statute books. 10 RICHARDSON 4808–10. See Note, *Power of Appointment to Public Office under the Federal Constitution*, 42 HARV.L.REV. 426, 430–31. See CORWIN, THE PRESIDENT 363–65.

Compare the President's objection to a provision that no compensation for service in the Executive Branch shall be paid to three named persons unless the President reappointed them with the consent of the Senate. H.R.Doc.No.264, 78th Cong., 1st Sess. (1943). The Supreme Court held the provision unconstitutional as a bill of attainder. See United States v. Lovett, 328 U.S. 303 (1946).

87. Compare Myers v. United States, 272 U.S. 52 (1926), with Humphrey's Ex'r v. United States, 295 U.S. 602 (1935), and Wiener v. United States, 357 U.S. 349 (1958), Chapter II, note 19. See also Morgan v. TVA, 28 F.Supp. 732 (E.D.Tenn.1939), *cert. denied*, 312 U.S. 701 (1941). Congress can limit the power to remove "inferior officers." United States v. Perkins, 116 U.S. 483 (1886).

88. Kendall v. United States *ex rel.* Stokes, 12 Pet. 524, 610 (U.S. 1838). The case in effect upheld also the power of a court of appropriate jurisdiction to mandamus federal officials. Compare 28 U.S.C. § 1361 (1970).

89. From the beginning Congress itself gave the President control of foreign affairs. The State Department has been a "Presidential Department" and Congress has generally refrained from directing its activities. The Act of July 27, 1789 established a Department of Foreign Affairs, entrusted it with diplomacy and "such other matters as the President shall assign" and directed that it conduct business "in such manner as the President of the United States shall from time to time order or instruct." Ch. 4, 1 Stat. 28–29, quoted in Chapter II, note 20. (The name of the Department was modified by Act of Sept. 15, 1789, 1 Stat. 68.) On the President's different relations to his different departments, compare ch. 4, 1 Stat. 28, and ch. 7, *id.* at 49, with ch. 12, *id.* at 65. And compare Corwin, The President 81, with Berger, *Executive Privilege v. Congressional Inquiry*, 12 U.C.L.A. L.Rev. 1044, 1062 (1965).

90. See United States *ex rel.* Ulrich v. Kellogg, 30 F.2d 984 (D.C. Cir. 1929); *cf.* Loza-Bedoya v. Immigration and Naturalization Service, 410 F.2d 343 (9th Cir. 1969). But the President may have executive authority to exclude an alien even if he bears a visa given by a consular officer. Compare Chapter II, note 31.

91. 19 U.S.C. §§ 1330 *et seq.* (1970). The National Security Council, for a different example, was also created and governed by statute. 50 U.S.C. § 402 (1970).

92. The regulation of communications satellites affords a striking modern example of complex relations between the President and administrative agencies related to foreign affairs. See generally Huszagh, *Relationships Between Foreign Policy, National Security and the Regulation of International Commerce: Variations With or Without a Theme?* 18 Am.U.L.Rev. 709 (1969).

93.  See Tariff Act of 1922, ch. 356, §§ 315, 316, 42 Stat. 941–46; Field v. Clark, 143 U.S. 649 (1892); Hampton & Co. v. United States, 276 U.S. 394 (1928); Chicago & Southern Air Lines v. Waterman S.S. Corp., 333 U.S. 103 (1948).  Compare: "All in all, if the President exercised every power delegated to him in section 315 of the Tariff Act of 1922, he could rewrite the entire bill as soon as the Congress had finished it."  J. LARKIN, THE PRESIDENT'S CONTROL OF THE TARIFF 2 (1926), quoted in CORWIN, THE PRESIDENT, 396 n. 19. On Presidential discretion in regard to foreign aid see p. 114, this chapter.

94.  Mr. Justice Jackson, concurring in Youngstown Sheet & Tube Co. v. Sawyer, 343 U.S. 579, 646, quoted p. 105, this chapter.  In a special sense, the President in turn may be said to "delegate" power to Congress when he seeks its consent for actions that he could probably take on his own constitutional authority.  See, *e. g.*, Chapter II, note 42, and note 50 this chapter.

95.  The doctrine that legislative power is not to be freely delegated is sometimes traced to Locke.  See THE SECOND TREATISE ON CIVIL GOVERNMENT, Chapter XI, § 141, at 118 (Gateway ed. 1960).  In this country, limits on delegation have been deemed to be rooted not only in the separation of powers, but also in common law concepts that deny to an agent the power to delegate his authority, and in notions of due process of law.  Compare Hampton & Co. v. United States, 276 U.S. 394, 405 (1928).  See generally, Jaffe, *An Essay on Delegation of Legislative Power*, 47 COLUM.L.REV. 339, 561 (1947).

The Supreme Court has not struck down any domestic delegation since 1935.  Panama Refining Co. v. Ryan, 293 U.S. 388 (1935) (delegation to the President); Schechter Poultry Corp. v. United States, 295 U.S. 495 (1935).  Compare Sunshine Anthracite Coal Co. v. Adkins, 310 U.S. 381 (1940); United States v. Rock Royal Cooperative, Inc., 307 U.S. 533 (1939); Currin v. Wallace, 306 U.S. 1 (1939); and particularly war-time delegations, Bowles v. Willingham, 321 U.S. 503 (1944); Yakus v. United States, 321 U.S. 414 (1944). The Supreme Court has said that delegation is permitted for "interstitial" legislation if Congress determines the basic policy and lays down guide lines.  Compare Chief Justice Marshall in Wayman v. Southard, 10 Wheat. 1, 43 (U.S.1825).  But the Court has accepted vague and general guidelines, *e. g.*, "public interest," "public convenience and necessity."  New York Central Securities Co. v. United States, 287 U.S. 12, 24 (1932); FCC v. Pottsville Broadcasting Co., 309 U.S. 134, 138 (1940).  See also the broad delegation in the Economic Stabilization Act of 1970, upheld by a three-judge court in *Amalgamated Meat Cutters*, Chapter III, note 7.  But see Kent v. Dulles, 357 U.S. 116, 129 (1958), note 97, this chapter; *cf.* L. JAFFE, JUDICIAL

CONTROL OF ADMINISTRATIVE ACTION 71–72 (1965). Although the Court has moved far from the earlier cases, they have not been over-ruled and the basic principle that the Constitution implies some limitations on delegation no doubt stands.

96. 299 U.S. 304 at 320. Compare Justice Lamar's statement that in foreign relations "even the internal adjustment of federal power, with its complex system of checks and balances, [is] unknown." *In re* Neagle, 135 U.S. 1, 85 (1890). Without announcing any special doctrine about the scope of delegation in foreign affairs, the Court upheld extensive delegations long before *Curtiss-Wright. E. g.,* The Aurora v. United States, 7 Cranch 382 (U.S.1813); The Thomas Gibbons, 8 Cranch 421, 429 (U.S.1814). Extensive delegations in regard to tariffs were upheld in Field v. Clark, 143 U.S. 649, 690 (1892), and Hampton & Co. v. United States, 276 U.S. 394 (1928); and see this chapter, note 93. See also United States *ex rel.* Knauff v. Shaughnessy, 338 U.S. 537, 542 (1950). But compare Zemel v. Rusk, 381 U.S. 1, 17–18 (1964): "[Curtiss-Wright] does not mean that simply because a statute deals with foreign relations, it can grant the Executive totally unrestricted freedom of choice." See Black, J., dissenting, *id.* at 20–23. And see note 97, this chapter.

97. In Kent v. Dulles, 357 U.S. 116 (1958), in considering Congressional delegation to the Secretary of State of authority to limit travel by citizens outside the United States, the Court said that "if that power is to be delegated, the standards must be adequate to pass scrutiny by the accepted tests." It cited *Panama Refining,* note 95, and did not mention *Curtiss-Wright.* Perhaps the Court's opinion alluded to that case and the tariff cases when it said: "If we were dealing with political questions entrusted to the Chief Executive by the Constitution we would have a different case. But there is more involved here." 357 U.S. at 129. The implication may be that as regards the delegation of power to regulate important individual rights, *Panama Refining* is applicable again, and in foreign as in domestic affairs. And compare *Zemel,* quoted note 96.

Subdelegation to other officials by the President, whether of his constitutional authority or of powers delegated to him by Congress, has not been seriously challenged. As regards his powers in foreign affairs, at least, there is little that the President must do in person. Compare, *e. g.,* Wilcox v. McConnell, 13 Pet. 498, 513 (U.S.1839); Williams v. United States, 1 How. 290, 296 (U.S.1843); McElrath v. United States, 102 U.S. 426, 436 (1880); United States *ex rel.* Knauff v. Shaughnessy, 338 U.S. 537, 543 (1950); also 7 OP.ATT'Y GEN. 453 (1871). See Marshall, quoted in Chapter VIII, n. 26.

98. Ch. 583, § 6, 59 Stat. 621, 22 U.S.C. § 287(d) (1970).

99.   Ch. 141, § 10, 65 Stat. 75 (1951).   The provision was repeated in later acts, *e. g.*, 69 Stat. 162, 163 (1955), 19 U.S.C. § 1351(a) (1) (A) (1970).

100.   This was done with the Federal Rules of Civil Procedure.   See Sibbach v. Wilson & Co., 312 U.S. 1, 14–16 (1941).   See 37 OP.ATT'Y GEN. 56, 63 (1933) ; 100 CONG.REC. 4879 (1954).

Section 123(c) of the Atomic Energy Act of 1954 provided that proposed bilateral agreements for cooperation with other nations shall not go into effect until "the proposed agreement for cooperation, together with the approval and the determination of the President, has been submitted to the Joint Committee [of Congress on Atomic Energy] and a period of thirty days has elapsed while Congress is in session . . . ." Ch. 1073, 68 Stat. 940, as amended, 42 U.S.C. 2153 (c) (1970).   A later amendment provided that the Joint Committee may by resolution waive all or part of the thirty day waiting period. Pub.L. 85–681, § 4, 72 Stat. 632 (1958).   (Another 1958 Amendment added that certain kinds of agreements had to lie before the Joint Committee for sixty days while Congress is in session and could not become effective if both Houses disapproved the agreement by concurrent resolution.   Pub.L. 85–479, § 4, 72 Stat. 277, 42 U.S.C. 2153 (d) (1970).   Compare the following notes, this chapter.)

101.   The actual form of the veto can vary greatly depending on the way in which three sets of variables are combined. First, the wielder of the device can vary.   The veto can be— and has been—vested in the whole Congress, in one House of Congress, in the committees, and even in a committee chairman.   Second, the manner in which the veto is expressed can vary.   It can be expressed in a negative, affirmative, or deliberative manner, and, in addition, it may be tied on to the appropriations process rather than defined as a condition on which the authorization of a proposal is made contingent.   In the first instance, a proposal of the executive goes into effect unless negated within a specified period.   In the second instance, a proposal of the executive does not go into effect unless it is affirmed.   In the third instance, a proposal of the executive does not go into effect until it has lain before Congress or some agent of Congress for a specified period.   Here, in contrast to the above instances where neither two-House action nor submission to the President is required, theoretically the actual disallowance of the proposal must take the form of regular legislation.   However, in reality many of the committees of Congress are so strong that the mere hint of their disapproval often is sufficient to convince the executive not to take the proposed step.   When the veto is attached to

the appropriations process, the provision restricts the use of appropriated funds or the appropriation of funds until some further form of legislative assent has been secured. Finally, the nature of the majority necessary to put the veto into effect can vary. Thus far, simple, absolute, and constitutional, i. e., two-thirds, majorities have been required. Cooper & Cooper, *The Legislative Veto and the Constitution*, 30 GEO. WASH.L.REV. 467, 468–69 (1962) (footnotes omitted).

For other examples of the use of the legislative veto in matters related to foreign affairs, see 8 U.S.C. § 1255b(c) (1970) (foreign diplomatic defectors); Pub.L.No.85–686, § 6, 72 Stat. 676 (1958), repealed, Pub.L.No.87–794, § 257(e) (1), 76 Stat. 882 (1962) (reciprocal trade; concurrent resolution to require two-thirds vote of each House).

102.   Ch. 11, § 3(c), 55 Stat. 32 (1941). See the provision in the Tonkin Resolution, note 31, this chapter, and in the Atomic Energy Act, note 100, this chapter.

Withdrawal by concurrent resolution was provided in one of the "Lodge Reservations" to United States adherence to the Versailles treaty, 58 CONG.REC. 8022 (1919) (reservation number 2).

103.   *E. g.*, the Greek-Turkish Aid Act of 1947, Ch. 81, § 6, 61 Stat. 105 (1947), repealed, ch. 937, § 542(a) (1), 68 Stat. 861 (1954); Foreign Assistance Act of 1961, Pub.L.No.87–195, § 617, 75 Stat. 444, 22 U.S.C. § 2367 (1970).

104.   Ch. 2, § 1, 54 Stat. 4 (1939), 22 U.S.C. § 441 (1970). A statute authorizing the deportation of aliens provided that the Attorney General could suspend deportation to avoid hardship to dependents, but he must inform Congress, which could veto the suspension by concurrent resolution. Ch. 439, § 20, 54 Stat. 672 (1940). Later legislation provided instead that the suspension should be lifted and the alien deported unless Congress affirmatively approved the suspension by concurrent resolution. See Ch. 783, 62 Stat. 120 (1948). Compare Ch. 477, § 244(b), 66 Stat. 216 (1952), 8 U.S.C. § 1254 (1970); Jay v. Boyd, 351 U.S. 345, 351 (1956).

105.   See the article quoted note 101 for numerous examples. A principal use of such a veto of Presidential action is in the Reorganization Acts. The 1939 Act provided that any plan for reorganization of an executive agency shall lie on the table for sixty days and shall then become effective unless disapproved by concurrent resolution. See Ch. 36, § 5(a), 53 Stat. 562–63 (1939). The 1949 Act provided for "veto" of a reorganization plan by resolution of either House. Ch. 226, § 6(a), 63 Stat. 205 (1949).

General legislative "oversight" of the execution of the laws is provided in 2 U.S.C. §§ 190b, 190d (1970). Each house has established a standing committee on Government Operations. Senate Rule XXV(1) (j); House Rule XI(8).

106. Corwin notes that the literal requirements of that provision have been long ago, and inevitably, disregarded. CORWIN, THE PRESIDENT 127–30.

That the concurrence of the President is not necessary to resolutions for amending the Constitution (Article V) has been upheld from our early history, Hollingsworth v. Virginia, 3 Dall. 378 (1798); the constitutional language lends itself to that interpretation. See the view that declarations of war do not require Presidential concurrence. Introduction to Chapter II, note 5.

107. Presidents have challenged the validity of various forms of Committee veto provisions. See *Hearings, Separation of Powers* 215–28 and especially 2 PUBLIC PAPERS OF THE PRESIDENTS: LYNDON B. JOHNSON 1963–64, at 1249, 1250 (1965), reprinted in *Hearings* at 224; Wilson's veto message reprinted *id.* at 203; see also Maass, *id.* at 187–188; Wozencraft, *id.* at 201; Bickel, *id.* at 245. See generally, Cooper and Cooper, note 101 this chapter; Ginnane, *The Control of Federal Administration by Congressional Resolutions and Committees*, 66 HARV.L.REV. 569 (1953), and an interesting footnote, Mr. Justice Jackson's *A Presidential Legal Opinion*, *id.* at 1353; Newman & Keeton, *Congress and the Faithful Execution of the Laws—Should Legislators Supervise Administrators?* 41 CALIF.L.REV. 568 (1953). And see 37 OP.ATT'Y GEN. 56 (1933).

108. Corwin gives some of the arguments for and against "repeal" of delegation by concurrent resolution; for him the arguments against "affront common sense". THE PRESIDENT 129–30 and accompanying notes.

NOTES, INTRODUCTION TO CHAPTER V, INTERNATIONAL
COOPERATION, pp. 127–28.

1. Chisholm v. Georgia, 2 Dall. 419, 474 (U.S.1793). Compare:
"When the United States declared their independence they were
bound to receive the law of nations, in its modern state of purity and
refinement." Wilson, J., in Ware v. Hylton, 3 Dall. 199, 281 (U.S.
1796).

NOTES, CHAPTER V, TREATIES, pp. 129 to 171.

1. "On July 11, 1776, the date on which the committee to draft a declaration of independence was chosen, the Congress resolved that committees to prepare a form of confederation and a plan of treaties to be proposed to foreign powers should be constituted. On the following day the two committees were chosen. Closely associated then in origin are these three features of our national life—independence, union, and treaty making." S. CRANDALL, TREATIES THEIR MAKING AND ENFORCEMENT 19 (2d ed. 1916) [hereinafter cited as CRANDALL, TREATIES], citing 2 JOURNALS OF CONGRESS (1800 ed.) 197, 198.

Compare Jay: "The power of making treaties is an important one, especially as it relates to war, peace, and commerce; and it should not be delegated but in such a mode, and with such precautions, as will afford the highest security that it will be exercised by men the best qualified for the purpose, and in the manner most conducive to the public good." THE FEDERALIST No. 64, at 420.

2. Clearly the prevailing mood at the Convention was that it should not be too easy to make treaties. Even the "nationalists" among them neither desired nor expected many treaties. Compare, *e. g.*, Morris and Madison, 2 FARRAND 393, 548. At the Pennsylvania Convention, Wilson said: "Neither the President nor the Senate, solely, can complete a treaty; they are checks upon each other, and are so balanced as to produce security to the people." 2 ELLIOT'S DEBATES 507. Later, Jefferson wrote: "On the subject of treaties, our system is to have none with any nation, as far as can be avoided." 11 T. JEFFERSON, WRITINGS 38–39 (Bergh ed. 1907). Compare Washington's Farewell Address, 1 RICHARDSON 205. Only six treaties were concluded under the Articles and the United States did not make many during the early years under the Constitution. As of 1967 the Department of State reported that the United States had made some 1250 treaties. See 62 AM.J.INT'L L. 162–63 (1968). And see Chapter VI, note 1.

Treaties and other international agreements that entered into force up to the end of 1949 were published in the United States Statutes-at-large. (An index to treaties and other international agreements printed in the statutes may be found at 64 Stat. B1107.) Beginning in 1950 they have been published in a new compilation by the Department of State, *U.S. Treaties and Other International Agreements*, (U.S.T.). The statutes and the later compilation are legal evidence of the authentic text.

372

3. Failure of States to observe the treaties made by the Congress was one of the principal impulses leading to the Constitutional Convention. See T. BAILEY, A DIPLOMATIC HISTORY OF THE AMERICAN PEOPLE, Chapter V (8th ed. 1968). At the Convention Madison said: "Will it prevent those violations of the law of nations & of Treaties which if not prevented must involve us in the calamities of foreign wars? The tendency of the States to these violations has been manifested in sundry instances. The files of Congs. contain complaints already, from almost every nation with which treaties have been formed. Hitherto indulgence has been shewn to us. This cannot be the permanent disposition of foreign nations. A rupture with other powers is among the greatest of national calamities. It ought therefore to be effectually provided that no part of a nation shall have it in its power to bring them on the whole. The existing confederacy does (not) sufficiently provide against this evil. The proposed amendment to it does not supply the omission. It leaves the will of the States as uncontrouled as ever." 1 FARRAND 316; also *id.* at 426, 513. See also THE FEDERALIST No. 15 at 156 (Hamilton); No. 22 at 197–98 (Hamilton), No. 42 at 302 (Madison).

4. The treaty-making process—as distinguished from the supremacy of treaties—received little consideration at the Convention. Early it was proposed that treaties be made by the Senate. Towards the end of the Convention the present version was proposed and accepted with little discussion. (Hamilton had suggested it earlier in the plan he originally submitted to the Convention but his proposal did not contain the two-thirds requirement.) It was obviously a compromise resulting from other compromises. "It was evident that the convention was getting tired. The Committee had recommended that the power of appointment and the making of treaties be taken from the senate and vested in the President 'by and with the advice and consent of the senate.' With surprising unanimity and surprisingly little debate, these important changes were agreed to." M. FARRAND, THE FRAMING OF THE CONSTITUTION OF THE UNITED STATES 171 (1913). Proposals to require the approval of the House of Representatives (as well as the Senate) were rejected because its fluctuating membership and the short-term of its members would preclude the development of expertise, and its numbers would render it incapable of quick action and of secrecy. Compare THE FEDERALIST No. 64 (Jay), No. 75 (Hamilton), and the views of "Marcos," (Iredell) and others, quoted in BUTLER, THE TREATY POWER §§ 253–54. See also 2 J. MADISON, JOURNAL OF THE CONSTITUTIONAL CONVENTION OF 1787 at 327 (Hunt ed. 1908); 4 ELLIOT'S DEBATES 253–67.

The choice of the Senate for the treaty-making process reflected also its character as the particular representative of state interests. It may not be irrelevant, too, that both President and Senate were only indirectly responsible to "the people," to popular vote. Compare Jay, THE FEDERALIST NO. 64. Madison wished to give the Senate alone the power to make peace because the President "would necessarily derive so much power and importance from a state of war that he might be tempted, if authorized, to impede a treaty of peace." 2 FARRAND 540. Compare Chapter IV, note 47.

The two-thirds requirement, however, was the subject of some debate. Among other suggestions, Madison proposed excepting peace treaties from that requirement so that a minority could not insist on continuing a war. There were also suggestions to require two-thirds of the entire Senate (rather than of those present and voting). A proposal for Senate approval by simple majority was defeated by one vote. See 2 FARRAND 532–54.

The two-thirds vote requirement can be seen as intended to approximate and perpetuate the situation in the Congress under the Articles. In 1789 the consent of two-thirds of the Senate, then consisting of representatives of thirteen States, would be roughly the same as the assent of nine states required under the Articles (Art. IX) in the Congress of thirteen States. (Compare Hamilton, THE FEDERALIST NO. 75.) Under the Articles, however, each state had one vote; in the Senate, Senators from the same State might not vote alike. In the Senate, also, a treaty requires only the consent of two-thirds of the Senators voting. For the growth of the treaty-making provisions at the Convention, see 1 BUTLER, THE TREATY POWER §§ 17 *et seq.*; CRANDALL, TREATIES, Chapter 4; W. HOLT, TREATIES DEFEATED BY THE SENATE, Chapter 1 (1933) [hereinafter cited as HOLT].

5. "The power in question seems therefore to form a distinct department, and to belong, properly, neither to the legislative nor to the executive. The qualities elsewhere detailed as indispensable in the management of foreign negotiations, point out the Executive as the most fit agent in those transactions; while the vast importance of the trust, and the operation of treaties as laws, plead strongly for the participation of the whole or a portion of the legislative body in the office of making them." Hamilton, THE FEDERALIST NO. 75 at 476–77. See also THE FEDERALIST NO. 64 (Jay). Hamilton was probably drawing on Locke who had written of a "federative branch" of government distinct from the executive. See Chapter II, note 10.

6. See THE FEDERALIST NO. 64 (Jay); also CORWIN, THE PRESIDENT 207–10.

7. "The wording of the Constitution itself visualizes treaty-making as one continuous process to be performed by a single authority, the

President acting throughout in consultation with the Senate. From the first, however, the Senate insisted upon asserting its independence of identity in the treaty-making business, thereby splitting the constitutional authority into two authorities, performing separate differentiated functions, a Presidential function of formulation and negotiation followed by a Senatorial function—completely legislative in character and motivation—of criticism and amendment, or of criticism and rejection." (Original in italics). E. CORWIN, THE CONSTITUTION AND WORLD ORGANIZATION 36 (1944).

Compare: "The President is the constitutional representative of the United States with regard to foreign nations. He manages our concerns with foreign nations and must necessarily be most competent to determine when, how, and upon what subjects negotiation may be urged with the greatest prospect of success. For his conduct he is responsible to the Constitution. The committee consider this responsibility the surest pledge for the faithful discharge of his duty. They think the interference of the Senate in the direction of foreign negotiations calculated to diminish that responsibility and thereby to impair the best security for the national safety. The nature of transactions with foreign nations, moreover, requires caution and unity of design, and their success frequently depends on secrecy and dispatch. U. S. Senate, Reports, Committee on Foreign Relations, vol. 8, p. 24." Quoted in *Curtiss-Wright,* 299 U.S. at 319.

For the developing role of the Senate, see R. HAYDEN, THE SENATE AND TREATIES, 1789–1817 (1920) [hereinafter cited as HAYDEN, TREATIES]. There are suggestions that the "advice" intended by the Constitution was to be as to whether or not to ratify. *Id.* at 6, 35.

8. Washington had told a Senate committee that oral communication seemed indispensable. 11 G. WASHINGTON, WRITINGS 417 (Ford ed. 1893). The Senate thereupon adopted a rule as to the procedure to be followed when the President met with the Senate. Senate Rule XXXVI(1). Once Washington apparently came seeking immediate yes-or-no answers to several questions about an Indian Treaty; the Senate insisted on a few days to refer it to committee and deliberate about it, not in the President's presence. The story is widely told, *e. g.,* in CORWIN, THE PRESIDENT 209–10.

The Jay Treaty was a particular source of difficulties between the President and the Senate. The Senate defeated a resolution asking Washington what Jay was off to negotiate about. In bitter public debate after the Jay Treaty was concluded, some urged the impeachment of Washington because, among other reasons, he had violated the Constitution in negotiating a treaty without the previous advice of the Senate. 5 J. MARSHALL, THE LIFE OF GEORGE WASHINGTON 229 (1926). See generally HAYDEN, TREATIES 58–94.

The Senate has often hidden treaties submitted to it, and what it was doing (or not doing) about them, by an injunction of secrecy, which Presidents for their part did not feel free to violate. Compare Senate Rules XXXVI(3), XXXVII(1); Hudson, *The "Injunction of Secrecy" with Respect to American Treaties*, 23 AM.J.INT'L L. 329 (1929).

9. Early Presidents sought such advice by message on some eighteen occasions, most of them by President Washington during the negotiation of the Jay Treaty. CRANDALL, TREATIES 68–75. In 1846 President Polk asked the Senate's advice as to an agreement to divide Oregon at the 49th parallel before he began negotiating. President Harding asked the Senate to approve U.S. adherence to the World Court in advance of executive negotiation of an agreement. Compare Secretary Kellogg who sent to the Senate Foreign Relations Committee a proposed Arbitration Agreement with France before it was negotiated. See D. BYRN-JONES, FRANK B. KELLOGG 248–49 (1937). Other instances of prior "consultation" are cited in the Appendix to H.R.REP.No. 1569, 68th Cong., 2d Sess. 19–20 (1925). Until 1815 Presidents often submitted to the Senate for confirmation the names of commissioners designated to negotiate treaties and advised the Senate of the general purpose of the negotiations. CRANDALL, TREATIES 75.

In 1953 Secretary Dulles assured the Senate: "It will be our effort to see that the Senate gets its opportunity to 'advise and consent' in time so that it does not have to choose between adopting treaties it does not like or embarrassing our international position by rejecting what has already been negotiated out with foreign governments." 28 DEP'T STATE BULL. 591–92 (1953). There is no evidence that he or other Secretaries have in fact formally sought the advice of the Senate (as distinguished from consultation with committees or individual Senators).

Early leaks by the Senate to a foreign government contributed to the development of the practice to tell the Senate nothing until negotiation was concluded. While there is nothing in the Constitution that precludes a secret treaty, especially as the Senate grew in membership it was accepted that secret agreements could not go to the Senate for formal consent. For examples of Senate leaks despite self-imposed injunctions of secrecy (this chapter, note 8), see HOLT at 16, 90 n. 32, 95, 138 n. 66, 139 n. 67, 167–68, 183, 193, 217. The Senate held secret hearings on treaties until the Versailles Treaty. *Id.* at 282. It now considers treaties generally in "open executive session," *i. e.*, in its executive capacity (as treaty maker, rather than as legislator) but usually not in secret. Compare Senate Rules XXXVI(3), XXXVII(1).

10. For the text of the Vandenberg Resolution see S.Res. 239, 80th Cong., 2d Sess., 94 Cong.Rec. 7791 (1948).

Congress has sometimes urged the President to make a treaty. See pp. 149–50 and note 80, this chapter.

11. Holt's book is a brief for that thesis. He ends his volume as follows (at 307):

"The fate of the treaty of Versailles turned the attention of thoughtful people to the treaty-making power of the United States. They saw that the exercise of that power had produced such bitter conflicts between the President and the Senate and had so increased the opportunities for political warfare unconnected with the merits of the question that many treaties had been lost. They knew that the ratification of nearly every important treaty had been endangered by a constitutional system which, instead of permitting a decision solely on the merits of the question, produces impotence and friction. They realized that if no disaster had resulted it was due partly to good fortune and chiefly to the relative unimportance of foreign relations in the history of the United States so that few treaties had contained vital issues. They also realized that, if the United States was to play the part in world affairs demanded by its interests and its strength, a deadlock between the President and the Senate over a treaty involving a really critical foreign problem may end in ruin."

Compare also D. Fleming, The Treaty Veto of the American Senate (1930). But *cf.* R. Dangerfield, In Defense of the Senate: a Study in Treaty-Making (1933).

12. 2 W. Thayer, The Life and Letters of John Hay 170 (1915). Hay also said: "A treaty entering the Senate is like a bull going into the arena: no one can say just how or when the final blow will fall—but one thing is certain it will never leave the arena alive." *Id.* at 393. He thought the Senate "veto" on treaties to be the "original mistake in the Constitution." 3 J. Hay, Letters of John Hay and Extracts from Diary 156 (Privately Printed 1908).

13. John W. Davis, 48 A.B.A.Rep. at 203 (1923). Compare: "It is a painful and humiliating state of things, but I see no escape from it, since the Fathers in their wisdom chose to assume that one-third of the Senate in opposition would always be right, and the President and the majority generally wrong." John Hay to President McKinley, Aug. 19, 1899, quoted in Holt 192. Dangerfield, this chapter, note 11, at 311–12, however, stresses that up to 1928 only seven treaties received a majority vote in the Senate but failed for lack of two-thirds.

There have been innumerable proposals to amend the Constitution to drop the two-thirds requirement but give the House of Representatives a voice in treaty-making equal to that of the Senate. Others have sought escape from the two-thirds requirement without constitutional amendment by promoting the approval of international agreements by simple majority in both houses. See Chapter VI.

Senate rules have made it possible for a minority of one-third-plus-one during debate to strike particular treaty provisions, thereby making the treaty as a whole less acceptable and unlikely later to attract the two-thirds vote. See HOLT 36–37. In the Versailles debates, the opposition exploited a different rule requiring only a simple majority to vote amendments to a treaty, and perhaps render the treaty less able to attract a two-thirds vote.

14. On June 15, 1934, the Senate approved twelve treaties in an hour. See 78 CONG.REC. 11561 *et seq.* For a graphic description of the Senate's record on treaties submitted for its consent between 1789 and 1967, see 62 AM.J.INT'L L. 162–63 (1968). See also U.S. DEP'T OF STATE, PUB.NO.2311, TREATIES SUBMITTED TO THE SENATE, 1935–1944 (1945).

15. See CRANDALL, TREATIES 94–99. The Eisenhower administration did not press for Senate consent to the Genocide Convention, sent to the Senate by President Truman, note 71, this chapter.

Presidents have also refused to proceed with treaties on the basis of Senate reservations. See CRANDALL, TREATIES 97–99.

16. CRANDALL, TREATIES 82–84. A treaty with Mexico was rejected by the Senate twice. See HOLT 132–33.

17. Compare the efforts of the Senate to withdraw its consent to a nomination of an officer, Chapter IV, note 84.

18. The Senate entered a reservation to the Jay Treaty, the first treaty made by the United States following the adoption of the Constitution. Senate Resolution of June 24, 1795, 1 S.EXEC.J. 64, quoted in D. MILLER, RESERVATIONS TO TREATIES 4–5 (1919).

In the days when the Senate approved instructions to negotiators it felt obligated to consent to a treaty concluded in accordance with the instructions. CRANDALL, TREATIES 79.

19. Monroe reported that Lord Harrowby, the British Foreign Minister, "censured in strong terms the practise into which we had fallen of ratifying treaties, with exceptions to parts of them, a practise which he termed new, unauthorized and not to be sanctioned." 3 AMERICAN STATE PAPERS, FOREIGN RELATIONS (Gales and Seaton eds. 1832–61) 93. See HAYDEN, TREATIES 150. See also Canning to Rush, Aug. 27, 1824, 5 AMERICAN STATE PAPERS, *supra* at 364–65. The treaty of Ghent provided that it shall become binding when ratified by both sides "without alteration by either of the contracting parties." 8 Stat. 218, 223 (1814).

20. The Supreme Court has expressly recognized the power of the Senate to give consent with reservations. See Haver v. Yaker, 9 Wall. 32, 35 (U.S.1869); Brown, J., concurring in Fourteen Diamond Rings

v. United States, 183 U.S. 176, 182 (1901). See generally, D. MILLER, RESERVATIONS TO TREATIES (1919). For what is described as an effort by a Senate committee to negotiate directly with a foreign government, see HOLT 107, 180–81.

21. See note 15, and text at note 22, this chapter. A reservation by another party, entered after the Senate had consented to the original treaty, presents the United States with a modified treaty and requires new consent. Such later reservations have in the past often (not always) been submitted for Senate consent. See, *e. g.*, the Treaty with France 1800, 1 MALLOY, TREATIES 496; HAYDEN, TREATIES 124. See generally CRANDALL, TREATIES 86–89; 5 MOORE, DIGEST 207. See MILLER, RESERVATIONS TO TREATIES 11–14 (1919). The principle has been reaffirmed recently by the Department of State in 60 AM.J.INT'L L. 562 (1966), but in fact foreign reservations have apparently not been submitted for Senate consent in many years. Perhaps that is because reservations by others after ratification by the United States are likely to occur in respect of multilateral treaties, and have not affected U.S. rights or obligations in ways deemed of major importance; perhaps, in these cases, the Executive concluded that, knowing the practice, the Senate had waived the need for its consent. Or that he could accept these modifications on his own authority. See Chapter VI.

22. See 36 Stat. 2199, 2240 (1909), 35 Stat. 1960 (1908); MALLOY, TREATIES 814, 2247. Presidents resisted these reservations. See CRANDALL, TREATIES 98–99. See HOLT 204 *et seq.*, 230 *et seq.*; WRIGHT 109–10; 1 WILLOUGHBY 541–43.

23. Particularly as to treaties which affect the revenue, *e. g.*, Treaty with Great Britain concerning Canada, 10 Stat. 1089, 1092 (1854); Treaty with Hawaii, 19 Stat. 625, 627 (1875); Treaty with Mexico, 24 Stat. 987, 988 (1883); Commercial Convention with Cuba, 33 Stat. 2136, 2143 (1903). See 2A HINDS, PRECEDENTS OF THE HOUSE OF REPRESENTATIVES §§ 1531–33, at 994–1002 (1907); 1 WILLOUGHBY, 558–60; S.DOC. NO. 47, 57th Cong., 2d Sess. (1902), reprinted in 2 HINDS, *supra* at 1001–02; see also United States v. American Sugar Co., 202 U.S. 563 (1906), where the Supreme Court gave effect to the Senate's reservation that the Cuba Convention should not take effect until it had been approved by Congress. Compare 42 Stat. 1946, 1949 (1921). And see the Niagara reservation, discussed at pp. 134–35.

The reservations to the Treaty of Versailles included several designed to ensure for Congress a major role in the implementation of the treaty. See Wright, *Validity of the Proposed Reservations to the Peace Treaty*, 20 COLUM.L.REV. 121, 125, 126, 138–42 (1920). One reservation would have authorized denunciation of the Treaty by concurrent resolution of Congress (without Presidential assent). See Chapter IV, p. 121.

24. The Senate Reservation to the Reciprocal Military Service Convention with Great Britain, June 3, 1918, 40 Stat. 1620, required the President, before ratifying the Convention, to issue a general certificate exempting from military service citizens of the United States in Great Britain who were outside the ages of military service specified in the laws of the United States. He complied in substance by an exchange of diplomatic notes. See S.EXEC.DOC. No. 5, presented as H.R.DOC. No. 1220, 65th Cong., 2d Sess. 2, 7 (1918).

In consenting to a treaty with Korea in 1883 the Senate resolved that it "does not admit or acquiesce" in any assertion of a right "to negotiate treaties or carry on diplomatic negotiations" other than by persons confirmed by the Senate. MALLOY, TREATIES 340. The Senate has lost that one.

Some of the Senate reservations to the Treaty of Versailles would have enhanced the powers of some organs of the federal government and limited the authority of others. See Wright, *Validity of the Proposed Reservations to the Peace Treaty*, 20 COLUM.L.REV. 121, 123–24 (1920).

25. See the previous note. Compare a recent, far-reaching expression by the Senate in consenting to ratification of the Convention on the Organization for Economic Cooperation and Development: ". . . with the interpretation and explanation of the intent of the Senate, that nothing in the convention, or the advice and consent of the Senate to the ratification thereof, confers any power on the Executive to bind the United States in substantive matters beyond what the Executive now has, or to bind the United States without compliance with applicable procedures imposed by domestic law, or confers any power on the Congress to take action in fields previously beyond the authority of Congress, or limits Congress in the exercise of any power it now has." 107 CONG.REC. 4149 (1961); [1961] 12 U.S.T. 1728, 1751, T.I.A.S. No. 4891. Compare analogous Congressional "reservations," Chapter IV, pp. 120–21.

26. See Uses of the Waters of the Niagara River, Convention Between the United States of America and Canada, Feb. 27, 1950, [1950] 1 U.S.T. 694, T.I.A.S. No. 2130. See generally Henkin, *The Treaty Makers and the Law Makers: The Niagara Reservation*, 56 COLUM.L. REV. 1151, 1154–58 (1956) [hereinafter cited as Henkin, *Niagara*]. The relevant portions of the treaty and the diplomatic exchanges are quoted there.

27. See, *e. g.*, the Memorandum of Law by Thomas F. Moore, Jr., counsel for the Power Authority of the State of New York, reproduced in N. Y. Times, Oct. 29, 1955, at 9, col. 1.

28. See Henkin, *Niagara* 1176–81. For this reason (and others, see pp. 160–61) I believe that the Court of Appeals for the District of Columbia erred in refusing to give effect to the Senate "reservation."

The court's judgment was vacated by the Supreme Court when the issue became moot because Congress adopted the legislation called for by the Senate. See Power Authority v. Federal Power Comm'n, 247 F. 2d 538 (D.C.Cir. 1957), vacated and remanded with directions to dismiss as moot, *sub nom.*, American Public Power Ass'n v. Power Authority, 355 U.S. 64 (1957).

New York Indians v. United States, 170 U.S. 1 (1898), is different. There the Supreme Court refused to let the President's non-compliance with the Senate's requirements (which the Court said were perhaps only directory not mandatory) defeat the claim of the Indians under the treaty. The rights of Indians, moreover, are different. *Cf.* Squire v. Capoeman, 351 U.S. 1, 6, 7 (1956); United States v. Shoshone Tribe, 304 U.S. 111, 117 (1938).

29.  Compare note 24, this chapter.  A very different condition couched as an understanding (p. 135 above) was that appended by the Senate in consenting to the London Treaty, 73 CONG.REC. 378 (1930):

> *Resolved further,* That in ratifying said treaty the Senate does so with the distinct and explicit understanding that there are no secret files, documents, letters, understandings, or agreements which in any way, directly or indirectly, modify, change, add to, or take away from any of the stipulations, agreements, or statements in said treaty; and that the Senate ratifies said treaty with the distinct and explicit understanding that, excepting the agreement brought about through the exchange of notes between the Governments of the United States, Great Britain, and Japan having reference to Article XIX, there is no agreement, secret or otherwise, expressed or implied, between any of the parties to said treaty as to any construction that shall hereafter be given to any statement or provision contained therein.

This "understanding" does not amend or interpret the treaty, nor does it require any action. Presumably it serves to deny Senate consent to any secret agreed construction that might exist. Perhaps, even, the Senate's consent would not be effective if a secret understanding in fact existed, and the President could not proceed to ratify.

30.  The Senate has sometimes taken the occasion of consent to a treaty to express policy in the form of a reservation or understanding. *E. g.,* Convention for the Pacific Settlement of International Disputes, July 29, 1899, 32 Stat. 1779, 1801 (1903), T.S. No. 392; General Act of the International Conference at Algeciras and An Additional Protocol, April 7, 1906, 34 Stat. 2905, 2946 (1907), T.S. No. 456. See MALLOY, TREATIES 2032, 2047, 2183; WRIGHT 282.

31.   The Senate has sometimes insisted that its understandings be mentioned in the ratification of the treaty "as conveying the true meaning of the treaty, and will in effect form a part of the treaty." Treaty with Mexico Respecting Utilization of Waters of the Colorado and Tijuana Rivers and the Rio Grande, 59 Stat. 1219, 1263–65 (1945), T.S. No. 994, at 53–55 (1946); Hidalgo County Water Control & Improvement Dist. v. Hedrick, 226 F.2d 1, 5, 8 (5th Cir. 1955), *cert. denied,* 350 U.S. 983 (1956).   The Senate has sometimes used "subject to the following understandings and reservations" without indicating which was which.

In some cases the other party expressly consented to the Senate understandings.   See, *e. g.,* the 1911 treaty with Japan, 37 Stat. 1508 (1913), T.S. No. 558.

32.   Compare the experience under the Headquarters Agreement between the U.S. and the UN which was not sent to the Senate for its consent as to a treaty, but concluded by the President under authority of a joint resolution of Congress. See 61 Stat. 756 (1947), T.I.A.S. No. 1676.   (See, generally, Chapter VI, p. 173 and note 11.)   Section 6 of the Joint Resolution contained a provision that:

> Nothing in the agreement shall be construed as in any way diminishing, abridging, or weakening the right of the United States to safeguard its own security and completely to control the entrance of aliens into any territory of the United States other than the headquarters district and its immediate vicinity, as to be defined and fixed in a supplementary agreement between the Government of the United States and the United Nations in pursuance of section 13(3) (e) of the agreement, and such areas as it is reasonably necessary to traverse in transit between the same and foreign countries. Moreover, nothing in section 14 of the agreement with respect to facilitating entrance into the United States by persons who wish to visit the headquarters district and do not enjoy the right of entry provided in section 11 of the agreement shall be construed to amend or suspend in any way the immigration laws of the United States or to commit the United States in any way to effect any amendment or suspension of such laws.
> 61 Stat. at 767–78.

The text of the resolution was communicated to the UN, but neither the Secretary General nor the General Assembly reacted to it, and the character of the security clause (as a reservation, understanding, or something else) and its purport were not agreed or discussed when the agreement was concluded, perhaps because neither the U.S. Executive Branch nor the UN wished to face its possible implications.   In 1953, however, the United States invoked the security provision to justify its refusal to admit to the U.S. for travel to UN Headquarters a representative of an approved non-governmental organization, whom the U.S. considered a threat to its security. The Secretary General claimed that the UN was not bound by that provision; the U.S. insisted that for its part under its Constitution there was no agreement except subject to that proviso. The issue was not resolved in principle. See Annual Report of Secretary General, 8 UN GAOR Supp. 1 at 144 (1953); 9 *id.* Supp. 1 at 100 (1954); 14 UN BULL. 339 (1953), 15 *id.* 102; [1953] UN YEAR BOOK 501–503.

33. William Rawle, one of the earliest expounders of the Constitution, and an ardent exponent of States' rights, noted that unlike the Articles of Confederation "[i]n our present Constitution no limitations [on the treaty power] were held necessary." W. RAWLE, A VIEW OF THE CONSTITUTION OF THE UNITED STATES 65 (2d ed. 1829).

34. But *cf.* Burdell v. Canadian Pacific Airlines, Ltd., Cir.Ct., Cook County, Ill., Nov. 7, 1968 noted in 63 AM.J.INT'L L. 339 (1969) (holding the venue and damage-limitation provisions of the Warsaw Convention unconstitutional). And *cf.* W. COWLES, TREATIES AND CONSTITUTIONAL LAW 294–95 (1941), whose thesis is that the Supreme Court has in fact declined to enforce treaty provisions where they infringed on private property rights. The case he makes is open to question.

35. Missouri v. Holland, 252 U.S. 416, 433 (1920), discussed p. 143. Shortly after that case was decided Professor Thomas Reed Powell said of the opinion: "Its hint that there may be no other test to be applied than whether the treaty has been duly concluded indicates that the court might hold that specific constitutional limitations in favor of individual liberty and property are not applicable to deprivations wrought by treaties." Powell, *Constitutional Law in 1919–20*, 19 MICH. L.REV. 1, 13 (1920). The possibility of such an interpretation was recognized also in Stinson, *The Treaty-Making Power and the Restraint of the Common Law*, 1 B.U.L.REV. 111, 112 (1921), and in 6 CORNELL L.Q. 91, 92 (1920). See also United States v. Reid, 73 F.2d 153, 155 (9th Cir. 1934), *cert. denied for untimeliness*, 299 U.S. 544 (1936); that case was rejected on other grounds in Perkins v. Elg, 307 U.S. 325, 349 n. 31 (1939). For earlier views to this effect compare PAMPHLETS ON THE CONSTITUTION OF THE UNITED STATES 279, 306 (Ford ed. 1888); H. DAVIS, THE JUDICIAL VETO 100 (1914).

That a treaty is not subject to constitutional limitation has been suggested, in addition, on the ground that under international law a sovereign nation may enter into any treaty and that this international law, antedating the Constitution, was not modified by the adoption of the Constitution. It has even been argued that the Constitution could not effectively limit the treaty powers of a sovereign nation. See

Potter, *Inhibitions Upon the Treaty-Making Power of the United States,* 28 AM.J.INT'L.L. 456 (1934).

A. Sutherland, *Restricting the Treaty Power,* 65 HARV.L.REV. 1305, 1319 (1952), notes that the President and the Senate evidently thought that they had the authority to contravene by treaty the Eighteenth Amendment of the Constitution when they ratified the Smuggling of Intoxicating Liquors Agreement, Jan. 23, 1924, 43 Stat. 1761, T.S. No. 685. There was, however, disagreement within the Executive Branch as to whether the Eighteenth Amendment limited diplomatic exemptions from baggage inspection. See 1 C. HYDE, INTERNATIONAL LAW 759 (1922).

The subject was much discussed in the various hearings on the Bricker Amendment. *Hearings on S.J. Res. 130 Before a Subcomm. of the Senate Comm. on the Judiciary,* 82d Cong., 2d Sess. 121, 132, 256, 313–16, 364, 413, 484, 486, 530 (1952); *Hearings on S.J. Res. 1 & 43 Before a Subcomm. of the Senate Comm. on the Judiciary,* 83d Cong., 1st Sess. 924, 959, 994, 999, 1010, 1070, 1123, 1130, 1136 (1953); *Hearings on S.J. Res. 1 Before a Subcomm. of the Senate Comm. on the Judiciary,* 84th Cong., 1st Sess. 185–86, 281–82, 297, 581–82 (1955). Some proponents of the Bricker Amendment argued that it was not clear whether a treaty was invalid if it was inconsistent with the Constitution, but they cited little authority for the view they feared. See, *e. g.,* statements of Frank Holman, *Bricker Hearings,* 1953, 142–49.

John Foster Dulles, shortly before he became Secretary of State, said: "The treaty making power is an extraordinary power, liable to abuse. Treaties make international law and also they make domestic law. Under our Constitution, treaties become the supreme law of the land. They are, indeed, more supreme than ordinary laws for congressional laws are invalid if they do not conform to the Constitution, whereas treaty law can overrule the Constitution. Treaties, for example, can take powers away from the Congress and give them to the President; they can take powers from the States and give them to the Federal Government or to some international body, and they can cut across the rights given the people by their constitutional Bill of Rights." Address at the regional meeting of the ABA, April 11, 1952, reprinted *id.* at 862.

Later, when Secretary of State, Mr. Dulles explained that he did not believe the treaty power could be unlimited and that the only personal rights which could be limited by treaties would be "property" rights through the exercise of eminent domain. *Bricker Hearings,* 1955, *supra* at 177–79.

There are other misleading statements, *e. g.,* "The treaty, then, as to the point in question, is of equal force with the Constitution itself;

and, certainly, with any law whatever." Cushing, J., in Ware v. Hylton, 3 Dall. 199, 284 (U.S.1796). Also that treaties have "the same effect as an act of Congress, and [are] of equal force with the Constitution." Pollard v. Kibbe, 14 Pet. 353, 415 (U.S.1840). In context such statements meant only that treaties were equally supreme to state law, not that they could disregard constitutional limitations.

36. See, *e. g.*, the opinion of the Court of Appeals of Virginia quoted in Martin v. Hunter's Lessee, 1 Wheat. 304, 323–24 (U.S.1816); also Marbury v. Madison, 1 Cranch 137, 180 (U.S.1803); Gibbons v. Ogden, 9 Wheat. 1, 210–11 (U.S.1824); *cf.* Field v. Clark, 143 U.S. 649, 669, 673 (1892); see R. BERGER, CONGRESS V. THE SUPREME COURT 228–36 (1969). But *cf.* 2 W. CROSSKEY, POLITICS AND THE CONSTITUTION IN THE HISTORY OF THE UNITED STATES 990–1007 (1953).

37. See 2 FARRAND 417; W. RAWLE, A VIEW OF THE CONSTITUTION OF THE UNITED STATES 66–67 (2d ed. 1829). See Reid v. Covert, 354 U.S. 1, 16 (1957), p. 139 above.

38. That indeed was the purpose of the phrase "made or which shall be made," 2 FARRAND 417, and that phrase alone achieves that meaning in Article III, section 2. Compare Worcester v. Georgia, 6 Pet. 515, 558 (U.S.1832).

39. It may be urged that in view of the possible international consequences of declaring a treaty provision unconstitutional, courts should not consider the validity of a treaty provision but treat that as a political question not for judicial determination. See Chapter VIII, p. 210. One commentator has said: "It is difficult to imagine anything more anomalous than a lawsuit between private litigants becoming the means of upsetting an international engagement." W. McCLURE, INTERNATIONAL EXECUTIVE AGREEMENTS 223 (1941). *Cf.* United States v. Reid, this chapter, note 35. Compare Mr. Justice Chase, in Ware v. Hylton, 3 Dall. 199, 237 (U.S.1796): "If the court possesses a power to declare treaties void, I shall never exercise it, but in a very clear case indeed." Article 60 of the Netherlands Constitution provides that judges shall not judge the constitutionality of treaties.

It has been argued that since for domestic purposes Congress can repeal treaty provisions (p. 163 above), there is a safeguard against abuse of the Treaty Power making it unnecessary to rely on judicial invalidation; if a treaty is to be nullified, with possible serious consequences to the nation, let it be done only by Congress which is the supreme political body (and has authority to court and make war). Some may see conceptual difficulties in a constitutional system under which treaties are not subject to constitutional limitations and judicial invalidation. Compare Mr. Justice Black, p. 139 above, and note 45, this chapter.

40. See Geofroy v. Riggs, 133 U.S. 258, 267 (1890) quoted p. 141, this chapter; The Cherokee Tobacco, 11 Wall. 616, 620–21 (U.S.1871) ("It need hardly be said that a treaty cannot change the Constitution or be held valid if it be in violation of that instrument"); Doe v. Braden, 16 How. 635, 657 (U.S.1853); Asakura v. Seattle, 265 U.S. 332, 341 (1924). And see Calhoun, quoted note 49, this chapter.

41. 252 U.S. at 433.

42. Judiciary Act of 1789, Ch. 20, 1 Stat. 73, 85–87. Of course, it may have referred to a claim of procedural invalidity, that a treaty was not properly made by the President with the consent of two-thirds of the Senators present. Or Congress may have had in mind only limitations on the subject matters of treaties, discussed below. On the other hand, the cases dealing with this phrase in the Judiciary Act, long after it was settled that federal statutes could be declared invalid, gave no indication that the validity of a treaty was to be tested in ways different from those for testing the validity of a statute. See, *e. g.,* Erie R. R. v. Hamilton, 248 U.S. 369 (1919).

43. For example, Secretary of State Hamilton Fish declined invitations for the United States to participate in international conferences on the enforcement of foreign judgments, in part because of supposed constitutional difficulties. Nadelmann, *Ignored State Interests: the Federal Government and International Efforts to Unify Rules of Private Law,* 102 U.PA.L.REV. 323–327 (1954). The State Department, U.S. negotiators, and the Senate have all asserted that there were constitutional limitations on the treaty power, notes 63, 67, 68, this chapter.

44. Compare, *e. g.,* the statement of Manion supporting the amendment, *Bricker Hearings,* 1955, this chapter note 35, at 263, with the statement of Perlman opposing the amendment, *id.* at 237–38. But *cf.* Dulles, note 35, this chapter.

45. Reid v. Covert, 354 U.S. 1, 16–17 (1957). That opinion also states: "It would be manifestly contrary to the objectives of those who created the Constitution, as well as those who were responsible for the Bill of Rights—let alone alien to our entire constitutional history and tradition—to construe Article VI [the Supremacy Clause] as permitting the United States to exercise power under an international agreement without observing constitutional prohibitions. In effect, such construction would permit amendment of that document in a manner not sanctioned by Article V." *Id.* at 17. Justice Black was writing for himself and three other Justices, but none of those who would have decided the case differently suggested that they disagreed with the views quoted. The Justices were fully aware of the recent Bricker Amendment, note 35, this

chapter, and perhaps they seized an occasion to allay the fears that supported it.

Justice Black continued: "This Court has repeatedly taken the position that an Act of Congress, which must comply with the Constitution, is on a full parity with a treaty, and that when a statute which is subsequent in time is inconsistent with a treaty, the statute to the extent of conflict renders the treaty null. It would be completely anomalous to say that a treaty need not comply with the Constitution when such an agreement can be overriden by a statute that must conform to that instrument." *Id.* at 18 (footnotes omitted). One might argue, however, that the anomaly is not as complete as Black said. A later inconsistent statute does not nullify a treaty but only prevents its implementation as domestic law; the doctrine Black cites, then, does not suggest that the Constitution limits also the international obligations that can be assumed. In fact, even as regards the domestic effect of treaties—to which, in general, the Bill of Rights is relevant—one might argue that although a treaty can be frustrated when the national legislature deems it desirable, it should not be invalidated by the courts at the behest of a private person to vindicate a private interest, even one which is protected by the Constitution in strictly domestic contexts.

A few months later the Supreme Court considered a claim that the Bill of Rights prohibited carrying out an agreement pursuant to the Japanese Security Treaty but found no violation. Wilson v. Girard, 354 U.S. 524 (1957).

46. See Chapter III, pp. 86–87 and note 79. Some of the prohibitions in Article I, section 9, were clearly not addressed to Congress, for example, that no officer of the United States may accept foreign office or employment without consent of Congress (*Cf.* 40 OP.ATT'Y GEN. 513 (1947)); or that "No Money shall be drawn from the Treasury, but in Consequence of Appropriations made by Law." Treaties are subject to the latter, p. 159 above; see Calhoun quoted note 49, this chapter. Presumably, too, before 1808, a treaty could not have prohibited the "Migration or Importation of such Persons as any of the States now existing shall think proper to admit." Calhoun expressly concedes this (in language omitted from the quotation).

47. I draw here on my articles *The Constitution, Treaties, and International Human Rights,* 116 U.PA.L.REV. 1012 (1968), and *"International Concern" and the Treaty Power of the United States,* 63 AM.J. INT'L L. 272 (1969).

48. Various statements going back to our early history are collected in H. TUCKER, LIMITATIONS ON THE TREATY-MAKING POWERS §§ 2–51 (1915), and Mikell, *The Extent of the Treaty-Making Power of the President and Senate of the United States,* 57 U.PA.L.REV. 435, 436–38

n. 1 (1909). Views of publicists on possible limitations on the treaty power are collected in BUTLER, THE TREATY POWER Chapter IX; for those who believed there were limitations see particularly 1 *id.* at 409, 413–15.

The debates on limitations do not distinguish between authority to make treaties or to give them effect as law in the United States. As regards treaties designed to have legal consequences in the United States, the distinction is academic. See this chapter, page 139. Presumably a treaty made in violation of any constitutional limitations would still bind the United States internationally, since other states are not bound to know our constitutional restrictions in detail. See page 137, this chapter; compare Chapter VI, note 21.

49. 133 U.S. 258, 267 (1890). Compare John C. Calhoun:

There appeared to him but two restrictions on its exercise; the one derived from the nature of our Government, and the other from that of the power itself. Most certainly all grants of power under the Constitution must be controlled by that instrument; for, having their existence from it, they must of necessity assume that form which the Constitution has imposed. This is acknowledged to be true of the legislative power, and it is doubtless equally so of the power to make treaties. The limits of the former are exactly marked; it was necessary to prevent collision with similar co-existing State powers. This country is divided into many distinct sovereignties. Exact enumeration here is necessary to prevent the most dangerous consequences. The enumeration of legislative powers in the Constitution has relation then, not to the treaty-power, but to the powers of the State. In our relation to the rest of the world the case is reversed. Here the States disappear. Divided within, we present the exterior of undivided sovereignty. The wisdom of the Constitution appears conspicuous. When enumeration was needed, there we find the powers enumerated and exactly defined; when not, we do not find what would be vain and pernicious. Whatever, then, concerns our foreign relations; whatever requires the consent of another nation, belongs to the treaty power; can only be regulated by it; and it is competent to regulate all such subjects; provided, and here are its true limits, such regulations are not inconsistent with the Constitution. If so they are void. No treaty can alter the fabric of our Government, nor can it do that which the Constitution has expressly forbad to be done; nor can it do that differently which is directed to be done in a given mode, and all other modes prohibited. For instance, the Constitution of the United States says, no money "shall be drawn out of the Treasury but by an appropriation made by law." Of course no subsidy can be granted without an act of law and a treaty of alliance could not involve the country in war without the consent of this House. . . . Besides these Constitutional limits, the treaty power, like all powers, has others derived from it object and nature. It has for its object contracts with foreign nations, as the powers of Congress have for their object whatever can be done in relation to the powers delegated to it without the consent of foreign nations. Each in its proper sphere operates with general influence; but when they became erratic, then they were portentous and dangerous. A treaty never can legitimately do that which can be done by law; and the converse is also true. Suppose the discriminating duties repealed on both sides by law, yet what is effected by this treaty would not even then be done; the pledged faith would be wanting. . . .

29 ANNALS OF CONGRESS 531–32 (1816) [1815–1816]. And see note 81, this chapter.

50. *E. g.*, Holden v. Joy, 17 Wall. 211, 243 (U.S.1872) ("all those objects which in the intercourse of nations, had usually been regarded as the proper subject of negotiation and treaty"); Asakura v. Seattle, 265 U.S. 332, 341 (1924) ("all proper subjects of negotiation between our government and other nations"); Santovincenzo v. Egan, 284 U.S. 30, 40 (1931) ("all subjects that properly pertain to our foreign relations"). Some general dicta suggesting limitations on the treaty power appear also in Taney's opinion in The Passenger Cases, 7 How. 283, 465 (U.S.1849), and in Daniel's in The License Cases, 5 How. 504, 613 (U.S.1847). And see note 76, this chapter.

51. Sec. LII. The manual is widely reprinted *e. g.*, in SENATE MANUAL, S.DOC. NO. 92–1, 92d Cong., 1st Sess. 435 *et seq.* (1971). The quoted section is there at 516–18.

52. Compare note 2, this chapter.

53. Under his final clause, a treaty cannot deal with matters that are within the enumerated powers of Congress (as to which the Constitution "gave a participation to the House of Representatives"). By the third limitation, the treaty power could not deal with matters reserved to the States—presumably, those not expressly conferred upon the national government or some branch of it, principally upon Congress by the enumeration, in Article I, section 8. If a treaty cannot deal with matters delegated to Congress, nor with matters not delegated to Congress, it can deal with very little, presumably only with matters that are in the President's sole domain apart from treaty. Joseph Story said: "Mr. Jefferson seems at one time to have thought,

that the constitution only meant to authorize the president and senate to carry into effect, by way of treaty, *any power they might constitutionally exercise*. At the same time, he admits, that he was sensible of the weak points of this position. 4 Jefferson's Corresp. 498. What are such powers given to the president and senate? Could they make appointments by treaty?" 2 STORY, COMMENTARIES § 1508, at 376 n. 3 (emphasis in original).

54. Harvard Law School Research in International Law, *Draft Convention on the Law of Treaties*, 29 AM.J.INT'L L., Supp., Pt. 3, 653, 686 (1935). The Supreme Court has quoted a similar definition: "a compact made between two or more independent nations with a view to the public welfare." B. Altman & Co. v. United States, 224 U.S. 583, 600 (1912).

55. See Art. 1, sec. 10. Compare Chapter IX, p. 228.

56. See note 4, this chapter.

57. This is the common interpretation of Jefferson's dictum. Of course, if one recognizes that the Treaty Power is one of the powers delegated to the federal government, and that what comes within it is therefore not reserved to the States, one could accept Jefferson's statement to mean that there may be some areas specially reserved to the States even as regards the Treaty Power, for example, that a treaty cannot cede territory of a State without its consent. See pp. 147–48.

Some—*e. g.*, Finch, *The Need to Restrain the Treaty-Making Power of the United States Within Constitutional Limits*, 48 AM.J.INT'L L. 57, 61 (1954)—contend that the majority of the Founding Fathers held the Jeffersonian view on this issue. Hayden, *The States' Rights Doctrine and the Treaty-Making Power*, 22 AM.HIST.REV. 556 (1917), presents evidence that the executive and legislative branches of the government in the period 1830–60 believed that treaties could not deal with matters not otherwise in the federal domain. A few commentators also adopted this narrow view of the Treaty Power. 5 MOORE DIGEST, 736; Mikell, *The Extent of the Treaty-Making Power of the President and Senate of the United States*, 57 U.PA.L.REV. 435, 528, 535 (1909).

Even before the Supreme Court settled the issue, in Missouri v. Holland, pp. 144–45, these authorities represented a minority view. Compilations of commentators may be found in Wright, *The Constitutionality of Treaties*, 13 AM.J.INT'L L. 242, 256 & n. 51, 257 (1919), and WRIGHT 92 & n. 97; see also 1 BUTLER, THE TREATY POWER 4–6.

In general, those who claimed limitations implied in federalism did not claim that the States were intended to have a voice or a veto in regard to foreign relations. Compare Chapter IX, p. 227. Their view, or feeling, was that although the States had no part in the conduct of foreign relations, treaties, *in their capacity as law of the land* (p. 156, above), like other federal law, could not "legislate" on matters reserved to the States. Strictly, the argument would not deny the treaty-makers power to incur international obligations on such matters, but they could not be made domestic law unless the States consented, or themselves acted to legislate them. (Compare the argument in Ware v. Hylton, 3 Dall. 199, 244–45 (U.S.1796).). Theoretically, then, such treaties could still be made by the United States with the consent of all of the States. Effectively, of course—especially as the nation grew and States multiplied—no one seriously suggested that procedure, and States' rights were asserted as obstacles to the Treaty Power in order to bar certain treaties from being made at all.

58.  252 U.S. 416 (1920).

59.  Ch. 145, 37 Stat. 847 (1913).

60.  United States v. Shauver, 214 F. 154 (D.C.E.D.Ark.1914); United States v. McCullagh, 221 F. 288 (D.C.Kan.1915). The courts also found that the birds were the property of the State and therefore immune to federal regulation. At the time the Supreme Court was taking a narrow view of the power of Congress, including its power to regulate commerce with foreign nations and among the several States. Compare, *e. g.*, Hammer v. Dagenhart, 247 U.S. 251 (1918), Holmes, J. (and others) dissenting.

61.  With Great Britain, then responsible for Canada's foreign relations. See Treaty of Aug. 16, 1916, 39 Stat. 1702. Congress implemented it in ch. 128, 40 Stat. 755 (1918), as amended, 16 U.S.C. § 703 (1970).

62.  252 U.S. at 432. See also Neely v. Henkel, 180 U.S. 109, 121 (1901). Compare Keller v. United States, 213 U.S. 138, 147 (1909). See this chapter, note 105. Some implementations of treaties can be based also on the "Offences clause," Chapter III, p. 72.

63.  252 U.S. at 432–434. I have omitted, among other things, Holmes's reading of the Supremacy Clause, quoted p. 137 above. Holmes also rejected the argument that the treaty could not constitutionally deal with the birds because they were property of the State. 252 U.S. at 434. Compare the Treaty of 1854 with Great Britain, Article IV, which provided: ". . . The Government of the United States further engages to urge upon the State Government to secure to the subjects of Her Britannic Majesty the use of the several State canals on terms of equality with the inhabitants of the United States." 1 MALLOY, TREATIES 668, 671. Presumably the U.S. negotiators assumed the U.S. could not promise that equal treatment because these were canals belonging to the State. Compare WRIGHT 90. While the "property rights" of the State in its canals are no doubt different from its "rights" in migratory birds (*cf.* Holmes, 252 U.S. at 434), the Court would today doubtless approve a treaty dealing with state canals as well. See the cases approving federal regulation of state properties

and activities, Chapter IX, note 70. The alleged limitation on ceding state territory, p. 147, above, is different, since that involves state sovereignty not its property rights.

64. I draw here on my article, *The Treaty Makers and the Law Makers: The Law of the Land and Foreign Relations*, 107 U.Pa.L.Rev. 903, 905–13 (1959).

65. The basic principles of *Missouri* v. *Holland* were laid down in the early years of the Republic. In 1796, in *Ware* v. *Hylton*, the Supreme Court held that a treaty with Great Britain reaffirming debts to British creditors superseded a Virginia statute (enacted during the War of Independence and valid when made) that canceled debts owed by its citizens to British subjects if they paid the sums into the state treasury. 3 Dall. 199 (U.S.1796). See Chapter X, p. 260. John Marshall appeared as counsel; this was apparently Marshall's only appearance before the Supreme Court, and he lost the case. *Cf.* Georgia v. Brailsford, 3 Dall. 1 (U.S.1794).

66. *E. g.*, Hauenstein v. Lynham, 100 U.S. 483 (1880); Asakura v. Seattle, 265 U.S. 332 (1924); and see the cases collected in 2 Butler, The Treaty Power 11–13 nn. 1 & 2.

Treaties of Friendship, Commerce, and Navigation have conferred on nationals of another country even the right to practice some professions, although those professions are normally regulated by the States. See, *e. g.*, the treaties with: Honduras, Dec. 7, 1927, Art. I, 45 Stat. 2618, T.S. No. 764; Italy, Feb. 2, 1948, Art. I, 63 Stat. 2255, T.I.A.S. No. 1965 (all professions except law). More recently, however, there has been a tendency to limit such reciprocal grants of national treatment for professionals. Thus, for example, although the treaty with Israel, Aug. 23, 1951, Art. VIII(2), [1954] 5 U.S.T. 550, T.I.A.S. No. 2948, as signed, provided that nationals of either party may not be barred from practicing the professions solely on account of alienage; and the treaty with Greece, Aug. 3, 1951, Art. XII(1), [1954] 5 U.S.T. 1829, T.I.A.S. No. 3057, guaranteed national and most-favored-nation treatment to professions (with some exceptions), the Senate ratifications contained reservations strictly limiting these provisions. The Senate declared these provisions inapplicable to "professions which, because they involve the performance of functions in a public capacity, or in the interest of public health and safety, are state-licensed and reserved by statute or constitution exclusively to citizens of the country." [1954] 5 U.S.T. at 603, 1918. It was not claimed, however, that such reservations were required by the Constitution. The treaty with the Federal Republic of Germany, Oct. 29, 1954, Art. VIII(2), [1956] 7 U.S.T. 1839, T.I.A.S. No. 3593—extends the national treatment guarantee to "scientific, educational, religious and philanthropic activities," but does not mention the professions.

Resident aliens may have the right to engage in at least some of these activities apart from treaty. See Chapter X, pp. 258–59, 270.

67. See, *e. g.*, LEAGUE OF NATIONS DOC. NO. C. 219 M. 142 (1927) IX, at 13; *id*. at No. C.F.A./2 Sess./P.V. 1 (1928), at 12; *id*. at No. A. 30 (1929) IX, at 7. This position was officially abandoned by the Department of State in 1932. BUREAU OF THE DISARMAMENT CONFERENCE, MINUTES OF THE 30TH MEETING, Nov. 18, 1932, I, at 100. Of course, the notion that, apart from the treaty, manufacture for interstate or foreign commerce is reserved to the States has long been exploded. See United States v. Darby, 312 U.S. 100 (1941); Wickard v. Filburn, 317 U.S. 111 (1942). See generally Chapter III, p. 69.

Even early Attorneys-General apparently misconceived the supremacy of the Treaty Power to state laws. *Cf*. 1 OP.ATT'Y GEN. 275 (1819), 2 *id*. at 426, 431–32, 436–37 (1831).

68. A United States reservation to the Charter of the OAS provided that nothing in the Charter should be considered as enlarging the powers of the federal government or limiting the powers of the States with respect to any matter recognized under the Constitution as being within the reserved powers of the States. See [1951] 2 U.S.T. 2394, 2484, T.I.A.S. No. 2361. Whether this effectively reserved anything is open to question.

Compare the federal-state clause proposed by the United States in 1950 for the draft covenant on human rights: "With respect to articles which are determined in accordance with the constitutional processes of that State to be appropriate in whole or in part for action by the constituent states, provinces, or cantons, the federal government shall bring such articles, with favorable recommendations to the notice of the authorities of the states, provinces or cantons at the earliest possible moment." Report of the Commission on Human Rights (6th Sess.) (U.N.Doc.E/1681) at 59 (1950). The key word "appropriate" was doubtless purposely ambiguous. The United States proposal was rejected. More recent federal-state clauses have admitted that they aim at a political rather than a constitutional obstacle.

The federal-state clause had early antecedents. Especially before the Civil War the United States often made treaties dependent on state law: *e. g.*, Article VII of the Treaty of 1853 with France, 10 Stat. 992, 1 MALLOY, TREATIES, 528, 531, allowing French citizens to possess land equally with American citizens "[i]n all states of the Union whose existing laws permit it, so long and to the same extent as the said laws shall remain in force." *Id*. at 996. As to other States "the President engages to recommend to them the passage of such laws as may be necessary for conferring the right." *Ibid*. But such deference to state law was not constitutionally required, and in-

creasingly other countries refused to accord it. For an earlier discussion see, generally N. MITCHELL, STATE INTERESTS IN AMERICAN
TREATIES, Chapter IV (1936).

69. See S.J.Res. 1, 83d Cong., 1st Sess., 99 CONG.REC. 6777 (1953).
See the extended arguments on both sides in the various Bricker Hearings, this chapter, note 35, *1952 Hearings* 121, 132, 256, 313–16, 364,
413, 484, 486, 530; *1953 Hearings* 924, 959, 994, 999, 1010, 1070,
1123, 1130, 1136; *1955 Hearings* 185–86, 281–82, 297, 581–82. For
articles supporting and opposing the amendment, see W. BISHOP, IN-
TERNATIONAL LAW 112 n. 39 (3d ed. 1971). The Bricker Amendment
would not have directly denied the treaty makers the power to make
such treaties but would have prevented their implementation in the
United States; of course, responsible treaty makers would not assume obligations that could not be carried out.

70. See, *e. g.*, Henkin, *The Treaty Makers and the Law Makers: The
Law of the Land and Foreign Relations,* 107 U.PA.L.REV. 903, 913 *et
seq.* (1959). See also Chapter III, p. 77 and note 53.

71. Having lost the constitutional battle Senator Bricker may yet
have won the political war to date, for in part because of "Brickerite"
opposition and the struggle it continues to wage, it seems unlikely that
the Executive Branch will propose, or that the Senate will consent to,
United States adherence to major human rights covenants. The Eisenhower Administration announced that it would not push for Senate
action on the Genocide Convention that had languished in the Senate
since 1949, and that it would not ratify other human rights covenants.
32 DEP'T STATE BULL. 820, 822 (1955). (Compare also U. S. DEP'T OF
STATE, DEP'T CIR. NO. 175 (1955), reprinted in 50 AM.J.INT'L L. 784
(1956), since revised; see note 89, this chapter.) When the Kennedy
Administration, reversing the Eisenhower policy, sent up three small
covenants (on slavery, forced labor, political rights of women), the Senate acted only on the first, the last two remaining on the shelf of the
Foreign Relations Committee. *Cf.* 113 CONG.REC. 8332 (1967). Inex-
plicably, however, in 1968 the U.S., with unanimous Senate consent,
ratified a protocol and in effect adhered to the Convention on the Status
of Refugees [1968] 19 U.S.T. 6223; T.I.A.S. No. 6577; perhaps this
was seen as relating largely to aliens, and requiring nothing that the
U.S. was not already doing. The Nixon Administration requested consent to ratification of the Genocide Convention and the Senate Foreign
Relations Committee recommended it. S.EXEC.REP. No. 92–6, 92nd
Cong., 1st Sess. (1971).

72. See *e. g.*, Geofroy v. Riggs, quoted p. 141 above. Some may see
support for that view by analogy from Article IV, section 3, forbidding
the alienation of state territory without its consent for the purpose of
creating a new state. Compare also the provision in Article 1, section 8,

clause 17, requiring state cession of the territory to become the capital of the United States, and the consent of state legislatures to the purchase of places for the erection of various "needful buildings."

The issue has never been resolved. Hamilton and Jefferson disagreed about it; Webster took the position expressed by Justice Field but Chancellor Kent disagreed. "The better opinion would seem to be that such a power of cession does reside exclusively in the treaty-making power under the Constitution of the United States, although a sound discretion would forbid the exercise of it without the consent" of any State. (Quoted in T. WOOLSEY, INTERNATIONAL LAW 161 (6th ed. 1899); See also KENT COMMENTARIES (14th ed. 1896) 166–67, and note; 1 WILLOUGHBY 576; CRANDALL, TREATIES § 99; 5 MOORE, DIGEST 171–75. *Cf.* Downes v. Bidwell, 182 U.S. 244, 316 (1901) (opinion of White, C. J.). But compare Worcester v. Georgia, 6 Pet. 515 (U.S. 1832) (upholding grant to Indian tribes of exclusive rights in reservations within state borders); 27 OP.ATT'Y GEN. 327 (1909) (consent of Minnesota not needed to treaty granting easement for dam). *Cf.* United States v. Rice, 4 Wheat. 246 (U.S.1819) (while occupied by the British, Maine ceased to be part of the United States).

There would seem to be little doubt that in case of necessity, *e. g.*, if the United States lost a war, a peace treaty ceding state territory could not be challenged on constitutional grounds. Letter of Jefferson, 1 AMERICAN STATE PAPERS: FOREIGN RELATIONS 252 (Gales and Seaton eds. 1833).

In the only two cases in which the United States in fact ceded territory, the settlement of the Northeast boundary, and the 1842 treaty with Mexico, the consent of the relevant States was obtained. In the Webster-Ashburton Treaty, Aug. 9, 1842, (8 Stat. 572 (1846); T.S. No. 119) the consent of Massachusetts and Maine was obtained to a boundary settlement and a provision to compensate them was included in the treaty, although the settlement of a boundary dispute is not strictly a cession of territory, there being doubt whether the States in question had ever had it. *Cf.* Lattimer' v. Poteet, 14 Pet. 4 (U.S.1840). The consent of Texas was not sought when the United States and Mexico settled the Chamizal dispute, though Senator Tower would have delayed until such consent was obtained. 109 CONG.REC. 24851 (1963). The legislature of New York authorized the Governor to cede to the United States jurisdiction over the territory of the UN headquarters, presumably in the expectation that the United States might in turn cede jurisdiction to the U.N. N.Y. STATE LAW § 59–l (McKinney 1952). Neither the governor nor the United States has executed such cession. To the extent that some cession by the United States is implicit in the terms of the UN Headquarters Agreement,

June 26, 1947 (61 Stat. 3416 (1947); T.I.A.S. No. 1676; 11 U.N.T.S. 11), the consent of New York was in effect obtained.

73. See Field, J., p. 141 above. Compare Calhoun note 49, this chapter. But what is essential to a republican form of government is hardly agreed, and the Supreme Court has considered that a political question not for judicial determination or review. Luther v. Borden, 7 How. 1 (U.S.1849); also, *e. g.*, Pacific Telephone Co. v. Oregon, 223 U.S. 118 (1912); Ohio *ex rel.* Bryant v. Akron Metropolitan Park District, 281 U.S. 74, 79–80 (1930); *cf.* Baker v. Carr, 369 U.S. 186 (1962), Chapter VIII, note 25.

74. See HENKIN, ARMS CONTROL 34–36.

75. See Chapter IX, p. 246. HENKIN, ARMS CONTROL, 33–37, 60–61. Old cases suggest that the United States cannot by treaty impose duties on state officials. See Chapter IX, p. 247. But the Headquarters Agreement with the United Nations seems to impose duties on both state and local officials. See Agreement Between the United States of America and the United Nations Regarding the Headquarters of the United Nations, June 26, 1947, §§ 3, 4(c), 11, 14, 16, 17, 18, 25, 61 STAT. 3416, T.I.A.S. No. 1676. International law, in effect, imposes duties on state officials to carry out the obligations of the United States that are in their care, for example, the responsibility to accord justice to aliens. Chapter IX, p. 245.

76. Jefferson's second clause would limit treaties to subjects "which are usually regulated by treaty, and can not be otherwise regulated." Later, perhaps echoing Jefferson, Chief Justice Taney said:

> The power to make treaties is given by the Constitution in general terms, without any description of the objects intended to be embraced by it; and, consequently, it was designed to include all those subjects, which in the ordinary intercourse of nations had usually been made subjects of negotiations and treaty; and which are consistent with the nature of our institutions, and the distribution of powers between the general and state governments.

Holmes v. Jennison, 14 Pet. 540, 569 (U.S.1840). And compare Holden v. Joy, 17 Wall. 211, 243 (U.S.1872). We do not know whether Jefferson's or Taney's "subjects" refer to the particular thing dealt with in the treaty (wheat, nuclear weapons), the rights or duties it establishes (quotas and prices, non-use of weapons), or its objective (trade, friendly relations, peace). Are human rights, for example, a new subject of international negotiation or the same subject as the traditional rights of aliens not to be denied justice? Or is the alleged object of new human rights covenants—friendly relations, international peace—as old as treaties? Taney's ambiguous tense is particularly troubling for it would seem to limit treaties of the United States to matters that had been the subject of treaty before 1787. It is difficult to find any basis for limiting the Treaty Power to eighteenth century needs, and the United States has in fact negotiated about subjects and for objectives not dreamed of by the Constitutional Fathers—*e. g.*, the United Nations Charter and the Nuclear Test Ban. Nor is there any reason for reading the Constitution as limiting the Treaty Power to matters "usually" regulated by treaty today. In any event, since the United States is hardly in the forefront seeking new subjects for international regulation, such a limitation would not in fact hamper the conduct of foreign affairs. It would not bar, in particular, U. S. accession to international human rights treaties: nations have been "usually" regulating human rights by treaty at least since the "minorities treaties" of a half century ago, surely in the UN Charter, in the various regional human rights arrangements now in effect, and in the human rights covenants that were under negotiation for almost 20 years under the auspices of the United Nations. See my article, *The Constitution, Treaties, and International Human Rights,* 116 U.PA.L.REV. 1012, 1019–22 (1968).

77. See Chapter IV, p. 94.

78. See Chapter III, p. 76. Calhoun made the point more than 100 years ago: "If this be the true view of the treaty-making power, it may be truly said that its exercise has been one continual series of habitual and uninterrupted infringements of the Constitution. From the beginning and throughout the whole existence of the Federal Government it has been exercised constantly on commerce, navigation, and other delegated powers." Letter of Secretary of State Calhoun to Wheaton, our minister to Prussia, June 28, 1844, reprinted in 5 MOORE, DIGEST 164, WRIGHT 344. He also stressed that a treaty could commit the United States to pay money, though he thought Congress could withhold the appropriation. See WRIGHT 121–22. Earlier Calhoun had said: "A treaty never can legitimately do that which can be done by law; and the converse is also true" (note 49 this chapter), but by that he apparently meant that treaties cannot legislate directly, they act only through international obligation.

Early in our history some treaties were rejected by the Senate because they dealt with matters deemed to belong exclusively to Congress. The Senate refused consent to a commercial treaty with the German States in 1844 because of lack of "constitutional competency." Senate Committee on Foreign Relations, *On The Convention With Prussia,* 8 REPORTS OF SENATE COMMITTEE ON FOREIGN RELATIONS, 28th Cong., 1st Sess. 36, 38 (1844), CRANDALL, TREATIES 189–90. There were questions in Congress about the validity of treaties that required an appropriation of funds. See, *e. g.*, Speech of Albert Gallatin in the House of Representatives, March 9, 1796, 5 ANNALS

OF CONG. 464, 467 (1796); see CRANDALL, TREATIES 164–82. Treaties on these and other subjects as to which questions were raised have been since made frequently by the United States.

79. Hence the occasional conflict between treaties and statutes, p. 163 above. The converse argument, that some matters can be regulated only by treaty not by Act of Congress has also not survived. See Chapter IV, pp. 93–94.

Jefferson privately considered his purchase of Louisiana "an act beyond the Constitution" but hoped Congress would overlook "metaphysical subtleties." See T. BAILEY, A DIPLOMATIC HISTORY OF THE AMERICAN PEOPLE 111–112 (8th ed. 1968). It is not clear whether the constitutional difficulty was that Jefferson had agreed to buy it before he obtained Senate consent; that he thought the treaty-makers could not agree to spend money until Congress appropriated it; or that he doubted the power of the United States to acquire new territory. Compare HAYDEN, TREATIES 143; Deutsch, *Constitutional Controversy over the Louisiana Purchase*, 53 A.B.A.J. 50 (1967). The last two doubts, at least, seem unwarranted today. See Chapter III, note 50.

Though wars are declared by Congress, no one has questioned the right to terminate war by treaty. The Wars of 1812 with England, of 1846 with Mexico, of 1898 with Spain were declared by Congress but terminated by treaty. Indeed, it has been argued that only a treaty (not an Act of Congress) can end war, presumably because international agreement is needed to end a war. That argument has not prevailed either. See Chapter III, p. 81, Chapter IV, p. 105 and note 37.

80. At various times, however, Presidents believed it might be easier to obtain a majority of both Houses than two-thirds of the Senate; for that and other reasons there developed the executive agreement approved by Congress as an alternative method for making international agreements. See Chapter VI, p. 173.

During almost 200 years Congress, and the House of Representatives in particular, sought to offset its exclusion from treaty-making in various ways. Sometimes it was content to support the treaty-makers, often purporting to "authorize" the negotiation of a treaty that would come to the Senate. For an early example see Act of March 3, 1815, 13th Cong., 3d Sess., 3 Stat. 224, authorizing conventions to provide for reciprocal termination of alien discriminations. Compare ch. 1079, § 4, 32 Stat. 373 (1902); ch. 3621, § 4, 34 Stat. 628 (1906); WRIGHT 281–82. In 1925 the House of Representatives resolved that it "desires to express its cordial approval of the [World Court] and an earnest desire that the United States give early adherance" to it with certain reservations. The House also expressed "its readiness to participate in the enactment of such legislation as will necessarily follow such approval." H.R.Res. 426, 68 Cong., 2d Sess., 66 CONG.REC. 5404–05 (1925). Sometimes it sought to forestall a treaty by legislating: to preserve its authority over commerce it sought to enact the provisions of a treaty with Great Britain. See 5 MOORE, DIGEST 223. On occasion it purported to prescribe that international agreements should go to Congress for approval rather than as a treaty to the Senate alone for its consent. Compare the United Nations Participation Act of 1945, 22 U.S.C. § 287d (1970), in regard to agreements under Article 43 of the UN Charter. Compare generally Chapter VI, pp. 173 *et seq.*

That Congress cannot prevent the President from making a treaty, see, *e. g.*, the famous remarks of Benjamin Curtis in his defense of Andrew Johnson at his impeachment trial. CONG.GLOBE (Supp.), 40th Cong., 2d Sess. 126–27 (1868).

81. Compare Mr. Justice Field, quoted p. 141 above. In fighting for ratification at the Virginia Convention, Madison answered Patrick Henry's fears by saying of the Treaty Power: "I do not conceive that power is given to the President and Senate to dismember the empire, or to alienate any great, essential right. I do not think the whole legislative authority have this power; the exercise of the power must be consistent with the object of the delegation." 3 ELLIOT'S DEBATES 501, 514. Also: "A treaty to change the organization of the government, or to annihilate its sovereignty, to overturn its republican form, or to deprive it of its constitutional powers, would be void." STORY, COMMENTARIES § 1508. Calhoun said: "It can enter into no stipulation calculated to change the character of the government; or to do that which can only be done by the constitution-making power; or which is inconsistent with the nature and structure of the government." *Discourse on Constitutional Government of the United States,* I WORKS, 203, quoted in 5 MOORE, DIGEST 166, WRIGHT 121–22. He also said: "No treaty can alter the fabric of our Government, nor can it do that which the Constitution has expressly forbad to be done; nor can it do that differently which is directed to be done in a given mode, and all other modes prohibited," quoted note 49, this chapter. Compare Willoughby quoted note 85, this chapter, though he found that limitation not in the separation of powers but in a requirement of "international concern", assuming apparently that no foreign government could possibly be interested in the distribution of our political powers or functions.

It has been assumed that constitutional limitations on delegation of legislative power apply as well to delegation by treaty. See WRIGHT 104 n. 48.

82. See note 57, this chapter.

83.   International law and practice know no such limitations.   See OPPENHEIM, INTERNATIONAL LAW § 501 (8th ed. Lauterpacht 1955). The only subject matter "limitation" now accepted is that declaring that the UN Charter shall prevail over conflicting treaties, UN Charter, Article 103.   The Vienna Convention on the Law of Treaties provides for the concept of *ius cogens* generally: a treaty is void if, at the time of its conclusion, it conflicts with a peremptory norm of general international law (Article 53); also Article 64; see 63 AM. J.INT'L L. at 891.

84.   See *Bricker Hearings*, 1953, note 15 this chapter, at 35–36; *American Bar Association, Report of the Standing Committee on Peace and Law Through United Nations: Human Rights Conventions and Recommendations*, 1 INT'L LAWYER 600 (1967); *Hearings on Human Rights Conventions Before a Subcommittee of the Senate Committee on Foreign Relations*, 90th Cong., 1st Sess. (1967).   Compare note 71 above.

85.   One might perhaps consider Jefferson one of them.   Limitations on the subject matter of treaties are implied in Jefferson's suggestion that treaties can properly deal only with matters "usually regulated by treaty," or Taney's statement that they can deal only with subjects "which in the ordinary intercourse of nations had usually been made subjects of negotiations and treaty."   See note 76 above.   But Jefferson's requirement that a treaty "concern the other nation" seems to imply only that there must be a bona fide contract not that it must deal with a subject that is "the other nation's business."   See pp. 153–54.   See, generally, Henkin, *The Constitution, Treaties, and International Human Rights*, 116 U.PA.L.REV. 1012, 1024–30 (1968).

Perhaps Hughes had consulted Willoughby:

"Briefly stated, the answer is that these limitations are to be found in the very nature of treaties.   That is, that the treaty-making power may not be used to secure a regulation or control of a matter not properly and fairly a matter of international concern.   It cannot be employed with reference to a matter not legitimately a subject for international agreement, any more than can the States under the claim of an exercise of their police powers regulate a matter not fairly comprehended within the field of police regulation.   Thus, while it might be appropriate for the United States, by treaty with England, to provide that English citizens living in the United States should have certain rights of property, or schooling privileges, etc., within the States, State law to the contrary notwithstanding, it would not be appropriate, and, therefore, would not be constitutional, for the United States by such a treaty to provide that all aliens, whether British subjects or not, should enjoy these rights within the States in which they might live.  So likewise, it would not be a proper or constitutional exercise of the treaty-making power to provide that Congress should have a general legislative authority over a subject which has not been given it by the Constitution;  or that a power now exercised by one of the departments of the General Government should be exercised by another department.  For these are matters of domestic National law with which foreign powers have no concern.  In short, the treaty-making power is to be exercised with constitutional *bona fides*.  1 WILLOUGHBY § 314.

Some of the examples Willoughby lists as inappropriate for treaties have in fact been the subject of bona fide treaties: for example, the treatment of aliens in another country is the subject of the minority treaties of post-World War I, of the Refugee Convention, of the human rights covenants.  And governments have long sought to determine the forms of other governments, not only in peace treaties.

86.  23 PROC.AM.SOC'Y INT'L L. 194–96 (1929).

87.  He spoke to the annual meeting of the American Society of International Law (of which he was then President), apparently extemporaneously, perhaps even impromptu, in response to urging from the floor.  He was attempting to justify a position taken earlier by the American Delegation (which he had headed) to the Sixth International Conference of American States, that, in part on constitutional grounds, the United States "could not join" in a treaty to establish uniform principles of private international law.  A year earlier he had attempted to justify that position in words that smacked of the Tenth Amendment, which suggests that he had not assimilated or accepted the implications of *Missouri* v. *Holland*.  Hughes, *The Outlook for Pan Americanism—Some Observations on the Sixth International Conference of American States*, 22 PROC.AM.SOC'Y INT'L L. 1, 12 (1928).  His 1929 statement also had some such undertones but this time he suggested that there might be a different constitutional limitation: a treaty is valid only if it deals with a matter of "international concern."

Surely the case that inspired Hughes's remarks hardly affords a realistic basis for his expressed concern.  Theoretically, his principle might bar a treaty that developed a "uniform law" where neither the United States nor the other party had any substantial interest in adopting such uniform law.  But even if nations should bother to have their experts join to develop those uniform laws, they would hardly incorporate such laws in a treaty unless they had some foreign policy interest in establishing common standards and binding other nations to these standards, and were willing to bind themselves in exchange. (For a discussion of some different kinds of concerns that may lead nations to negotiate a treaty or include a particular provision, see Henkin, *Niagara* 1164–69, note 91 below.)

There is no indication that Hughes's critics were persuaded by his 1929 statement. Today, few would accept—on any theory—the conclusion he was justifying, that the United States could not adhere to a convention establishing uniform principles of private international law. The United States has adhered to the Hague Conference on Private International Law. Today, principles of conflicts of law between nations are probably subject to federal, not state, law, precisely because they affect the foreign relations of the United States. See Banco Nacional de Cuba v. Sabbatino, 376 U.S. 398, 425–26 (1964); Henkin, *The Foreign Affairs Power of the Federal Courts: Sabbatino,* 64 COLUM.L.REV. 805, 820–21 n. 51 (1964). Compare Chapter VIII, p. 219, and note 47.

88. Power Authority v. Federal Power Commission, note 28, this chapter.

89. Some have confused the "doctrine" of "international concern" and "relation to American foreign policy," with a very different concept, claiming, in effect, that a treaty cannot deal with matters that are "essentially within the domestic jurisdiction of the United States." See *American Bar Association, Report of the Standing Committee on Peace and Law Through United Nations: Human Rights Conventions and Recommendations,* 1 INT'L LAWYER 600, 601 (1967). (Compare the U. S. reservation to its acceptance of the compulsory jurisdiction of the International Court of Justice, 61 STAT. 1218 (1946), T.I.A.S. No. 1598, Chapter VII, note 24; *cf.* UN charter art. 2(7).) "Domestic jurisdiction" is unknown to American constitutional doctrine but it is well known to international law. Under international law, a matter is deemed to be within a country's domestic jurisdiction if it is not governed by customary international law or by any treaty obligation. What is within the domestic jurisdiction of a state in the absence of treaty ceases to be so when that state enters into an international agreement on the subject. See Advisory Opinion on Nationality Decrees Issued in Tunis and Morocco, [1923] P.C.I.J. ser. B, No. 4. To suggest that the Constitution forbids treaties as to matters that are "essentially within the domestic jurisdiction of the United States," is to bar any treaty on any matter not already governed by customary international law or previous agreement. That would invalidate common provisions in common treaties of commerce, friendship and navigation, treaties on disarmament, extradition, nationality, the prevention of double taxation and a host of other subjects. It would prevent the United States from participating in the

development of new law by multilateral convention—the principal form of international legislation today. It seems patently absurd. In any event, it is a limitation which no one has suggested before, and has no basis anywhere, surely not in Hughes's "international concern." It cannot be derived from the character and purpose of the Treaty Power as an instrument of foreign relations; it has no support even in the early writings about the Constitution; it is contradicted by the history of American treaty practice. In the absence of treaty, this country's armaments, its nationality laws, its immigration policies, all lie within its domestic jurisdiction; the United States has had agreements on these subjects of international concern from the beginning of its history to this day.

In part, responsibility for this confusion may be traced to old "Circular 175" promulgated by Secretary of State Dulles, apparently in an effort to console the Bricker forces after the defeat of their efforts to amend the Constitution. See note 71 above. The Circular —an instruction to the State Department—provided:

> Treaties should be designed to promote United States interests by securing action by foreign governments in a way deemed advantageous to the United States. Treaties are not to be used as a device for the purposes of affecting internal social changes or to try to circumvent the constitutional procedures established in relation to what are essentially matters of domestic concern.

The Circular, it should be noted, spoke not of "domestic jurisdiction" but of "domestic concern". The Circular may have used "domestic concern" in contradistinction to Hughes's "international concern," but that is a misleading play on words. "Domestic concern" and "international concern" are not closed, exclusive categories. To say that something is essentially a matter of domestic concern may be merely a way of expressing a determination not to negotiate about it. But what is essentially a matter of "domestic concern" becomes a matter of "international concern" if nations do, in fact, decide to bargain about it. In any event the Circular announced policy, not constitutional doctrine. Indeed, it was probably designed to impose as policy what the Bricker Amendment would have written into the Constitution, but which, it was realized, was not the law of the Constitution unamended. The quoted language in the Circular has since been eliminated. Compare Dulles, *Bricker Hearings*, 1953, 824–25.

90. Compare the Convention between the American republics regarding the status of aliens in their respective territories, Feb. 20, 1928, 46 Stat. 2753, T.S.No.815. Even when United States law already conforms to the treaty obligation, the treaty makes the domestic law of international concern and subjects it to international scrutiny;

the United States will not henceforth be free to modify its domestic law at will.

91.   The lack of "international concern" was also raised as an objection to the Senate Reservation to the Niagara treaty, pp. 134–35 above.   The claim was that the provision postponing use by the United States of its treaty waters until Congress acted was not of "international concern" because it did not concern Canada, and was therefore not properly part of the treaty.   I have suggested that Canada had an interest in how the U. S. developed its share of the Niagara waters; she also had an interest in satisfying the U. S. Senate since Senate consent was essential to make the treaty effective.   See Henkin, *Niagara* at 1164–69.   In any event, in that case the question was not whether the provision constituted a valid international obligation as between the United States and Canada, but whether it was effective as law of the land in the United States, a different issue which I consider at p. 160.

Opponents of human rights conventions have also sought support in the case that disregarded that reservation, Power Authority v. Federal Power Commission, note 28, this chapter.   That case, I believe, was wrongly decided, but in any event it lends no support to the view that the United States cannot adhere to human rights covenants.   The case suggests that only provisions that are "contractual," *i. e.*, part of the agreement with the foreign nation, can be law of the land.   Nothing in that case suggests any limitations on the kinds of provisions that can be made the subject of a contract with other nations.   In a human rights convention, the provisions are "contractual," imposing obligations upon the parties.   The majority opinion in the case adopted the views of Professor Jessup, counsel for the Power Authority in the case, and author of an earlier legal memorandum on the issues.   Professor (later Judge) Jessup has been one of the leading exponents of the view that the individual should be a subject of international law, and has expressly favored multilateral conventions to promote human rights.   P. JESSUP, A MODERN LAW OF NATIONS 87–93 (1948).

92.   There are now substantial volumes of such international agreements, *e. g.*, I. BROWNLIE, (ed.), BASIC DOCUMENTS ON HUMAN RIGHTS (1971);   see also Part IX, INTERNATIONAL ORGANIZATION AND INTEGRATION (Van Panhuys *et al.* eds. 1968)

Modern universal treaties generally sometimes deal with matters that are not the concern of other nations in some narrow sense;   even the UN Charter can be said to make many once domestic or bilateral matters into everybody's business, for example, threats to peace in some distant place or colonialism in Asia or Africa.

93.   International agreements, like private contracts, may be parallel as well as reciprocal: parties may bind themselves to do, or not to do, for each other; or a nation may undertake to do nor not to do in its own land and to its own people, in consideration of a similar (or some other) undertaking by the other party.  Such agreements are not novel phenomena or made only by other countries; the United States, too, has undertaken obligations in regard to its own citizens or inhabitants and to domestic activities.  When we acquired Louisiana, Florida, Mexico, Alaska, we promised the ceding country that we would continue to give the inhabitants, after they become ours, rights of citizenship and other personal liberties.  See, *e. g.*, CRANDALL, TREATIES 210–12.  The United States adhered to ILO Conventions establishing minimum labor standards for some of its citizens, *e. g.*, the conventions relating to masters and seamen.  (Conventions with Members of the International Labor Organization, Oct. 24, 1936, 54 Stat. 1683, 1693, 1705, T.S.No.950, 951, 952.)  It agreed to control raw and manufactured opium and other drugs within the United States.   (International Opium Convention, Jan. 23, 1912, 38 Stat. 1912, T.S.No.612, and Convention for Limiting the Manufacture and Regulating the Distribution of Narcotic Drugs, July 13, 1931, 48 Stat. 1543, T.S.No.863, implemented by the Opium Poppy Control Act, 56 Stat. 1045 (1942), 21 U.S.C. § 188 (1970)); to apply to its own vessels accepted load lines and common standards for safety at sea (International Load Line Convention, July 5, 1930, 47 Stat. 2228, T.S.No.858; International Convention and Regulation for Promoting Safety of Life at Sea, June 10, 1948 [1952] 3 U.S.T. & O.I.A. 3450, T.I.A.S.No.2495, replacing the Convention of May 31, 1929, 50 Stat. 1121, T.S.No.910); not to bring to trial an American soldier if he had been tried for the same offense by the courts of an allied NATO country (NATO Status of Forces Agreement, June 19, 1951, art. VII, para. 8, [1953] 2 U.S.T. & O.I.A. 1792, T.I.A.S.No.2846); to limit its taxes on American citizens.  (See, *e. g.*, Convention with France about Double Taxation and Fiscal Assistance, Oct. 18, 1946, Supplementary Protocol, May 17, 1948, art. 5, 64 Stat. B3, T.I.A.S.No.1982.)  And the United States has agreed to limit its own armaments; it continues to strive for far-reaching controls on arms and armies, that would impose strict limitations on activities by Americans within the United States; it sought, for years, agreement for the control of atomic energy that would have governed strictly many domestic activities by Americans in the United States.  See HENKIN, ARMS CONTROL 4–9, 104, 161–62 n. 5.

The United States has in fact adhered to several contemporary human rights treaties as well.  See note 71, this chapter.

94. For a comparison of treaties and treaty-making in Great Britain, France and the United States, see F. A. M. ALTING VON GEUSAU, EUROPEAN ORGANIZATION AND FOREIGN RELATIONS OF STATES Part I (1962).

95. Foster v. Neilson, 2 Pet. 253, 314 (U.S.1829). Compare Mr. Justice Miller in Head Money Cases, 112 U.S. 580, 598 (1884): "A treaty is primarily a compact between independent nations. It depends for the enforcement of its provisions on the interest and the honor of the governments which are parties to it. If these fail, its infraction becomes the subject of international negotiations and reclamations, so far as the injured party chooses to seek redress, which may in the end be enforced by actual war. It is obvious that with all this, the judicial courts have nothing to do and can give no redress. But a treaty may also contain provisions which confer certain rights upon the citizens or subjects of one of the nations residing in the territorial limits of the other, which partake of the nature of municipal law, and which are capable of enforcement as between private parties in the courts of the country. An illustration of this character is found in treaties which regulate the mutual rights of citizens and subjects of the contracting nations in regard to rights of property by descent or inheritance, when the individuals concerned are aliens."

96. That was the purpose of the provision in Article IV that the treaty should be "carried out by the Parties in accordance with their respective constitutional processes." North Atlantic Treaty, April 4, 1949, 63 Stat. 2241, 2246, T.I.A.S. No. 1964. Compare pp. 159–60, 192.

97. See, *e. g.*, the Niagara reservation, pp. 134–35 above. See, generally, Henkin, *Niagara* 1169 *et seq.*

Once the House sought to treat a treaty as non-self-executing but the Senate disagreed. 29 ANNALS OF CONGRESS 1022, 1057 [1815–1816].

98. Turner v. American Baptist Missionary Union, 24 F.Cas. 344 (No. 14251) (C.C.Mich.1852). But the treaty can apparently serve as legislation authorizing the subsequent appropriation. See note 102, this chapter.

99. Before the Constitution, a Philadelphia court convicted a person for assaulting the French Consul-General, on the ground that he had violated the law of nations which was part of the municipal law of Philadelphia. Respublica v. De Longchamps, 1 Dall. 111 (Pa.O. & T. 1784). It is now accepted that there is no federal criminal common law and such an offense could not be punished in the federal courts unless defined by Congress. Compare United States v. Hudson & Goodwin, 7 Cranch 32 (U.S.1812); United States v. Coolidge, 1 Wheat. 415 (U.S.1816); *cf.* The Estrella, 4 Wheat. 298 (U.S.1819). *But see* Warren, *New Light on the History of the Federal Judiciary Act of 1789,* 37 HARV.L.REV. 49, 73 (1923); also 2 MOORE, DIGEST 978.

In Cotzhausen v. Nazro, 107 U.S. 215 (1882), a provision in the Treaty of Berne that certain articles "shall not be admitted for conveyance by the post" was said to constitute law of the United States prohibiting such importation, within the meaning of a statute providing criminal penalties and forfeiture for bringing articles into the United States "contrary to law." But the case did not involve criminal prosecution of the importer; it only affirmed dismissal of a suit for conversion brought by the importer against the customs officer who had forfeited the article.

100. In his testimony before the Senate Foreign Relations Committee on the North Atlantic Treaty, Secretary of State Acheson asserted that the treaty would not put the United States automatically into war. "Under our Constitution, the Congress alone has the power to declare war." *Hearings on the North Atlantic Treaty Before the Senate Committee on Foreign Relations,* 81st Cong., 1st Sess., pt. 1 at 11 (1949). *Cf.* D. ACHESON, PRESENT AT THE CREATION (1969) 282–83. See Calhoun, note 49 above. And see Chapter VII, p. 192.

S. 2956, 92d Cong., 2nd Sess., Chapter IV, p. 102 above, includes: ". . . authority to introduce the Armed Forces of the United States in hostilities or in any such situation shall not be inferred . . . from any treaty hereinafter ratified unless such treaty is implemented by legislation specifically authorizing the introduction of the Armed Forces . . . and specifically exempting the introduction of such Armed Forces from compliance with the provisions of this Act. . . . No treaty in force at the time of the enactment of this Act shall be construed as specific statutory authorization for, or a specific exemption permitting, the introduction of the Armed Forces of the United States in hostilities or in any such situation. . . ." Insofar as this bill, if it becomes law, applies to hostilities and situations "short of war" the President might feel free to disregard it. Compare Chapter IV, p. 103.

101. Parties to a treaty are presumably masters as to what they wish to agree to and what they consider an obligation: undertakings that might seem illusory in a private contract might yet serve the purposes of states and constitute a treaty "undertaking." See Henkin, *Niagara* 1164–69. Compare the provisions in older extradition treaties of the United States that "the executive authority of each shall have the power to deliver [their own nationals] up, if in its discretion, it be deemed proper to do so." The Supreme Court has implied that though that language contained no binding obligation, such a provision gave the President power to extradite American citizens which he would not otherwise have. See Valentine v. United States *ex rel.* Neidecker, 299 U.S. 5, 12–16 (1936); Henkin, *Niagara* 1168–69. (In *Neidecker,* however, the Court denied the President's power because

the treaty in that case did not contain that provision but provided only that "Neither of the contracting parties shall be bound to deliver up its own citizens.")

102.   Such provisions have rarely come to court but it is commonly accepted that they will be given effect.   The provision in the Webster-Ashburton Treaty that money shall be paid to Massachusetts and Maine (for their consent to a boundary settlement), note 72 this chapter, was apparently treated as an authorization to appropriate and money was later appropriated.   5 Stat. 623 (1850).   See Henkin, *Niagara* 1166–67.   Compare Calhoun, note 49, this chapter.   Other non-contractual provisions—*e. g.*, that particular arbitration agreements pursuant to a general arbitration convention shall require the consent of the Senate (note 22, this chapter), or that officials appointed pursuant to a treaty shall require Senate confirmation (note 24, this chapter) have also been honored by the Executive, but it is not clear whether because they were treated as law of the land or as conditions to Senate consent which had to be complied with.   See pp. 135–36 above. But *cf.* Power Authority v. Federal Power Comm., note 28, this chapter.

103.   Downes v. Bidwell, 182 U.S. 244 (1901); Dorr v. United States, 195 U.S. 138, 143 (1904); see Henkin, *Niagara* 1174–75.   See Chapter X, p. 268.   Compare the Senate reservations providing that nothing in the treaties shall be deemed to increase the powers of the President or Congress, p. 134 above.

104.   See Henkin, *Niagara*, especially 1169–75, 1182.

105.   See p. 144 above.   The "necessary and proper" clause originally contained expressly the power "to enforce treaties" but it was stricken as superfluous.   See 2 FARRAND 382; 1 BUTLER, THE TREATY POWER 318.   Earlier Story had said that the power of Congress to implement treaties "has been supposed to result from the duty of the national government to fulfil all the obligations of treaties."   Prigg v. Pennsylvania, 16 Pet. 539, 619 (U.S.1842).

Only a constitutionally valid treaty would support implementing legislation by Congress: In *Missouri* v. *Holland,* for example, whether the act of Congress implementing the Migratory Bird Treaty was valid law in the United States turned on whether the treaty itself was within the Treaty Power.   See p. 144 above.   Presumably a treaty must be valid and binding under international law to support legislation as necessary and proper to implement it.   Compare p. 160 above.

Although the question has never been raised, in principle legislation to implement a treaty might cease to be valid if the treaty lost its effect, unless it found support in other powers of Congress.   *Cf.* United States v. Chambers, 291 U.S. 217, 222–26 (1934), and United States v. Constantine, 296 U.S. 287 (1935), holding the National Prohibition

Act and related taxes inoperative when the 18th Amendment which supported them was repealed. Today other powers of Congress are ample for any such situation (p. 76 above), but even where the legislation is not in terms dependent on an effective treaty an argument might be made that the statute should fall because Congress intended to legislate only on the basis of a treaty obligation.

106.   The issue arose even before the Jay Treaty when Washington contemplated ransoming Americans captured by the Barbary Pirates and making a treaty with Algiers. Since money would have to be appropriated for the ransom, Jefferson advised getting advance sanction of the House as well as the Senate, but the Senate objected that it would give the House "a handle always to claim it," and "would let them into a participation of the power to make treaties." Jefferson agreed that if a treaty were made it would be the duty of the House to furnish the money, but that it might decline to do its duty. His fears proved unfounded. 1 WRITINGS OF THOMAS JEFFERSON 183–84, 190–92 (Ford ed. 1892). In accordance with his advice to Washington, Jefferson later considered putting the treaties consummating the Louisiana Purchase before both houses of Congress, but he was dissuaded by members of his cabinet lest he offend the Senate. See HAYDEN, TREATIES, 141–45; 1 RICHARDSON 357.

107.   Works of Alexander Hamilton 566 (J.C. Hamilton ed. 1851), quoted in CRANDALL, TREATIES 170–71. See also 6 OP.ATT'Y GEN. 291 (1854); WRIGHT 353–56.

The arguments against Congressional discretion might seem even stronger where it is required to do something which it can do only because it is necessary and proper to implement a treaty (*Missouri* v. *Holland*), than when the implementing legislation is within some enumerated power of Congress. Whatever merits such a distinction might have had, it has virtually disappeared now that Congress can legislate independently on all matters which might also appear in treaties. Compare C. III, p. 76 above.

108.   4 ANNALS OF CONGRESS 519 (1796); also CORWIN, THE PRESIDENT 423–24. Compare also Calhoun, note 78, this chapter.

109.   5 ANNALS OF CONGRESS 771 (1796) [1795–1796]. (The resolution was reaffirmed in 1871, CONG.GLOBE, 42d Cong., 1st Sess. 835 (1871).) On the day it adopted that resolution the House passed another maintaining its "constitutional right to deliberate and determine the propriety or impropriety of passing such laws, and to act thereon as the public good shall require." 5 ANNALS OF CONGRESS 769 (1796) [1795–1796]. For contemporary views not unlike Madison's, see note 51, Chapter IV.

Language to similar effect was adopted by the House when it appropriated funds to implement the treaty acquiring Alaska. CONG.GLOBE,

40th Cong., 2d Sess. 4055 (1868). But a phrase expressing "the assent of Congress" to the treaty was stricken out in conference. Language denying the power of the treaty makers to acquire territory before Congress appropriated the funds therefor failed by 2 votes. See CRAN-DALL, TREATIES 175–77.

110. In 1925 a Report of the House Foreign Affairs Committee lined up the champions on each side of the issue and concluded: "There have been numerous collisions over this matter between the Senate and the House and the question cannot be regarded as definitely settled." H.R.REP.NO.1569, 68th Cong., 2d Sess. 8 (1925). The Report noted that the House had always appropriated funds to implement treaties: "While it would be in the power of the House to refuse, that comity which exists between the respective departments of Government and the delicate nature of our foreign relations have led to the prompt enactment of legislation carrying appropriations." *Id.* at 9. In regard to treaties affecting revenue legislation and tariffs, the House has often insisted on the need of its concurrence and the Senate has acquiesced; such treaties have often provided for the concurrence of the Congress to make them effective. *Ibid.* (Compare pp. 149–50, this chapter.) The Report also lists occasions on which the House took initiative in foreign affairs matters, usually by resolution, including several expressions of views and requests for Presidential action. *Id.* at 11–16.

111. Whitney v. Robertson, 124 U.S. 190, 194 (1888). This view of the relation between the legislative power and the treaty power has been explained as an application of the maxim *leges posteriores priores contraries abrogant* ("the last expression of the sovereign will must control"). The Chinese Exclusion Case, 130 U.S. 581, 600 (1889). Implicit is the view that, in the area of jurisdiction common to both, the treaty power and the legislative power are distinct but equal. Either may enter the field but may be superseded by the other.

Prior treaty provisions have been held to have been superseded in numerous cases: in addition to The Chinese Exclusion Case, and Whitney v. Robertson, see, *e. g.,* Head Money Cases, 112 U.S. 580 (1884); The Cherokee Tobacco, 11 Wall. 616 (U.S.1871); and see Moser v. United States, 341 U.S. 41 (1951). Also Foster & Elam v. Neilson, 2 Pet. 253 (U.S.1829). But *cf.* Reichert v. Felps, 6 Wall. 160, 165–66 (U.S.1868). That giving effect to later legislation results in a violation of international law by the United States is constitutionally irrelevant. See p. 188 above.

In the Head Money Cases, 112 U.S. at 599, Justice Miller said:

. . . The Constitution gives [a treaty] no superiority over an act of Congress in this respect, which may be repealed or modified by an act of a later date. Nor is there anything in its essential character, or in the branches of the government by which the treaty is made, which gives it this superior sanctity.

A treaty is made by the President and the Senate. Statutes are made by the President, the Senate and the House of Representatives. The addition of the latter body to the other two in making a law certainly does not render it less entitled to respect in the matter of its repeal or modification than a treaty made by the other two. If there be any difference in this regard, it would seem to be in favor of an act in which all three of the bodies participate. And such is, in fact, the case in a declaration of war, which must be made by Congress, and which, when made, usually suspends or destroys existing treaties between the nations thus at war.

In short, we are of opinion that, so far as a treaty made by the United States with any foreign nation can become the subject of judicial cognizance in the courts of this country, it is subject to such acts as Congress may pass for its enforcement, modification, or repeal.

In *Baker* v. *Carr*, the Court said that "a court will not undertake to construe a treaty in a manner inconsistent with a subsequent federal statute." 369 U.S. 186, 212 (1962). But "the meaning of treaty provisions so construed is not restricted by any necessity of avoiding possible conflict with state legislation . . . ." Nielsen v. Johnson, 279 U.S. 47, 52 (1929).

As to some subjects at least the Court has seemed to treat lawmaking by treaty as at best concurrent and inferior to Congressional legislation. Rights granted to aliens by treaty, for example, were not permanent but only at the sufferance of the legislature. Fong Yue Ting v. United States, 149 U.S. 698, 720 (1893). In *The Chinese Exclusion Case,* too, the Supreme Court spoke of the power to exclude aliens as a sovereign power that cannot be abandoned or surrendered. 130 U.S. at 609. But all treaty undertakings "surrender" the right to do what the United States could otherwise do as a "sovereign right." See p. 150 above. No one asserts that the Constitution deprives the Federal Government of the power to breach a treaty; the question is whether it is Congress that has the power, and can act under its enumerated powers just as though no treaty had been made.

112. See, *e. g.*, E. CORWIN (ed)., THE CONSTITUTION OF THE UNITED STATES OF AMERICA, S. DOC. NO. 170, 82d Cong., 2d Sess. 422–23 (1953); 1 WILLOUGHBY § 306 at 555. Compare Mr. Justice Miller, note 111 this chapter.

113. Cook v. United States, 288 U.S. 102 (1933). Compare United States v. The Schooner Peggy, 1 Cranch 103 (U.S.1801), where the

Court gave effect to a treaty requiring the restoration of captured property not definitively condemned, although it had been seized as prize under a commission issued pursuant to an act of Congress authorizing such seizures. The relation between the act of Congress and the treaty was not discussed. Compare also La Ninfa, 75 F. 513 (5th Cir.1896); see also 23 OP.ATT'Y GEN. 545 (1901); 21 OP.ATT'Y GEN. 68 (1894), and 21 OP.ATT'Y GEN. 347 (1896), ruling that a treaty with China superseded a statute requiring Chinese laborers returning to the U.S. to present certain certificates. *Cf.* 6 OP.ATT'Y GEN. 291 (1854).

114.   That, generally, is the result prescribed by Article 55 of the French Constitution of 1958, and Articles 65–66 of the Constitution of the Netherlands.   See Sasse, *The Common Market: Between International and Municipal Law,* 75 YALE L.J. 695, 705–14 (1966).   As regards statutes inconsistent with customary international law, compare Chapter VIII, pp. 221–22.

115.   Compare THE FEDERALIST No. 64 (at 424) in which Jay said that:

> .   .   .   .   a treaty is only another name for a bargain, and that it would be impossible to find a nation who would make any bargain with us, which should be binding on them *absolutely,* but on us only so long and so far as we may think proper to be bound by it.   They who make laws may without doubt, amend or repeal them; and it will not be disputed that they who make treaties may alter or cancel them; but still let us not forget that treaties are made, not by only one of the contracting parties, but by both; and consequently, that as the consent of both was essential to their formation at first, so must it ever afterwards be to alter or cancel them.   The proposed Constitution, therefore, has not in the least extended the obligation of treaties.   They are just as binding, and just as far beyond the lawful reach of legislative acts now, as they will be at any future period, or under any form of government.

Hamilton's statement declaring the obligation of Congress to implement treaties, p. 161 above, has been interpreted as asserting the supremacy of treaties over statutes.   See E. CORWIN, THE CONSTITUTION AND WORLD ORGANIZATION 27–28 (1944); compare, generally, W. MCCLURE, WORLD LEGAL ORDER 81–132 (1960).

That Congress can join with the President to make international agreements fully equivalent to a treaty (Chapter VI, p. 173) does not suggest that Congress ought to be able unilaterally to undo what the treaty-makers have done.   Even if one accepted a concurrent power in Congress to abrogate treaties in their international effect, p. 169 above, the power to repeal their domestic character as law would not necessarily follow: Congress might have power to affect our international obligations but not necessarily to chip away at them piecemeal by indirection.

116. An explicit undertaking in a treaty that Congress would not legislate contrary to its provisions would, of course, change nothing, since Congress could disregard that provision as well. It might, however, have some psychological effect as a further deterrent to Congress and as an earnest of U.S. sincerity. Such provisions are generally hypothetical. See HENKIN, ARMS CONTROL 31–32. But, in GATT, for example, the United States has in effect agreed not to adopt certain legislation and the agreement indicates the international consequences if Congress should do so nonetheless. See General Agreement on Tariffs and Trade, Oct. 1947, 61 Stat. A3, T.I.A.S. No. 1700. (GATT is not a treaty but an executive agreement which may have congressional authorization in general legislation authorizing trade agreements. See § 350 of the Tariff Act of 1930, as amended, 19 U.S.C. § 1351 (1970); but compare the reference to GATT in the Trade Agreement Extension Act of 1955, 69 Stat. 162, 163, quoted Chapter IV, pp. 120–21.)

117. Even the Supreme Court has written—I think loosely—of Congress "repealing" a treaty: Head Money Cases, 112 U.S. 580, 599 (1884), note 111, this chapter ("subject to such acts as Congress may pass for its enforcement, modification, or repeal"). See also La Abra Silver Mining Co. v. United States, 175 U.S. 423, 460 (1899) ("Congress by legislation, and so far as the people and authorities of the United States are concerned, could abrogate a treaty"). The Court was more careful (and more accurate) in Pigeon River Co. v. Cox Co., 291 U.S. 138, 160 (1934).

There is a different kind of error in saying even that Congress has power to repeal any treaty provision in its capacity as law of the land. In a famous opinion approved by the Supreme Court, Mr. Justice Curtis, sitting in the circuit court, said that Congress can repeal a treaty provision so far as it is domestic law *provided the subject matter were within the legislative power of Congress.* Taylor v. Morton, 23 F.Cas. 784, 786 (No. 13,799) (C.C.Mass.1855), *aff'd,* 2 Black 481 (U.S.1862). In *The Chinese Exclusion Case,* Justice Field, too, recognized the power of Congress to repeal a treaty provision only when it "relates to a subject within the powers of Congress." 130 U.S. at 600.

If, as *Missouri v. Holland* and the Bricker Amendment both assumed, treaties can deal with matters which are not within the domain of Congress apart from the treaty, where would Congress get the power to repeal such a treaty? Under *Missouri v. Holland* Congress has the power to *implement* such treaties by legislation "necessary and proper for carrying [it] into execution," but surely repealing a treaty is not necessary and proper for carrying it into execution. Congress would have the power to repeal any treaty only if one assumes that under the sum of its various powers it can legislate on any matter which might be the subject of a treaty. See Chapter III, p. 76. Or, perhaps the power to enact a law implies an inherent power to repeal it.

118. Compare Valentine v. United States *ex rel.* Neidecker, 299 U.S. 5 (1936), Chapter IV, p. 98, which held that the President could not extradite an American national on his own authority, but suggested that he could do so if authorized by treaty or act of Congress. *Cf. In re* Metzger, 5 How. 176, 188–89 (U.S.1847). Compare also the authority asserted by the President to "govern" in the Panama Canal Zone, pursuant to "sovereignty" acquired by treaty, in the absence of an act of Congress. 26 OP.ATT'Y GEN. 113 (1907). See Chapter II, note 56.

119. Theodore Roosevelt stated that he had planned to use troops to protect treaty rights of Japanese in San Francisco. T. BAILEY, THEODORE ROOSEVELT AND THE JAPANESE-AMERICAN CRISES 28–29, 45, 80–84, 100–101 (1934). But *cf.* CORWIN, THE PRESIDENT 408 n. 106. Compare 10 U.S.C. §§ 332–34 (1970); 41 OP.ATT'Y GEN. 313 (1957); *In re* Debs, 158 U.S. 564 (1895); Alabama v. United States, 373 U.S. 545 (1963).

120. The need for a federal judiciary for the purpose, *inter alia,* of enforcing treaties is a theme of THE FEDERALIST No. 22 at 197–198 (Hamilton). Courts have given effect to intervening treaties even in a pending case. The Schooner Peggy, 1 Cranch 103 (U.S.1801).

The federal district courts have jurisdiction "of all civil actions wherein the matter in controversy exceeds the sum or value of $10,-000, exclusive of interest and costs, and arises under the Constitution, laws, or treaties of the United States." 28 U.S.C. § 1331(a) (1970). A suit to enjoin a state official from enforcing an act violating a treaty might be said to arise under the Constitution as well as under "treaties," since the state action would violate the Supremacy Clause. It is not barred as a suit against the State (under the Eleventh Amendment), but is considered a suit against the officer only. *Ex parte* Young, 209 U.S. 123 (1908). As regards some treaty obligations, implemented by Congress, a suit to enjoin state violation might qualify as one to "redress the deprivation, under color of any State law . . . of any right, privilege or immunity secured by the Constitution of the United States or by any Act of Congress providing for equal rights of citizens or of all persons within the jurisdiction of the United States." 28 U.S.C. § 1343(3). The Supreme Court has rejected the suggestion that it applies only to "personal" rights, not to "property" rights. Lynch v. Household Finance Corp., 405 U.S. 538

(1972). That basis of jurisdiction does not require the $10,000 minimum jurisdictional amount. Compare 42 U.S.C. § 1983.

In addition to many state provisions for declaratory judgments, the Federal Declaratory Judgment Act provides for relief "[i]n a case of actual controversy within its [the district court's] jurisdiction," 28 U.S.C. § 2201 (1970).

121. 3 Dall. 199 (U.S.1796), note 65, this chapter, Chapter X, p. 260.

122. *E. g.*, Hauenstein v. Lynham, 100 U.S. 483 (1880); Nielsen v. Johnson, 279 U.S. 47 (1929); *cf.* Kolovrat v. Oregon, 366 U.S. 187 (1961); Chirac v. Chirac, 2 Wheat. 259 (U.S.1817).

123. Asakura v. Seattle, 265 U.S. 332, 341 (1924).

124. See 34 DEP'T STATE BULL. 728 (1956). The Department of State was apparently of the opinion that the Government could not seek a judicial remedy against the States. But see p. 167, this chapter.

125. Congress could authorize the Attorney General (or the Secretary of State) to seek injunctive or other relief against treaty violations by state officials or others. See H. HART AND H. WECHSLER, THE FEDERAL COURTS AND THE FEDERAL SYSTEM, Chapter 9 (1953). Presidents have repeatedly asked Congress to make it a federal crime to violate treaty rights of aliens. See W. H. TAFT, THE UNITED STATES AND PEACE 74 (1914); see generally, 6 MOORE, DIGEST, 810, 837–41; compare Baldwin v. Franks, 120 U.S. 678 (1887). But Congress has afforded only a "civil action by an alien for a tort only, committed in violation of the law of nations or a treaty of the United States." See 28 U.S.C. § 1350 (1970). This would presumably permit an alien to seek an injunction as well as to recover money damages.

126. In a suit by the United States against a state agency to enforce treaty limitations on the amount of water to be diverted from Lake Michigan, the Court said that the United States Government "has a standing in this suit not only to remove obstruction to interstate and foreign commerce, the main ground . . . but also to carry out treaty obligations to a foreign power." Sanitary Dist. v. United States, 266 U.S. 405, 425 (1925). See also United States v. Minnesota, 270 U.S. 181 (1926), involving a suit to obtain return to Indian tribes of title to certain lands alleged to have been mistakenly granted to Minnesota. The tribes claimed title to the land pursuant to a treaty with the United States. The Court said that the United States had "the right to invoke the aid of a court of equity in removing unlawful obstacles to the fulfillment of its obligations." *Id.* at 194–95.

The Court has upheld suits by the United States, or in its behalf, to enjoin state violations of various laws of the United States, *e. g.*, voting laws. Katzenbach v. Morgan, 384 U.S. 641 (1966). Compare *In re* Debs, 158 U.S. 564 (1895); New York Times Co. v. United

States, 403 U.S. 713 (1971); United States v. California, 332 U.S. 19 (1947); also United Steelworkers v. United States, 361 U.S. 39, 43–44 (1960); United States v. Raines, 362 U.S. 17, 27 (1960). *Cf.* South Carolina v. Katzenbach, 383 U.S. 301 (1966) (original proceeding by a State in the Supreme Court to enjoin the Attorney General from enforcing the Voting Act of 1965). See generally, 32 N.Y.U.L.REV. 870 (1957); 42 CORNELL L.Q. 418 (1957).

Private interests in a foreign country aggrieved by an alleged treaty violation might also have standing to seek relief in our courts; the foreign government itself might also have standing to sue to protect an economic interest, but there is some question whether it could sue to vindicate political interests only. Compare Massachusetts v. Mellon, 262 U.S. 447 (1923); Stanton v. Georgia, 6 Wall. 50, 64 (U.S. 1868). Foreign governments might also be reluctant to appear as suitors in our courts for this purpose.

127. In passing the Panama Canal Act of 1912 Congress apparently interpreted the Hay-Pauncefote Treaty as exempting American vessels engaged in coastwise trade from paying canal tolls, as did President Taft. Wilson later interpreted the Treaty differently and induced Congress to repeal the statutory exemption. See 37 Stat. 560 (1912), 51 CONG.REC. 4313 (1914), 38 Stat. 385 (1914).

128. *E. g.*, Factor v. Laubenheimer, 290 U.S. 276 (1933). In early cases the Court seemed to consider itself bound by Executive interpretation of a treaty. Foster & Elam v. Neilson, 2 Pet. 253, 307 (U.S.1829). A Congressional "misinterpretation" would of course be binding as U.S. law because Congress can legislate regardless of what the treaty-makers intended, p. 163 above. Compare United States v. Lynde, 11 Wall. 632 (U.S.1870). But in a case involving rights under an Indian Treaty, the Court said that interpretation of treaties is "the peculiar province of the judiciary," and not of Congress or the Secretary of the Interior. Jones v. Meehan, 175 U.S. 1 (1899).

The Court has interpreted a treaty differently than did the Executive Branch in a case in which the U.S. was party, Perkins v. Elg, 307 U.S. 325 (1939), but there was no issue with a foreign government in the case. Compare Pearcy v. Stranahan, 205 U.S. 257 (1907).

It seems unlikely that a court would feel free to interpret a treaty differently if the Executive has taken a formal position on its meaning. Compare the deference to the Executive in the immunity cases, Chapter II, pp. 56 *et seq.*

Of course, later interpretations whether by the President or the courts do not have the consent of the Senate. Judicial "misinterpretation" of a treaty, of course, does not compel the Executive to adopt that interpretation internationally and it can be rectified presumably by a new treaty or a less formal agreement.

129.   Art. IV, 14 U.S.T. 1313, T.I.A.S. No. 5433, 480 U.N.T.S. 43.

130.   See, *e. g.*, the Vienna Convention on the Law of Treaties, Art. 62, reprinted in 63 AM.J.INT'L L. 875, 894–95 (1969).

131.   See 5 HACKWORTH, DIGEST OF INTERNATIONAL LAW (1943) 330; WRIGHT 258–260.   Compare Riesenfeld, *The Power of Congress and the President in International Relations*, 25 CALIF.L.REV. 643, 658–65 (1937); Nelson, *The Termination of Treaties and Executive Agreements by the United States*, 42 MINN.L.REV. 879 (1958).   *Cf.* Van der Weyde v. Ocean Transport Co., Ltd., 297 U.S. 114, 117 (1936), discussed by Riesenfeld, *supra*, at 663–65.

132.   See 9 STATE DEPT. PRESS RELEASES 257–58 (1933); letter from the Secretary of State to Japanese Ambassador [1931–41] 2 FOREIGN REL. U. S.: JAPAN 189 (1943), DEPT.STATE BULL. 81 (1939).   At the time Congress was considering resolutions to the same effect.   Compare Franklin Roosevelt's suspension of the International Load Line Convention, in 1941, "for the duration of the present emergency."   6 FED.REG. 3999 (1941), relying on 40 OP.ATT'Y GEN. 119 (1941).

President Lincoln was apparently the first President to terminate a treaty without prior Congressional endorsement, although he subsequently received its approval.   See 5 MOORE, DIGEST 323.   Hamilton (Pacificus), Chapter II, note 9, noted that, by his power to recognize or not recognize governments, the President can continue or suspend treaty relations with that country.

On the President's power to decide not to terminate even when warranted, see pp. 170–71, 224 above, and note 138 below.

133.   In Techt v. Hughes, 229 N.Y. 222, 243, 128 N.E. 185, 192 (1920), *cert. denied*, 254 U.S. 643 (1920), Judge Cardozo said in a dictum: "President and senate may denounce the treaty, and thus terminate its life."   John Jay said that "they who make treaties may alter or cancel them."   THE FEDERALIST NO. 64 at 424.   Compare, "the obligations of the treaty could not be changed or varied, but by the same formalities with which they were introduced; or, at least, by some act of as high an import, and of as unequivocal an authority."   The Amiable Isabella, 6 Wheat. 1, 75 (U.S.1821) (Story, J.).   And see Riesenfeld, note 131, this chapter.   Compare *Presidential Amendment and Termination of Treaties: The Case of the Warsaw Convention*, 34 U.CHI.L.REV. 580 (1967), for the view that the President cannot terminate a treaty alone where private rights are affected.   Compare also Riggs, *Termination of Treaties by the Executive Without Congressional Approval*, 32 J. AIR LAW AND COMMERCE 526, 533–34 (1966) (courts should require "some Congressional approval" for Executive termination of treaty that is law of the land).

134.   For U.S. practice as regards the effect of war on treaties, see 2 C.C.HYDE, INTERNATIONAL LAW 547 *et seq.* (2d ed. 1945).   Compare,

for example, Cardozo, J., in Techt v. Hughes, 229 N.Y. 222, 128 N.E. 185 (1920), *cert. denied,* 254 U.S. 643 (1920); also Society for the Propagation of the Gospel in Foreign Parts v. New Haven, 8 Wheat. 464 (U.S.1823); Clark v. Allen, 331 U.S. 503 (1947); Karnuth v. United States *ex rel.* Albro, 279 U.S. 231 (1929). See Rank, *Modern War and the Validity of Treaties,* 38 CORNELL L.Q. 321, 511 (1953); S. MCINTYRE, LEGAL EFFECT OF WORLD WAR II ON TREATIES OF THE UNITED STATES (1958); Arts. 62, 73, Vienna Convention on the Law of Treaties, 63 AM.J.INT'L L. 875, 894–95, 896 (1969). Some multilateral treaties specifically provide for their continued effect in time of war, *e. g.,* Art. 89 of the Convention on International Civil Aviation, December 7, 1944, 61 Stat. 1180, T.I.A.S. No. 1591, 15 U.N.T.S. 295, 356. See, generally, H. TOBIN, TERMINATION OF MULTIPARTITE TREATIES 85–87, 122 (1933). The effect of the UN Charter outlawing war is uncertain. *Cf.* Articles 73 and 75 of the Vienna Convention on the Law of Treaties, 63 AM.J.INT'L L. 875, 898 (1969).

On the other hand, of course, war brings into play the laws of war and treaties applicable between belligerents, for example, the Geneva Conventions on treatment of prisoners, on civilian populations, on forbidden weapons. Compare also the Nuremberg principles, Chapter VII, note 25.

135. See Chapter III, p. 83, and note 136, this chapter. Jefferson said that since treaties are supreme law of the land equally with laws, "an act of the legislature alone can declare them infringed and rescinded." Manual of Parliamentary Practice, Sec. LII, note 51, this chapter; compare Iredell, J., note 138, this chapter. Individual members of Congress have recurrently asserted Congressional authority, *e. g.,* Senator Austin's statement that only Congress not the President can denounce treaties, 86 CONG.REC. 3574 (1940). Compare: "It is the right and province of the legislative power of this country to repeal treaties where they are found to contravene the best interests or the general welfare of the people." Senator Morgan, 13 CONG.REC. 3268 (1882). That statement, like many others, is ambiguous, it not being clear whether it asserts a right to abrogate a treaty on behalf of the United States, or merely to adopt domestic legislation inconsistent with the treaty, p. 163 above.

136. Congress abrogated treaties with France, 1 Stat. 578 (1798), 2 Stat. 7 (1800). In context, those acts, with others, were seen as constituting a declaration of war. Bas v. Tingy, 4 Dall. 37 (U.S.1800). See 5 MOORE, DIGEST 356–58. Later, French claims against the United States on account of such unilateral abrogations were in effect set-off against the claims of the United States and of American citizens arising out of French spoliations. The story is told in Gray v. United States, 21 Ct.Cl. 340, 367 *et seq.* (1886). See Chapter X, p. 264.

*Notes, Chapter V*

Later in the Nineteenth Century Congress also denounced treaties with Great Britain and with Belgium, apparently at Presidential request or with his concurrence. Lincoln ignored Congressional directions to terminate the Rush-Bagot Agreement disarming the Great Lakes; Wilson ignored a directive in the Jones Act to terminate certain conventions on customs and tonnage duties. Earlier he had complied with a similar directive contained in the LaFollette Seaman's Act of 1915. See Reeves, *The Jones Act and the Denunciation of Treaties*, 15 AM.J.INT'L L. 331 (1921); CORWIN, THE PRESIDENT 190–91. See, generally, WRIGHT 258–59; CRANDALL, TREATIES 458–65. For a case involving Presidential compliance with a direction to terminate a treaty, compare Van Der Weyde v. Ocean Transport Co. Ltd., 297 U.S. 114 (1936), note 131, this chapter. Compare the President's renunciation of treaty rights of extraterritoriality in Morocco, pursuant to a Congressional resolution probably inspired by the Executive Branch. 70 Stat. 773 (1956), 35 DEP'T STATE BULL. 844 (1956).

137. Compare: "Or the Chief Executive or the Congress may have formulated a national policy quite inconsistent with the enforcement of a treaty in whole or in part." Clark v. Allen, 331 U.S. 503, 508–09 (1947).

138. Charlton v. Kelly, 229 U.S. 447 (1913). Put another way, breach by a foreign government may render a treaty voidable at the option of the United States to be exercised by the President; if he chooses not to void it, the courts will give it effect. Compare Marshall's opinions in The Nereide, 9 Cranch 388, 422–23 (U.S.1815); see Terlinden v. Ames, 184 U.S. 270, 288 (1902); The Schooner Exchange v. M'Faddon, 7 Cranch 116, 146 (U.S.1812); Foster & Elam v. Neilson, 2 Pet. 253, 307 (U.S.1829); Clark v. Allen, 331 U.S. 503, 514 (1947); Taylor v. Morton, 23 F.Cas. 784, 787 (No. 13,799) (C.C.Mass. 1855), *affirmed*, 2 Black 481 (U.S.1862).

Iredell, J., in an opinion delivered in the court below in *Ware* v. *Hylton*, set forth in 3 Dall. at 256, thought Congress alone had the power to declare a treaty "vacated" by breach of the other party.

Compare the discussion of U.S. responses to other violations of international law, p. 224 above.

139. In upholding a statute inconsistent with a treaty, the Court said: "This court is not a censor of the morals of the other departments of the government." The Chinese Exclusion Case, 130 U.S. 581, 602–603 (1889).

NOTES, CHAPTER VI, OTHER INTERNATIONAL AGREE-
MENTS, pp. 173 to 188.


1.  The number of executive agreements to which the United States
has been party depends on how an executive agreement is defined.  One
writer counted "well over 1,250" as of February, 1941.  MCCLURE, IN-
TERNATIONAL EXECUTIVE AGREEMENTS: DEMOCRATIC PROCEDURE UN-
DER THE CONSTITUTION OF THE UNITED STATES xii–xiii (1941)
[hereinafter cited as MCCLURE, INTERNATIONAL EXECUTIVE AGREE-
MENTS].  On January 1, 1969, there were officially considered as in
force for the United States 909 treaties and 3973 executive agreements.
See 14 M. WHITEMAN, DIGEST OF INTERNATIONAL LAW 210 (1970).
The office of the Legal Adviser of the Department of State reports
368 treaties and 5590 other international agreements concluded by
the United States between January 1, 1946 and April 1, 1972.  Secretary of State John Foster Dulles, applying a more liberal definition,
said at the Bricker Amendment hearings that "every time we open a
new privy, we have to have an executive agreement."  Pointing out
that with every treaty or agreement listed in the Executive Agreement Series there were numerous concomitant unlisted agreements, he
estimated that about 10,000 such informal agreements accompanied
the North Atlantic Treaty alone.  Probably the number was picked
out of the air, but Dulles was doubtless including informal understandings in letters, notes, even oral conversations, and routine transactions
reflecting some element of consensus.  See *Bricker Hearings* 1953, at
877; also *id.* at 828, 866.

For a recent essay, including some additional statistics, see the state-
ment by John Stevenson, the Legal Adviser of the Department of State,
*Constitutional Aspects of the Executive Agreement Procedure*, 66
DEP'T STATE BULL. 840 (1972).

2.  See, *e. g.*, Pub.L. 86–682, § 505, 74 Stat. 581 (1960), 39 U.S.C.
§ 505 (1970) (authority to Postmaster General "by and with the
advice and consent of the President" to make postal agreements); ch.
169, § 3, 69 Stat. 162 (1955), as amended, 19 U.S.C. § 1351(a) (1) (A)
(1970) (trade agreements); Pub.L. 87–195, Pt. III, § 635, 75 Stat. 456
(1961), 22 U.S.C. § 2395(b) (1970) (President may make "agreements and contracts" relating to foreign assistance); ch. 1073, § 1,
68 Stat. 940 (1954), as amended, 42 U.S.C. §§ 2153–54 (1970) (nuclear
cooperation); compare ch. 391, § 1, 61 Stat. 652 (1947), 17 U.S.C.
§ 9(b) (1970) (international copyrights).

3.  See the joint resolution authorizing conclusion of the Headquarters Agreement with the United Nations, ch. 482, 61 Stat. 756

(1947) (text of agreement included in resolution); U.N.R.R.A. Act of March 28, 1944, ch. 135, 58 Stat. 122; Bretton Woods Agreement Act (providing for participation in the International Monetary Fund and the International Bank for Reconstruction and Development), ch. 339, 59 Stat. 512 (1945); joint resolutions providing for membership and participation in the International Refugee Organization, ch. 185, 61 Stat. 214 (1947); F.A.O., ch. 342, 59 Stat. 529 (1945); U.N.E. S.C.O., ch. 700, 60 Stat. 712 (1946); W.H.O., ch. 469, 62 Stat. 441 (1948). Earlier, Congress had approved United States adherence to that part of the Versailles Treaty which established the International Labor Office, ch. 676, 48 Stat. 1182, 1183 (1934).

The UN Charter was approved as a treaty, but implementation was left largely to Congressional-Executive cooperation. See the United Nations Participation Act of 1945, ch. 583, 59 Stat. 619 (1945), *as amended*, 22 U.S.C. §§ 287–287e (1970); even "Article 43 agreements" to put forces at the disposal of the Security Council were to be approved by Congress, not consented to by the Senate only. See § 6, 59 Stat. 621, 22 U.S.C. 287d.

4. For example, U.S. participation in the Pan American Union. See, for example, ch. 104, 48 Stat. 534 (1934), and subsequent Congressional appropriations; compare 25 Stat. 155 (1888); *id.* at 957 (1889); 26 Stat. 272, 275 (1890), and others. An unconditional most-favored nation clause was included in an agreement with Albania before Congress in effect approved such agreements. See McClure, International Executive Agreements 176 (1941).

5. The argument that the Constitution permits international agreements by treaty only was long ago rejected. See, for example, as to postal agreements, 19 Op.Att'y Gen. 513 (1890); *cf.* 29 Op.Att'y Gen. 380 (1912); see, generally, 19 Op.Att'y Gen. 513 (1890).

For an extended debate of the constitutionality of executive agreements see Borchard, *Shall the Executive Agreement Replace the Treaty?* 53 Yale L.J. 664 (1944); McDougal and Lans, *Treaties and Congressional-Executive or Presidential Agreements: Interchangeable Instruments of National Policy*, 54 Yale L.J. 181, 534 (1945); Borchard, *Treaties and Executive Agreements—A Reply, id.* at 616.

6. J. B. Moore, 60 *Proceedings of The American Philosophical Society, Minutes* XV–XVI (1921), quoted in Wright 375: "As Congress possesses no power whatever to make international agreements, it has no such power to delegate." If seen as delegation of Congressional authority, the often total absence of guidelines might also raise issues. See Chapter IV, p. 119. Moore saw Congress as implementing the President's agreements, often in advance.

7. *Cf.* Wright at 105, 375. See also McClure, International Executive Agreements 371–72.

8. See the debate cited note 5, this chapter.

9. Compare United States v. Curtiss-Wright Export Corp., 299 U.S. 304 (1936); Introduction to Chapter II, p. 32, and note 4, and Chapter IV, p. 118. There are also arguments to support joint Executive-Congressional power in this context in particular. Before the Constitution all international agreements were made by Congress. The Constitutional Convention considered proposals to require the advice and consent of both houses to the making of treaties, and rejected them largely because that would have made the process too difficult and cumbersome. The requirement of consent of the Senate only can be seen, then, as "settling for less", and the two-thirds requirement in the Senate as a lesser substitute for the consent of the House of Representatives also. If so, the consent of both houses (even if only by simple majority) is an even greater safeguard and should surely be no less effective than the consent of the Senate alone (even by two-thirds). Compare especially Head Money Cases, 112 U.S. 580, 599 (1884), quoted Chapter V, note 111. For this suggestion that Congress was really the preferred "treaty-maker" there is some support in that Congress, not the President, nor the President-and-Senate, was given authority to authorize agreements (other than treaties) by the States with foreign powers. Art. I, sec. 10, cl. 2. See Chapter IX.

While often an agreement approved or authorized by Congress in fact obtains the consent of two-thirds of the Senate, the Trade Agreements Act of 1934, for an important example, passed the Senate by 57–33, less than the two-thirds required for consent to a treaty. 78 CONG.REC. 10395 (1934). And compare Chapter V, note 13.

Of course, those who find a broad power in the President to make international agreements alone (note 19, this chapter) might see Congressional approval as politically welcome (and disarming Senate resentment) but constitutionally unnecessary; or perhaps as needed only to give legal effect to the agreement in the United States. See p. 184 above.

It has been argued that all Presidential agreements are essentially Congressional-Executive agreements, since, in effect, they have the acquiescence of Congress, if only in that Congress does not legislate to supersede them. That suggestion does not take account of the realities of the legislative process; in any event it could not apply where Congress does not know of the agreement, or when the agreement does not deal with a matter of domestic import as to which Congress could legislate.

10. See, *e. g.*, President Truman's message to Congress in regard to the agreement for the Trust Territory of the Pacific Islands: "I have given special consideration to whether the attached trusteeship agreement should be submitted to the Congress for action by

422

joint resolution or by the treaty process. I am satisfied that either method is constitutionally permissible and that the agreement resulting will be of the same effect internationally and under the supremacy clause of the Constitution whether advised and consented to by the Senate or whether approval is authorized by a joint resolution. The interest of both Houses of Congress in the execution of this agreement is such, however, that I think it would be appropriate for the Congress, in this instance, to take action by joint resolution authorizing the Government to bring the agreement into effect." Message of the President to Congress, H.DOC.NO. 378, 80th Cong., 1st Sess. (July 3, 1947). See also the opinion of the Attorney General in note 11, this chapter.

The legislative branch has also recognized Congressional-Executive agreements as alternatives to treaties. After the First World War a House Committee Report asserted the propriety of adherence to the World Court by Congressional Resolution instead of treaty, citing precedents. H.R.REP.NO.1569, 68th Cong., 2nd Sess. 16 (1925). And see note 3 this chapter.

The Executive had apparently planned to conclude the UNRRA agreement, *ibid.*, on his own authority rather than seek Senate consent to it as a treaty, but "compromised" with a subcommittee of the Senate Foreign Relations Committee which agreed to support approval of the agreement by a joint resolution of Congress. See *Hearings on H.R.J. Res. 192 Before the House Comm. on Foreign Affairs*, 78th Cong., 1st and 2d Sess., at 158–59 (1943–44) (remarks of Mr. Sayre of Department of State). See, generally, 90 CONG.REC. 1727–53 (1944).

The courts have approved Congressional-Executive agreements in a few cases involving matters within the delegated powers of Congress. In 1882 the Supreme Court held that postal conventions have equal status with treaties as part of the law of the land. Cotzhausen v. Nazro, 107 U.S. 215 (1882). (See comments, S.DOC. No. 244, SEN.MISC.DOC., 78th Cong., 2d Sess. (1944); 19 OP.ATT'Y GEN. 513 (1882).) See also B. Altman & Co. v. United States, 224 U.S. 583 (1912), where the Supreme Court considered a Congressional-Executive agreement to be a "treaty" within the meaning of a federal statute.

In 1943 Representative Fulbright argued the full equality, and the inherent superiority, of Congressional-Executive agreements in *The New York Herald-Tribune* Nov. 3, 1943, reprinted in CORWIN, THE CONSTITUTION AND WORLD ORGANIZATION 49–50 (1944). Corwin supported that position generally, and in effect favored a constitutional amendment to replace Senate consent to treaties with approval by Congress. *Id.* at 49, 54. There have been innumerable bills to amend the Constitution to give the House a voice in treaties, and many to replace the treaty power with Congressional-Executive agreement.

An agreement may be approved by resolution of Congress although it bears the description "treaty" internationally. Congress has itself referred to "any treaty or convention" approved by the President on the authorization of Congress. 5 U.S.C. § 372 (1970).

11. When the Executive Branch decided to seek approval of the UN Headquarters Agreement by joint resolution, it provided concerned foreign governments with an opinion of the Attorney General assuring them that the Congressional-Executive agreement would be the equivalent of a treaty and supreme law of the land. 40 OP.ATT'Y GEN. 469 (1946). While his opinion purported to speak only for the agreement in question, the arguments and authorities cited would seem to apply as well to any agreement.

A Congressional-Executive agreement would supersede an earlier statute, and a later statute would supersede an earlier Congressional-Executive agreement as it does a treaty, Chapter V, p. 163.

The control of Congress over such executive agreements is at least as strong as that of the Senate over treaties. In 1962, Congress required the inclusion of members of prescribed Congressional committees on delegations for trade agreement negotiations. See Trade Expansion Act of 1962, Pub.L. 87–794, § 243, 76 Stat. 878, 19 U.S.C. § 1873 (1970). In approving agreements by joint resolution Congress has sometimes entered conditions or reservations; see, *e. g.*, the resolution approving U. S. adherence to the International Refugee Organization, ch. 185, 61 Stat. 214 (1947); also the resolution authorizing the UN Headquarters Agreement, ch. 482, 61 Stat. 756, 758, 767–68 (1947), discussed in Chapter V, note 32.

Who has the power to terminate a Congressional-Executive agreement is unresolved, but the President's authority seems no weaker than in regard to treaties. See Chapter V, p. 168. In some cases Congress purported to reserve for itself an equal right to annul authorized arrangements independently of the President. See, *e. g.*, The Postal Service Act of 1960, Pub.L. No. 86–682, § 6103, 74 Stat. 688. The Postal Reorganization Act of 1970 does not contain such a provision. Pub.L. No. 91–375, ch. 50, § 5002, 84 Stat. 719, 766, 39 U.S.C. § 5002 (1970).

12. See Chapter V, note 4.

13. *E. g.*, the executive agreement to lease the Guantanamo base was concluded pursuant to the 1903 treaty with Cuba, 1 MALLOY, TREATIES 358, 360 (1938). For other examples see CRANDALL, TREATIES 117. An executive agreement pursuant to a security treaty with Japan was given effect by the Supreme Court in Wilson v. Girard, 354 U.S. 524 (1957); see the following note. The peace treaty with Italy

was also supplemented by executive agreements; *e. g.*, Memorandum Agreement with Italy on Financial and Economic Relations, August 14, 1947, T.I.A.S. No. 1757. Compare Dulles, note 1, this chapter.

It is difficult to see why there was ever any doubt as to the power by general arbitration treaty to authorize the President later to submit claims to arbitration. See WRIGHT 108–109. Probably he could submit claims to arbitration on his own authority even without an antecedent treaty; *ibid.*, and note 30 this chapter; compare Chapter II, p. 49. But where the Senate has insisted otherwise, the President, by accepting their consent on that condition, is presumably bound by it. Compare the Hague Convention of 1907, 2 MALLOY, TREATIES, at 2247–48, and the General Arbitration Treaty of 1908, Art. II, 1 MALLOY, TREATIES at 814. Compare Chapter V, pp. 135–36.

14. In Wilson v. Girard, 354 U.S. 524, 528–29 (1957), the Supreme Court said:

> In light of the Senate's ratification of the Security Treaty after consideration of the Administrative Agreement, which had already been signed, and its subsequent ratification of the NATO Agreement, with knowledge of the commitment to Japan under the Administrative Agreement, we are satisfied that the approval of Article III of the Security Treaty authorized the making of the Administrative Agreement and the subsequent Protocol embodying the NATO Agreement provisions governing jurisdiction to try criminal offenses.

Numerous executive agreements have been made pursuant to NATO, see Dulles, note 1, this chapter. In view of the important consequences and obligations which every new member entails, however, it was assumed that the addition of new members to NATO required consent of the Senate. *Hearings on the North Atlantic Treaty Before the Senate Comm. on Foreign Relations*, 81st Cong., 1st Sess. 26 (1949); D. ACHESON, PRESENT AT THE CREATION 285 (1969). See Chapter VII, note 12. There has been no practice of seeking Senate consent in regard to membership in organizations like the UN, the Specialized Agencies or other multilateral organizations in which additional members would not importantly modify U. S. obligations and which have "parliamentary" procedures for admission of new members and contemplate "open membership." Senate consent to the original treaty can be deemed to imply consent to the procedures for admitting new members.

15. See The Conferences at Malta and Yalta, [1945] FOREIGN REL. U.S. 549, 968–87 (1955), E.A.S. No. 498; 2 Conference of Berlin (Potsdam), [1945] FOREIGN REL. U.S. 1462–99 (1960). See note 16, this chapter.

Some executive agreements have been communicated to the Senate for information: *e. g.*, Secretary of State Root offered to apprise the Senate of the substance and effect of the Root-Takahira Agreement, 1908. See P. JESSUP, 2 ELIHU ROOT 43 (1964). Compare note 32, this chapter.

16. Senators have often accused Presidents of usurping the Treaty Power. See, for example, Senator Teller's attack on Theodore Roosevelt, 40 CONG.REC. 1475–80 (1906). When it became clear that the Senate would not consent to a protocol whereby the United States would take over the customs houses of the Dominican Republic, Roosevelt concluded it as an executive agreement "pending the action of the United States Senate upon the treaty." [1905] FOREIGN REL. U.S. 360 (1906); see HOLT 212 *et seq.* The issue produced a famous constitutional debate. See, for example, 40 CONG.REC. 433–36, 1173–80, 1417–31, 2125–48 (1905–06).

An executive agreement with Panama supplementing the Hay-Varilla Treaty and establishing a *modus vivendi* for the co-occupation of the Zone was "attacked vigorously in the Senate as a usurpation of the treaty-making power." W. H. TAFT, OUR CHIEF MAGISTRATE AND HIS POWERS 112 (1916). See also Senator Robert Taft's admonition that an "important matter" such as then-pending agreements with Panama, is inappropriate for executive agreements and should be submitted for Senate approval as treaties. 88 CONG.REC. 9276–77 (1942). On the anniversary of the Yalta agreement in 1952, several Senators excoriated that agreement as "shameful", "infamous", and a Presidential usurpation of power. See, *e. g.*, Sen. Ives, 98 CONG.REC. 900 (1952). For a more recent example, see *Hearings on H.R. 9042 Before the Senate Comm. on Finance on the United States-Canadian Automobile Agreement*, 89th Cong., 1st Sess., 85–86 (1965). President Lincoln was severely criticized when without support in statute or treaty, he agreed to extradite to Spain a man named Arguelles accused of illegitimate slave trading. See, *e. g.*, 9 NICOLAY AND HAY, ABRAHAM LINCOLN 45–47 (1890). Compare Chapter IV, p. 98.

In 1972 the Senate adopted the Case Resolution urging the President to submit the Azores and the Bahrain base agreements for Senate consent. S.Res. 214, 92d Cong., 1st Sess., 118 CONG.REC. 3290 (daily ed. March 3, 1972). When the Executive did not comply, Senator Case proposed that Congress refuse to appropriate for the aid provided in these agreements. See New York Times, April 3, 1972, p. 7, col. 1. Earlier Senator Fulbright had sought to compel disclosure, discussion, and submission for Senate consent of the extension of the military-base agreement with Spain. 116 CONG.REC. 26968–72 (1970). Compare note 32 below.

17. 301 U.S. 324, 330–31 (1937); the facts of the case are given above at p. 184. See also United States v. Pink, 315 U.S. 203 (1942).

18. In *Curtiss-Wright* Sutherland included "the power to make such international agreements as do not constitute treaties in the constitutional sense" as one of those powers which though not "expressly affirmed by the Constitution, nevertheless exist as inherently inseparable from the conception of nationality." United States v. Curtiss-Wright Export Corp., 299 U.S. 304, 318 (1936), quoted Chapter I, p. 21 above.

19. See *e. g.*, McCLURE, INTERNATIONAL EXECUTIVE AGREEMENTS 330, 363, 371; Mathews, *The Constitutional Power of the President to Conclude International Agreements,* 64 YALE L.J. 345, 370 *et seq.* (1955); Wright, *The United States and International Agreements,* 38 AM. J. INT'L. 341, 348 (1944); *cf.* McDougal and Lans, 54 Yale L.J. at 246. Theodore Roosevelt's discussion of his action in regard to the San Domingo customs houses (note 16, this chapter) implies that the Constitution does not limit the President's power to make executive agreements. T. ROOSEVELT, AUTOBIOGRAPHY 551–52 (1912).

20. See Chapter V, note 4. In *The Federalist,* Hamilton makes much of the fact that while the King of Great Britain could himself make treaties, the President could not. "In this respect, therefore, there is no comparison between the intended power of the President and the actual power of the British sovereign." THE FEDERALIST NO. 69, at 448.

21. A different issue is whether under international law the United States could ever claim it was not bound by an agreement because it was made without Senate consent. Whether a state can escape obligation on the ground that those who incurred it in her behalf acted *ultra vires* under the national constitution is not wholly agreed. See H. BLIX, THE TREATY-MAKING POWER 370–74 (1960). Compare Art. 46(1) of the Vienna Convention on the Law of Treaties, 63 AM.J.INT'L L. 875, 890 (1969), which provides that a state can not invoke failure to comply with its internal law as a defense "unless that violation was manifest and concerned a rule of its internal law of fundamental importance." Senate consent has been cited as an example of a fundamental requirement. A. McNAIR, THE LAW OF TREATIES 63 (1961). But the power of the President to make many agreements without the Senate casts some doubt on the "fundamental importance" of Senate consent; in any event, failure to obtain such consent cannot be a "manifest" violation of the Constitution since no one can say with certainty when it is required. Compare Chapter V, p. 137.

22. In the language quoted p. 178, Sutherland might leave the impression that what matters is whether an agreement is called a treaty or something else, but surely constitutional power does not hang on those labels. Even international practice is hardly firm and clear about them: there is nothing to prevent nations from calling

something a treaty instead of a *modus vivendi,* or vice versa, and international law accords all these agreements the same binding effect.

Borchard proposed that "in case of doubt, and in the event that there should be any substantial opinion in the Senate insisting that the arrangement should be made by treaty, no President should hesitate in adopting the method provided in the Constitution of seeking Senate approval instead of resolving the doubt in his own favor." Borchard, *Treaties and Executive Agreements—A Reply, supra* note 5, at 625. See, also the remarks of Senator Taft, note 16 *supra.*

On the difficulty of distinguishing executive agreements from treaties, see, *e. g.,* Dulles, *Bricker Hearings,* 1953, at 866. It does not seem unreasonable to suggest that the Bricker Amendment might have succeeded in limiting or regulating executive agreements if its proponents had been able effectively to define them and distinguish their scope clearly from that of treaties.

23. Some of the examples that follow are derived from a long series listed in CRANDALL, TREATIES Chapter VIII. The agreements mentioned in the text are: Rush-Bagot Agreement, 8 Stat. 231 (1817), T.S. No. 110½; Root-Takahira Agreement, [1908] FOREIGN REL. U.S. 510–12 (1912), T.S. No. 511½; Lansing-Ishii Agreement, 3 MALLOY, TREATIES 2720–22, T.S. No. 630; Gentlemen's Agreement with Japan, 1907 (substance of this agreement, never published verbatim, is in a letter from the Japanese Ambassador to the United States to Secretary of State Hughes, April 10, 1924, 63 CONG.REC. 6073–74 (1924)); Correspondence Relating to the Protocol of Agreement with the Dominican Republic Providing for the Collection and Disbursement of Customs Revenues in that Republic, [1905], FOREIGN REL.U.S. 298–391 (1906) note 16 above; for McKinley's Agreement to provide troops during the Boxer Rebellion see generally 13 RICHARDSON 6417–25 (1897); Boxer Indemnity Protocol, 1901, 2 MALLOY, TREATIES 2006, [1901] FOREIGN REL.U.S., App. 312 (1902); Destroyer exchange with England, 1940, E.A.S. No. 181; Potsdam and Yalta agreements, note 15, this chapter.

24. The Rush-Bagot agreement was concluded by exchange of notes April 28–29, 1817. Nearly a year later, on April 6, 1818, President Monroe submitted the correspondence to the Senate and asked it to consider whether the agreement was under the President's constitutional power or required Senate consent. The Senate gave consent, but there was no formal exchange of ratifications thereafter; and President Monroe had acted under the agreement before the Senate consented. See CRANDALL, TREATIES 102–103. Rush-Bagot may have been substantially a Congressional-Executive agreement since Congress had earlier authorized the President to sell or lay up all the armed vessels on the Great Lakes. See ch. 62, §§ 4, 6, 3 Stat. 217, 218 (1815). Compare, *e. g.,* 5 MOORE, DIGEST 214–15.

25. For a list of such agreements, see, *e. g.*, CRANDALL, TREATIES 109–11. For more recent examples, see FOREIGN CLAIMS SETTLEMENT COMMISSION OF THE UNITED STATES: DECISIONS AND ANNOTATIONS 731–64 (1968). Compare Chapter X, note 52.

26. United States v. Guy W. Capps, Inc., 204 F.2d 655 (4th Cir. 1953), *aff'd on other grounds*, 348 U.S. 296 (1955). In that case the Acting Secretary of State and the Canadian Ambassador had exchanged notes in which it was agreed that Canada would permit the export of potatoes into the United States only if the importer agreed that they would be used exclusively for seed. The Capps Company gave such assurances but later sold the potatoes to a grocery chain. The United States sued for damages and the lower court directed a verdict for the Company on the ground that the United States had shown no breach of contract and no damage. The Court of Appeals affirmed on the ground that the executive agreement was void; the Supreme Court affirmed the judgments below but did so on the grounds given by the trial court.

27. 204 F.2d at 659.

28. Judge Parker himself reduced his suggestion to dictum by leaving open "whatever the power of the executive with respect to making executive trade agreements regulating foreign commerce in the absence of action by Congress." *Ibid.*

29. *E. g.*, the International Antidumping Code. See *Hearings on the International Antidumping Code Before the Senate Comm. on Finance*, 90th Cong., 2d Sess. 13 (1968). United States participation in G.A.T.T. (Oct. 30, 1947, 61 Stat. A3, T.I.A.S.No.1700), may also be wholly on Presidential authority: compare the provision in the Trade Agreements Extension Act, Chapter IV, pp. 120–21.

In 1965 the Acting Legal Adviser of the State Department took the position that trade agreements may be concluded either by executive agreement or by treaty, and that Congressional authorization is clearly needed only when the agreement is inconsistent with prior legislation. Letter from Leonard C. Meeker to Senator Fulbright, Feb. 24, 1965, in *Hearings on the United States—Canada Automotive Products Agreement Before the House Comm. on Ways and Means*, 89th Cong., 1st Sess. 226–27 (1965); compare *id.* at 227–30.

30. See, *e. g.*, T. Roosevelt, note 19, this chapter; Borchard, note 5 this chapter, at 678–79; *cf.* 88 CONG.REC. 9276 (1942) (remarks of Senator Taft). A related suggestion would have it that agreements that can be consummated immediately and do not require legislative implementation need not be submitted for Senate approval. 39 OP. ATT'Y GEN. 484, 487 (1940). Such alleged limitations have been widely criticized. See, *e. g.*, Levitan, *Executive Agreements*, 35 ILL.L.REV. at 376–78; McDougal and Lans, 54 YALE L.J. at 331–48; CORWIN, THE

PRESIDENT 214; Lissitzyn, *Duration of Executive Agreements,* 54 AM. J.INT'L L. 860–70 (1960).

It has also been suggested that Senate consent is not necessary for agreements that involve only obligations or concessions by the other side. See 30 OP.ATT'Y GEN. 484, 487 (1940). Compare, *e. g.,* Smallwood v. Clifford, 286 F.Supp. 97, 100 (D.C.D.C.1968). That case upheld an executive agreement establishing the status of U.S. forces in Korea; a basis for that executive agreement might be found in a treaty between the United States and the Republic of Korea. See Korean Mutual Defense Treaty of 1953, art. IV, [1954] 5 U.S.T. 2368, T.I.A.S. No. 3097.

Some other assumed limitations on the President's agreement-making authority have also not survived. It was suggested that while the President could arbitrate claims by the United States on his own authority, an agreement to arbitrate claims against the United States required Senate consent. 5 MOORE, DIGEST 211. There is little theoretical basis for that distinction and Presidents have agreed to arbitrate claims against the United States. See WRIGHT 108–109, note 13 this chapter.

31.  Compare Senator Taft note 16, this chapter. But compare: "In some instances we have come close to reversing the traditional distinction between the treaty as the instrument of a major commitment and the executive agreement as the instrument of a minor one." SENATE COMM. ON FOREIGN RELATIONS, NATIONAL COMMITMENTS, S.REP. NO. 129, 91st Cong., 1st Sess. 28 (1969).

In 1939 an Assistant Secretary of State wrote:

> "International agreements involving political issues or changes of national policy and those involving international arrangements of a permanent character usually take the form of treaties. But international agreements embodying adjustments of detail carrying out well-established national policies and traditions and those involving arrangements of a more or less temporary nature usually take the form of executive agreements.

Sayre, *The Constitutionality of the Trade Agreements Act,* 39 COLUM. L.REV. 751, 755 (1939). That distinction, too, is not consistently reflected in practice.

32.  Compare Chapter V, note 9. Senate committees or individual Senators are sometimes informed of confidential agreements privately. Sometimes constitutional formalities are satisfied by making an unclassified covering treaty to which the Senate's consent is obtained, and classified executive agreements pursuant to the treaty. Compare Dulles, this chapter, note 1.

In 1972 the Senate unanimously adopted S. 596 requiring the President to transmit to congress all international agreements other than treaties, within 60 days after their execution. If the President deemed that public disclosure of the agreement would be prejudicial to national security, he shall transmit it instead to the foreign affairs committees of both houses of Congress under injunction of secrecy to be removed only upon due notice from the President. Cong.Rec. S 1901, S 1904–11, Feb. 16, 1972. See S.REP.No.591, 92d Cong., 2d Sess. (1972).

33. See S.Res. 85, 90th Cong. 1st Sess., 115 CONG.REC. 2603 (1969). The same resolution was originally introduced in 1967 (S.Res. 151, 113 CONG.REC. 20702), and was modified by the Senate Foreign Relations Committee after extensive hearings. See S.REP.No.797, 90th Cong., 1st Sess. (1967); *Hearings on S.Res. 151 Before the Senate Comm. on Foreign Relations*, 90th Cong., 1st Sess. (1967). Senator Fulbright reintroduced his original resolution in 1969, and this time it was approved by the Senate Foreign Relations Committee without modification. S.REP.No.129, 91st Cong., 1st Sess. (1969). The Senate also sought to require the President to obtain its consent to all base agreements but in conference the House of Representatives refused to accede.

In December, 1950, while Prime Minister Attlee was visiting in the United States, twenty-four Republican senators introduced and debated a resolution requiring Senate advice and consent to any agreement that might be made by President Truman and the Prime Minister. See 96 CONG.REC. 16173 (1950).

34. See 115 CONG.REC. 17245 (1969).

35. The suggestion has been frequently made, recently by Senator Morse. See *Hearings, Separation of Powers* 75; also *id.* at 63. Compare Attorney General Jackson's statement that agreements requiring Congressional implementation "are customarily submitted" for Senate approval as treaties. 39 OP.ATT'Y GEN. 484, 487 (1940).

36. See, *e. g.*, Russian Socialist Federated Soviet Republic v. Cibrario, 235 N.Y. 255, 263, 139 N.E. 259, 262 (1923); James & Co. v. Second Russian Ins. Co., 239 N.Y. 248, 257, 146 N.E. 369, 371 (1925); Vladikavkazsky Ry. Co. v. New York Trust Co., 263 N.E. 369, 378, 189 N.E. 456, 460 (1934); Moscow Fire Ins. Co. v. Bank of New York & Trust Co., 280 N.Y. 286, 20 N.E.2d 758 (1939), *aff'd by an equally divided court*, 309 U.S. 624 (1940). The Act of State doctrine, Chapter VIII, p. 217, does not apply where the assets confiscated by a foreign government are situated here. See, *e. g.*, Republic of Iraq v. First National City Bank, 353 F.2d 47 (2d Cir. 1965), *cert. denied*, 382 U.S. 1027 (1966).

37. 301 U.S. at 331.

38. United States v. Pink, 315 U.S. 203 (1942).

A California Court invalidated California Buy-American provisions as inconsistent with GATT. Baldwin-Lima-Hamilton Corp. v. Superior Court, 25 Cal.Rptr. 798, 208 Cal.App.2d 803 (D.Ct.App.1962). GATT may be a sole executive agreement. See note 29, this chapter. Other courts have held that such Buy American acts violate the Commerce Clause.

39. In 1883 the Attorney General concluded that the President could not, on his own authority, extend to the German Government the privilege of taking testimony of prisoners in state prisons. 17 OP.ATT'Y GEN. 565 (1883). It is questionable whether that opinion survives *Belmont* and *Pink*.

Whether an agreement is self-executing is considered a matter of interpretation, first for the President then for the courts. See Chapter V, p. 158. As a matter of interpretation, however, *ad hoc* agreements governing some single instance would rarely be intended to await congressional action, especially if the agreement is to be carried out immediately; indeed some agreements exist solely by implication in the President's act of executing them. Compare the suggestion that some agreements cannot be made, surely cannot be executed, without Congressional approval, if they impinge on preferred individual rights, p. 187.

40. For criticism of *Capps*, see Matthews, *The Constitutional Power of the President to Conclude International Agreements*, 64 YALE L.J. 345, 386–87 (1955). Compare South Puerto Rico Sugar Co. Trading Corp. v. United States, 334 F.2d 622, 634 (Ct.Cl.1964), where the Court of Claims suggested that the Supreme Court's affirmance of *Capps* on other grounds "neutralized" the views of the Court of Appeals on executive agreements.

41. Of course, those who argue that a treaty should not be law in the face of an earlier statute, would hold that view as to executive agreements, *a fortiori*. See Chapter V, p. 163. It has been argued that a power in the President to "overrule" Congressional legislation is irreconcilable with the "entire tenor" of the Constitution. See McCLURE, INTERNATIONAL EXECUTIVE AGREEMENTS 343. Compare United States v. Clarke, 20 Wall. 92, 112–13 (U.S.1874) ("No power was ever vested in the President to repeal an act of Congress."), Chapter IV, note 40.

42. *Cf.* THE FEDERALIST NO. 64 (Jay) cited in *Pink*: "All constitutional acts of power, whether in the executive or in the judicial department, have as much legal validity and obligation as if they proceeded from the legislature." 315 U.S. at 230.

An argument can perhaps be made that even if unilateral acts of the President do not have effect as law, sole executive agreements stand better. Like a treaty an executive agreement has the "seriousness" of an international act and an international obligation, clearly engaging international interests of the United States.

For a judicial suggestion that, like a treaty, an executive agreement might supersede an earlier act of Congress, see Etlimar Société Anonyme of Casablanca v. United States, 106 F.Supp. 191 (Ct.Cl.1952). And see an early case from the Territory of Washington that appears to give effect to an executive agreement to modify the government of the territory as earlier provided by Congress. Watts v. United States, 1 Wash.Terr. 288 (1870).

It has been suggested that F.D.R.'s destroyer agreement with Great Britain, (p. 180 this chapter) was inconsistent with existing statutes and represents an assertion of the power to supersede an act of Congress by sole executive agreement. See E. CORWIN, THE CONSTITUTION AND WORLD ORGANIZATION 42 (1944); also CORWIN, THE PRESIDENT 238. But Attorney General Jackson thought that the agreement was not inconsistent with any statute, and indeed expressed the opinion that the President could not transfer certain mosquito boats because it was forbidden by statute. 39 OP.ATT'Y GEN. 484, 494 (1940).

Franklin Roosevelt also entered into agreements to station troops in Greenland and Iceland apparently in disregard of Congressional legislation limiting conscripted troops to service in the Western Hemisphere and the territorial possessions of the United States. See Defense of Iceland by United States Forces, July 1, 1941, 55 Stat. 1547 (1941), E.A.S. No. 232; Defense of Greenland, April 9, 1941, 55 Stat. 1245 (1941), E.A.S. No. 204. Compare the Selective Training and Service Act of 1940, ch. 720, § 3(e), 54 Stat. 885, 886 (1940). See Chapter IV, p. 106. Perhaps the President believed that agreements under this power as Commander-in-Chief could disregard Congressional limitations, even if executive agreements generally could not.

Another instance is cited in a recent Congressional committee report:

> This was illustrated in 1968, in the course of a controversy between the Senate and the President over the International Anti-Dumping Code agreed to by the President as an adjunct to the Kennedy round of negotiations on reciprocal trade. The conflict arose because of congressional expressions of opinion against the negotiation and signature of such a code during the Paris meetings, the execution of such an agreement by the President, the alleged conflict between the terms of the code and preexisting statutory law, and the suggestion by the executive branch that executive agreements, like treaties were superior in law to prior, inconsistent statutes.

*Separation of Powers* S.REP.NO.549, 91st Cong., 1st Sess. 16 (1969).

43.   Valentine v. United States *ex rel.* Neidecker, 299 U.S. 5 (1936), Chapter IV, p. 98.

44.   A century earlier several Justices held that when the Governor of Vermont sought to extradite one Holmes to Canada he was entering into an agreement with Canada which Vermont could not do without Congressional consent.   Holmes v. Jennison, 14 Pet. 540 (U.S.1840), discussed in Chapter IX, p. 231.

45.   Some of this customary law is now being codified and developed by multilateral treaty, principally through the efforts of the International Law Commission.   See, *e. g.*, the 1958 conventions adopted April 28, 1958, which codified, clarified, and somewhat modified the law of the seas.   Convention on the High Seas, 450 U.N.T.S. 82, T.I.A.S. No. 5200; Convention on the Continental Shelf, 499 U.N.T.S. 311, T.I.A.S. No. 5578; Convention on the Territorial Sea and the Contiguous Zone, 516 U.N.T.S. 205, T.I.A.S. No. 5639; Convention on Fishing and Conservation of the Living Resources of the High Seas, 599 U.N.T.S. 285, T.I.A.S. No. 5969.   See also the Vienna Convention on Diplomatic Relations, *done* April 18, 1961, 500 U.N.T.S. 95; Vienna Convention on the Law of Treaties, printed in 63 AM.J.INT'L L. 875 (1969).

For the suggestion that for our Constitutional Fathers "the law of nations" included also private international law, see Chapter III, note 22.   Today the rules of conflicts are largely domestic law except insofar as they may be modified by treaty.   But compare Chapter VIII, p. 219, and Chapter V, note 87.

NOTES, CHAPTER VII, INTERNATIONAL ORGANIZATION, pp. 189 to 201.

1. This multilateral "organization" was established in 1865 to direct, administer, and financially support the lighthouse that had been built by the Moroccan government at Cape Spartel. See Convention concerning the Cape Spartel Lighthouse, May 31, 1865, 14 Stat. 679-81 (1868), T.S. No. 245. The Convention was terminated by protocol on March 31, 1958 [1958] 9 U.S.T. 527, T.I.A.S. No. 4029; 320 U.N.T.S. 103. Control was returned to the government of Morocco.

2. United Nations Charter, June 26, 1945, 59 Stat. 1031; T.S. No. 993; United Nations Participation Act of 1945, ch. 583, 59 Stat. 619, *as amended*, 22 U.S.C. §§ 287–287e (1964). Compare the International Organizations Immunities Act, ch. 652, 59 Stat. 669 (1945), 22 U.S.C. § 288 (1952).

No one pressed constitutional objections to U.S. adherence to the UN Charter, whereas proposals for participation in the League of Nations had run into many such objections. See WRIGHT, 113–115; also, Wright, *Validity of the Proposed Reservations to the Peace Treaty*, 20 COLUM.L.REV. 121 (1920). Political change apart, major constitutional change (or clarification) had intervened, *e. g., Curtiss-Wright, Missouri v. Holland* and the New Deal cases. Compare CORWIN, THE PRESIDENT 217 *et seq.*

3. UN Charter, articles 23, 27; see generally *id.* Chapters V–VII.

4. *Id.* article 2(4); compare article 51. Article 2 is a treaty undertaking independent of the UN Organization established elsewhere in the Charter. Compare L. HENKIN, HOW NATIONS BEHAVE: LAW AND FOREIGN POLICY, Chapters X and XI (1968); Henkin, *Force, Intervention, and Neutrality in Contemporary International Law*, [1963] PROC.AM.SOC.INT'L L. 147–53.

5. UN Charter, articles 55, 56.

6. It has been urged, indeed, that the legal concept of war and the traditional laws of war have been abolished. See, *e. g.,* Henkin, *Force, Intervention, and Neutrality in Contemporary International Law*, note 4 this chapter at 147, 159–61. But *cf.* Déak, *Neutrality Revisited* in TRANSNATIONAL LAW IN A CHANGING SOCIETY (Friedmann, Henkin, & Lissitzyn, eds.) 137 (1972).

7. "The powers of government are delegated in trust to the United States, and are incapable of transfer to any other parties. They cannot be abandoned or surrendered." The Chinese Exclusion Case, 130 U.S. 581, 609 (1889).

8. UN Charter, articles 43–47.

9. Article 27(3), as amended, [1965] 16 U.S.T. 1134, T.I.A.S. No. 5857, 557 U.N.T.S. 143: "Decisions of the Security Council on all other matters shall be made by an affirmative vote of nine members including the concurring votes of the permanent members. . . ."

The General Assembly, in which resolutions can be adopted by majority vote, or two-thirds vote on "important questions," (Article 18 (2)), can only recommend action, not command it. See UN Charter, Chapter IV. Compare the Uniting for Peace Resolution, November 3, 1950, Ga.Res. 377A, 5 UN GAOR, Supp. 20 (A/1775), at 10.

10. The United Nations Participation Act confirms the power of the President to act for the United States in the Security Council, thus lending the support of Congressional authority to his own. The Act requires Congressional approval for article 43 agreements and expressly supports the President's authority (without further approval by Congress) to act for the United States in determining their use by the Council. See 22 U.S.C. §§ 287a, 287d (1970).

11. Compare the decision of Congress to flout UN sanctions against Rhodesia by requiring the President to permit the importation of Rhodesian chrome. See Pub.L. 92–156, § 503, 85 Stat. 423 (1971). Compare 21 U.N. SCOR, 1340th meeting 7 (1966); 23 U.N. SCOR, 1428th meeting 5 (1968); 24 U.N. SCOR 1535th meeting 4 (1970); U.N.S.C. Res. 314 (adopted February 20, 1972); G.A. Res. 2262, 22 U.N. GAOR Supp. 16, at 45, U.N. Doc. A/6716 (1967); see also G.A. Res. 2765 (XXVI) (Nov. 17, 1971).

12. North Atlantic Treaty, April 4, 1949, 63 Stat. 2241, T.I.A.S. No. 1964, 34 U.N.T.S. 243. The United States later accepted additional membership (Greece, Turkey, the Federal Republic of Germans), with Senate consent. [1951] T.I.A.S. No. 2390, 126 U.N.T.S. 350; [1955] T.I.A.S. No. 3428, 243 U.N.T.S. 308.

13. North Atlantic Treaty, articles 5 and 11.

14. Constitutional "niceties" were met also by a two-hat arrangement: the NATO Council asked the United States to make available a U. S. officer as Supreme Commander; the President designated General Eisenhower, whom he also appointed Commander of U. S. Forces in Europe. In this way the President in effect commanded U. S. forces assigned to NATO through his appointee, a U. S. officer. See D. ACHESON, PRESENT AT THE CREATION 486 (1969).

15. I draw here on HENKIN, ARMS CONTROL Chapter VII; see also Henkin, *International Organization and the Rule of Law*, 23 INTERNATIONAL ORGANIZATION 656 (1969).

16. UN Charter, articles 83, 85.

17. See International Monetary Fund Articles of Agreement, 1944, art. IV, 60 Stat. 1401, T.I.A.S. No. 1501.

18. Convention on International Civil Aviation, 1944, Art. 37, 61 Stat. 1180, 1190, T.I.A.S. No. 1591.

19. International Wheat Agreement, March 23, 1949, 63 Stat. 2173, T.I.A.S. No. 1957; International Sugar Agreement, December 1, 1958, T.I.A.S. No. 4389, 385 U.N.T.S. 137; International Coffee Agreement, Sept. 28, 1962, T.I.A.S. No. 5505, 469 U.N.T.S. 169 (1963); also Articles of Agreement of International Cotton Institute, Jan. 17, 1966, T.I.A.S. No. 5964, 592 U.N.T.S. 171.

The World Health Organization and the Universal Postal Union also develop rules and practices in their respective fields, and international officials have propounded cooperative practices for the international control of narcotics. There is regulation also by regional, even by bilateral bodies, especially of fishing. See, *e. g.*, International Convention for the Regulation of Whaling, December 2, 1946, 62 Stat. 1716 (1948); T.I.A.S. No. 1849, 161 U.N.T.S. 72, implemented by the Whaling Convention Act of 1950, ch. 653, 64 Stat. 421 (1950), 16 U.S.C. §§ 916–916*l* (1970). See HENKIN, ARMS CONTROL 107–108 and notes, and my article *International Organization and the Rule of Law*, note 15, this chapter, at 657–661.

20. Compare Wilson v. Girard, 354 U.S. 524, 528–29 (1957), quoted Chapter VI, note 14.

21. These are the conclusions of my book ARMS CONTROL, as summed up in its Chapter IX.

22. U. S. Dep't of State Special Committee on Atomic Energy, *A Report on the International Control of Atomic Energy*, U.S.DEP'T OF STATE PUB.NO.2498 (1946). See also *International Control of Atomic Energy*, U.S.DEP'T OF STATE PUB.NOS. 2702 (1946), 3161 (1948). *Cf.* "Findings on the Safeguards to Ensure the Use of Atomic Energy Only for Peaceful Purposes," in *The International Control of Atomic Energy: First Report of the United Nations Atomic Energy Commission to the Security Council*, U.N.DOC.NO.AEC/18/Rev.1 (1947), also reprinted in U.S.DEP'T OF STATE PUB.NO.2737 (1947). This plan substantially embodied the United States proposal known as the "Baruch Plan," which, in turn, was based on the proposals of the Acheson-Lilienthal Report.

23. I draw here on HENKIN, ARMS CONTROL, Chapter VIII.

24. "All Members of the United Nations are *ipso facto* parties to the Statute of the International Court of Justice." UN Charter, article 93(1). The jurisdiction of the Court depends on consent of the parties in each case unless the parties had committed themselves to accept its jurisdiction for the solution of disputes in particular treaties or conventions. I.C.J. Statute, Article 36(1). Parties may also accept compulsory jurisdiction of the Court by declaration under Article 36 (2) of the Statute. In numerous instances the United States has ac-

cepted the jurisdiction of the Court for issues arising out of particular treaties. See 106 CONG.REC. 11194 (1960); Bishop and Myers, *Unwarranted Extension of Connally Amendment Thinking*, 55 AM.J.INT'L L. 135 (1961). It has also filed a declaration under Article 36(2) although the reservation imposed by the Senate (including the "Connally Amendment") may have rendered it largely illusory. See 61 Stat. 1218 (1946). But *cf.* Henkin, *The Connally Reservation Revisited and, Hopefully, Contained*, 65 AM.J.INT'L L. 374 (1971).

25. See DEP'T STATE PUB. NO. 2420 (1945), 39 AM.J.INT'L L. (Supp.) 257 (1945). The Nuremberg Charter established a tribunal for the trial of war criminals. That charter does not itself legally commit the United States to submit to the jurisdiction of similar tribunals in future. The principles of international law recognized by the Nuremberg Charter were unanimously affirmed by the U.N. General Assembly, Res. 95(I) December 11, 1946, 1 UN GAOR, 2d pt., Verbatim Record 1144 (1946).

26. See, for example, the International Covenant on Civil and Political Rights, article 41, and the optional protocol to the Covenant, Annex to G.A. Res. 2200 (XXI), Dec. 16, 1966; the International Convention on the Elimination of all Forms of Racial Discrimination, Annex to G.A.Res. 2106–A (XX), Jan. 19, 1965; the European Convention for the Protection of Human Rights and Fundamental Freedoms, Nov. 4, 1950, 213 U.N.T.S. 221, and its subsequent protocols; the American Convention on Human Rights, OAS Official Records, OEA/Ser. K/XVI/I.I, Doc. 65, Rev. 1, Corr. 2, Jan. 7, 1970.

27. That in some circumstances suits between the United States and another power might come before American courts as well is immaterial; such suits might be concurrently within the judicial power of one or more particular countries as well as of extra-national bodies established by agreement. Nor does it matter that the International Court itself decides whether it has jurisdiction, (Statute of the International Court of Justice, Article 36(6), 59 Stat. 1055, 1060 (1945); T.S. No. 933), though at one time a Senate Committee considered it to be unconstitutional to give to a joint commission authority to determine whether a dispute is subject to arbitration under a treaty. S.DOC.NO.98, 62d Cong., 1st Sess. 6 (1911), 47 CONG.REC. 3935 (1911); see WRIGHT 111–12.

28. Compare Hirota v. MacArthur, 338 U.S. 197 (1948), note 44, this chapter.

29. Compare the European Convention, note 26, this chapter, which provides for proceedings against a state by the European Commission or by another State, not by the individual himself. 213 U.N.T.S. 221, article 48; but compare article 25. Compare also the optional protocol

to the International Covenant on Civil and Political Rights, note 26, this chapter.

30. See the Hague International Prize Court Convention, October 18, 1907, in 3 G. CHARLES, TREATIES, CONVENTIONS, INTERNATIONAL ACTS, PROTOCOLS, AND AGREEMENTS 248 (1913). For the proposed protocol to avoid appeal from the U. S. Supreme Court, see [1909] FOREIGN REL.U.S. 303, 318 (1914); CHARLES, *supra* at 263. Although the Senate consented the United States did not ratify the Convention and it never came into effect. See CHARLES, *id.*; 2 OPPENHEIM, INTERNATIONAL LAW 876 (Lauterpacht 7th ed. 1952).

31. It was also argued that if there were an appeal from a federal court to an international tribunal, the domestic proceeding would cease to be a case or controversy of judicial character and be inappropriate for a federal court. See WRIGHT 117–18. The argument, and its reliance on Gordon v. United States, 2 Wall. 561 (U.S.1865), also 117 U.S. 697 (Appendix), are not persuasive. In any event Congress could provide for such proceedings to begin not in the regular federal courts but in "legislative courts," special courts established by Congress pursuant to its legislative powers (hence frequently called "Article I courts," after the article of the Constitution vesting legislative power in Congress. The term "legislative courts" originated apparently in American Ins. Co. v. Canter, 1 Pet. 516 (U.S.1828).) Such "courts" are not subject to the requirement in Article III that there be a "case or controversy," to the requirements relating to tenure and compensation of judges, or other limitations which may be implicit in that article. In addition to the *Canter* case, see *Ex parte* Bakelite Corp., 279 U.S. 438 (1929); Williams v. United States, 289 U.S. 553 (1933); compare O'Donoghue v. United States, 289 U.S. 516 (1933); National Mutual Ins. Co. v. Tidewater Transfer Co., 337 U.S. 582 (1949); Glidden Co. v. Zdanok, 370 U.S. 530 (1962). See, generally, *Legislative and Constitutional Courts: What Lurks Ahead for Bifurcation,* 71 YALE L.J. 979 (1962); H. HART & H. WECHSLER, THE FEDERAL COURTS AND THE FEDERAL SYSTEM 340–371 (1953); Katz, *Federal Legislative Courts,* 43 HARV.L.REV. 894 (1930); Note, *The Judicial Power of Federal Tribunals Not Organized Under Article Three,* 34 COLUM.L.REV. 746 (1934).

For a defense of the constitutional right of the United States to submit to an international prize court's jurisdiction, see H.R.REP.NO. 1569, 68th Cong.2d Sess. 10 (1925).

32. See Butte, *The "Protocole Additionnel" to the International Prize Court Convention,* 6 AM.J.INT'L L. 799 (1912).

33. That device was used in the Convention for the Pacific Settlement of Disputes Between Sweden and Finland, Jan. 29, 1926, 49

L.N.T.S. 367. See also similar treaties between Denmark and Sweden, Jan. 14, 1926, 51 L.N.T.S. 251; Denmark and Finland, Jan. 30, 1926, 51 L.N.T.S. 367; Norway and Sweden, Nov. 25, 1925, 60 L.N.T.S. 295.

34. *E. g.*, UN Committee on International Criminal Jurisdiction, *Draft Statute for an International Criminal Court*, UN Doc. A/AC. 48/4 (1951) reprinted in 46 AM.J.INT'L L. (Supp.) 1 (1952). Wright, *Proposal for an International Criminal Court*, 46 AM.J.INT'L L. 60 (1952).

The Convention on the Prevention and Punishment of the Crime of Genocide, December 9, 1948, 78 U.N.T.S. 578, is directed at individual offenders (Art. 4), and provides that persons charged with genocide may be tried by "such international penal tribunal as may have jurisdiction with respect to those Contracting Parties which shall have accepted its jurisdiction." (Art. 6). The international criminal court apparently contemplated by the treaty has never been seriously considered. (The United States has not ratified the Genocide Convention itself but in 1972, after more the twenty years delay, a Senate Committee recommended Senate consent to U. S. adherence. Sen.Ex.Rep. No. 6, 92d Cong., 1st sess. (1971). See Chapter V, note 71.)

35. See Valentine v. United States *ex rel.* Neidecker, 299 U.S. 5 (1936); Charlton v. Kelly, 229 U.S. 447 (1913); compare 18 U.S.C. § 3184 (1970). The power to extradite American citizens under a treaty was upheld in an early case that aroused wide public interest. United States v. Robins, 27 F.Cas. 825, No. 16175 (D.S.C. 1799). (There is some doubt as to whether Robins was in fact an American citizen, but it was apparently assumed that he was.) See Chapter II, note 18.

36. That only courts ordained and established by Congress can exercise the judicial power of the United States, see Martin v. Hunter's Lessee, 1 Wheat. 304, 330–31 (U.S.1816); *Ex parte* Milligan, 4 Wall. 2, 121 (U.S.1866); Williams v. United States, 289 U.S. 553, 566 (1933); *cf.* Robertson v. Baldwin, 165 U.S. 275, 278–79 (1897). It is accepted that federal criminal law can be enacted only by Congress, not by treaty. See Chapter V, p. 159, and note 99.

37. For the suggestion that a person accused of crime in the United States has a constitutional right to trial by a judge enjoying the independence that comes with life tenure and assured compensation, see United States *ex rel.* Toth v. Quarles, 350 U.S. 11, 15–17 (1955); *Ex parte* Milligan, 4 Wall. 2, 121–22 (U.S.1866); compare the court-martial cases, Chapter III, note 42.

One of the grievances in the Declaration of Independence was that the King had "made Judges dependent on his Will alone, for the tenure of their offices, and the amount and payment of their salaries." Compare THE FEDERALIST No. 78 (Hamilton).

38.  To meet these objections, there have been suggestions that the United States agree instead to a system that provides trial in American courts with appeal to an international tribunal. That would raise questions as difficult as those it would eliminate. It would involve appeal from U.S. courts to a body other than the Supreme Court, p. 198 above. And if an appeal by the prosecution were permitted after an acquittal in a U.S. court, there would be a serious issue under the double jeopardy clause of the Fifth Amendment. United States v. Ball, 163 U.S. 662, 671 (1896); Peters v. Hobby, 349 U.S. 331, 344–45 (1955); Green v. United States, 355 U.S. 184, 188 (1957); *cf.* Kepner v. United States, 195 U.S. 100 (1914); United States v. Sanges, 144 U.S. 310 (1892); Benton v. Maryland, 395 U.S. 784 (1969); Price v. Georgia, 398 U.S. 323 (1970).

If trial by a U.S. court is constitutionally required, trial by an international court with appeal to a U.S. court might not satisfy the requirement, perhaps even if the U.S. court gave the accused a trial *de novo*. Compare Callan v. Wilson, 127 U.S. 540, 556–57 (1888); but *cf.* Crowell v. Benson, 285 U.S. 22 (1932), and Brandeis, J., dissenting *id.* at 86–87; Ng Fung Ho v. White, 259 U.S. 276, 283 (1922); Colten v. Kentucky, 407 U.S. 104 (1972).

For an unusual instance, in extraordinary circumstances, of a treaty providing judicial review in U.S. courts of determinations of an international body, see Abrey v. Reusch, 153 F.Supp. 337 (S.D.N.Y.1957).

39.  Indeed, foreign consuls have had the right to call upon officials and courts of the United States for assistance in arresting, interrogating, and imprisoning persons subject to their jurisdiction. See, *e. g.,* Convention Between the United States of America and Greece Defining the Rights, Privileges and Immunities of Consular Officers in the Two Countries, Nov. 19, 1902, arts. II, IX, XII, 33 Stat. 2122, T.S. No. 424; Consular Convention between the United States of America and Ireland, May 1, 1950, arts. 21–27, [1954] 5 U.S.T. 949, T.I.A.S. No. 2984; Consular Convention and Protocol Between the United States of America and the Union of Soviet Socialist Republics, June 1, 1964, art. 13(2), [1968] 19 U.S.T. 5018, T.I.A.S. No. 6503; and the enabling legislation in 22 U.S.C. §§ 256–58a (1970). 22 U.S.C. § 256 confers jurisdiction on a consul only where by treaty the nation he represents gives reciprocal rights to United States consuls in its territory. 22 U.S.C. § 258a provides for enforcement by federal courts or commissioners of consular awards and decrees in differences between captains and crews of the vessels of the nation the consul represents.

Lower federal courts have given effect to foreign consular jurisdiction: The Koenigin Luise, 184 F. 170 (D.N.J.1910) (denying court's jurisdiction of alien seaman's libel against vessel, because of exclusive jurisdiction of consul) ; but *cf.* The Neck, 138 F. 144 (W.D. Wash.1905) (refusing to dismiss suit for wages by United States citizen who had served as seaman under flag of country whose consul claimed exclusive jurisdiction under a treaty). See also Glass v. The Betsey, 3 Dall. 6 (U.S.1794) (implying that the United States has the power by treaty to permit foreign countries to establish courts in United States) ; *cf.* The Belgenland, 114 U.S. 355, 364 (1884).

40. North Atlantic Treaty Status of Forces Agreement, June 19, 1951, Art. VII, [1953] 4 U.S.T. 1792, T.I.A.S. No. 2846, 199 U.N.T.S. 67.

41. Service Courts of Friendly Foreign Forces Act, ch. 326, 58 Stat. 643 (1944), 22 U.S.C. §§ 701–706 (1970). The statute also authorized United States military officials to arrest members of the foreign forces at the request of their commanding officer.

42. While not involving criminal law, the disposition of claims of American citizens by international claims commissions affords some analogy. Although judicial or quasi-judicial in character, and deciding cases that might be decided by American courts, they are *ad hoc* tribunals of a special bi-national authority created by international agreement, and are exercising only its "judicial power." See, *e. g.,* Convention Between the United States of America and the Republic of Mexico for the Adjustment of Claims, July 4, 1868, art. II, 15 Stat. 679, 681–82, T.S. No. 212; Agreement Between the United States and Germany for a Mixed Commission, Aug. 10, 1922, 42 Stat. 2200, T.S. No. 665. Professor Hudson, writing in 1944, stated that the United States had participated in twenty-six such tribunals in the past one hundred years. M. HUDSON, INTERNATIONAL TRIBUNALS 196 (1944). There have been a number of them since.

Congress has also authorized international and foreign officials to act within this country and to use American courts and processes to support their activities. For example, the United States-Canadian International Joint Commission, under a treaty with Canada as implemented by Congress, is authorized to administer oaths and take evidence in the United States in proceedings within the Commission's jurisdiction. Treaty between the United States and Great Britain Relating to Boundary Waters Between the United States and Canada, Jan. 11, 1909, 36 Stat. 2448, T.S. No. 548, as implemented 22 U.S.C. § 268 (1970), and 22 C.F.R. §§ 401.1 (1972). By application to the United States court in the district within which the Commission is sitting, the Commission may compel the attendance of witnesses and the production of evidence and invoke the court's contempt power to insure compliance (FED.R.CIV.P. 45(f); 18 U.S.C. § 401 (1970)).

Congress has also given even broader authority to any international tribunal or commission to which the U. S. is party, considering a

442

claim in which the United States or any of its nationals is interested, to administer oaths under penalty of perjury and to require the attendance of witnesses and the production of evidence enforcible by contempt proceedings. Ch. 851, § 1, 46 Stat. 1005 (1930). Subsequent amendment permitted the United States agent before such tribunals to invoke the aid of a federal court to order witnesses to appear before the court for examination by the agent. Ch. 50, 48 Stat. 117 (1933). The legislation was repealed in 1964, Pub.L. 88–619, § 3, 78 Stat. 995 (1964), but federal district courts now may order testimony for use in a proceeding in a foreign or international tribunal. *Id.* at 997, 28 U.S.C. § 1782 (1970).

43. United States "services" to such tribunals would also seem acceptable, although constitutional difficulties might be further attenuated if convicted individuals were imprisoned in some international facility rather than in one under the authority of the United States. Seamen convicted by foreign consuls, note 39, this chapter, may be confined in United States prisons, 22 U.S.C. § 258 (1970). Compare also Art. VII, § 7(b) of the NATO Status of Forces Treaty, note 40, this chapter.

44. In Hirota v. MacArthur, 338 U.S. 197 (1948), the Supreme Court was asked to review on habeas corpus the constitutionality of the trial of several Japanese for "war crimes" before an international commission which the Allied military commander, who was also United States commander, had established on behalf of the Allied Powers. The Court held *per curiam* that the military tribunal was not a "tribunal of the United States" whose judgments could be subject to review by the Supreme Court or by other federal courts. Mr. Justice Douglas, concurring in the result, was of the opinion that there was no power of review because the military tribunal "was solely an instrument of political power" as to which the President, spokesman for the United States in its foreign affairs, had the final say. *Id.* at 199, 215.

Even if these arguments were accepted in principle, it is unlikely that the courts would tolerate any exercise in the United States of a foreign criminal jurisdiction that entailed violations of fundamental fairness or "shocked the conscience." Compare Chapter X.

NOTES, CHAPTER VIII, THE COURTS, pp. 205 to 224.

1. Marbury v. Madison, 1 Cranch 137 (U.S.1803); Cooper v. Aaron, 358 U.S. 1, 17–20 (1958). See Introduction, notes 5, 6.

It remains disputed whether the grant of power over "cases arising under the Constitution," and the declaration in the Supremacy Clause that the Constitution and the laws "in pursuance thereof" are law of the land, were intended as a grant to the courts of the power to declare acts of Congress unconstitutional, or whether the courts developed that power on their own. Compare, *e. g.*, Wechsler, *Toward Neutral Principles of Constitutional Law*, 73 HARV.L.REV. 1 (1959), and R. BERGER, CONGRESS v. THE SUPREME COURT cc. 7, 8 (1969), with L. HAND, THE BILL OF RIGHTS (1958), and 2 W. CROSSKEY, POLITICS AND THE CONSTITUTION IN THE HISTORY OF THE UNITED STATES c. XXVIII (1953).

2. Since *Erie R. R. v. Tompkins*, 304 U.S. 64 (1938), a federal court in a diversity of citizenship case applies the common law as "found" by the courts of the State in which it sits. See this chapter, notes 39, 65.

3. See Holmes, J., dissenting in Southern Pacific Co. v. Jensen, 244 U.S. 205, 218, 222 (1917): "Judges do and must legislate but they can only do so interstitially; they are confined from molar to molecular motions". Compare: "Congress acts . . . against the background of the total *corpus juris* of the states in much the same way that a state legislature acts against the background of the common law, assumed to govern unless changed by legislation." H. HART & H. WECHSLER, THE FEDERAL COURTS AND THE FEDERAL SYSTEM 435 (1953). See, generally, Hart, *The Relations Between State and Federal Law*, 54 COLUM.L.REV. 489 (1954). Federal courts, then, make law in the interstices of the interstices which federal law generally occupies in the American legal system.

4. See, *e. g.*, Henkin, *Some Reflections on Current Constitutional Controversy*, 109 U.PA.L.REV. 637, 650 *et seq.* (1961).

5. *Cf.* L. BOUDIN, GOVERNMENT BY JUDICIARY (1932).

6. Alexander Hamilton's phrase popularized by Professor Alexander Bickel, THE LEAST DANGEROUS BRANCH (1962).

7. The judicial power extends to cases arising under the Constitution, laws and treaties, no matter who the parties. Cases affecting foreign diplomats, and diversity cases to which a foreign state or an alien is party, can come to the federal courts regardless of the subject matter of the case. See Cohens v. Virginia, 6 Wheat. 264, 378 (U.S.1821).

Issues related to foreign affairs often come before state courts which interpret and apply federal statutes and review their constitutionality. State courts derive their jurisdiction from their own constitutions and laws and are not subject to the case or controversy requirement of the Federal Constitution, but must, of course, provide due process of law and other constitutional requirements applicable to the States. See Chapters IX and X. But a state proceeding that did not involve a case or controversy cannot be reviewed by the Supreme Court. Doremus v. Board of Education, 342 U.S. 429 (1952). Federal questions in state cases are subject to federal law and to review by the Supreme Court. 28 U.S.C. § 1257 (1970).

While the jurisdiction of state courts is governed by state law, Congress has also provided for the use of state courts to enforce federal regulatory acts. In earlier days States sometimes claimed the right to refuse, *e. g.*, United States v. Lathrop, 17 Johns. 4, 8 (N. Y. 1819). But the Supreme Court has since held that state courts of appropriate jurisdiction could not properly refuse a Congressional assignment. Testa v. Katt, 330 U.S. 386 (1947). Especially when federal courts were few and their jurisdiction not fully extended by Congress, Congress relied on States and state courts to punish offenses against the law of nations. See this chapter, note 67. For the role of state courts in federal matters see generally H. HART AND H. WECHSLER, THE FEDERAL COURTS AND THE FEDERAL SYSTEM (1953), especially at 391–99.

8. Since the Judiciary Act of 1789, ch. 20, § 13, 1 Stat. 73, 80–81, now, as amended, 28 U.S.C. § 1251 (1970). Generally, suits against an accredited diplomat are consistent with the law of nations only when his government waives immunity.

The lower federal courts can exercise only the jurisdiction which Congress grants them. Cary v. Curtis, 3 How. 236, 245 (U.S.1845); Sheldon v. Sill, 8 How. 441 (U.S.1850); also, Kline v. Burke Construction Co., 260 U.S. 226, 233–34 (1922). There is an old controversy as to whether Congress was obligated to confer on federal courts all the judicial power vested by Article III. Story's view that Congress was so obligated has not prevailed. Compare Martin v. Hunter's Lessee, 1 Wheat. 304, 328–32 (U.S.1816) (Story, J.), with Turner v. Bank of North-America, 4 Dall. 8, 10n. (U.S.1799) (Chase, J.).

While Congress cannot add to the original jurisdiction of the Supreme Court (Marbury v. Madison, 1 Cranch 137 (U.S. 1803)), or take any of it away, it can give to other federal courts concurrent jurisdiction of matters that are within the Supreme Court's original jurisdiction. Börs v. Preston, 111 U.S. 252 (1884); Ames v. Kansas, 111 U.S. 449, 469 (1884). Congress left exclusively to the Supreme Court only suits against Ambassadors, ministers, and their servants, but the lower federal courts have jurisdiction of suits by them, and others affecting them. See Judiciary Act of 1789, *supra*. (The Court will commonly decline to exercise original jurisdiction in cases in which lower federal courts are available. Compare, for example, Washington v. General Motors Corp., 406 U.S. 109 (1972); Illinois v. City of Milwaukee, 406 U.S. 91 (1972). Compare Massachusetts v. Missouri, 308 U.S. 1, 19 (1939), and Ohio v. Wyandotte Chemicals Corp., 401 U.S. 493 (1971), where the Court declined jurisdiction although no other federal tribunal was clearly available.) The Constitutional grant of original jurisdiction to the Supreme Court does not preclude suits against consuls in state courts. Popovici v. Agler, 280 U.S. 379, 383–84 (1930).

9. Muskrat v. United States, 219 U.S. 346 (1911); Massachusetts v. Mellon, 262 U.S. 447 (1923); Frothingham v. Mellon, 262 U.S. 447 (1923), as modified by Flast v. Cohen, 392 U.S. 83 (1968); Tileston v. Ullmann, 318 U.S. 44 (1943); Lampasas v. Bell, 180 U.S. 276 (1901); Braxton County Court v. West Virginia *ex rel.* Dillon, 208 U.S. 192 (1908). The vitality of some of these cases is now open to question. *Cf.* Griswold v. Connecticut, 381 U.S. 479 (1965).

10. The United States, also, cannot be sued without its consent. See Chisholm v. Georgia, 2 Dall. 419, 478 (U.S.1793); Cohens v. Virginia, 6 Wheat. 264, 412 (U.S.1821); cf. United States v. Lee, 106 U.S. 196 (1882). The President is personally immune to judicial jurisdiction. Mississippi v. Johnson, 4 Wall. 475 (U.S.1867). But a suit will lie to enjoin a lesser official on the ground that he is acting under an unconstitutional statute; that is deemed not a suit against the United States but rather against the official personally. Compare *Ex parte* Young, 209 U.S. 123 (1908).

11. The Justices refused to construe treaties and advise on other questions of international law arising out of the French wars. See 3 THE CORRESPONDENCE AND PUBLIC PAPERS OF JOHN JAY 486–89 (Johnston ed. 1890); See 1 C. WARREN, THE SUPREME COURT IN UNITED STATES HISTORY 110–111 (1922).

12. Massachusetts v. Mellon, 262 U.S. 447 (1923); *cf.* Massachusetts v. Laird, 400 U.S. 886 (1970), Chapter XI, p. 274; also Lee v. Humphrey, 352 U.S. 904 (1956) (denying motion of Governor of Utah for leave to file original proceeding to prevent expenditures for defense and foreign affairs). A State can sometimes test federal "usurpation" in upholding its own authority against private challenge. When Maryland convicted McCulloch of failing to pay a tax, he challenged the Maryland tax as inconsistent with an act of Congress, and Maryland defended its tax on the ground that the federal act was beyond the power of Congress. McCulloch v. Maryland, 4 Wheat. 316

(U.S.1819). Compare the various cases in which States resisted the asserted supremacy of a treaty, *e. g.*, Asakura v. Seattle, 265 U.S. 332 (1924), Chapter V, p. 166.

On the other hand the Court regularly monitors state encroachment on the federal domain, as in the commerce cases, Chapter IX, p. 234.

13. Compare Doremus v. Board of Education, 342 U.S. 429 (1952); also Frothingham v. Mellon, 262 U.S. 447 (1923), largely reaffirmed in Flast v. Cohen, 392 U.S. 83 (1968), note 9, this chapter, which, with small exception, bars taxpayer suits to challenge spending even on the ground that it is unconstitutional. Compare Sierra Club v. Morton, 405 U.S. 727 (1972).

14. He will usually allege that because the action is unconstitutional he is deprived of liberty or property without due process of law in violation of the Fifth Amendment. See, *e. g.*, Carter v. Carter Coal Co., 298 U.S. 238 (1936); Youngstown Sheet & Tube Co. v. Sawyer, 343 U.S. 579 (1952).

15. See this chapter, note 32.

16. See Chapter I, p. 26. It is fair to say that since that time the Court has invalidated only one act of Congress as beyond its powers, Oregon v. Mitchell, 400 U.S. 112 (1970) (voting for 18-year-olds in state elections); and only a few as infringing the Bill of Rights or other safeguards for individual rights, *e. g.*, Tot v. United States, 319 U.S. 463 (1943); United States v. Lovett, 328 U.S. 303 (1946); Trop v. Dulles, 356 U.S. 86 (1958); Schneider v. Rusk, 377 U.S. 163 (1964); Aptheker v. Secretary of State, 378 U.S. 500 (1964); Afroyim v. Rusk, 387 U.S. 253 (1967). Reid v. Covert, 354 U.S. 1 (1957), and related cases held that Congress cannot prescribe trial by court martial for those not in the military, Chapter III, note 42. While these cases speak in terms of the limits of the necessary and proper clause the Court was really protecting the right to a jury trial. See Chapter III, note 54.

17. Compare, *e. g.*, Missouri v. Holland, 252 U.S. 416 (1920), Chapter V. Persons accused of violating federal statutes have sometimes challenged federal authority, without success, *e. g.*, United States v. Arjona, 120 U.S. 479 (1887) (conviction for counterfeiting foreign currency), Chapter III, p. 73. And compare the Commerce Power cases, Chapter III.

18. See 28 U.S.C. §§ 1254, 1257 (1970). Compare the Vietnam cases this chapter, note 32. The Court also exercises discretion as to whether to entertain original suits. See notes 8 and 12, this chapter. Even as to cases on appeal, which in principle are entitled to review as of right, the Supreme Court has developed doctrines and procedures for giving them short shrift, as by dismissing for want of a sub-

stantial federal question. Zucht v. King, 260 U.S. 174 (1922); U.S. Sup.Ct. Rule 15(e). Unlike denials of certiorari, however, such dismissals decide the federal issue. But *cf.* Poe v. Ullman, 367 U.S. 497 (1961).

The appellate jurisdiction of the Supreme Court is subject to comprehensive Congressional control. At least that seems to be the import of *Ex parte* McCardle, 7 Wall. 506 (U.S.1869); but *cf.* United States v. Klein, 13 Wall. 128 (U.S.1871). While *McCardle* is cited in Glidden Co. v. Zdanok, 370 U.S. 530, 567, 605 (1962), at least Mr. Justice Douglas, dissenting, suggested that the case would not be followed today and that the power of Congress to make exceptions and regulations for the appellate jurisdiction of the Supreme Court (Art. III, sec. 2, cl. 2) might yet be limited. For the view that the clause was intended to give Congress only very limited authority, see R. BERGER, CONGRESS v. THE SUPREME COURT 285–96 (1969); Ratner, *Congressional Power Over the Appellate Jurisdiction of the Supreme Court*, 109 U.PA.L.REV. 157 (1960). Compare Hart, *The Power of Congress to Limit the Jurisdiction of Federal Courts: An Exercise in Dialectic*, 66 HARV.L.REV. 1362 (1953), with Wechsler, *The Courts and The Constitution*, 65 COLUM.L.REV. 1001 (1965).

19. See, *e. g.*, the travel and passport cases Chapter X, p. 257. That courts will construe a statute to avoid declaring it unconstitutional, even to avoid a serious constitutional question, see Crowell v. Benson, 285 U.S. 22, 62 (1932). For a list of "canons" developed by the Supreme Court to avoid invalidating Acts of Congress, see Mr. Justice Brandeis concurring in Ashwander v. Tennessee Valley Authority, 297 U.S. 288, 346–48 (1936). A more "activist" Supreme Court in recent years seemed far less loath, and indeed some Justices seemed to consider it their duty to reach and decide constitutional issues. *Cf.* Douglas, J., concurring in Flast v. Cohen, 392 U.S. 83, 107 (1968); Fortas, J., *id.* at 115–16; and Brennan, J., concurring in Abington School Dist. v. Schempp, 374 U.S. 203, 230, 266–67 n. 30 (1963). And *cf.* the dissenting Justices in the Vietnam cases this chapter, note 32.

20. I draw here on my comment, *Vietnam in the Courts of the United States: "Political Questions,"* 63 AM.J.INT'L L. 284 (1969). For a recent general discussion see Scharpf, *Judicial Review and the Political Question: A Functional Analysis*, 75 YALE L.J. 517 (1966). See also Nathanson, *The Supreme Court as a Unit of the National Government: Herein of Separation of Powers and Political Questions*, 6 J.PUBLIC L. 331 (1957). For earlier discussions see Finkelstein, *Judicial Self-Limitation*, 37 HARV.L.REV. 338 (1924); C. POST, THE SUPREME COURT AND POLITICAL QUESTIONS (1936).

21. Compare, *e. g.*, Wechsler, *Toward Neutral Principles of Constitutional Law*, 73 HARV.L.REV. 1, 9 (1959), with Bickel, *The Supreme*

*Court, 1960 Term—Foreword: The Passive Virtues,* 75 HARV.L. REV. 40, 46 (1961). Later (at p. 75) Bickel says:

> . . . Such is the basis of the political-question doctrine: the court's sense of lack of capacity, compounded in unequal parts of the strangeness of the issue and the suspicion that it will have to yield more often and more substantially to expediency than to principle; the sheer momentousness of it, which unbalances judgment and prevents one from subsuming the normal calculations of probabilities; the anxiety not so much that judicial judgment will be ignored, as that perhaps it should be, but won't; finally and in sum ("in a mature democracy"), the inner vulnerability of an institution which is electorally irresponsible and has no earth to draw strength from.

22.  See his dissent in Baker v. Carr, 369 U.S. 186, 266, 267 (1962); compare his opinion in Colegrove v. Green, 328 U.S. 549 (1946).

23.  369 U.S. 186 (1962).

24.  369 U.S. at 210.

25.  Compare Wechsler, this chapter, note 21. So, for example, the Court will not hear that there has been a failure to carry out the constitutional obligation that "The United States shall guarantee to every State in this Union a Republican Form of Government" (Art. IV, Sec. 4). Luther v. Borden, 7 How. 1 (U.S.1849); the discussion in *Baker* v. *Carr* seems to reaffirm that case. The courts would probably refuse to review a judgment of impeachment since the Constitution provides that "The Senate shall have the sole Power to try all Impeachments." (Art. 1, Sec. 3). Clearly the Court would not review impeachment proceedings on a simple writ of error; I doubt that the Court would consider even claims that a particular impeachment proceeding denied due process.

26.  The courts have often used words like "political question" in this very different sense and context, in all kinds of cases. They have said, for example, that their concern is only whether the political branches of government, federal or state, have exceeded constitutional limitations; as long as they act within their Constitutional powers, the desirability or wisdom of what they do is a "political question" which is not for the courts to consider. Such statements imply no special doctrine of judicial abstention; in that sense there are political questions in virtually every case, whenever a court reads and applies the Constitution or an act of Congress.

Marshall was speaking of such political questions in Marbury v. Madison, 1 Cranch 137, 165–66 (1803):

> By the constitution of the United States, the president is invested with certain important political powers, in the exer-

cise of which he is to use his own discretion, and is accountable only to his country in his political character, and to his own conscience. To aid him in the performance of these duties, he is authorized to appoint certain officers, who act by his authority, and in conformity with his orders. In such cases, their acts are his acts; and whatever opinion may be entertained of the manner in which executive discretion may be used, still there exists, and can exist, no power to control that discretion. The subjects are political: they respect the nation, not individual rights, and being entrusted to the executive, the decision of the executive is conclusive. The application of this remark will be perceived, by adverting to the act of congress for establishing the department of foreign affairs. This officer, as his duties were prescribed by that act, is to conform precisely to the will of the president: he is the mere organ by whom that will is communicated. The acts of such an officer, as an officer, can never be examinable by the courts.

\* \* \*

The conclusion from this reasoning is, that where the heads of departments are the political or confidential agents of the executive, merely to execute the will of the president, or rather to act in cases in which the executive possesses a constitutional or legal discretion, nothing can be more perfectly clear, than that their acts are only politically examinable. . . .

*Baker* v. *Carr* does not seem to recognize the distinction I stress. See, *e. g.*, 369 U.S. at 211 n. 31, where the Court cites an example of "sweeping statements to the effect that all questions touching foreign relations are political questions." The example reads: "The conduct of the foreign relations of our Government is committed by the Constitution to the Executive and Legislative—'the political'— Departments of the Government, and the propriety of what may be done in the exercise of this political power is not subject to judicial inquiry or decision." Oetjen v. Central Leather Co., 246 U.S. 297, 302 (1918). But if, as is probable, "propriety" there did not mean constitutionality, the statement is unexceptionable and commonplace: so long as the political branches are acting within their constitutional powers, "wisdom," "desirability," "propriety," are not for the courts to review.

27. See, *e. g.*, Williams v. Suffolk Ins. Co., 13 Pet. 415, 420 (U.S. 1839):

And can there be any doubt, that when the executive branch of the government, which is charged with our foreign relations, shall, in its correspondence with a foreign nation, assume a fact in regard to the sovereignty of any island or country, it is conclusive on the judicial department? And in this view it is not material to inquire, nor is it the province of the court to determine, whether the executive be right or wrong. It is enough to know, that in the exercise of his constitutional functions, he had decided the question. Having done this, under the responsibilities which belong to him, it is obligatory on the people and government of the Union.

See also Jones v. United States, 137 U.S. 202, 212 (1890): "Who is the sovereign, *de jure* or *de facto,* of a territory is not a judicial, but a political question, the determination of which by the legislative and executive departments of any government conclusively binds the judges . . . ." *Cf.* Cordova v. Grant, 248 U.S. 413 (1919); Foster & Elam v. Neilson, 2 Pet. 253, 306, 309 (U.S.1829); Garcia v. Lee, 12 Pet. 511 (U.S.1838); Kennett v. Chambers, 14 How. 38, 50–51 (U.S.1852).

28. Rose v. Himely, 4 Cranch 241, 272 (U.S.1808); Gelston v. Hoyt, 3 Wheat. 246, 322 (U.S.1818); United States v. Palmer, 3 Wheat. 610, 634–35 (U.S.1818); Guaranty Trust Co. v. United States, 304 U.S. 126, 137–38 (1938); *cf.* Terlinden v. Ames, 184 U.S. 270 (1902); Oetjen v. Central Leather Co., 246 U.S. 297 (1918). See Chapter II, p. 47. Compare RESTATEMENT § 111, Reporters' Note no. 1; 7 Op.ATT'Y GEN. 186, 217 (1855). In the Federal Reserve Act of 1941, 12 U.S.C. § 632 (1970), Congress provided that a certificate of the Secretary of State that a foreign government is recognized is binding on the bank.

Similarly, it is a political question only in this sense when the courts say that how the United States shall respond to a breach of international law or treaty by another state is not for the courts to decide. See Chapter V, p. 170 and this chapter, p. 224. In the sovereign immunity and Act of State cases, too, Chapter II, p. 57, the courts are not abstaining but are giving effect to "legislation" by the President or Congress. See note 45, this Chapter.

29. The Court was not saying anything different in cases like Chicago & Southern Air Lines v. Waterman S. S. Corp., 333 U.S. 103, 111–14 (1948):

. . . But even if courts could require full disclosure, the very nature of executive decisions as to foreign policy is political, not judicial. Such decisions are wholly confided by our Constitution to the political departments of the government, Executive and Legislative. They are delicate, complex, and involve large elements of prophecy. They are and should be undertaken only by those directly responsible to the people whose welfare they advance or imperil. They are decisions of a kind for which the Judiciary has neither aptitude, facilities nor responsibility and which has long been held to belong in the domain of political power not subject to judicial intrusion or inquiry.

Compare also: "It is pertinent to observe that any policy towards aliens is vitally and intricately interwoven with contemporaneous policies in regard to the conduct of foreign relations, the war power, and the maintenance of a republican form of government. Such matters are so exclusively entrusted to the political branches of government as to be largely immune from judicial inquiry or interference." Mr. Justice Jackson in Harisiades v. Shaughnessy, 342 U.S. 580, 588–89 (1952).

See also United States v. Curtiss-Wright Export Corp., 299 U.S. 304, 319–21 (1936). In that case, the Court held that an action by the President pursuant to delegation by Congress was amply within their powers; it did not say that the constitutional validity of the action could not be examined.

Whether the Court would hear claims that in reaching such foreign decisions the President violated some general prohibition in the Constitution—*e. g.*, that he denied due process of law—is a different question and one to which the Court has not addressed itself. Refusal to do so would require something closer to what I call a strict "political question" doctrine, although the doctrine might well contemplate abstention as to some constitutional claims, not others. Compare Gomillion v. Lightfoot, 364 U.S. 339 (1960).

30. International Treaty Providing For the Renunciation of War, 46 Stat. 2343 [1929–1931]; UN Charter, article 2(4), Chapter VII, note 4.

31. See Chapter V, p. 171, Chapter VI, p. 188. This issue, then, raises a political question only in my second sense—a question within the constitutional powers of the political branches to decide.

In Mitchell v. United States, 369 F.2d 323 (2d Cir. 1966), *cert. denied,* 386 U.S. 972 (1967), the petitioner apparently argued that the war was a violation of international law, and that he would be guilty of an offense because the Nuremberg Charter imposed individual responsibility for waging a war of aggression and denied the defense of "superior orders." In dissenting from the denial of certiorari Justice Douglas urged that the Court should decide, *inter alia,* whether the question as to waging of aggressive war is justiciable and whether the Nuremberg Charter was a defense.

32. *E. g.*, Luftig v. McNamara, 373 F.2d 664 (D.C.Cir.), *cert. denied,* 387 U.S. 945 (1967); Mora v. McNamara, 387 F.2d 862 (D.C.

Cir.), *cert. denied,* 389 U.S. 934 (1967). (Stewart and Douglas, JJ., dissented in opinions urging that the justiciability of the constitutional issues, and other questions, be decided). Compare Orlando v. Laird, 443 F.2d 1039 (2d Cir. 1971), *cert. denied,* 404 U.S. 869 (1971), Douglas and Brennan, JJ., dissenting; also Da Costa v. Laird, 448 F.2d 1368 (2d Cir. 1971), *cert. denied,* 405 U.S. 979 (1972).

33. Without apparent hesitation the Court decided that President Truman exceeded his constitutional powers (and invaded those of Congress) when he seized the steel mills. Youngstown Sheet & Tube Co. v. Sawyer, 343 U.S. 579 (1952). The Court also decided that the President usurped Congressional powers in other cases, Chapter IV, p. 96. For other cases where the court considered separation of powers issues, compare Myers v. United States, 272 U.S. 52 (1926); United States v. Klein, 13 Wall. 128 (U.S.1871).

34. In several instances the Supreme Court found that in establishing a federal regulatory system Congress had in effect directed the courts to supply federal common law for the interstices, as in regard to bankruptcy; or even to develop a body of law, *e. g.,* to govern labor relations within the framework of federal labor laws, or to protect uniquely federal interests that should not be subject to the vagaries and diversities of the different laws of the different states. Textile Workers Union of America v. Lincoln Mills, 353 U.S. 448 (1957); United States v. Standard Oil Co., 332 U.S. 301, 308 (1947); Clearfield Trust Co. v. United States, 318 U.S. 363 (1943); D'Oench, Duhme & Co. v. F.D.I.C., 315 U.S. 447, 469 (1942); compare Illinois v. City of Milwaukee, 406 U.S. 91 (1972). It seems unlikely that the Court would find constitutional obstacles to such delegations. But *cf.* Hill, *The Law-Making Power of the Federal Courts: Constitutional Preemption,* 67 COLUM.L.REV. 1024, 1030 n. 33 (1967).

The Supreme Court has also found that the Constitution itself implies power for the federal courts to make law—to maintain and develop the judge-made maritime law inherited from England, or to govern relationships between States in regard to boundary disputes, respective water rights, or other quasi-"international" issues of the kind that come for original adjudication before the Supreme Court. See, *e. g.,* Southern Pac. Co. v. Jensen, 244 U.S. 205 (1917); Connecticut v. Massachusetts, 282 U.S. 660 (1931); Hinderlider v. La Plata River Co., 304 U.S. 92 (1938); Texas v. New Jersey, 379 U.S. 674 (1965). *Cf.* West Virginia *ex rel.* Dyer v. Sims, 341 U.S. 22, 28 (1951) (construction of interstate compact). And see the *Sabbatino* case discussed this chapter. In developing law for cases between States the Court has sometimes looked to the common law; see, *e. g.,* Missouri v. Illinois, 180 U.S. 208, 243–48 (1901). See Note, *What*

*Rule of Decision Should Control in Interstate Controversies?*, 21
HARV.L.REV. 132 (1907).

Ultimately of course all that federal courts do derives authority
from the Constitution which conceived them and ordained their power,
and from the Congress which created them and fixed their jurisdiction (within constitutional limits). One might argue, then, that the
federal courts have some law-making authority inherent in their judicial character, that the laws so made are supported by the Constitution and Congress, perhaps, too, that they are supreme to state
law. But what explicit law-making is inherent in the judicial function is hardly agreed. Surely, it does not include the power to make
law on any subject within their jurisdiction. Compare *Erie R. R.
v. Tompkins*, 304 U.S. 64 (1938), denying that power for cases of
diversity jurisdictions, note 39, this chapter. And compare the cases
that held there is no common-law criminal jurisdiction in the federal
courts. United States v. Hudson & Goodwin, 7 Cranch 32 (U.S.1812),
Chapter V, note 99.

See, generally, Hill, *supra*. But *cf.* Note, *The Federal Common
Law*, 82 HARV.L.REV. 1512 (1969). While Hill took a broad view of
the law-making power of the federal courts, he might have taken an
even broader view after the Supreme Court decided Zschernig v.
Miller, 389 U.S. 429 (1968), Chapter IX, holding that the Constitution bars the States from "intruding" on foreign relations even when
the political branches have not acted. Compare Hill at 1056–57.

35. Except insofar as Congress expressly left to the courts the determination and application of "the law of nations." See, *e. g.*, United
States v. Smith, 5 Wheat. 153, 160–62 (U.S.1820); *Ex parte* Quirin,
317 U.S. 1, 27–28 (1942), Chapter III, note 21.

36. See, *e. g.*, Southern Pac. Co. v. Jensen, 244 U.S. 205 (1917);
Romero v. International Terminal Operating Co., 358 U.S. 354, 360–61
(1959); G. GILMORE & C. BLACK, THE LAW OF ADMIRALTY 40–46,
374–86 (1957). Indeed, the power of Congress to legislate on maritime
matters has been inferred from the grant of judicial power to the
courts. See Chapter III, p. 77. Other law made by the courts on
authority inferred from constitutional grants of jurisdiction might
also have relevance for foreign affairs, for example the law to be applied in original suits in the Supreme Court and the law of construing
compacts. See this chapter, note 34.

37. The exact meaning and constitutional status of international
comity are uncertain. The Supreme Court has said that comity is
"neither a matter of absolute obligation, on the one hand, nor of mere
courtesy and good will, upon the other." Hilton v. Guyot, 159 U.S.
113, 163–64 (1895), quoted in Banco Nacional de Cuba v. Sabbatino,
376 U.S. 398, 409 (1964). For the constitutional status of comity in

the past compare with Hilton v. Guyot, *supra*, Cowans v. Ticonderoga Pulp & Paper Co., 219 App.Div. 120, 219 N.Y.S. 284, *aff'd mem.*, 246 N.Y. 603, 159 N.E. 669 (1927); *cf.* Vladikavkazsky Ry. v. New York Trust Co., 263 N.Y. 369, 378, 189 N.E. 456, 460 (1934); also Johnston v. Compagnie Générale Transatlantique, 242 N.Y. 381, 152 N.E. 121 (1926). See the following note. See Henkin, *The Foreign Affairs Power of the Federal Courts: Sabbatino,* 64 COLUM.L.REV. 805, 820 n. 49 (1964).

38. See, *e. g.*, Johnston v. Compagnie Générale Transatlantique, 242 N.Y. 381, 152 N.E. 121 (1926), which chose not to follow the rule laid down by the Supreme Court in Hilton v. Guyot, 159 U.S. 113 (1895), that, with some exceptions, foreign judgments should be executed only on the basis of reciprocity. But see this chapter, note 47, and p. 219.

39. For a hundred years, federal courts applied the common law, as they saw and developed it, in suits between citizens of different states, which can come to the federal courts even if they involve no federal question. Art. III, sec. 2; Swift v. Tyson, 16 Pet. 1 (U.S. 1842). That case was overruled in Erie R. R. v. Tompkins, 304 U.S. 64 (1938), which held that in diversity of citizenship cases a federal court must apply the common law as determined by the courts of the State in which it sits. On the early application of the *Erie* doctrine to customary international law, see this chapter, p. 223. As regards its application to issues of the conflict of laws and the effect to be given to foreign judgments, see this chapter, note 47.

40. Banco Nacional de Cuba v. Sabbatino, 376 U.S. 398 (1964), discussed also in Chapter II, p. 62.

41. The District Court granted summary judgment for the Defendant principally because the Cuban Government had not granted prompt, adequate and effective compensation. 193 F.Supp. 375 (S.D. N.Y.1961) (alternative holding). The Court of Appeals affirmed, finding a violation of international law in particular in that the nationalization was not for a proper public purpose and was designed to retaliate and discriminate against the United States and its citizens. 307 F.2d 845 (2d Cir. 1962).

42. 376 U.S. at 421, 423–25.

43. See Chapter II, p. 60 and note 71.

44. Justice Harlan seemed to find the power in the fact that foreign relations are "intrinsically federal" and that the Judiciary is a separate, independent branch. Neither of these facts nor both combined, however, necessarily require or support an independent legislative power in the courts. Harlan's reference to the intrinsically federal character of foreign relations perhaps echoes *Curtiss-Wright,* but that case did not tell us how the inherent sovereign powers of the United States are distributed among the branches; if it be deemed

to imply a "judicial foreign affairs power" it hardly suggests that the courts must have legislative power in regard to foreign affairs. With Henkin, *The Foreign Affair Power of the Federal Courts: Sabbatino*, 64 COLUM.L.REV. at 814–19 (1964), compare Hill, this chapter, note 34 at 1062–67.

45.  376 U.S. at 426.  Despite superficial similarities, Act of State (under *Sabbatino*) differs fundamentally from the sovereign immunity cases, Chapter II, p. 57.  Here the court declares national policy where international law is assumed to be silent; in the immunity cases the court recognizes the authority of the Executive to make national policy regardless of international law.  The consequences are also different: immunity results in dismissing the proceeding and preventing judicial determination; Act of State is a rule of law applied to reach a substantive decision in the case.  These distinctions were blurred by both Mr. Justice Rehnquist and Mr. Justice Brennan in First National City Bank v. Banco Nacional de Cuba, 406 U.S. 759, 760, 776 (1972), Chapter II, p. 62.

46.  376 U.S. at 426.  Justice Harlan went out of his way to establish this power in the federal courts, and Act of State as supreme federal law; as he recognized, New York law apparently also accepted the doctrine, and the result in the case could have been reached as well under state law.  See 376 U.S. at 424–25.

Sabbatino did not purport to deny the States the power to make similar law where there was no federal law, or where the State law was not inconsistent with federal law, or where the federal law did not reveal a purpose to exclude the States.  (Compare the preemption doctrine, Chapter IX.)  Justice Harlan said expressly that the Constitution does not require the Act of State doctrine, apparently even of the States.  But compare Zschernig v. Miller, 389 U.S. 429 (1968), Chapter IX, p. 238, barring a state inheritance law as an intrusion into foreign affairs.  In *Zschernig*, the Supreme Court was not making federal law about alien inheritance; the States were held excluded not by federal judge-made law but by the Constitution itself.

47.  Compare Cheatham, *Federal Control of Conflict of Laws*, 6 VAND.L.REV. 581 n. 2 (1953), citing Clark v. Allen, 331 U.S. 503 (1947), and the *Johnston* case this chapter, note 38, with Reese, *The Status in this Country of Judgments Rendered Abroad*, 50 COLUM.L. REV. 783, 786–88 (1950), and Note, *Application by Federal Courts of State Rules on Conflict of Laws*, 41 COLUM.L.REV. 1403, 1405–09 (1941).  Strong argument for broad federal judicial power and supremacy, particularly on matters like respect for foreign judgments, is made by Moore, *Federalism and Foreign Relations*, 1965 DUKE L.J. 248, 262–63; compare Hill, note 34 this chapter, at 1044–46 (1967).  In my view Congress could legislate on these matters under

its foreign affairs power (Chapter III, p. 74) and the President can make treaties about them (Chapter V, note 87); in the absence of political action, the federal courts, under *Sabbatino*, can also make law and make it binding on the States as well. See Henkin, *The Foreign Affairs Power of the Federal Courts:* Sabbatino, 64 COLUM. L.REV. 805, 820–21, n. 51 (1964). See generally Friendly, *In Praise of Erie—and of the New Federal Common Law*, 39 N.Y.U.L.REV. 383 (1964); Hill, *supra*.

The federal courts could presumably also promote other forms of judicial cooperation with foreign courts; and perhaps, like Congress, they can even impose new duties on the state courts consistent with their jurisdiction. *Cf.* Testa v. Katt, 330 U.S. 386 (1947).

*Sabbatino* suggests that the standing of foreign governments to sue in American courts, even in state courts, is a question of national policy, implying, I believe, that the States must follow rules made by the federal courts, perhaps also by the Executive. 376 U.S. at 408. Compare Hill, *supra*, at 1068.

48. Federal common law is supreme if one reads "the Laws of the United States" in the Supremacy Clause (Art. VI, sec. 2) as including federal judge-made law. For the federal courts to have jurisdiction of cases raising such issues one would have to find also that they are cases "arising under this Constitution" or under "the Laws of the United States." Article III, sec. 2. The Supreme Court would have jurisdiction to review state cases refusing supremacy to federal judge-made law if in these cases the validity of a State statute can be said to be drawn into question on the ground of its being "repugnant to the Constitution" (*i. e.*, the Supremacy Clause) or repugnant to "laws of the United States." 28 U.S.C. § 1257(2), (3) (1970). There is authority to support such jurisdiction. Compare Hinderlider v. La Plata River Co., 304 U.S. 92, 110 (1938); compare also Illinois v. City of Milwaukee, 406 U.S. 91 (1972) (interpreting similar language in 28 U.S.C. § 1331(a), for purposes of district court jurisdiction). Compare Hill, note 34, this chapter at 1073–79; Note, *Federal Common Law and Article III, A Jurisdictional Approach to Erie*, 74 YALE L.J. 325 (1964); Hart, *The Relations between State and Federal Law*, 54 COLUM.L.REV. 489, 500 (1954).

49. 376 U.S. at 423.

50. *Ibid.* Act of State itself has uncertainties which courts might feel less than confident to resolve in the light of foreign policy needs. Compare Henkin, *Sabbatino*, note 47, this chapter, at 826–30 (1964).

51. Act of State itself is essentially a special rule of conflicts denying the state of the forum its usual freedom to assert its own public policies and refuse to apply the law of the state where a transaction "occurred." See Henkin, *id.* at 808–10 (1964). Compare Mr.

Justice Rehnquist in First National City Bank v. Banco Nacional de Cuba, 406 U.S. 759, 768 (1972).

52. A broad judicial foreign affairs power is supported by Hill, this chapter, note 34, and an even broader one, apparently, by Moore, *Federalism and Foreign Relations*, 1965 DUKE L.J. 248, but how broad is not clear.

53. See Chapter II, note 71.

54. It is suggested, even, that judicial legislative power exists only to the extent of federal political power, and the authority of political branches to supersede the courts follows. Hill, note 34, this chapter, at 1046–56 (1967).

55. See the Second Hickenlooper Amendment, 22 U.S.C. 2370(e), (2) (1970), upheld and applied in the aftermath of *Sabbatino* itself: Banco Nacional de Cuba v. Farr, 243 F.Supp. 957, 966, 972 (S.D.N.Y. 1965), *aff'd*, 383 F.2d 166 (2d Cir. 1967), *cert. denied*, 390 U.S. 956 (1968), *rehearing denied* 390 U.S. 1037 (1968). I have never seen much substance in the arguments that Congress could not modify the judicial doctrine. See Henkin, *Act of State Today: Recollections in Tranquility*, 6 COLUM.J.TRANSNATIONAL L. 175, 177–78 (1967); but *cf.* Cardozo, *Congress Versus Sabbatino: Constitutional Considerations*, 4 COLUM.J.TRANSNATIONAL L. 297 (1966); R. FALK, THE AFTERMATH OF SABBATINO (1965).

The Hickenlooper Amendment apparently directs the courts not to apply the Act of State doctrine to expropriations for which prompt, adequate and effective compensation is not provided, unless the President certifies that the doctrine is nonetheless required by the foreign relations of the United States. By this statute, incidentally, Congress seems to have given legislative approval to the Act of State doctrine generally, rendering it no longer dependent on judicial legislation alone. Compare the effort of the State department to go beyond the Hickenlooper Amendment and assert additional exceptions, Chapter II, p. 62.

56. See Henkin, *Sabbatino*, note 47 this chapter, at 826–28.

57. Compare, Chapter VI, p. 187. See generally R. FALK, THE ROLE OF DOMESTIC COURTS IN THE INTERNATIONAL LEGAL ORDER (1964).

58. No doubt American judges followed their British ancestors who had earlier said that the law of nations was part of the law of England. See, *e. g.*, Lord Mansfield in Triquet and Others v. Bath, 97 Eng.Rep. 936, 938, 3 Burr. 1478 (K.B.1764). Numerous statements speak of the law of nations as being part of the common law received in the United States from England, *e. g.*, Iredell, J., in Talbot v. Jansen, 3 Dall. 133, 161 (U.S.1795). See generally, Sprout, *Theories as to the Applicability of International Law in the Federal Courts of*

*the United States*, 26 AM.J.INT'L L. 280 (1932). Compare Hill, note 34 this chapter, at 1042 *et seq.*

59. 175 U.S. 677, 700 (1900).

Before the Constitution, the Continental Congress recognized the force of international law and in 1779 it resolved that the United States would cause the "law of nations to be strictly observed." 14 J.CONT. CONG. 635. In 1781 it recommended that the States adopt laws to punish offenses against that law, 21 J.CONT.CONG. 1136–37.

Since the Constitution, Congress has implemented obligations under international law by statute: see, *e. g.*, WRIGHT 179–86 for various old statutes punishing offenses against foreign governments or persons protected by international law, or those committed on the high seas, or violations of neutrality laws or international boundaries or treaties. International law is sometimes incorporated by reference in federal law. See, *e. g.*, Act of April 10, 1806, ch. 20, § 2, 2 Stat. 359, 371; Act of March 3, 1819, ch. 76, § 5, 3 Stat. 510, 513–14; for a more recent example see 18 U.S.C. § 1651 (1970). See also WRIGHT 179–83. Compare United States v. Repentigny, 5 Wall. 211 (U.S.1866); United States v. Smith, 5 Wheat. 153 (U.S.1820); *Ex parte* Quirin, 317 U.S. 1 (1942).

Since 1789 the federal courts have had jurisdiction "where an alien sues for a tort only in violation of the law of nations or a treaty of the United States." 1 Stat. 73, 77 (1789), as amended, 28 U.S.C. § 1350 (1970). This grant was independent of the diversity jurisdiction of the federal courts and suggests that the first Congress took the view that the law of nations was part of the laws of the United States (not of the States) for purposes of Article III. See Note, *Federal Common Law and Article III: A Jurisdictional Approach to Erie*, 74 YALE L.J. 325, 335–37 (1965). See this chapter, p. 223. In a number of instances Congress has left it to the state courts to enforce sanctions for violations of international law, even after it had enacted laws to punish such offenses. Thus, once, at least, it was assumed that treason and sedition against a foreign government might be punished by the States. See 2 MOORE, DIGEST 432. Perhaps that would now be an impermissible intrusion in foreign relations under *Zschernig v. Miller*, Chapter IX, p. 238.

Even without a statute some States treated violations of international law as violations of state law: *e. g.*, in 1784, in Respublica v. De Longchamps, 1 Dall. 111, a Philadelphia court found the accused guilty of assault on the Secretary of the French legation, "a crime against the whole world." (*Id.* at 116.) States can continue to enforce international law unless barred by federal law. Compare Fox v. Ohio, 5 How. 410, 417 (U.S.1847); see p. 223 above. Compare Washington's first neutrality proclamation of April 22, 1793, in which

459

he announced that he had given instructions to prosecute persons who violate the law of nations, 11 Stat. 753 (App.1859). It is now established, however, that the federal courts can punish violations only pursuant to statute. See United States v. Hudson & Goodwin, 7 Cranch 32 (U.S.1812). Compare Chapter V, p. 159.

60. *E. g.*, Berizzi Bros. Co. v. S. S. Pesaro, 271 U.S. 562 (1926), Chapter II, p. 57. See also, The Nereide, 9 Cranch 388 (U.S.1815); The Exchange v. M'Faddon, 7 Cranch 116 (U.S.1812).

61. Compare Chapter V, p. 171, Chapter VI, p. 187. In *The Paquete Habana* Justice Gray said: "This rule of international law is one which prize courts, administering the law of nations, are bound to take judicial notice of, and to give effect to, *in the absence of any treaty or other public act of their own government in relation to the matter.*" (Emphasis added.) 175 U.S. at 708. The Court also said that it will look to customary law "where there is no treaty, and no controlling executive or legislative act or judicial decision." 175 U.S. at 700. Earlier, Chief Justice Marshall said: "Till such an act [of Congress] be passed, the Court is bound by the law of nations which is part of the law of the land." The Nereide, 9 Cranch 388, 423 (U.S.1815). The Supreme Court in effect also so held when it applied acts of Congress inconsistent with treaty obligations (Chapter V, p. 163 *supra*), since violation of a treaty is essentially a violation of the principle of customary international law requiring that treaties be observed. But "an Act of Congress ought never to be construed to violate the law of nations, if any other possible construction remains." Marshall, C. J., in Murray v. The Charming Betsey, 2 Cranch 64, 118 (U.S.1804).

There are no clear Supreme Court holdings, or even explicit dicta, upholding the power of the President to act contrary to international law, but the principle is, I believe, the same. Compare the "political question" cases, p. 213 above. Justice Story once suggested that the law of nations limits Presidential discretion in time of war:

> He has a discretion vested in him, as to the manner and extent; but he cannot lawfully transcend the rules of warfare established among civilized nations. He cannot lawfully exercise powers or authorize proceedings which the civilized world repudiates and disclaims.

Brown v. United States, 8 Cranch 110, 153 (U.S.1814). Perhaps by "lawfully" Story meant only "under international law." Chief Justice Marshall in that case recognized the sovereign power to violate that law:

> [U]sage [of the law of nations] is a guide which the sovereign follows or abandons at his will. The rule, like other precepts of morality, of humanity, and even of wisdom, is

addressed to the judgment of the sovereign; and although it cannot be disregarded by him, without obloquy, yet it may be disregarded.

*Id.* at 128. Compare the power of the President to denounce or terminate treaties even in violation of their terms, or to act under other Constitutional power inconsistently with treaty obligations. Chapter V, p. 167. See Tag v. Rogers, 267 F.2d 664 (App.D.C.1959), *cert. denied,* 362 U.S. 904 (1960); The Over the Top, 5 F.2d 838 (D.Conn. 1925).

62. As in *The Paquete Habana* itself, 175 U.S. 677 (1900).

63. See note 58 *supra.*

64. At one time the Supreme Court denied review of state determinations of customary international law on the ground that they did not raise federal questions. New York Life Ins. Co. v. Hendren, 92 U.S. 286 (1875); Oliver American Trading Co. v. Mexico, 264 U.S. 440 (1924); Wulfsohn v. Russian Socialist Federated Soviet Republic, 266 U.S. 580 (1924) *(semble), per curiam dismissing a writ of error for want of jurisdiction,* 234 N.Y. 372, 138 N.E. 24 (1923), *rev'g* 202 App.Div. 421, 195 N.Y.S. 472 (1922), *aff'g* 118 Misc. 28, 192 N.Y.S. 282 (1922). Compare Wright: "A state constitution or legislative provision in violation of customary international law is valid unless in conflict with a Federal constitutional provision or an act of Congress as would usually be the case." WRIGHT 161.

As regards international "comity," international conflicts of laws, and related subjects see notes 37, 38 and 47, this chapter.

65. Erie R. R. v. Tompkins, 304 U.S. 64 (1938), this chapter note 39. The *Erie* doctrine, however, applies to questions of local law: on federal questions, federal courts, like state courts, must apply federal law, including federal law made by the federal courts. See Friendly, *In Praise of* Erie—*And of the New Federal Common Law,* 39 N.Y.U.L.REV. 383 (1964); Hill, *supra* note 34.

In Bergman v. De Sieyes, 170 F.2d 360 (2d Cir. 1948), Judge Learned Hand held that in cases based on diversity of citizenship, the state courts' interpretation of international law is binding on the federal courts. However, he did not consider whether an avowed refusal to accept a well-established doctrine of international law or a plain misapprehension of it would also be binding on the federal court. Perhaps Judge Hand felt bound by the cases holding that international law did not raise a federal question, note 64. Perhaps he thought that if a question of international law was sufficiently uncertain there was obviously no uniform or federal view and until one was achieved it was important that the parties to a particular case should not be able to achieve a different result by "forum shopping," by going to a federal rather than a state court.

66.  There is confusion, too, as to the obligation of the courts to follow the Executive on questions of customary international law. See Hill, note 34 this chapter, at 1051–54.  See also Note, *The Relationship Between Executive and Judiciary: The State Department as the Supreme Court of International Law*, 53 MINN.L.REV. 389 (1968). It would seem that the courts ought to follow the Executive at least when he has taken an international position on an issue of international law not only for the obvious practical reasons but because the practices and policies of executives, including our own, are major ingredients of customary international law, and Executive statements on international law make foreign policy and are legislative in some measure.  Compare:

> When articulating principles of international law in its relations with other states, the Executive Branch speaks not only as an interpreter of generally accepted and traditional rules, as would the courts, but also as an advocate of standards it believes desirable for the community of nations and protective of national concerns.

Banco Nacional de Cuba v. Sabbatino, 376 U.S. 398, 432–33 (1964). See also Hill, *supra*, at 1046–49, 1057–59.

67.  In *Sabbatino* Mr. Justice Harlan said:

> [W]e are constrained to make it clear that an issue concerned with a basic choice regarding the competence and function of the Judiciary and the National Executive in ordering our relationships with other members of the international community must be treated exclusively as an aspect of federal law.  It seems fair to assume that the Court did not have rules like the act of state doctrine in mind when it decided *Erie R. Co. v. Tompkins*.  Soon thereafter, Professor Philip C. Jessup, now a judge of the International Court of Justice, recognized the potential dangers were *Erie* extended to legal problems affecting international relations.  .  .  .  He cautioned that rules of international law should not be left to divergent and perhaps parochial state interpretations.

Banco Nacional de Cuba v. Sabbatino, 376 U.S. 398, 425 (1964).  See Hill, *supra* note 58, at 1042–59; Henkin, note 64 this chapter, at 820–21 n. 51.  For earlier suggestions to similar effect, see Jessup, *The Doctrine of Erie Railroad v. Tompkins Applied to International Law*, 33 AM.J.INT'L L. 740, 742–43 (1939).  See Bradley, J., dissenting in New York Life Ins. Co. v. Hendren, 92 U.S. 286, 287–88, note 64, this chapter.  In Chisholm v. Georgia, 2 Dall. 419, 474 (U.S.1793) Chief Justice Jay said that the "United States were responsible to foreign nations for the conduct of each state, relative to the laws of nations, and the performance of treaties," that it would be inexpedient to leave such issues to state courts, particularly the courts of the delinquent state, and it was the proper responsibility of a national judiciary. That the Framers expected federal courts to enforce state court observance of the law of nations, see THE FEDERALIST NO. 3 (Jay) and No. 80 (Hamilton). See also, Dickinson, *The Law of Nations as Part of the National Law of the United States,* 101 U.PA.L. REV. 26, 792 (1952) especially at 34–46, 55–56; 1 W. CROSSKEY, POLITICS AND THE CONSTITUTION IN THE HISTORY OF THE UNITED STATES 651–52 (1953). Compare Note, *The Federal Common Law and Article III,* 74 YALE L.J. 325, 335–336 (1964).

It has been suggested also that principles of international conflicts of law also raise federal questions and those developed by the federal courts should be binding on the States. See Henkin, this note.

Compare the Supreme Court's holding that, even where the federal government has taken no relevant action, the States and their courts may not intrude in matters affecting the foreign relations of the United States. Zschernig v. Miller, 389 U.S. 429 (1968), Chapter IX.

68. See, *e. g., The Effect to be Given in the United States to Foreign Nationalization Decrees: Banco Nacional de Cuba v. Sabbatino,* 19 RECORD OF THE ASS'N OF THE BAR OF THE CITY OF N. Y., Report by the Committee on International Law, No. 1, at 12–14 (Supp., Jan. 1964). Compare the lower court opinion in *Sabbatino,* 193 F.Supp. 375, 381–82 (S.D.N.Y.1961). But *cf.* generally Henkin, *Act of State Today: Recollections in Tranquility,* 6 COLUM.J.TRANSNATIONAL L. 175, 181–82 (1967).

69. Compare Banco Nacional de Cuba v. Sabbatino, 376 U.S. 398, 423 (1964); Charlton v. Kelly, 229 U.S. 447, 474, 476 (1913), Chapter V, note 138. See Henkin, note 68, this chapter. That the courts of the United States will not apply international law to acts of foreign governments was held in *Sabbatino* and in other Act of State cases: Oetjen v. Central Leather Co., 246 U.S. 297, 304 (1918); Ricaud v. American Metal Co., 246 U.S. 304, 310 (1918); Shapleigh v. Mier, 299 U.S. 468, 471 (1937). Compare Williams v. Armroyd (The Fortitude), 7 Cranch 423, 432 (U.S.1813). See Dickinson, note 67 this chapter, at 44–45 and his discussion of THE FEDERALIST NO. 3 (Jay) and 80 (Hamilton).

70. As in the Second Hickenlooper Amendment, note 55, this chapter. See Henkin, note 68, at 181–85. Of course, the federal courts might themselves, perhaps, venture to legislate remedies under the authority to make law in foreign relations matters established in *Sabbatino.*

NOTES, CHAPTER IX, THE STATES, pp. 227 to 248.

1. Gibbons v. Ogden, 9 Wheat. 1, 228 (U.S.1824) (Johnson, J., concurring); Holmes v. Jennison, 14 Pet. 540, 575–76 (U.S.1840) (Taney, C. J.); United States v. Belmont, 301 U.S. 324, 331 (1937) (Sutherland, J.) Taney's opinion in *Holmes* v. *Jennison* includes an extensive denigration of the authority of the States in foreign affairs.

2. For example: "For local interests the several States of the Union exist; but for national purposes, embracing our relations with foreign nations, we are but one people, one nation, one power." The Chinese Exclusion Case, 130 U.S. 581, 606 (1889). And United States v. Pink: "Power over external affairs is not shared by the States; it is vested in the national government exclusively". 315 U.S. 203, 233 (1942). Compare Marshall, C. J., in Cohens v. Virginia, 6 Wheat. 264, 413–14 (U.S.1821). Compare also Calhoun: "In our relation to the rest of the world . . . the States disappear," quoted in Chapter V, note 49.

The need for national control and the dangers of state interference in foreign affairs are emphasized in several of the Federalist papers, notably Nos. 3, 4, 5, 42, and 80. In No. 42 Madison said, "If we are to be one nation in any respect, it clearly ought to be in respect to other nations."

Even the Constitution of the Confederate States during the Civil War retained virtually the same limitations on the States in regard to foreign relations that are in the United States Constitution. See The Constitution of the Confederate States, March 11, 1861, Art. I, sec. 10, quoted 1 BUTLER, THE TREATY POWER 229–31 n.

3. United States v. Curtiss-Wright Export Corp., 299 U.S. 304 (1936), quoted in Chapter I, pp. 19–20.

4. Brown v. Maryland, 12 Wheat. 419 (U.S.1827); Hooven & Allison Co. v. Evatt, 324 U.S. 652 (1945); *cf.* Youngstown Sheet & Tube Co. v. Bowers, 358 U.S. 534 (1959); Dept. of Revenue v. James Beam Distilling Co., 377 U.S. 341 (1964). See Note, *State Taxation of Imports—When Does an Import Cease to be an Import?*, 58 HARV.L.REV. 858 (1945).

5. Empresa Siderurgica v. Merced County, 337 U.S. 154 (1949); Joy Oil Co. v. State Tax Commission, 337 U.S. 286 (1949); *cf.* Richfield Oil Corp. v. State Board, 329 U.S. 69 (1946).

6. Consent to state agreements can probably also be given by treaty. Compare Art. IX of the 1899 Treaty with Mexico under which some States would extradite directly to Mexico. 31 Stat. 1818, 1824–25 (1899), T.S. 242. (That extradition inevitably involves "agreement," see pp. 231–32, this chapter).

464

In 1839, the Secretary of State agreed with the British minister to leave the regulation of issues in disputed territory to the State of Maine and the Province of New Brunswick, pending the final settlement of the boundary dispute. See CRANDALL, TREATIES 113.

7. But compare the State Department's communication, note 27, this chapter.

8. Taney insisted on the distinction between treaties and agreements but appears to suggest that the difference is formal: "For when we speak of 'a treaty,' we mean an instrument written and executed with the formalities customary among nations . . . ." Holmes v. Jennison, 14 Pet. 540, 571 (U.S.1840). Formality might indeed be a sufficient reason for excluding the States since it implies international sovereignty and involves the States in diplomatic intercourse and negotiation. Taney further suggests, quoting Vattel, that a principal difference between treaties and compacts is that the former are "for perpetuity, or for a considerable time". *Id.* at 572.

9. See 2 STORY, COMMENTARIES § 1402. He adds:
Perhaps the language of the former clause may be more plausibly interpreted from the terms used, "treaty, alliance, or confederation" and upon the ground, that the sense of each is best known by its association (*noscitur a sociis*) to apply to treaties of a political character; such as treaties of alliance for purposes of peace and war; and treaties of confederation, in which the parties are leagued for mutual government, political cooperation, and the exercise of political sovereignty; and treaties of cession of sovereignty, or conferring internal political jurisdiction, or external political dependence, or general commercial privileges. The latter clause, "compacts and agreements," might then very properly apply to such as regarded what might be deemed mere private rights of sovereignty; such as questions of boundary; interests in land situate in the territory of each other; and other internal regulations for the mutual comfort and convenience of States bordering on each other. . . . In such cases, the consent of Congress may be properly required, in order to check any infringement of the rights of the national government; and, at the same time, a total prohibition to enter into any compact or agreement might be attended with permanent inconvenience or public mischief. *Id.* at § 1403.

Frankfurter and Landis expressed a different view: "There is no self-executing test differentiating 'compact' from 'treaty.' Story and other writers have attempted an analytical classification. . . . The attempt is bound to go shipwreck for we are in a field in which political judgment is, to say the least, one of the important factors."

They conclude that it must be left to Congress "to circumscribe the area of agreement open to the States." Frankfurter and Landis, *The Compact Clause of the Constitution—A Study In Interstate Adjustments,* 34 YALE L.J. 685, 695 n. 37 (1925). Compare Naujoks, *Compacts and Agreements Between States and Between States and a Foreign Power,* 36 MARQUETTE L.REV. 219, 231–33 (1952).

10. Especially since Congress has acquired the equivalent of a treaty-making authority through Congressional-Executive agreements, Chapter VI, p. 173. Compare F. ZIMMERMAN & M. WENDELL, *The Interstate Compact Since 1925* 74, 75 (1951).

11. See ch. 758, 70 Stat. 701 (1956), repealed, Pub.L.No. 85–145, 71 Stat. 367 (1957), but the repealing statute gave consent to an agreement providing for the continued existence of the Buffalo and Fort Erie Public Bridge Authority. These and similar grants of consent contain clauses expressly reserving the right of Congress to amend, alter or repeal the authorization.

12. 72 Stat. 1701 (1958).

13. Ch. 246, 63 Stat. 271 (1949), ch. 267, 66 Stat. 71 (1952).

14. Federal Civil Defense Act of 1950, ch. 1228, § 203, 64 Stat. 1251 (1951), 50 U.S.C.App. § 2283 (1970). (The functions of the Civil Defense Administrator have since been transferred to the President.)

15. Ch. 201, 68 Stat. 92 (1954), 33 U.S.C. §§ 981 *et seq.* (1970).

16. ". . . we do not perceive any difference in the meaning, except that the word 'compact' is generally used with reference to more formal and serious engagements than is usually implied in the term 'agreement' . . . ." Mr. Justice Field in Virginia v. Tennessee, 148 U.S. 503, 520 (1893).

The law of compacts is meager and virtually all of it has been developed in regard to interstate compacts; the law of foreign compacts would probably be the same in many respects but the foreign element and the relevance to American foreign relations might sometimes suggest a difference. In regard to interstate compacts, the court held that the consent of Congress need not be given in advance or in any particular form, and can even be implied. See *id.* at 517, 521; Virginia v. West Virginia, 11 Wall. 39 (U.S.1871); Wharton v. Wise, 153 U.S. 155, 172–73 (1894); Green v. Biddle, 8 Wheat. 1, 85–87 (U.S.1823); Poole v. Fleeger, 11 Pet. 185, 209 (U.S.1837). And the consent of Congress may be conditional. *Cf.* James v. Dravo Contracting Co., 302 U.S. 134 (1937). Congress has authority to compel compliance with such compacts. Virginia v. West Virginia, 246 U.S. 565, 601 (1918).

The classic discussion of the compact clause (again, principally, in regard to interstate compacts) is Frankfurter and Landis, this chapter, note 9. See also ZIMMERMAN & WENDELL, this chapter, note 10; Dunbar, *Interstate Compacts and Congressional Consent,* 36 VA. L.REV. 753 (1950); Weinfield, *What Did the Framers of the Federal Constitution Mean by 'Agreements or Compacts?,'* 3 U.CHI.L.REV. 453 (1936).

"The compact . . . adapts to our Union of sovereign States the age-old treaty-making power of independent sovereign nations." Hinderlider v. La Plata River Co., 304 U.S. 92, 104 (1938). In colonial days boundary disputes were usually settled by negotiation, their agreement subject to approval of the Crown. See Frankfurter and Landis, *supra* at 692. Under the Articles of Confederation boundary disputes between States were to be appealed to the Congress. Article IX.

17. 14 Pet. 540 (U.S.1840).

18. After the writ of error was dismissed, the Supreme Court of Judicature of the State of Vermont discharged Holmes. "The judges of that court were satisfied, on an examination of the opinions delivered by the justices of the supreme court, that by a majority of the court it was held, that the power claimed to deliver up George Holmes did not exist." Reporter's Note, 14 Pet. at 598.

19. 14 Pet. at 572–74. Taney's conclusion that Governor Jennison had entered into an agreement that was invalid for want of Congressional consent was an alternative ground of decision, probably in an effort to base it on an express constitutional prohibition. He went on to find also that because the power to extradite was granted to the federal government it was denied to the States. See this chapter, note 44.

The Taney position that a State may not extradite to a foreign country was later adopted in dictum in United States v. Rauscher, 119 U.S. 407, 414 (1886).

20. 14 Pet. at 596.

21. Justice Thompson seemed to admit that the Governor had no authority to act as he did, but found that the Supreme Court nevertheless had no jurisdiction. *Id.* at 579–81.

22. Taney found indeed that it was apparently the policy of the United States not to extradite persons to foreign governments and state extradition would be inconsistent with that policy. *Id.* at 574.

23. Virginia v. Tennessee, 148 U.S. 503, 519 (1893). The Court held that preliminary arrangements to ascertain and adjust the boundary between the two States did not constitute an agreement requiring Congressional consent. Later agreement to accept the boundary probably required consent if it effected important change since it increased the political power of the enlarged State, but the Court found

such consent in that Congress had acted on the new boundaries. *Id.* at 521–22.

24. A number of unpublicized agreements are reported in Rodgers, *The Capacity of States of The Union to Conclude International Agreements: The Background and Some Recent Developments*, 61 AM.J.INT'L L. 1021, 1025–27 (1967). He describes, *inter alia*, proposals for a Mexican-Gulf South Association, to include Mexico and six States of the United States, to promote education, commerce and tourism, and a proposed cultural agreement between Louisiana and Quebec (which later came to fruition in 1970. See Rodgers, *Conclusion of Quebec-Louisiana Agreement on Cultural Co-operation*, 64 AM.J.INT'L L. 380 (1970)).

McHenry County v. Brady, 37 N.D. 59, 163 N.W. 540 (1917), upheld an arrangement whereby a county in North Dakota constructed a drainage ditch in cooperation with a Canadian town. The state court held that it did not require the consent of Congress since it did not increase the "political power" of the State.

25. Perhaps authority for these is deemed to be implied in the Agreement Between the United States of America and the United Nations Regarding the Headquarters of the United Nations, June 26, 1947, 61 Stat. 3416, T.I.A.S. No. 1676; the agreement was authorized by Congress, ch. 482, 61 Stat. 756 (1947). See Chapter V, note 32.

26. See 14 MAINE REV.STAT.ANN. § 6352 (1965); N.J.STAT.ANN. 2A:41A (Supp.1971); 12 PA.STAT.ANN. § 591 (Supp.1971); N.Y. SESS.LAWS ch. 237 (McKinney 1962).

27. In some instances State authorities have sought the advice of the State Department. In 1936, the Legal Adviser of the State Department informed the Director of the Department of Motor Vehicles of California that an arrangement with its counterpart across the Mexican border for reciprocal exemption of motor vehicles from registration and fees would require the consent of Congress and might infringe the Treaty Power. In regard to a proposed compact for the promotion of trade between Florida and Cuba, the State Department wrote in 1937 that the "Department's policy in regard to promotion of commerce with foreign countries and the negotiation of commercial treaties does not contemplate the conclusion of special agreements or pacts between separate states and foreign governments even if the consent of Congress to such special agreements could be obtained." 5 HACKWORTH, DIGEST OF INTERNATIONAL LAW 25 (1943).

28. Surely clauses that give Congress power to legislate in regard to national courts, national armed forces, the national capital, deny such power to the States. Other grants of power to Congress have also been held to exclude the States. A State cannot naturalize or denaturalize persons. See Chirac v. Chirac, 2 Wheat. 259, 269 (U.S.1817). (But a state court held that a State may grant the right to vote to resi-

dent aliens who have declared their intention to become citizens. See Spragins v. Houghton, 3 Ill. 377 (1840).) The States are not forbidden to define and punish piracies and offenses against the law of nations, especially if international law be deemed part of the common law of the State (Chapter VIII, p. 222). Congress, in fact, left many offenses to be punished by the State. See this chapter, note 63. The States can have bankruptcy laws if Congress does not act. Sturges v. Crowninshield, 4 Wheat. 122, 195–97 (U.S.1819); Ogden v. Saunders, 12 Wheat. 213, 368–69 (U.S.1827). A state may also punish the issuance of counterfeit coins. Fox v. Ohio, 5 How. 410 (U.S.1847). And in the absence of federal legislation a state might regulate patent rights. *Cf.* Allen v. Riley, 203 U.S. 347 (1906).

29. The principal case establishing the doctrine was Cooley v. Board of Wardens of the Port of Philadelphia, 12 How. 299 (U.S.1851). Compare Southern Pacific Co. v. Arizona, 325 U.S. 761 (1945), and H. P. Hood & Sons v. Du Mond, 336 U.S. 525 (1949).

It has been suggested that it was not the Constitution itself that denied powers to the States in regard to interstate or foreign commerce, but Congress, whether by action or inaction. On this view, when the Supreme Court concluded that a state burden on commerce was forbidden it was deciding that Congressional silence in that instance implied a prohibition, while in other cases Congressional silence implied that the States were free to act. Doctrines like *Cooley* and the others, then, were guides to interpreting Congressional silence. The suggestion was inspired, no doubt, by a desire to find a basis for a prohibition on the States in an affirmative grant to Congress, even more, to justify holding the grant to Congress "concurrent" with state power in some cases, exclusive in others; it would also help explain how Congress could authorize the States to do what they could not do if Congress were silent (this chapter, p. 237). See Dowling, *Interstate Commerce and State Power*, 27 VA.L.REV. 1 (1940), cited in Southern Pacific Co. v. Arizona, *supra*, at 768. See also Dowling, *Interstate Commerce and State Power—Revised Version*, 47 COLUM.L.REV. 547 (1947). *Cf.* Field, J., concurring in Bowman v. Chicago and Northwestern Ry. Co., 125 U.S. 465, 507–508 (1888). The difficulties with the suggestion are obvious. *Cf.* T. R. POWELL, VAGARIES AND VARIETY IN CONSTITUTIONAL INTERPRETATION 161–64 (1956). And the courts have found prohibitions on the States implied in other affirmative grants to Congress. See this chapter, note 28.

The Twenty-first Amendment substantially relieved the States of the prohibitions of the Commerce Clause (and other provisions of the Constitution) as regards intoxicating liquors. State Board v. Young's Market Co., 299 U.S. 59 (1936); Mahoney v. Triner Corp., 304 U.S. 401 (1938); Indianapolis Brewing Co. v. Liquor Control Commission,

305 U.S. 391 (1939). But *cf.* Collins v. Yosemite Park & Curry Co., 304 U.S. 518 (1938). The Amendment did not, however, repeal the Export-Import Clause and the "original package" doctrine as regards liquor. Dept. of Revenue v. James Beam Distilling Co., 377 U.S. 341 (1964); *cf.* Hostetter v. Idlewild Bon Voyage Liquor Corp., 377 U.S. 324 (1964).

30. In our time, as earlier, some Justices have continued to insist that the Commerce Clause implies no limitation on the States and they can regulate commerce unless Congress says that they shall not, either directly or by enacting its own regulations which supersede inconsistent state laws. Compare Chief Justice Taney in the License Cases, 5 How. 504, 573 (U.S.1847); Mr. Justice Black dissenting in Southern Pacific Co. v. Arizona, 325 U.S. 761, 784 (1945). Mr. Justice Douglas urged that the Commerce Clause itself forbids only state discrimination against interstate or foreign commerce, *id.* at 795; McCarroll v. Dixie Greyhound Lines, Inc., 309 U.S. 176, 183–89 (1940). The Court, however, has never accepted these views, perhaps because it considered that the inertia of government made it unlikely that Congress could consider and overcome all the obstructions to interstate commerce. "The practical result is that in default of action by us [the States] will go on suffocating and retarding and Balkanizing American commerce, trade and industry." Mr. Justice Jackson concurring in Duckworth v. Arkansas, 314 U.S. 390, 400 (1941). Even Black and Douglas joined in striking down a state regulation inconsistent with that of other states and thus creating burdens on interstate traffic. Bibb v. Navajo Freight Lines, Inc., 359 U.S. 520 (1959), this chapter, note 39.

31. The judicial applications of the Commerce Clause against the States were no doubt large in the mind of Mr. Justice Holmes when he said: "I do not think the United States would come to an end if we lost our power to declare an act of Congress void. I do think the Union would be imperiled if we could not make that declaration as to the law of the several States." O. W. Holmes, *Law and the Court,* in Collected Legal Papers, 291, 295–96 (1920).

32. *E. g.,* Willson v. Black-Bird Creek Marsh Co., 2 Pet. 245 (U.S. 1829). But the Supreme Court sometimes seemed to decide what the States cannot do by asking what Congress can; and it denied power to Congress to do what it could not bring itself to forbid to the States. It sowed confusion in deciding cases exploring the reach of Congressional power by citing cases on the limits of state power, and vice versa. Strange distinctions were drawn between what is "commerce" and what is not, what is a regulation of commerce and what merely an exercise of "police power" affecting commerce, which led to other strange distinctions, *e. g.,* between direct and indirect burdens on

commerce. Most of this, happily, is history. Stern, *The Commerce Clause and the National Economy, 1933–1946,* 59 HARV.L.REV. 645, 883 (1946).

33. Cooley v. Board of Wardens of the Port of Philadelphia, 12 How. 299, 319 (U.S.1851). The Court held that pilotage laws did not "admit only of one uniform system" and upheld the local law. In that case Congress had in fact adopted the pilotage laws of the States, but the Court assumed that if, had Congress been silent, these would have been forbidden by the Constitution, Congress could not "validate" them. *Id.* at 318. Now, we know, Congress can permit what would be forbidden if it were silent. See this chapter, p. 237.

34. Compare Carter v. Carter Coal Co., 298 U.S. 238, 307–308 (1936); Schechter Poultry Corp. v. United States, 295 U.S. 495, 546–47 (1935); also Heisler v. Thomas Colliery Co., 260 U.S. 245, 259–60 (1922); Kidd v. Pearson, 128 U.S. 1, 20–21 (1888).

35. Southern Pacific Co. v. Arizona, 325 U.S. 761, 768 (1945).

36. No doubt the Court has not been above including unarticulated factors in the balance, as when it found regulations that discriminated on account of race more burdensome to interstate or foreign commerce than those that forbade such discrimination. Compare Morgan v. Virginia, 328 U.S. 373 (1946), with Bob-Lo Excursion Co. v. Michigan, 333 U.S. 28 (1948).

In commerce cases there is little presumption of constitutionality and the "balancing" done by state legislatures is given little weight. But compare Black, J., dissenting in Southern Pacific Co. v. Arizona, 325 U.S. 761, 784 (1945).

37. Compare, for example, Southern Railway Co. v. King, 217 U.S. 524 (1910), with Seaboard Airline R.R. Co. v. Blackwell, 244 U.S. 310 (1917); H.P. Hood & Sons v. Du Mond, 336 U.S. 525 (1949), with Frankfurter's dissenting opinion there, at 564.

38. See Mr. Justice Cardozo in Baldwin v. G.A.F. Seelig, Inc., 294 U.S. 511, 523 (1935):

> . . . Economic welfare is always related to health . . . . Let such an exception be admitted, and all that a state will have to do in times of stress and strain is to say that its farmers and merchants and workmen must be protected against competition from without, lest they go upon the poor relief lists or perish altogether. . . . . The Constitution was framed under the dominion of a political philosophy less parochial in range. It was framed upon the theory that the peoples of the several states must sink or swim together, and that in the long run prosperity and salvation are in union and not division.

Compare Mr. Justice Brandeis in Buck v. Kuykendall, 267 U.S. 307 (1925). Also, H. P. Hood & Sons v. Du Mond, 336 U.S. 525 (1949).

That overt discrimination against foreign or interstate commerce is barred by the Constitution even when Congress has not acted is now accepted by all, even, *e. g.,* Mr. Justice Douglas in Southern Pacific Co. v. Arizona, 325 U.S. 761, 795 (1945). See this chapter, note 30.

In recent years, the Court has increasingly tolerated local regulation "which does not discriminate against interstate commerce or operate to disrupt its required uniformity." Huron Portland Cement Co. v. City of Detroit, 362 U.S. 440 (1960); see also Brotherhood of Locomotive Firemen v. Chicago, R.I. & P.R.R. Co., 393 U.S. 129 (1968).

The States may, however, exclude foreign corporations and require them to incorporate in the state. See Lafayette Ins. Co. v. French, 18 How. 404, 407 (U.S.1856); Atlantic Refining Co. v. Virginia, 302 U.S. 22, 26 (1937); Hemphill v. Orloff, 277 U.S. 537, 548 (1928); Asbury Hospital v. Cass County, 326 U.S. 207, 211–12 (1945). But *cf.* Western Union Tel. Co. v. Kansas, 216 U.S. 1 (1910); Terral v. Burke Construction Co., 257 U.S. 529, 532–33 (1922). Alien corporations stand no better and States have in fact required that corporate directors or even large shareholders be American citizens. Compare FLA.GEN.CORP.LAW § 608.09(1), ch. 717, § 27, [1951] NEW YORK LAWS, 174th Sess. 1670, *as amended,* NEW YORK SESSION LAWS, ch. 803, § 25 (McKinney 1965).

39. The Court struck down a city ordinance of Madison, Wisconsin, that forbade the sale of milk unless pasteurized within five miles of the city, because it considered that reasonable alternatives were available which would protect local health without discriminating against out-of-state milk. Dean Milk Co. v. City of Madison, 340 U.S. 349 (1951). In Bibb v. Navajo Freight Lines, Inc., 359 U.S. 520 (1959), the Court invalidated an Illinois regulation requiring that trucks using its highways employ a particular mudguard different from one required by other States, because it was not shown that its safety advantages warranted the heavy burden on companies whose trucks traveled in many States.

40. Perhaps *a fortiori,* and perhaps the limitations on the States would be more stringent in regard to foreign commerce. Compare Chapter III, note 9; the additional limitations on the States in regard to foreign commerce, *e. g.,* the "original package" doctrine, this chapter, p. 229, and *Zschernig v. Miller,* this chapter, p. 238.

Some of the cases that define what the Commerce Clause required of the States in fact involved foreign commerce. *E. g.,* City of New York v. Miln, 11 Pet. 102 (U.S.1837), and The Passenger Cases, 7 How. 283 (U.S.1849), *distinguished in* Henderson v. Mayor of New York, 92 U.S. 259 (1876); The License Cases, 5 How. 504 (U.S.1847);

*Notes, Chapter IX*

Chy Lung v. Freeman, 92 U.S. 275 (1875); New York *ex rel.* Silz v. Hesterberg, 211 U.S. 31 (1908); Sanitary District v. United States, 266 U.S. 405 (1925); Bayside Fish Flour Co. v. Gentry, 297 U.S. 422 (1936); Kelly v. Washington, 302 U.S. 1 (1937); Hale v. Bimco Trading, Inc., 306 U.S. 375 (1939); Huron Portland Cement Co. v. City of Detroit, 362 U.S. 440 (1960).

41. The Court has struck down taxes on "the interstate transaction itself," Freeman v. Hewit, 329 U.S. 249 (1946); taxes that obviously discriminate against interstate or foreign commerce; and even those that seem "neutral" but weigh particularly on out-of-state commerce, for example a tax on "drummers" as applied to companies that engage in no other local activity in the State. Robbins v. Shelby County Taxing District, 120 U.S. 489 (1887). But it has permitted States to select subjects for taxation in ways that might entail hidden discrimination against out-of-state goods, as when a dairy state decides to tax margarine. States have substantial lee-way as to types and rates of tax including formulae for apportioning the local part of a complex interstate or international enterprise; and, increasingly, the Court finds some local incident of an interstate or foreign transaction to support a state tax so that interstate or foreign commerce would "pay its way". See, generally, Brown, *The Open Economy: Justice Frankfurter and the Position of the Judiciary*, 67 YALE L.J. 219 (1957), and P. HARTMAN, STATE TAXATION OF INTERSTATE COMMERCE (1953). Congress has commissioned studies of the field but good reports have not yet produced comprehensive overhauling. See SUBCOM. OF THE HOUSE COMM. ON THE JUDICIARY, STATE TAXATION OF INTERSTATE COMMERCE, H.R.REP. NO. 565, 89th Cong., 1st Sess. (1965).

42. While the Constitution is read to protect interstate and foreign commerce against multiple taxation by several States, presumably it would not be held to bar state taxation merely because the object is also subject to tax by one or more foreign governments.

For taxes invalidated as burdens on foreign commerce, see, *e. g.*, McGoldrick v. Gulf Oil Corp., 309 U.S. 414 (1939); Joseph v. Carter & Weekes Co., 330 U.S. 422 (1947). Usually a state tax burdening foreign commerce is invalidated under the Import or Export Clauses, see notes 4 and 5 this chapter.

43. See Leisy v. Hardin, 135 U.S. 100 (1890). Congress could also regulate in support of state law, forbidding commerce into States that bar it. *In re* Rahrer, 140 U.S. 545 (1891). The Supreme Court, however, held that Congress could not similarly adopt state laws that would modify the maritime law. Knickerbocker Ice Co. v. Stewart, 253 U.S. 149 (1920); Washington v. W. C. Dawson & Co., 264 U.S. 219 (1924). Although never overruled it is unlikely that those cases still express constitutional limits on Congressional authority, since

the Court later allowed Congress to adopt state laws in other areas. Compare Davis v. Department of Labor and Industries, 317 U.S. 249 (1942); Prudential Insurance Co. v. Benjamin, 328 U.S. 408 (1946).

44. In *Holmes* v. *Jennison*, this chapter, p. 231, Taney suggested that, even when the Federal Government had not acted, the States were excluded from one kind of incursion into foreign relations, extradition to foreign countries. While for him the attempt by the Governor of Vermont to extradite Holmes was an "agreement" with Canada prohibited to the States unless Congress consented, he offered an alternative objection: extradition policy was entrusted to the federal government and concurrent jurisdiction in the States would be ". . . totally contradictory and repugnant to the power granted to the United States." (*Id.* at 574). That conclusion apparently reflected the view that in regard to extradition federal silence was itself a policy, that from "its nature," the power to extradite "can never be dormant in the hands of the general government." (*Id.* at 576). Extradition, moreover, inevitably involved communication with a foreign government and it "was one of the main objects of the Constitution . . . to cut off all communications between foreign governments, and the several state authorities." (*Id.* at 575–76). Whether there were other matters which were exclusively federal, as to which federal silence barred the States, he did not say; but he did not appear to be suggesting a general principle that even when the political branches had not acted the States could not adopt laws or perform other acts of local government that impinge on the foreign relations of the United States. Taney indeed denied that the Commerce Power, even, implied any prohibitions on the States if Congress had not acted. See his opinion in The License Cases, 5 How. 504, 573 (U.S. 1847).

In 1941, the Supreme Court said: "And whether or not registration of aliens is of such a nature that the Constitution permits only of one uniform national system, it cannot be denied that the Congress might validly conclude that such uniformity is desirable." Hines v. Davidowitz, 312 U.S. 52, 73 (1941), discussed p. 243, above. That statement might be read to imply that there may be matters forbidden to the States even when Congress is silent, because a "uniform national system" is required, echoing the Cooley Doctrine as to implied prohibitions on state regulation of commerce, p. 235, above. But in *Hines* Congress had acted, and the question was whether Pennsylvania's alien registration system could coexist with the federal system, not whether the State could register aliens if Congress did not register them. The Court expressly left open the contention that " . . . the federal power in this field, whether exercised or unexercised, is exclusive." *Id.* at 62. Compare also the language quoted in this chapter, note 61.

45. But *cf.* Chapter VIII, note 47. To date at least, the federal Act of State doctrine has not been applied in the circumstances cited. Compare Henkin, *The Foreign Affairs Power of the Federal Courts;* Sabbatino, 64 COLUMB.L.REV. 805, 826–830 (1964).

There is the possibility for state impingement on foreign relations also in that a state can regulate the conduct of its citizens on the high seas. See Skiriotes v. Florida, 313 U.S. 69 (1941) ; *cf.* The Hamilton, 207 U.S. 398 (1907) ; and a State has jurisdiction over its absent domiciliaries for purposes of a personal judgment. Milliken v. Meyer, 311 U.S. 457, 462 (1940).

46. Compare the debates that raged as to whether the United States could prevent New York courts from trying for murder Alexander McLeod, a British soldier who allegedly killed someone in the course of the *Caroline* incident. McLeod was acquitted by the New York courts but the question of state-federal power was never decided. For the whole story see 1 WHARTON, DIGEST OF INTERNATIONAL LAW, § 21, and 3 *id.* § 350 (1886).

Compare: The Department of State "does not believe that the States should decline to enact statutes concerning recognition of foreign judgments on the ground that the United States may at some future date become a party to the Hague Convention on the Recognition and Enforcement of Foreign Judgments." Letter from Ambassador Kearney to Professor Homburger, dated March 14, 1969, reprinted in 63 AM.J. INT'L L. 816–17 (1969).

One might suggest that when a State acts in a matter that affects foreign relations and could be regulated by the federal government, the State is making federal law, subject to later rejection or modification by federal authority. In a sense this is what happens when a state court decides issues of maritime law or international law (see Chapter VIII, p. 223) not previously decided by the federal courts, or newly interprets and applies a federal statute. Usually, however, it is assumed that the State merely presumes to apply state law and it can do so except to the extent that the Constitution bars it, as in some regulations of foreign commerce, or in some intrusions into foreign relations under the doctrine of *Zschernig v. Miller* discussed at pp. 238–41.

47. 331 U.S. 503 (1947). In Blythe v. Hinckley, 180 U.S. 333 (1901), it was argued that a California provision permitting aliens to inherit real property invaded the Treaty Power. The Court said: "If [the plaintiff] means that it has never heretofore been asserted, that in the absence of any treaty whatever upon the subject, the State had no right to pass a law in regard to the inheritance of property within its borders by an alien, counsel may be correct. The absence of such a claim is not so extraordinary as is the claim itself." *Id.* at 340. Referring to Blythe v. Hinckley, the Court in *Allen* said: "The

Court rejected the argument as being an extraordinary one. The objection to the present statute is equally far-fetched. . . . What California has done will have some incidental or indirect effect in foreign countries. But that is true of many state laws which none would claim cross the forbidden line." 331 U.S. at 517.

Five years before *Zschernig* the Court dismissed a substantially similar claim for want of a substantial federal question. Ioannou v. New York, 371 U.S. 30 (1962); *cf.* 391 U.S. 604 (1968).

48. 389 U.S. 429 (1968).

49. *Id.* at 434.

50. *Id.* at 432.

51. The Court did not build sturdy underpinnings for its constitutional doctrine or face substantial arguments against it. Critics might insist that even if the federal foreign relations power is largely extra-constitutional, inherent in sovereignty (Chapter I, p. 21), sovereignty implies nothing about the distribution of responsibility between nation and state in a federal system. What the Constitution says about foreign affairs also provides little basis for the Court's doctrine. Article I indeed forbids the States to make treaties and do other specified acts in foreign relations, but these, singly or together, do not support the general exclusion announced in *Zschernig*; and the prohibition to the States of some things might even imply that others are permitted. Nor is the *Zschernig* doctrine the natural inference from the expressed grants to the federal branches or from "the Constitution as a whole," for in other matters even explicit grant of power to the federal government does not necessarily foreclose state action where federal power has not been exercised. See this chapter, note 28. Nor is there support for *Zschernig* in the history of the Constitution in practice.

Perhaps the Court considered that sovereignty as it relates to foreign affairs implies exclusive, central control even in a federal system. Perhaps the majority thought that what the Constitution expressly forbade to the States in regard to foreign relations implied wider prohibitions as well. Perhaps it concluded that the power to conduct foreign relations (like the power to extradite for Taney, this chapter, note 44) "can never be dormant in the hands of the general government" and that its concurrent exercise by the States would be "totally contradictory and repugnant."

Perhaps, too, the Court was impressed by the Commerce Clause cases where in the absence of Congressional regulation the courts protect the national interest against what it considers undue invasion by the States. See this chapter, p. 234. But in those cases, the Court has felt, and Congress has agreed, that the courts should intervene because it could not be left to Congress to anticipate or deal with all the possible state encroachments on the national interest; and federal administrative agencies could not effectively do so in all cases. See note 30, this chapter. In foreign affairs, one might argue, the President is "in continuous session" and has full authority, and there are executive agencies, principally the State Department, expert and informed, which could consider whether a state action unduly interferes with foreign relations. Perhaps the Court was not prepared to reaffirm that the Department of State had constitutional authority to supersede state law. See Chapter II, pp. 56 *et seq.*

52. 389 U.S. at 433–436.

53. In *Sabbatino*, the Court had said that the Constitution itself did not require the Act of State doctrine and did not therefore forbid courts (either state or federal, presumably) to sit in judgment on the acts of foreign governments in regard to property in their own territory. See Chapter VIII, p. 218. Perhaps a State's legitimate interest in refusing to give effect to a foreign act of state is greater than Oregon's here, for while a State's interest in regulating inheritance is long recognized, and insistence on reciprocity may help some Oregon citizen obtain an inheritance, the other limitations in this case reflected a desire to attack communism—an element in foreign policy that might well be left to the national government. But the only authority cited by the Court is language in *Hines* v. *Davidowitz,* note 44, this chapter, where the Court invalidated (because Congress had acted in the matter) Pennsylvania's alien registration statute which involved no judgments or reflections on any foreign government, did not directly "intrude" on foreign relations, and had no apparent purpose of doing so.

On the other hand, as Justice Harlan, concurring in the result in *Zschernig* on other grounds, points out, States have been allowed to "sit in judgment" on foreign countries in other contexts. Under the Uniform Foreign Money-judgments Recognition Act, for example, a foreign judgment is not to be recognized if it "was rendered under a system which does not provide impartial tribunals or procedures compatible with the requirements of due process of law." Under the rules of the conflict-of-laws generally, "the tort law of a foreign country will not be applied if that country is shown to be 'uncivilized.'" 389 U.S. at 461–62.

Compare the Florida Territorial Waters Act which requires a license for aliens to fish in the State's territorial waters, but denies licenses to any vessels owned by a Communist state, to an alien Communist, or to other alien vessels "on the basis of reciprocity or retorsion" unless the State Department transmits a formal suggestion that the state of the vessel is a friendly ally or neutral. [1963] Fla. Laws, ch. 63–202, at 457, *as amended*, FLA.STAT.ANN. § 370.21(3)

(Supp.1971); see Moore, *Federalism and Foreign Relations,* (1965) DUKE L.J. 248, 311–19. A conviction under the statute was apparently affirmed. See *id.* at 312–13 and notes; 3 INT'L LEG. MAT. 317 (1964).

54. It has been suggested that all should turn on whether the purpose of the state regulation is to influence foreign relations. But while in some cases such a purpose is obvious often it is not, and in other contexts the Court has been reluctant to probe legislative purpose. Compare, *e. g.,* United States v. Kahriger, 345 U.S. 22 (1953), *overruled on other grounds.* Marchetti v. United States, 390 U.S. 39 (1968).

Some believe that the Court may already have limited the promise of *Zschernig* when it affirmed *per curiam* in Gorun v. Fall, 393 U.S. 398 (1968), and dismissed for want of a substantial federal question in Gorun v. Montana, 399 U.S. 901 (1970). See, generally, Maier, *The Bases and Range of Federal Common Law in Private International Matters,* 5 VAND.J.TRANSNATIONAL L. 133 (1971).

55. Compare the express right of States to make agreements with the consent of Congress, Art. 1, § 10, p. 229, and the instance cited in note 6 this chapter. Compare the statutes leaving to the States the punishment of offenses against the law of nations, this chapter, note 63, Chapter VIII, note 59.

56. Takahashi v. Fish & Game Commission, 334 U.S. 410 (1948), Chapter X, note 80.

57. Missouri v. Holland, 252 U.S. 416 (1920); Ware v. Hylton, 3 Dall. 199 (U.S.1796); Hauenstein v. Lynham, 100 U.S. 483 (1880); Asakura v. Seattle, 265 U.S. 332 (1924). See Chapter V.

58. In one instance at one time the Constitution may have prevented federal preemption. Compare Section 2 of the Eighteenth Amendment to the Constitution: "The Congress and the several States shall have concurrent power to enforce this article by appropriate legislation."

59. Rice v. Santa Fe Elevator Corp., 331 U.S. 218, 230 (1947).

60. 312 U.S. 52 (1941).

61. 312 U.S. at 66–67, 73, 74 (footnotes omitted). Mr. Justice Black also said: ". . . this legislation is in a field which affects international relations, the one aspect of our government that from the first has been most generally conceded imperatively to demand broad national authority. Any concurrent state power that may exist is restricted to the narrowest of limits . . .." *Id.* at 68.

62. Under "long-arm statutes," States have asserted jurisdiction to adjudicate claims against aliens and alien corporations that do business in the State or have "minimum contacts" with it. Compare Velandra v. Regie Nationale des Usines Renault, 336 F.2d 292 (6th Cir. 1964), with Duple Motor Bodies, Ltd. v. Hollingsworth, 417 F.2d 231 (9th

Cir. 1969). *Cf.* TACA International Airlines, S.A. v. Rolls-Royce of England, Ltd. 15 N.Y.2d 97, 204 N.E.2d 329 (1965); Aquascutum of London, Inc. v. SS American Champion, 426 F.2d 205 (2d Cir. 1970).

63. Under the Articles of Confederation Congress urged the States to provide for the punishment of offenses against the law of nations. See Chapter VIII, note 59. And compare the *De Longchamps* case, *ibid.* Under the Constitution Congress enacted laws to punish some offenses against the law of nations and gave the federal courts exclusive jurisdiction of them (e. g. Judicial Code of 1911, § 256, 36 Stat. 1087, 1160–61, and see this chapter, note 64. Chapter III, pp. 72–74; but the States remained free to pass additional laws enforceable in their courts. See Fox v. Ohio, 5 How. 410, 416 (1847). And some offenses against the law of nations, not having been defined and legislated by Congress, remain for the States alone to enforce. See WRIGHT 178–79. The general protection of aliens, for which the United States is responsible under international law, is still left largely to state law, state officials and state courts. See p. 238; *cf.* Chapter VIII, note 3.

That treaties would sometimes be relevant to decisions in state courts was, of course, the reason for the express reference to them in the Supremacy Clause, Article VI, section 2. Some treaties have been left largely to enforcement by the States, *e. g.*, those relating to migratory bird conservation. See Koenig, *Federal and State Cooperation under the Constitution*, 36 MICH.L.REV. 752, 775–76 (1938).

In general, Congress has from the beginning left enforcement of many national policies to state officials and state courts. Early federal regulatory acts provided for enforcement proceedings in state courts. See, *e. g.*, Carriage Tax Act § 10, 1 Stat. 373 (1794); Alien Enemies Act, § 2, 1 STAT. 577 (1798). And in 1815 Congress conferred upon the state courts jurisdiction over federal tax claims, including prosecutions for fines, penalties, forfeitures, and regulated state judicial proceedings in such cases. 3 STAT. 244 (1815). The States have been generally willing to accept this function and it is now accepted that Congress could require it of them. Compare Testa v. Katt, 330 U.S. 386 (1947); Claflin v. Houseman, 93 U.S. 130, 136–37 (1876); McKnett v. St. Louis & S. F. Ry., 292 U.S. 230 (1934). But it was held long ago that Congress could not impose duties on other state officials. See note 74 below. On state and local cooperation in national policy, see generally HENKIN, ARMS CONTROL, Chapter VI and notes.

64. The federal courts have exclusive jurisdiction of actions brought against ambassadors, public ministers, consuls and vice consuls of foreign states, 28 U.S.C. §§ 1251, 1351 (1970), but where exclusive federal jurisdiction is not expressly reserved, it is retained by the States, as in suits brought by ambassadors or consuls, or in suits brought against foreign governments (if they waive immunity). Com-

pare Popovici v. Agler, 280 U.S. 379, 383–84 (1930); Chapter VIII, note 8. State courts also have substantial concurrent jurisdiction in regard to maritime matters. See Madruga v. Superior Court of California, 346 U.S. 556, 560–61 (1954).

65. United States v. Darby, 312 U.S. 100, 124 (1941).

66. The Tenth Amendment was invoked recently by Mr. Justice Douglas dissenting in United States v. Oregon, 366 U.S. 643, 654 (1961), and in Maryland v. Wirtz, 392 U.S. 183, 205 (1968). Compare Oregon v. Mitchell, 400 U.S. 112 (1971).

67. Expressly in Missouri v. Holland, 252 U.S. 416, 433–34 (1920), Chapter V, pp. 143 *et seq.*

68. The Hartford Convention in 1812 was perhaps the only occasion when States rights' were urged in protest against a declaration of war. See, T. DWIGHT, HISTORY OF THE HARTFORD CONVENTION 352–79 (1833), partially reprinted in DOCUMENTS OF AMERICAN HISTORY, Commager, ed., DOC.No.115 at 209 (1968). Compare Massachusetts v. Laird, 400 U.S. 886 (1970), Chapter XI, p. 274.

69. Monaco v. Mississippi, 292 U.S. 313, 330 (1934):
> We perceive no ground upon which it can be said that any waiver or consent by a State of the Union has run in favor of a foreign State. As to suits brought by a foreign State, we think that the States of the Union retain the same immunity that they enjoy with respect to suits by individuals whether citizens of the United States or citizens or subjects of a foreign State. The foreign State enjoys a similar sovereign immunity and without her consent may not be sued by a State of the Union.

70. State-owned liquor and mineral waters are subject to federal tax, New York v. United States, 326 U.S. 572 (1946); railroads and wharves owned by the State are subject to regulation under the Commerce Power, California v. Taylor, 353 U.S. 553 (1957); United States v. California, 297 U.S. 175 (1936); California v. United States, 320 U.S. 577 (1944); timber owned and sold by the State is subject to federal price regulation under the war powers, Case v. Bowles, 327 U.S. 92 (1946); state hospitals and schools are subject to federal fair labor standards, Maryland v. Wirtz, 392 U.S. 183 (1968); a state university must pay federal customs duties, University of Illinois v. United States, 289 U.S. 48 (1933); state property can be taken for federal use subject to compensation, *cf.* St. Louis v. Western Union Tel. Co., 148 U.S. 92, 101 (1893); Missouri *ex rel.* Camden County v. Union Electric Light & Power Co., 42 F.2d 692 (W.D.Mo.1930); the federal power to regulate commerce extends to control navigable waters within United States jurisdiction, even if state water sup-

plies may be adversely affected, Sanitary District v. United States, 266 U.S. 405 (1925).

71. New York v. United States, 326 U.S. 572, 582 (1946). Justice Frankfurter was not speaking for the Court but a majority expressed similar views (*id.* at 586) and the dissenting opinion of Douglas, J., asserted even greater immunity for the States (*id.* at 590, 598). See also Douglas, J., dissenting in Maryland v. Wirtz, 392 U.S. 183, 201 (1968). But compare St. Louis v. Western Union Tel. Co., 148 U.S. 92, 101 (1893), implying that federal eminent domain might be available even against "statehouse grounds."

Some claims of state immunity to federal regulation might raise "political questions" which the courts will not adjudicate. In *New York* v. *United States,* (*supra* at 581–82), Mr. Justice Frankfurter suggested that "the claim of implied immunity by States from federal taxation raises questions not wholly unlike provisions of the Constitution, such as that of Art. IV, § 4, guaranteeing States a republican form of government . . . which this Court has deemed not within its duty to adjudicate." But Justice Frankfurter was a leading exponent of judicial abstention in political questions, and the Court has since refused to follow his lead. See Baker v. Carr, 369 U.S. 186 (1962); and Chapter VIII, p. 210.

72. Metcalf & Eddy v. Mitchell, 269 U.S. 514, 523–24 (1926).

73. Say, a disarmament treaty that provides for international inspection of the State-house or interrogation of state officials about their functions. See Chapter V, p. 148. HENKIN, ARMS CONTROL 60–61.

74. In Kentucky v. Dennison, 24 How. 66 (U.S.1861), Chief Justice Taney held it to be the moral obligation of the governor of a State to perform a duty (extradition of a fugitive) imposed upon him by Congress, but found no power in the federal government to compel the governor to do so should he fail to do so. Taney added that were the federal government to possess this power, "it might overload the officer with duties which would fill up all his time, and disable him from performing his obligations to the State, and might impose on him duties of a character incompatible with the rank and dignity to which he was elevated by the State." *Id.* at 108. See also Mr. Justice Story in Prigg v. Pennsylvania, 16 Pet. 539, 615–16 (U.S.1842). Taney's views, however, seem to contradict those of the Founding Fathers. For Hamilton, speaking to the States, said: "Thus the legislatures, courts, and magistrates, of the respective members, will be incorporated into the operations of the national government *as far as its just and constitutional authority extends*; and will be rendered auxiliary to the enforcement of its laws." THE FEDERALIST No. 27, at 221–22. See also *id.* Nos. 44–45 (Madison); Holcombe, *The States as Agents of the Na-*

*tion,* reprinted in 3 SELECTED ESSAYS ON CONSTITUTIONAL LAW 1187, 1189 (1938). The Supreme Court later upheld an act of Congress imposing duties on state officials in regard to Congressional elections. *Ex parte* Siebold, 100 U.S. 371 (1880). (In the Voting Rights Act of 1965 Congress provided for federal registrars, but not apparently from any doubt as to its power to require state officials to register qualified voters. See Pub.L.No. 89–110, 79 Stat. 437 (1965) 42 U.S.C. § 1973 *et seq.* (1970).) And the Court has held that Congress can require state courts to enforce federal obligations. See Testa v. Katt, 330 U.S. 386 (1947) this chapter, note 63. The UN Headquarters Agreement seems to impose duties on state officials. See Chapter V, note 75. But even if the rule expressed by Taney is rejected, the problem of enforcing affirmative action by a recalcitrant state government would remain. It has been said that the Framers of the Constitution were aware of the delicacy and difficulty of enforcing the affirmative mandates of the federal government against the States, so that the Constitution's provisions and most subsequent legislation directed at the states have generally been framed in the form of "Do not do . . ." (thus leaving alternative methods of doing open) rather than in the command form of "Do this . . .," Hart, *The Relations Between State and Federal Law,* 54 COLUM.L.REV. 489, 515 (1954).

75. In one famous unhappy instance the United States indemnified the Italian Government when a mob lynched Italian nationals in New Orleans. See 6 MOORE, DIGEST 837–41. For other instances in which the United States was held internationally responsible for actions (or inactions) of States, see BUTLER, THE TREATY POWER 142–159 (1902). See also WRIGHT 30, 265; Hale Memorandum, S.DOC.NO.56, 54th Cong., 2d Sess. 5 (1897). For more recent cases, see the cases before the claims commission with Mexico in W. BISHOP, INTERNATIONAL LAW, CASES AND MATERIALS c. 9 (3d ed. 1971).

States cannot be sued by foreign countries or nationals on the States' bonds or other obligations. See p. 246. For obstacles to the enforcement of treaties against violation by the States, see Chapter V, p. 166.

In Hauenstein v. Lynham, 100 U.S. 483 (1880), for example, it was almost 20 years after Hauenstein died before the Supreme Court decided that, under the applicable treaty, Virginia could not escheat his property but had to permit Swiss heirs to inherit.

76. See Chapter V, notes 66, 71. And when the Supreme Court found that the territorial sea and the resources of its sea-bed are of great importance to the nation in its international relations and belong to the United States rather than the coastal State, United States v. California, 332 U.S. 19 (1947), Congress gave resources of the sea and

submerged land to the States. Submerged Lands Act of 1953, ch. 65, 67 Stat. 29 (1953), 43 U.S.C. §§ 1301–15 (1970).

77. Compare Marshall, C. J., in Cohens v. Virginia, 6 Wheat. 264, 413–14 (U.S.1821).

78. Wechsler, *The Political Safeguards of Federalism: The Role of the States in the Composition and Selection of the National Government*, 54 COLUM.L.REV. 543, 544, 558. He also said:

> National action has thus always been regarded as exceptional in our polity, an intrusion to be justified by some necessity, the special rather than the ordinary case . . . .
> National power may be quite unquestioned in a given situation; those who would advocate its exercise must none the less answer the preliminary question why the matter should not be left to the states . . .
>
> .  .  .  .  .  .  .  .  .  .  .
>
> If I have drawn too much significance from the mere fact of the existence of the states, the error surely will be rectified by pointing also to their crucial rôle in the selection and the composition of national authority. More is involved here than that aspect of the compromise between the larger and the smaller states that yielded their equality of status in the Senate. Representatives no less than Senators are allotted by the Constitution to the states, although their number varies with state population as determined by the census . . . .
> And with the President, as with Congress, the crucial instrument of the selection—whether through electors or, in the event of failure of majority, by the House voting as state units—is again the states. The consequence, of course, is that the states are the strategic yardsticks for the measurement of interest and opinion, the special centers of political activity, the separate geographical determinants of national as well as local politics. *Id.* at 544–45, 546.

NOTES, CHAPTER X, INDIVIDUAL RIGHTS, pp. 251 to 270.

1. Ours is an Eighteenth Century constitution reflecting the prevailing "Enlightened" views. The Constitution did not give the people their rights for these antedate and are independent of it; the Constitution recognizes and takes account of these rights and denies to government the authority to infringe them. Thus, for example, the Bill of Rights confers no freedom of speech but forbids Congress to make law abridging it. The Second Amendment confers no right to bear arms but "the right of the people to keep and bear Arms, shall not be infringed." Or Amendment IV: "The right of the people to be secure in their persons . . . shall not be violated . . . ." And Amendment IX: "The enumeration in the Constitution, of certain rights, shall not be construed to deny or disparage others retained by the people." Certain rights might be said to have been conferred by the Constitution and its Amendments, *e. g.*, those to be enjoyed by persons accused of crime (Amendments V, VI), but these relate to governmental action; "the privileges or immunities of citizens of the United States" (Amendment XIV) are also protected only against governmental, "state action." Only the Thirteenth Amendment, apparently, confers a new absolute right, freedom from slavery. A right to travel freely within the United States has now been accepted although the Justices are not agreed as to whence it derives. See United States v. Guest, 383 U.S. 745, 757 (1966); Shapiro v. Thompson, 394 U.S. 618, 629–31 (1969); Oregon v. Mitchell, 400 U.S. 112, 237–38 (1970) (opinion of Brennan, J.)

2. See Introduction to Chapter II, note 2.

3. Only the prohibitions on *ex post facto* laws and bills of attainder (Art. I, secs. 9, 10), the provision that the writ of habeas corpus shall not be suspended (Art. 1, sec. 9), the local jury trial for those accused of crime (Art. III, sec. 2), and the special safeguards for those accused of treason (Art. III, sec. 3). One might include also the prohibition on impairment of contract obligations, Art. I, sec. 10, and the limitation on direct taxes (Art. I, sec. 9). The provision for jury trial in criminal cases is largely duplicated in the Sixth Amendment, and others—*e. g.*, those against *ex post facto* laws—are probably subsumed in the due process clauses of the Fifth and Fourteenth Amendments. Compare the suggestion that trial before a judge assured of life tenure and guaranteed compensation is also a "right" of the accused. Chapter VII, note 37.

4. See Chapters VIII, IX above. See, generally, Henkin, *Some Reflections on Current Constitutional Controversy,* 109 U.PA.L.REV. 637 (1961).

5. That indeed was one of the objections of Sutherland's critics. See Levitan, Chapter I, note 9; *cf.* WRIGHT 134 n. 13.

Hamilton perhaps implies that national defense and "the public peace" ought to know no constitutional limitations:

> "As the duties of superintending the national defence and of securing the public peace against foreign or domestic violence involve a provision for casualties and dangers to which no possible limits can be assigned, the power of making that provision ought to know no other bounds than the exigencies of the nation and the resources of the community." THE FEDERALIST NO. 31 at 238.

There was a theory that the powers deriving from sovereignty were limited "not by Constitutional provisions, but by those fundamental principles upon which the Government of the United States, and of its people, is based." See discussion and authorities cited in 1 BUTLER, THE TREATY POWER 62 *et seq.* The Supreme Court cases he cited, however, find fundamental principles as limiting the authority of the United States in governing acquired territory, and even those were derived "by inference and the general spirit of the Constitution." Mormon Church v. United States, 136 U.S. 1, 42–44 (1890). They do not suggest that only these implied limitations govern powers inherent in sovereignty exercised within the United States. Later cases found limitations in "fundamental principles" implied in "due process of law," but as regards the federal government these were in addition to other rights enumerated in the Bill of Rights. Compare Palko v. Connecticut, 302 U.S. 319 (1938), *overruled,* Benton v. Maryland, 395 U.S. 784 (1969). Compare also what courts have poured into substantive due process, pp. 255–57 above.

6. Perez v. Brownell, 356 U.S. 44, 58 (1958). In 1967, the Court overruled that case, holding that the Constitution prohibits deprivation of citizenship, but not even the sharp dissent suggested that legislation relating to foreign affairs is not subject to constitutional limitation. Afroyim v. Rusk, 387 U.S. 253 (1967). *Afroyim* was narrowed somewhat in Rogers v. Bellei, 401 U.S. 815 (1971), which held that Congress can take away statutory citizenship, but that case, too, does not deny that naturalization statutes are subject to the full panoply of constitutional limitations. See also Reid v. Covert, 354 U.S. 1, 16–17 (1957); compare Burnet v. Brooks, 288 U.S. 378 (1933); Mr. Justice Brewer dissenting in Fong Yue Ting v. United States, 149 U.S. 698, 737–38 (1893). And compare the decision by a three-judge court invalidating a requirement that a naturalized citizen have been a citizen for ten years to be eligible for the Foreign Service. See

Faruki v. Rogers, D.D.C. Oct. 6, 1972, reported in New York Times, Oct. 12, 1972, p. 6.

*Afroyim* and other cases also confirm that "it is error to suppose that every case or controversy which touches foreign relations lies beyond judicial cognizance." Baker v. Carr, 369 U.S. 186, 211 (1962). The Supreme Court has never invoked the political question doctrine to dismiss an individual's claim that a foreign relations action deprived him of constitutional rights. See Chapter VIII, p. 210.

7. This is now generally assumed, although there appears to be no clear holding by the Supreme Court, and no discussion of the issue as it relates to foreign affairs. The First Amendment was one of a number invoked in Joint Anti-Fascist Refugee Comm. v. McGrath, 341 U.S. 123 (1951), but the Court's judgment did not necessarily rest on it, and the opinions did not examine the applicability of the amendment to the Executive. In his concurring opinion, however, Mr. Justice Black said: ". . . [I]n my judgment the executive has no constitutional authority, with or without a hearing, officially to prepare and publish the lists challenged by petitioners. . . . This cannot be reconciled with the First Amendment as I interpret it." *Id.* at 143. Mr. Justice Reed's dissent dealt with the First Amendment so as to imply that in a proper case the amendment would limit the powers of the Executive. *Id.* at 199. That the First Amendment was in play was not questioned by any of the parties or any of the Justices in the *Pentagon Papers Case*, note 9, this chapter. And compare the references to the First Amendment in United States v. U. S. District Court, Eastern Michigan, 407 U.S. 297 (1972); also Laird v. Tatum, 408 U.S. 1 (1972). Compare Mr. Justice Jackson: "If there is any fixed star in our constitutional constellation, it is that no official, high or petty, can prescribe what shall be orthodox in politics, nationalism, religion, or other matters of opinion or force citizens to confess by word or act their faith therein." West Virginia State Bd. of Educ. v. Barnette, 319 U.S. 624, 642 (1943). (The case itself involved state action, not action by the Federal Executive but, in addition to the Fourteenth, the First Amendment is much mentioned in the opinion.) Also Mr. Justice Douglas dissenting, in Beauharnais v. Illinois, 343 U.S. 250, 284, 286 (1952): "The First Amendment says that freedom of speech, freedom of press, and the free exercise of religion shall not be abridged. That is a negation of power on the part of each and every department of government." Compare also Mr. Justice Black, in Reid v. Covert, 354 U.S. 1 (1957); Mr. Justice Douglas dissenting in Gravel v. United States, 408 U.S. 606, 633 (1972). See generally Maslow, "Is the President Bound by the First Amendment," *Hearings on S.J.Res. 1 and 43 Before a Subcomm. on Treaties and Executive Agreements of the Senate Comm. on the Judiciary,* 83d Cong., 1st Sess., at 314 (1953).

In any event the Fifth Amendment denies to the Executive, as well as to other branches, authority to deprive a citizen of "liberty" without due process of law, and that "liberty" would doubtless be held to include the freedoms specified in the First Amendment.

8. See, *e. g.* International Convention on the Elimination of All Forms of Racial Discrimination, 1966, cited Chapter VII, note 26. The Supreme Court has drawn a line between speech that incites to illegal action and that which merely advocates it or teaches its desirability. Yates v. United States, 354 U.S. 298 (1957); *cf.* Scales v. United States, 367 U.S. 203 (1961).

9. New York Times Co. v. United States, 403 U.S. 713 (1971). In a brief *per curiam* opinion the Court held that the Government had failed to sustain its burden of overcoming a heavy presumption against the constitutional validity of "prior restraints of expression." Some of the concurring opinions, however, suggest that there was a majority of the Court for only a very narrow doctrine. Three of the concurring Justices seemed to imply that the injunction might have issued if Congress had authorized it. Stewart and White, JJ., thought that it was the constitutional duty of the Executive "to protect the confidentiality necessary to carry out its responsibilities in the fields of international relations and national defense." But in the absence of an act of Congress authorizing an injunction (or even specific Executive regulations), the First Amendment bars the injunction at least when the courts are not persuaded that disclosure "will surely result in direct, immediate and irreparable damage to our Nation or its people." *Id.* at 727–30. Marshall, J., considered it would "be utterly inconsistent with the concept of separation of powers for this Court to use its power of contempt to prevent behavior that Congress has specifically declined to prohibit." *Id.* at 742. Mr. Justice White, in an opinion which Stewart, J., joined, stressed that Congress had apparently been satisfied to rely on criminal sanctions and their deterrent effect, implied that criminal statutes in effect were here relevant, and asserted that he "would have no difficulty in sustaining convictions under these sections on facts that would not justify the intervention of equity and the imposition of a prior restraint." *Id.* at 737. Harlan, J., dissenting in an opinion joined by Burger, C. J., and Blackmun, J., would apparently grant an injunction where the Court was satisfied that "the subject matter of the dispute does lie within the proper compass of the President's foreign relations power," and if the determination that disclosure would "irreparably impair the national security be made by the head of the Executive Department concerned—here the Secretary of State or the Secretary of Defense—after actual personal consideration by that officer." *Id.* at 757. See, generally, Henkin, *The Right to Know and the Duty*

*to Withhold: The Case of the Pentagon Papers,* 120 U.PA.L.REV. 271 (1971).

10. *Cf.* Abel v. United States, 362 U.S. 217, 219–20 (1960).

11. Wong Wing v. United States, 163 U.S. 228 (1896). An alien, of course, is not entitled to the rights, privileges and immunities of citizenship under the Fourteenth Amendment, but what these are is still highly uncertain. Compare, as regards an alien's rights to equality generally, pp. 258, 269–70.

Corporations, too, are entitled to the protection of the Bill of Rights but with some differences. Security against search and seizure may be different, for "corporations can claim no equality with individuals in the enjoyment of a right to privacy." United States v. Morton Salt Co., 338 U.S. 632, 652 (1950). Corporations do not enjoy the privilege against self-incrimination, and corporate officers may not refuse to surrender corporate books or documents on the ground that they might incriminate the corporation or its officers. Hale v. Henkel, 201 U.S. 43 (1906); Wilson v. United States, 221 U.S. 361 (1911); see also Oklahoma Press Publishing Co. v. Walling, 327 U.S. 186, 205–208 (1946); *cf.* United States v. White, 322 U.S. 694 (1944); Curcio v. United States, 354 U.S. 118 (1957). Corporations do not enjoy privileges and immunities of citizenship. Orient Insurance Co. v. Daggs, 172 U.S. 557, 561 (1899); *cf.* Paul v. Virginia, 18 Wall. 168 (U.S. 1869).

That a corporation is a "person" under the Fourteenth Amendment was considered so obvious that it was a question on which "the court [did] not wish to hear argument"—when it first arose in relation to the equal protection clause. Santa Clara County v. Southern Pac. R.R., 118 U.S. 394, 396 (1886). This was soon applied also in regard to corporate property under the due process clause of the Fourteenth Amendment. Covington and Lexington Turnpike Road Co. v. Sandford, 164 U.S. 578 (1896); Smyth v. Ames, 169 U.S. 466 (1898); Grosjean v. American Press Co., 297 U.S. 233 (1936). While Mr. Justice Black at one time sought to have this interpretation overruled—see dissenting opinion, Connecticut Gen. Life Ins. Co. v. Johnson, 303 U.S. 77, 83, 85 (1938)—it appears to be firmly fixed. That a corporation is a "person" whose property is protected by the due process clause of the Fifth Amendment does not appear to have been seriously questioned and has been held, in effect, in numerous cases. In Sinking-Fund Cases, 99 U.S. 700, 718–19 (1879), the Court said that the United States "equally with the States . . . are prohibited from depriving persons or corporations of property without due process of law."

12. See L. OPPENHEIM, INTERNATIONAL LAW § 320 at 687–89 (Lauterpacht 8th ed. 1958); RESTATEMENT § 179 (1965). Compare Universal Declaration of Human Rights, G.A.Res. 217 (III), Arts. 2,

3, 5–13 (1948); International Covenant on Civil and Political Rights, Annex to G.A.Res. 2200(XXI), 21 U.N. GAOR Supp. 16, Articles 9, 10, 14, U.N.Doc.A/6316 (1966).

13. North Atlantic Treaty, Status of Forces, [1951] 4 U.S.T. 1792, T.I.A.S. No. 2846, Art. VII, § 9.

14. But wiretapping might infringe rights of the other party to a conversation with the Embassy. Katz v. United States, 389 U.S. 347 (1967).

15. See United States v. Carolene Products Co., 304 U.S. 144, 152 n. 4 (1938). See the cases collected by Frankfurter, J., concurring in Kovacs v. Cooper, 336 U.S. 77, 90–97 (1949).

16. The First Amendment has not precluded punishment for violation—by speech or publication—of military censorship or other security regulations, of laws against interfering with the administration of justice, against individual or group libel, public obscenity, inciting to crime, unlawful picketing, or disrupting the Selective Service System by "symbolic speech" like burning a draft card in protest against the Vietnam War. See Schenck v. United States, 249 U.S. 47 (1919); Beauharnais v. Illinois, 343 U.S. 250 (1952); Roth v. United States, 354 U.S. 476 (1957); Giboney v. Empire Storage & Ice Co., 336 U.S. 490 (1949); United States v. O'Brien, 391 U.S. 367 (1968). Compare Dennis v. United States, 341 U.S. 494 (1951); also the various opinions in New York Times v. United States, note 9, this chapter.

17. *E. g.*, Frend v. United States, 100 F.2d 691 (D.C.Cir. 1938), *cert. denied*, 306 U.S. 640 (1939); see Chapter III, note 27.

18. Mr. Justice Frankfurter suggested that research and scholarship can not be barred "except for reasons that are exigent and obviously compelling." Sweezy v. New Hampshire, 354 U.S. 234, 262 (1957); see HENKIN, ARMS CONTROL 45, 185–86.

19. Generally a search is not unreasonable if pursuant to a warrant meeting the requirements of the Amendment—"upon probable cause, supported by Oath or affirmation, and particularly describing the place to be searched, and the persons or things to be seized." In some cases a search may be valid even though without a warrant. Compare United States v. Rabinowitz, 339 U.S. 56 (1950), with Chimel v. California, 395 U.S. 752 (1969), and Coolidge v. New Hampshire, 403 U.S. 443 (1971) (search incident to arrest); Carroll v. United States, 267 U.S. 132 (1925), and Henry v. United States, 361 U.S. 98 (1959) (moving vehicle); compare Terry v. Ohio, 392 U.S. 1 (1968), with Sibron v. New York, 392 U.S. 40 (1968), and Adams v. Williams, 407 U.S. 143 (1972) ("stop and frisk"); Warden v. Hayden, 387 U.S. 294 (1967) ("hot pursuit"); *cf.* Schmerber v. California, 384 U.S. 757 (1966) (compulsory blood test).

The Fourth Amendment is particularly important in criminal cases since the courts will exclude evidence obtained in violation of the Amendment (applicable also to the States by virtue of the Fourteenth Amendment). Weeks v. United States, 232 U.S. 383 (1914); Mapp v. Ohio, 367 U.S. 643 (1961). The Amendment can also be the basis for civil suit against officials who violate it. 42 U.S.C. § 1983 (1970), Monroe v. Pape, 365 U.S. 167 (1961) (state official); Bivens v. Six Unknown Named Agents, 403 U.S. 388 (1971) (judicially created remedy against federal officials). Willful violation of the Amendment could also be a criminal offense under 18 U.S.C. § 242 (1970); *cf.* Screws v. United States, 325 U.S. 91 (1945) (state official); the language of the statute would seem to cover federal officials as well. But see the attack on the exclusion doctrine by Burger, C. J., in his dissent in *Bivens, supra.*

20. See HENKIN, ARMS CONTROL, c. IV. The privilege against self-incrimination (Amendment V) would also be relevant to such a disarmament inspection system especially if it involved interrogation of persons. See *id.* at 59–63, 79–81 and notes.

Other hypothetical cases suggest other hypothetical issues: an agreement for general and complete disarmament forbids the bearing of arms even by State militia, in the face of the Second Amendment (see *id.* at 34–36); an allied command on peace-time maneuvers is quartered in private homes without the owner's consent (Amendment III).

21. See Wong Wing v. United States, 163 U.S. 228 (1896) (alien); *cf.* Sinking Fund Cases, 99 U.S. 700, 718–19 (1879) (corporation); Edison Co. v. Labor Board, 305 U.S. 197 (1938); Gonzales v. United States, 348 U.S. 407, 417–18 (1955) (administrative proceeding); *cf.* Goldberg v. Kelly, 397 U.S. 254 (1970); Bell v. Burson, 402 U.S. 535 (1971); Fuentes v. Shevin, 407 U.S. 67 (1972); Morrissey v. Brewer, 408 U.S. 471 (1972). But not to alien enemies abroad in time of war. Johnson v. Eisentrager, 339 U.S. 763, 771 (1950); compare *In re* Yamashita, 327 U.S. 1 (1946), with dissenting opinion *id.* at 26, 42.

Generally, but not universally, due process "implies and includes *actor, reus, judex,* regular allegations, opportunity to answer, and a trial according to some settled course of judicial proceedings . . . ." Murray's Lessee v. Hoboken Land & Improvement Co., 18 How. 272, 280 (U.S. 1856); see also *Ex parte* Wall, 107 U.S. 265, 289 (1883).

But not all administrative actions require similar proceedings. See, *e. g.,* Opp Cotton Mills v. Administrator, 312 U.S. 126, 152–53 (1949); *cf.* Bowles v. Willingham, 321 U.S. 503, 519–21 (1944) (upholding war-time orders without hearing since judicial review available); Richardson v. Perales, 402 U.S. 389 (1971).

22.   Nishimura Ekiu v. United States, 142 U.S. 651 (1892); United States v. Ju Toy, 198 U.S. 253, 263 (1905); U. S. *ex rel.* Knauff v. Shaughnessy, 338 U.S. 537 (1950).   The Supreme Court has held that under general statutory authority to exclude in the national interest (formerly 22 U.S.C. § 223, now 8 U.S.C. § 1185(a) (1970)), even a resident alien who leaves can be excluded upon return without a hearing and on undisclosed evidence and could be detained if there is no country that will accept him.   Shaughnessy v. U. S. *ex rel.* Mezei, 345 U.S. 206 (1953).   It is not unlikely that in less fearful days at least, Mr. Justice Jackson's eloquent dissent requiring procedural due process will prevail.   But the entrant is entitled to a fair hearing on his claim that he is a citizen.   Kwock Jan Fat v. White, 253 U.S. 454, 457 (1920).   Congress has enacted special procedures, including judicial review for those with a substantial, *bona fide* claim that they are U. S. nationals.   C. 477, Title III, Ch. 3, § 360, 66 Stat. 273 (1952), 8 U.S.C. § 1503 (1970).

23.   Woodby v. Immigration and Naturalization Service, 385 U.S. 276 (1966).   The standard of proof is higher than in ordinary civil cases but not as high as that required in criminal cases ("beyond a reasonable doubt"; see *In re* Winship, 397 U.S. 358, 361–64 (1970)). The Court long ago held that the alien is not constitutionally entitled to judicial review of a deportation order.   Zakonaite v. Wolf, 226 U.S. 272 (1912);   Fong Yue Ting v. United States, 149 U.S. 698 (1893); also Carlson v. Landon, 342 U.S. 524, 537–38 (1952); *cf.* Jay v. Boyd, 351 U.S. 345 (1956).   But he is entitled to procedural due process. The Japanese Immigrant Case, 189 U.S. 86, 100–101 (1903); Kwong Hai Chew v. Colding, 344 U.S. 590, 596–97 (1952).   He can bring habeas corpus to challenge a deportation order for lack of fair hearing or any support in evidence.   U. S. *ex rel.* Vajtauer v. Comm'r of Immigration, 273 U.S. 103, 106 (1927).   And he can get a day in court on his claim that he is not an alien.   Ng Fung Ho v. White, 259 U.S. 276, 281 (1922).   Congress has provided judicial review.   8 U.S.C. § 1105 (a) (1970); *cf.* Cheng Fan Kwok v. Immigration and Naturalization Service, 392 U.S. 206 (1968).

Since deportation is not a criminal punishment the alien is not denied due process because the immigration officers are not given power to compel witnesses in his behalf.   Low Wah Suey v. Backus, 225 U.S. 460 (1912).   When a search and seizure is made pursuant to an administrative arrest by immigration officials rather than a criminal arrest, the search and seizure do not violate the Fourth or Fifth Amendment and the use in evidence of the article seized does not invalidate the petitioner's conviction.   Abel v. United States, 362 U.S. 217 (1960).   A lower court has held that an alien is not entitled to "Miranda" warnings when he is arrested pursuant to an Immigration order.   Jolley v. Immigration and Naturalization Service, 441

F.2d 1245 (1971). The government need not supply an attorney for an indigent alien in deportation proceedings. *Cf.* 8 U.S.C. § 1252(b) (1970).

"When the Constitution requires a hearing, it requires a fair one, one before a tribunal which meets at least currently prevailing standards of impartiality." Wong Yang Sung v. McGrath, 339 U.S. 33, 50 (1950). To avoid the constitutional question the Court interpreted the law as precluding a deportation hearing presided over by an immigration inspector. But a divided court held that an enemy alien in time of war is not entitled to any hearing and cannot complain of the inadequacy of one he is given gratutitously. Ludecke v. Watkins, 335 U.S. 160 (1948).

24. See, *e. g.*, Bowles v. Willingham, 321 U.S. 503, 519 (1944); Bi-Metallic Investment Co. v. Colorado, 239 U.S. 441, 445 (1915); Bragg v. Weaver, 251 U.S. 57, 58 (1919).

25. Compare, for example, the Tate letter declaring the restrictive theory of sovereign immunity, Chapter II, note 81, with the Executive determination on immunity in *Peru* and *Hoffman*, Chapter II, p. 58; some might consider the latter more "judicial" than "legislative" in character. In the *First National City Bank Case*, Chapter II, p. 62, the State Department letter was issued in the context of a particular case but purported to establish a general principle. Compare the provision for *ad hoc* Presidential intervention in the Second Hickenlooper Amendment, Chapter II, n. 83.

26. For recent suggestions urging a right to a hearing see Leigh and Atkeson, *Due Process in the Emerging Foreign Relations Law of the United States,* 21 BUSINESS LAWYER 853 (1966); 22 BUSINESS LAWYER 3 (1966); compare Timberg, *Wanted: Administrative Safeguards for the Protection of the Individual in International Economic Regulation,* 17 ADMIN.L.REV. 159 (1965). Also Cardozo, *Sovereign Immunity: The Plaintiff Deserves a Day in Court,* 67 HARV.L.REV. 608 (1954). The claim to a hearing is stronger if the State Departments intervenes in a particular case with a "suggestion" that is conclusive on the courts. Chapter II, p. 58.

27. That day is epitomized probably by Lochner v. New York, 198 U.S. 45 (1905), and Adkins v. Children's Hospital, 261 U.S. 525 (1923), and had its last gasps in Morehead v. New York *ex rel.* Tipaldo, 298 U.S. 587 (1935). Although the doctrine grew primarily and ramified pursuant to the Fourteenth Amendment and has been invoked more frequently in regard to state action, substantive due process had been frequently sought and applied under the Fifth Amendment in regard to acts of Congress. A single famous instance, before the Fourteenth Amendment existed, was Scott v. Sandford, 19 How. 393 (U.S.1857), p. 252, this chapter; also Adair v. United States, 208 U.S. 161

(1908); and see *Adkins, supra,* as applied to an act of Congress for the District of Columbia. The doctrine was laid to rest in West Coast Hotel Co. v. Parrish, 300 U.S. 379 (1937).

28. Nebbia v. New York, 291 U.S. 502, 525 (1934).

29. The contemporary judicial attitude is represented by *Nebbia,* perhaps even more by Williamson v. Lee Optical, Inc., 348 U.S. 483 (1955), and Day-Brite Lighting, Inc. v. Missouri, 342 U.S. 421 (1952). It remains to be seen whether the economic rights of the poor, in welfare or consumer-protection cases, might yet restore a measure of substantive due process in such "economic" cases. See Henkin, *Foreword: On Drawing Lines,* 82 HARV.L.REV. 63, 91 n. 92 (1968). Compare the development of new "equal protection" for the poor, this chapter, note 39.

For the special attitude requiring "reasonableness" in fixing the rates of public utilities, compare Power Commission v. Hope Gas Co., 320 U.S. 591 (1944).

30. See HENKIN, ARMS CONTROL 39–43.

31. For a discussion of the "double standard" of substantive due process, see G. GUNTHER and N. DOWLING, CASES AND MATERIALS ON CONSTITUTIONAL LAW 1051–56 (8th ed. 1970). Henkin, *Some Reflections on Current Constitutional Controversy,* 109 U.PA.L.REV. 637, 658–60 (1961). Compare this chapter, note 15.

The court has sought to mitigate the conceptual difficulties of its double standard by finding additional rights implied in the "specifics" of the Bill of Rights, some also in their "penumbra". Compare Griswold v. Connecticut, 381 U.S. 479 (1965). The Court's opinion, and particularly Justice Goldberg concurring, also invoked the "retained" rights referred to in the Ninth Amendment. As regards the States it has sought to avoid substantive due process by finding most of the provisions of the Bill of Rights (and their penumbra) "incorporated" in the Fourteenth Amendment and therefore applicable to the States exactly as the Bill of Rights governs the Federal Government. See p. 269, this chapter.

32. Kent v. Dulles, 357 U.S. 116, 129 (1958). *Cf.* United States v. Laub, 385 U.S. 475 (1967). The Supreme Court has not considered the validity of additional restrictions on the departure of aliens. See 8 U.S.C. § 1185(a) (1970).

33. Aptheker v. Secretary of State, 378 U.S. 500, 505 (1964).

34. See Korematsu v. United States, 323 U.S. 214 (1944). Compare an interesting dissent by Justice Jackson refusing to approve the action but asserting a kind of "political question" doctrine for military decisions in time of war. "A military commander may overstep the bounds of constitutionality, and it is an incident. But if we review and approve, that passing incident becomes the doctrine of the Con-

493

stitution." *Id.* at 246. It seems unlikely that the courts would limit even the power of the President acting alone. Compare *Ex parte Quirin*, 317 U.S. 1 (1942). See CORWIN, THE PRESIDENT 256–61 (1957).

While he was still a senator Sutherland said that the War Power is subject only to express prohibitions "and such fundamental restraints upon governmental action, as are obviously and clearly intended to apply at all times and under all conditions." CONSTITUTIONAL POWER AND WORLD AFFAIRS 94 (1919). Compare Hamilton, quoted note 5, this chapter.

35. Harisiades v. Shaughnessy, 342 U.S. 580 (1952); Galvan v. Press, 347 U.S. 522, 529–32 (1954). But see Bullitt, *Deportation as a Denial of Substantive Due Process*, 28 GEO.WASH.L.REV. 205 (1953), and Hesse, *The Constitutional Status of the Lawfully Admitted Permanent Resident Alien*, 68 YALE L.J. 1578 (1959), 69 YALE L.J. 262 (1959), who suggested that there ought to be and are constitutional limitations on the power of Congress to expel lawfully admitted resident aliens. See also Scharpf, Chapter VIII, note 21, at 580–83, who treats the cases upholding expulsion as asserting an unreviewable political question.

A three judge court had held that an alien cannot be excluded when the effect would be to deny First Amendment rights to citizens, Mandel v. Mitchell, 325 F.Supp. 620 (E.D.N.Y.1971), but the Supreme Court reversed. Kleindienst v. Mandel, 408 U.S. 753 (1972).

The Kentucky Resolutions of November 10, 1798, drafted by Jefferson, notorious as a vain attempt by a State to "nullify" national action, were directed against the alien and sedition laws and include an attack on the constitutionality of the provisions giving the President authority to expel aliens. See H.R.REP. No. 43, 21st Cong., 2d Sess. (1831).

36. While the Fifth Amendment contains no explicit guarantee of the equal protection of the laws, "discrimination may be so unjustifiable as to be violative of due process." Bolling v. Sharpe, 347 U.S. 497, 499 (1954). *Cf.* Hurd v. Hodge, 334 U.S. 24 (1948); Thiel v. Southern Pacific Co., 328 U.S. 217 (1946). See also Mr. Justice Jackson, concurring, in Railway Express Agency, Inc. v. New York, 336 U.S. 106, 112 (1949). It is safe to say that, despite its aversion to "substantive due process," p. 256 above, the Supreme Court will now strike down under the due process clause federal discriminations which it would have invalidated under an equal protection clause if one were contained in the Bill of Rights.

37. Holmes, J., in Buck v. Bell, 274 U.S. 200, 208 (1927).

38. See, *e. g.*, Railway Express Agency v. New York, 336 U.S. 106 (1949); Jackson, J., concurring, *id.* at 111; Williamson v. Lee Optical

494

Inc., 348 U.S. 483 (1955); compare Morey v. Doud, 354 U.S. 457 (1959); McGowan v. Maryland, 366 U.S. 420, 426 (1961); Dandridge v. Williams, 397 U.S. 471 (1970). See, generally, GUNTHER AND DOWLING, note 31 this chapter, Chapter 14.

At no time was equal protection without importance for protecting against racial discrimination. Strauder v. West Virginia, 100 U.S. 303 (1880); Yick Wo v. Hopkins, 118 U.S. 356 (1886); Brown v. Board of Education, 347 U.S. 483 (1954).

39.  See Levy v. Louisiana, 391 U.S. 68 (1968); Williams v. Rhodes, 393 U.S. 23 (1968); Shapiro v. Thompson, 394 U.S. 618 (1969); see the development of the new doctrine which Justice Harlan traces and rejects, in his dissent, *id.* at 658–63. See also Dunn v. Blumstein, 405 U.S. 330 (1972). The Court has been particularly solicitous when the interests of the poor and of minority groups are involved. Compare *Shapiro, supra;* Harper v. Virginia Board of Elections, 383 U. S. 663 (1966); James v. Strange, 407 U.S. 128 (1972). But the Court may already be retreating to some extent from the sweep of its new equal protection doctrine. Compare Dandridge v. Williams, 397 U.S. 471 (1970); Labine v. Vincent, 401 U.S. 532 (1971); James v. Valtierra, 402 U.S. 137 (1971); Jefferson v. Hackney, 406 U.S. 535 (1972).

40.  Yick Wo v. Hopkins, 118 U.S. 356 (1886); Truax v. Raich, 239 U.S. 33 (1915); Graham v. Richardson, 403 U.S. 365 (1971).

41.  See, in particular, Yick Wo v. Hopkins, in the previous note.

42.  For example, the U.S. Civil Service Commission has limited eligibility for competitive examination to citizens or persons who owe permanent allegiance to the United States. 5 C.F.R. § 338.101 (1971), authorized by Executive Order 10577 (1967), 5 U.S.C.A. § 3301 notes, pursuant to 5 U.S.C. §§ 3301 (1970). And compare the limitations in Public Works Appropriation Act, P.L. 91–144, 83 Stat. 1336–337 (1970) and in cases dealing with state discrimination against aliens, notes 40, 78, 82, this chapter.

43.  The property of aliens, like that of citizens, can be taken only for a public use and subject to just compensation, even if their government does not reciprocate. Russian Volunteer Fleet v. United States, 282 U.S. 481 (1931).

Marshall had "no doubt" that the United States could confiscate property of alien enemies. See Brown v. United States, 8 Cranch 110, 122 *et seq.* (U.S.1814), Chapter IV, p. 96. See also United States v. Chemical Foundation, 272 U.S. 1, 11 (1926); Miller v. United States, 11 Wall. 268 (U.S.1870). For the legality of blockade and capture of neutral ships that run the blockade, see The Prize Cases, 2 Black 635 (U.S.1862).

44. "That provision [in the Fifth Amendment] has always been understood as referring only to a direct appropriation, and not to consequential injuries resulting from the exercise of lawful power. It has never been supposed to have any bearing upon, or to inhibit laws that indirectly work harm or loss to individuals." Legal Tender Cases, 12 Wall. 457, 551 (U.S.1870). Holmes has called this "the petty larceny of the police power," 1 HOLMES-LASKI LETTERS 457 (Howe ed. 1953). See Holmes's dissent in Tyson and Brother v. Banton, 273 U.S. 418, 445–46 (1927). Compare generally the opinions of Holmes and Brandeis on opposite sides in Pennsylvania Coal Co. v. Mahon, 260 U.S. 393, 412, 416 (1922). Also Goldblatt v. Hempstead, 369 U.S. 590 (1962). For instances in which the Supreme Court held that federal or state regulations did not require compensation see HENKIN, ARMS CONTROL 42 and notes.

45. United States v. Caltex, Inc., 344 U.S. 149 (1952). Compare Juragua Iron Co. v. United States, 212 U.S. 297 (1909). The Court also found no compensable "taking" by the United States when the War Production Board ordered the closing of non-essential gold mines to release personnel, equipment, and materials for essential defense production. United States v. Central Eureka Mining Co., 357 U.S. 155 (1958). Compare also National Board of YMCA v. United States, 395 U.S. 85 (1969) (suit for damage inflicted by rioters after U. S. troops retreated into buildings).

46. 328 U.S. 256 (1946). Later cases extended the principle to other "takings" by aviation. Griggs v. County of Allegheny, 369 U.S. 84 (1962). But *cf.* Laird v. Nelms, 406 U.S. 797 (1972).

47. 3 Dall. 199 (U.S.1796).

48. 3 Dall. at 281, 283.

49. *Id.* at 245 (emphasis in original). Chase continued: "Although Virginia is not bound to make compensation to the debtors, yet it is evident that they ought to be indemnified, and it is not to be supposed, that those whose duty it may be to make the compensation, will permit the rights of our citizens to be sacrificed to a public object, without the fullest indemnity."

Compare W. COWLES, TREATIES AND CONSTITUTIONAL LAW 292–95 (1941), suggesting that this case would not be followed today. His argument, however, does not lead to the conclusion that the treaty is invalid, but rather than to bring it into effect domestically in the United States Congress would have to meet the requirements of the Fifth Amendment and provide compensation. A court, therefore, might well follow *Ware v. Hylton* and give effect to the treaty, leaving the debtor to an action in the Court of Claims on a claim "founded upon the Constitution." *Cf.* Cities Serv. Co. v. McGrath, 342 U.S. 330

(1952), discussed this chapter, pp. 261–62. And see HENKIN, ARMS CONTROL 230–31 n. 20.

If in a situation like that in *Ware v. Hylton* the courts were to decide in favor of the American citizen whose property rights are involved, the United States might fulfill its international obligations by compensating the foreign claimant. Compare the treaties discussed above in Chapter VII, note 33.

50. 342 U.S. 330 (1952).

51. 342 U.S. at 336. *Cf.* Yearsley v. W. A. Ross Constr. Co., 309 U.S. 18, 21 (1940); Hurley v. Kincaid, 285 U.S. 95 (1932).

52. See M. HUDSON, INTERNATIONAL TRIBUNALS 196 (1944). In some cases private claims were adjudicated by joint claims commissions. See, *e. g.*, Convention Between the United States of America and the Republic of Mexico for the Adjustment of Claims, July 4, 1868, art. II, 15 Stat. 682, T.S.No. 212; compare the Agreement Between the United States and Canada Concerning the Establishment of an International Arbitral Tribunal to Dispose of United States Claims Relating to Gut Dam, March 25, 1965, [1966] 17 U.S.T. 1566, T.I.A.S. No. 6114, 52 DEP'T STATE BULL. 643 (1965). Many claims settlements have been by executive agreement. Compare Chapter VI, note 25. Congress authorized the establishment of the Foreign Claims Settlement Commission to adjudicate American claims and determine their validity and amount. International Claims Settlement Act of 1949, ch. 54, 64 Stat. 12 (1950), 22 U.S.C. § 1621 *et seq.*, as amended, Foreign Claims Settlement Commission Act, ch. 645, 69 Stat. 562 (1955), pursuant to Reorganization Plan No. 1 of 1954, 68 Stat. 1279 (1954). See also the Cuban Claims Act [also applicable to Communist China], Pub.L.No.88–666, 78 Stat. 1110 (1964), as amended, 22 U.S.C. § 1643 *et seq.* (1970). There is no appeal from the Commission to the courts, 22 U.S.C. § 1623h (1970).

53. But *cf.* Meade v. United States, 9 Wall. 691 (U.S.1869), where the Court struggled with whether the claimant had authorized the United States to deal with his claim. See generally HENKIN, ARMS CONTROL 109–10 and notes.

54. See Article V, Convention of Peace, Commerce and Navigation, Sept. 30, 1800, 1 MALLOY 496, 498.

55. Congress adopted three bills to provide for payment, but the first two were vetoed, one by Polk, another by Pierce. The whole story is told at length in Gray v. United States, 21 Ct.Cl. 340 (1886). In that case the Court of Claims dismissed the claim because the claim for compensation was not enforceable without Congressional legislation. See also Buchanan v. United States, 24 Ct.Cl. 74, 82 (1889). Congress later paid, no doubt partly in response to the pleas of the Court of Claims quoted p. 264.

56. The Constitutional provision prohibiting impairment of the obligation of contracts (Art. 1, sec. 10) is directed to the States, but similar limitations have been held to apply to the federal government by virtue of the due process clause of the Fifth Amendment. Lynch v. United States, 292 U.S. 571 (1934); Perry v. United States, 294 U.S. 330 (1935).

57. Compare Meade v. United States, 9 Wall. 691 (U.S. 1869); Comegys v. Vasse, 1 Pet. 193 (U.S.1803); Alling v. United States, 114 U.S. 562 (1885).

58. The Supreme Court has referred to Congressional payments in such a case "as of grace and not of right." Blagge v. Balch, 162 U.S. 439, 457 (1896). Compare a recent case, Aris Gloves, Inc. v. United States, 420 F.2d 1386 (Ct.Cl. 1970). The Supreme Court held also that even payments received "on behalf of" an American claimant do not legally belong to him, and the Executive Branch could refuse to remit payments received from the Mexican Government (allegedly because it suspected the claimants of fraud). La Abra Silver Mining Co. v. United States, 175 U.S. 423 (1899); United States *ex rel.* Boynton v. Blaine, 139 U.S. 306 (1891); Frelinghuysen v. Key, 110 U.S. 63 (1884). *Cf.* Z. & F. Assets Realization Corp. v. Hull, 311 U.S. 470 (1941).

59. Compare Chief Justice Marshall: " . . . but in great national concerns, where individual rights, acquired by war, are sacrificed for national purposes, the contract making the sacrifice ought always to receive a construction conforming to its manifest import; and if the nation has given up the vested rights of its citizens, it is not for the court, but for the government, to consider whether it be a case proper for compensation." United States v. Schooner Peggy, 1 Cranch 103, 110 (U.S.1801).

60. Gray v. United States, 21 Ct.Cl. 340, 392–93 (1886).

61. For the jurisdiction of the Court of Claims, see 28 U.S.C. § 1491 (1970). There is, however, an ambiguous limitation barring the Court of Claims from hearing any claim against the United States "growing out of or dependent upon any treaty." 28 U.S.C. § 1502. *Cf.* Alling v. United States, 114 U.S. 562 (1885).

62. See Leigh and Atkeson, *Due Process in the Emerging Foreign Relations Law of the United States,* 22 BUSINESS LAWYER 3, 23–26 (1966), suggesting that there may be a substantive right to compensation when, in the interests of achieving national foreign policy objectives, one's property rights are abridged, one's foreign claim is settled over his objection, or one is compelled to release an attachment of property of a foreign sovereign. These authors have also proposed that future claims settlements go to the Senate for ratification, thus affording private claimants an opportunity to be heard there. 21

BUSINESS LAWYER at 875–876. Compare generally Sax, *Takings and the Police Power*, 74 YALE L.J. 36, 63 (1964).

63. International organizations and their officials generally enjoy only "functional immunity", those privileges and immunities needed for carrying out their official functions. Compare the Convention on Privileges and Immunities of the United Nations, 1 U.N.T.S. 15 (1946); *cf.* also the International Organizations Immunities Act, 22 U.S.C. § 288 *et seq.* (1970). Representatives of Members to the U. N. enjoy full diplomatic privileges and immunities. Agreement between the United States of America and the United Nations regarding the Headquarters of the United Nations, June 26, 1947, 61 Stat. 3416, T.I.A.S. No. 1676.

64. Diplomatic immunity might raise other questions. For example, an accused is entitled "to have compulsory process for obtaining witnesses in his favor" (U.S.Const., Amend. VI), but international law denies the United States the right to compel a diplomat to testify. The international immunity has been considered a historical exception to the constitutional requirement, and recent extensions of immunity to new categories (*e. g.*, international officials or member representatives to the UN, note 63 this chapter) would also prevail despite the constitutional language. In 1854 Secretary of State Marcy said that the constitutional right to compulsory testimony was at its inception limited by diplomatic immunity to subpoena and other compulsory process, but consuls had no such immunity under international law and a grant of immunity by treaty was unconstitutional. See 5 MOORE, DIGEST OF INTERNATIONAL LAW § 736 at 167. A lower federal court, however, held the treaty exemption for consuls valid, interpreting the Sixth Amendment as satisfied when both the prosecution and the defendant are subject to the same limitations. See *In re* Dillon, 7 F.Cas. 710 (No. 3914) (N.D.Cal.1854). (The United States has long discontinued such consular exemptions.) Compare the Supreme Court's view that the United States may have to choose between making "privileged" evidence available to an accused or foregoing the prosecution. Jencks v. United States, 353 U.S. 657 (1957), Chapter IV, note 63.

65. *In re* Ross, 140 U.S. 453, 464 (1891).

Consular courts exercised jurisdiction over offenses by American citizens in many "uncivilized" countries under treaties that granted exclusive jurisdiction to the United States. *Ross* upheld their constitutionality. A brief history of these consular courts can be found in Justice Frankfurter's concurring opinion in Reid v. Covert, 354 U.S. 1, 56–64 (1957).

66. 354 U.S. 1 (1957).

67. *Id.* at 12; also at 1. Black used other language suggesting that the Constitution might govern almost all acts of the United States anywhere. Justice Frankfurter also emphasized the historical context of *Ross*, but said only that the Constitution applied in some situations, leaving further refinement of that doctrine to the future. *Id.* at 41, 64. Justice Harlan found that *Ross* did not apply to the case before him but emphasized that the applicability of constitutional requirements to United States action abroad would depend on the "particular circumstances, the practical necessities, and the possible alternatives which Congress had before it." *Id.* at 65, 75. The implications of *Reid v. Covert* were confirmed and extended in other cases invalidating court martial jurisdiction over civilians abroad, Chapter III, note 42.

The *Insular Cases* and the case of U.S. occupation courts, pp. 52, 105 above, were distinguished by Justice Black in his *Reid* opinion. The Status of Forces Agreements distributing jurisdiction over visiting forces between the host and the sending state do not raise these issues. See Chapter VII, n. 40. As regards an American in an allied country, it is not the Agreement that subjects him to the jurisdiction of foreign courts where he does not enjoy the protections of the Bill of Rights. He is subject to foreign jurisdiction because he is in foreign territory, by virtue of the domestic laws of that country and the accepted international principle of territorial sovereignty. The Agreement merely confirms that principle and modifies it to the extent that the host country agrees that in some circumstances a visiting soldier will not be subject to local jurisdiction, but only, or primarily, to that of his military authorities. Equally flimsy is the argument that the United States can not constitutionally send troops abroad against their will and thereby expose them to foreign laws and lesser safeguards than they enjoy under the Constitution. A few months after *Reid v. Covert*, the Supreme Court unanimously rejected such arguments. Wilson v. Girard, 354 U.S. 524 (1957). One might note too that it is not sending a soldier abroad that deprives him of the particular constitutional rights in question—jury trial and other elements of due process; the soldier does not enjoy them even in the United States since military justice does not provide them. But *cf.* O'Callahan v. Parker, 395 U.S. 258 (1969), where the Court held that a soldier cannot be tried by court-martial for non-service-connected crimes committed in the United States in time of peace. See also Flemings v. Chafee, 458 F.2d 544 (2d Cir. 1972), *cert. granted*, 407 U.S. 919 (1972).

68. 354 U.S. at 6.

69. The opinions in *Reid*, note 67 this chapter, leave doubt as to whether abroad, as in the United States, the Bill of Rights protects
500

all who are subject to an exercise of U.S. authority, or whether it protects only the United States citizen. While there is language in Justice Black's opinion implying that the United States can never act free of constitutional limitations, he stressed that American citizens were involved in the case before him. For the Justices who took a more limited view of constitutional rights abroad, the citizenship of the claimant might be a critical factor.

"Extra-territorial" legislation by one of the States would probably violate due process. Compare Pennoyer v. Neff, 95 U.S. 714 (1878); Union Refrigerator Transit Co. v. Kentucky, 199 U.S. 194, 204 (1905); United States v. Bevans, 3 Wheat. 336, 386–87 (U.S.1818); but *cf*. Skiriotes v. Florida, 313 U.S. 69 (1941).

No one has suggested that it is a denial of due process for the United States to apply its laws to acts of American nationals abroad or to others whom it can reach under one of the bases of prescriptive jurisdiction accepted under international law. See Chapter II, note 55.

70. Compare note 11, this chapter; but *cf*. note 22.

71. Compare note 22, this chapter.

72. Johnson v. Eisentrager, 339 U.S. 763 (1950). See pp. 255, 258 above. And compare the *Mandel* case, note 35, this chapter.

73. Dorr v. United States, 195 U.S. 138 (1904); Balzac v. Puerto Rico, 258 U.S. 298 (1922); Hawaii v. Mankichi, 190 U.S. 197 (1903); *cf*. Downes v. Bidwell, 182 U.S. 244 (1901).

74. 354 U.S. at 14.

75. Palko v. Connecticut, 302 U.S. 319 (1937); Snyder v. Massachusetts, 291 U.S. 97 (1934); Rochin v. California, 342 U.S. 165 (1952). See note 77, this chapter.

76. Barron v. Baltimore, 7 Pet. 243 (U.S.1833).

77. As regards the States, the liberty protected by the due process clause has long included all the "preferred freedoms" which the First Amendment safeguards against undue federal encroachment. See note 15, this chapter. Until the 1960's, however, the Court eschewed the doctrine propounded by Mr. Justice Black in his dissent in Adamson v. California, 332 U.S. 46, 68, 92 (1947), that the Fourteenth Amendment "incorporated" all of the Bill of Rights and made it applicable to the States. Instead, the Court was deciding case by case whether the procedure in a State case was basically unfair; whether the same procedure if applied by the Federal Government would have violated one of the specific provisions of the Bill of Rights was not determinative. In the 1960's, however, the Court adopted a modified version of Black's doctrine, "selective incorporation": those provisions of the Bill of Rights that are "fundamental" are incorporated in the Fourteenth Amendment and applicable to the States exactly as to the Federal Government. Compare Henkin, *"Selective Incorporation"*

*in the Fourteenth Amendment,* 73 YALE L.J. 74 (1963). By 1969 all the principal provisions governing criminal procedure except the grand jury requirement (Amendment VI) had been held fundamental and incorporated. Mapp v. Ohio, 367 U.S. 643 (1961) (exclusion of evidence obtained by unlawful search and seizure); Malloy v. Hogan, 378 U.S. 1 (1964) (privilege against self-incrimination); Gideon v. Wainwright, 372 U.S. 335 (1965) (right to counsel); Klopfer v. North Carolina, 386 U.S. 213 (1967); Pointer v. Texas, 380 U.S. 400 (1965) (confrontation of witnesses); Washington v. Texas, 388 U.S. 14 (1967) (compulsory process for obtaining witnesses); Duncan v. Louisiana, 391 U.S. 145 (1968) (jury trial in criminal cases); Benton v. Maryland, 395 U.S. 784 (1969) (double jeopardy); also *In re* Oliver, 333 U.S. 257 (1948) (public trial). Perhaps because these provisions had been extended to the States, however, the Court was recently moved to reduce their content. See *e. g.,* Williams v. Florida, 399 U.S. 78 (1970) (jury of fewer than 12 permissible); Apodaca v. Oregon, 406 U.S. 404 (1972) (jury verdict need not be unanimous); Colten v. Kentucky, 407 U.S. 104 (1972) (double jeopardy); *cf.* Kastigar v. United States, 406 U.S. 441 (1972) (Fifth Amendment guarantees only "functional immunity").

During the heyday of selective incorporation the Court looked to the Bill of Rights (as incorporated) to protect rights against State infringement. It went to great lengths to find safeguards in the Bill of Rights rather than invoke "substantive due process" (p. 256 above): compare Griswold v. Connecticut, 381 U.S. 479 (1965), where a majority of the Court found a right of marital privacy in the "penumbra" of several provisions of the Bill of Rights and incorporated it in the Fourteenth Amendment. It also revitalized the equal protection clause, p. 258 above. As the composition of the Court changed in 1969–72 new Justices were also looking over the doctrine of incorporation and of substantive due process. Compare Mr. Justice Powell concurring in Apodaca v. Oregon, *supra.*

78. Yick Wo v. Hopkins, 118 U.S. 356 (1886); Truax v. Raich, 239 U.S. 33 (1915); Wong Wing v. United States, 163 U.S. 228 (1896); Takahashi v. Fish and Game Commission, 334 U.S. 410 (1948); see also the concurring opinions in Oyama v. California, 332 U.S. 633, 647, 650 (1948). See Comment, *The Alien and the Constitution,* 20 U.CHI. L.REV. 547 (1953).

Although a State cannot bar an immigrant alien from employment, p. 270 above, an alien has no right to work in the face of restrictions imposed by the United States as conditions of his entry in non-immigrant status. Pilapil v. Immigration and Naturalization Service, 424 F.2d 6 (10th Cir. 1970), *cert. denied,* 400 U.S. 908 (1970); Wei v.

Robinson, 246 F.2d 739 (7th Cir. 1957), *cert. denied*, 355 U.S. 879 (1957).

79. Compare this chapter, notes 39, 40.

80. The Civil Rights Act of 1870 granted basic rights to aliens as well as citizens, note 78 this chapter, ch. 114, 16 Stat. 144 (1870), 42 U.S.C. § 1981 *et seq.* (1970). *Takahashi* also held that state laws barring aliens from common employments were inconsistent with the Immigration Laws admitting aliens to residence. Earlier cases upholding some State discriminations against aliens (Ohio *ex rel.* Clarke v. Deckebach, 274 U.S. 392 (1927); Terrace v. Thompson, 263 U.S. 197 (1923); Heim v. McCall, 239 U.S. 175 (1915)), are now of dubious validity, for "the power of a state to apply its laws exclusively to its alien inhabitants as a class is confined within narrow limits." *Takahashi, supra,* at 420. That power has been further narrowed, no doubt, by Hines v. Davidowitz, 312 U.S. 52 (1941) (Congressional preemption), and Zschernig v. Miller, 389 U.S. 429 (1968), Chapter IX, pp. 238, 243 above. And see the following note.

81. Graham v. Richardson, 403 U.S. 365 (1971).

82. Compare Crane v. New York, 239 U.S. 195 (1915), upholding the exclusion of aliens from employment on public works. Relying on more recent cases, notably *Graham* (see the previous note), lower courts have reached the opposite result. See, *e. g.,* Teitscheid v. Leopold, 342 F.Supp. 299 (D.Vt.1971); compare Dougall v. Sugarman, 339 F.Supp. 906 (S.D.N.Y.1971), *probable jurisdiction noted,* 407 U.S. 908 (1972); also Purdy & Fitzpatrick v. State, 79 Cal. 77, 456 P.2d 645 (1969).

NOTES, CHAPTER XI, CONCLUSION, pp. 271 to 281.

1. Letter to H. S. Randall, May 23, 1857, in 2 G. O. TREVELYAN, THE LIFE AND LETTERS OF LORD MACAULAY 409–10 (1875).

2. Holmes, J., Missouri v. Holland, 252 U.S. 416, 433 (1920).

3. "Great cases like hard cases make bad law." Holmes, J., dissenting in Northern Securities Co. v. United States, 193 U.S. 197, 400–401 (1904). But compare Henkin, *The Right to Know and the Duty to Withhold: The Case of the Pentagon Papers*, 120 U.PA.L.REV. 271 (1971).

4. Compare Senator Fulbright's earlier view that "for the existing requirements of American foreign policy we have hobbled the President by too niggardly a grant of power," Fulbright, *American Foreign Policy in the 20th Century under an 18th Century Constitution*, 47 CORNELL L.Q. 1, 2 (1961), and Fulbright, *Foreign Policy—Old Myths and New Realities*, 53 KY.L.J. 13, 33 (1964–65), with his later views as expressed in *Hearings, Separation of Powers*, and *Hearings, National Commitments*, Chapter III, note 70; Chapter IV, note 30; Chapter V, notes 16 and 33.

5. For example, the suggestion for a Congressional Force Committee that would share with the President any decision to use force short of war. See *Hearings, Separation of Powers* at 164. Compare Chapter IV, pp. 102–103.

6. Mr. Justice Jackson concurring in Youngstown Sheet & Tube Co. v. Sawyer, 343 U.S. 579, 654 (1952).

7. For reflections by a contemporary, renowned Secretary of State on relations between President and Congress in foreign relations and on bi-partisan and non-partisan foreign policy, see D. ACHESON, PRESENT AT THE CREATION (1969) especially at 95–101, 318. Note in particular his report of Senator Taft's view that the purpose of an Opposition is to oppose. *Id.* at 95–97.

Compare President Truman: "I've always said that the President who didn't have a fight with the Congress wasn't any good anyhow. And that's no reflection on the Congress. They are always looking after their rights. You needn't doubt that." Speech, May 8, 1954 reprinted in R. HIRSCHFELD, THE POWER OF THE PRESIDENCY 111, 113 (1968).

8. Chancellor Kent, quoted in Myers v. United States, 272 U.S. 52, 149 (1926).

9. Holmes, J., dissenting in Tyson & Brother v. Banton, 273 U.S. 418, 445 (1927).

10. *The Treaty Makers and the Law Makers: The Law of the Land in Foreign Relations,* 107 U.PA.L.REV. 903, 936 (1959).

11. Gladstone, *Kin Beyond Sea,* 127 NORTH AMERICAN REVIEW 185 (1878).

# CASES CITED

Abby Dodge, The, 223 U.S. 166 (1912): p. 319 (c. III, n. 9)

Abel v. United States, 362 U.S. 217 (1960): pp. 488 (c. X, n. 10), 491 (c. X, n. 23)

Abington School Dist. v. Schempp, 374 U.S. 203 (1963): p. 448 (c. VIII, n. 19)

Abrey v. Reusch, 153 F.Supp. 337 (S.C.N.Y.1957): p. 441 (c. VII, n. 38)

Adair v. United States, 208 U.S. 161 (1908): p. 492 (c. X, n. 27)

Adams v. Williams, 407 U.S. 143 (1972): p. 489 (c. X, n. 19)

Adamson v. California, 332 U.S. 46 (1947): p. 501 (c. X, n. 77)

Adkins v. Children's Hospital, 261 U.S. 525 (1923): p. 492 (c. X, n. 27)

Afroyim v. Rusk, 387 U.S. 253 (1967): pp. 292 (c. I, nn. 14, 17), 326 (c. III, n. 39), 447 (c. VIII, n. 16), 485 (c. X, n. 6), 486 (c. X, n. 6)

Alabama v. Texas, 347 U.S. 272 (1954): pp. 330 (c. III, n. 51), 331 (c. III, n. 52)

Alabama v. United States, 373 U.S. 545 (1963): p. 414 (c. V, n. 119)

Allen v. Riley, 203 U.S. 347 (1906): p. 469 (c. IX, n. 28)

Alling v. United States, 114 U.S. 562 (1885): p. 498 (c. X, nn. 57, 61)

Amalgamated Meat Cutters & Butcher Workmen of North America v. Connally, 337 F.Supp. 737 (D.C.D.C.1971): p. 319 (c. III, n. 7)

American Banana Co. v. United Fruit Co., 213 U.S. 347 (1909): p. 326 (c. III, n. 41)

American Ins. Co. v. Canter, 1 Pet. 516 (U.S.1828): pp. 288 (c. I, n. 3), 321 (c. III, n. 15), 329 (c. III, n. 50), 439 (c. VII, n. 31)

American Public Power Ass'n v. Power Authority, 355 U.S. 64 (1957): p. 381 (c. V, n. 28)

Ames v. Kansas, 111 U.S. 449 (1884): p. 445 (c. VIII, n. 8)

Anderson v. Dunn, 6 Wheat. 204 (U.S.1821): p. 358 (c. IV, n. 66)

Anderson v. N. V. Transandine Handelmaatschappij, 289 N.Y. 9, 43 N. E.2d 502 (1942): p. 313 (c. II, n. 67)

Apodaca v. Oregon, 406 U.S. 404 (1972): p. 502 (c. X, n. 77)

Aptheker v. Secretary of State, 378 U.S. 500 (1964): pp. 447 (c. VIII, n. 16), 493 (c. X, n. 33)

Aquascutum of London, Inc. v. SS American Champion, 426 F.2d 205 (2d Cir. 1970): p. 479 (c. IX, n. 62)

Aris Gloves, Inc. v. United States, 420 F.2d 1386 (Ct.Cl.1970): p. 498 (c. X, n. 58)

Cook v. United States, 288 U.S. 102 (1933): p. 411 (c. V, n. 113)

Cooley v. Board of Wardens of the Port of Philadelphia, 12 How. 299 (U.S.1851): pp. 469 (c. IX, n. 29), 471 (c. IX, n. 33)

Coolidge v. New Hampshire, 403 U.S. 443 (1971): p. 489 (c. X, n. 19)

Cooper v. Aaron, 358 U.S. 1 (1958): pp. 287 (c. I, n. 6), 444 (c. VIII, n. 1)

Cordova v. Grant, 248 U.S. 413 (1919): p. 451 (c. VIII, n. 27)

Cotzhausen v. Nazro, 107 U.S. 215 (1882): pp. 407 (c. V, n. 99), 423 (c. VI, n. 10)

Covington and Lexington Turnpike Road Co. v. Sandford, 164 U.S. 578 (1896): p. 488 (c. X, n. 11)

Cowans v. Ticonderoga Pulp & Paper Co., 219 App.Div. 120, 219 N.Y.S. 284, aff'd mem., 246 N.Y. 603, 159 N.E. 669 (1927): p. 455 (c. VIII, n. 37)

Cox v. Wood, 247 U.S. 3 (1918): p. 307 (c. II, n. 45)

Crane v. New York, 239 U.S. 195 (1915): p. 503 (c. X, n. 82)

Cross v. Harrison, 16 How. 164 (U.S.1853): p. 305 (c. II, n. 37)

Crowell v. Benson, 285 U.S. 22 (1932): pp. 441 (c. VII, n. 38), 448 (c. VIII, n. 19)

Curcio v. United States, 354 U.S. 118 (1957): p. 488 (c. X, n. 11)

Currin v. Wallace, 306 U.S. 1 (1939): p. 366 (c. IV, n. 95)


Da Costa v. Laird, 448 F.2d 1368 (2d Cir. 1971), cert. denied, 405 U.S. 979 (1972): pp. 351 (c. IV, n. 47), 453 (c. VIII, n. 32)

Dandridge v. Williams, 397 U.S. 471 (1970): p. 495 (c. X, nn. 38, 39)

Davis v. Department of Labor and Industries, 317 U.S. 249 (1942): p. 474 (c. IX, n. 43)

Day-Brite Lighting, Inc. v. Missouri, 342 U.S. 421 (1952): p. 493 (c. X, n. 29)

Dean Milk Co. v. City of Madison, 340 U.S. 349 (1951): p. 472 (c. IX, n. 39)

In re Debs, 158 U.S. 564 (1895): p. 415 (c. V, n. 126)

Dennis v. United States, 341 U.S. 494 (1951): p. 489 (c. X, n. 16)

Dept. of Revenue v. James Beam Distilling Co., 377 U.S. 341 (1964): pp. 464 (c. IX, n. 4), 470 (c. IX, n. 29)

In re Dillon, 7 F.Cas. 710 (No.3914) (N.D.Cal.1854): p. 499 (c. X, n. 64)

Doe v. Braden, 16 How. 635 (U.S.1853): p. 386 (c. V, n. 40)

D'Oench, Duhme & Co. v. E.D.I.C., 315 U.S. 447 (1942): p. 453 (c. VIII, n. 34)

Dooley v. United States, 182 U.S. 222 (1901): pp. 305 (c. II, n. 37), 340 (c. IV, n. 8)

Doremus v. Board of Education, 342 U.S. 429 (1952): pp. 445 (c. VIII, n. 7), 447 (c. VIII, n. 13)

Dorr v. United States, 195 U.S. 138 (1904): pp. 268, 330 (c. III, n. 50), 408 (c. V, n. 103), 500 (c. X, n. 67), 501 (c. X, n. 73)

Dougall v. Sugarman, 339 F.Supp. 906 (S.D.N.Y.1971), probable jurisdiction noted, 407 U.S. 908 (1972): p. 503 (c. X, n. 82)

Downes v. Bidwell, 182 U.S. 244 (1901): pp. 268, 330 (c. III, n. 50), 395 (c. V, n. 72), 408 (c. V, n. 103), 500 (c. X, n. 67), 501 (c. X, n. 73)

Duckworth v. Arkansas, 314 U.S. 390 (1941): p. 470 (c. IX, n. 30)

Duncan v. Louisiana, 391 U.S. 145 (1968): p. 502 (c. X, n. 77)

Dunn v. Blumstein, 405 U.S. 330 (1972): p. 495 (c. X, n. 39)

Duple Motor Bodies, Ltd. v. Hollingsworth, 417 F.2d 231 (9th Cir. 1969): p. 478 (c. IX, n. 62)

Durand v. Hollins, 8 F.Cas. 111 (No.4186) (C.C.S.D.N.Y.1860): p. 308 (c. II, n. 47)


Edison v. Labor Board, 305 U.S. 197 (1938): p. 490 (c. X, n. 21)

Electric Bond & Share Co. v. SEC, 303 U.S. 419 (1938): p. 319 (c. III, n. 7)

Empresa Siderurgica v. Merced County, 337 U.S. 154 (1949): p. 464 (c. IX, n. 5)

Ex parte Endo, 323 U.S. 283 (1944): p. 334 (c. III, n. 61)

Erie R. R. v. Hamilton, 248 U.S. 369 (1919): p. 386 (c. V, n. 42)

Erie R. R. v. Tompkins, 304 U.S. 64 (1938): pp. 217, 444 (c. VIII, n. 2), 454 (c. VIII, n. 34), 455 (c. VIII, n. 39), 461 (c. VIII, n. 65)

Estrella, The, 4 Wheat. 298 (U.S.1819): p. 406 (c. V, n. 99)

Etlimar Société Anonyme of Casablanca v. United States, 106 F.Supp. 191 (Ct.Cl.1952): p. 433 (c. VI, n. 42)

Exchange, The Schooner v. M'Faddon, 7 Cranch 116 (U.S.1812): pp. 419 (c. V, n. 138), 460 (c. VIII, n. 60)


Factor v. Laubenheimer, 290 U.S. 276 (1933): p. 416 (c. V, n. 128)

Fairbank v. United States, 181 U.S. 283 (1901): p. 337 (c. III, n. 79)

Faruki v. Rogers (D.D.C.1972): p. 486 (c. X, n. 6)

FCC v. Pottsville Broadcasting Co., 309 U.S. 134 (1940): p. 366 (c. IV, n. 95)

Field v. Clark, 143 U.S. 649 (1892): pp. 366 (c. IV, n. 93), 367 (c. IV, n. 96), 385 (c. V, n. 36)

First National City Bank v. Banco Nacional de Cuba, 406 U.S. 759 (1972): pp. 63, 64, 220, 315 (c. II, n. 77), 456 (c. VIII, n. 45), 458 (c. VIII, n. 51), 492 (c. X, n. 25)

Flast v. Cohen, 392 U.S. 83 (1968): pp. 329 (c. III, n. 48), 446 (c. VIII, n. 9), 447 (c. VIII, n. 13), 448 (c. VIII, n. 19)

Fleming v. Mohawk Wrecking & Lumber Co., 331 U.S. 111 (1947): p. 334 (c. III, n. 61)

Humphrey's Ex'r v. United States, 295 U.S. 602 (1935): pp. 300 (c. II, n. 19), 365 (c. IV, n. 87)

Hurd v. Hodge, 334 U.S. 24 (1948): p. 494 (c. X, n. 36)

Hurley v. Kincaid, 285 U.S. 95 (1932): p. 497 (c. X, n. 51)

Huron Portland Cement Co. v. City of Detroit, 362 U.S. 440 (1960): pp. 472 (c. IX, n. 38), 473 (c. IX, n. 40)

Illinois v. City of Milwaukee, 406 U.S. 91 (1972): pp. 446 (c. VIII, n. 8), 453 (c. VIII, n. 34), 457 (c. VIII, n. 48)

Indianapolis Brewing Co. v. Liquor Control Commission, 305 U.S. 391 (1939): p. 469 (c. IX, n. 29)

Ioannou v. New York, 371 U.S. 30 (1962): p. 476 (c. IX, n. 47)

Ioannou v. New York, 391 U.S. 604 (1968): p. 476 (c. IX, n. 47)

Isabella, The Amiable, 6 Wheat. 1 (U.S.1821): p. 417 (c. V, n. 133)

Isbrandtsen-Moller Co. v. United States, 300 U.S. 139 (1937): p. 334 (c. III, n. 61)

James v. Dravo Contracting Co., 302 U.S. 134 (1937): p. 466 (c. IX, n. 16)

James v. Strange, 407 U.S. 128 (1972): p. 495 (c. X, n. 39)

James v. Valtierra, 402 U.S. 137 (1971): p. 495 (c. X, n. 39)

James & Co. v. Second Russian Ins. Co., 239 N.Y. 248, 146 N.E. 369 (1925): p. 431 (c. VI, n. 36)

Japanese Immigrant Case, 189 U.S. 86 (1903): p. 491 (c. X, n. 23)

Jay v. Boyd, 351 U.S. 345 (1956): pp. 369 (c. IV, n. 104), 491 (c. X, n. 23)

Jefferson v. Hackney, 406 U.S. 535 (1972): p. 495 (c. X, n. 39)

Jencks v. United States, 353 U.S. 657 (1957): pp. 357 (c. IV, n. 63), 499 (c. X, n. 64)

Johnson v. Eisentrager, 339 U.S. 763 (1950): pp. 490 (c. X, n. 21), 501 (c. X, n. 72)

Johnston v. Compagnie Générale Transatlantique, 242 N.Y. 381, 152 N.E. 121 (1926): pp. 455 (c. VIII, nn. 37, 38), 456 (c. VIII, n. 47)

Joint Anti-Fascist Refugee Comm. v. McGrath, 341 U.S. 123 (1951): p. 486 (c. X, n. 7)

Jolley v. Immigration and Naturalization Service, 441 F.2d 1245 (1971): p. 492 (c. X, n. 23)

Jones v. Alfred H. Mayer Co., 392 U.S. 409 (1968): pp. 292 (c. I, n. 18), 331 (c. III, n. 53)

Jones v. Meehan, 175 U.S. 1 (1899): p. 416 (c. V, n. 128)

Jones v. United States, 137 U.S. 202 (1890): pp. 288 (c. I, n. 5), 292 (c. I, n. 15), 330 (c. III, n. 50), 451 (c. VIII, n. 27)

Joseph v. Carter & Weeks Co., 330 U.S. 422 (1947): p. 473 (c. IX, n. 42)

519

## Cases Cited

NLRB v. Jones & Laughlin Steel Corp., 301 U.S. 1 (1937): pp. 277, 292 (c. I, n. 18), 318 (c. III, nn. 6, 8)

Northern Securities Co. v. United States, 193 U.S. 197 (1904): p. 504 (c. XI, n. 3)

O'Callahan v. Parker, 395 U.S. 258 (1969): pp. 327 (c. III, n. 42), 500 (c. X, n. 67)

O'Donoghue v. United States, 289 U.S. 516 (1933): p. 439 (c. VII, n. 31)

Oetjen v. Central Leather Co., 246 U.S. 297 (1918): pp. 311 (c. II, n. 57), 450 (c. VIII, n. 26), 451 (c. VIII, n. 28), 463 (c. VIII, n. 69)

Ogden v. Saunders, 12 Wheat. 213 (U.S.1827): p. 469 (c. IX, n. 28)

Ohio v. Wyandotte Chemicals Corp., 401 U.S. 493 (1971): p. 446 (c. VIII, n. 8)

Ohio ex rel. Bryant v. Akron Metropolitan Park District, 281 U.S. 74 (1930): p. 396 (c. V, n. 73)

Ohio ex rel. Clarke v. Deckebach, 274 U.S. 392 (1927): p. 503 (c. X, n. 80)

Oklahoma Press Publishing Co. v. Walling, 327 U.S. 186 (1946): p. 488 (c. X, n. 11)

In re Oliver, 333 U.S. 257 (1948): p. 502 (c. X, n. 77)

Oliver American Trading Co. v. Mexico, 264 U.S. 440 (1924): p. 461 (c. VIII, n. 64)

Opp Cotton Mills v. Administrator, 312 U.S. 126 (1949): p. 490 (c. X, n. 21)

Oregon v. Mitchell, 400 U.S. 112 (1970): pp. 293 (c. I, n. 18), 331 (c. III, n. 53), 447 (c. VIII, n. 16), 480 (c. IX, n. 66), 484 (c. X, n. 1)

Orient Insurance Co. v. Daggs, 172 U.S. 557 (1899): p. 488 (c. X, n. 11)

Orlando v. Laird, 443 F.2d 1039 (2d Cir.), cert. denied, 404 U.S. 869 (1971): pp. 347 (c. IV, n. 28), 453 (c. VIII, n. 32)

Orono, The, 18 F.Cas. 830 (No. 10,585) (C.C.Mass.1812): p. 349 (c. IV, n. 41)

Over the Top, The, 5 F.2d 838 (D.Conn.1925): p. 461 (c. VIII, n. 61)

Oyama v. California, 332 U.S. 633 (1948): p. 502 (c. X, n. 78)

Pacific Telephone Co. v. Oregon, 223 U.S. 118 (1912): p. 396 (c. V, n. 73)

Palko v. Connecticut, 302 U.S. 319 (1938), overruled: pp. 485 (c. X, n. 5), 501 (c. X, n. 75)

Panama Refining Co. v. Ryan, 293 U.S. 388 (1935): pp. 366 (c. IV, n. 95), 367 (c. IV, n. 97)

Paquete Habana, The, 175 U.S. 677 (1900): pp. 221 (c. VIII), 310 (c. II, n. 55), 311 (c. II, n. 58), 459 (c. VIII, n. 59), 460 (c. VIII, n. 61), 461 (c. VIII, n. 62)

Ex parte Quirin, 317 U.S. 1 (1942): pp. 291 (c. I, n. 12), 305 (c. II, n. 36), 322 (c. III, n. 24), 333 (c. III, n. 59), 339 (c. IV, n. 1), 454 (c. VIII, n. 35), 459 (c. VIII, n. 59), 494 (c. X, n. 34)

In re Rahrer, 140 U.S. 545 (1891): p. 473 (c. IX, n. 43)

Railway Express Agency, Inc. v. New York, 336 U.S. 106 (1949): p. 494 (c. X, nn. 36, 38)

Reed v. Pennsylvania R. R., 351 U.S. 502 (1956): p. 318 (c. III, n. 7)

Reichert v. Felps, 6 Wall. 160 (U.S.1868): p. 410 (c. V, n. 111)

Reid v. Covert, 354 U.S. 1 (1957): pp. 266–268, 327 (c. III, n. 42), 385 (c. V, n. 37), 386 (c. V, n. 45), 447 (c. VIII, n. 16), 485 (c. X, n. 6), 486 (c. X, n. 7), 499 (c. X, nn. 65, 66), 500 (c. X, nn. 67–69), 501 (c. X, n. 74)

Relford v. Commandant, U. S. Disciplinary Barracks, 401 U.S. 355 (1971): pp. 327 (c. III, n. 42), 332 (c. III, n. 54)

Republic of Iraq v. First National City Bank, 353 F.2d 47 (2d Cir. 1965), cert. denied, 382 U.S. 1027 (1966): p. 431 (c. VI, n. 36)

Republic of Mexico v. Hoffman, 324 U.S. 30 (1945): pp. 58, 312 (c. II, n. 62)

Ex parte Republic of Peru, 318 U.S. 578, 589 (1943): pp. 58, 63, 312 (c. II, n. 61)

Respublica v. De Longchamps, 1 Dall. 111 (Pa. O. & T.1784): pp. 406 (c. V, n. 99), 459 (c. VIII, n. 59), 479 (c. IX, n. 63)

Ricaud v. American Metal Co., 246 U.S. 304 (1918): p. 463 (c. VIII, n. 69)

Rice v. Santa Fe Elevator Corp., 331 U.S. 218 (1947): p. 478 (c. IX, n. 59)

Richardson v. Perales, 402 U.S. 389 (1971): p. 490 (c. X, n. 21)

Richfield Oil Corp. v. State Board, 329 U.S. 69 (1946): p. 464 (c. IX, n. 5)

Robbins v. Shelby County Taxing District, 120 U.S. 489 (1887): p. 473 (c. IX, n. 41)

Robertson v. Baldwin, 165 U.S. 275 (1897): p. 440 (c. VII, n. 36)

Robertson v. General Electric Co., 32 F.2d 495 (4th Cir.), cert. denied, 280 U.S. 571 (1929): p. 328 (c. III, n. 46)

Robertson v. R. R. Labor Board, 268 U.S. 619 (1925): p. 326 (c. III, n. 41)

Rochin v. California, 342 U.S. 165 (1952): p. 501 (c. X, n. 75)

Rogers v. Bellei, 401 U.S. 815 (1971): pp. 326 (c. III, n. 39), 485 (c. X, n. 6)

Romero v. International Terminal Operating Co., 358 U.S. 354 (1959): p. 454 (c. VIII, n. 36)

Rose v. Himely, 4 Cranch 241 (U.S.1808): p. 451 (c. VIII, n. 28)

In re Ross, 140 U.S. 453 (1891): pp. 499 (c. X, n. 65), 500 (c. X, n. 67)

526

# Cases Cited

Smallwood v. Clifford, 286 F.Supp. 97 (D.C.D.C.1968): p. 430 (c. VI, n. 30)

Smith v. Allwright, 321 U.S. 649 (1944): p. 287 (c. I, n. 7)

Smith v. Whitney, 116 U.S. 167 (1886): p. 305 (c. II, n. 35)

Smyth v. Ames, 169 U.S. 466 (1898): p. 488 (c. X, n. 11)

Snyder v. Massachusetts, 291 U.S. 97 (1934): p. 501 (c. X, n. 75)

Society for the Propagation of the Gospel in Foreign Parts v. New Haven, 8 Wheat. 464 (U.S.1823): p. 418 (c. V, n. 134)

South Carolina v. Katzenbach, 383 U.S. 301 (1966): pp. 292 (c. I, n. 18), 331 (c. III, n. 53), 416 (c. V, n. 126)

Southern Pac. Co. v. Arizona, 325 U.S. 761 (1945): pp. 299 (c. II, n. 17), 469 (c. IX, n. 29), 470 (c. IX, n. 30), 471 (c. IX, nn. 35, 36), 472 (c. IX, n. 38)

Southern Pacific Co. v. Jensen, 244 U.S. 205 (1917): pp. 331 (c. III, n. 52), 444 (c. VIII, n. 3), 453 (c. VIII, n. 34), 454 (c. VIII, n. 36)

Southern Ry. Co. v. King, 217 U.S. 524 (1910): p. 471 (c. IX, n. 37)

South Puerto Rico Sugar Co. Trading Corp. v. United States, 334 F.2d 622 (Ct.Cl.1964): p. 432 (c. VI, n. 40)

Spragins v. Houghton, 3 Ill. 377 (1840): p. 469 (c. IX, n. 28)

Springer v. Philippine Islands, 277 U.S. 189 (1928): p. 294 (c. II, n. 3)

Squire v. Capoeman, 351 U.S. 1 (1956): p. 381 (c. V, n. 28)

S.S. "Lotus," [1927] P.C.I.J., ser. A, No. 9: p. 311 (c. II, n. 56)

Stanton v. Georgia, 6 Wall. 50 (U.S.1868): p. 416 (c. V, n. 126)

State Board v. Young's Market Co., 299 U.S. 59 (1936): p. 469 (c. IX, n. 29)

Steele v. Bulova Watch Co., 344 U.S. 280 (1952): p. 326 (c. III, n. 41)

Steward Machinery Co. v. Davis (Social Security Case), 301 U.S. 548 (1937): p. 115 (c. IV)

Strauder v. West Virginia, 100 U.S. 303 (1880): p. 495 (c. X, n. 38)

Sturges v. Crowninshield, 4 Wheat. 122 (U.S.1819): p. 469 (c. IX, n. 28)

Sunshine Anthracite Coal Co. v. Adkins, 310 U.S. 381 (1940): p. 366 (c. IV, n. 95)

Sweezy v. New Hampshire, 354 U.S. 234 (1957): p. 489 (c. X, n. 18)

Swift v. Tyson, 16 Pet. 1 (U.S.1842): pp. 217 (c. VIII), 455 (c. VIII, n. 39)


TACA International Airlines, S. A. v. Rolls-Royce of England, Ltd., 15 N.Y.2d 97, 204 N.E.2d 329 (1965): p. 479 (c. IX, n. 62)

Tag v. Rogers, 267 F.2d 664 (App.D.C.1959), cert. denied, 362 U.S. 904 (1960): p. 461 (c. VIII, n. 61)

Takahashi v. Fish & Game Commission, 334 U.S. 410 (1948): pp. 325 (c. III, n. 37), 478 (c. IX, n. 56), 502 (c. X, n. 78), 503 (c. X, n. 80)

Talbot v. Jansen, 3 Dall. 133 (U.S.1795): p. 458 (c. VIII, n. 58)

Talbot v. Seeman, 1 Cranch 1 (U.S.1801): pp. 333 (c. III, n. 60), 334 (c. III, n. 61), 352 (c. IV, n. 49)

Talbot v. The Commanders, 1 Dall. 95 (High Ct. of Err. and App., Pa. 1784): p. 290 (c. I, n. 10)

Taylor v. Morton, 23 F.Cas. 784 (No. 13,799) (C.C.Mass.1855), aff'd, 2 Black 481 (U.S.1862): pp. 413 (c. V, n. 117), 419 (c. V, n. 138)

Techt v. Hughes, 229 N.Y. 222, 128 N.E. 185, cert. denied, 254 U.S. 643 (1920): pp. 332 (c. III, n. 58), 417 (c. V, n. 133), 418 (c. V, n. 134)

Teitscheid v. Leopold, 342 F.Supp. 299 (D.Vt.1971): p. 503 (c. X, n. 82)

Terlinden v. Ames, 184 U.S. 270 (1902): pp. 419 (c. V, n. 138), 451 (c. VIII, n. 28)

Terrace v. Thompson, 263 U.S. 197 (1923): p. 503 (c. X, n. 80)

Terral v. Burke Construction Co., 257 U.S. 529 (1922): p. 472 (c. IX, n. 38)

Terry v. Ohio, 392 U.S. 1 (1968): p. 489 (c. X, n. 19)

Testa v. Katt, 330 U.S. 386 (1947): pp. 445 (c. VIII, n. 7), 457 (c. VIII, n. 47), 479 (c. IX, n. 63), 482 (c. IX, n. 74)

Texas v. New Jersey, 379 U.S. 674 (1965): p. 453 (c. VIII, n. 34)

Textile Workers Union of America v. Lincoln Mills, 353 U.S. 448 (1957): p. 453 (c. VIII, n. 34)

Thames & Mersey Marine Ins. Co. v. United States, 237 U.S. 19 (1915): p. 337 (c. III, n. 79)

Thiel v. Southern Pac. Co., 328 U.S. 217 (1946): p. 494 (c. X, n. 36)

Thomas Gibbons, The, 8 Cranch 421 (U.S.1814): p. 367 (c. IV, n. 96)

Tileston v. Ullmann, 318 U.S. 44 (1943): p. 446 (c. VIII, n. 9)

Ex parte Toscano, 208 F. 938 (S.D.Cal.1913): p. 308 (c. II, n. 51)

Tot v. United States, 319 U.S. 463 (1943): p. 447 (c. VIII, n. 16)

Totten v. United States, 92 U.S. 105 (1875): pp. 305 (c. II, n. 36), 342 (c. IV, n. 13), 357 (c. IV, n. 63)

Trade-Mark Cases, 100 U.S. 82 (1879): p. 329 (c. III, n. 49)

Triquet and Others v. Bath, 97 Eng.Rep. 936, 3 Burr. 1478 (K.B.1764): p. 458 (c. VIII, n. 58)

Truax v. Raich, 239 U.S. 33 (1915): pp. 495 (c. X, n. 40), 502 (c. X, n. 78)

Trop v. Dulles, 356 U.S. 86 (1958): p. 447 (c. VIII, n. 16)

Trustees of University of Illinois v. United States, 289 U.S. 48 (1933): p. 319 (c. III, n. 9)

Tucker v. Alexandroff, 183 U.S. 424 (1902): p. 303 (c. II, n. 30)

Turner v. American Baptist Missionary Union, 24 F.Cas. 344 (No. 14251) (C.C.Mich.1852): p. 406 (c. V, n. 98)

Turner v. Bank of North-America, 4 Dall. 8 (U.S.1799): p. 445 (c. VIII, n. 8)

Tyson & Brother v. Banton, 273 U.S. 418 (1927): pp. 496 (c. X, n. 44), 505 (c. XI, n. 9)

## Cases Cited

Uebersee Finanz-Korp. v. McGrath, 343 U.S. 205 (1952): p. 342 (c. IV, n. 15)

Union Refrigerator Transit Co. v. Kentucky, 199 U.S. 194 (1905): p. 501 (c. X, n. 69)

United States v. American Sugar Co., 202 U.S. 563 (1906): p. 379 (c. V, n. 23)

United States v. Arjona, 120 U.S. 479 (1887): pp. 323 (c. III, n. 26), 332 (c. III, n. 55), 447 (c. VIII, n. 17)

United States v. Ball, 163 U.S. 662 (1896): p. 441 (c. VII, n. 38)

United States v. Belmont, 301 U.S. 324 (1937): pp. 59, 63, 177, 178, 184–187, 242, 312 (c. II, n. 65), 426 (c. VI, n. 17), 431 (c. VI, n. 37), 432 (c. VI, n. 39), 464 (c. IX, n. 1)

United States v. Bevans, 3 Wheat. 336 (U.S.1818): pp. 331 (c. III, n. 52), 501 (c. X, n. 69)

United States v. Bowman, 260 U.S. 94 (1922): pp. 292 (c. I, n. 16), 326 (c. III, n. 41)

United States v. Butler, 297 U.S. 1 (1936): pp. 71, 115, 328 (c. III, n. 48)

United States v. California, 297 U.S. 175 (1936): p. 480 (c. IX, n. 70)

United States v. California, 332 U.S. 19 (1947): pp. 331 (c. III, n. 52), 416 (c. V, n. 126), 482 (c. IX, n. 76)

United States v. Caltex, Inc., 344 U.S. 149 (1952): pp. 259, 260, 496 (c. X, n. 45)

United States v. Carolene Products Co., 304 U.S. 144 (1938): p. 489 (c. X, n. 15)

United States v. Central Eureka Mining Co., 357 U.S. 155 (1958): p. 496 (c. X, n. 45)

United States v. Chambers, 291 U.S. 217 (1934): p. 408 (c. V, n. 105)

United States v. Chemical Foundation, 272 U.S. 1 (1926): p. 495 (c. X, n. 43)

United States v. Clarke, 20 Wall. 92 (U.S.1874): pp. 349 (c. IV, n. 40), 432 (c. VI, n. 41)

United States v. Constantine, 296 U.S. 287 (1935): p. 408 (c. V, n. 105)

United States v. Coolidge, 1 Wheat. 415 (U.S.1816): p. 406 (c. V, n. 99)

United States v. Curtiss-Wright Export Corp., 299 U.S. 304 (1936): pp. 19, 24–26, 31, 32, 119, 185, 209, 227, 228, 252, 253, 289 (c. I, nn. 6–8, 10), 291 (c. I, n. 12), 292 (c. I, nn. 14, 15), 294 (c. II, n. 1), 296 (c. II, n. 1), 300 (c. II, n. 18), 303 (c. II, n. 26), 328 (c. III, n. 45), 339 (c. IV, n. 1), 340 (c. IV, n. 9), 357 (c. IV, n. 63), 358 (c. IV, n. 64), 359 (c. IV, n. 67), 367 (c. IV, nn. 96, 97), 375 (c. V, n. 7), 422 (c. VI, n. 9), 427 (c. VI, n. 18), 435 (c. VII, n. 2), 452 (c. VIII, n. 29), 455 (c. VIII, n. 44), 464 (c. IX, n. 3)

*Cases Cited*

Washington v. Texas, 388 U.S. 14 (1967): p. 502 (c. X, n. 77)

Washington v. W. C. Dawson & Co., 264 U.S. 219 (1924): p. 473 (c. IX, n. 43)

Watkins v. United States, 354 U.S. 178 (1957): p. 337 (c. III, n. 77)

Watts v. United States, 1 Wash.Terr. 288 (1870): p. 433 (c. VI, n. 42)

Wayman v. Southard, 10 Wheat. 1 (U.S.1825): p. 366 (c. IV, n. 95)

Weber v. Freed, 239 U.S. 325 (1915): p. 319 (c. III, n. 9)

Weeks v. United States, 232 U.S. 383 (1914): p. 490 (c. X, n. 19)

Wei v. Robinson, 246 F.2d 739 (7th Cir.), cert. denied, 355 U.S. 879 (1957): p. 502 (c. X, n. 78)

West Coast Hotel Co. v. Parrish, 300 U.S. 379 (1937): pp. 292 (c. I, n. 18), 493 (c. X, n. 27)

Western Union Tel. Co. v. Kansas, 216 U.S. 1 (1910): p. 472 (c. IX, n. 38)

West Virginia ex rel. Dyer v. Sims, 341 U.S. 22 (1951): p. 453 (c. VIII, n. 34)

West Virginia State Bd. of Educ. v. Barnett, 319 U.S. 624 (1943): p. 486 (c. X, n. 7)

Wharton v. Wise, 153 U.S. 155 (1894): p. 466 (c. IX, n. 16)

Whitney v. Robertson, 124 U.S. 190 (1888): p. 410 (c. V, n. 111)

Wickard v. Filburn, 317 U.S. 111 (1942): pp. 292 (c. I, n. 18), 318 (c. III, nn. 6, 7), 393 (c. V, n. 67)

Wiener v. United States, 357 U.S. 349 (1958): pp. 300 (c. II, n. 19), 365 (c. IV, n. 87)

Wilcox v. McConnell, 13 Pet. 498 (U.S.1839): p. 367 (c. IV, n. 97)

Williams v. Armroyd (The Fortitude), 7 Cranch 423 (U.S.1813): p. 463 (c. VIII, n. 69)

Williams v. Florida, 399 U.S. 78 (1970): p. 502 (c. X, n. 77)

Williams v. Rhodes, 393 U.S. 23 (1968): p. 495 (c. X, n. 39)

Williams v. Suffolk Ins. Co., 13 Pet. 415 (U.S.1839): p. 450 (c. VIII, n. 27)

Williams v. United States, 1 How. 290 (U.S.1843): p. 367 (c. IV, n. 97)

Williams v. United States, 289 U.S. 553 (1933): pp. 439 (c. VII, n. 31), 440 (c. VII, n. 36)

Williamson v. Lee Optical, Inc., 348 U.S. 483 (1955): pp. 493 (c. X, n. 29), 494 (c. X, n. 38)

Wilson v. Black-Bird Creek Marsh Co., 2 Pet. 245 (U.S.1829): p. 470 (c. IX, n. 32)

Wilson v. Girard, 354 U.S. 524 (1957): pp. 130, 387 (c. V, n. 45), 424 (c. VI, n. 13), 425 (c. VI, n. 14), 437 (c. VII, n. 20), 500 (c. X, n. 67)

Wilson v. Shaw, 204 U.S. 24 (1907): pp. 295 (c. II, n. 4), 334 (c. III, n. 61)

Wilson v. United States, 221 U.S. 361 (1911): p. 488 (c. X, n. 11)

In re Winship, 397 U.S. 358 (1970): p. 491 (c. X, n. 23)

Wong Wing v. United States, 163 U.S. 228 (1896): pp. 488 (c. X, n. 11), 490 (c. X, n. 21), 502 (c. X, n. 78)

Wong Yang Sung v. McGrath, 339 U.S. 33 (1950): p. 492 (c. X, n. 23)

Woodby v. Immigration and Naturalization Service, 385 U.S. 276 (1966): p. 491 (c. X, n. 23)

Woods v. Miller Co., 333 U.S. 138 (1948): p. 321 (c. III, n. 17)

Worcester v. Georgia, 6 Pet. 515 (U.S.1832): pp. 385 (c. V, n. 38), 395 (c. V, n. 72)

Wulfsohn v. Russian Socialist Federated Soviet Republic, 266 U.S. 580 (1924), per curiam dismissing a writ of error for want of jurisdiction, 234 N.Y. 372, 138 N.E. 24 (1923), rev'g 202 App.Div. 421, 195 N.Y.S. 472 (1922), aff'g 118 Misc. 28, 192 N.Y.S. 282 (1922): p. 461 (c. VIII, n. 64)

Yakus v. United States, 321 U.S. 414 (1944): p. 366 (c. IV, n. 95)

In re Yamashita, 327 U.S. 1 (1946): pp. 305 (c. II, n. 36), 322 (c. III, n. 24), 490 (c. X, n. 21)

Yates v. United States, 354 U.S. 298 (1957): p. 487 (c. X, n. 8)

Yearsley v. W. A. Ross Constr. Co., 309 U.S. 18 (1940): p. 497 (c. X, n. 51)

Yick Wo v. Hopkins, 118 U.S. 356 (1886): p. 495 (c. X, nn. 38, 40, 41), 502 (c. X, n. 78)

Ex parte Young, 209 U.S. 123 (1908): pp. 414 (c. V, n. 120), 446 (c. VIII, n. 10)

Youngstown Sheet & Tube Co. v. Bowers, 358 U.S. 534 (1959): p. 464 (c. IX, n. 4)

Youngstown Sheet & Tube Co. v. Sawyer, 343 U.S. 579 (1952): pp. 40, 98, 99, 275, 287 (c. I, n. 2), 292 (c. I, n. 14), 293 (c. I, n. 20), 294 (c. II, nn. 2, 3), 297 (c. II, n. 7), 299 (c. II, nn. 15–17), 307 (c. II, n. 45), 329 (c. II, n. 50), 340 (c. IV, nn. 9, 11), 341 (c. IV, n. 11), 343 (c. IV, n. 20), 349 (c. IV, nn. 39, 40), 353 (c. IV, n. 50), 354 (c. IV, n. 57), 366 (c. IV, n. 94), 447 (c. VIII, n. 14), 453 c. VIII, n. 33), 504 (c. XI, n. 6)

Zakonaite v. Wolfe, 226 U.S. 272 (1912): p. 491 (c. X, n. 23)

Z. & F. Assets Realization Corp. v. Hull, 311 U.S. 470 (1941): p. 498 (c. X, n. 58)

Zemel v. Rusk, 381 U.S. 1 (1965): pp. 257, 292 (c. I, n. 17), 339 (c. IV, n. 4), 343 (c. IV, n. 20), 357 (c. IV, n. 63), 367 (c. IV, nn. 96, 97)

Zschernig v. Miller, 389 U.S. 429 (1968): pp. 61–63, 238–241, 314 (c. II, nn. 72, 73), 315 (c. II, n. 75), 454 (c. VIII, n. 34), 456 (c. VIII, n. 46), 459 (c. VIII, n. 59), 463 (c. VIII, n. 67), 472 (c. IX, n. 40), 475 (c. IX, n. 46), 476 (c. IX, nn. 47–51), 477 (c. IX, nn. 52, 53), 478 (c. IX, n. 54), 503 (c. X, n. 80)

Zucht v. King, 260 U.S. 174 (1922): p. 448 (c. VIII, n. 18)

\*

# The Constitution of
# the United States of America

We the people of the United States, in Order to form a more perfect Union, establish Justice, insure domestic Tranquility, provide for the common defence, promote the general Welfare, and secure the Blessings of Liberty to ourselves and our Posterity, do ordain and establish this Constitution for the United States of America.

## ARTICLE I

SECTION 1. All legislative Powers herein granted shall be vested in a Congress of the United States, which shall consist of a Senate and House of Representatives.

SECTION 2. The House of Representatives shall be composed of Members chosen every second Year by the People of the several States, and the Electors in each State shall have the Qualifications requisite for Electors of the most numerous Branch of the State Legislature.

No person shall be a Representative who shall not have attained to the Age of twenty-five Years, and been seven Years a Citizen of the United States, and who shall not, when elected, be an Inhabitant of that State in which he shall be chosen.

Representatives and direct Taxes shall be apportioned among the several States which may be included within this Union, according to their respective Numbers, which shall be determined by adding to the whole Number of free Persons, including those bound to Service for a Term of Years, and excluding Indians not taxed, three fifths of all other Persons. The actual Enumeration shall be made within three Years after the first Meeting of the Congress of the United States, and within every subsequent Term of ten Years, in such Manner as they shall by Law direct. The Number of Representatives shall not exceed one for every thirty Thousand, but each State shall have at Least one Representative; and until such enumeration shall be made, the State of New Hampshire shall be entitled to chuse three, Massachusetts eight, Rhode-Island and Providence Plantations one, Connecticut five, New York six, New Jersey four, Pennsylvania eight, Delaware one,

Maryland six, Virginia ten, North Carolina five, South Carolina five, and Georgia three.

When vacancies happen in the Representation from any State, the Executive Authority thereof shall issue Writs of Election to fill such Vacancies.

The House of Representatives shall choose their Speaker and other Officers; and shall have the sole Power of Impeachment.

SECTION 3. The Senate of the United States shall be composed of two Senators from each State, chosen by the Legislature thereof, for six Years; and each Senator shall have one Vote.

Immediately after they shall be assembled in Consequence of the first Election, they shall be divided as equally as may be into three Classes. The Seats of the Senators of the first Class shall be vacated at the Expiration of the second Year, of the second Class at the Expiration of the fourth Year, and of the third Class at the Expiration of the sixth Year, so that one third may be chosen every second Year; and if Vacancies happen by Resignation, or otherwise, during the Recess of the Legislature of any State, the Executive thereof may make temporary Appointments until the next Meeting of the Legislature, which shall then fill such Vacancies.

No Person shall be a Senator who shall not have attained to the Age of thirty Years, and been nine Years a Citizen of the United States, and who shall not, when elected, be an Inhabitant of that State for which he shall be chosen.

The Vice President of the United States shall be President of the Senate, but shall have no Vote, unless they be equally divided.

The Senate shall chuse their other Officers, and also a President pro tempore, in the absence of the Vice President, or when he shall exercise the Office of President of the United States.

The Senate shall have the sole Power to try all Impeachments. When sitting for that Purpose, they shall be on Oath or Affirmation. When the President of the United States is tried, the Chief Justice shall preside: And no Person shall be convicted without the Concurrence of two thirds of the Members present.

Judgment in Cases of Impeachment shall not extend further than to removal from Office, and disqualification to hold and enjoy any Office of honor, Trust or Profit under the United States: but the Party convicted shall nevertheless be liable and subject to Indictment, Trial, Judgment and Punishment, according to Law.

SECTION 4. The Times Places and Manner of holding Elections for Senators and Representatives, shall be prescribed in each State by the Legislature thereof; but the Congress may at any time by Law make or alter such Regulations, except as to the Places of Chusing Senators.

The Congress shall assemble at least once in every Year, and such Meeting shall be on the first Monday in December, unless they shall by Law appoint a different Day.

SECTION 5. Each House shall be the Judge of the Elections, Returns and Qualifications of its own Members, and a Majority of each shall constitute a Quorum to do Business; but a smaller Number may adjourn from day to day, and may be authorized to compel the Attendance of absent Members, in such Manner, and under such Penalties as each House may provide.

Each House may determine the Rules of its Proceedings, punish its Members for disorderly Behavior, and, with the Concurrence of two thirds, expel a Member.

Each House shall keep a Journal of its Proceedings, and from time to time publish the same, excepting such Parts as may in their Judgment require Secrecy; and the Yeas and Nays of the Members of either House on any question shall, at the Desire of one fifth of those Present, be entered on the journal.

Neither House, during the Session of Congress, shall, without the Consent of the other, adjourn for more than three days, nor to any other Place than that in which the two Houses shall be sitting.

SECTION 6. The Senators and Representatives shall receive a Compensation for their Services, to be ascertained by Law, and paid out of the Treasury of the United States. They shall in all Cases, except Treason, Felony and Breach of the Peace, be privileged from Arrest during their Attendance at the Session of their respective Houses, and in going to and returning from the same; and for any Speech or Debate in either House, they shall not be questioned in any other Place.

No Senator or Representative shall, during the Time for which he was elected, be appointed to any civil Office under the Authority of the United States, which shall have been created, or the Emoluments whereof shall have been encreased during such time; and no Person holding any Office under the United States, shall be a Member of either House during his Continuance in Office.

SECTION 7. All Bills for raising Revenue shall originate in the House of Representatives; but the Senate may propose or concur with Amendments as on other Bills.

Every Bill which shall have passed the House of Representatives and the Senate, shall, before it become a Law, be presented to the President of the United States; If he approve he shall sign it, but if not he shall return it, with his Objections to that House in which it shall have originated, who shall enter the Objections at large on their Journal, and proceed to reconsider it. If after such Reconsideration two thirds of that House shall agree to pass the Bill, it shall be sent, together with the Objections, to the other House, by which it shall likewise be reconsidered, and if approved by two thirds of that House, it shall become a Law. But in all such Cases the Votes of both Houses shall be determined by Yeas and Nays, and the Names of the Persons voting for and against the Bill shall be entered on the Journal of each House respectively. If any Bill shall not be returned by the President within ten Days (Sundays excepted) after it shall have been presented to him, the Same shall be a Law, in like Manner as if he had signed it, unless the Congress by their Adjournment prevent its Return, in which Case it shall not be a Law.

Every Order, Resolution, or Vote to which the Concurrence of the Senate and House of Representatives may be necessary (except on a question of Adjournment) shall be presented to the President of the United States; and before the Same shall take Effect, shall be approved by him, or being disapproved by him, shall be repassed by two thirds of the Senate and House of Representatives, according to the Rules and Limitations prescribed in the Case of a Bill.

SECTION 8. The Congress shall have Power To lay and collect Taxes, Duties, Imposts and Excises, to pay the Debts and provide for the common Defence and general Welfare of the United States; but all Duties, Imposts and Excises shall be uniform throughout the United States;

To borrow Money on the Credit of the United States;

To regulate Commerce with foreign Nations, and among the several States, and with the Indian Tribes;

To establish an uniform Rule of Naturalization, and uniform Laws on the subject of Bankruptcies throughout the United States;

To coin Money, regulate the Value thereof, and of foreign Coin, and fix the Standard of Weights and Measures;

To provide for the Punishment of counterfeiting the Securities and current Coin of the United States;

To establish Post Offices and post Roads;

To promote the Progress of Science and useful Arts, by securing for limited Times to Authors and Inventors the exclusive Right to their respective Writings and Discoveries;

To constitute Tribunals inferior to the supreme Court;

To define and punish Piracies and Felonies committed on the high Seas, and Offenses against the Law of Nations;

To declare War, grant Letters of Marque and Reprisal, and make Rules concerning Captures on Land and Water;

To raise and support Armies, but no Appropriation of Money to that Use shall be for a longer Term than two Years;

To provide and maintain a Navy;

To make Rules for the Government and Regulation of the land and naval Forces;

To provide for calling forth the Militia to execute the Laws of the Union, suppress Insurrections and repel Invasions;

To provide for organizing, arming, and disciplining the Militia, and for governing such Part of them as may be employed in the Service of the United States, reserving to the States respectively, the Appointment of the Officers, and the Authority of training the Militia according to the discipline prescribed by Congress.

To exercise exclusive Legislation in all Cases whatsoever, over such District (not exceeding ten Miles square) as may, by Cession of particular States, and the acceptance of Congress, become the Seat of the Government of the United States, and to exercise like Authority over all Places purchased by the Consent of the Legislature of the State in which the Same shall be, for the Erection of Forts, Magazines, Arsenals, dock-Yards, and other needful Buildings; — And

To make all Laws which shall be necessary and proper for carrying into Execution the foregoing Powers, and all other Powers vested by this Constitution in the Government of the United States, or in any Department or Officer thereof.

SECTION 9. The Migration or Importation of such Persons as any of the States now existing shall think proper to admit, shall not be prohibited by the Congress prior to the Year one thousand eight hundred and eight, but a Tax or duty may be imposed on such Importation, not exceeding ten dollars for each Person.

The privilege of the Writ of Habeas Corpus shall not be suspended, unless when in Cases of Rebellion or Invasion the public Safety may require it.

No Bill of Attainder or ex post facto Law shall be passed.

No capitation, or other direct, Tax shall be laid, unless in Proportion to the Census or Enumeration herein before directed to be taken.

No Tax or Duty shall be laid on Articles exported from any State.

No Preference shall be given by any Regulation of Commerce or Revenue to the Ports of one State over those of another; nor shall Vessels bound to, or from, one State, be obliged to enter, clear, or pay Duties in another.

No Money shall be drawn from the Treasury, but in Consequence of Appropriations made by Law; and a regular Statement and Account of the Receipts and Expenditures of all public Money shall be published from time to time.

No Title of Nobility shall be granted by the United States: And no Person holding any Office or Profit or Trust under them, shall, without the Consent of the Congress, accept of any present, Emolument, Office, or Title, of any kind whatever, from any King, Prince, or foreign State.

SECTION 10. No State shall enter into any Treaty, Alliance, or Confederation; grant Letters of Marque and Reprisal; coin Money; emit Bills of Credit; make any Thing but gold and silver Coin a Tender in Payment of Debts; pass any Bill of Attainder, ex post facto Law, or Law impairing the Obligation of Contracts, or grant any Title of Nobility.

No State shall, without the Consent of the Congress, lay any Imposts or Duties on Imports or Exports, except what may be absolutely necessary for executing its inspection Laws: and the net Produce of all Duties and Imposts, laid by any State on Imports or Exports, shall be for the Use of the Treasury of the United States; and all such Laws shall be subject to the Revision and Controul of the Congress.

No State shall, without the Consent of Congress, lay any duty of Tonnage, keep Troops, or Ships of War in time of Peace, enter into any Agreement or Compact with another State, or with a foreign Power, or engage in War, unless actually invaded, or in such imminent Danger as will not admit of delay.

### ARTICLE II

SECTION 1. The executive Power shall be vested in a President of the United States of America. He shall hold his Office during the Term of four Years, and, together with the Vice President, chosen for the same Term, be elected, as follows

Each State shall appoint, in such Manner as the Legislature thereof may direct, a Number of Electors, equal to the whole Number of Senators and Representatives to which the State may be entitled in the Congress: but no Senator or Representative, or Person holding an Office of Trust or Profit under the United States, shall be appointed an Elector.

The Electors shall meet in their respective States, and vote by Ballot for two persons, of whom one at least shall not be an Inhabitant of the same State with themselves. And they shall make a List of all the Persons voted for, and of the Number of Votes for each; which List they shall sign and certify, and transmit sealed to the Seat of the Government of the United States, directed to the President of the Senate. The President of the Senate shall, in the Presence of the Senate and House of Representatives, open all the Certificates, and the Votes shall then be counted. The Person having the greatest Number of Votes shall be the President, if such Number be a Majority of the whole Number of Electors appointed; and if there be more than one who have such Majority, and have an equal Number of Votes, then the House of Representatives shall immediately chuse by Ballot one of them for President; and if no Person have a Majority, then from the five highest on the List the said House shall in like Manner chuse the President. But in chusing the President, the Votes shall be taken by States, the Representation from each State having one Vote; A quorum for this Purpose shall consist of a Member or Members from two thirds of the States, and a Majority of all the States shall be necessary to a Choice. In every Case, after the Choice of the President, the Person having the greatest Number of Votes of the Electors shall be the Vice President. But if there should remain two or more who have equal Votes, the Senate shall chuse from them by Ballot the Vice President.

The Congress may determine the Time of chusing the Electors, and the Day on which they shall give their Votes; which Day shall be the same throughout the United States.

No person except a natural born Citizen, or a Citizen of the United States, at the time of the Adoption of this Constitution, shall be eligible to the Office of President; neither shall any Person be eligible to that Office who shall not have attained to the Age of thirty-five Years, and been fourteen Years a Resident within the United States.

In Case of the Removal of the President from Office, or of his Death, Resignation, or Inability to discharge the Powers and Duties of the said Office, the same shall devolve on the Vice President, and the Congress may by Law provide for the Case of Removal, Death, Resignation or Inability, both of the President and Vice President, declaring what Officer shall then act as President, and such Officer shall act accordingly, until the Disability be removed, or a President shall be elected.

The President shall, at stated Times, receive for his Services, a Compensation, which shall neither be encreased nor diminished during the Period for which he shall have been elected, and he shall not receive within that Period any other Emolument from the United States, or any of them.

Before he enter on the Execution of his Office, he shall take the following Oath or Affirmation: "I do solemnly swear (or affirm) that I will faithfully execute the Office of President of the United States, and will to the best of my Ability, preserve, protect and defend the Constitution of the United States."

SECTION 2. The President shall be Commander in Chief of the Army and Navy of the United States, and of the Militia of the several States, when called into the actual Service of the United States; he may require the Opinion in writing, of the principal Officer in each of the executive Departments, upon any subject relating to the Duties of their respective Offices, and he shall have Power to Grant Reprieves and Pardons for Offenses against the United States, except in Cases of Impeachment.

He shall have Power, by and with the Advice and Consent of the Senate, to make Treaties, provided two thirds of the Senators present concur; and he shall nominate, and by and with the Advice and Consent of the Senate, shall appoint Ambassadors, other public Ministers and Consuls, Judges of the supreme Court, and all other Officers of the United States, whose Appointments are not herein otherwise provided for, and which shall be established by Law: but the Congress may by Law vest the Appointment of such inferior Officers, as they think proper, in the President alone, in the Courts of Law, or in the Heads of Departments.

The President shall have Power to fill up all Vacancies that may happen during the Recess of the Senate, by granting Commissions which shall expire at the End of their next Session.

SECTION 3. He shall from time to time give to the Congress Information of the State of the Union, and recommend to their Consideration such Measures as he shall judge necessary and expedient; he may, on extraordinary Occasions, convene both Houses, or either of them, and in Case of Disagreement between them, with Respect to the Time of Adjournment, he may adjourn them to such Time as he shall think proper; he shall receive Ambassadors and other public Ministers; he shall take Care that the Laws be faithfully executed, and shall Commission all the Officers of the United States.

SECTION 4. The President, Vice President and all civil Officers of the United States, shall be removed from Office on Impeachment for, and Conviction of, Treason, Bribery, or other high Crimes and Misdemeanors.


ARTICLE III

SECTION 1. The judicial Power of the United States, shall be vested in one supreme Court, and in such inferior Courts as the Congress may from time to time ordain and establish. The Judges, both of the supreme and inferior Courts, shall hold their Offices during good Behaviour, and shall, at stated Times, receive for their Services a Compensation which shall not be diminished during their Continuance in Office.

SECTION 2. The judicial Power shall extend to all Cases, in Law and Equity, arising under this Constitution, the Laws of the United States, and Treaties made, or which shall be made, under their Authority; — to all Cases affecting Ambassadors, other public Ministers and Consuls; — to all Cases of admiralty and maritime Jurisdiction; — to Controversies to which the United States shall be a Party; — to Controversies between two or more States; — between a State and Citizens of another State; — between Citizens of different States; — between Citizens of the same State claiming Lands under Grants of different States, and between a State, or the Citizens thereof, and foreign States, Citizens or Subjects.

In all Cases affecting Ambassadors, other public Ministers and Consuls, and those in which a State shall be Party, the supreme Court shall have original Jurisdiction. In all the other Cases before mentioned, the supreme Court shall have appellate Jurisdiction, both as to Law and Fact, with such Exceptions, and under such Regulations as the Congress shall make.

The trial of all Crimes, except in Cases of Impeachment, shall be by Jury; and such Trial shall be held in the State where the said Crimes shall have been committed; but when not committed within any State, the Trial shall be at such Place or Places as the Congress may by Law have directed.

SECTION 3. Treason against the United States, shall consist only in levying War against them, or in adhering to their Enemies, giving them Aid and Comfort. No Person shall be convicted of Treason unless on the Testimony of two Witnesses to the same overt Act, or on Confession in open Court.

The Congress shall have power to declare the Punishment of Treason, but no Attainder of Treason shall work Corruption of Blood, or Forfeiture except during the Life of the Person attainted.

## ARTICLE IV

SECTION 1. Full Faith and Credit shall be given in each State to the public Acts, Records, and judicial Proceedings of every other State. And the Congress may by general Laws prescribe the Manner in which such Acts, Records and Proceedings shall be proved, and the Effect thereof.

SECTION 2. The Citizens of each State shall be entitled to all Privileges and Immunities of Citizens in the several States.

A Person charged in any State with Treason, Felony, or other Crime, who shall flee from Justice, and be found in another State, shall on demand of the executive Authority of the State from which he fled, be delivered up, to be removed to the State having Jurisdiction of the Crime.

No Person held to Service or Labour in one State, under the Laws thereof, escaping into another, shall, in Consequence of any Law or Regulation therein, be discharged from such Service or Labour, but shall be delivered up on Claim of the Party to whom such Service or Labour may be due.

SECTION 3. New States may be admitted by the Congress into this Union; but no new State shall be formed or erected within the Jurisdiction of any other State; nor any State be formed by the Junction of two or more States, or parts of States, without the Consent of the Legislatures of the States concerned as well as of the Congress.

The Congress shall have Power to dispose of and make all needful Rules and Regulations respecting the Territory or other Property belonging to the United States; and nothing in this Constitution shall be so construed as to Prejudice any Claims of the United States, or of any particular State.

SECTION 4. The United States shall guarantee to every State in this Union a Republican Form of Government, and shall protect each of them against Invasion; and on Application of the Legislature, or of the Executive (when the Legislature cannot be convened) against domestic Violence.

## ARTICLE V

The Congress, whenever two thirds of both Houses shall deem it necessary, shall propose Amendments to this Constitution, or, on the Application of the Legislatures of two thirds of the several States, shall call a Convention for proposing Amendments, which, in either Case, shall be valid to all Intents and Purposes, as part of this Constitution, when ratified by the Legislatures of three fourths of the several States, or by Conventions in three fourths thereof, as the one or the other Mode of Ratification may be proposed by the Congress; Provided that no Amendment which may be made prior to the Year One thousand eight hundred and eight shall in any Manner affect the first and fourth Clauses in the Ninth Section of the first Article; and that no State, without its Consent, shall be deprived of its equal Suffrage in the Senate.

## ARTICLE VI

All Debts contracted and Engagements entered into, before the Adoption of this Constitution, shall be as valid against the United States under this Constitution, as under the Confederation.

This Constitution, and the Laws of the United States which shall be made in Pursuance thereof; and all Treaties made, or which shall be made, under the Authority of the United States, shall be the supreme Law of the Land; and the Judges in every State shall be bound thereby, any Thing in the Constitution or Laws of any State to the Contrary notwithstanding.

The Senators and Representatives before mentioned, and the Members of the several State Legislatures, and all executive and judicial Officers, both of the United States and of the several States, shall be bound by Oath or Affirmation, to support this Constitution; but no religious Test shall ever be required as a Qualification to any Office or public Trust under the United States.

## ARTICLE VII

The Ratification of the Conventions of nine States shall be sufficient for the Establishment of this Constitution between the States so ratifying the Same.[a]

Done in Convention by the Unanimous Consent of the States present the Seventeenth Day of September in the Year of our Lord one thousand seven hundred and Eighty seven and of the Independence of the United States of America the Twelfth. In Witness whereof We have hereunto subscribed our Names. [Signatures omitted.]

ARTICLES IN ADDITION TO, AND AMENDMENT OF, THE CONSTITUTION OF THE UNITED STATES OF AMERICA, PROPOSED BY CONGRESS, AND RATIFIED BY THE LEGISLATURES

[a] By July 26, 1788, eleven states had ratified the Constitution. On September 13, 1788, the Continental Congress (which had continued to function at irregular intervals) passed a resolution to put the new Constitution into operation. The first Wednesday, or January 17, 1789, was fixed as the day for choosing presidential electors, the first Wednesday of February for the meeting of electors, and the first Wednesday of March, i.e., March 4, 1789, for the opening of the new Congress. — ED.

OF THE SEVERAL STATES, PURSUANT TO THE FIFTH ARTICLE OF THE ORIGINAL CONSTITUTION.

## AMENDMENT I

Congress shall make no law respecting an establishment of religion, or prohibiting the free exercise thereof; or abridging the freedom of speech, or of the press; or the right of the people peaceably to assemble, and to petition the Government for a redress of grievances.

## AMENDMENT II

A well regulated Militia, being necessary to the security of a free State, the right of the people to keep and bear Arms, shall not be infringed.

## AMENDMENT III

No Soldier shall, in time of peace be quartered in any house, without the consent of the Owner, nor in time of war, but in a manner to be prescribed by law.

## AMENDMENT IV

The right of the people to be secure in their persons, houses, papers, and effects, against unreasonable searches and seizures, shall not be violated, and no Warrants shall issue, but upon probable cause, supported by Oath or affirmation, and particularly describing the place to be searched, and the persons or things to be seized.

## AMENDMENT V

No person shall be held to answer for a capital, or otherwise infamous crime, unless on a presentment or indictment of a Grand Jury, except in cases arising in the land or naval forces, or in the Militia, when in actual service in time of War or public danger; nor shall any person be subject for the same offence to be twice put in jeopardy of life or limb; nor shall be compelled in any criminal case to be a witness against himself, nor be deprived of life, liberty, or property, without due process of law; nor shall private property be taken for public use, without just compensation.

## AMENDMENT VI

In all criminal prosecutions, the accused shall enjoy the right to a speedy and public trial, by an impartial jury of the State and district wherein the crime shall have been committed, which district shall have been previously ascertained by law, and to be informed of the nature and cause of the accusation; to be confronted with the witnesses against him; to have compulsory process for obtaining witnesses in his favor, and to have the Assistance of Counsel for his defence.

## AMENDMENT VII

In suits at common law, where the value in controversy shall exceed twenty dollars, the right of trial by jury shall be preserved, and no fact tried by a jury, shall be otherwise re-examined in any Court of the United States, than according to the rules of the common law.

## AMENDMENT VIII

Excessive bail shall not be required, nor excessive fines imposed, nor cruel and unusual punishments inflicted.

## AMENDMENT IX

The enumeration in the Constitution, of certain rights, shall not be construed to deny or disparage others retained by the people.

## AMENDMENT X

The powers not delegated to the United States by the Constitution, nor prohibited by it to the States, are reserved to the States respectively, or to the people.[b]

## AMENDMENT XI [1798]

The Judicial power of the United States shall not be construed to extend to any suit in law or equity, commenced or prosecuted against one of the United States by Citizens of another State, or by Citizens or Subjects of any Foreign State.

## AMENDMENT XII [1804]

The Electors shall meet in their respective states and vote by ballot for President and Vice President, one of whom, at least, shall not be an inhabitant of the same state with themselves; they shall name in their ballots the person voted for as President, and in distinct ballots the person voted for as Vice President, and they shall make distinct lists of all persons voted for as President, and of all persons voted for as Vice President, and of the number of votes for each, which lists they shall sign and certify, and transmit sealed to the seat of the government of the United States, directed to the President of the Senate; — The President of the Senate shall, in presence of the Senate and House of Representatives, open all the certificates and the votes shall then be counted; — The person having the greatest number of votes for President, shall be the President, if such number be a majority of the whole number of Electors appointed; and if no person have such majority, then from the persons having the highest numbers not exceeding three on the list of those voted for as President, the House of Representatives shall choose immediately, by ballot, the President. But in choosing the President, the votes shall be taken by states, the representation from each state having one vote; a quorum for this purpose shall consist of a member or members from two-thirds of the states, and a majority of all the states shall be necessary to a choice. And if the House of Representatives shall not choose a President whenever the right of choice shall devolve upon them, before the fourth day of March next following, then the Vice President shall act as President, as in the case of the death or other constitutional disability of the President. — The person having the greatest number of votes as Vice President, shall be the Vice President, if such number be a majority of the whole number of Electors appointed, and

[b] The first ten amendments went into effect November 3, 1791. — Ed.

if no person have a majority, then from the two highest numbers on the list, the Senate shall choose the Vice President; a quorum for the purpose shall consist of two-thirds of the whole number of Senators, and a majority of the whole number shall be necessary to a choice. But no person constitutionally ineligible to the office of President shall be eligible to that of Vice President of the United States.

## AMENDMENT XIII [1865]

SECTION 1.   Neither slavery nor involuntary servitude, except as a punishment for crime whereof the party shall have been duly convicted, shall exist within the United States, or any place subject to their jurisdiction.

SECTION 2.   Congress shall have power to enforce this article by appropriate legislation.

## AMENDMENT XIV [1868]

SECTION 1.   All persons born or naturalized in the United States, and subject to the jurisdiction thereof, are citizens of the United States and of the State wherein they reside. No State shall make or enforce any law which shall abridge the privileges or immunities of citizens of the United States; nor shall any State deprive any person of life, liberty, or property, without due process of law; nor deny to any person within its jurisdiction the equal protection of the laws.

SECTION 2.   Representatives shall be apportioned among the several States according to their respective numbers, counting the whole number of persons in each State, excluding Indians not taxed. But when the right to vote at any election for the choice of electors for President and Vice President of the United States, Representatives in Congress, the Executive and Judicial officers of a State, or the members of the Legislature thereof, is denied to any of the male inhabitants of such State, being twenty-one years of age, and citizens of the United States, or in any way abridged, except for participation in rebellion, or other crime, the basis of representation therein shall be reduced in the proportion which the number of such male citizens shall bear to the whole number of male citizens twenty-one years of age in such State.

SECTION 3.   No person shall be a Senator or Representative in Congress, or elector of President and Vice President, or hold any office, civil or military, under the United States, or under any State, who, having previously taken an oath, as a member of Congress, or as an officer of the United States, or as a member of any State legislature, or as an executive or judicial officer of any State, to support the Constitution of the United States, shall have engaged in insurrection or rebellion against the same, or given aid or comfort to the enemies thereof. But Congress may by a vote of two-thirds of each House, remove such disability.

SECTION 4.   The validity of the public debt of the United States, authorized by law, including debts incurred for payment of pensions and bounties for services in suppressing insurrection or rebellion  shall not be questioned. But neither the United States nor any State shall assume or pay any debt or obligation incurred in aid of insurrection or rebellion against the United States, or any claim for the loss or emancipation of any slaves; but all such debts, obligations and claims shall be held illegal and void.

SECTION 5.   The Congress shall have power to enforce, by appropriate legislation, the provisions of this article.

## AMENDMENT XV [1870]

SECTION 1. The right of citizens of the United States to vote shall not be denied or abridged by the United States or by any State on account of race, color, or previous condition of servitude.

SECTION 2. The Congress shall have power to enforce this article by appropriate legislation.

## AMENDMENT XVI [1913]

The Congress shall have power to lay and collect taxes on incomes, from whatever source derived, without apportionment among the several States, and without regard to any census or enumeration.

## AMENDMENT XVII [1913]

The Senate of the United States shall be composed of two Senators from each State, elected by the people thereof, for six years; and each Senator shall have one vote. The electors in each State shall have the qualifications requisite for electors of the most numerous branch of the State legislatures.

When vacancies happen in the representation of any State in the Senate, the executive authority of such State shall issue writs of election to fill such vacancies: *Provided*, That the legislature of any State may empower the executive thereof to make temporary appointments until the people fill the vacancies by election as the legislature may direct.

This amendment shall not be so construed as to affect the election or term of any Senator chosen before it becomes valid as part of the Constitution.

## AMENDMENT XVIII [1919]

SECTION 1. After one year from the ratification of this article the manufacture, sale, or transportation of intoxicating liquors within, the importation thereof into, or the exportation thereof from the United States and all territory subject to the jurisdiction thereof for beverage purposes is hereby prohibited.

SECTION 2. The Congress and the several States shall have concurrent power to enforce this article by appropriate legislation.

SECTION 3. This article shall be inoperative unless it shall have been ratified as an amendment to the Constitution by the legislatures of the several States, as provided in the Constitution, within seven years from the date of the submission hereof to the States by the Congress.

## AMENDMENT XIX [1920]

The right of citizens of the United States to vote shall not be denied or abridged by the United States or by any State on account of sex.

Congress shall have power to enforce this article by appropriate legislation.

## AMENDMENT XX [1933]

SECTION 1. The terms of the President and Vice President shall end at noon on the 20th day of January, and the terms of Senators and Representatives at noon on the 3d day of January, of the years in which such terms would have ended if this article had not been ratified; and the terms of their successors shall then begin.

SECTION 2. The Congress shall assemble at least once in every year, and such meeting shall begin at noon on the 3d day of January, unless they shall by law appoint a different day.

SECTION 3. If, at the time fixed for the beginning of the term of the President, the President elect shall have died, the Vice President elect shall become President. If a President shall not have been chosen before the time fixed for the beginning of his term, or if the President elect shall have failed to qualify, then the Vice President elect shall act as President until a President shall have qualified; and the Congress may by law provide for the case wherein neither a President elect nor a Vice President elect shall have qualified, declaring who shall then act as President, or the manner in which one who is to act shall be selected, and such person shall act accordingly until a President or Vice President shall have qualified.

SECTION 4. The Congress may by law provide for the case of the death of any of the persons from whom the House of Representatives may choose a President whenever the right of choice shall have devolved upon them, and for the case of the death of any of the persons from whom the Senate may choose a Vice President whenever the right of choice shall have devolved upon them.

SECTION 5. Sections 1 and 2 shall take effect on the 15th day of October following the ratification of this article.

SECTION 6. This article shall be inoperative unless it shall have been ratified as an amendment to the Constitution by the legislatures of three-fourths of the several States within seven years from the date of its submission.

## AMENDMENT XXI [1933]

SECTION 1. The eighteenth article of amendment to the Constitution of the United States is hereby repealed.

SECTION 2. The transportation or importation into any State, Territory, or Possession of the United States for delivery or use therein of intoxicating liquors, in violation of the laws thereof, is hereby prohibited.

SECTION 3. This article shall be inoperative unless it shall have been ratified as an amendment to the Constitution by conventions in the several States, as provided in the Constitution, within seven years from the date of the submission hereof to the States by the Congress.

## AMENDMENT XXII [1951]

SECTION 1. No person shall be elected to the office of the President more than twice, and no person who has held the office of President, or acted as President, for more than two years of a term to which some other person was elected President shall be elected to the office of the President more than once. But this Article shall not apply to any person holding the office of President when this Article was proposed by the Congress, and shall not prevent any person who may be holding the office of President, or acting as President, during the term within which this Article becomes operative from holding the office of President or acting as President during the remainder of such term.

SECTION 2. This article shall be inoperative unless it shall have been ratified as an amendment to the Constitution by the legislatures of three-fourths of the several States within seven years from the date of its submission to the States by the Congress.

## AMENDMENT XXIII [1961]

SECTION 1. The District constituting the seat of Government of the United States shall appoint in such manner as Congress may direct:

A number of electors of President and Vice President equal to the whole number of Senators and Representatives in Congress to which the District would be entitled if it were a State, but in no event more than the least populous State; they shall be in addition to those appointed by the States, but they shall be considered, for the purposes of the election of President and Vice President, to be electors appointed by a State; and they shall meet in the District and perform such duties as provided by the twelfth article of amendment.

SECTION 2. The Congress shall have power to enforce this article by appropriate legislation.

## AMENDMENT XXIV [1964]

SECTION 1. The right of citizens of the United States to vote in any primary or other election for President or Vice President, for electors for President or Vice President, or for Senator or Representative in Congress, shall not be denied or abridged by the United State or any State by reason of failure to pay any poll tax or other tax.

SECTION 2. The Congress shall have power to enforce this article by appropriate legislation.

## AMENDMENT XXV [1967]

SECTION 1. In case of the removal of the President from office or of his death or resignation, the Vice President shall become President.

SECTION 2. Whenever there is a vacancy in the office of the Vice President, the President shall nominate a Vice President who shall take office upon confirmation by a majority vote of both Houses of Congress.

SECTION 3. Whenever the President transmits to the President pro tempore of the Senate and the Speaker of the House of Representatives his written declaration that he is unable to discharge the powers and duties of his office, and until he transmits to them a written declaration to the contrary, such powers and duties shall be discharged by the Vice President as Acting President.

SECTION 4. Whenever the Vice President and a majority of either the principal officers of the executive departments or of such other body as Congress may by law provide, transmit to the President pro tempore of the Senate and the Speaker of the House of Representatives their written declaration that the President is unable to discharge the powers and duties of his office, the Vice President shall immediately assume the powers and duties of the office as Acting President.

Thereafter, when the President transmits to the President pro tempore of the Senate and the Speaker of the House of Representatives his written declaration that no inability exists, he shall resume the powers and duties of his office unless the Vice President and a majority of either the principal officers of the executive department or of such other body as Congress may by law provide, transmit within four days to the President pro tempore of the Senate and the Speaker of the House of Representatives their written declaration that the President is unable to discharge the powers and duties of his office. Thereupon Congress shall decide the issue, assembling within forty-eight hours for that purpose if not in session. If the Congress, within twenty-one days after receipt of the latter written declaration, or, if Congress is not in session, within twenty-one days after Congress is required to assemble, determines by two-thirds vote of both Houses that the President is unable to discharge the powers and duties of his office, the Vice President shall continue to discharge the same as Acting President; otherwise, the President shall resume the powers and duties of his office.

## AMENDMENT XXVI [1971]

SECTION 1. The right of citizens of the United States, who are eighteen years of age or older, to vote shall not be denied or abridged by the United States or by any State on account of age.

SECTION 2. The Congress shall have power to enforce this article by appropriate legislation.

# INDEX

553

# *Index*

# Index

**GOVERNMENT**
See also Congressional Powers;
Federal Government; Presidential Powers; Separation of Powers
Constitutional limitations, 3
Express, 3, 4
Implied, 3

**GRANT, PRESIDENT**
Reference to, 49, 86, 112, 113

*GRAY CASE*
Quoted, 264

**GRAY, JUSTICE**
Quoted, 221, 460

**HAGUE CONFERENCES**
Reference to, 198

**HAMILTON**
Quoted, 50, 161, 298, 300, 344, 374, 485
Reference to, 7, 41, 42, 43, 48, 82, 99,
130, 162, 297, 304, 328, 334, 343,
412, 417, 427, 481

**HAND, JUDGE**
Reference to, 59, 60, 312, 313, 461

**HARLAN, JUSTICE**
Reference to, 61

**HARRIMAN, AVERELL**
Reference to, 118

**HAY, JOHN**
Quoted, 377
Reference to, 132

*HEAD MONEY CASES*
Quoted, 406, 410, 411

**HENKIN, LOUIS**
Quoted, 280–281

**HICKENLOOPER AMENDMENT**
"Act of State" doctrine, 317, 325, 362,
458, 463, 492
First Hickenlooper Amendment, 114

*HINES v. DAVIDOWITZ CASE*
Quoted, 243, 244

**HOLMES, JUSTICE**
Quoted, 137, 138, 144–146, 294, 295, 391
Reference to, 139

*HOLMES v. JENNISON CASE*
Quoted, 231, 232

**HOPKINS, HARRY**
Reference to, 46

**HUGHES, JUSTICE**
Quoted, 152–155
Reference to, 401

**HUMAN RIGHTS**
International interest of U. S., 155

**IMMIGRATION LAWS**
Aliens, 270

**IMPLIED POWERS**
President, 41–44

**INDIVIDUAL RIGHTS**
Generally, 251–270
Bill of rights protection, 253–255, 484,
485, 493, 500, 501, 502
Constitutional protection abroad, 266–
269
Crimes committed abroad, 266, 267
Establishment of courts abroad,
267
Territories, 268, 269
*Insular Cases*, 268, 269
Constitutional safeguards, applicability of, 251–266
Bill of rights, 253–255
"Due Process" clause, 255–257
Aliens, 255, 257
Personal liberties, 256, 257
States, 269–270
Equal protection of the laws, 257–
259
Aliens, 258, 259
States, 269–270
"Due Process" clause, 255–257
States, 269–270
Equal protection of the laws, 257–259,
495
Aliens, 258, 259
States, 269–270
States and individual rights, 269, 270
Alien residents, 269, 270
Constitutional protection against
state infringement, 269, 270
Equal Protection Clause, 269
Fourteenth Amendment, 269
Taking of private property for public
use, just compensation, 259–266
Aliens, 259, 261
Constitutional authority, 259
Court of Claims, jurisdiction over,
264, 265

559

*Index*

**WAR POWERS ACT**
Nature and scope, 102, 103

**WAR PRODUCTION BOARD**
Reference to, 496

*WARE* v. *HYLTON CASE*
Quoted, 261
Reference to, 166, 260, 262, 263, 419, 496, 497

**WARSAW CONVENTION**
Reference to, 207

**WASHINGTON, PRESIDENT**
Neutrality proclamations, 53
Reference to, 46, 48, 57, 85, 99, 112, 131, 161, 302, 375

**WEBSTER–ASHBURTON TREATY**
Reference to, 408

**WECHSLER, PROFESSOR**
Quoted, 248, 483

**WILSON, PRESIDENT**
Quoted, 304
Reference to, 49, 52, 99, 132, 306, 416, 419

*WILSON* v. *GERARD CASE*
Quoted, 425

**WORLD HEALTH ORGANIZATION**
Reference to, 437

**YALTA AGREEMENT**
Reference to, 8, 177, 180, 182, 209, 425, 426

*ZSCHERNIG CASE*
Quoted, 61, 239, 240
Reference to, 60, 63, 238, 239, 241, 456, 476–478